TEACHING the BOOK of MORMON

PART TWO

ALMA 17–MORONI

TEACHING the BOOK of MORMON

PART TWO

ALMA 17–MORONI

JOHN S. BUSHMAN, REED ROMNEY,
JOHN R. MANIS & CURT R. WAKEFIELD

CFI
An Imprint of Cedar Fort, Inc.
Springville, Utah

© 2013 John S. Bushman, Reed Romney, John R. Manis, and Curt R. Wakefield

All rights reserved.

No part of this book may be reproduced in any form whatsoever, whether by graphic, visual, electronic, film, microfilm, tape recording, or any other means, without prior written permission of the publisher, except in the case of brief passages embodied in critical reviews and articles.

This is not an official publication of The Church of Jesus Christ of Latter-day Saints. The opinions and views expressed herein belong solely to the author and do not necessarily represent the opinions or views of Cedar Fort, Inc. Permission for the use of sources, graphics, and photos is also solely the responsibility of the author.

ISBN 13: 978-1-4621-1249-4

Published by CFI, an imprint of Cedar Fort, Inc., 2373 W. 700 S., Springville, UT 84663
Distributed by Cedar Fort, Inc., www.cedarfort.com

The Library of Congress has cataloged Teaching the Book of Mormon, Part One, as follows:

Bushman, John S. (John Sanford), 1971- author.
Teaching the Book of Mormon / John S. Bushman, Reed Romney, John R. Manis, Curt R. Wakefield.
  pages cm
Includes bibliographical references and index.
Summary: Designed specifically for teachers of the Book of Mormon.
ISBN 978-1-4621-1217-3 (alk. paper)
  1. Book of Mormon--Study and teaching. I. Romney, Reed, 1980- author. II. Manis, John R., author. III. Wakefield, Curt Ryan, author. IV. Title.

BX8627.B87 2013
289.3'22071--dc23

2013007035

Cover design by Rebecca J. Greenwood and Shawnda T. Craig
Cover design © 2013 Lyle Mortimer
Interior book design by Emily Chambers
Edited by Summer Romney and Emily Chambers
Typeset by Shawnda T. Craig
Printed in the United States of America

10 9 8 7 6 5 4 3 2 1

Printed on acid-free paper

To the dedicated teachers and students
of scripture everywhere.

CONTENTS

Introduction 1

The Book of Alma (17) 5

The Book of Helaman 155

The Third Book of Nephi 207

The Fourth Book of Nephi 283

The Book of Mormon 289

The Book of Ether 313

The Book of Moroni 353

Index 373

About the Authors 375

INTRODUCTION

"Remember the New Covenant, Even the Book of Mormon"

In September 1832, several missionaries returned from their fields of labor to Kirtland, Ohio. They had been preaching the message of the restored gospel of Jesus Christ as they had been commissioned by revelation through the Prophet Joseph Smith. After reporting their missionary labors, the Lord gave another revelation to the Prophet Joseph, now recorded as Section 84 of the Doctrine and Covenants. Speaking to the group of elders, the Lord explained that the elders' "minds in times past have been darkened because of unbelief, . . . and [the whole church] shall remain under this condemnation until they repent and remember the new covenant, even the Book of Mormon." (See Doctrine and Covenants 84:54–57.)

While these missionaries had not been completely unsuccessful in their preaching, it seemed they had not achieved all the success possible or expected. The Lord indicates that this "darkness" was because of their indifference toward a former commandment given to all teachers of the Church in Doctrine and Covenants 42:12, "And again, the elders, priests and teachers of this church shall teach the principles of my gospel, which are in the Bible and the Book of Mormon, in the which is the fulness of the gospel."

Since the beginning of this dispensation, the Lord has emphasized the importance of the Book of Mormon in gospel teaching. Ezra Taft Benson famously reiterated the same message in a general conference of the Church when he taught, "If the early Saints were rebuked for treating the Book of Mormon lightly, are we under any less condemnation if we do the same? The Lord Himself bears testimony that it is of eternal significance" (Ezra Taft Benson, "The Book of Mormon—The Keystone of Our Religion," *Ensign,* November 1986).

As Latter-day Saints, we must make the effort to utilize the Book of Mormon in our personal gospel study and while teaching gospel principles to others. Since many publications assist with personal Book of Mormon study, the purpose of this book is to help overcome obstacles inhibiting the latter effort—teaching others the principles of the gospel. *Teaching the Book of Mormon* provides several major advantages to Latter-day Saint teachers.

An All-in-One Resource

As many teachers know, instruction materials can be cumbersome. Scriptures, manuals, magazines, references, lesson outlines, and other materials can quickly become a disorganized mess. *Teaching the Book of Mormon* provides lesson plans, supporting quotations, explanatory references, and the scriptural text in one easy-to-view volume.

Lesson Plans for Complete Book of Mormon Courses. Many teachers are assigned to sequentially teach the entire content of the Book of Mormon. Official Church curriculum is generally provided to these teachers and should be used as the primary resources for lesson plans.

INTRODUCTION

However, as many teachers understand, some lesson ideas don't seem to be the right approach for a certain class. *Teaching the Book of Mormon* provides strong additional resources for useful lesson plans and ideas. A teacher may choose to utilize an entire lesson plan from this book or may simply glean questions, object lessons, or activities to enhance plus adapt Church curriculum.

Teaching Ideas for Using the Book of Mormon in Topical Instruction. While some courses focus solely on the Book of Mormon, Latter-day Saint teachers are also frequently involved in topical instruction. Seminary courses excluded, much of the primary and youth-oriented curriculum approaches gospel teaching in this manner. Topical teaching also occurs in priesthood and Relief Society meetings, family home evenings, and informally throughout the Church. The Lord expects us to continue to utilize the Book of Mormon in this type of teaching. For this purpose, *Teaching the Book of Mormon* contains a topical index. If a lesson centers on the topic of faith, for example, a teacher may use the index to find ideas on how to teach the doctrine of faith as it is found within the Book of Mormon.

Use for Personal Study. *Teaching the Book of Mormon* may also be an excellent study aid for personal scripture study. Members of the Church will find the ideas, questions, insights, and invitations found within this book an engaging way to study the scriptures on their own.

As Latter-day Saint teachers endeavor to teach the principles of the gospel from the Book of Mormon, they will find greater success in their classes, experience the enlightenment of the Holy Ghost, and bring the gospel into the hearts of their class members. *Teaching the Book of Mormon* is an attempt to help teachers fulfill this commission.

How to Use This Book

Principles and Doctrines. You must have a clear understanding of ***what*** you want to teach before you can decide ***how*** you want to teach it. Principles and doctrines are short statements of truth that encapsulate the main lesson you want your class to learn. In *Teaching the Book of Mormon*, the principles and doctrines are in bold text and indicate the verse(s) they are derived from. Principles generally 1) describe an action, 2) are personal, and 3) have a result. Some examples of how a principle might be written at the beginning of a lesson idea are:

v. 10 When I make righteous choices, I will be happier.

v. 3 Studying the scriptures will give me guidance.

Doctrines generally are statements of belief that you would want your class to understand and have a testimony of. In this book, they look like this:

vv. 25–26 The Fall was necessary for our growth and happiness.

vv. 24–28 God loves His children and wants every one of them to be saved.

⚡ **Lesson Starter.** When you start teaching a lesson or a different set of verses, you will want to do something to get or regain the class's attention and help them prepare to learn. Teachers sometimes call this a "starter." The lesson starter will grab class members' interest so that they will want to turn to their scriptures and learn more. It also prepares the class members' hearts and minds so that they may learn by the Holy Ghost. Often a starter is an object lesson or a compelling question that shows the relevancy of what you will be studying. In this book, the lesson starter icon will show you the starter you might want to use to help stimulate interest in what you will be teaching.

🔍 **Look For.** Once you have captured class members' interest with a starter, you will want to direct them to the scriptures. Before asking someone to read, you will want to give them something to **look for** in those verses so that they will be engaged and focused. The look for icon will also be used before a long quote is read or sometimes even before watching a video. Italicized text indicates questions or statements that you may choose to use word for word.

INTRODUCTION

? Questions. Effective teaching is most often centered around powerful discussion questions. Again, italicized phrases indicate that you could ask those questions of your class exactly as they appear in the book. In addition, there are different types of questions to be used at different points during a discussion. This book outlines two types of questions: analyze and apply. Analyze questions are designed to help the learner analyze and ponder the scriptures being discussed. Once the doctrine or principle has been effectively analyzed and understood, the teacher can ask the apply questions, which helps the learners apply the analyzed doctrines and principles.

Group Work. Class members often enjoy getting into smaller groups and working with each other on a task you have given them. This provides variety in teaching methods and also allows more class members the opportunity to share their thoughts.

Participation Activities. Similar to group work, participation activities get the class members participating in more ways than just a class discussion.

Writing Activities. Here the class members have the opportunity to either write in a journal or annotate their scriptures.

To assist with understanding the content of each scripture chapter, this book also provides Insights and Quotations.

Insights. This icon adds historical and contextual information that may add depth to the understanding of a chapter.

Quotations. Often a quote by a prophet or Church leader can greatly enhance a lesson.

♥ Deep into Their hearts. Henry B. Eyring taught, "The pure gospel of Jesus Christ must go down into the hearts of students by the power of the Holy Ghost" (*We Must Raise Our Sights*, CES Conference on the Book of Mormon, August 14, 2001, Brigham Young University). These icons help the learner feel the promptings of the Holy Ghost, make applications to their lives, and commit to live those principles.

Topical Index. The Book of Mormon "contains the fulness of the everlasting gospel" (introduction to the Book of Mormon) and can be used in any teaching situation. *Teaching the Book of Mormon* offers teaching ideas and suggestions to be used in various settings—from the classroom to a family home evening lesson, or even for personal study. This book provides a topical index to aid in your lesson preparation. If you are preparing a lesson on the Godhead, for example, refer to the index for references to the Godhead taught in the Book of Mormon. You can then turn to that page and have a lesson outline ready to teach from.

> **Teaching Tips from Prophets' Lips** Teaching tips will be found within various chapters of the book to give both general and specific principles of teaching and learning. Though not every quote will be from a prophet, all sources come from Church publications. Additionally, these quotes will be tied to the specific lesson to enhance your ability to teach with power and understanding.

THE BOOK OF ALMA

ALMA SUMMARY

Time Period: About 91–53 BC (39 years)

Major Contributors: Moroni, Alma the Younger, Amulek, Ammon, Aaron, Zenos, Zenock

Source: Large plates of Nephi

Abridged by: Mormon

Synopsis:

Chapters 17–28: The missions of the sons of Mosiah to the Lamanites: their preachings, sufferings, deliverance, and the affairs concerning the people of Ammon

Chapter 29: A psalm of Ammon

Chapter 30: An account of Korihor, an antichrist

Chapters 31–35: The mission to the Zoramites

Chapters 36–42: The commandments of Alma to his sons

Chapters 43–62: The wars and political unrest between the Nephites and Lamanites

Chapter 63: Hagoth builds and sails ships; the sacred records are passed to Helaman

ALMA 17

Ammon and His Brethren Begin Their Missions

About 91 BC

1–4, Alma meets the sons of Mosiah at the end of their mission; 5–17, The sons of Mosiah separate to different Lamanite lands for their missions; 18–25, Ammon goes to the land of King Lamoni and offers to be his servant and is given a commission over the sheep; 26–39, Ammon defends the king's flocks by chopping off the arms of the invading Lamanites.

1 And now it came to pass that as Alma was journeying from the land of Gideon southward, away to the land of Manti, behold, to his astonishment, he met with the sons of Mosiah journeying towards the land of Zarahemla.

2 Now these sons of Mosiah were with Alma at the time the angel first appeared unto him; therefore

Notes

ALMA 17

Alma did rejoice exceedingly to see his brethren; and what added more to his joy, they were still his brethren in the Lord; yea, and they had waxed strong in the knowledge of the truth; for they were men of a sound understanding and they had searched the scriptures diligently, that they might know the word of God.

3 But this is not all; they had given themselves to much prayer, and fasting; therefore they had the spirit of prophecy, and the spirit of revelation, and when they taught, they taught with power and authority of God.

4 And they had been teaching the word of God for the space of fourteen years among the Lamanites, having had much success in bringing many to the knowledge of the truth; yea, by the power of their words many were brought before the altar of God, to call on his name and confess their sins before him.

5 Now these are the circumstances which attended them in their journeyings, for they had many afflictions; they did suffer much, both in body and in mind, such as hunger, thirst and fatigue, and also much labor in the spirit.

6 Now these were their journeyings: Having taken leave of their father, Mosiah, in the first year of the judges; having refused the kingdom which their father was desirous to confer upon them, and also this was the minds of the people;

vv. 1–8 Missions can be challenging endeavors, but proper preparation and hard work lead to great spiritual blessings for missionaries.

- Prepare copies of the following to distribute to class members or consider copying it on the board for all to see: "MEN WANTED: FOR HAZARDOUS JOURNEY. SMALL WAGES, BITTER COLD, LONG MONTHS OF COMPLETE DARKNESS, CONSTANT DANGER, SAFE RETURN DOUBTFUL. HONOUR AND RECOGNITION IN CASE OF SUCCESS."
- Explain that this want ad was rumored to have been published by Ernest Shackleton, an Antarctic explorer, who was seeking to gather a crew for a dangerous polar expedition. Tell the class that in Alma 17, they will begin discussing the mission of the sons of Mosiah to the Lamanites. Ask, *How might such an advertisement be similar to serving a mission, particularly among a hostile people? How might it differ?*
- Ask the class to read Alma 17:1–6 and mark some of the preparation, hazards, efforts, and benefits of serving a mission for the Lord. Based on what they read about the sons of Mosiah, invite them to write a short "want ad" summarizing what the Lord is looking for in His missionaries and what benefits those who are worthy will receive. Share and discuss their results, emphasizing the verses from Alma that they used to create their ads.
- The Prophet Joseph Smith taught, "Let the Saints remember that great things depend on their individual exertion, and that they are called to be coworkers with us and the Holy Spirit in accomplishing the great work of the last days" (*Teachings of the Prophet Joseph Smith*, 178–79).
- Testify that as members of the Church labor diligently, they can be granted sufficient spiritual gifts to accomplish the missions that the Lord has called them to fulfill. Consider sharing a personal missionary experience of when you saw the blessings detailed in this chapter realized in your own life.

7 Nevertheless they departed out of the land of Zarahemla, and took their swords, and their spears, and their bows, and their arrows, and their slings; and this they did that they might provide food for themselves while in the wilderness.

8 And thus they departed into the wilderness with their numbers which they had selected, to go up to the land of Nephi, to preach the word of God unto the Lamanites.

9 And it came to pass that they journeyed many days in the wilderness, and they fasted much

Notes

and prayed much that the Lord would grant unto them a portion of his Spirit to go with them, and abide with them, that they might be an instrument in the hands of God to bring, if it were possible, their brethren, the Lamanites, to the knowledge of the truth, to the knowledge of the baseness of the traditions of their fathers, which were not correct.

10 And it came to pass that the Lord did visit them with his Spirit, and said unto them: Be comforted. And they were comforted.

11 And the Lord said unto them also: Go forth among the Lamanites, thy brethren, and establish my word; yet ye shall be patient in longsuffering and afflictions, that ye may show forth good examples unto them in me, and I will make an instrument of thee in my hands unto the salvation of many souls.

12 And it came to pass that the hearts of the sons of Mosiah, and also those who were with them, took courage to go forth unto the Lamanites to declare unto them the word of God.

13 And it came to pass when they had arrived in the borders of the land of the Lamanites, that they separated themselves and departed one from another, trusting in the Lord that they should meet again at the close of their harvest; for they supposed that great was the work which they had undertaken.

14 And assuredly it was great, for they had undertaken to preach the word of God to a wild and a hardened and a ferocious people; a people who delighted in murdering the Nephites, and robbing and plundering them; and their hearts were set upon riches, or upon gold and silver, and precious stones; yet they sought to obtain these things by murdering and plundering, that they might not labor for them with their own hands.

15 Thus they were a very indolent people, many of whom did worship idols, and the curse of God had fallen upon them because of the traditions of their fathers; notwithstanding the promises of the Lord were extended unto them on the conditions of repentance.

16 Therefore, this was the cause for which the sons of Mosiah had undertaken the work, that perhaps they might bring them unto repentance; that perhaps they might bring them to know of the plan of redemption.

17 Therefore they separated themselves one from another, and went forth among them, every man alone, according to the word and power of God which was given unto him.

vv. 9–17 The righteous serve missions because of their desire to bring others to salvation and be instruments in the Lord's hands.

- Bring a copy of *Preach My Gospel* to class. Hold up the manual and ask, *Does anyone know how the purpose of missionary work is defined in this book?* If no one responds, invite a class member to read from page 1: "Invite others to come unto Christ by helping them receive the restored gospel through faith in Jesus Christ and His Atonement, repentance, baptism, receiving the gift of the Holy Ghost, and enduring to the end." Explain that while the sons of Mosiah worded it differently, the scriptures give us details concerning how they defined the purpose of their mission—bringing the Lord's children to repentance.

- *Read Alma 17:9–17 and look for phrases that define the purpose of the mission of the sons of Mosiah. Ask class members to share and explain the phrases that stood out to them.*

- Analyze:
  - *What types of things were keeping the Lamanites from coming unto Christ (vv. 14–15)?*
  - *What degree of success would you guess a missionary would experience with such a people?*
  - *How do you think the sons of Mosiah felt about their chances of success as missionaries?*
  - *Verse 16 uses the word "perhaps" twice. Why do you think the likelihood of "perhaps"*

Notes

ALMA 17

was good enough for the sons of Mosiah to labor the way they did?
- Why would the word "instrument" in verses 9 and 11 give the sons of Mosiah hope to be successful in their purpose?
- What does the word "instrument" teach us about Heavenly Father's role in missionary work?

❓ Apply: *What do these verses teach about missionary work in our day?*

♥ Testify that when we put forth the effort to bring someone closer to Christ, even when we think chances of acceptance are low, we allow the Father to work through us to work miracles in the lives of His children.

18 Now Ammon being the chief among them, or rather he did administer unto them, and he departed from them, after having blessed them according to their several stations, having imparted the word of God unto them, or administered unto them before his departure; and thus they took their several journeys throughout the land.

19 And Ammon went to the land of Ishmael, the land being called after the sons of Ishmael, who also became Lamanites.

20 And as Ammon entered the land of Ishmael, the Lamanites took him and bound him, as was their custom to bind all the Nephites who fell into their hands, and carry them before the king; and thus it was left to the pleasure of the king to slay them, or to retain them in captivity, or to cast them into prison, or to cast them out of his land, according to his will and pleasure.

21 And thus Ammon was carried before the king who was over the land of Ishmael; and his name was Lamoni; and he was a descendant of Ishmael.

22 And the king inquired of Ammon if it were his desire to dwell in the land among the Lamanites, or among his people.

23 And Ammon said unto him: Yea, I desire to dwell among this people for a time; yea, and perhaps until the day I die.

24 And it came to pass that king Lamoni was much pleased with Ammon, and caused that his bands should be loosed; and he would that Ammon should take one of his daughters to wife.

25 But Ammon said unto him: Nay, but I will be thy servant. Therefore Ammon became a servant to king Lamoni. And it came to pass that he was set among other servants to watch the flocks of Lamoni, according to the custom of the Lamanites.

26 And after he had been in the service of the king three days, as he was with the Lamanitish servants going forth with their flocks to the place of water, which was called the water of Sebus, and all the Lamanites drive their flocks hither, that they may have water—

27 Therefore, as Ammon and the servants of the king were driving forth their flocks to this place of water, behold, a certain number of the Lamanites, who had been with their flocks to water, stood and scattered the flocks of Ammon and the servants of the king, and they scattered them insomuch that they fled many ways.

28 Now the servants of the king began to murmur, saying: Now the king will slay us, as he has our brethren because their flocks were scattered by the wickedness of these men. And they began to weep exceedingly, saying: Behold, our flocks are scattered already.

29 Now they wept because of the fear of being slain. Now when Ammon saw this his heart was swollen within him with joy; for, said he, I will show forth my power unto these my fellow-servants, or the power which is in me, in restoring these flocks unto the king, that I may win the hearts of these my fellow-servants, that I may lead them to believe in my words.

30 And now, these were the thoughts of Ammon, when he saw the afflictions of those whom he termed to be his brethren.

31 And it came to pass that he flattered them by his words, saying: My brethren, be of good cheer and let us go in search of the flocks, and

Notes

we will gather them together and bring them back unto the place of water; and thus we will preserve the flocks unto the king and he will not slay us.

vv. 18–31 Service is an essential element of missionary work.

⚡ *Have you ever had an experience when you saw the helpfulness, kindness, or service of an individual lead someone to come closer to the Savior?*

🔍 Summarize verses 18–20 and invite the class to read verses 21–25, looking for Ammon's approach to missionary work and its effects on Lamoni the king.

❓ Analyze:
- *How can you tell that Ammon's request was sincere and not just a method to manipulate the king?*
- *Read verses 26–31 and ask, Why does Ammon rejoice when he hears the problem confronting the servants?*
- *Was this something that Ammon could have planned out?*
- *What would have happened if he had missed the opportunity?*

💡 Regarding unplanned service, *Preach My Gospel* reads, "This type of service involves listening to the Spirit to recognize opportunities for small, simple acts of kindness that you can offer to God's children. Pray and be aware of opportunities throughout each day to do good. As you seek to do good, you will be led to people who are being prepared for the restored gospel" (page 168).

32 And it came to pass that they went in search of the flocks, and they did follow Ammon, and they rushed forth with much swiftness and did head the flocks of the king, and did gather them together again to the place of water.

33 And those men again stood to scatter their flocks; but Ammon said unto his brethren: Encircle the flocks round about that they flee not; and I go and contend with these men who do scatter our flocks.

34 Therefore, they did as Ammon commanded them, and he went forth and stood to contend with those who stood by the waters of Sebus; and they were in number not a few.

35 Therefore they did not fear Ammon, for they supposed that one of their men could slay him according to their pleasure, for they knew not that the Lord had promised Mosiah that he would deliver his sons out of their hands; neither did they know anything concerning the Lord; therefore they delighted in the destruction of their brethren; and for this cause they stood to scatter the flocks of the king.

36 But Ammon stood forth and began to cast stones at them with his sling; yea, with mighty power he did sling stones amongst them; and thus he slew a certain number of them insomuch that they began to be astonished at his power; nevertheless they were angry because of the slain of their brethren, and they were determined that he should fall; therefore, seeing that they could not hit him with their stones, they came forth with clubs to slay him.

37 But behold, every man that lifted his club to smite Ammon, he smote off their arms with his sword; for he did withstand their blows by smiting their arms with the edge of his sword, insomuch that they began to be astonished, and began to flee before him; yea, and they were not few in number; and he caused them to flee by the strength of his arm.

38 Now six of them had fallen by the sling, but he slew none save it were their leader with his sword; and he smote off as many of their arms as were lifted against him, and they were not a few.

39 And when he had driven them afar off, he returned and they watered their flocks and returned them to the pasture of the king, and then went in unto the king, bearing the arms which had been smitten off by the sword of Ammon, of those who sought to slay him; and

Notes

they were carried in unto the king for a testimony of the things which they had done.

vv. 32–39 The Lord empowers His servants with strength beyond their own.

♥ Although verses 32–39 contain one of the most famous stories within the Book of Mormon, avoid the urge to simply summarize. Consider reading these verses to your class with the enthusiasm and excitement it deserves. There is power when a faithful teacher reads directly from the scriptures. As prompted, bear your testimony that Ammon was able to perform this mighty miracle because the Lord was with him. Testify that the Lord will strengthen your class members as they seek to perform His work.

> **Teaching Tips from Prophets' Lips** "One of the dangers of the times we are passing into is that we might be tempted to lower our expectations for ourselves and for those young people we serve. As the world darkens, even a partial conversion and a few spiritual experiences may seem more and more remarkable, compared to the world. We might be tempted to expect less. The Lord has given another signal, clear and powerful. It is that we can expect more, not less, of youth. . . . It begins with expectations, yours and theirs." (Henry B. Eyring, "Raising Expectations," CES satellite training broadcast, August 4, 2004, 1–2.)

Index Topics: missionary work, service, preparation, labor

ALMA 18

The Conversion of King Lamoni
About 90 BC

1–11, King Lamoni and his servants deliberate who Ammon is, concluding that he is the Great Spirit; 12–18, Ammon is able to discern the thoughts of the king; 19–39, Ammon unfolds the scriptures to the king and teaches him; 40–43, King Lamoni prays to God and falls to the earth.

Note: Alma chapters 17–19 are one continuous story and can be taught together.

Overarching Principle: Conversion can be a result of our hearing the word of God and our willingness to accept it.

⚡ Discuss with your class the relationship between desire and action. Some of the discussion could include what comes first, the desire or action, or why desire is necessary for action. Explain that the class will use Lamoni's conversion as an example of the need to have a desire to believe, which will motivate a person to righteous action.

🔍 Read Alma 18:21–23, 40–41 to look for King Lamoni's desire. Once identified, use the following chart to allow class members to read the story and identify the lesson learned from King Lamoni.

What does King Lamoni desire?	Alma 18:21–23, 40–41
Why is King Lamoni interested in learning about God?	Alma 17
What does King Lamoni believe about God?	Alma 18:2–5
What does King Lamoni think about Ammon?	Alma 18:8–11
What and how does Ammon teach King Lamoni?	Alma 18:12–39
How does King Lamoni show his desire to believe?	Alma 18:40–41
What happens to King Lamoni?	Alma 18:42–43

Notes

- 💬 Elder Dallin H. Oaks said, "Desires dictate our priorities, priorities shape our choices, and choices determine our actions. The desires we act on determine our changing, our achieving, and our becoming" (Dallin H. Oaks, "Desire," *Ensign*, May 2011, 42.)
- ❓ Apply: Once you have given class members enough time to study the following chart, discuss together what lesson they learned from King Lamoni.
- ♥ Help the class to recognize the important relationship that desire and action have on their journey toward conversion.

Note: The verses below are broken up according to the chart above. Each question from the chart is also placed above their selected verses in bold.

vv. 1–5 What does King Lamoni believe about God?

1 And it came to pass that king Lamoni caused that his servants should stand forth and testify to all the things which they had seen concerning the matter.

2 And when they had all testified to the things which they had seen, and he had learned of the faithfulness of Ammon in preserving his flocks, and also of his great power in contending against those who sought to slay him, he was astonished exceedingly, and said: Surely, this is more than a man. Behold, is not this the Great Spirit who doth send such great punishments upon this people, because of their murders?

3 And they answered the king, and said: Whether he be the Great Spirit or a man, we know not; but this much we do know, that he cannot be slain by the enemies of the king; neither can they scatter the king's flocks when he is with us, because of his expertness and great strength; therefore, we know that he is a friend to the king. And now, O king, we do not believe that a man has such great power, for we know he cannot be slain.

4 And now, when the king heard these words, he said unto them: Now I know that it is the Great Spirit; and he has come down at this time to preserve your lives, that I might not slay you as I did your brethren. Now this is the Great Spirit of whom our fathers have spoken.

5 Now this was the tradition of Lamoni, which he had received from his father, that there was a Great Spirit. Notwithstanding they believed in a Great Spirit, they supposed that whatsoever they did was right; nevertheless, Lamoni began to fear exceedingly, with fear lest he had done wrong in slaying his servants;

6 For he had slain many of them because their brethren had scattered their flocks at the place of water; and thus, because they had had their flocks scattered they were slain.

7 Now it was the practice of these Lamanites to stand by the waters of Sebus to scatter the flocks of the people, that thereby they might drive away many that were scattered unto their own land, it being a practice of plunder among them.

vv. 8–11 What does King Lamoni think about Ammon?

8 And it came to pass that king Lamoni inquired of his servants, saying: Where is this man that has such great power?

9 And they said unto him: Behold, he is feeding thy horses. Now the king had commanded his servants, previous to the time of the watering of their flocks, that they should prepare his horses and chariots, and conduct him forth to the land of Nephi; for there had been a great feast appointed at the land of Nephi, by the father of Lamoni, who was king over all the land.

10 Now when king Lamoni heard that Ammon was preparing his horses and his chariots he was more astonished, because of the faithfulness of Ammon, saying: Surely there has not been any servant among all my servants that has been so faithful as this man; for even he doth remember all my commandments to execute them.

Notes

11 Now I surely know that this is the Great Spirit, and I would desire him that he come in unto me, but I durst not.

vv. 12–39 What and how does Ammon teach King Lamoni?

12 And it came to pass that when Ammon had made ready the horses and the chariots for the king and his servants, he went in unto the king, and he saw that the countenance of the king was changed; therefore he was about to return out of his presence.

13 And one of the king's servants said unto him, Rabbanah, which is, being interpreted, powerful or great king, considering their kings to be powerful; and thus he said unto him: Rabbanah, the king desireth thee to stay.

14 Therefore Ammon turned himself unto the king, and said unto him: What wilt thou that I should do for thee, O king? And the king answered him not for the space of an hour, according to their time, for he knew not what he should say unto him.

15 And it came to pass that Ammon said unto him again: What desirest thou of me? But the king answered him not.

16 And it came to pass that Ammon, being filled with the Spirit of God, therefore he perceived the thoughts of the king. And he said unto him: Is it because thou hast heard that I defended thy servants and thy flocks, and slew seven of their brethren with the sling and with the sword, and smote off the arms of others, in order to defend thy flocks and thy servants; behold, is it this that causeth thy marvelings?

17 I say unto you, what is it, that thy marvelings are so great? Behold, I am a man, and am thy servant; therefore, whatsoever thou desirest which is right, that will I do.

18 Now when the king had heard these words, he marveled again, for he beheld that Ammon could discern his thoughts; but notwithstanding this, king Lamoni did open his mouth, and said unto him: Who art thou? Art thou that Great Spirit, who knows all things?

19 Ammon answered and said unto him: I am not.

20 And the king said: How knowest thou the thoughts of my heart? Thou mayest speak boldly, and tell me concerning these things; and also tell me by what power ye slew and smote off the arms of my brethren that scattered my flocks—

21 And now, if thou wilt tell me concerning these things, whatsoever thou desirest I will give unto thee; and if it were needed, I would guard thee with my armies; but I know that thou art more powerful than all they; nevertheless, whatsoever thou desirest of me I will grant it unto thee.

22 Now Ammon being wise, yet harmless, he said unto Lamoni: Wilt thou hearken unto my words, if I tell thee by what power I do these things? And this is the thing that I desire of thee.

23 And the king answered him, and said: Yea, I will believe all thy words. And thus he was caught with guile.

24 And Ammon began to speak unto him with boldness, and said unto him: Believest thou that there is a God?

25 And he answered, and said unto him: I do not know what that meaneth.

26 And then Ammon said: Believest thou that there is a Great Spirit?

27 And he said, Yea.

28 And Ammon said: This is God. And Ammon said unto him again: Believest thou that this Great Spirit, who is God, created all things which are in heaven and in the earth?

29 And he said: Yea, I believe that he created all things which are in the earth; but I do not know the heavens.

30 And Ammon said unto him: The heavens is a place where God dwells and all his holy angels.

31 And king Lamoni said: Is it above the earth?

32 And Ammon said: Yea, and he looketh down

Notes

upon all the children of men; and he knows all the thoughts and intents of the heart; for by his hand were they all created from the beginning.

33 And king Lamoni said: I believe all these things which thou hast spoken. Art thou sent from God?

34 Ammon said unto him: I am a man; and man in the beginning was created after the image of God, and I am called by his Holy Spirit to teach these things unto this people, that they may be brought to a knowledge of that which is just and true;

35 And a portion of that Spirit dwelleth in me, which giveth me knowledge, and also power according to my faith and desires which are in God.

36 Now when Ammon had said these words, he began at the creation of the world, and also the creation of Adam, and told him all the things concerning the fall of man, and rehearsed and laid before him the records and the holy scriptures of the people, which had been spoken by the prophets, even down to the time that their father, Lehi, left Jerusalem.

37 And he also rehearsed unto them (for it was unto the king and to his servants) all the journeyings of their fathers in the wilderness, and all their sufferings with hunger and thirst, and their travail, and so forth.

38 And he also rehearsed unto them concerning the rebellions of Laman and Lemuel, and the sons of Ishmael, yea, all their rebellions did he relate unto them; and he expounded unto them all the records and scriptures from the time that Lehi left Jerusalem down to the present time.

39 But this is not all; for he expounded unto them the plan of redemption, which was prepared from the foundation of the world; and he also made known unto them concerning the coming of Christ, and all the works of the Lord did he make known unto them.

vv. 40–41 How does King Lamoni show his desire to believe?

40 And it came to pass that after he had said all these things, and expounded them to the king, that the king believed all his words.

41 And he began to cry unto the Lord, saying: O Lord, have mercy; according to thy abundant mercy which thou hast had upon the people of Nephi, have upon me, and my people.

vv. 42–43 What happens to King Lamoni?

42 And now, when he had said this, he fell unto the earth, as if he were dead.

43 And it came to pass that his servants took him and carried him in unto his wife, and laid him upon a bed; and he lay as if he were dead for the space of two days and two nights; and his wife, and his sons, and his daughters mourned over him, after the manner of the Lamanites, greatly lamenting his loss.

ALMA 19

The Conversion of King Lamoni's People
About 90 BC

1–10, The queen inquires of Ammon about her husband, Ammon teaches the queen and she has faith; 11–16, King Lamoni arises, teaches his servants who then all fall to the earth, including Ammon; 17–28, Abish calls for the Lamanites to come see what has happened, they deliberate about Ammon, Ammon is protected while he is asleep; 29–36, Lamoni and the others wake up and teach the people.

⚡ Alma chapter 19 is a continuation of the previous chapter's story and could be taught together. If you choose to do so, then you can continue with the theme of conversion and desiring to believe. You can use the following chart to study the story with your class. As an alternate idea, tell the story yourself or have class members tell the story. Additionally, you could have class members act the story out.

Notes

What is the queen's desire?	Alma 19:1–5
How does the queen express her belief?	Alma 19:6–11
What happens next?	Alma 19:12–27
Once converted, what do King Lamoni and his wife do?	Alma 19:28–36
What is the definition of conversion?	Alma 19:33
What is Mormon's concluding point? How does it apply to us?	Alma 19:36

Note: The verses below are broken up according to the chart above. Each question from the chart is also placed above their selected verses in bold.

vv. 1–5 What is the queen's desire?

1 And it came to pass that after two days and two nights they were about to take his body and lay it in a sepulchre, which they had made for the purpose of burying their dead.

2 Now the queen having heard of the fame of Ammon, therefore she sent and desired that he should come in unto her.

3 And it came to pass that Ammon did as he was commanded, and went in unto the queen, and desired to know what she would that he should do.

4 And she said unto him: The servants of my husband have made it known unto me that thou art a prophet of a holy God, and that thou hast power to do many mighty works in his name;

5 Therefore, if this is the case, I would that ye should go in and see my husband, for he has been laid upon his bed for the space of two days and two nights; and some say that he is not dead, but others say that he is dead and that he stinketh, and that he ought to be placed in the sepulchre; but as for myself, to me he doth not stink.

vv. 6–11 How does the queen express her belief?

6 Now, this was what Ammon desired, for he knew that king Lamoni was under the power of God; he knew that the dark veil of unbelief was being cast away from his mind, and the light which did light up his mind, which was the light of the glory of God, which was a marvelous light of his goodness—yea, this light had infused such joy into his soul, the cloud of darkness having been dispelled, and that the light of everlasting life was lit up in his soul, yea, he knew that this had overcome his natural frame, and he was carried away in God—

7 Therefore, what the queen desired of him was his only desire. Therefore, he went in to see the king according as the queen had desired him; and he saw the king, and he knew that he was not dead.

8 And he said unto the queen: He is not dead, but he sleepeth in God, and on the morrow he shall rise again; therefore bury him not.

9 And Ammon said unto her: Believest thou this? And she said unto him: I have had no witness save thy word, and the word of our servants; nevertheless I believe that it shall be according as thou hast said.

10 And Ammon said unto her: Blessed art thou because of thy exceeding faith; I say unto thee, woman, there has not been such great faith among all the people of the Nephites.

11 And it came to pass that she watched over the bed of her husband, from that time even until that time on the morrow which Ammon had appointed that he should rise.

vv. 12–27 What happens next?

12 And it came to pass that he arose, according to the words of Ammon; and as he arose, he stretched forth his hand unto the woman, and said: Blessed be the name of God, and blessed art thou.

13 For as sure as thou livest, behold, I have seen my Redeemer; and he shall come forth, and be born of a woman, and he shall redeem all mankind

Notes

who believe on his name. Now, when he had said these words, his heart was swollen within him, and he sunk again with joy; and the queen also sunk down, being overpowered by the Spirit.

14 Now Ammon seeing the Spirit of the Lord poured out according to his prayers upon the Lamanites, his brethren, who had been the cause of so much mourning among the Nephites, or among all the people of God because of their iniquities and their traditions, he fell upon his knees, and began to pour out his soul in prayer and thanksgiving to God for what he had done for his brethren; and he was also overpowered with joy; and thus they all three had sunk to the earth.

15 Now, when the servants of the king had seen that they had fallen, they also began to cry unto God, for the fear of the Lord had come upon them also, for it was they who had stood before the king and testified unto him concerning the great power of Ammon.

16 And it came to pass that they did call on the name of the Lord, in their might, even until they had all fallen to the earth, save it were one of the Lamanitish women, whose name was Abish, she having been converted unto the Lord for many years, on account of a remarkable vision of her father—

17 Thus, having been converted to the Lord, and never having made it known, therefore, when she saw that all the servants of Lamoni had fallen to the earth, and also her mistress, the queen, and the king, and Ammon lay prostrate upon the earth, she knew that it was the power of God; and supposing that this opportunity, by making known unto the people what had happened among them, that by beholding this scene it would cause them to believe in the power of God, therefore she ran forth from house to house, making it known unto the people.

18 And they began to assemble themselves together unto the house of the king. And there came a multitude, and to their astonishment, they beheld the king, and the queen, and their servants prostrate upon the earth, and they all lay there as though they were dead; and they also saw Ammon, and behold, he was a Nephite.

19 And now the people began to murmur among themselves; some saying that it was a great evil that had come upon them, or upon the king and his house, because he had suffered that the Nephite should remain in the land.

20 But others rebuked them, saying: The king hath brought this evil upon his house, because he slew his servants who had had their flocks scattered at the waters of Sebus.

21 And they were also rebuked by those men who had stood at the waters of Sebus and scattered the flocks which belonged to the king, for they were angry with Ammon because of the number which he had slain of their brethren at the waters of Sebus, while defending the flocks of the king.

22 Now, one of them, whose brother had been slain with the sword of Ammon, being exceedingly angry with Ammon, drew his sword and went forth that he might let it fall upon Ammon, to slay him; and as he lifted the sword to smite him, behold, he fell dead.

23 Now we see that Ammon could not be slain, for the Lord had said unto Mosiah, his father: I will spare him, and it shall be unto him according to thy faith—therefore, Mosiah trusted him unto the Lord.

24 And it came to pass that when the multitude beheld that the man had fallen dead, who lifted the sword to slay Ammon, fear came upon them all, and they durst not put forth their hands to touch him or any of those who had fallen; and they began to marvel again among themselves what could be the cause of this great power, or what all these things could mean.

25 And it came to pass that there were many among them who said that Ammon was the Great Spirit, and others said he was sent by the Great Spirit;

26 But others rebuked them all, saying that he was

Notes

a monster, who had been sent from the Nephites to torment them.

27 And there were some who said that Ammon was sent by the Great Spirit to afflict them because of their iniquities; and that it was the Great Spirit that had always attended the Nephites, who had ever delivered them out of their hands; and they said that it was this Great Spirit who had destroyed so many of their brethren, the Lamanites.

vv. 28–36 Once converted, what do King Lamoni and his wife do?

28 And thus the contention began to be exceedingly sharp among them. And while they were thus contending, the woman servant who had caused the multitude to be gathered together came, and when she saw the contention which was among the multitude she was exceedingly sorrowful, even unto tears.

29 And it came to pass that she went and took the queen by the hand, that perhaps she might raise her from the ground; and as soon as she touched her hand she arose and stood upon her feet, and cried with a loud voice, saying: O blessed Jesus, who has saved me from an awful hell! O blessed God, have mercy on this people!

30 And when she had said this, she clasped her hands, being filled with joy, speaking many words which were not understood; and when she had done this, she took the king, Lamoni, by the hand, and behold he arose and stood upon his feet.

31 And he, immediately, seeing the contention among his people, went forth and began to rebuke them, and to teach them the words which he had heard from the mouth of Ammon; and as many as heard his words believed, and were converted unto the Lord.

32 But there were many among them who would not hear his words; therefore they went their way.

33 And it came to pass that when Ammon arose he also administered unto them, and also did all the servants of Lamoni; and they did all declare unto the people the selfsame thing—that their hearts had been changed; that they had no more desire to do evil.

34 And behold, many did declare unto the people that they had seen angels and had conversed with them; and thus they had told them things of God, and of his righteousness.

35 And it came to pass that there were many that did believe in their words; and as many as did believe were baptized; and they became a righteous people, and they did establish a church among them.

36 And thus the work of the Lord did commence among the Lamanites; thus the Lord did begin to pour out his Spirit upon them; and we see that his arm is extended to all people who will repent and believe on his name.

Teaching Tips from Prophets' Lips "Be patient, and above all do not lose the Spirit. We can't in any way be offended or get angry or disappointed that we've worked so hard on our lesson, and it doesn't seem the students are with us. We just have to be patient and loving. More is happening in their hearts than we think." (Jeffrey R. Holland, "Teaching and Learning in the Church", *Ensign*, June 2007, 88–105.)

ALMA 20

Ammon Meets Lamoni's Father
About 90 BC

1–7, Lamoni goes with Ammon to release his brethren; 8–27, Ammon contends with Lamoni's father; 28–30, Ammon's brethren are released.

1 And it came to pass that when they had established a church in that land, that king Lamoni desired that Ammon should go with him to the land of Nephi, that he might show him unto his father.

Notes

v. 1 When we experience the sweetness of the gospel, we want to share it with our families and others.

- ⚡ Show a piece of fruit and ask, *What Book of Mormon story might this fruit relate to? In Lehi's dream, when Lehi partook of the fruit, who did he want share it with first?*

- 🔍 *In Alma 20:1, look for how King Lamoni's feelings are similar to how Lehi felt at the tree of life (1 Nephi 8:12).*

- ❓ *Why did Lamoni want to share what he discovered?*

- ♥ Ask class members to write a list of people they care about and would want to have the gospel change and bless their lives. Challenge them to share the goodness of the gospel with others. Give the class time to write down a plan of how they might share the gospel with one of those people.

2 And the voice of the Lord came to Ammon, saying: Thou shalt not go up to the land of Nephi, for behold, the king will seek thy life; but thou shalt go to the land of Middoni; for behold, thy brother Aaron, and also Muloki and Ammah are in prison.

3 Now it came to pass that when Ammon had heard this, he said unto Lamoni: Behold, my brother and brethren are in prison at Middoni, and I go that I may deliver them.

4 Now Lamoni said unto Ammon: I know, in the strength of the Lord thou canst do all things. But behold, I will go with thee to the land of Middoni; for the king of the land of Middoni, whose name is Antiomno, is a friend unto me; therefore I go to the land of Middoni, that I may flatter the king of the land, and he will cast thy brethren out of prison. Now Lamoni said unto him: Who told thee that thy brethren were in prison?

5 And Ammon said unto him: No one hath told me, save it be God; and he said unto me—Go and deliver thy brethren, for they are in prison in the land of Middoni.

6 Now when Lamoni had heard this he caused that his servants should make ready his horses and his chariots.

7 And he said unto Ammon: Come, I will go with thee down to the land of Middoni, and there I will plead with the king that he will cast thy brethren out of prison.

8 And it came to pass that as Ammon and Lamoni were journeying thither, they met the father of Lamoni, who was king over all the land.

9 And behold, the father of Lamoni said unto him: Why did ye not come to the feast on that great day when I made a feast unto my sons, and unto my people?

10 And he also said: Whither art thou going with this Nephite, who is one of the children of a liar?

11 And it came to pass that Lamoni rehearsed unto him whither he was going, for he feared to offend him.

12 And he also told him all the cause of his tarrying in his own kingdom, that he did not go unto his father to the feast which he had prepared.

13 And now when Lamoni had rehearsed unto him all these things, behold, to his astonishment, his father was angry with him, and said: Lamoni, thou art going to deliver these Nephites, who are sons of a liar. Behold, he robbed our fathers; and now his children are also come amongst us that they may, by their cunning and their lyings, deceive us, that they again may rob us of our property.

14 Now the father of Lamoni commanded him that he should slay Ammon with the sword. And he also commanded him that he should not go to the land of Middoni, but that he should return with him to the land of Ishmael.

15 But Lamoni said unto him: I will not slay Ammon, neither will I return to the land of Ishmael, but I go to the land of Middoni that I may release the brethren of Ammon, for I know that they are just men and holy prophets of the true God.

Notes

ALMA 20

16 Now when his father had heard these words, he was angry with him, and he drew his sword that he might smite him to the earth.

17 But Ammon stood forth and said unto him: Behold, thou shalt not slay thy son; nevertheless, it were better that he should fall than thee, for behold, he has repented of his sins; but if thou shouldst fall at this time, in thine anger, thy soul could not be saved.

18 And again, it is expedient that thou shouldst forbear; for if thou shouldst slay thy son, he being an innocent man, his blood would cry from the ground to the Lord his God, for vengeance to come upon thee; and perhaps thou wouldst lose thy soul.

19 Now when Ammon had said these words unto him, he answered him, saying: I know that if I should slay my son, that I should shed innocent blood; for it is thou that hast sought to destroy him.

20 And he stretched forth his hand to slay Ammon. But Ammon withstood his blows, and also smote his arm that he could not use it.

21 Now when the king saw that Ammon could slay him, he began to plead with Ammon that he would spare his life.

22 But Ammon raised his sword, and said unto him: Behold, I will smite thee except thou wilt grant unto me that my brethren may be cast out of prison.

23 Now the king, fearing he should lose his life, said: If thou wilt spare me I will grant unto thee whatsoever thou wilt ask, even to half of the kingdom.

24 Now when Ammon saw that he had wrought upon the old king according to his desire, he said unto him: If thou wilt grant that my brethren may be cast out of prison, and also that Lamoni may retain his kingdom, and that ye be not displeased with him, but grant that he may do according to his own desires in whatsoever thing he thinketh, then will I spare thee; otherwise I will smite thee to the earth.

25 Now when Ammon had said these words, the king began to rejoice because of his life.

26 And when he saw that Ammon had no desire to destroy him, and when he also saw the great love he had for his son Lamoni, he was astonished exceedingly, and said: Because this is all that thou hast desired, that I would release thy brethren, and suffer that my son Lamoni should retain his kingdom, behold, I will grant unto you that my son may retain his kingdom from this time and forever; and I will govern him no more—

27 And I will also grant unto thee that thy brethren may be cast out of prison, and thou and thy brethren may come unto me, in my kingdom; for I shall greatly desire to see thee. For the king was greatly astonished at the words which he had spoken, and also at the words which had been spoken by his son Lamoni, therefore he was desirous to learn them.

vv. 7–27 We should trust in God even when we might not understand His reasons.

- Write on the board, "Friend's Advice" and next to it, "God's Advice." Ask, *If God specifically told you to do one thing, but a friend advised you to do another, which would you choose? Why might following God's advice work out better?*

- In verses 1–7, look for where King Lamoni and Ammon traveled. What were their reasons for going?

- Analyze:
  - Was Lamoni's plan bad?
  - Was Ammon's plan bad?
  - How was God able to help them accomplish what they desired?
  - What do you learn about God's knowledge and power from this example?

- Invite someone to summarize what happens along the journey to release Ammon's brethren.

- Analyze: *How might the situation have been different if they had met with the king before his throne? Did God know they would meet the king while traveling?*

- Apply: *What lesson does this teach?*

- Have class members cross-reference Isaiah 55:8–9 in their margins. Read the verse

Notes

together. Testify and challenge class members to trust in God even when His reasons are not understood.

vv. 10–13 Grudges keep happiness and healing from our lives.

- 🔎 *In verses 10–13, look for how the Lamanites usually felt about the Nephites.*
- ❓ Analyze: *Why did the king and the Lamanites have such hard feelings toward Nephites?*
- ✏️ Invite class members to cross-reference Mosiah 10:12–17 in their margins. Have a class member read the verse aloud.
- ❓ Apply: *What results from holding grudges? What is the solution to holding grudges?*
- 💬 "Resentment is like taking poison and waiting for the other person to die." —Malachy McCourt
- ♥ Being sensitive of the personal subject matter, encourage someone in the class to share an appropriate experience when forgiveness healed their bad feelings. Invite the class to forgive in order to bring greater happiness and healing in their lives.

28 And it came to pass that Ammon and Lamoni proceeded on their journey towards the land of Middoni. And Lamoni found favor in the eyes of the king of the land; therefore the brethren of Ammon were brought forth out of prison.

29 And when Ammon did meet them he was exceedingly sorrowful, for behold they were naked, and their skins were worn exceedingly because of being bound with strong cords. And they also had suffered hunger, thirst, and all kinds of afflictions; nevertheless they were patient in all their sufferings.

30 And, as it happened, it was their lot to have fallen into the hands of a more hardened and a more stiffnecked people; therefore they would not hearken unto their words, and they had cast them out, and had smitten them, and had driven them from house to house, and from place to place, even until they had arrived in the land of Middoni; and there they were taken and cast into prison, and bound with strong cords, and kept in prison for many days, and were delivered by Lamoni and Ammon.

Index Topics: missionary work, trusting in God, grudges, forgiveness

ALMA 21

"They Brought Many to the Knowledge of the Truth"
About 91–81 BC

1–13, Aaron and his brethren preach of Christ to the hardened Lamanites and are imprisoned; 14–17, Aaron and his brethren are freed from prison and preach with success; 18–23, King Lamoni builds synagogues, and allows all to worship freely.

1 Now when Ammon and his brethren separated themselves in the borders of the land of the Lamanites, behold Aaron took his journey towards the land which was called by the Lamanites, Jerusalem, calling it after the land of their fathers' nativity; and it was away joining the borders of Mormon.

2 Now the Lamanites and the Amalekites and the people of Amulon had built a great city, which was called Jerusalem.

3 Now the Lamanites of themselves were sufficiently hardened, but the Amalekites and the Amulonites were still harder; therefore they did cause the Lamanites that they should harden their hearts, that they should wax strong in wickedness and their abominations.

4 And it came to pass that Aaron came to the city of Jerusalem, and first began to preach to the Amalekites. And he began to preach to them in their synagogues, for they had built synagogues

Notes

after the order of the Nehors; for many of the Amalekites and the Amulonites were after the order of the Nehors.

5 Therefore, as Aaron entered into one of their synagogues to preach unto the people, and as he was speaking unto them, behold there arose an Amalekite and began to contend with him, saying: What is that thou hast testified? Hast thou seen an angel? Why do not angels appear unto us? Behold are not this people as good as thy people?

6 Thou also sayest, except we repent we shall perish. How knowest thou the thought and intent of our hearts? How knowest thou that we have cause to repent? How knowest thou that we are not a righteous people? Behold, we have built sanctuaries, and we do assemble ourselves together to worship God. We do believe that God will save all men.

7 Now Aaron said unto him: Believest thou that the Son of God shall come to redeem mankind from their sins?

8 And the man said unto him: We do not believe that thou knowest any such thing. We do not believe in these foolish traditions. We do not believe that thou knowest of things to come, neither do we believe that thy fathers and also that our fathers did know concerning the things which they spake, of that which is to come.

9 Now Aaron began to open the scriptures unto them concerning the coming of Christ, and also concerning the resurrection of the dead, and that there could be no redemption for mankind save it were through the death and sufferings of Christ, and the atonement of his blood.

10 And it came to pass as he began to expound these things unto them they were angry with him, and began to mock him; and they would not hear the words which he spake.

11 Therefore, when he saw that they would not hear his words, he departed out of their synagogue, and came over to a village which was called Ani-Anti, and there he found Muloki preaching the word unto them; and also Ammah and his brethren. And they contended with many about the word.

12 And it came to pass that they saw that the people would harden their hearts, therefore they departed and came over into the land of Middoni. And they did preach the word unto many, and few believed on the words which they taught.

13 Nevertheless, Aaron and a certain number of his brethren were taken and cast into prison, and the remainder of them fled out of the land of Middoni unto the regions round about.

14 And those who were cast into prison suffered many things, and they were delivered by the hand of Lamoni and Ammon, and they were fed and clothed.

15 And they went forth again to declare the word, and thus they were delivered for the first time out of prison; and thus they had suffered.

16 And they went forth whithersoever they were led by the Spirit of the Lord, preaching the word of God in every synagogue of the Amalekites, or in every assembly of the Lamanites where they could be admitted.

17 And it came to pass that the Lord began to bless them, insomuch that they brought many to the knowledge of the truth; yea, they did convince many of their sins, and of the traditions of their fathers, which were not correct.

18 And it came to pass that Ammon and Lamoni returned from the land of Middoni to the land of Ishmael, which was the land of their inheritance.

19 And king Lamoni would not suffer that Ammon should serve him, or be his servant.

20 But he caused that there should be synagogues built in the land of Ishmael; and he caused that his people, or the people who were under his reign, should assemble themselves together.

21 And he did rejoice over them, and he did teach them many things. And he did also declare unto them that they were a people who were under him, and that they were a free people, that they were

Notes

free from the oppressions of the king, his father; for that his father had granted unto him that he might reign over the people who were in the land of Ishmael, and in all the land round about.

22 And he also declared unto them that they might have the liberty of worshiping the Lord their God according to their desires, in whatsoever place they were in, if it were in the land which was under the reign of king Lamoni.

23 And Ammon did preach unto the people of king Lamoni; and it came to pass that he did teach them all things concerning things pertaining to righteousness. And he did exhort them daily, with all diligence; and they gave heed unto his word, and they were zealous for keeping the commandments of God.

vv. 3–23 The preaching of "all things pertaining to righteousness" leads to lasting conversion.

- Ask class members the following questions: *Which mission in the entire Church do you think has the lowest success rate? Which mission do you think has the highest success rate?* Allow class members to respond and ask a few of them which mission they would rather go to as a missionary and why. Inform the class that Aaron and his brethren found themselves in a more difficult mission.

- After informing the class of the difficult mission of Aaron and his brethren, write the following quote on the board by Elder Francisco J. Viñas. "Teaching our members and families about the things pertaining to righteousness is essential in the process of achieving an enduring conversion since it can lead them to obtain a correct knowledge of the Lord's commandments, the principles and doctrines of the gospel, and the requirements and ordinances with which we must comply in order to achieve salvation in the Lord's kingdom" ("Things Pertaining to Righteousness," *Ensign*, April 2010, 107).

- *According to Elder Viñas what is one of the keys of conversion?* Underline from the quote or write on the board the class's response.

- Tell the class that there are three groups who react differently to the word of God being preached unto them. Invite class members to read about each of the groups and mark in the scriptures how they react to the preaching of all things pertaining to righteousness.

    Amalekites and Amulonites—vv. 3–11

    Those convinced of sins—vv. 16–17

    King Lamoni's people—vv. 19–23

- Apply: You may want to consider focusing on the word "zealous" in your discussion using the following questions.
    - *Why do some receive the word of God while others do not?*
    - *What does it mean to be zealous? (v. 23)*
    - *What does "daily" in the verse have to do with being zealous? (v. 23)*
    - *What is the difference between someone who is zealous and someone who is overzealous?*

- Testify of the power of the word of God in helping all of us become converted to the gospel of Christ. Invite class members to teach, learn, and understand all things pertaining to righteousness so that we may be converted to the gospel.

> **Teaching Tips from Prophets' Lips** President Henry B. Eyring: "You will teach with the Spirit of God when you teach the word of God.... If you will qualify to be taught by the Spirit, you will be able to teach by the Spirit" ("To Know and To Love God," Address to Religious Educators, Feb 27, 2010).

Index Topics: missionary work, power of the word

Notes

ALMA 22

"I Will Give Away All My Sins to Know Thee"
About 91–81 BC

1–3 Aaron is led by the Spirit to Lamoni's Father; 4–14, Aaron teaches Lamoni's father about the Creation, Fall, and Atonement; 15–18, King Lamoni's father is born of God; 19–26, The king's household is converted to the gospel; 27–35, Nephite and Lamanite geography is set forth.

1 Now, as Ammon was thus teaching the people of Lamoni continually, we will return to the account of Aaron and his brethren; for after he departed from the land of Middoni he was led by the Spirit to the land of Nephi, even to the house of the king which was over all the land save it were the land of Ishmael; and he was the father of Lamoni.

2 And it came to pass that he went in unto him into the king's palace, with his brethren, and bowed himself before the king, and said unto him: Behold, O king, we are the brethren of Ammon, whom thou hast delivered out of prison.

3 And now, O king, if thou wilt spare our lives, we will be thy servants. And the king said unto them: Arise, for I will grant unto you your lives, and I will not suffer that ye shall be my servants; but I will insist that ye shall administer unto me; for I have been somewhat troubled in mind because of the generosity and the greatness of the words of thy brother Ammon; and I desire to know the cause why he has not come up out of Middoni with thee.

4 And Aaron said unto the king: Behold, the Spirit of the Lord has called him another way; he has gone to the land of Ishmael, to teach the people of Lamoni.

5 Now the king said unto them: What is this that ye have said concerning the Spirit of the Lord? Behold, this is the thing which doth trouble me.

6 And also, what is this that Ammon said—If ye will repent ye shall be saved, and if ye will not repent, ye shall be cast off at the last day?

7 And Aaron answered him and said unto him: Believest thou that there is a God? And the king said: I know that the Amalekites say that there is a God, and I have granted unto them that they should build sanctuaries, that they may assemble themselves together to worship him. And if now thou sayest there is a God, behold I will believe.

8 And now when Aaron heard this, his heart began to rejoice, and he said: Behold, assuredly as thou livest, O king, there is a God.

9 And the king said: Is God that Great Spirit that brought our fathers out of the land of Jerusalem?

10 And Aaron said unto him: Yea, he is that Great Spirit, and he created all things both in heaven and in earth. Believest thou this?

11 And he said: Yea, I believe that the Great Spirit created all things, and I desire that ye should tell me concerning all these things, and I will believe thy words.

12 And it came to pass that when Aaron saw that the king would believe his words, he began from the creation of Adam, reading the scriptures unto the king—how God created man after his own image, and that God gave him commandments, and that because of transgression, man had fallen.

13 And Aaron did expound unto him the scriptures from the creation of Adam, laying the fall of man before him, and their carnal state and also the plan of redemption, which was prepared from the foundation of the world, through Christ, for all whosoever would believe on his name.

14 And since man had fallen he could not merit anything of himself; but the sufferings and death of Christ atone for their sins, through faith and repentance, and so forth; and that he breaketh the bands of death, that the grave shall have no victory, and that the sting of death should be

Notes

swallowed up in the hopes of glory; and Aaron did expound all these things unto the king.

15 And it came to pass that after Aaron had expounded these things unto him, the king said: What shall I do that I may have this eternal life of which thou hast spoken? Yea, what shall I do that I may be born of God, having this wicked spirit rooted out of my breast, and receive his Spirit, that I may be filled with joy, that I may not be cast off at the last day? Behold, said he, I will give up all that I possess, yea, I will forsake my kingdom, that I may receive this great joy.

16 But Aaron said unto him: If thou desirest this thing, if thou wilt bow down before God, yea, if thou wilt repent of all thy sins, and will bow down before God, and call on his name in faith, believing that ye shall receive, then shalt thou receive the hope which thou desirest.

17 And it came to pass that when Aaron had said these words, the king did bow down before the Lord, upon his knees; yea, even he did prostrate himself upon the earth, and cried mightily, saying:

18 O God, Aaron hath told me that there is a God; and if there is a God, and if thou art God, wilt thou make thyself known unto me, and I will give away all my sins to know thee, and that I may be raised from the dead, and be saved at the last day. And now when the king had said these words, he was struck as if he were dead.

vv. 1–18 The word leads to repentance, which brings a desire to change.

Role-play verses 1–18 by inviting two class members to read the dialogue of the two main characters in this chapter, Aaron and King Lamoni's father. Additionally, you may invite a class member to be a narrator or you may want to do this yourself to help the flow of the reading. Read verse 1 as a way to introduce the context and then have the class member who is reading the part of Aaron begin in verse 2. You may also consider reminding the class of what had happened in the encounter the king had with his son King Lamoni and with Ammon in Alma chapter 20. It might be helpful to make two or three separate copies of the text and highlight each part to facilitate the role-play. Before the two class members begin reading, hand out the following questions to the remaining class members. Give only one question to each class member. Most likely more than one class member will have the same question. Invite them to think about the answer and be prepared to share their insights with the class.

1. What change came upon the king?

2. Why was the king willing to listen?

3. Why do you think the king was willing to give up his kingdom?

4. Why do you think the king was willing to give away all of his sins?

5 What role did Aaron have in the king's conversion?

6. What part of Aaron's message do you think had the greatest impact on the king's conversion?

7. What do you think is the overall message of this story?

Invite class members to discuss the answers to their questions. Use appropriate follow-up questions to deepen the discussion. Consider using the quote below.

Elder Ringwood of the Seventy stated, "When Aaron arrived to teach the king, his heart had changed and he had an easiness to believe, as he said to Aaron, 'Behold I will believe' (Alma 22:7). He then expressed a willingness to give up all he possessed, even to forsake his kingdom, to have the joy of the Lord (Alma 22:15). When he first prayed, he offered that which Heavenly Father wanted when he said, 'I will give away all my sins to know thee' (Alma 22:18). An easiness and willingness to believe the word of God will come from repentance and obedience" ("An Easiness and Willingness to Believe," *Ensign*, October 2009, 101).

Notes

ALMA 22

- ✋ Invite class members to highlight and number the steps to being saved in their scriptures based on Elder Ringwood's words (verse 7, believe; verse 15, give up all possessions; verse 18, give up all sins to know God). Indicate that they could also write in the margin of their scriptures near these verses, "How to receive eternal life."

- ♥ Ask class members to think about the following question. *What are we willing to give up for the gospel?* Invite them to write down and complete the following, "I will give away _____ to know God." Invite them to evaluate their lives, to commit to change, and to repent that they may come to know God.

19 And it came to pass that his servants ran and told the queen all that had happened unto the king. And she came in unto the king; and when she saw him lay as if he were dead, and also Aaron and his brethren standing as though they had been the cause of his fall, she was angry with them, and commanded that her servants, or the servants of the king, should take them and slay them.

20 Now the servants had seen the cause of the king's fall, therefore they durst not lay their hands on Aaron and his brethren; and they pled with the queen saying: Why commandest thou that we should slay these men, when behold one of them is mightier than us all? Therefore we shall fall before them.

21 Now when the queen saw the fear of the servants she also began to fear exceedingly, lest there should some evil come upon her. And she commanded her servants that they should go and call the people, that they might slay Aaron and his brethren.

22 Now when Aaron saw the determination of the queen, he, also knowing the hardness of the hearts of the people, feared lest that a multitude should assemble themselves together, and there should be a great contention and a disturbance among them; therefore he put forth his hand and raised the king from the earth, and said unto him: Stand. And he stood upon his feet, receiving his strength.

23 Now this was done in the presence of the queen and many of the servants. And when they saw it they greatly marveled, and began to fear. And the king stood forth, and began to minister unto them. And he did minister unto them, insomuch that his whole household were converted unto the Lord.

24 Now there was a multitude gathered together because of the commandment of the queen, and there began to be great murmurings among them because of Aaron and his brethren.

25 But the king stood forth among them and administered unto them. And they were pacified towards Aaron and those who were with him.

26 And it came to pass that when the king saw that the people were pacified, he caused that Aaron and his brethren should stand forth in the midst of the multitude, and that they should preach the word unto them.

vv. 19–26 The impact of a missionary is great.

- ✋ Have a class member summarize the ending of the story by explaining what they remember.

- 🔍 Invite class members to find the two results of the miraculous conversion of the king. (v. 23, the king's household was converted; v. 26, Aaron and his brethren were allowed to preach the word unto all the people round about the land.)

27 And it came to pass that the king sent a proclamation throughout all the land, amongst all his people who were in all his land, who were in all the regions round about, which was bordering even to the sea, on the east and on the west, and which was divided from the land of Zarahemla by a narrow strip of wilderness, which ran from the sea east even to the sea west, and round about on the borders of the seashore, and the borders of the wilderness which was on the north by the land of Zarahemla, through the borders of Manti, by the head of the river Sidon, running

Notes

from the east towards the west—and thus were the Lamanites and the Nephites divided.

28 Now, the more idle part of the Lamanites lived in the wilderness, and dwelt in tents; and they were spread through the wilderness on the west, in the land of Nephi; yea, and also on the west of the land of Zarahemla, in the borders by the seashore, and on the west in the land of Nephi, in the place of their fathers' first inheritance, and thus bordering along by the seashore.

29 And also there were many Lamanites on the east by the seashore, whither the Nephites had driven them. And thus the Nephites were nearly surrounded by the Lamanites; nevertheless the Nephites had taken possession of all the northern parts of the land bordering on the wilderness, at the head of the river Sidon, from the east to the west, round about on the wilderness side; on the north, even until they came to the land which they called Bountiful.

30 And it bordered upon the land which they called Desolation, it being so far northward that it came into the land which had been peopled and been destroyed, of whose bones we have spoken, which was discovered by the people of Zarahemla, it being the place of their first landing.

31 And they came from there up into the south wilderness. Thus the land on the northward was called Desolation, and the land on the southward was called Bountiful, it being the wilderness which is filled with all manner of wild animals of every kind, a part of which had come from the land northward for food.

32 And now, it was only the distance of a day and a half's journey for a Nephite, on the line Bountiful and the land Desolation, from the east to the west sea; and thus the land of Nephi and the land of Zarahemla were nearly surrounded by water, there being a small neck of land between the land northward and the land southward.

33 And it came to pass that the Nephites had inhabited the land Bountiful, even from the east unto the west sea, and thus the Nephites in their wisdom, with their guards and their armies, had hemmed in the Lamanites on the south, that thereby they should have no more possession on the north, that they might not overrun the land northward.

34 Therefore the Lamanites could have no more possessions only in the land of Nephi, and the wilderness round about. Now this was wisdom in the Nephites—as the Lamanites were an enemy to them, they would not suffer their afflictions on every hand, and also that they might have a country whither they might flee, according to their desires.

35 And now I, after having said this, return again to the account of Ammon and Aaron, Omner and Himni, and their brethren.

? Ask, *Why would Mormon take up space in the Book of Mormon to explain the geography of the land? How does an understanding of the geography help us as we study the Book of Mormon?*

Index Topics: missionary work, conversion, power of the word

ALMA 23

The Anti-Nephi-Lehies
About 91–81 BC

1–7, Ammon and his brethren are allowed to preach to all the Lamanites and have great success; 8–15, The seven lands of the converted Lamanites are named; 16–18, They become industrious and the curse is taken away.

1 Behold, now it came to pass that the king of the Lamanites sent a proclamation among all his people, that they should not lay their hands on Ammon, or Aaron, or Omner, or Himni, nor either of their brethren who should go forth preaching the word of God, in whatsoever place they should be, in any part of their land.

Notes

2 Yea, he sent a decree among them, that they should not lay their hands on them to bind them, or to cast them into prison; neither should they spit upon them, nor smite them, nor cast them out of their synagogues, nor scourge them; neither should they cast stones at them, but that they should have free access to their houses, and also their temples, and their sanctuaries.

3 And thus they might go forth and preach the word according to their desires, for the king had been converted unto the Lord, and all his household; therefore he sent his proclamation throughout the land unto his people, that the word of God might have no obstruction, but that it might go forth throughout all the land, that his people might be convinced concerning the wicked traditions of their fathers, and that they might be convinced that they were all brethren, and that they ought not to murder, nor to plunder, nor to steal, nor to commit adultery, nor to commit any manner of wickedness.

4 And now it came to pass that when the king had sent forth this proclamation, that Aaron and his brethren went forth from city to city, and from one house of worship to another, establishing churches, and consecrating priests and teachers throughout the land among the Lamanites, to preach and to teach the word of God among them; and thus they began to have great success.

5 And thousands were brought to the knowledge of the Lord, yea, thousands were brought to believe in the traditions of the Nephites; and they were taught the records and prophecies which were handed down even to the present time.

6 And as sure as the Lord liveth, so sure as many as believed, or as many as were brought to the knowledge of the truth, through the preaching of Ammon and his brethren, according to the spirit of revelation and of prophecy, and the power of God working miracles in them—yea, I say unto you, as the Lord liveth, as many of the Lamanites as believed in their preaching, and were converted unto the Lord, never did fall away.

7 For they became a righteous people; they did lay down the weapons of their rebellion, that they did not fight against God any more, neither against any of their brethren.

vv. 1–7 If we are diligent missionaries, we can help God change a person's heart.

- Before class, have the following question written on the board: "What is harder, God healing someone's physical body or God changing someone's heart?" Discuss their responses.

- Elder Dallin H. Oaks stated, "Changing bodies or protecting temples are miracles, but an even greater miracle is a mighty change of heart by a son or daughter of God (Mosiah 5:2). A change of heart, including new attitudes, priorities, and desires, is greater and more important than any miracle involving the body. I repeat, the body will be resurrected in any event, but a change affecting what the scripture calls the 'heart' of a spirit son or daughter of God is a change whose effect is eternal. If of the right kind, this change opens the door to the process of repentance that cleanses us to dwell in the presence of God" (Dallin H. Oaks, "Miracles," *Ensign*, June 2001).

- In verses 1–7, look for what circumstances helped this miracle of changing hearts to occur.

- Analyze: *What might have happened if Ammon and his brethren had decided not to serve missions? What might have happened if they had returned home after facing some difficulties?*

- Apply: *What is the lesson for us from these verses?*

- Invite class members to write down one way they can be faithful in missionary work. Challenge the class to be diligent in sharing the gospel with others, whether as member missionaries or as full-time missionaries.

8 Now, these are they who were converted unto the Lord:

Notes

9 The people of the Lamanites who were in the land of Ishmael;

10 And also of the people of the Lamanites who were in the land of Middoni;

11 And also of the people of the Lamanites who were in the city of Nephi;

12 And also of the people of the Lamanites who were in the land of Shilom, and who were in the land of Shemlon, and in the city of Lemuel, and in the city of Shimnilom.

13 And these are the names of the cities of the Lamanites which were converted unto the Lord; and these are they that laid down the weapons of their rebellion, yea, all their weapons of war; and they were all Lamanites.

14 And the Amalekites were not converted, save only one; neither were any of the Amulonites; but they did harden their hearts, and also the hearts of the Lamanites in that part of the land wheresoever they dwelt, yea, and all their villages and all their cities.

15 Therefore, we have named all the cities of the Lamanites in which they did repent and come to the knowledge of the truth, and were converted.

vv. 8–15 A hard heart prohibits conversion.

- Read verses 8–15 and note the name of any city or land whose people were converted.

- Note to the class that some people were not converted. Ask, *Why were the people in some cities not converted according to verse 14?*

- Invite class members to cross-reference Alma 24:30. Note: The next chapter covers this principle so you may want to combine these verses with Alma chapter 24.

16 And now it came to pass that the king and those who were converted were desirous that they might have a name, that thereby they might be distinguished from their brethren; therefore the king consulted with Aaron and many of their priests, concerning the name that they should take upon them, that they might be distinguished.

17 And it came to pass that they called their names Anti-Nephi-Lehies; and they were called by this name and were no more called Lamanites.

18 And they began to be a very industrious people; yea, and they were friendly with the Nephites; therefore, they did open a correspondence with them, and the curse of God did no more follow them.

vv. 16–18 The Meaning of Anti-Nephi-Lehi.

- Read verses 16–18 and look for the name these new converts wanted to take upon themselves.

- Share the following quote that explains what the name Anti-Nephi-Lehi could mean: "The name Anti-Nephi-Lehi may mean that the new converts desired to become like Nephi and Lehi and may have chosen a new name that reflected their righteous desires. Studies show that in some languages there is a common root corresponding to the word 'anti' that means 'in the face of' or 'facing,' like you would face a mirror. It may have a meaning similar to the word 'imitation.' In this light the name Anti-Nephi-Lehies might refer to those who desire to imitate what the descendants of Nephi and Lehi taught" (Daniel H. Ludlow, *A Companion to Your Study of the Book of Mormon* [1976], 210).

- Note with the class the phrase, "the curse of God did no more follow them" (v. 18). Some think the curse of the Lamanites was their dark skin. It is actually a sign of their curse, but the curse itself was manifest in the hardness of their hearts (see 2 Nephi 5:21). Therefore the phrase "the curse of God did no more follow them" means that the converted Lamanites hearts' were changed and they became industrious and friendly with the Nephites. On the other hand, 3 Nephi 2:14–16 is an example of their skins being changed.

Teaching Tips from Prophets' Lips "Our instruction ought to be so provocative, so spiritually sweet, so new and interesting that the students say to themselves, 'I felt so much that I will think about it this afternoon and tomorrow and next week and next month.' In

Notes

that way, our lesson will take on a life of its own and bring new thoughts" (Jeffrey R. Holland, "Teaching and Learning in the Church," *Ensign*, June 2007, 88–105).

Index Topics: missionary work; conversion; rebellion; curse

ALMA 24

"They Buried Their Weapons of War"
About 91–81 BC

1–6, The unconverted desire to destroy the Anti-Nephi-Lehies who will not fight back and the kingdom is conferred on another; 7–16, The new king explains why they will not fight again; 17–20, They bury their weapons in covenant; 21–27, Many are martyred and more Lamanites believe; 28–30, The Amulonites and Amalekites become more hardened.

1 And it came to pass that the Amalekites and the Amulonites and the Lamanites who were in the land of Amulon, and also in the land of Helam, and who were in the land of Jerusalem, and in fine, in all the land round about, who had not been converted and had not taken upon them the name of Anti-Nephi-Lehi, were stirred up by the Amalekites and by the Amulonites to anger against their brethren.

2 And their hatred became exceedingly sore against them, even insomuch that they began to rebel against their king, insomuch that they would not that he should be their king; therefore, they took up arms against the people of Anti-Nephi-Lehi.

3 Now the king conferred the kingdom upon his son, and he called his name Anti-Nephi-Lehi.

4 And the king died in that selfsame year that the Lamanites began to make preparations for war against the people of God.

5 Now when Ammon and his brethren and all those who had come up with him saw the preparations of the Lamanites to destroy their brethren, they came forth to the land of Midian, and there Ammon met all his brethren; and from thence they came to the land of Ishmael that they might hold a council with Lamoni and also with his brother Anti-Nephi-Lehi, what they should do to defend themselves against the Lamanites.

6 Now there was not one soul among all the people who had been converted unto the Lord that would take up arms against their brethren; nay, they would not even make any preparations for war; yea, and also their king commanded them that they should not.

7 Now, these are the words which he said unto the people concerning the matter: I thank my God, my beloved people, that our great God has in goodness sent these our brethren, the Nephites, unto us to preach unto us, and to convince us of the traditions of our wicked fathers.

8 And behold, I thank my great God that he has given us a portion of his Spirit to soften our hearts, that we have opened a correspondence with these brethren, the Nephites.

9 And behold, I also thank my God, that by opening this correspondence we have been convinced of our sins, and of the many murders which we have committed.

10 And I also thank my God, yea, my great God, that he hath granted unto us that we might repent of these things, and also that he hath forgiven us of those our many sins and murders which we have committed, and taken away the guilt from our hearts, through the merits of his Son.

11 And now behold, my brethren, since it has been all that we could do (as we were the most lost of all mankind) to repent of all our sins and the many murders which we have committed, and to get God to take them away from our hearts, for it was all we could do to repent sufficiently before God that he would take away our stain—

12 Now, my best beloved brethren, since God hath taken away our stains, and our swords have

Notes

become bright, then let us stain our swords no more with the blood of our brethren.

13 Behold, I say unto you, Nay, let us retain our swords that they be not stained with the blood of our brethren; for perhaps, if we should stain our swords again they can no more be washed bright through the blood of the Son of our great God, which shall be shed for the atonement of our sins.

14 And the great God has had mercy on us, and made these things known unto us that we might not perish; yea, and he has made these things known unto us beforehand, because he loveth our souls as well as he loveth our children; therefore, in his mercy he doth visit us by his angels, that the plan of salvation might be made known unto us as well as unto future generations.

15 Oh, how merciful is our God! And now behold, since it has been as much as we could do to get our stains taken away from us, and our swords are made bright, let us hide them away that they may be kept bright, as a testimony to our God at the last day, or at the day that we shall be brought to stand before him to be judged, that we have not stained our swords in the blood of our brethren since he imparted his word unto us and has made us clean thereby.

16 And now, my brethren, if our brethren seek to destroy us, behold, we will hide away our swords, yea, even we will bury them deep in the earth, that they may be kept bright, as a testimony that we have never used them, at the last day; and if our brethren destroy us, behold, we shall go to our God and shall be saved.

17 And now it came to pass that when the king had made an end of these sayings, and all the people were assembled together, they took their swords, and all the weapons which were used for the shedding of man's blood, and they did bury them up deep in the earth.

18 And this they did, it being in their view a testimony to God, and also to men, that they never would use weapons again for the shedding of man's blood; and this they did, vouching and covenanting with God, that rather than shed the blood of their brethren they would give up their own lives; and rather than take away from a brother they would give unto him; and rather than spend their days in idleness they would labor abundantly with their hands.

vv. 1–17

- To summarize the verses, assign each class member one verse. Give them one minute to read their verse and prepare to summarize it in one sentence. Then, in order, have each person quickly summarize their verse.

vv. 16–18 Forsaking our sins is pleasing to God. Sometimes to overcome a sin, we need to remove our access to that sin.

- Give each class member a small piece of paper and something to write with. Ask, *In verses 16–18, what sin did the Lamanites struggle with the most?* With great assurances of privacy, ask class members to write a sin they struggle with on the piece of paper. Explain that they need to retain it for later in the lesson. Note: the class will get the opportunity to bury their sin.

- *In verses 16–17, look for what the converted Lamanites did so they would not be tempted to return to their sins.*

- Analyze:
  - *Why do you think the Lamanites chose to bury their weapons?*
  - *What could the burying of weapons represent for them?*
  - *Were the weapons their actual sins?*

- Apply: *How does this story apply today? What weapons could a person "bury" today?* (Consider providing examples of sins the class can discuss such as Word of Wisdom, immorality, and pornography.)

Note with the class that the weapons of the Anti-Nephi-Lehies weren't the actual sin, but rather the means of sinning. Ask, *In what ways can people today remove the means of sinning in their lives?*

Notes

ALMA 24

❤ Before class, locate a suitable place outdoors in which you can dig a hole to "bury" the sins, or if you feel that is not feasible, you could bring a container of dirt into the classroom instead. Refer class members to the paper their sin is written on. Discuss together if they would be willing to bury their sins, similar to the Anti-Nephi-Lehies, as evidence of their willingness to forsake them. Invite class members to bury their pieces of paper (sins), then replace the dirt to make the area appear as if it was untouched. Consider inviting class members to pray and seek the Lord's help to overcome their sins.

19 And thus we see that, when these Lamanites were brought to believe and to know the truth, they were firm, and would suffer even unto death rather than commit sin; and thus we see that they buried their weapons of peace, or they buried the weapons of war, for peace.

20 And it came to pass that their brethren, the Lamanites, made preparations for war, and came up to the land of Nephi for the purpose of destroying the king, and to place another in his stead, and also of destroying the people of Anti-Nephi-Lehi out of the land.

21 Now when the people saw that they were coming against them they went out to meet them, and prostrated themselves before them to the earth, and began to call on the name of the Lord; and thus they were in this attitude when the Lamanites began to fall upon them, and began to slay them with the sword.

22 And thus without meeting any resistance, they did slay a thousand and five of them; and we know that they are blessed, for they have gone to dwell with their God.

23 Now when the Lamanites saw that their brethren would not flee from the sword, neither would they turn aside to the right hand or to the left, but that they would lie down and perish, and praised God even in the very act of perishing under the sword—

24 Now when the Lamanites saw this they did forbear from slaying them; and there were many whose hearts had swollen in them for those of their brethren who had fallen under the sword, for they repented of the things which they had done.

25 And it came to pass that they threw down their weapons of war, and they would not take them again, for they were stung for the murders which they had committed; and they came down even as their brethren, relying upon the mercies of those whose arms were lifted to slay them.

26 And it came to pass that the people of God were joined that day by more than the number who had been slain; and those who had been slain were righteous people, therefore we have no reason to doubt but what they were saved.

27 And there was not a wicked man slain among them; but there were more than a thousand brought to the knowledge of the truth; thus we see that the Lord worketh in many ways to the salvation of his people.

vv. 21–27 "The Lord worketh in many ways to the salvation of his people."

🔍 *In verses 21–24, look for how many Anti-Nephi-Lehies died on this day of martyrdom. In verses 25–27, what effect did their deaths have on many of the attacking Lamanites?*

❓ Analyze: *How many were converted that day? (vv. 22, 26–27)*

Note with the class that previous to this martyrdom, the attacking Lamanites were not converted to the gospel even though they had been taught by missionaries. Ask, *Why do they now become converted? In your own words, what is the principle of verses 26 and 27?*

28 Now the greatest number of those of the Lamanites who slew so many of their brethren were Amalekites and Amulonites, the greatest number of whom were after the order of the Nehors.

29 Now, among those who joined the people of the Lord, there were none who were Amalekites or

Notes

Amulonites, or who were of the order of Nehor, but they were actual descendants of Laman and Lemuel.

30 And thus we can plainly discern, that after a people have been once enlightened by the Spirit of God, and have had great knowledge of things pertaining to righteousness, and then have fallen away into sin and transgression, they become more hardened, and thus their state becomes worse than though they had never known these things.

Index Topics: conversion, rebellion, repentance, additions

ALMA 25

The Final Destruction of the Priests of King Noah
About 81–77 BC

1–3, The Lamanites turn their aggression from the Anti-Nephi-Lehies toward the Nephites; 4–7, More Lamanites are converted; 8–17, The priests of King Noah are hunted down and killed, fulfilling Abinadi's words.

Note: Alma chapter 25 concludes the story from Alma 23–24.

1 And behold, now it came to pass that those Lamanites were more angry because they had slain their brethren; therefore they swore vengeance upon the Nephites; and they did no more attempt to slay the people of Anti-Nephi-Lehi at that time.

2 But they took their armies and went over into the borders of the land of Zarahemla, and fell upon the people who were in the land of Ammonihah and destroyed them.

3 And after that, they had many battles with the Nephites, in the which they were driven and slain.

4 And among the Lamanites who were slain were almost all the seed of Amulon and his brethren, who were the priests of Noah, and they were slain by the hands of the Nephites;

5 And the remainder, having fled into the east wilderness, and having usurped the power and authority over the Lamanites, caused that many of the Lamanites should perish by fire because of their belief—

6 For many of them, after having suffered much loss and so many afflictions, began to be stirred up in remembrance of the words which Aaron and his brethren had preached to them in their land; therefore they began to disbelieve the traditions of their fathers, and to believe in the Lord, and that he gave great power unto the Nephites; and thus there were many of them converted in the wilderness.

7 And it came to pass that those rulers who were the remnant of the children of Amulon caused that they should be put to death, yea, all those that believed in these things.

8 Now this martyrdom caused that many of their brethren should be stirred up to anger; and there began to be contention in the wilderness; and the Lamanites began to hunt the seed of Amulon and his brethren and began to slay them; and they fled into the east wilderness.

9 And behold they are hunted at this day by the Lamanites. Thus the words of Abinadi were brought to pass, which he said concerning the seed of the priests who caused that he should suffer death by fire.

10 For he said unto them: What ye shall do unto me shall be a type of things to come.

11 And now Abinadi was the first that suffered death by fire because of his belief in God; now this is what he meant, that many should suffer death by fire, according as he had suffered.

12 And he said unto the priests of Noah that their seed should cause many to be put to death, in the like manner as he was, and that they should be scattered abroad and slain, even as a sheep having no shepherd is driven and slain by wild beasts; and now behold, these words were verified, for

Notes

they were driven by the Lamanites, and they were hunted, and they were smitten.

vv. 1–12 The prophet's words will always be fulfilled.

- ↯ Refer class members to Matthew 5:17–18 to discuss what the Savior is teaching about the words of the prophets. Conduct an Internet search on the phrase "jot and tittle" to learn more about what this phrase means. Explain your research to the class and tell them that they will see two instances of the fulfillment of prophets' words.

- 🔎 **Prophecy**: Alma 8:16; 16:9. **Fulfillment**: Read Alma 25:1–3 to learn what happens to the city of Ammonihah.

- 🔎 **Prophecy**: Alma 13:10; 17:15–20. **Fulfillment**: Alma 25:4–12 to find out what happens to the wicked priests of King Noah.

- ❤ Help class members feel the importance of following a prophet since all of his words will be fulfilled. Refer to "The Family: A Proclamation to the World" and discuss the prophetic council and warnings that are contained in that document.

13 And it came to pass that when the Lamanites saw that they could not overpower the Nephites they returned again to their own land; and many of them came over to dwell in the land of Ishmael and the land of Nephi, and did join themselves to the people of God, who were the people of Anti-Nephi-Lehi.

14 And they did also bury their weapons of war, according as their brethren had, and they began to be a righteous people; and they did walk in the ways of the Lord, and did observe to keep his commandments and his statutes.

15 Yea, and they did keep the law of Moses; for it was expedient that they should keep the law of Moses as yet, for it was not all fulfilled. But notwithstanding the law of Moses, they did look forward to the coming of Christ, considering that the law of Moses was a type of his coming, and believing that they must keep those outward performances until the time that he should be revealed unto them.

16 Now they did not suppose that salvation came by the law of Moses; but the law of Moses did serve to strengthen their faith in Christ; and thus they did retain a hope through faith, unto eternal salvation, relying upon the spirit of prophecy, which spake of those things to come.

17 And now behold, Ammon, and Aaron, and Omner, and Himni, and their brethren did rejoice exceedingly, for the success which they had had among the Lamanites, seeing that the Lord had granted unto them according to their prayers, and that he had also verified his word unto them in every particular.

vv. 13–17 More Lamanites are converted.

- 💡 Note with class members that even more Lamanites are converted and become Anti-Nephi-Lehies due to the example of the faithful new converts. Ask class members if they are striving to be good examples to people who are not currently interested in the Church.

> **Teaching Tips from Prophets' Lips** "Learning by faith cannot be transferred from an instructor to a student through a lecture, a demonstration, or an experiential exercise; rather, a student must exercise faith and act in order to obtain the knowledge for himself or herself" (David A. Bednar, "Seek Learning by Faith," address to CES religious educators, February 3, 2006, 3).

Index: prophets, role of

ALMA 26

The Sons of Mosiah Rejoice in Their Success
About 81–77 BC

Notes

1–10, Ammon rejoices with his brethren in their missionary success; 11–26, Ammon acknowledges that God has been merciful to him and the Lamanites; 27–37, He recounts their success among the Lamanites.

Overarching Principle: We can experience great joy as we reflect on our service in the Lord's kingdom, see our brothers and sisters come to the truth of the gospel, and recognize the Lord's hand in our labors.

1 And now, these are the words of Ammon to his brethren, which say thus: My brothers and my brethren, behold I say unto you, how great reason have we to rejoice; for could we have supposed when we started from the land of Zarahemla that God would have granted unto us such great blessings?

2 And now, I ask, what great blessings has he bestowed upon us? Can ye tell?

3 Behold, I answer for you; for our brethren, the Lamanites, were in darkness, yea, even in the darkest abyss, but behold, how many of them are brought to behold the marvelous light of God! And this is the blessing which hath been bestowed upon us, that we have been made instruments in the hands of God to bring about this great work.

4 Behold, thousands of them do rejoice, and have been brought into the fold of God.

5 Behold, the field was ripe, and blessed are ye, for ye did thrust in the sickle, and did reap with your might, yea, all the day long did ye labor; and behold the number of your sheaves! And they shall be gathered into the garners, that they are not wasted.

6 Yea, they shall not be beaten down by the storm at the last day; yea, neither shall they be harrowed up by the whirlwinds; but when the storm cometh they shall be gathered together in their place, that the storm cannot penetrate to them; yea, neither shall they be driven with fierce winds whithersoever the enemy listeth to carry them.

7 But behold, they are in the hands of the Lord of the harvest, and they are his; and he will raise them up at the last day.

8 Blessed be the name of our God; let us sing to his praise, yea, let us give thanks to his holy name, for he doth work righteousness forever.

9 For if we had not come up out of the land of Zarahemla, these our dearly beloved brethren, who have so dearly beloved us, would still have been racked with hatred against us, yea, and they would also have been strangers to God.

vv. 1–9 Missionary work brings joy.

⚡ Prior to the lesson, contact a member of your class who has a relative or close friend currently serving a mission. Ask the individual to share with the class some of the correspondence with the missionary that demonstrates that person's excitement for the work they are engaged in. If possible and appropriate, consider reading a portion of a letter from the missionary that demonstrates the joy of missionary service. Ask, *What stands out to you in this missionary letter?*

❓ Analyze: Invite class members to read Alma 26:1–9 and ask, *If you had to choose one word to describe the emotion that Ammon is expressing the most, what would it be and why?* List a few of the class members' responses on the board. Then ask, *What is it about missionary work that creates these types of emotions?*

❓ Apply: *Can you think of a time when you felt similar emotions while serving the Lord?*

10 And it came to pass that when Ammon had said these words, his brother Aaron rebuked him, saying: Ammon, I fear that thy joy doth carry thee away unto boasting.

11 But Ammon said unto him: I do not boast in my own strength, nor in my own wisdom; but behold, my joy is full, yea, my heart is brim with joy, and I will rejoice in my God.

Notes

ALMA 26

12 Yea, I know that I am nothing; as to my strength I am weak; therefore I will not boast of myself, but I will boast of my God, for in his strength I can do all things; yea, behold, many mighty miracles we have wrought in this land, for which we will praise his name forever.

13 Behold, how many thousands of our brethren has he loosed from the pains of hell; and they are brought to sing redeeming love, and this because of the power of his word which is in us, therefore have we not great reason to rejoice?

14 Yea, we have reason to praise him forever, for he is the Most High God, and has loosed our brethren from the chains of hell.

15 Yea, they were encircled about with everlasting darkness and destruction; but behold, he has brought them into his everlasting light, yea, into everlasting salvation; and they are encircled about with the matchless bounty of his love; yea, and we have been instruments in his hands of doing this great and marvelous work.

16 Therefore, let us glory, yea, we will glory in the Lord; yea, we will rejoice, for our joy is full; yea, we will praise our God forever. Behold, who can glory too much in the Lord? Yea, who can say too much of his great power, and of his mercy, and of his long-suffering towards the children of men? Behold, I say unto you, I cannot say the smallest part which I feel.

17 Who could have supposed that our God would have been so merciful as to have snatched us from our awful, sinful, and polluted state?

18 Behold, we went forth even in wrath, with mighty threatenings to destroy his church.

19 Oh then, why did he not consign us to an awful destruction, yea, why did he not let the sword of his justice fall upon us, and doom us to eternal despair?

20 Oh, my soul, almost as it were, fleeth at the thought. Behold, he did not exercise his justice upon us, but in his great mercy hath brought us over that everlasting gulf of death and misery, even to the salvation of our souls.

21 And now behold, my brethren, what natural man is there that knoweth these things? I say unto you, there is none that knoweth these things, save it be the penitent.

22 Yea, he that repenteth and exerciseth faith, and bringeth forth good works, and prayeth continually without ceasing—unto such it is given to know the mysteries of God; yea, unto such it shall be given to reveal things which never have been revealed; yea, and it shall be given unto such to bring thousands of souls to repentance, even as it has been given unto us to bring these our brethren to repentance.

vv. 11–22 We must praise the Lord for the great works He performs in our lives.

- *Read verses 10–11 and look for Aaron's concern with Ammon's discussion of missionary work. What careful distinction does Ammon make?*

- Analyze: *What are some events on his mission that Ammon might have been able to boast about? What is the difference between boasting of one's strength and boasting in the Lord?*

- Read verse 16 together as a class. Point out that while Ammon doesn't feel like he can adequately express the glorious nature of the Lord, he does recount a few of the things that have been glorious to him during his mission. Invite class members to read verses 12–22 and make a list of the glorious works of the Lord as recounted by Ammon. Instruct class members to identify one thing from Ammon's words that they feel has also happened in their own lives. Ask them to consider how they could show greater praise for those blessings.

23 Now do ye remember, my brethren, that we said unto our brethren in the land of Zarahemla, we go up to the land of Nephi, to preach unto our brethren, the Lamanites, and they laughed us to scorn?

24 For they said unto us: Do ye suppose that ye can bring the Lamanites to the knowledge of

Notes

the truth? Do ye suppose that ye can convince the Lamanites of the incorrectness of the traditions of their fathers, as stiffnecked a people as they are; whose hearts delight in the shedding of blood; whose days have been spent in the grossest iniquity; whose ways have been the ways of a transgressor from the beginning? Now my brethren, ye remember that this was their language.

25 And moreover they did say: Let us take up arms against them, that we destroy them and their iniquity out of the land, lest they overrun us and destroy us.

26 But behold, my beloved brethren, we came into the wilderness not with the intent to destroy our brethren, but with the intent that perhaps we might save some few of their souls.

27 Now when our hearts were depressed, and we were about to turn back, behold, the Lord comforted us, and said: Go amongst thy brethren, the Lamanites, and bear with patience thine afflictions, and I will give unto you success.

28 And now behold, we have come, and been forth amongst them; and we have been patient in our sufferings, and we have suffered every privation; yea, we have traveled from house to house, relying upon the mercies of the world—not upon the mercies of the world alone but upon the mercies of God.

29 And we have entered into their houses and taught them, and we have taught them in their streets; yea, and we have taught them upon their hills; and we have also entered into their temples and their synagogues and taught them; and we have been cast out, and mocked, and spit upon, and smote upon our cheeks; and we have been stoned, and taken and bound with strong cords, and cast into prison; and through the power and wisdom of God we have been delivered again.

30 And we have suffered all manner of afflictions, and all this, that perhaps we might be the means of saving some soul; and we supposed that our joy would be full if perhaps we could be the means of saving some.

31 Now behold, we can look forth and see the fruits of our labors; and are they few? I say unto you, Nay, they are many; yea, and we can witness of their sincerity, because of their love towards their brethren and also towards us.

32 For behold, they had rather sacrifice their lives than even to take the life of their enemy; and they have buried their weapons of war deep in the earth, because of their love towards their brethren.

33 And now behold I say unto you, has there been so great love in all the land? Behold, I say unto you, Nay, there has not, even among the Nephites.

34 For behold, they would take up arms against their brethren; they would not suffer themselves to be slain. But behold how many of these have laid down their lives; and we know that they have gone to their God, because of their love and of their hatred to sin.

35 Now have we not reason to rejoice? Yea, I say unto you, there never were men that had so great reason to rejoice as we, since the world began; yea, and my joy is carried away, even unto boasting in my God; for he has all power, all wisdom, and all understanding; he comprehendeth all things, and he is a merciful Being, even unto salvation, to those who will repent and believe on his name.

36 Now if this is boasting, even so will I boast; for this is my life and my light, my joy and my salvation, and my redemption from everlasting wo. Yea, blessed is the name of my God, who has been mindful of this people, who are a branch of the tree of Israel, and has been lost from its body in a strange land; yea, I say, blessed be the name of my God, who has been mindful of us, wanderers in a strange land.

37 Now my brethren, we see that God is mindful of every people, whatsoever land they may be in; yea, he numbered his people, and his bowels of mercy are over all the earth. Now this is my joy, and my great thanksgiving; yea, and I will give thanks unto my God forever. Amen.

Notes

vv. 23–37 Great joy comes from our efforts to bring others unto Christ.

- ✏ Invite class members to note Doctrine and Covenants 18:10, 15–16 in their scriptures.

- ❓ Read Doctrine and Covenants 18:10, 15–16 as a class and ask, *What have you learned from Alma 26 that demonstrates that these verses are true? How have you seen the truth of these verses in your own life?*

- ♥ Testify of the joy that can be ours when we immerse ourselves in missionary service.

ALMA 27

The People of Anti-Nephi-Lehi Move to Zarahemla
About 81–77 BC

1–9, The people of Anti-Nephi-Lehi council together regarding moving to the land of Zarahemla; 10–15, Ammon seeks the Lord for guidance and they move away from their homeland toward Zarahemla; 16–19, Alma meets Ammon as they travel; 20–30, The people of Anti-Nephi-Lehi are welcomed by the Nephites and given the land of Jershon to settle.

Overarching Principle: When individuals truly repent, they should forgive themselves, join the people of God, and be completely embraced by Church members without hesitation.

1 Now it came to pass that when those Lamanites who had gone to war against the Nephites had found, after their many struggles to destroy them, that it was in vain to seek their destruction, they returned again to the land of Nephi.

2 And it came to pass that the Amalekites, because of their loss, were exceedingly angry. And when they saw that they could not seek revenge from the Nephites, they began to stir up the people in anger against their brethren, the people of Anti-Nephi-Lehi; therefore they began again to destroy them.

3 Now this people again refused to take their arms, and they suffered themselves to be slain according to the desires of their enemies.

4 Now when Ammon and his brethren saw this work of destruction among those whom they so dearly beloved, and among those who had so dearly beloved them—for they were treated as though they were angels sent from God to save them from everlasting destruction—therefore, when Ammon and his brethren saw this great work of destruction, they were moved with compassion, and they said unto the king:

5 Let us gather together this people of the Lord, and let us go down to the land of Zarahemla to our brethren the Nephites, and flee out of the hands of our enemies, that we be not destroyed.

6 But the king said unto them: Behold, the Nephites will destroy us, because of the many murders and sins we have committed against them.

7 And Ammon said: I will go and inquire of the Lord, and if he say unto us, go down unto our brethren, will ye go?

8 And the king said unto him: Yea, if the Lord saith unto us go, we will go down unto our brethren, and we will be their slaves until we repair unto them the many murders and sins which we have committed against them.

9 But Ammon said unto him: It is against the law of our brethren, which was established by my father, that there should be any slaves among them; therefore let us go down and rely upon the mercies of our brethren.

10 But the king said unto him: Inquire of the Lord, and if he saith unto us go, we will go; otherwise we will perish in the land.

11 And it came to pass that Ammon went and inquired of the Lord, and the Lord said unto him:

12 Get this people out of this land, that they perish not; for Satan has great hold on the hearts of the

Notes

Amalekites, who do stir up the Lamanites to anger against their brethren to slay them; therefore get thee out of this land; and blessed are this people in this generation, for I will preserve them.

13 And now it came to pass that Ammon went and told the king all the words which the Lord had said unto him.

14 And they gathered together all their people, yea, all the people of the Lord, and did gather together all their flocks and herds, and departed out of the land, and came into the wilderness which divided the land of Nephi from the land of Zarahemla, and came over near the borders of the land.

15 And it came to pass that Ammon said unto them: Behold, I and my brethren will go forth into the land of Zarahemla, and ye shall remain here until we return; and we will try the hearts of our brethren, whether they will that ye shall come into their land.

16 And it came to pass that as Ammon was going forth into the land, that he and his brethren met Alma, over in the place of which has been spoken; and behold, this was a joyful meeting.

vv. 1–16 Because the people Anti-Nephi-Lehi continue to suffer persecution at the hands of the Lamanites, Ammon seeks to bring them into the land of Zarahemla.

Note: It is often useful to recapitulate the storyline of the scriptures. Remind your class of the situation the people of Anti-Nephi-Lehi are experiencing and the destruction they had endured at the hands of the Lamanites. Consider summarizing Alma 27:1–4.

🔎 *Read Alma 26:5–14 and look for evidence that the people of Anti-Nephi-Lehi had truly repented for their earlier sins against the Nephites.* Depending on your approach to this chapter, consider extending this Look For activity to verses 27–30 as well.

❓ Analyze: *Why do you think that moving to the land of Zarahemla was a difficult decision for the people of Anti-Nephi-Lehi even though their lives were in danger?*

💬 Explain that Ammon was confident that the Nephites would be merciful to the people of Anti-Nephi-Lehi, but the king was still hesitant to move forward with the migration. Invite class members to listen to the following quote and ponder whether it might apply to this situation. President Dieter F. Uchtdorf said, "Refusing to forgive is a grievous sin—one the Savior warned against. . . . When the Lord requires that we forgive all men—that includes forgiving ourselves" ("The Merciful Obtain Mercy," *Ensign*, May 2012, 77).

17 Now the joy of Ammon was so great even that he was full; yea, he was swallowed up in the joy of his God, even to the exhausting of his strength; and he fell again to the earth.

18 Now was not this exceeding joy? Behold, this is joy which none receiveth save it be the truly penitent and humble seeker of happiness.

19 Now the joy of Alma in meeting his brethren was truly great, and also the joy of Aaron, of Omner, and Himni; but behold their joy was not that to exceed their strength.

20 And now it came to pass that Alma conducted his brethren back to the land of Zarahemla; even to his own house. And they went and told the chief judge all the things that had happened unto them in the land of Nephi, among their brethren, the Lamanites.

21 And it came to pass that the chief judge sent a proclamation throughout all the land, desiring the voice of the people concerning the admitting their brethren, who were the people of Anti-Nephi-Lehi.

22 And it came to pass that the voice of the people came, saying: Behold, we will give up the land of Jershon, which is on the east by the sea, which joins the land Bountiful, which is on the south of the land Bountiful; and this land Jershon is the land which we will give unto our brethren for an inheritance.

23 And behold, we will set our armies between

Notes

ALMA 27

the land Jershon and the land Nephi, that we may protect our brethren in the land Jershon; and this we do for our brethren, on account of their fear to take up arms against their brethren lest they should commit sin; and this their great fear came because of their sore repentance which they had, on account of their many murders and their awful wickedness.

24 And now behold, this will we do unto our brethren, that they may inherit the land Jershon; and we will guard them from their enemies with our armies, on condition that they will give us a portion of their substance to assist us that we may maintain our armies.

25 Now, it came to pass that when Ammon had heard this, he returned to the people of Anti-Nephi-Lehi, and also Alma with him, into the wilderness, where they had pitched their tents, and made known unto them all these things. And Alma also related unto them his conversion, with Ammon and Aaron, and his brethren.

26 And it came to pass that it did cause great joy among them. And they went down into the land of Jershon, and took possession of the land of Jershon; and they were called by the Nephites the people of Ammon; therefore they were distinguished by that name ever after.

27 And they were among the people of Nephi, and also numbered among the people who were of the church of God. And they were also distinguished for their zeal towards God, and also towards men; for they were perfectly honest and upright in all things; and they were firm in the faith of Christ, even unto the end.

28 And they did look upon shedding the blood of their brethren with the greatest abhorrence; and they never could be prevailed upon to take up arms against their brethren; and they never did look upon death with any degree of terror, for their hope and views of Christ and the resurrection; therefore, death was swallowed up to them by the victory of Christ over it.

29 Therefore, they would suffer death in the most aggravating and distressing manner which could be inflicted by their brethren, before they would take the sword or cimeter to smite them.

30 And thus they were a zealous and beloved people, a highly favored people of the Lord.

vv. 17–30 We have a duty to accept those who repent and join the Church, welcoming them into full fellowship.

- *What evidences are there that the Nephites fully forgave and accepted the people of Anti-Nephi-Lehi in verses 21–26?*

- Analyze: *How do you think the actions of the Nephites made the people of Anti-Nephi-Lehi feel?*

- Apply: *What similar circumstances might we experience in the Church today? How can we follow the examples of the Nephites?*

- Elder Carl B. Pratt of the Seventy taught, "In building the kingdom of God, every positive act, every friendly greeting, every warm smile, every thoughtful, kind note contributes to the strength of the whole. It is my prayer that we may be open and outgoing, friendly, and helpful to all who come among us. But let us give special care and concern for the new converts to the Church. When we detect a halting step or a stumble as they begin their journey on the gospel path, let us be there to lift and support with words of kindness and concern; let us be available to give gentle, loving counsel that will strengthen and sustain. Let us conscientiously look for occasions to show that love which the Savior admonished us to have when He said, 'A new commandment I give unto you, that ye love one another' " ("Care for New Converts," *Ensign*, November 1997, 11).

- Invite class members to make a special effort to reach out to new converts in the Church.

Teaching Tips from Prophets' Lips "I am not the teacher, and you are not the teachers. We all need to be receptive to the Holy Spirit, to the guidance of heaven, which is the teacher.

Notes

> We are 'to preach [the] gospel by the Spirit, even the Comforter which was sent forth to teach the truth'" (Jeffrey R. Holland, "Teaching and Learning in the Church", *Ensign*, June 2007, 88–105).

ALMA 28

The Light of Christ Brings Joy
77–76 BC

1–9, Nephites defend the people of Ammon by defeating the Lamanites; 10–14, Mormon summarizes the state of the righteous verses the wicked.

1 And now it came to pass that after the people of Ammon were established in the land of Jershon, and a church also established in the land of Jershon, and the armies of the Nephites were set round about the land of Jershon, yea, in all the borders round about the land of Zarahemla; behold the armies of the Lamanites had followed their brethren into the wilderness.

2 And thus there was a tremendous battle; yea, even such an one as never had been known among all the people in the land from the time Lehi left Jerusalem; yea, and tens of thousands of the Lamanites were slain and scattered abroad.

3 Yea, and also there was a tremendous slaughter among the people of Nephi; nevertheless, the Lamanites were driven and scattered, and the people of Nephi returned again to their land.

4 And now this was a time that there was a great mourning and lamentation heard throughout all the land, among all the people of Nephi—

5 Yea, the cry of widows mourning for their husbands, and also of fathers mourning for their sons, and the daughter for the brother, yea, the brother for the father; and thus the cry of mourning was heard among all of them, mourning for their kindred who had been slain.

6 And now surely this was a sorrowful day; yea, a time of solemnity, and a time of much fasting and prayer.

7 And thus endeth the fifteenth year of the reign of the judges over the people of Nephi;

8 And this is the account of Ammon and his brethren, their journeyings in the land of Nephi, their sufferings in the land, their sorrows, and their afflictions, and their incomprehensible joy, and the reception and safety of the brethren in the land of Jershon. And now may the Lord, the Redeemer of all men, bless their souls forever.

9 And this is the account of the wars and contentions among the Nephites, and also the wars between the Nephites and the Lamanites; and the fifteenth year of the reign of the judges is ended.

10 And from the first year to the fifteenth has brought to pass the destruction of many thousand lives; yea, it has brought to pass an awful scene of bloodshed.

11 And the bodies of many thousands are laid low in the earth, while the bodies of many thousands are moldering in heaps upon the face of the earth; yea, and many thousands are mourning for the loss of their kindred, because they have reason to fear, according to the promises of the Lord, that they are consigned to a state of endless wo.

12 While many thousands of others truly mourn for the loss of their kindred, yet they rejoice and exult in the hope, and even know, according to the promises of the Lord, that they are raised to dwell at the right hand of God, in a state of never-ending happiness.

13 And thus we see how great the inequality of man is because of sin and transgression, and the power of the devil, which comes by the cunning plans which he hath devised to ensnare the hearts of men.

14 And thus we see the great call of diligence of men to labor in the vineyards of the Lord; and thus we see the great reason of sorrow, and also of

Notes

rejoicing—sorrow because of death and destruction among men, and joy because of the light of Christ unto life.

vv. 1–14 Those who know the promises of the Lord have great reason to hope and rejoice even in the face of death and destruction.

- ⚡ Discuss with the class the difference between the final destination of the righteous versus the final destination of the wicked in the plan of salvation. Explain that this lesson will discuss the two contrasting outcomes of the wicked and the righteous.

- 🔍 After establishing that the Lamanites had followed the people of Ammon (as found in verse 1), invite class members to find phrases or words that describe the battle and the aftermath between the Lamanites and the Nephites in verses 2–6.

- 🔍 Invite class members to read verses 11 and 12 and look for the differences between those who die in righteousness and those who die in wickedness. Discuss what class members found, specifically asking what Mormon states as the main reason the righteous had reason to hope.

- ❓ Analyze: *What does the phrase "promises of the Lord" mean in verse 12? We know that the blessings of the Lord are great; therefore, why do you think some choose to live in a way that disqualifies them from having the promises of the Lord in their lives?*

- ♥ Create a two-column chart on the board entitled "Thus we see." Label one title "Verse 13" and the other "Verse 14." In his abridging, Mormon would use the phrase "thus we see" to teach a principle from the lives of the Nephites and Lamanites. Invite class members to identify phrases from those verses they feel best summarize this chapter and explain their choices. Consider writing their answers in the appropriate columns. After a few class members have discussed their thoughts, ask, *Which of these statements best describes the account of the sons of Mosiah (chapters 17–28) and why?* Testify of the joy that comes from righteousness and knowing the promises of the Lord.

Index Topics: plan of salvation, judgment

ALMA 29
"O That I Were an Angel"
About 76 BC

1–9, Alma proclaims his desire to be an angel so he can cry repentance unto the earth; 10–17, Alma glories in what God has done for him and his brethren.

1 O that I were an angel, and could have the wish of mine heart, that I might go forth and speak with the trump of God, with a voice to shake the earth, and cry repentance unto every people!

2 Yea, I would declare unto every soul, as with the voice of thunder, repentance and the plan of redemption, that they should repent and come unto our God, that there might not be more sorrow upon all the face of the earth.

3 But behold, I am a man, and do sin in my wish; for I ought to be content with the things which the Lord hath allotted unto me.

4 I ought not to harrow up in my desires the firm decree of a just God, for I know that he granteth unto men according to their desire, whether it be unto death or unto life; yea, I know that he allotteth unto men, yea, decreeth unto them decrees which are unalterable, according to their wills, whether they be unto salvation or unto destruction.

5 Yea, and I know that good and evil have come before all men; he that knoweth not good from evil is blameless; but he that knoweth good and evil, to him it is given according to his desires, whether he desireth good or evil, life or death, joy or remorse of conscience.

Notes

6 Now, seeing that I know these things, why should I desire more than to perform the work to which I have been called?

7 Why should I desire that I were an angel, that I could speak unto all the ends of the earth?

8 For behold, the Lord doth grant unto all nations, of their own nation and tongue, to teach his word, yea, in wisdom, all that he seeth fit that they should have; therefore we see that the Lord doth counsel in wisdom, according to that which is just and true.

9 I know that which the Lord hath commanded me, and I glory in it. I do not glory of myself, but I glory in that which the Lord hath commanded me; yea, and this is my glory, that perhaps I may be an instrument in the hands of God to bring some soul to repentance; and this is my joy.

vv. 1–9 We should be content with what the Lord has allotted unto us.

- Write the following on the board prior to the start of class:
  - I am grateful for what the Lord has given me.
  - I feel satisfied with my calling and my role in the Church.
  - I am confident I can bless the lives of those I interact with.
  - I believe I have a purpose for being on the earth at this time.

  Ask class members to consider the statements on the board and rate the degree to which they agree with each one on a scale from 1 to 5—5 being "strongly agree" and 1 being "strongly disagree."

- Read Alma 29:1–2 and look for a desire of Alma's heart.

- Analyze:
  - *What do you think of Alma's desire—is it righteous or not?*
  - *What events in Alma's life may have caused this desire to grow within him?*
  - *What might be good about his desire? What might not be good?*
  - *What does Alma think of his own desire according to verse 3?*
  - *Read Alma 29:4. What is Alma's reasoning for determining that he commits "sin in his wish"?*

- Speaking to the youth of the Church, the First Presidency has stated, "Our Father in Heaven has placed great trust in you. He has a work for you to do. . . . It is our fervent prayer that you will remain steadfast and valiant throughout your lives and that you will trust in the Savior and His promises. As you do this, you will be an influence for good in helping to build the kingdom of God and prepare the world for the Second Coming of the Savior." (*For the Strength of Youth*, 1) Ask, *Why is it important that we understand that the Lord has a work for us to do in His kingdom now?*

- Read Alma 29:9 to the class. Testify that the Lord has allotted each of us a work and time to do it and that if we are faithful, we will be joyful and will bring joy to those around us.

10 And behold, when I see many of my brethren truly penitent, and coming to the Lord their God, then is my soul filled with joy; then do I remember what the Lord has done for me, yea, even that he hath heard my prayer; yea, then do I remember his merciful arm which he extended towards me.

11 Yea, and I also remember the captivity of my fathers; for I surely do know that the Lord did deliver them out of bondage, and by this did establish his church; yea, the Lord God, the God of Abraham, the God of Isaac, and the God of Jacob, did deliver them out of bondage.

12 Yea, I have always remembered the captivity of my fathers; and that same God who delivered them out of the hands of the Egyptians did deliver them out of bondage.

vv. 11–12 Remembering how God helped those in the scriptures helps us recognize how He can help us now.

Notes

- Look for what Alma has always done in verses 11–12.

- **Analyze:** *Why does Alma feel it is important to "remember"?*

- Divide the class into three groups and give each group one of the following cross references to read and later share what they learn with the class: Alma 36:2; Alma 5:6; Helaman 5:12.

- Invite class members to mark the word "remember" in Alma 29:11–12 and note these cross-references in their scriptures. Testify that remembering God's works in the past brings blessings in the present.

13 Yea, and that same God did establish his church among them; yea, and that same God hath called me by a holy calling, to preach the word unto this people, and hath given me much success, in the which my joy is full.

14 But I do not joy in my own success alone, but my joy is more full because of the success of my brethren, who have been up to the land of Nephi.

15 Behold, they have labored exceedingly, and have brought forth much fruit; and how great shall be their reward!

16 Now, when I think of the success of these my brethren my soul is carried away, even to the separation of it from the body, as it were, so great is my joy.

vv. 14–16 True disciples take joy in the success of others.

- *Read verses 14–16 and look for a great characteristic of Alma that is sometimes lacking in the world today.*

- **Analyze:** *Why is it sometimes difficult to rejoice in the success of others? How does pride relate with how a person feels about another's success?*

- "Pride is ugly. It says, 'If you succeed, I am a failure'" (President Ezra Taft Benson, "Beware of Pride," *Ensign*, May 1989).

- C. S. Lewis stated: "Pride gets no pleasure out of having something, only out of having more of it than the next man. . . . It is the comparison that makes you proud: the pleasure of being above the rest. Once the element of competition has gone, pride has gone" (*Mere Christianity* [New York: Macmillan, 1952], 109–10).

- Invite class members to reflect on how they currently feel about the success of others. Invite them to evaluate—and change if necessary—their feelings about this gospel principle they have learned.

17 And now may God grant unto these, my brethren, that they may sit down in the kingdom of God; yea, and also all those who are the fruit of their labors that they may go no more out, but that they may praise him forever. And may God grant that it may be done according to my words, even as I have spoken. Amen.

vv. 10–17 The gospel brings great joy to those who remember the Lord and recognize His hand in all things.

- Read Alma 29:10–17. Make a list of everything that Alma remembers and brings him joy. Discuss the results as a class. Ask, *In what ways can we find similar joy in the gospel today?*

> **Teaching Tips from Prophets' Lips** "Make your objective to help students understand, retain, and use divine truth. Keep that objective foremost in every aspect of your preparation and teaching" (Elder Richard G. Scott, "To Understand and Live Truth," Address to CES Religious Educators, Feb 4, 2005, 2).

ALMA 30

The Anti-Christ Korihor
About 76–74 BC

Notes

ALMA 30

1–5, The general affairs of the Nephites; 6–11, Religious freedom is explained; 12–18, The manner of Korihor's preaching; 19–29, His interactions with the people and the chief judge; 30–50, Korihor demands a sign from Alma for proof that there is a God, and is struck dumb; 51–60, Korihor recants but the curse remains with him and he is killed while among the Zoramites.

1 Behold, now it came to pass that after the people of Ammon were established in the land of Jershon, yea, and also after the Lamanites were driven out of the land, and their dead were buried by the people of the land—

2 Now their dead were not numbered because of the greatness of their numbers; neither were the dead of the Nephites numbered—but it came to pass after they had buried their dead, and also after the days of fasting, and mourning, and prayer, (and it was in the sixteenth year of the reign of the judges over the people of Nephi) there began to be continual peace throughout all the land.

3 Yea, and the people did observe to keep the commandments of the Lord; and they were strict in observing the ordinances of God, according to the law of Moses; for they were taught to keep the law of Moses until it should be fulfilled.

vv. 2–3 Following the Lord brings peace.

- *In verses 2–3, look for the connection between the peace the Nephites had in verse 2 and what they did in verse 3.*

- Invite class members to cross-reference Mosiah 29:43 and Isaiah 48:18. Ask them to read the verses and write down the principle that is taught.

4 And thus the people did have no disturbance in all the sixteenth year of the reign of the judges over the people of Nephi.

5 And it came to pass that in the commencement of the seventeenth year of the reign of the judges, there was continual peace.

6 But it came to pass in the latter end of the seventeenth year, there came a man into the land of Zarahemla, and he was Anti-Christ, for he began to preach unto the people against the prophecies which had been spoken by the prophets, concerning the coming of Christ.

v. 6 Anti-Christ.

- Anti-Christ is defined in the Bible Dictionary under "Antichrist" and also in 1 John 2:22. Note with the class that there are three anti-Christ's in the Book of Mormon: Sherem (Jacob 7), Nehor (Alma 1), and Korihor (Alma 30).

7 Now there was no law against a man's belief; for it was strictly contrary to the commands of God that there should be a law which should bring men on to unequal grounds.

8 For thus saith the scripture: Choose ye this day, whom ye will serve.

9 Now if a man desired to serve God, it was his privilege; or rather, if he believed in God it was his privilege to serve him; but if he did not believe in him there was no law to punish him.

10 But if he murdered he was punished unto death; and if he robbed he was also punished; and if he stole he was also punished; and if he committed adultery he was also punished; yea, for all this wickedness they were punished.

11 For there was a law that men should be judged according to their crimes. Nevertheless, there was no law against a man's belief; therefore, a man was punished only for the crimes which he had done; therefore all men were on equal grounds.

vv. 7–11 Principles of religious freedom.

- Next to verses 7–11, invite your class to cross-reference Doctrine and Covenants 135:4, which references religious freedom.

12 And this Anti-Christ, whose name was Korihor, (and the law could have no hold upon him)

Notes

began to preach unto the people that there should be no Christ. And after this manner did he preach, saying:

13 O ye that are bound down under a foolish and a vain hope, why do ye yoke yourselves with such foolish things? Why do ye look for a Christ? For no man can know of anything which is to come.

14 Behold, these things which ye call prophecies, which ye say are handed down by holy prophets, behold, they are foolish traditions of your fathers.

15 How do ye know of their surety? Behold, ye cannot know of things which ye do not see; therefore ye cannot know that there shall be a Christ.

16 Ye look forward and say that ye see a remission of your sins. But behold, it is the effect of a frenzied mind; and this derangement of your minds comes because of the traditions of your fathers, which lead you away into a belief of things which are not so.

17 And many more such things did he say unto them, telling them that there could be no atonement made for the sins of men, but every man fared in this life according to the management of the creature; therefore every man prospered according to his genius, and that every man conquered according to his strength; and whatsoever a man did was no crime.

18 And thus he did preach unto them, leading away the hearts of many, causing them to lift up their heads in their wickedness, yea, leading away many women, and also men, to commit whoredoms—telling them that when a man was dead, that was the end thereof.

vv. 13–18 The Book of Mormon fortifies us against the false teachings of the world.

- Show the class a syringe or picture of a syringe. Ask class members if they know the medical science of how inoculations work. Explain that the shot contains a dead or weakened form of a disease. The body overcomes the weakened disease and creates antibodies so that, if it is exposed to it again, it will not contract the disease. Explain that you will give the class a "spiritual inoculation." In Alma 30, Korihor's false teachings are very similar to the false teachings of today.

- Share the following quote by Ezra Taft Benson, "The Book of Mormon exposes the enemies of Christ. It confounds false doctrines and lays down contention. (See 2 Ne. 3:12.) It fortifies the humble followers of Christ against the evil designs, strategies, and doctrines of the devil in our day. The type of apostates in the Book of Mormon are similar to the type we have today. God, with his infinite foreknowledge, so molded the Book of Mormon that we might see the error and know how to combat false educational, political, religious, and philosophical concepts of our time" ("The Book of Mormon Is the Word of God," *Ensign*, May 1975, 63).

- Explain to class members that Korihor uses worldly logic to try and disprove the reality of God. Read verses 13–18 as a class to look for each argument Korihor makes against religion. Consider writing their findings on the board.

- Analyze: *How could this type of logic persuade someone against religion?*

- Consider sharing the following examples with class members and ask how they would respond in defense of religion and faith. After talking about the statements, look in verses 13–18 for how each of those statements are said in different words.

  - "You Mormons aren't allowed to do anything fun. Commandments limit your freedoms."
  - "The feelings you say are from the 'Holy Ghost' are just delusions."
  - "It's only wrong if you think it is wrong."
  - "You only believe in your church because you have been taught that all of your lives."
  - "Seeing is believing. How can you believe something is true which you haven't seen?"
  - "It doesn't matter what we do because we all die in the end."

- Heber C. Kimball said, "The time will come when no man nor woman will be able to

Notes

endure on borrowed light. Each will have to be guided by the light within himself" (*Life of Heber C. Kimball*, 449–50).

♥ Refer back to the syringe and challenge them to think of what they might say if the situation arises. Note that Alma responds to Korihor's objections in verses 37–44 of this chapter.

19 Now this man went over to the land of Jershon also, to preach these things among the people of Ammon, who were once the people of the Lamanites.

20 But behold they were more wise than many of the Nephites; for they took him, and bound him, and carried him before Ammon, who was a high priest over that people.

21 And it came to pass that he caused that he should be carried out of the land. And he came over into the land of Gideon, and began to preach unto them also; and here he did not have much success, for he was taken and bound and carried before the high priest, and also the chief judge over the land.

22 And it came to pass that the high priest said unto him: Why do ye go about perverting the ways of the Lord? Why do ye teach this people that there shall be no Christ, to interrupt their rejoicings? Why do ye speak against all the prophecies of the holy prophets?

23 Now the high priest's name was Giddonah. And Korihor said unto him: Because I do not teach the foolish traditions of your fathers, and because I do not teach this people to bind themselves down under the foolish ordinances and performances which are laid down by ancient priests, to usurp power and authority over them, to keep them in ignorance, that they may not lift up their heads, but be brought down according to thy words.

24 Ye say that this people is a free people. Behold, I say they are in bondage. Ye say that those ancient prophecies are true. Behold, I say that ye do not know that they are true.

25 Ye say that this people is a guilty and a fallen people, because of the transgression of a parent. Behold, I say that a child is not guilty because of its parents.

26 And ye also say that Christ shall come. But behold, I say that ye do not know that there shall be a Christ. And ye say also that he shall be slain for the sins of the world—

27 And thus ye lead away this people after the foolish traditions of your fathers, and according to your own desires; and ye keep them down, even as it were in bondage, that ye may glut yourselves with the labors of their hands, that they durst not look up with boldness, and that they durst not enjoy their rights and privileges.

28 Yea, they durst not make use of that which is their own lest they should offend their priests, who do yoke them according to their desires, and have brought them to believe, by their traditions and their dreams and their whims and their visions and their pretended mysteries, that they should, if they did not do according to their words, offend some unknown being, who they say is God—a being who never has been seen or known, who never was nor ever will be.

29 Now when the high priest and the chief judge saw the hardness of his heart, yea, when they saw that he would revile even against God, they would not make any reply to his words; but they caused that he should be bound; and they delivered him up into the hands of the officers, and sent him to the land of Zarahemla, that he might be brought before Alma, and the chief judge who was governor over all the land.

30 And it came to pass that when he was brought before Alma and the chief judge, he did go on in the same manner as he did in the land of Gideon; yea, he went on to blaspheme.

31 And he did rise up in great swelling words before Alma, and did revile against the priests and teachers, accusing them of leading away the people after the silly traditions of their fathers, for the sake of glutting on the labors of the people.

Notes

32 Now Alma said unto him: Thou knowest that we do not glut ourselves upon the labors of this people; for behold I have labored even from the commencement of the reign of the judges until now, with mine own hands for my support, notwithstanding my many travels round about the land to declare the word of God unto my people.

33 And notwithstanding the many labors which I have performed in the church, I have never received so much as even one senine for my labor; neither has any of my brethren, save it were in the judgment-seat; and then we have received only according to law for our time.

34 And now, if we do not receive anything for our labors in the church, what doth it profit us to labor in the church save it were to declare the truth, that we may have rejoicings in the joy of our brethren?

35 Then why sayest thou that we preach unto this people to get gain, when thou, of thyself, knowest that we receive no gain? And now, believest thou that we deceive this people, that causes such joy in their hearts?

36 And Korihor answered him, Yea.

vv. 23 & 27–36 False teachings of Satan.

- Look for three false teachings of Korihor in verse 23 and in verses 27–28. After class members have shared what they found, have them look for what counters the false doctrine in verses 31–35.

37 And then Alma said unto him: Believest thou that there is a God?

38 And he answered, Nay.

39 Now Alma said unto him: Will ye deny again that there is a God, and also deny the Christ? For behold, I say unto you, I know there is a God, and also that Christ shall come.

40 And now what evidence have ye that there is no God, or that Christ cometh not? I say unto you that ye have none, save it be your word only.

41 But, behold, I have all things as a testimony that these things are true; and ye also have all things as a testimony unto you that they are true; and will ye deny them? Believest thou that these things are true?

42 Behold, I know that thou believest, but thou art possessed with a lying spirit, and ye have put off the Spirit of God that it may have no place in you; but the devil has power over you, and he doth carry you about, working devices that he may destroy the children of God.

43 And now Korihor said unto Alma: If thou wilt show me a sign, that I may be convinced that there is a God, yea, show unto me that he hath power, and then will I be convinced of the truth of thy words.

44 But Alma said unto him: Thou hast had signs enough; will ye tempt your God? Will ye say, Show unto me a sign, when ye have the testimony of all these thy brethren, and also all the holy prophets? The scriptures are laid before thee, yea, and all things denote there is a God; yea, even the earth, and all things that are upon the face of it, yea, and its motion, yea, and also all the planets which move in their regular form do witness that there is a Supreme Creator.

vv. 37–44 Evidence that there is a God.

- Explain that all of the false teachings of Korihor could be derived from one central idea. Review Korihor's false teachings with the class from earlier in this chapter to analyze what the central idea is.

- Read verses 37–44 as a class and look for Alma's response to Korihor's false teachings.

- Analyze: *What is the first thing Alma did to show there is a God in verse 39? What does he wisely do in verse 40?*

- In verses 43–44, have class members look for at least five evidences that there is a God. After each one of the answers, discuss with the class how each example proves there is a God.

- You may also want to demonstrate how the

Notes

false teachings in verses 13–18 derive from the false idea that there is no God. Consider bearing your testimony of God's omniscience.

45 And yet do ye go about, leading away the hearts of this people, testifying unto them there is no God? And yet will ye deny against all these witnesses? And he said: Yea, I will deny, except ye shall show me a sign.

46 And now it came to pass that Alma said unto him: Behold, I am grieved because of the hardness of your heart, yea, that ye will still resist the spirit of the truth, that thy soul may be destroyed.

47 But behold, it is better that thy soul should be lost than that thou shouldst be the means of bringing many souls down to destruction, by thy lying and by thy flattering words; therefore if thou shalt deny again, behold God shall smite thee, that thou shalt become dumb, that thou shalt never open thy mouth any more, that thou shalt not deceive this people any more.

48 Now Korihor said unto him: I do not deny the existence of a God, but I do not believe that there is a God; and I say also, that ye do not know that there is a God; and except ye show me a sign, I will not believe.

49 Now Alma said unto him: This will I give unto thee for a sign, that thou shalt be struck dumb, according to my words; and I say, that in the name of God, ye shall be struck dumb, that ye shall no more have utterance.

50 Now when Alma had said these words, Korihor was struck dumb, that he could not have utterance, according to the words of Alma.

51 And now when the chief judge saw this, he put forth his hand and wrote unto Korihor, saying: Art thou convinced of the power of God? In whom did ye desire that Alma should show forth his sign? Would ye that he should afflict others, to show unto thee a sign? Behold, he has showed unto you a sign; and now will ye dispute more?

52 And Korihor put forth his hand and wrote, saying: I know that I am dumb, for I cannot speak; and I know that nothing save it were the power of God could bring this upon me; yea, and I always knew that there was a God.

53 But behold, the devil hath deceived me; for he appeared unto me in the form of an angel, and said unto me: Go and reclaim this people, for they have all gone astray after an unknown God. And he said unto me: There is no God; yea, and he taught me that which I should say. And I have taught his words; and I taught them because they were pleasing unto the carnal mind; and I taught them, even until I had much success, insomuch that I verily believed that they were true; and for this cause I withstood the truth, even until I have brought this great curse upon me.

v. 53 Sin can cause us to justify that there is no God so that we do not feel guilty.

🔎 Summarize what happens after Korihor seeks a sign in verses 45–52. Ask, *In verse 53, look for why Korihor wanted to teach these false ideas.*

❓ Analyze: *What do you think the phrase "pleasing unto the carnal mind" means?* Consider reviewing the false teachings of Korihor and why those might be pleasing to the carnal mind.

❓ Apply: *How might this situation apply in our day?*

54 Now when he had said this, he besought that Alma should pray unto God, that the curse might be taken from him.

55 But Alma said unto him: If this curse should be taken from thee thou wouldst again lead away the hearts of this people; therefore, it shall be unto thee even as the Lord will.

56 And it came to pass that the curse was not taken off of Korihor; but he was cast out, and went about from house to house begging for his food.

57 Now the knowledge of what had happened unto Korihor was immediately published throughout all the land; yea, the proclamation was sent forth

Notes

by the chief judge to all the people in the land, declaring unto those who had believed in the words of Korihor that they must speedily repent, lest the same judgments would come unto them.

58 And it came to pass that they were all convinced of the wickedness of Korihor; therefore they were all converted again unto the Lord; and this put an end to the iniquity after the manner of Korihor. And Korihor did go about from house to house, begging food for his support.

59 And it came to pass that as he went forth among the people, yea, among a people who had separated themselves from the Nephites and called themselves Zoramites, being led by a man whose name was Zoram—and as he went forth amongst them, behold, he was run upon and trodden down, even until he was dead.

60 And thus we see the end of him who perverteth the ways of the Lord; and thus we see that the devil will not support his children at the last day, but doth speedily drag them down to hell.

vv. 59–60 "The devil will not support his children at the last day."

- Look for the lesson about Satan that Mormon teaches in verses 59–60.
- Apply: What can we learn from that lesson?
- Contrast God's desire for our happiness with Satan's desire for our misery.

Index Topics: religious freedom, peace, godhead, anti-Mormon teachings, testimony, commandments

ALMA 31

Mission to the Zoramites
About 74 BC

1–7, Alma enlists missionaries to help restore the apostate Zoramites to the faith; 8–23, Descriptions of the perversion of their religion; 24–38, Alma's reaction to their perverse ways and prayer for strength.

- Write on the board the question, "Which is worse: No religion or corrupt religion?" After class members offer their opinions to this question, explain that Alma 30 was about someone promoting no religion, while Alma 31–35 is about missionaries trying to help those with a corrupt religion

1 Now it came to pass that after the end of Korihor, Alma having received tidings that the Zoramites were perverting the ways of the Lord, and that Zoram, who was their leader, was leading the hearts of the people to bow down to dumb idols, his heart again began to sicken because of the iniquity of the people.

2 For it was the cause of great sorrow to Alma to know of iniquity among his people; therefore his heart was exceedingly sorrowful because of the separation of the Zoramites from the Nephites.

3 Now the Zoramites had gathered themselves together in a land which they called Antionum, which was east of the land of Zarahemla, which lay nearly bordering upon the seashore, which was south of the land of Jershon, which also bordered upon the wilderness south, which wilderness was full of the Lamanites.

4 Now the Nephites greatly feared that the Zoramites would enter into a correspondence with the Lamanites, and that it would be the means of great loss on the part of the Nephites.

5 And now, as the preaching of the word had a great tendency to lead the people to do that which was just—yea, it had had more powerful effect upon the minds of the people than the sword, or anything else, which had happened unto them—therefore Alma thought it was expedient that they should try the virtue of the word of God.

v. 5 Preaching the word of God can change a society.

Notes

> ⚡ Ask class members, *What types of things could change the world for good? While many things can bring change to the world, are there things that may be more effective than others?*
>
> 🔍 After the discussion above, ask class members to look at a related principle in verse 5.
>
> ❓ *Why do you think preaching the word of God could have a greater impact than any other thing?*
>
> 💬 Ezra Taft Benson stated, "The Lord works from the inside out. The world works from the outside in. The world would take people out of the slums. Christ takes the slums out of people, and then they take themselves out of the slums. The world would mold men by changing their environment. Christ changes men, who then change their environment. The world would shape human behavior, but Christ can change human nature" ("Born of God," *Ensign*, July 1989, 4).
>
> ❤ Ask class members, *How can we apply this lesson in our lives?* Encourage them to share the gospel with others. You might consider discussing ways to share the gospel with others.

6 Therefore he took Ammon, and Aaron, and Omner; and Himni he did leave in the church in Zarahemla; but the former three he took with him, and also Amulek and Zeezrom, who were at Melek; and he also took two of his sons.

7 Now the eldest of his sons he took not with him, and his name was Helaman; but the names of those whom he took with him were Shiblon and Corianton; and these are the names of those who went with him among the Zoramites, to preach unto them the word.

8 Now the Zoramites were dissenters from the Nephites; therefore they had had the word of God preached unto them.

9 But they had fallen into great errors, for they would not observe to keep the commandments of God, and his statutes, according to the law of Moses.

10 Neither would they observe the performances of the church, to continue in prayer and supplication to God daily, that they might not enter into temptation.

11 Yea, in fine, they did pervert the ways of the Lord in very many instances; therefore, for this cause, Alma and his brethren went into the land to preach the word unto them.

12 Now, when they had come into the land, behold, to their astonishment they found that the Zoramites had built synagogues, and that they did gather themselves together on one day of the week, which day they did call the day of the Lord; and they did worship after a manner which Alma and his brethren had never beheld;

13 For they had a place built up in the center of their synagogue, a place for standing, which was high above the head; and the top thereof would only admit one person.

14 Therefore, whosoever desired to worship must go forth and stand upon the top thereof, and stretch forth his hands towards heaven, and cry with a loud voice, saying:

15 Holy, holy God; we believe that thou art God, and we believe that thou art holy, and that thou wast a spirit, and that thou art a spirit, and that thou wilt be a spirit forever.

16 Holy God, we believe that thou hast separated us from our brethren; and we do not believe in the tradition of our brethren, which was handed down to them by the childishness of their fathers; but we believe that thou hast elected us to be thy holy children; and also thou hast made it known unto us that there shall be no Christ.

17 But thou art the same yesterday, today, and forever; and thou hast elected us that we shall be saved, whilst all around us are elected to be cast by thy wrath down to hell; for the which holiness, O God, we thank thee; and we also thank thee that thou hast elected us, that we may not be led away after the foolish traditions of our brethren, which doth bind them down to a belief of Christ, which doth lead their hearts to wander far from thee, our God.

Notes

18 And again we thank thee, O God, that we are a chosen and a holy people. Amen.

19 Now it came to pass that after Alma and his brethren and his sons had heard these prayers, they were astonished beyond all measure.

20 For behold, every man did go forth and offer up these same prayers.

21 Now the place was called by them Rameumptom, which, being interpreted, is the holy stand.

22 Now, from this stand they did offer up, every man, the selfsame prayer unto God, thanking their God that they were chosen of him, and that he did not lead them away after the tradition of their brethren, and that their hearts were not stolen away to believe in things to come, which they knew nothing about.

23 Now, after the people had all offered up thanks after this manner, they returned to their homes, never speaking of their God again until they had assembled themselves together again to the holy stand, to offer up thanks after their manner.

vv. 13–23 The Zoramites offer prayers from the Rameumptom.

⚡ Before class, take verses 15–18 and modify the words of the Zoramite prayer to refer to your class in some way, and copy it down onto a piece of paper. Be cautious to maintain a reverence regarding the doctrine of prayer and any references to the Godhead. Then in a joking way, refer back to the opening prayer, remark that you have had thoughts about how to change the prayers in class. Bring out a ladder and say that you have been thinking it might be better to have the person pray standing on the ladder with his hands stretched out, and always include a few statements you have written down in the prayer. Read what you have written and ask the class what they think of the proposed change. After acknowledging the insincere nature of your comments ask, *How might such action interfere with the efficacy of our prayers?*

🔍 *Read verses 15–23 and underline aspects of their prayer that would interfere with the power of prayer.*

❓ *In contrast, what practices bring a spiritual power to our prayers? List the answers on the board. How are sincere prayers a part of our worship of God?*

🔍 *In verse 23, look for what else was happening that could negatively impact an individual's worship of God?*

❓ Apply:
- *In what ways might limiting prayer to once a week keep us from receiving the full blessings of faithful prayer?*
- *What difficulties arise when an individual only thinks of God on Sunday and not throughout the week?*
- *What blessings do we miss out on if we become so-called "Sunday Mormons"?*
- *What part should God play in our lives?*

💚 Testify that sincere daily prayer and worship can increase our spirituality and strengthen our relationship with God.

24 Now when Alma saw this his heart was grieved; for he saw that they were a wicked and a perverse people; yea, he saw that their hearts were set upon gold, and upon silver, and upon all manner of fine goods.

25 Yea, and he also saw that their hearts were lifted up unto great boasting, in their pride.

26 And he lifted up his voice to heaven, and cried, saying: O, how long, O Lord, wilt thou suffer that thy servants shall dwell here below in the flesh, to behold such gross wickedness among the children of men?

27 Behold, O God, they cry unto thee, and yet their hearts are swallowed up in their pride. Behold, O God, they cry unto thee with their mouths, while they are puffed up, even to greatness, with the vain things of the world.

28 Behold, O my God, their costly apparel, and their ringlets, and their bracelets, and their ornaments

Notes

of gold, and all their precious things which they are ornamented with; and behold, their hearts are set upon them, and yet they cry unto thee and say—We thank thee, O God, for we are a chosen people unto thee, while others shall perish.

29 Yea, and they say that thou hast made it known unto them that there shall be no Christ.

30 O Lord God, how long wilt thou suffer that such wickedness and infidelity shall be among this people? O Lord, wilt thou give me strength, that I may bear with mine infirmities. For I am infirm, and such wickedness among this people doth pain my soul.

31 O Lord, my heart is exceedingly sorrowful; wilt thou comfort my soul in Christ. O Lord, wilt thou grant unto me that I may have strength, that I may suffer with patience these afflictions which shall come upon me, because of the iniquity of this people.

32 O Lord, wilt thou comfort my soul, and give unto me success, and also my fellow laborers who are with me—yea, Ammon, and Aaron, and Omner, and also Amulek and Zeezrom, and also my two sons—yea, even all these wilt thou comfort, O Lord. Yea, wilt thou comfort their souls in Christ.

33 Wilt thou grant unto them that they may have strength, that they may bear their afflictions which shall come upon them because of the iniquities of this people.

34 O Lord, wilt thou grant unto us that we may have success in bringing them again unto thee in Christ.

35 Behold, O Lord, their souls are precious, and many of them are our brethren; therefore, give unto us, O Lord, power and wisdom that we may bring these, our brethren, again unto thee.

36 Now it came to pass that when Alma had said these words, that he clapped his hands upon all them who were with him. And behold, as he clapped his hands upon them, they were filled with the Holy Spirit.

37 And after that they did separate themselves one from another, taking no thought for themselves what they should eat, or what they should drink, or what they should put on.

38 And the Lord provided for them that they should hunger not, neither should they thirst; yea, and he also gave them strength, that they should suffer no manner of afflictions, save it were swallowed up in the joy of Christ. Now this was according to the prayer of Alma; and this because he prayed in faith.

vv. 30–38 With prayer, God can strengthen us to bear our burdens.

- In verses 30–38, look for what Alma is praying for.

- Ask:
  - How is Alma's prayer different than the prayers on the Rameumptom?
  - Why was he praying for comfort?
  - How can missions become discouraging?
  - Who does Alma see as the source of comfort?
  - How is a priesthood blessing inferred in that prayer? (v. 36 and see the footnote.)
  - Did God remove all their afflictions? (v. 38)
  - Did this mean it would no longer be difficult?

- Ask, *What does this teach we should do when facing afflictions in life?* Invite class members to go to the Lord in prayer and seek a priesthood blessing when facing afflictions.

Teaching Tips from Prophets' Lips "It's better to take just a few good ideas and get good discussion—and good learning—than to be frenzied, trying to teach every word in the manual" (Jeffrey R. Holland, "Teaching and Learning in the Church," *Ensign*, June 2007, 88–105).

Index Topics: missionary work, scriptures, prayer, trials or afflictions

Notes

ALMA 32

The Seed of Faith: Hope, Belief, Knowledge
About 74 BC

1–7, Alma begins to have success in teaching the poor because their circumstances have humbled them; 8–16, blessed are those who are compelled to be humble; 17–43, Alma discourses on faith—faith is not a perfect knowledge; exercise a particle of faith; faith is like a seed.

Overarching Principle: In order to exercise faith we need to prepare our hearts and experiment upon the word; then, we will reap the rewards of our faith.

1 And it came to pass that they did go forth, and began to preach the word of God unto the people, entering into their synagogues, and into their houses; yea, and even they did preach the word in their streets.

2 And it came to pass that after much labor among them, they began to have success among the poor class of people; for behold, they were cast out of the synagogues because of the coarseness of their apparel—

3 Therefore they were not permitted to enter into their synagogues to worship God, being esteemed as filthiness; therefore they were poor; yea, they were esteemed by their brethren as dross; therefore they were poor as to things of the world; and also they were poor in heart.

4 Now, as Alma was teaching and speaking unto the people upon the hill Onidah, there came a great multitude unto him, who were those of whom we have been speaking, of whom were poor in heart, because of their poverty as to the things of the world.

5 And they came unto Alma; and the one who was the foremost among them said unto him: Behold, what shall these my brethren do, for they are despised of all men because of their poverty, yea, and more especially by our priests; for they have cast us out of our synagogues which we have labored abundantly to build with our own hands; and they have cast us out because of our exceeding poverty; and we have no place to worship our God; and behold, what shall we do?

6 And now when Alma heard this, he turned him about, his face immediately towards him, and he beheld with great joy; for he beheld that their afflictions had truly humbled them, and that they were in a preparation to hear the word.

7 Therefore he did say no more to the other multitude; but he stretched forth his hand, and cried unto those whom he beheld, who were truly penitent, and said unto them:

8 I behold that ye are lowly in heart; and if so, blessed are ye.

9 Behold thy brother hath said, What shall we do?—for we are cast out of our synagogues, that we cannot worship our God.

10 Behold I say unto you, do ye suppose that ye cannot worship God save it be in your synagogues only?

11 And moreover, I would ask, do ye suppose that ye must not worship God only once in a week?

12 I say unto you, it is well that ye are cast out of your synagogues, that ye may be humble, and that ye may learn wisdom; for it is necessary that ye should learn wisdom; for it is because that ye are cast out, that ye are despised of your brethren because of your exceeding poverty, that ye are brought to a lowliness of heart; for ye are necessarily brought to be humble.

13 And now, because ye are compelled to be humble blessed are ye; for a man sometimes, if he is compelled to be humble, seeketh repentance; and now surely, whosoever repenteth shall find mercy; and he that findeth mercy and endureth to the end the same shall be saved.

14 And now, as I said unto you, that because ye were compelled to be humble ye were blessed, do

Notes

ye not suppose that they are more blessed who truly humble themselves because of the word?

15 Yea, he that truly humbleth himself, and repenteth of his sins, and endureth to the end, the same shall be blessed—yea, much more blessed than they who are compelled to be humble because of their exceeding poverty.

16 Therefore, blessed are they who humble themselves without being compelled to be humble; or rather, in other words, blessed is he that believeth in the word of God, and is baptized without stubbornness of heart, yea, without being brought to know the word, or even compelled to know, before they will believe.

vv. 1–16 Our hearts need to be prepared in order to exercise faith.

- Alma realizes that the hearts of the people he is teaching are prepared to hear the word of God—an essential first step to start exercising faith. To help class members understand this preparation process, discuss the following quote and how it applies to preparation: "In the process of making concrete, precise amounts of sand, gravel, cement, and water are used in order to achieve maximum strength. An incorrect amount or exclusion of any portion of these elements would make the concrete weak and not able to perform its important function" (Dean M. Davies, "A Sure Foundation," *Ensign*, May 2013, 9).

- Invite class members to answer the questions in the following chart:

What is the story?	Alma 32:1–5
What does Alma realize?	Alma 32:6–8
What principle does Alma teach about preparation?	Alma 32:9–16

Depending on the size of the class, consider breaking them into groups to work on it together.

- Analyze: Once the chart is completed, analyze the principle that Alma is trying to teach. Consider using the following questions:
  - *What do you think it means to be compelled to be humble?*
  - *Why is it better to humble one's self, rather than to be compelled?*
  - *How does humility relate to gospel learning?*
  - *Why do people's hearts need to be prepared in order to hear and learn the word of God?*

- Apply: *How does this situation apply to gospel learning in our day?*

- Share the following quote from President Ezra Taft Benson: "God will have a humble people. Either we can choose to be humble or we can be compelled to be humble. Alma said, 'Blessed are they who humble themselves without being compelled to be humble.' Let us choose to be humble" ("Beware of Pride," *Ensign*, May 1989, 6).

- *What can you do to humble yourself in preparation to hear the word of God?* Consider discussing opportunities when we can hear the word of God—general conference, stake and ward conferences, personal scripture study, etc.

Note: Throughout the rest of this chapter, Alma discusses faith. Notice that the principles found in verses 1–16 set the context for how to prepare ourselves to exercise faith. If you are teaching all of Alma 32 for a lesson, consider using verses 1–16 to establish the context of Alma's great discourse regarding exercising faith.

17 Yea, there are many who do say: If thou wilt show unto us a sign from heaven, then we shall know of a surety; then we shall believe.

18 Now I ask, is this faith? Behold, I say unto you, Nay; for if a man knoweth a thing he hath no cause to believe, for he knoweth it.

19 And now, how much more cursed is he that knoweth the will of God and doeth it not, than he that only believeth, or only hath cause to believe, and falleth into transgression?

Notes

ALMA 32

20 Now of this thing ye must judge. Behold, I say unto you, that it is on the one hand even as it is on the other; and it shall be unto every man according to his work.

21 And now as I said concerning faith—faith is not to have a perfect knowledge of things; therefore if ye have faith ye hope for things which are not seen, which are true.

vv. 17–21 The Triad of Faith: Hope is the first step in exercising faith.

Note: All of chapter 32 is one sermon on faith. Notice that the principles found in verses 1–16 set the context for how to prepare ourselves to exercise faith. If you are teaching all of Alma 32 for a lesson, consider using verses 1–16 to establish the context of Alma's great discourse regarding exercising faith. For example, what do the people's prepared and humbled hearts have to do with exercising faith and learning the gospel?

- Explain to class members that a triad is a grouping of three things that are interconnected. In this case the three aspects of faith are hope, belief, and knowledge. Each of the three aspects are dependent upon the others. Consider drawing the stool diagram on the board as a visual as you discuss the principles of faith found in the remaining chapter.

- Invite class members to read verses 17–21 and look for the following: What faith is and What faith is not. Consider writing these statements on the board to guide their reading.

- Analyze: Discuss with the class the concept of hope and how it could apply to faith. You could ask the following: *What do you think should come first—hope or faith?* (Refer class members back to verse 21 to consider their answers.) *Why would God expect us to hope for something we can't see?*

- *Preach My Gospel* teaches the following about hope: "Hope is an abiding trust that the Lord will fulfill His promises to you. It is manifest in confidence, optimism, enthusiasm, and patient perseverance. It is believing and expecting that something will occur. When you have hope, you work through trials and difficulties with the confidence and assurance that all things will work together for your good. Hope helps you conquer discouragement. The scriptures often describe hope in Jesus Christ as the assurance that you will inherit eternal life in the celestial kingdom" (*Preach My Gospel* [2004], 163).

- Elder Jeffrey R. Holland has taught, "So how does one 'come unto Christ' in response to this constant invitation? The scriptures give scores of examples and avenues. You are well acquainted with the most basic ones. The easiest and the earliest comes simply with the desire of our heart, the most basic form of faith that we know. . . . Just believing, just having a 'molecule' of faith—simply hoping for things which are not yet seen in our lives, but which are nevertheless truly there to be bestowed—that simple step, when focused on the Lord Jesus Christ, has ever been and always will be the first principle of His eternal gospel, the first step out of despair" ("Broken Things to Mend," *Ensign*, May 2006, 71).

- Note with class members that Elder Jeffrey R. Holland refers to hope as the "first step." Refer them to the following set of verses to help them discover the next step after hope.

22 And now, behold, I say unto you, and I would that ye should remember, that God is merciful unto all who believe on his name; therefore he desireth, in the first place, that ye should believe, yea, even on his word.

Notes

23 And now, he imparteth his word by angels unto men, yea, not only men but women also. Now this is not all; little children do have words given unto them many times, which confound the wise and the learned.

24 And now, my beloved brethren, as ye have desired to know of me what ye shall do because ye are afflicted and cast out—now I do not desire that ye should suppose that I mean to judge you only according to that which is true—

25 For I do not mean that ye all of you have been compelled to humble yourselves; for I verily believe that there are some among you who would humble themselves, let them be in whatsoever circumstances they might.

26 Now, as I said concerning faith—that it was not a perfect knowledge—even so it is with my words. Ye cannot know of their surety at first, unto perfection, any more than faith is a perfect knowledge.

27 But behold, if ye will awake and arouse your faculties, even to an experiment upon my words, and exercise a particle of faith, yea, even if ye can no more than desire to believe, let this desire work in you, even until ye believe in a manner that ye can give place for a portion of my words.

28 Now, we will compare the word unto a seed. Now, if ye give place, that a seed may be planted in your heart, behold, if it be a true seed, or a good seed, if ye do not cast it out by your unbelief, that ye will resist the Spirit of the Lord, behold, it will begin to swell within your breasts; and when you feel these swelling motions, ye will begin to say within yourselves—It must needs be that this is a good seed, or that the word is good, for it beginneth to enlarge my soul; yea, it beginneth to enlighten my understanding, yea, it beginneth to be delicious to me.

29 Now behold, would not this increase your faith? I say unto you, Yea; nevertheless it hath not grown up to a perfect knowledge.

vv. 22–29 The Triad of Faith: Belief is a product of hope and causes us to act on what we hope for and believe in.

- Use the picture of the stool from the previous section to continue your discussion about faith.

- Explain to class members that belief is the next step in the faith process. Invite them to read verses 22–29 and look for how belief relates to faith.

- Analyze: Verses 27–28 are used often to teach people about faith. Consider spending time with your class analyzing what Alma is teaching in those two verses and how it applies to us. Consider asking:
  - *Why a seed?*
  - *What do you think the swelling motions represent?*
  - *How can someone's soul be enlarged?*

- Elder David A. Bednar has taught, "A testimony is a gift from God and is available to all of His children. Any honest seeker of truth can obtain a testimony by exercising the necessary 'particle of faith' in Jesus Christ to 'experiment upon' and 'try the virtue of the word' (see Alma 31:5), to yield 'to the enticings of the Holy Spirit' (see Mosiah 3:19), and to awaken unto God (see Alma 5:7). Testimony brings increased personal accountability and is a source of purpose, assurance, and joy. Seeking for and obtaining a testimony of spiritual truth requires asking, seeking, and knocking (see Matthew 7:7; 3 Nephi 14:7) with a sincere heart, real intent, and faith in the Savior" ("Converted Unto the Lord," *Ensign*, November 2012, 106).

- Ask, *When have you felt that you desired to believe? What does it feel like to experiment upon the word and then find out for yourself that it is true?* Before class you might consider choosing someone to share a personal experience regarding testimony and have him or her share that now.

Notes

30 But behold, as the seed swelleth, and sprouteth, and beginneth to grow, then you must needs say that the seed is good; for behold it swelleth, and sprouteth, and beginneth to grow. And now, behold, will not this strengthen your faith? Yea, it will strengthen your faith: for ye will say I know that this is a good seed; for behold it sprouteth and beginneth to grow.

31 And now, behold, are ye sure that this is a good seed? I say unto you, Yea; for every seed bringeth forth unto its own likeness.

32 Therefore, if a seed groweth it is good, but if it groweth not, behold it is not good, therefore it is cast away.

33 And now, behold, because ye have tried the experiment, and planted the seed, and it swelleth and sprouteth, and beginneth to grow, ye must needs know that the seed is good.

34 And now, behold, is your knowledge perfect? Yea, your knowledge is perfect in that thing, and your faith is dormant; and this because you know, for ye know that the word hath swelled your souls, and ye also know that it hath sprouted up, that your understanding doth begin to be enlightened, and your mind doth begin to expand.

35 O then, is not this real? I say unto you, Yea, because it is light; and whatsoever is light, is good, because it is discernible, therefore ye must know that it is good; and now behold, after ye have tasted this light is your knowledge perfect?

36 Behold I say unto you, Nay; neither must ye lay aside your faith, for ye have only exercised your faith to plant the seed that ye might try the experiment to know if the seed was good.

vv. 30–36 The Triad of Faith: Our belief turns into knowledge and causes us to have great faith.

- Continue to use the picture of the three-legged stool as you teach these verses.

- *Once a person has planted "the seed," look for what happens next in verses 30–36.*

- Analyze: *How does faith become real? (Refer to verses 34–35.) What do you think Alma means in verse 36?*

- President Boyd K. Packer taught, "My experience has been that a testimony does not burst upon us suddenly. Rather it grows, as Alma said, from a seed of faith. 'It will strengthen your faith: for ye will say I know that this is a good seed; for behold it sprouteth and beginneth to grow.' If you nourish it, it will grow; and if you do not nourish it, it will wither. Do not be disappointed if you have read and reread and yet have not received a powerful witness. You may be somewhat like the disciples spoken of in the Book of Mormon who were filled with the power of God in great glory 'and they knew it not' (see 3 Ne. 9:20). Do the best you can. Think of this verse: 'See that all these things are done in wisdom and order; for it is not requisite that a man should run faster than he has strength. And again, it is expedient that he should be diligent, that thereby he might win the prize; therefore, all things must be done in order' (see Mosiah 4:27)" ("The Book of Mormon: Another Testament of Jesus Christ—Plain and Precious Things," *Ensign*, May 2005, 6).

- Consider asking a class member or two before class to be prepared to share the process they went through to gain the testimony they now have. You may also consider sharing your own experience. Invite class members to use the principles from Alma 32 to increase their own faith.

37 And behold, as the tree beginneth to grow, ye will say: Let us nourish it with great care, that it may get root, that it may grow up, and bring forth fruit unto us. And now behold, if ye nourish it with much care it will get root, and grow up, and bring forth fruit.

38 But if ye neglect the tree, and take no thought

Notes

for its nourishment, behold it will not get any root; and when the heat of the sun cometh and scorcheth it, because it hath no root it withers away, and ye pluck it up and cast it out.

39 Now, this is not because the seed was not good, neither is it because the fruit thereof would not be desirable; but it is because your ground is barren, and ye will not nourish the tree, therefore ye cannot have the fruit thereof.

40 And thus, if ye will not nourish the word, looking forward with an eye of faith to the fruit thereof, ye can never pluck of the fruit of the tree of life.

41 But if ye will nourish the word, yea, nourish the tree as it beginneth to grow, by your faith with great diligence, and with patience, looking forward to the fruit thereof, it shall take root; and behold it shall be a tree springing up unto everlasting life.

42 And because of your diligence and your faith and your patience with the word in nourishing it, that it may take root in you, behold, by and by ye shall pluck the fruit thereof, which is most precious, which is sweet above all that is sweet, and which is white above all that is white, yea, and pure above all that is pure; and ye shall feast upon this fruit even until ye are filled, that ye hunger not, neither shall ye thirst.

43 Then, my brethren, ye shall reap the rewards of your faith, and your diligence, and patience, and long-suffering, waiting for the tree to bring forth fruit unto you.

vv. 37–43 The Triad of Faith: The final step of increasing your faith is to nourish it with great diligence.

- To conclude the lesson, consider bringing a basketball to bounce in front of the class. Ask, *What will happen if I stop bouncing the ball while it is in the air?*

- Invite class members to read verse 37–43 and look for how the basketball object lesson applies to faith.

- President Dieter F. Uchtdorf has taught, "Too often we approach the gospel like a farmer who places a seed in the ground in the morning and expects corn on the cob by the afternoon. When Alma compared the word of God to a seed, he explained that the seed grows into a fruit-bearing tree gradually, as a result of our 'faith, and [our] diligence, and patience, and long-suffering.' It's true that some blessings come right away: soon after we plant the seed in our hearts, it begins to swell and sprout and grow, and by this we know that the seed is good. From the very moment we set foot upon the pathway of discipleship, seen and unseen blessings from God begin to attend us. But we cannot receive the fulness of those blessings if we 'neglect the tree, and take no thought for its nourishment.' Knowing that the seed is good is not enough. We must 'nourish it with great care, that it may get root.' Only then can we partake of the fruit that is 'sweet above all that is sweet, and . . . pure above all that is pure' and 'feast upon this fruit even until [we] are filled, that [we] hunger not, neither shall [we] thirst' " ("The Way of the Disciple," *Ensign*, May 2009, 78).

- Analyze: *In what ways can faith become 'scorched'? How can someone continue to nourish their faith?*

- Apply: *Who do you know that seems to always be nourishing their faith?*

- If you taught all of chapter 32, consider asking class members to summarize what they have learned either by writing it down or by raising their hand to share. Invite them to apply Alma's lesson regarding faith into their own lives.

Notes

ALMA 33

How to Plant the Seed of Faith
About 74 BC

1–2, The people ask Alma how to plant the seed he spoke of in Alma 32; 3–14, Alma quotes the prophet Zenos, who glories in God's mercy; 15–23, Moses lifts up the serpent in the wilderness, which serves as a type of the salvation that comes through Christ.

Overarching Principle: When we have faith in God's mercy, we cry unto Him in our afflictions and find joy in Him.

⚡ Note that Alma 33 is a continuation of the sermon from Alma 32. The people Alma was teaching ask him a question—how they should plant the seed, or in what manner they should begin to exercise their faith. Consider bringing a seed to class and discussing with class members how to plant seeds to ensure they grow. Assuming you taught Alma 32 previously, refer the class to Alma 33:1 to look for the people's question. Then have class members read Alma 33:23 and look for Alma's concluding remarks. Note that he says, "I desire that ye shall plant this word in your hearts." Everything in between the first verse and the last verse is Alma's answer to the people's initial question. Consider using the following chart on the board as you teach this chapter:

Their question (v. 1)	Alma's answer (vv. 2–22)	Alma's conclusion (v. 23)

1 Now after Alma had spoken these words, they sent forth unto him desiring to know whether they should believe in one God, that they might obtain this fruit of which he had spoken, or how they should plant the seed, or the word of which he had spoken, which he said must be planted in their hearts; or in what manner they should begin to exercise their faith.

2 And Alma said unto them: Behold, ye have said that ye could not worship your God because ye are cast out of your synagogues. But behold, I say unto you, if ye suppose that ye cannot worship God, ye do greatly err, and ye ought to search the scriptures; if ye suppose that they have taught you this, ye do not understand them.

3 Do ye remember to have read what Zenos, the prophet of old, has said concerning prayer or worship?

4 For he said: Thou art merciful, O God, for thou hast heard my prayer, even when I was in the wilderness; yea, thou wast merciful when I prayed concerning those who were mine enemies, and thou didst turn them to me.

5 Yea, O God, and thou wast merciful unto me when I did cry unto thee in my field; when I did cry unto thee in my prayer, and thou didst hear me.

6 And again, O God, when I did turn to my house thou didst hear me in my prayer.

7 And when I did turn unto my closet, O Lord, and prayed unto thee, thou didst hear me.

8 Yea, thou art merciful unto thy children when they cry unto thee, to be heard of thee and not of men, and thou wilt hear them.

9 Yea, O God, thou hast been merciful unto me, and heard my cries in the midst of thy congregations.

10 Yea, and thou hast also heard me when I have been cast out and have been despised by mine enemies; yea, thou didst hear my cries, and wast angry with mine enemies, and thou didst visit them in thine anger with speedy destruction.

11 And thou didst hear me because of mine afflictions and my sincerity; and it is because of thy

Notes

Son that thou hast been thus merciful unto me, therefore I will cry unto thee in all mine afflictions, for in thee is my joy; for thou hast turned thy judgments away from me, because of thy Son.

vv. 2–11 The Lord God is always merciful.

⚡ Use the chart suggested at the beginning of this chapter. As class members discover principles from these verses, write them on the board under the "Alma's Answer" column.

🔎 Note with the class that Alma quotes the writing of a prophet named Zenos. Ask, *Look for and note each time the Lord showed mercy to Zenos.*

❓ Analyze: *In your own words, how often does the Lord show mercy? What lesson is Alma trying to teach from quoting these verses?* Consider writing class members' responses on the board.

🔎 After acknowledging the Lord's mercy in his life, what is Zenos's conclusion in verse 11?

❓ Apply: *How has the Lord shown mercy in your life?* Consider using the examples Zenos gave and relate them to modern-day examples.

12 And now Alma said unto them: Do ye believe those scriptures which have been written by them of old?

13 Behold, if ye do, ye must believe what Zenos said; for, behold he said: Thou hast turned away thy judgments because of thy Son.

14 Now behold, my brethren, I would ask if ye have read the scriptures? If ye have, how can ye disbelieve on the Son of God?

15 For it is not written that Zenos alone spake of these things, but Zenock also spake of these things—

16 For behold, he said: Thou art angry, O Lord, with this people, because they will not understand thy mercies which thou hast bestowed upon them because of thy Son.

v. 16 We must understand and acknowledge the mercies the Lord has bestowed upon us because of His Son.

🔎 *Look in verse 16 for what angers the Lord.*

❓ Analyze: *Why do you think that would make the Lord angry? What does this teach about God's mercy?*

17 And now, my brethren, ye see that a second prophet of old has testified of the Son of God, and because the people would not understand his words they stoned him to death.

18 But behold, this is not all; these are not the only ones who have spoken concerning the Son of God.

19 Behold, he was spoken of by Moses; yea, and behold a type was raised up in the wilderness, that whosoever would look upon it might live. And many did look and live.

20 But few understood the meaning of those things, and this because of the hardness of their hearts. But there were many who were so hardened that they would not look, therefore they perished. Now the reason they would not look is because they did not believe that it would heal them.

21 O my brethren, if ye could be healed by merely casting about your eyes that ye might be healed, would ye not behold quickly, or would ye rather harden your hearts in unbelief, and be slothful, that ye would not cast about your eyes, that ye might perish?

22 If so, wo shall come upon you; but if not so, then cast about your eyes and begin to believe in the Son of God, that he will come to redeem his people, and that he shall suffer and die to atone for their sins; and that he shall rise again from the dead, which shall bring to pass the resurrection, that all men shall stand before him, to

Notes

be judged at the last and judgment day, according to their works.

vv. 17–22 The manifestation of God's mercy is the Atonement of Jesus Christ.

- ⚡ Continue to use the chart from the beginning of the lesson.
- 🔍 Read verses 19–22 as a class and invite class members to consider how these verses relate to God's mercy.
- ❤ Once you have completed the entire chapter, allow the class time to consider what the overall lesson from this chapter is and how it applies in our day. Testify of God's mercy in your own life.

23 And now, my brethren, I desire that ye shall plant this word in your hearts, and as it beginneth to swell even so nourish it by your faith. And behold, it will become a tree, springing up in you unto everlasting life. And then may God grant unto you that your burdens may be light, through the joy of his Son. And even all this can ye do if ye will. Amen.

> **Teaching Tips from Prophet's Lips** "No greater responsibility can rest upon any man [or woman], than to be a teacher of God's children" (David O. McKay, in Conference Report, Oct. 1916, 57).

ALMA 34

"Now Is the Time to Prepare to Meet God"

About 74 BC

1–16, Amulek teaches about the Atonement and faith unto repentance; 17–27, Amulek teaches the importance of crying unto the Lord; 28–29, Remember to be charitable; 30–36, Do not procrastinate the day of your repentance; 37–41, Amulek exhorts the Zoramites to bear their afflictions with patience and hope.

1 And now it came to pass that after Alma had spoken these words unto them he sat down upon the ground, and Amulek arose and began to teach them, saying:

2 My brethren, I think that it is impossible that ye should be ignorant of the things which have been spoken concerning the coming of Christ, who is taught by us to be the Son of God; yea, I know that these things were taught unto you bountifully before your dissension from among us.

3 And as ye have desired of my beloved brother that he should make known unto you what ye should do, because of your afflictions; and he hath spoken somewhat unto you to prepare your minds; yea, and he hath exhorted you unto faith and to patience—

4 Yea, even that ye would have so much faith as even to plant the word in your hearts, that ye may try the experiment of its goodness.

5 And we have beheld that the great question which is in your minds is whether the word be in the Son of God, or whether there shall be no Christ.

6 And ye also beheld that my brother has proved unto you, in many instances, that the word is in Christ unto salvation.

7 My brother has called upon the words of Zenos, that redemption cometh through the Son of God, and also upon the words of Zenock; and also he has appealed unto Moses, to prove that these things are true.

8 And now, behold, I will testify unto you of myself that these things are true. Behold, I say unto you, that I do know that Christ shall come among the children of men, to take upon him the transgressions of his people, and that he shall atone for the sins of the world; for the Lord God hath spoken it.

9 For it is expedient that an atonement should be

Notes

made; for according to the great plan of the Eternal God there must be an atonement made, or else all mankind must unavoidably perish; yea, all are hardened; yea, all are fallen and are lost, and must perish except it be through the atonement which it is expedient should be made.

10 For it is expedient that there should be a great and last sacrifice; yea, not a sacrifice of man, neither of beast, neither of any manner of fowl; for it shall not be a human sacrifice; but it must be an infinite and eternal sacrifice.

11 Now there is not any man that can sacrifice his own blood which will atone for the sins of another. Now, if a man murdereth, behold will our law, which is just, take the life of his brother? I say unto you, Nay.

12 But the law requireth the life of him who hath murdered; therefore there can be nothing which is short of an infinite atonement which will suffice for the sins of the world.

13 Therefore, it is expedient that there should be a great and last sacrifice, and then shall there be, or it is expedient there should be, a stop to the shedding of blood; then shall the law of Moses be fulfilled; yea, it shall be all fulfilled, every jot and tittle, and none shall have passed away.

14 And behold, this is the whole meaning of the law, every whit pointing to that great and last sacrifice; and that great and last sacrifice will be the Son of God, yea, infinite and eternal.

15 And thus he shall bring salvation to all those who shall believe on his name; this being the intent of this last sacrifice, to bring about the bowels of mercy, which over powereth justice, and bringeth about means unto men that they may have faith unto repentance.

16 And thus mercy can satisfy the demands of justice, and encircles them in the arms of safety, while he that exercises no faith unto repentance is exposed to the whole law of the demands of justice; therefore only unto him that has faith unto repentance is brought about the great and eternal plan of redemption.

Notes

vv. 1–16 The infinite Atonement of Christ.

- Put the phrase, "Encircles them in the arms of safety" (v. 16) on the board or on a large piece of paper and hide or cover it before class starts. As you begin class, tell the class members that you are going to share a phrase with them and ask them to tell you the first thing that comes to mind when they read this phrase. Reveal the phrase above and then write on the board their initial responses. Inform class members that today you will be discussing and learning how this phrase, as described by Amulek, teaches of the Atonement of Christ.

- Ask the following question to help class members discover the context of the chapter: *What is the question that Amulek is addressing to the Zoramites? (v. 5)*

- Explain that one of the roles of the gospel learner is to analyze and ask questions about truths of the gospel. Invite class members to study verses 8–10 and be prepared to share a question and/or insight they had as they studied these three doctrinal-based verses. Have class members share what they found and what questions they may have had.

- Elder Nelson said, "In preparatory times of the Old Testament, the practice of atonement was finite—meaning it had an end. It was a symbolic forecast of the definitive Atonement of Jesus the Christ. His Atonement is infinite—without an end. It was also infinite in that all humankind would be saved from never-ending death. It was infinite in terms of His immense suffering. It was infinite in time, putting an end to the preceding prototype of animal sacrifice. It was infinite in scope—it was to be done once for all. And the mercy of the Atonement extends not only to an infinite number of people, but also to an infinite number of worlds created by Him. It was infinite beyond any human scale of measurement or mortal comprehension. Jesus was the only one who could offer such an infinite atonement, since He was born of a mortal mother and an immortal Father. Because of that unique birthright, Jesus was an infinite Being" (Russell M. Nelson, "The Atonement," *Ensign*, November 1996, 36).

💬 Elder Holland stated, "This infinite Atonement of Christ was possible because (1) He was the only sinless man ever to live on this earth and therefore was not subject to the spiritual death resulting from sin, (2) He was the Only Begotten of the Father and therefore possessed the attributes of godhood that gave Him power over physical death, and (3) He was apparently the only one sufficiently humble and willing in the premortal council to be foreordained to that service" (Jeffrey R. Holland, "The Atonement of Jesus Christ," *Ensign*, March 2008, 32–38).

❓ Analyze: Read verses 15–16 as a class and ask, *What does it mean to have faith unto repentance? What does "bowels of mercy" mean?*

💡 According the 1828 Edition of Webster's American Dictionary of the English Language the word "bowel"—as used in the context of this verse—is defined as, "The seat of pity or kindness; hence, tenderness, compassion, a scriptural sense."

17 Therefore may God grant unto you, my brethren, that ye may begin to exercise your faith unto repentance, that ye begin to call upon his holy name, that he would have mercy upon you;

18 Yea, cry unto him for mercy; for he is mighty to save.

19 Yea, humble yourselves, and continue in prayer unto him.

20 Cry unto him when ye are in your fields, yea, over all your flocks.

21 Cry unto him in your houses, yea, over all your household, both morning, mid-day, and evening.

22 Yea, cry unto him against the power of your enemies.

23 Yea, cry unto him against the devil, who is an enemy to all righteousness.

24 Cry unto him over the crops of your fields, that ye may prosper in them.

25 Cry over the flocks of your fields, that they may increase.

26 But this is not all; ye must pour out your souls in your closets, and your secret places, and in your wilderness.

27 Yea, and when you do not cry unto the Lord, let your hearts be full, drawn out in prayer unto him continually for your welfare, and also for the welfare of those who are around you.

28 And now behold, my beloved brethren, I say unto you, do not suppose that this is all; for after ye have done all these things, if ye turn away the needy, and the naked, and visit not the sick and afflicted, and impart of your substance, if ye have, to those who stand in need—I say unto you, if ye do not any of these things, behold, your prayer is vain, and availeth you nothing, and ye are as hypocrites who do deny the faith.

29 Therefore, if ye do not remember to be charitable, ye are as dross, which the refiners do cast out, (it being of no worth) and is trodden under foot of men.

vv. 17–29 Faith unto repentance is accomplished by prayer and charity.

🔍 *What are the two things that Amulek suggests that we must do to have faith unto repentance in verses 18–29?*

❓ Analyze:
• *From these verses, what would you say the phrase "faith unto repentance" means?*
• *What is true faith?*
• *What is the relationship between faith and repentance?*

30 And now, my brethren, I would that, after ye have received so many witnesses, seeing that the holy scriptures testify of these things, ye come forth and bring fruit unto repentance.

31 Yea, I would that ye would come forth

Notes

and harden not your hearts any longer; for behold, now is the time and the day of your salvation; and therefore, if ye will repent and harden not your hearts, immediately shall the great plan of redemption be brought about unto you.

32 For behold, this life is the time for men to prepare to meet God; yea, behold the day of this life is the day for men to perform their labors.

33 And now, as I said unto you before, as ye have had so many witnesses, therefore, I beseech of you that ye do not procrastinate the day of your repentance until the end; for after this day of life, which is given us to prepare for eternity, behold, if we do not improve our time while in this life, then cometh the night of darkness wherein there can be no labor performed.

34 Ye cannot say, when ye are brought to that awful crisis, that I will repent, that I will return to my God. Nay, ye cannot say this; for that same spirit which doth possess your bodies at the time that ye go out of this life, that same spirit will have power to possess your body in that eternal world.

35 For behold, if ye have procrastinated the day of your repentance even until death, behold, ye have become subjected to the spirit of the devil, and he doth seal you his; therefore, the Spirit of the Lord hath withdrawn from you, and hath no place in you, and the devil hath all power over you; and this is the final state of the wicked.

36 And this I know, because the Lord hath said he dwelleth not in unholy temples, but in the hearts of the righteous doth he dwell; yea, and he has also said that the righteous shall sit down in his kingdom, to go no more out; but their garments should be made white through the blood of the Lamb.

vv. 30–36 This life is the time to prepare to meet God.

- Ask the following question of the class and have class members respond to someone next to them. *What does it mean "to prepare to meet God"?* Invite class members to share and discuss their responses.

- *What does Amulek teach in verses 32–34?*

- Analyze: Connect the teachings of Amulek (vv. 1–16) with the end of the chapter by asking, *How does Amulek's explanation of the Atonement teach us about the need for repentance in this life?*

- Invite all to prepare to return to their Heavenly Father. Testify that now is the time. Consider sharing a story or having a class member share an experience when they came to understand that now is the time to prepare to meet God.

37 And now, my beloved brethren, I desire that ye should remember these things, and that ye should work out your salvation with fear before God, and that ye should no more deny the coming of Christ;

38 That ye contend no more against the Holy Ghost, but that ye receive it, and take upon you the name of Christ; that ye humble yourselves even to the dust, and worship God, in whatsoever place ye may be in, in spirit and in truth; and that ye live in thanksgiving daily, for the many mercies and blessings which he doth bestow upon you.

39 Yea, and I also exhort you, my brethren, that ye be watchful unto prayer continually, that ye may not be led away by the temptations of the devil, that he may not overpower you, that ye may not become his subjects at the last day; for behold, he rewardeth you no good thing.

40 And now my beloved brethren, I would exhort you to have patience, and that ye bear with all manner of afflictions; that ye do not revile against those who do cast you out because of your exceeding poverty, lest ye become sinners like unto them;

41 But that ye have patience, and bear with those afflictions, with a firm hope that ye shall one day rest from all your afflictions.

Notes

ALMA 35

Index Topics: atonement, faith, repentance, prayer, charity

Zoramite Believers Are Cast Out
About 74 BC

1–6, The Zoramites find out who believes in the word and that group is cast out; 7–9, The people of Ammon receive them and administer to them; 10–16, The Zoramites stir up the Lamanites to war and Alma is grieved for the wickedness of the people.

1 Now it came to pass that after Amulek had made an end of these words, they withdrew themselves from the multitude and came over into the land of Jershon.

2 Yea, and the rest of the brethren, after they had preached the word unto the Zoramites, also came over into the land of Jershon.

3 And it came to pass that after the more popular part of the Zoramites had consulted together concerning the words which had been preached unto them, they were angry because of the word, for it did destroy their craft; therefore they would not hearken unto the words.

4 And they sent and gathered together throughout all the land all the people, and consulted with them concerning the words which had been spoken.

5 Now their rulers and their priests and their teachers did not let the people know concerning their desires; therefore they found out privily the minds of all the people.

6 And it came to pass that after they had found out the minds of all the people, those who were in favor of the words which had been spoken by Alma and his brethren were cast out of the land; and they were many; and they came over also into the land of Jershon.

7 And it came to pass that Alma and his brethren did minister unto them.

8 Now the people of the Zoramites were angry with the people of Ammon who were in Jershon, and the chief ruler of the Zoramites, being a very wicked man, sent over unto the people of Ammon desiring them that they should cast out of their land all those who came over from them into their land.

9 And he breathed out many threatenings against them. And now the people of Ammon did not fear their words; therefore they did not cast them out, but they did receive all the poor of the Zoramites that came over unto them; and they did nourish them, and did clothe them, and did give unto them lands for their inheritance; and they did administer unto them according to their wants.

10 Now this did stir up the Zoramites to anger against the people of Ammon, and they began to mix with the Lamanites and to stir them up also to anger against them.

11 And thus the Zoramites and the Lamanites began to make preparations for war against the people of Ammon, and also against the Nephites.

vv. 1–11 It is our covenant responsibility to care for each other in times of need.

- Before class, think of a topic that you know class members will have differing opinions about. This could be as simple as those who like fish and those who do not. Refrain from choosing a topic that will become a heated debate. At the beginning of class, present the topic and request class members to choose a side. After they have made their choice, ask them what they would think if those who choose the differing opinion were kicked out of class. After a very brief discussion, explain what this has to do with Alma 35.

- Divide the class into two groups. (If you prefer, you could use the groups that were formed in teaching suggestion above). Invite one

Notes

group to imagine themselves in the position of those who have been cast out of the land of the Zoramites and the other group to imagine themselves in the position of the people of Ammon. Have everyone silently read the chapter with the perspective that has been assigned to them.

❓ Analyze: Ask the following questions to each group.

Questions for those cast out:

- *What emotions would you have after finding out that you were to be cast out because of your belief of the gospel?*
- *What would your feelings be toward the people of Ammon?*
- *How would you feel knowing that, because of your actions, there is a war that is beginning between the Lamanites and the Nephites?*

Questions for the people of Ammon:

- *What would your reaction be to those who came to your land seeking refuge?*
- *Consider the history of the people of Ammon. Why do you think they were so happy to help?*

❓ Apply: *What can we learn from this story?*

♥ Invite the class to care for all those around them as they experience trials and tribulations.

12 And thus ended the seventeenth year of the reign of the judges over the people of Nephi.

13 And the people of Ammon departed out of the land of Jershon, and came over into the land of Melek, and gave place in the land of Jershon for the armies of the Nephites, that they might contend with the armies of the Lamanites and the armies of the Zoramites; and thus commenced a war betwixt the Lamanites and the Nephites, in the eighteenth year of the reign of the judges; and an account shall be given of their wars hereafter.

14 And Alma, and Ammon, and their brethren, and also the two sons of Alma returned to the land of Zarahemla, after having been instruments in the hands of God of bringing many of the Zoramites to repentance; and as many as were brought to repentance were driven out of their land; but they have lands for their inheritance in the land of Jershon, and they have taken up arms to defend themselves, and their wives, and children, and their lands.

15 Now Alma, being grieved for the iniquity of his people, yea for the wars, and the bloodsheds, and the contentions which were among them; and having been to declare the word, or sent to declare the word, among all the people in every city; and seeing that the hearts of the people began to wax hard, and that they began to be offended because of the strictness of the word, his heart was exceedingly sorrowful.

16 Therefore, he caused that his sons should be gathered together, that he might give unto them every one his charge, separately, concerning the things pertaining unto righteousness. And we have an account of his commandments, which he gave unto them according to his own record.

Teaching Tips from Prophets' Lips "The pure gospel of Jesus Christ must go down into the hearts of young people by the power of the Holy Ghost. It will not be enough for them to have had a spiritual witness of the truth and to want good things later. It will not be enough for them to hope for some future cleansing and strengthening. Our aim must be for them to become truly converted to the restored gospel of Jesus Christ while they are young" (Elder Eyring, "We Must Raise Our Sights," *Ensign*, Sept. 2004).

Index Topics: covenant

ALMA 36

Alma Recounts His Conversion
About 74 BC

1–5, Alma counsels his son Helaman; 6–16, Recounts the appearing of the angel and the torment of his soul;

Notes

ALMA 36

17–23, Calls upon the Lord and is forgiven; 24–30, Lives a life of faithfulness.

Overarching Principle: Alma Chapters 36–42 include the words of Alma the younger to his three sons. Similar to the lesson idea at the beginning of 2 Nephi chapter 1, you could write "Life Lessons for Happiness and Success" on the board as a way to guide your class discussion. Consider creating a chart similar to the one below in order to present an overview of the next seven chapters.

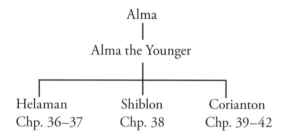

1 My son, give ear to my words; for I swear unto you, that inasmuch as ye shall keep the commandments of God ye shall prosper in the land.

2 I would that ye should do as I have done, in remembering the captivity of our fathers; for they were in bondage, and none could deliver them except it was the God of Abraham, and the God of Isaac, and the God of Jacob; and he surely did deliver them in their afflictions.

3 And now, O my son Helaman, behold, thou art in thy youth, and therefore, I beseech of thee that thou wilt hear my words and learn of me; for I do know that whosoever shall put their trust in God shall be supported in their trials, and their troubles, and their afflictions, and shall be lifted up at the last day.

vv. 1–3 Leading by example helps others to follow the path of righteousness.

🔎 As mentioned above, write on the board, "Life Lessons for Happiness and Success" and have class members look in verses 1–3 for principles and ideas that, when applied in our lives, lead to greater happiness and success. After they share what they have found, write on the board, "Do as I say; not as I do" and ask, *Why doesn't that work with raising children?* After they have shared, ask them to look for the idea of "Do as I have done" in chapter 36 verses 1 and 29, and also in chapter 37 verse 2.

♥ Ask, *Why does this make your actions important?* Invite class members to live exemplary lives so they can say "Do as I have done" to their children. It may be helpful to point out that Alma, like all parents, had not lived a perfect life, but because of repentance he could say, "Do as I have done" (see Alma 36:6).

4 And I would not that ye think that I know of myself—not of the temporal but of the spiritual, not of the carnal mind but of God.

5 Now, behold, I say unto you, if I had not been born of God I should not have known these things; but God has, by the mouth of his holy angel, made these things known unto me, not of any worthiness of myself;

6 For I went about with the sons of Mosiah, seeking to destroy the church of God; but behold, God sent his holy angel to stop us by the way.

7 And behold, he spake unto us, as it were the voice of thunder, and the whole earth did tremble beneath our feet; and we all fell to the earth, for the fear of the Lord came upon us.

8 But behold, the voice said unto me: Arise. And I arose and stood up, and beheld the angel.

9 And he said unto me: If thou wilt of thyself be destroyed, seek no more to destroy the church of God.

10 And it came to pass that I fell to the earth; and it was for the space of three days and three nights that I could not open my mouth, neither had I the use of my limbs.

Notes

11 And the angel spake more things unto me, which were heard by my brethren, but I did not hear them; for when I heard the words—If thou wilt be destroyed of thyself, seek no more to destroy the church of God—I was struck with such great fear and amazement lest perhaps I should be destroyed, that I fell to the earth and I did hear no more.

12 But I was racked with eternal torment, for my soul was harrowed up to the greatest degree and racked with all my sins.

13 Yea, I did remember all my sins and iniquities, for which I was tormented with the pains of hell; yea, I saw that I had rebelled against my God, and that I had not kept his holy commandments.

14 Yea, and I had murdered many of his children, or rather led them away unto destruction; yea, and in fine so great had been my iniquities, that the very thought of coming into the presence of my God did rack my soul with inexpressible horror.

15 Oh, thought I, that I could be banished and become extinct both soul and body, that I might not be brought to stand in the presence of my God, to be judged of my deeds.

16 And now, for three days and for three nights was I racked, even with the pains of a damned soul.

vv. 11–16 The consequences of sin are great.

- Ask: *Is it ever worth it to sin?* After some discussion, explain that because Alma was rebellious against God, he did not realize how awful the consequences of sin are, so God gave him a clear conception of them through the experience recorded in these verses.

- Look for and mark in your scriptures words and phrases in verses 11–16 describing how awful the consequences of sin were for Alma. Have your class share what they marked.

- Ask:
  - *How might these verses be similar to a description of hell?*
  - *What is a "rack"?* (It is a torture device used to stretch the body.)
  - *What does that add to the description of Alma's sufferings?*
  - *What is a "harrow"?* (It is a farming instrument with sharp spikes used to tear up hard soil before planting.)
  - *What does that add to the description of Alma's sufferings?*
  - *What brought the "inexpressible horror" to Alma?* (v. 14)
  - *Why would that cause such torment?*
  - *In light of these verses, what impressions are you left with regarding sin?*
  - *What two things do these verses suggest we all do?* (Avoid sin and repent when we do sin.)

- Invite class members to avoid these awful consequences by avoiding sin and committing to repent when necessary.

17 And it came to pass that as I was thus racked with torment, while I was harrowed up by the memory of my many sins, behold, I remembered also to have heard my father prophesy unto the people concerning the coming of one Jesus Christ, a Son of God, to atone for the sins of the world.

18 Now, as my mind caught hold upon this thought, I cried within my heart: O Jesus, thou Son of God, have mercy on me, who am in the gall of bitterness, and am encircled about by the everlasting chains of death.

vv. 16–18 Some of the most powerful gospel lessons are taught by parents.

- Hand out small pieces of paper to the class. Ask, *Who has the greatest influence on you for good?* Have them write the response on their papers and collect the papers. Later, calculate how often responses like parents, siblings, family members, friends, coaches, or any other responses appear. Then share what the class's results were and ask what can be learned from the results.

- Prior to reading verses 16–18 ask, *When Alma was in this torment of soul, whose teachings did he remember?* Read verses 16–18 and look for

Notes

whose words came to him at the critical moment.

❓ Analyze:
- *What important lesson might a parent learn from these verses?*
- *Why might this surprise some parents?*
- *Do you think Alma's father ever thought his son wasn't listening to his counsel?*

✏️ Invite class members to note the following cross-references in their scriptures: Enos 1:2–3; Alma 56:47–48; 2 Timothy 1:5; 3:15. Read the verses together and discuss the impact these parents had in their children's lives. Discuss with your class how parents share their faith with their children.

♥ Invite class members to be parents who are strong enough to share their faith with their children directly.

19 And now, behold, when I thought this, I could remember my pains no more; yea, I was harrowed up by the memory of my sins no more.

20 And oh, what joy, and what marvelous light I did behold; yea, my soul was filled with joy as exceeding as was my pain!

21 Yea, I say unto you, my son, that there could be nothing so exquisite and so bitter as were my pains. Yea, and again I say unto you, my son, that on the other hand, there can be nothing so exquisite and sweet as was my joy.

22 Yea, methought I saw, even as our father Lehi saw, God sitting upon his throne, surrounded with numberless concourses of angels, in the attitude of singing and praising their God; yea, and my soul did long to be there.

23 But behold, my limbs did receive their strength again, and I stood upon my feet, and did manifest unto the people that I had been born of God.

24 Yea, and from that time even until now, I have labored without ceasing, that I might bring souls unto repentance; that I might bring them to taste of the exceeding joy of which I did taste; that they might also be born of God, and be filled with the Holy Ghost.

25 Yea, and now behold, O my son, the Lord doth give me exceedingly great joy in the fruit of my labors;

26 For because of the word which he has imparted unto me, behold, many have been born of God, and have tasted as I have tasted, and have seen eye to eye as I have seen; therefore they do know of these things of which I have spoken, as I do know; and the knowledge which I have is of God.

27 And I have been supported under trials and troubles of every kind, yea, and in all manner of afflictions; yea, God has delivered me from prison, and from bonds, and from death; yea, and I do put my trust in him, and he will still deliver me.

28 And I know that he will raise me up at the last day, to dwell with him in glory; yea, and I will praise him forever, for he has brought our fathers out of Egypt, and he has swallowed up the Egyptians in the Red Sea; and he led them by his power into the promised land; yea, and he has delivered them out of bondage and captivity from time to time.

29 Yea, and he has also brought our fathers out of the land of Jerusalem; and he has also, by his everlasting power, delivered them out of bondage and captivity, from time to time even down to the present day; and I have always retained in remembrance their captivity; yea, and ye also ought to retain in remembrance, as I have done, their captivity.

30 But behold, my son, this is not all; for ye ought to know as I do know, that inasmuch as ye shall keep the commandments of God ye shall prosper in the land; and ye ought to know also, that inasmuch as ye will not keep the commandments of God ye shall be cut off from his presence. Now this is according to his word.

vv. 19–28 How to know if you have been forgiven.

⚡ Ask class members, *How can a person know if he or she has been forgiven of sins?* Discuss various ways an individual can gain that knowledge. Explain that Alma 36:19–28

Notes

ALMA 36

shares insights of how to know you have been forgiven.

✋ Assign the verses below to the class, and have them look for what in that verse would have signified to Alma that he had received forgiveness.

v. 19

vv. 20–21

v. 22 (Contrast with vv. 14–15)

v. 23

v. 24

v. 27

v. 28

♥ Explain that if an individual is unsure if he or she has been forgiven, they should confirm whether or not these elements apply.

vv. 1–30 Alma was convinced, converted, and committed.

🔍 Explain that some people feel that Alma's conversion was too easy because an angel appeared to him. Write the words "Convinced, Converted, and Committed" on the board. Have class members review the chapter and try to identify in which verses each of those actions occurred. In the end, they should see that the angel only convinced Alma, but his conversion happened days later when he called on the Lord for mercy.

vv. 1–30 "Chiasmus" is a proof of the Book of Mormon's authenticity.

💡 Explain that chiasmus is an ancient literary form in which the author writes using specific ideas and words that will be paralleled in reversed order. Examples of chiasmus are frequent and numerous in the Hebrew bible, particularly in the more poetic writings such as the books of Psalms and Isaiah. Often, an author would use chaiastic structure to emphasize thoughts or principles by placing them in the center or turning point of the chiasm. This literary form was not widely recognized in ancient records until the late 1920s (after Joseph Smith's day) and is thus an internal evidence for the authenticity of the Book of Mormon. A striking example of chiasmus can be found throughout Alma 36. Using chiastic structure, Alma illustrates the impact of the central turning point of his life—his acceptance of Jesus Christ as his Savior (see vv. 17–18).

Words v. 1

  Prosper v. 1

    As I v. 2

      Captivity v. 2

      Deliver v. 2

        Trust v. 3

          Support v. 3

        Know v. 4

          Born of God v. 5

          Church v. 6

            Limbs v. 10

              Presence v. 14

                Pain v. 16

                  Jesus—Son v. 17

                  Jesus—Son v. 18

                Joy (no pain) v. 20

              Presence (alt. word) v. 22

            Limbs v. 23

            People v. 23

          Born of God v. 23

        Know v. 26

          Supported v. 27

        Trust v. 27

      Deliver v. 28

      Captivity v. 28

    As I v. 29

  Prosper v. 30

Word v. 30

Notes

Index Topics: conversion, forgiveness, sin, hell, parenting

ALMA 37

"Small and Simple Things"
About 74 BC

1–20, Alma entrusts Helaman with the sacred records and explains their power; 21–32, He is not to share the works of darkness contained in the record; 33–37, He is to teach faithfulness and counseling with the Lord; 38–47, The Liahona is a shadow of the assistance we can have on our spiritual journey in life.

1 And now, my son Helaman, I command you that ye take the records which have been entrusted with me;

2 And I also command you that ye keep a record of this people, according as I have done, upon the plates of Nephi, and keep all these things sacred which I have kept, even as I have kept them; for it is for a wise purpose that they are kept.

3 And these plates of brass, which contain these engravings, which have the records of the holy scriptures upon them, which have the genealogy of our forefathers, even from the beginning—

4 Behold, it has been prophesied by our fathers, that they should be kept and handed down from one generation to another, and be kept and preserved by the hand of the Lord until they should go forth unto every nation, kindred, tongue, and people, that they shall know of the mysteries contained thereon.

5 And now behold, if they are kept they must retain their brightness; yea, and they will retain their brightness; yea, and also shall all the plates which do contain that which is holy writ.

6 Now ye may suppose that this is foolishness in me; but behold I say unto you, that by small and simple things are great things brought to pass; and small means in many instances doth confound the wise.

7 And the Lord God doth work by means to bring about his great and eternal purposes; and by very small means the Lord doth confound the wise and bringeth about the salvation of many souls.

8 And now, it has hitherto been wisdom in God that these things should be preserved; for behold, they have enlarged the memory of this people, yea, and convinced many of the error of their ways, and brought them to the knowledge of their God unto the salvation of their souls.

9 Yea, I say unto you, were it not for these things that these records do contain, which are on these plates, Ammon and his brethren could not have convinced so many thousands of the Lamanites of the incorrect tradition of their fathers; yea, these records and their words brought them unto repentance; that is, they brought them to the knowledge of the Lord their God, and to rejoice in Jesus Christ their Redeemer.

10 And who knoweth but what they will be the means of bringing many thousands of them, yea, and also many thousands of our stiffnecked brethren, the Nephites, who are now hardening their hearts in sin and iniquities, to the knowledge of their Redeemer?

vv. 1–10 The scriptures change people's lives for good.

- Hold up a small seed that comes from a large fruit, such as a watermelon. As you show the seed, ask, *How is this an example of verse 6?*
- Analyze: *What are some examples of "small and simple things" that make a big difference?*
- *What is the small and simple thing referred to in verses 1–5?*
- Analyze:
  - *How do the scriptures make a big difference in someone's life?*
  - *How do people often underestimate the power of the scriptures in their lives?*

Notes

- *What are some reasons people may neglect studying the scriptures?*

💬 Ezra Taft Benson stated, "Often we spend great effort in trying to increase the activity levels in our stakes. We work diligently to raise the percentages of those attending sacrament meetings. We labor to get a higher percentage of our young men on missions. We strive to improve the numbers of those marrying in the temple. All of these are commendable efforts and important to the growth of the kingdom. But when individual members and families immerse themselves in the scriptures regularly and consistently, these other areas of activity will automatically come. Testimonies will increase. Commitment will be strengthened. Families will be fortified. Personal revelation will flow" ("The Power of the Word," *Ensign*, May 1986, Priesthood Leadership Meeting, 79).

🔍 *In verses 7–10, look for examples of how the scriptures had helped the people in the Book of Mormon.* After each example, ask, *How is that similar today?*

❤ Invite class members to apply this "small and simple thing" in their lives and look for the great things that will come to pass.

11 Now these mysteries are not yet fully made known unto me; therefore I shall forbear.

12 And it may suffice if I only say they are preserved for a wise purpose, which purpose is known unto God; for he doth counsel in wisdom over all his works, and his paths are straight, and his course is one eternal round.

13 O remember, remember, my son Helaman, how strict are the commandments of God. And he said: If ye will keep my commandments ye shall prosper in the land—but if ye keep not his commandments ye shall be cut off from his presence.

14 And now remember, my son, that God has entrusted you with these things, which are sacred, which he has kept sacred, and also which he will keep and preserve for a wise purpose in him, that he may show forth his power unto future generations.

15 And now behold, I tell you by the spirit of prophecy, that if ye transgress the commandments of God, behold, these things which are sacred shall be taken away from you by the power of God, and ye shall be delivered up unto Satan, that he may sift you as chaff before the wind.

16 But if ye keep the commandments of God, and do with these things which are sacred according to that which the Lord doth command you, (for you must appeal unto the Lord for all things whatsoever ye must do with them) behold, no power of earth or hell can take them from you, for God is powerful to the fulfilling of all his words.

v. 16 "No power of earth or hell can take them from you."

💡 With your class, compare verse 16 to the charge Joseph Smith was given in Joseph Smith History 1:59.

17 For he will fulfil all his promises which he shall make unto you, for he has fulfilled his promises which he has made unto our fathers.

18 For he promised unto them that he would preserve these things for a wise purpose in him, that he might show forth his power unto future generations.

19 And now behold, one purpose hath he fulfilled, even to the restoration of many thousands of the Lamanites to the knowledge of the truth; and he hath shown forth his power in them, and he will also still show forth his power in them unto future generations; therefore they shall be preserved.

20 Therefore I command you, my son Helaman, that ye be diligent in fulfilling all my words, and that ye be diligent in keeping the commandments of God as they are written.

21 And now, I will speak unto you concerning

Notes

those twenty-four plates, that ye keep them, that the mysteries and the works of darkness, and their secret works, or the secret works of those people who have been destroyed, may be made manifest unto this people; yea, all their murders, and robbings, and their plunderings, and all their wickedness and abominations, may be made manifest unto this people; yea, and that ye preserve these interpreters.

22 For behold, the Lord saw that his people began to work in darkness, yea, work secret murders and abominations; therefore the Lord said, if they did not repent they should be destroyed from off the face of the earth.

23 And the Lord said: I will prepare unto my servant Gazelem, a stone, which shall shine forth in darkness unto light, that I may discover unto my people who serve me, that I may discover unto them the works of their brethren, yea, their secret works, their works of darkness, and their wickedness and abominations.

24 And now, my son, these interpreters were prepared that the word of God might be fulfilled, which he spake, saying:

25 I will bring forth out of darkness unto light all their secret works and their abominations; and except they repent I will destroy them from off the face of the earth; and I will bring to light all their secrets and abominations, unto every nation that shall hereafter possess the land.

26 And now, my son, we see that they did not repent; therefore they have been destroyed, and thus far the word of God has been fulfilled; yea, their secret abominations have been brought out of darkness and made known unto us.

27 And now, my son, I command you that ye retain all their oaths, and their covenants, and their agreements in their secret abominations; yea, and all their signs and their wonders ye shall keep from this people, that they know them not, lest peradventure they should fall into darkness also and be destroyed.

28 For behold, there is a curse upon all this land, that destruction shall come upon all those workers of darkness, according to the power of God, when they are fully ripe; therefore I desire that this people might not be destroyed.

29 Therefore ye shall keep these secret plans of their oaths and their covenants from this people, and only their wickedness and their murders and their abominations shall ye make known unto them; and ye shall teach them to abhor such wickedness and abominations and murders; and ye shall also teach them that these people were destroyed on account of their wickedness and abominations and their murders.

30 For behold, they murdered all the prophets of the Lord who came among them to declare unto them concerning their iniquities; and the blood of those whom they murdered did cry unto the Lord their God for vengeance upon those who were their murderers; and thus the judgments of God did come upon these workers of darkness and secret combinations.

31 Yea, and cursed be the land forever and ever unto those workers of darkness and secret combinations, even unto destruction, except they repent before they are fully ripe.

32 And now, my son, remember the words which I have spoken unto you; trust not those secret plans unto this people, but teach them an everlasting hatred against sin and iniquity.

vv. 21–32 It is better not to know all the details of sin and perversion.

- As a class, turn to Romans 16:19 and invite someone to read the verse. Ask, *What does it mean to be "wise unto that which is good, and simple concerning evil"?* (You may need to explain that "simple" can mean "unknowledgeable.")

- *Why might it be good to be ignorant regarding the details of how people sin?* Explain that in Alma 37:21–32, Alma tells his son not to share the details of the works of darkness that are contained on some of the plates.

Notes

33 Preach unto them repentance, and faith on the Lord Jesus Christ; teach them to humble themselves and to be meek and lowly in heart; teach them to withstand every temptation of the devil, with their faith on the Lord Jesus Christ.

34 Teach them to never be weary of good works, but to be meek and lowly in heart; for such shall find rest to their souls.

35 O, remember, my son, and learn wisdom in thy youth; yea, learn in thy youth to keep the commandments of God.

36 Yea, and cry unto God for all thy support; yea, let all thy doings be unto the Lord, and whithersoever thou goest let it be in the Lord; yea, let all thy thoughts be directed unto the Lord; yea, let the affections of thy heart be placed upon the Lord forever.

37 Counsel with the Lord in all thy doings, and he will direct thee for good; yea, when thou liest down at night lie down unto the Lord, that he may watch over you in your sleep; and when thou risest in the morning let thy heart be full of thanks unto God; and if ye do these things, ye shall be lifted up at the last day.

vv. 36–37 Continual communication with the Lord is a critical part of our relationship with Him.

- Look for what verses 36–37 are teaching about the nature of our relationship with the Lord.

- Analyze:
  - What words are used instead of "prayer"?
  - What do such words add to your understanding of prayer?
  - According to the verses, how should we feel about the Lord?
  - What benefits of prayer are promised in those verses?

- Apply: When are times we can "cry" and "council" with the Lord?

- If journals are available, invite class members to write about a time when they cried unto the Lord and felt supported. Ask a few individuals to share appropriate experiences. Invite class members to communicate continually with the Lord.

38 And now, my son, I have somewhat to say concerning the thing which our fathers call a ball, or director—or our fathers called it Liahona, which is, being interpreted, a compass; and the Lord prepared it.

39 And behold, there cannot any man work after the manner of so curious a workmanship. And behold, it was prepared to show unto our fathers the course which they should travel in the wilderness.

40 And it did work for them according to their faith in God; therefore, if they had faith to believe that God could cause that those spindles should point the way they should go, behold, it was done; therefore they had this miracle, and also many other miracles wrought by the power of God, day by day.

41 Nevertheless, because those miracles were worked by small means it did show unto them marvelous works. They were slothful, and forgot to exercise their faith and diligence and then those marvelous works ceased, and they did not progress in their journey;

42 Therefore, they tarried in the wilderness, or did not travel a direct course, and were afflicted with hunger and thirst, because of their transgressions.

43 And now, my son, I would that ye should understand that these things are not without a shadow; for as our fathers were slothful to give heed to this compass (now these things were temporal) they did not prosper; even so it is with things which are spiritual.

44 For behold, it is as easy to give heed to the word of Christ, which will point to you a straight course to eternal bliss, as it was for our fathers to give heed to this compass, which would point unto them a straight course to the promised land.

45 And now I say, is there not a type in this thing?

Notes

For just as surely as this director did bring our fathers, by following its course, to the promised land, shall the words of Christ, if we follow their course, carry us beyond this vale of sorrow into a far better land of promise.

46 O my son, do not let us be slothful because of the easiness of the way; for so was it with our fathers; for so was it prepared for them, that if they would look they might live; even so it is with us. The way is prepared, and if we will look we may live forever.

47 And now, my son, see that ye take care of these sacred things, yea, see that ye look to God and live. Go unto this people and declare the word, and be sober. My son, farewell.

vv. 38–47 The scriptures will guide us on our spiritual journey back to God.

- Show a picture displaying the Liahona. Read verse 38 and explain that this is the only verse in which the word "Liahona" is used.

- Assign verses 39–42 in the Book of Mormon to different individuals in the class. After each person reads their verse ask, *What in that verse is similar to the effect the scriptures can have on our journey back to God?* Then look for any additional insights in verses 43–47.

- Invite class members to "look to God" by doing the simple act of studying their scriptures each day.

Teaching Tips from Prophets' Lips "Any honest seeker of truth, regardless of educational background, can successfully employ . . . simple approaches. You and I do not need sophisticated study aids and should not rely extensively upon the spiritual knowledge of others. We simply need to have a sincere desire to learn, the companionship of the Holy Ghost, the Holy Scriptures, and an active and inquiring mind" (Elder Bednar, "A Reservoir of Living Water," CES Fireside for Young Adults, Feb. 4, 2007, Brigham Young University).

Index Topics: scriptures, prayer

Notes

ALMA 38

Alma's Counsel to Shiblon
About 74 BC

1–3, Alma's commendation to Shiblon; 4–5, Those who put their trust in God shall be lifted up at the last day; 6–15, Alma gives counsel to Shiblon about how to be a missionary.

Note: Shiblon is the second of three sons Alma counsels.

Overarching Principle: Alma teaches what skills and attributes are needed to be a successful missionary.

- Bring a box of cake mix and the required ingredients to class. Discuss with the class what ingredients are necessary to make the cake. Explain that Alma will teach his son Shiblon about some essential "ingredients" required to becoming a successful missionary.

1 My son, give ear to my words, for I say unto you, even as I said unto Helaman, that inasmuch as ye shall keep the commandments of God ye shall prosper in the land; and inasmuch as ye will not keep the commandments of God ye shall be cut off from his presence.

2 And now, my son, I trust that I shall have great joy in you, because of your steadiness and your faithfulness unto God; for as you have commenced in your youth to look to the Lord your God, even so I hope that you will continue in keeping his commandments; for blessed is he that endureth to the end.

3 I say unto you, my son, that I have had great joy in thee already, because of thy faithfulness and thy diligence, and thy patience and thy long-suffering among the people of the Zoramites.

4 For I know that thou wast in bonds; yea, and I also know that thou wast stoned for the word's sake; and thou didst bear all these things with patience because the Lord was with thee; and

now thou knowest that the Lord did deliver thee.

vv. 1–4 Attributes of a missionary.

- ⚡ Ask a member of the class to draw a picture that represents Shiblon (a stick figure would be perfectly acceptable) on the board. You may also find one online or draw one yourself. Write "Getting to Know Shiblon" above the picture.

- 🔍 Read verses 1–3 to get to know Shiblon. What are some attributes he has? (You may want to list the answers on the board beneath the picture.) Note: In order for class members to better understand the principles in this chapter, it is important to identify the preceding attributes of Shiblon.

5 And now my son, Shiblon, I would that ye should remember, that as much as ye shall put your trust in God even so much ye shall be delivered out of your trials, and your troubles, and your afflictions, and ye shall be lifted up at the last day.

6 Now, my son, I would not that ye should think that I know these things of myself, but it is the Spirit of God which is in me which maketh these things known unto me; for if I had not been born of God I should not have known these things.

7 But behold, the Lord in his great mercy sent his angel to declare unto me that I must stop the work of destruction among his people; yea, and I have seen an angel face to face, and he spake with me, and his voice was as thunder, and it shook the whole earth.

8 And it came to pass that I was three days and three nights in the most bitter pain and anguish of soul; and never, until I did cry out unto the Lord Jesus Christ for mercy, did I receive a remission of my sins. But behold, I did cry unto him and I did find peace to my soul.

9 And now, my son, I have told you this that ye may learn wisdom, that ye may learn of me that there is no other way or means whereby man can be saved, only in and through Christ. Behold, he is the life and the light of the world. Behold, he is the word of truth and righteousness.

vv. 5–9 A good missionary relies on the Atonement of Jesus Christ and teaches others to do the same.

- ⚡ Refer to the box of ingredients required for the cake mix. Explain that even though the ingredients and instructions may vary depending on the cake mix, there are some elements that remain the same regardless (such as the eggs, oil, etc.). Discuss with your class how this could relate to missionary work.

- 🔍 Explain that even though missionary skills and attributes may vary from person to person, there is one element of a successful missionary that will remain constant for everyone. Invite class members to read verse 5 to discover what that constant element could be.

- ❓ Analyze: *Why or how does putting our trust in God deliver us from trials, troubles, and afflictions?*

- 🔍 Alma continues in verses 6–9 to explain how and why he puts his trust in God. Read these verses with class members and create a list of how we can trust in God. Note: Be sure to explain that Alma's experience in these verses is unique; therefore, an identical experience should not be expected. Teach the principle and the process of what Alma went through to trust God.

- ❓ Analyze: Analyze your list with the class by asking questions to ensure their understanding.

- ❓ Apply: *What experiences have you had where you have learned to trust God?*

- ❤ Encourage class members to trust in the Lord and to seek Him in all they do.

10 And now, as ye have begun to teach the word even so I would that ye should continue to teach; and I would that ye would be diligent and temperate in all things.

Notes

ALMA 39

11 See that ye are not lifted up unto pride; yea, see that ye do not boast in your own wisdom, nor of your much strength.

12 Use boldness, but not overbearance; and also see that ye bridle all your passions, that ye may be filled with love; see that ye refrain from idleness.

13 Do not pray as the Zoramites do, for ye have seen that they pray to be heard of men, and to be praised for their wisdom.

14 Do not say: O God, I thank thee that we are better than our brethren; but rather say: O Lord, forgive my unworthiness, and remember my brethren in mercy—yea, acknowledge your unworthiness before God at all times.

15 And may the Lord bless your soul, and receive you at the last day into his kingdom, to sit down in peace. Now go, my son, and teach the word unto this people. Be sober. My son, farewell.

vv. 10–15 Skills of an effective missionary.

- Read verses 10–15 looking for skills a missionary could use. Create a list on the board based on these verses.

- Analyze: Once the list is created, analyze the skills with your class so they can understand what each skill is and how the skill would help a missionary.

- Elder Robert D. Hales made this point about being bold but not overbearing: "This is not to suggest that we compromise our principles or dilute our beliefs. We cannot change the doctrines of the restored gospel, even if teaching and obeying them makes us unpopular in the eyes of the world. Yet even as we feel to speak the word of God with boldness, we must pray to be filled with the Holy Ghost. We should never confuse boldness with Satan's counterfeit: overbearance. True disciples speak with quiet confidence, not boastful pride" ("Christian Courage: The Price of Discipleship," *Ensign*, November 2008, 73).

- Elder Dallin H. Oaks said the following about prayers: "Literary excellence is not our desire. We do not advocate flowery and wordy prayers. We do not wish to be among those who 'pray to be heard of men, and to be praised for their wisdom.' We wish to follow the Savior's teaching, 'When ye pray, use not vain repetitions, as the heathen do: for they think that they shall be heard for their much speaking.' Our prayers should be simple, direct, and sincere" ("The Language of Prayer," *Ensign*, May 1993, 17).

Index Topics: missionary work

ALMA 39
"Most Abominable Above All Sins"
About 74 BC

Verses 1–4, Alma counsels his son Corianton, who had left the ministry to follow after a harlot; 5–6, Sexual immorality, murder, and denying the Holy Ghost are listed as the three most serious sins; 7–14, Alma encourages his son to repent; 15–19, In a future day to the Nephites, Christ will come to redeem mankind.

Note: Alma chapters 39–42 comprise Alma's council to his third son, Corianton.

1 And now, my son, I have somewhat more to say unto thee than what I said unto thy brother; for behold, have ye not observed the steadiness of thy brother, his faithfulness, and his diligence in keeping the commandments of God? Behold, has he not set a good example for thee?

2 For thou didst not give so much heed unto my words as did thy brother, among the people of the Zoramites. Now this is what I have against thee; thou didst go on unto boasting in thy strength and thy wisdom.

3 And this is not all, my son. Thou didst do that which was grievous unto me; for thou didst forsake the ministry, and did go over into the land of Siron among the borders of the Lamanites, after the harlot Isabel.

Notes

4 Yea, she did steal away the hearts of many; but this was no excuse for thee, my son. Thou shouldst have tended to the ministry wherewith thou wast entrusted.

5 Know ye not, my son, that these things are an abomination in the sight of the Lord; yea, most abominable above all sins save it be the shedding of innocent blood or denying the Holy Ghost?

6 For behold, if ye deny the Holy Ghost when it once has had place in you, and ye know that ye deny it, behold, this is a sin which is unpardonable; yea, and whosoever murdereth against the light and knowledge of God, it is not easy for him to obtain forgiveness; yea, I say unto you, my son, that it is not easy for him to obtain a forgiveness.

vv. 1–6 Sexual immorality is a grievous sin.

⚡ *Do you have a sibling who is a good example—someone to look up to?* Invite a class member to read Alma 39:1. Explain that Alma instructs his third son, Corianton, to follow the good examples of Helaman and Shiblon because Corianton had fallen into transgression.

🔍 *Read Alma 39:2–3 and look for what Alma has against Corianton.*

❓ Analyze:
- Alma mentions two very different shortcomings of Corianton (boasting in his own strength and sexual transgression). How might these two issues be related?
- What do you think Alma means in verse 4?
- Why does Corianton's calling as a missionary make his transgression more grievous?

💡 Have a class member read Alma 39:5. Explain that Elder Jeffrey R. Holland has given an explanation of the "ranking system" used in this verse: "By assigning such rank to a physical appetite so conspicuously evident in all of us, what is God trying to tell us about its place in his plan for all men and women in mortality? I submit to you he is doing precisely that—commenting about the very plan of life itself. Clearly God's greatest concerns regarding mortality are how one gets into this world and how one gets out of it. . . . These are the two matters that he has repeatedly told us he wants us never to take illegally, illicitly, unfaithfully, without sanction" (Jeffrey R. Holland, *Of Souls, Symbols, and Sacraments* [Salt Lake City: Deseret Book], 2001).

7 And now, my son, I would to God that ye had not been guilty of so great a crime. I would not dwell upon your crimes, to harrow up your soul, if it were not for your good.

8 But behold, ye cannot hide your crimes from God; and except ye repent they will stand as a testimony against you at the last day.

9 Now my son, I would that ye should repent and forsake your sins, and go no more after the lusts of your eyes, but cross yourself in all these things; for except ye do this ye can in nowise inherit the kingdom of God. Oh, remember, and take it upon you, and cross yourself in these things.

10 And I command you to take it upon you to counsel with your elder brothers in your undertakings; for behold, thou art in thy youth, and ye stand in need to be nourished by your brothers. And give heed to their counsel.

11 Suffer not yourself to be led away by any vain or foolish thing; suffer not the devil to lead away your heart again after those wicked harlots. Behold, O my son, how great iniquity ye brought upon the Zoramites; for when they saw your conduct they would not believe in my words.

12 And now the Spirit of the Lord doth say unto me: Command thy children to do good, lest they lead away the hearts of many people to destruction; therefore I command you, my son, in the fear of God, that ye refrain from your iniquities;

13 That ye turn to the Lord with all your mind, might, and strength; that ye lead away the hearts of no more to do wickedly; but rather return unto them, and acknowledge your faults and that wrong which ye have done.

Notes

14 Seek not after riches nor the vain things of this world; for behold, you cannot carry them with you.

15 And now, my son, I would say somewhat unto you concerning the coming of Christ. Behold, I say unto you, that it is he that surely shall come to take away the sins of the world; yea, he cometh to declare glad tidings of salvation unto his people.

16 And now, my son, this was the ministry unto which ye were called, to declare these glad tidings unto this people, to prepare their minds; or rather that salvation might come unto them, that they may prepare the minds of their children to hear the word at the time of his coming.

17 And now I will ease your mind somewhat on this subject. Behold, you marvel why these things should be known so long beforehand. Behold, I say unto you, is not a soul at this time as precious unto God as a soul will be at the time of his coming?

18 Is it not as necessary that the plan of redemption should be made known unto this people as well as unto their children?

19 Is it not as easy at this time for the Lord to send his angel to declare these glad tidings unto us as unto our children, or as after the time of his coming?

vv. 7–19 Alma's discussion with Corianton teaches us about taking steps toward repentance.

- After discussing the nature of Corianton's sins, invite class members to silently study Alma 39:7–19 and look for anything that Alma counsels Corianton to do to begin the repentance process. After giving them time, allow class members to share what they have found in partnerships or in small groups. Ask several individuals to share what they learned from the activity.

- Read Alma 39:9 to the class. Testify that repentance from sexual transgression is possible through the Atonement of Christ, and that with His help, we can overcome such sins and temptations.

> **Teaching Tips from Prophets' Lips** "President John Taylor said, "It is true intelligence for a man to take a subject that is mysterious and great in itself and to unfold and simplify it so that a child can understand it" ("Discourse," *Deseret News*, Sept. 30, 1857, 238).

ALMA 40

The Resurrection of the Dead
About 74 BC

1–5, All men and women will rise from the dead; 6–11, Where the spirits of men go when they die; 12–21, The state of the righteous and wicked after death; 22–26, In the resurrection, righteousness and wickedness will be restored unto man according to their works.

1 Now my son, here is somewhat more I would say unto thee; for I perceive that thy mind is worried concerning the resurrection of the dead.

2 Behold, I say unto you, that there is no resurrection—or, I would say, in other words, that this mortal does not put on immortality, this corruption does not put on incorruption—until after the coming of Christ.

3 Behold, he bringeth to pass the resurrection of the dead. But behold, my son, the resurrection is not yet. Now, I unfold unto you a mystery; nevertheless, there are many mysteries which are kept, that no one knoweth them save God himself. But I show unto you one thing which I have inquired diligently of God that I might know—that is concerning the resurrection.

4 Behold, there is a time appointed that all shall come forth from the dead. Now when this time cometh no one knows; but God knoweth the time which is appointed.

Notes

5 Now, whether there shall be one time, or a second time, or a third time, that men shall come forth from the dead, it mattereth not; for God knoweth all these things; and it sufficeth me to know that this is the case—that there is a time appointed that all shall rise from the dead.

6 Now there must needs be a space betwixt the time of death and the time of the resurrection.

7 And now I would inquire what becometh of the souls of men from this time of death to the time appointed for the resurrection?

8 Now whether there is more than one time appointed for men to rise it mattereth not; for all do not die at once, and this mattereth not; all is as one day with God, and time only is measured unto men.

9 Therefore, there is a time appointed unto men that they shall rise from the dead; and there is a space between the time of death and the resurrection. And now, concerning this space of time, what becometh of the souls of men is the thing which I have inquired diligently of the Lord to know; and this is the thing of which I do know.

10 And when the time cometh when all shall rise, then shall they know that God knoweth all the times which are appointed unto man.

11 Now, concerning the state of the soul between death and the resurrection—Behold, it has been made known unto me by an angel, that the spirits of all men, as soon as they are departed from this mortal body, yea, the spirits of all men, whether they be good or evil, are taken home to that God who gave them life.

12 And then shall it come to pass, that the spirits of those who are righteous are received into a state of happiness, which is called paradise, a state of rest, a state of peace, where they shall rest from all their troubles and from all care, and sorrow.

13 And then shall it come to pass, that the spirits of the wicked, yea, who are evil—for behold, they have no part nor portion of the Spirit of the Lord; for behold, they chose evil works rather than good; therefore the spirit of the devil did enter into them, and take possession of their house—and these shall be cast out into outer darkness; there shall be weeping, and wailing, and gnashing of teeth, and this because of their own iniquity, being led captive by the will of the devil.

14 Now this is the state of the souls of the wicked, yea, in darkness, and a state of awful, fearful looking for the fiery indignation of the wrath of God upon them; thus they remain in this state, as well as the righteous in paradise, until the time of their resurrection.

15 Now, there are some that have understood that this state of happiness and this state of misery of the soul, before the resurrection, was a first resurrection. Yea, I admit it may be termed a resurrection, the raising of the spirit or the soul and their consignation to happiness or misery, according to the words which have been spoken.

16 And behold, again it hath been spoken, that there is a first resurrection, a resurrection of all those who have been, or who are, or who shall be, down to the resurrection of Christ from the dead.

17 Now, we do not suppose that this first resurrection, which is spoken of in this manner, can be the resurrection of the souls and their consignation to happiness or misery. Ye cannot suppose that this is what it meaneth.

vv. 9–17 After death, and prior to the resurrection, men and women dwell in the world of spirits.

- Invite a class member to read the following story from the life of President Thomas S. Monson: "Many years ago I stood at the bedside of a young father as he hovered between life and death. His distraught wife and their two children stood nearby. He took my hand in his and, with a pleading look, said, 'Bishop, I know I am about to die. Tell me what happens to my spirit when I do.'

Notes

ALMA 40

I offered a silent prayer for heavenly guidance and noticed on his bedside table a copy of the triple combination. I reached for the book and fanned the pages. Suddenly I discovered that I had, with no effort on my part, stopped at the 40th chapter of Alma in the Book of Mormon" (Thomas S. Monson, "Precious Promises of the Book of Mormon," *Ensign*, Nov. 2011). Inform the class that President Monson then read Alma 40:11–12 to the man.

❓ *How can a knowledge of what happens after death affect a person? What would it be like if you didn't know what happens to a person when he or she dies?*

🔍 *Read Alma 40:9–17 and look for the two descriptions about life after death.*

❓ *Analyze: What stands out to you most from these passages? Which of the two descriptions sounds the most desirable?*

💡 Explain that these verses describe the spirit world—prison and paradise—which are temporary situations for spirits awaiting the resurrection and final judgment. Use the following quote to clarify the doctrine of these verses: "In the scriptures, the word paradise is used in different ways. First, it designates a place of peace and happiness in the post–mortal spirit world, reserved for those who have been baptized and who have remained faithful. Those in spirit prison have the opportunity to learn the gospel of Jesus Christ, repent of their sins, and receive the ordinances of baptism and confirmation through the work we do in temples (see Doctrine and Covenants 138:30–35). When they do, they may enter paradise" (*True to the Faith: A Gospel Reference* [2004], 111).

💬 President Thomas S. Monson concluded the story quoted above by saying, "As I continued to read about the Resurrection, a glow came to the young man's face and a smile graced his lips. As I concluded my visit, I said good-bye to this sweet family. I next saw the wife and children at the funeral. I think back to that night when a young man pleaded for truth and, from the Book of Mormon, heard the answer to his question" ("Precious Promises of the Book of Mormon," *Ensign*, Nov. 2011).

💗 Testify of the truthfulness of this message from Book of Mormon. Express your gratitude for valuable doctrines regarding life after death that are available through the restored gospel.

18 Behold, I say unto you, Nay; but it meaneth the reuniting of the soul with the body, of those from the days of Adam down to the resurrection of Christ.

19 Now, whether the souls and the bodies of those of whom has been spoken shall all be reunited at once, the wicked as well as the righteous, I do not say; let it suffice, that I say that they all come forth; or in other words, their resurrection cometh to pass before the resurrection of those who die after the resurrection of Christ.

20 Now, my son, I do not say that their resurrection cometh at the resurrection of Christ; but behold, I give it as my opinion, that the souls and the bodies are reunited, of the righteous, at the resurrection of Christ, and his ascension into heaven.

21 But whether it be at his resurrection or after, I do not say; but this much I say, that there is a space between death and the resurrection of the body, and a state of the soul in happiness or in misery until the time which is appointed of God that the dead shall come forth, and be reunited, both soul and body, and be brought to stand before God, and be judged according to their works.

22 Yea, this bringeth about the restoration of those things of which has been spoken by the mouths of the prophets.

23 The soul shall be restored to the body, and the body to the soul; yea, and every limb and joint shall be restored to its body; yea, even a hair of

Notes

the head shall not be lost; but all things shall be restored to their proper and perfect frame.

24 And now, my son, this is the restoration of which has been spoken by the mouths of the prophets—

25 And then shall the righteous shine forth in the kingdom of God.

26 But behold, an awful death cometh upon the wicked; for they die as to things pertaining to things of righteousness; for they are unclean, and no unclean thing can inherit the kingdom of God; but they are cast out, and consigned to partake of the fruits of their labors or their works, which have been evil; and they drink the dregs of a bitter cup.

vv. 1–26 Truths of the Resurrection.

- Discuss the following:
  - *Do prophets know everything?*
  - *What types of things do they know?*
  - *Are there some things they should know that are more important than others?*

- *Read Alma 40:3 and look for Alma's description of his knowledge as a prophet.*

- Invite class members to read Alma 40 looking for the things that Alma knows for certain about the resurrection and those things that are unknown or his opinion. Instruct class members to look for phrases like "it mattereth not," "I know not," or "my opinion." Have class members mark the "known truths" of the resurrection in one color and the "unknowns" in another. As an alternative approach you may consider making two lists on the board. To narrow the search, guide class members toward Alma 40:2, 4–8, 19–23—particularly if you have spent time on previous principles for verses 11–17.

- Testify that while prophets may not have all knowledge, God does, and He commands His prophets to teach the doctrines that are more important for us to know. Everything else will be revealed in the Lord's time.

Notes

ALMA 41

"Wickedness Never Was Happiness"
About 74 BC

1–3, In the resurrection the body will be restored; 4–8, Men will be judged according to their works and desires; 9–15, Man cannot be restored from sin to happiness because it is contrary to the nature of God.

1 And now, my son, I have somewhat to say concerning the restoration of which has been spoken; for behold, some have wrested the scriptures, and have gone far astray because of this thing. And I perceive that thy mind has been worried also concerning this thing. But behold, I will explain it unto thee.

2 I say unto thee, my son, that the plan of restoration is requisite with the justice of God; for it is requisite that all things should be restored to their proper order. Behold, it is requisite and just, according to the power and resurrection of Christ, that the soul of man should be restored to its body, and that every part of the body should be restored to itself.

3 And it is requisite with the justice of God that men should be judged according to their works; and if their works were good in this life, and the desires of their hearts were good, that they should also, at the last day, be restored unto that which is good.

4 And if their works are evil they shall be restored unto them for evil. Therefore, all things shall be restored to their proper order, everything to its natural frame—mortality raised to immortality, corruption to incorruption—raised to endless happiness to inherit the kingdom of God, or to endless misery to inherit the kingdom of the devil, the one on one hand, the other on the other—

5 The one raised to happiness according to his desires of happiness, or good according to his desires of good; and the other to evil according to his desires of evil; for as he has desired to do

evil all the day long even so shall he have his reward of evil when the night cometh.

6 And so it is on the other hand. If he hath repented of his sins, and desired righteousness until the end of his days, even so he shall be rewarded unto righteousness.

7 These are they that are redeemed of the Lord; yea, these are they that are taken out, that are delivered from that endless night of darkness; and thus they stand or fall; for behold, they are their own judges, whether to do good or do evil.

8 Now, the decrees of God are unalterable; therefore, the way is prepared that whosoever will may walk therein and be saved.

vv. 3–8 Men will be judged according to their works and desires.

- *What are three synonyms of the word "restore" or "restoration"?* Write the answers on the board and inform class members that Alma is teaching his son the principles of restoration in connection with the Final Judgment at the last day.

- Have class members summarize verses 3–6 in one statement. This will allow them to write down what they feel is the most important aspect of restoration.

- Consider asking one or all of the following questions:
  - Why do you feel Alma includes "good desires" was well as "good works"?
  - Why do you think Alma is choosing to teach this to his son Corianton?
  - Is the concept of being restored to righteousness and happiness only a concept that applies after we die? Why or why not?

- Elder Oaks stated, "The law of God can reward a righteous desire because an omniscient God can discern it. As revealed through the prophet of this dispensation, God 'is a discerner of the thoughts and intents of the heart' (Doctrine and Covenants 33:1). If a person refrains from a particular act because he is genuinely unable to perform it, but truly would if he could, our Heavenly Father will know this and can reward that person accordingly" (Dallin H. Oaks, "The Desires of Our Hearts," BYU Devotional, October 8, 1985).

- Apply: *How does the doctrine taught by Elder Oaks give you hope?*

- To discuss more about how our desires influence our judgment at the last days, have class members refer to Doctrine and Covenants 137:9.

9 And now behold, my son, do not risk one more offense against your God upon those points of doctrine, which ye have hitherto risked to commit sin.

10 Do not suppose, because it has been spoken concerning restoration, that ye shall be restored from sin to happiness. Behold, I say unto you, wickedness never was happiness.

11 And now, my son, all men that are in a state of nature, or I would say, in a carnal state, are in the gall of bitterness and in the bonds of iniquity; they are without God in the world, and they have gone contrary to the nature of God; therefore, they are in a state contrary to the nature of happiness.

12 And now behold, is the meaning of the word restoration to take a thing of a natural state and place it in an unnatural state, or to place it in a state opposite to its nature?

13 O, my son, this is not the case; but the meaning of the word restoration is to bring back again evil for evil, or carnal for carnal, or devilish for devilish—good for that which is good; righteous for that which is righteous; just for that which is just; merciful for that which is merciful.

14 Therefore, my son, see that you are merciful unto your brethren; deal justly, judge righteously, and do good continually; and if ye do all these things then shall ye receive your reward; yea, ye shall have mercy restored unto you again;

Notes

ye shall have justice restored unto you again; ye shall have a righteous judgment restored unto you again; and ye shall have good rewarded unto you again.

15 For that which ye do send out shall return unto you again, and be restored; therefore, the word restoration more fully condemneth the sinner, and justifieth him not at all.

vv. 9–15 Wickedness never was happiness.

- ⚡ Invite class members to tell you the opposite of each of the following items. Ask them to say the first thing that comes to mind when you say the word. Skunk, Salt, Flower, Light, Book, Wickedness, Happiness. Choose as many as you feel appropriate, or make up your own. After this activity ask, *Is the opposite of happiness wickedness? Why or why not?*

- 🔍 *In verses 9–11, what is Alma concerned that Corianton will think because of the doctrine of restoration?*

- ❓ Analyze: *What does the phrase "contrary to the nature of God" mean in verse 11? How does this phrase relate with restoration?*

- ❓ Apply: *If wickedness never was happiness, why are people wicked?* Consider asking the following question and discussing the difference between fun and lasting happiness. *Is sin fun?*

- 💬 Recount the following talk by Elder Mervyn B. Arnold, "In the inspired pamphlet *For the Strength of Youth*, we read that freedom of choice is a God-given, eternal principle that carries with it moral responsibilities for the choices made. 'While [we] are free to choose for [ourselves], [we] are not free to choose the consequences of [our] actions. When [we] make a choice, [we] will receive the consequences of that choice.'" Elder Arnold went on to share the following experience from his wife Devonna when she was fifteen years old: "This particular summer, one of my jobs was to ensure that the cows grazing on the mountain pasture did not break through the fence and get into the wheat field. A cow grazing on the growing wheat can bloat, causing suffocation and death. One cow in particular was always trying to stick her head through the fence. One morning, as I was riding my horse along the fence line checking on the cattle, I found that the cow had broken through the fence and gotten into the wheat field. To my dismay, I realized that she had been eating wheat for quite some time because she was already bloated and looked much like a balloon. I thought, 'You stupid cow! That fence was there to protect you, yet you broke through it and you have eaten so much wheat that your life is in danger.'

   "I raced back to the farmhouse to get my dad. However, when we returned, I found her lying dead on the ground. I was saddened by the loss of that cow. We had provided her with a beautiful mountain pasture to graze in and a fence to keep her away from the dangerous wheat, yet she foolishly broke through the fence and caused her own death.

   "As I thought about the role of the fence, I realized that it was a protection, just as the commandments and my parents' rules were a protection. The commandments and rules were for my own good. I realized that obedience to the commandments could save me from physical and spiritual death. That enlightenment was a pivotal point in my life." Sister Arnold learned that our kind, wise, and loving Heavenly Father has given us commandments not to restrict us, as the adversary would have us believe, but to bless our lives and to protect our good name and our legacy for future generations—as they had for Lehi and Nephi. Just like the cow that received the consequences of her choice, each one of us must learn that the grass is never greener on the other side of the fence—nor will it ever be, for "wickedness never was happiness." Each one of us will receive the consequences of our choices when this life is over. The commandments are clear, they are protective—they are not restrictive—and the wonderful blessings of

Notes

obedience are numberless! ("What Have You Done with My Name," *Ensign*, Nov. 2010, 107).

- ❤ Invite class members to make the choices that lead to happiness. Help them realize that the happiness spoken of is not only when we return to our Heavenly Father, but can be obtained in this life. Share how you personally have come to know that wickedness never was happiness. Consider inviting others to share how they know this as well. You may want to invite a few class members to think about this question at the beginning of class in order to allow them time to generate a response.

> **Teaching Tips from Prophets' Lips** "For you teachers of the Church, the principal goal of your lessons is the conversion of hearts. The quality of a lesson is not measured by the number of new pieces of information that you give your students. It comes from your capacity to invite the presence of the Spirit and to motivate your students to make commitments. It is by exercising their faith by putting into practice the lessons taught that they will increase their spiritual knowledge" (Elder Gerald Causse, "Even a Child Can Understand," *Ensign*, Nov. 2008, 32–34).

Index Topics: judgment, agency

ALMA 42

A Just and Merciful God
About 74 BC

1–11, This life is a probationary time; 12–28, How God is just and merciful; 29–31, Alma exhorts his son to repent and do his duty.

1 And now, my son, I perceive there is somewhat more which doth worry your mind, which ye cannot understand—which is concerning the justice of God in the punishment of the sinner; for ye do try to suppose that it is injustice that the sinner should be consigned to a state of misery.

v. 1 Some people excuse their own sins by finding fault with God or the Church.

- ⚡ Refer class members to Alma 39:3 and ask, *What sin was Corianton guilty of?*
- 🔎 Refer the class back to Alma 42:1. Say, *Look for what Corianton is worried about and what he considers unjust.*
- ❓ Analyze: *Why would Corianton consider God's punishment of sinners to be unjust? How is Corianton finding fault with God?*
- 💬 Elder Dallin H. Oaks stated, "Some seem to value God's love because of their hope that His love is so great and so unconditional that it will mercifully excuse them from obeying His laws. In contrast, those who understand God's plan for His children know that God's laws are invariable, which is another great evidence of His love for His children. Mercy cannot rob justice, and those who obtain mercy are 'they who have kept the covenant and observed the commandment' (Doctrine and Covenants 54:6)" ("Love and Law," *Ensign*, Nov. 2009, 27).
- ❓ Apply: *How do we see a similar mentality in some people today?*

2 Now behold, my son, I will explain this thing unto thee. For behold, after the Lord God sent our first parents forth from the garden of Eden, to till the ground, from whence they were taken—yea, he drew out the man, and he placed at the east end of the garden of Eden, cherubim, and a flaming sword which turned every way, to keep the tree of life—

3 Now, we see that the man had become as God, knowing good and evil; and lest he should put forth his hand, and take also of the tree of life, and eat and live forever, the Lord God placed cherubim and the flaming sword, that he should not partake of the fruit—

Notes

4 And thus we see, that there was a time granted unto man to repent, yea, a probationary time, a time to repent and serve God.

5 For behold, if Adam had put forth his hand immediately, and partaken of the tree of life, he would have lived forever, according to the word of God, having no space for repentance; yea, and also the word of God would have been void, and the great plan of salvation would have been frustrated.

6 But behold, it was appointed unto man to die—therefore, as they were cut off from the tree of life they should be cut off from the face of the earth—and man became lost forever, yea, they became fallen man.

7 And now, ye see by this that our first parents were cut off both temporally and spiritually from the presence of the Lord; and thus we see they became subjects to follow after their own will.

8 Now behold, it was not expedient that man should be reclaimed from this temporal death, for that would destroy the great plan of happiness.

9 Therefore, as the soul could never die, and the fall had brought upon all mankind a spiritual death as well as a temporal, that is, they were cut off from the presence of the Lord, it was expedient that mankind should be reclaimed from this spiritual death.

10 Therefore, as they had become carnal, sensual, and devilish, by nature, this probationary state became a state for them to prepare; it became a preparatory state.

vv. 4–10 By being obedient to God, we show Him we are prepared to live with Him again.

- Ask, *What does it mean when a person is put on probation by a judge?*
- Read verses 4 and 10 to determine if we are on probation.
- Analyze:
  - *In what sense are we on probation?*
  - *What do we need to prove while we are on probation?*
- *When will our probation end?*
- Bruce R. McConkie stated, "This life is the time that is appointed as a probationary estate for men to prepare to meet God, and as far as faithful people are concerned, if they are in line of their duty, if they are doing what they ought to do, although they may not have been perfect in this sphere, their probation is ended. Now there will be some probation for some other people hereafter. But for the faithful Saints of God, now is the time and the day, and their probation is ended with their death, and they will not thereafter depart from the path" (address given at the funeral of Elder S. Dilworth Young, July 13, 1981, 5).
- Challenge class members to live the best they can and repent when they make mistakes so that when they leave this mortal life they can have eternal life.

11 And now remember, my son, if it were not for the plan of redemption, (laying it aside) as soon as they were dead their souls were miserable, being cut off from the presence of the Lord.

12 And now, there was no means to reclaim men from this fallen state, which man had brought upon himself because of his own disobedience;

13 Therefore, according to justice, the plan of redemption could not be brought about, only on conditions of repentance of men in this probationary state, yea, this preparatory state; for except it were for these conditions, mercy could not take effect except it should destroy the work of justice. Now the work of justice could not be destroyed; if so, God would cease to be God.

14 And thus we see that all mankind were fallen, and they were in the grasp of justice; yea, the justice of God, which consigned them forever to be cut off from his presence.

15 And now, the plan of mercy could not be brought about except an atonement should be made; therefore God himself atoneth for the sins of the world, to bring about the plan of mercy, to

Notes

ALMA 42

appease the demands of justice, that God might be a perfect, just God, and a merciful God also.

16 Now, repentance could not come unto men except there were a punishment, which also was eternal as the life of the soul should be, affixed opposite to the plan of happiness, which was as eternal also as the life of the soul.

17 Now, how could a man repent except he should sin? How could he sin if there was no law? How could there be a law save there was a punishment?

18 Now, there was a punishment affixed, and a just law given, which brought remorse of conscience unto man.

19 Now, if there was no law given—if a man murdered he should die—would he be afraid he would die if he should murder?

20 And also, if there was no law given against sin men would not be afraid to sin.

21 And if there was no law given, if men sinned what could justice do, or mercy either, for they would have no claim upon the creature?

22 But there is a law given, and a punishment affixed, and a repentance granted; which repentance, mercy claimeth; otherwise, justice claimeth the creature and executeth the law, and the law inflicteth the punishment; if not so, the works of justice would be destroyed, and God would cease to be God.

23 But God ceaseth not to be God, and mercy claimeth the penitent, and mercy cometh because of the atonement; and the atonement bringeth to pass the resurrection of the dead; and the resurrection of the dead bringeth back men into the presence of God; and thus they are restored into his presence, to be judged according to their works, according to the law and justice.

24 For behold, justice exerciseth all his demands, and also mercy claimeth all which is her own; and thus, none but the truly penitent are saved.

25 What, do ye suppose that mercy can rob justice? I say unto you, Nay; not one whit. If so, God would cease to be God.

26 And thus God bringeth about his great and eternal purposes, which were prepared from the foundation of the world. And thus cometh about the salvation and the redemption of men, and also their destruction and misery.

27 Therefore, O my son, whosoever will come may come and partake of the waters of life freely; and whosoever will not come the same is not compelled to come; but in the last day it shall be restored unto him according to his deeds.

28 If he has desired to do evil, and has not repented in his days, behold, evil shall be done unto him, according to the restoration of God.

vv. 14–28 It is by the mercy of God that we are able to return to His presence.

- Ask, *On Judgment day, how many of you want God to be perfectly just with you?* Ask class members to respond why or why not.

- Ask:
  - *In verse 14, look for why it would be a bad thing if God were perfectly just with you.*
  - *Look in verse 15 for what we should seek on Judgment Day.*
  - *In verses 22–25, look for who paid the price of justice so you could have mercy.*

- Analyze: *How did Jesus make it possible for us to have mercy? How did he settle the demands of justice?*

- Write on the board, "When have you felt the Lord's mercy as you have repented?" Invite class members to write down their feelings in response to this question.

- Testify of the goodness of God and His mercy that made it possible for you to repent.

29 And now, my son, I desire that ye should let these things trouble you no more, and only let your sins trouble you, with that trouble which shall bring you down unto repentance.

30 O my son, I desire that ye should deny the justice of God no more. Do not endeavor to excuse

Notes

yourself in the least point because of your sins, by denying the justice of God; but do you let the justice of God, and his mercy, and his long-suffering have full sway in your heart; and let it bring you down to the dust in humility.

31 And now, O my son, ye are called of God to preach the word unto this people. And now, my son, go thy way, declare the word with truth and soberness, that thou mayest bring souls unto repentance, that the great plan of mercy may have claim upon them. And may God grant unto you even according to my words. Amen.

v. 31 Corianton helped others find the same mercy he received.

- Ask, *After being counseled by Alma, did Corianton repent and remain faithful?* To find the answer, ask half of the class to search Alma 48:18 and the other half to search Alma 49:30.
- Analyze: *Why did Corianton want to teach others?*
- Apply: *What is the lesson we can learn from his change?*

Index Topics: justice and mercy, obedience, personal apostasy

ALMA 43

The Beginning of the Battle with Zerahemnah
About 74 BC

1–8, Zerahemnah is made the leader of the Lamanite army and incites the Lamanites against the Nephites; 9–14, the first battle begins in the land of Jershon; 15–24, the Nephite army is led by Captain Moroni, who seeks council from Alma; 25–54, the Nephites surround the Lamanites and cease fighting.

Overarching Principle: As a protection against Satan's influence in the world today, we should be armed with righteousness and follow the prophet.

Note: Alma 43–62 are often referred to as "The War Chapters" in the Book of Mormon. These chapters which describe their warfare give great insights into the spiritual warfare we fight in our day.

- To help teach the overarching principle, have an object that could be used as a means of protection, such as a helmet, and ask a volunteer to put the helmet on. Invite other class members to throw lightweight objects at the helmet. Use this activity to explain the need for protection against Satan's influence and that Alma 43 will offer two suggestions of types of "helmets" to wear as protection.

1 And now it came to pass that the sons of Alma did go forth among the people, to declare the word unto them. And Alma, also, himself, could not rest, and he also went forth.

2 Now we shall say no more concerning their preaching, except that they preached the word, and the truth, according to the spirit of prophecy and revelation; and they preached after the holy order of God by which they were called.

3 And now I return to an account of the wars between the Nephites and the Lamanites, in the eighteenth year of the reign of the judges.

4 For behold, it came to pass that the Zoramites became Lamanites; therefore, in the commencement of the eighteenth year the people of the Nephites saw that the Lamanites were coming upon them; therefore they made preparations for war; yea, they gathered together their armies in the land of Jershon.

5 And it came to pass that the Lamanites came with their thousands; and they came into the land of Antionum, which is the land of the Zoramites; and a man by the name of Zerahemnah was their leader.

Notes

ALMA 43

6 And now, as the Amalekites were of a more wicked and murderous disposition than the Lamanites were, in and of themselves, therefore, Zerahemnah appointed chief captains over the Lamanites, and they were all Amalekites and Zoramites.

7 Now this he did that he might preserve their hatred towards the Nephites, that he might bring them into subjection to the accomplishment of his designs.

8 For behold, his designs were to stir up the Lamanites to anger against the Nephites; this he did that he might usurp great power over them, and also that he might gain power over the Nephites by bringing them into bondage.

9 And now the design of the Nephites was to support their lands, and their houses, and their wives, and their children, that they might preserve them from the hands of their enemies; and also that they might preserve their rights and their privileges, yea, and also their liberty, that they might worship God according to their desires.

10 For they knew that if they should fall into the hands of the Lamanites, that whosoever should worship God in spirit and in truth, the true and the living God, the Lamanites would destroy.

11 Yea, and they also knew the extreme hatred of the Lamanites towards their brethren, who were the people of Anti-Nephi-Lehi, who were called the people of Ammon—and they would not take up arms, yea, they had entered into a covenant and they would not break it—therefore, if they should fall into the hands of the Lamanites they would be destroyed.

12 And the Nephites would not suffer that they should be destroyed; therefore they gave them lands for their inheritance.

13 And the people of Ammon did give unto the Nephites a large portion of their substance to support their armies; and thus the Nephites were compelled, alone, to withstand against the Lamanites, who were a compound of Laman and Lemuel, and the sons of Ishmael, and all those who had dissented from the Nephites, who were Amalekites and Zoramites, and the descendants of the priests of Noah.

14 Now those descendants were as numerous, nearly, as were the Nephites; and thus the Nephites were obliged to contend with their brethren, even unto bloodshed.

15 And it came to pass as the armies of the Lamanites had gathered together in the land of Antionum, behold, the armies of the Nephites were prepared to meet them in the land of Jershon.

16 Now, the leader of the Nephites, or the man who had been appointed to be the chief captain over the Nephites—now the chief captain took the command of all the armies of the Nephites—and his name was Moroni;

17 And Moroni took all the command, and the government of their wars. And he was only twenty and five years old when he was appointed chief captain over the armies of the Nephites.

vv. 1–17 The first battle begins.

⚡ Using the object lesson from the overarching principle, explain that the class will create a chart to help track and apply the battle found in chapter 43 to our day. You may want to draw the following chart on the board, or give one to the class as a handout.

How were the Lamanites stirred up against the Nephites?	Alma 43:2–8
How are people stirred up in our own day?	
What is the Nephite motivation to fight back?	Alma 43:9–10
Who is the Nephite general?	Alma 43:16–17

Notes

ALMA 43

🔍 *Look for the name of the Lamanite leader in verse 5. Then give the class time to look for the categories in the boxes above.*

❓ Analyze: *Why do you think anger and hatred is a motivating factor for people to fight? What can we learn from the example of the Nephites in verses 9–10?*

❓ Apply: *What principle is being taught in these verses that could be like a "helmet" or protection (referring to the object lesson) for us?*

18 And it came to pass that he met the Lamanites in the borders of Jershon, and his people were armed with swords, and with cimeters, and all manner of weapons of war.

19 And when the armies of the Lamanites saw that the people of Nephi, or that Moroni, had prepared his people with breast plates and with arm-shields, yea, and also shields to defend their heads, and also they were dressed with thick clothing—

20 Now the army of Zerahemnah was not prepared with any such thing; they had only their swords and their cimeters, their bows and their arrows, their stones and their slings; and they were naked, save it were a skin which was girded about their loins; yea, all were naked, save it were the Zoramites and the Amalekites;

21 But they were not armed with breastplates, nor shields—therefore, they were exceedingly afraid of the armies of the Nephites because of their armor, notwithstanding their number being so much greater than the Nephites.

22 Behold, now it came to pass that they durst not come against the Nephites in the borders of Jershon; therefore they departed out of the land of Antionum into the wilderness, and took their journey round about in the wilderness, away by the head of the river Sidon, that they might come into the land of Manti and take possession of the land; for they did not suppose that the armies of Moroni would know whither they had gone.

vv. 18–22 We can protect ourselves against Satan's temptations by having better armor.

🔍 Explain that the first battle began in the borders of Jershon. Have class members look in verses 18–22 for what happened when the Nephites and Lamanites met on the battlefield for the first time.

❓ Analyze: *Why do you think the Lamanites were scared of the Nephites?*

❓ Apply: *How would this example from the Nephites apply to today? What are some standards that could be considered armor? Allow class members time to discuss these questions and consider how they are a protection against the temptations of Satan.*

♥ Consider discussing how the standards of the Church can help in overcoming Satan's temptations.

23 But it came to pass, as soon as they had departed into the wilderness Moroni sent spies into the wilderness to watch their camp; and Moroni, also, knowing of the prophecies of Alma, sent certain men unto him, desiring him that he should inquire of the Lord whither the armies of the Nephites should go to defend themselves against the Lamanites.

24 And it came to pass that the word of the Lord came unto Alma, and Alma informed the messengers of Moroni, that the armies of the Lamanites were marching round about in the wilderness, that they might come over into the land of Manti, that they might commence an attack upon the weaker part of the people. And those messengers went and delivered the message unto Moroni.

25 Now Moroni, leaving a part of his army in the land of Jershon, lest by any means a part of the Lamanites should come into that land and take possession of the city, took the remaining part of his army and marched over into the land of Manti.

Notes

26 And he caused that all the people in that quarter of the land should gather themselves together to battle against the Lamanites, to defend their lands and their country, their rights and their liberties; therefore they were prepared against the time of the coming of the Lamanites.

vv. 23–26 We can protect ourselves against Satan's temptations by seeking the guidance of our prophet and other Church leaders.

- Invite class members to look for a lesson we can learn from the Nephites about protecting ourselves against Satan's temptations in verses 23–26.
- Analyze: *Whose help did Moroni seek? Why would Moroni seek the help of a prophet?*
- Apply: *How does this example apply to our day?* Allow class members to discuss various application scenarios.
- Consider sharing recent council from the prophet, his counselors, or members of the Quorum of the Twelve that you feel may be applicable to the class.

27 And it came to pass that Moroni caused that his army should be secreted in the valley which was near the bank of the river Sidon, which was on the west of the river Sidon in the wilderness.

28 And Moroni placed spies round about, that he might know when the camp of the Lamanites should come.

29 And now, as Moroni knew the intention of the Lamanites, that it was their intention to destroy their brethren, or to subject them and bring them into bondage that they might establish a kingdom unto themselves over all the land;

30 And he also knowing that it was the only desire of the Nephites to preserve their lands, and their liberty, and their church, therefore he thought it no sin that he should defend them by stratagem; therefore, he found by his spies which course the Lamanites were to take.

31 Therefore, he divided his army and brought a part over into the valley, and concealed them on the east, and on the south of the hill Riplah;

32 And the remainder he concealed in the west valley, on the west of the river Sidon, and so down into the borders of the land Manti.

33 And thus having placed his army according to his desire, he was prepared to meet them.

34 And it came to pass that the Lamanites came up on the north of the hill, where a part of the army of Moroni was concealed.

35 And as the Lamanites had passed the hill Riplah, and came into the valley, and began to cross the river Sidon, the army which was concealed on the south of the hill, which was led by a man whose name was Lehi, and he led his army forth and encircled the Lamanites about on the east in their rear.

36 And it came to pass that the Lamanites, when they saw the Nephites coming upon them in their rear, turned them about and began to contend with the army of Lehi.

37 And the work of death commenced on both sides, but it was more dreadful on the part of the Lamanites, for their nakedness was exposed to the heavy blows of the Nephites with their swords and their cimeters, which brought death almost at every stroke.

38 While on the other hand, there was now and then a man fell among the Nephites, by their swords and the loss of blood, they being shielded from the more vital parts of the body, or the more vital parts of the body being shielded from the strokes of the Lamanites, by their breastplates, and their arm shields, and their head-plates; and thus the Nephites did carry on the work of death among the Lamanites.

39 And it came to pass that the Lamanites became frightened, because of the great destruction among them, even until they began to flee towards the river Sidon.

40 And they were pursued by Lehi and his men;

Notes

and they were driven by Lehi into the waters of Sidon, and they crossed the waters of Sidon. And Lehi retained his armies upon the bank of the river Sidon that they should not cross.

41 And it came to pass that Moroni and his army met the Lamanites in the valley, on the other side of the river Sidon, and began to fall upon them and to slay them.

42 And the Lamanites did flee again before them, towards the land of Manti; and they were met again by the armies of Moroni.

43 Now in this case the Lamanites did fight exceedingly; yea, never had the Lamanites been known to fight with such exceedingly great strength and courage, no, not even from the beginning.

44 And they were inspired by the Zoramites and the Amalekites, who were their chief captains and leaders, and by Zerahemnah, who was their chief captain, or their chief leader and commander; yea, they did fight like dragons, and many of the Nephites were slain by their hands, yea, for they did smite in two many of their head-plates, and they did pierce many of their breastplates, and they did smite off many of their arms; and thus the Lamanites did smite in their fierce anger.

45 Nevertheless, the Nephites were inspired by a better cause, for they were not fighting for monarchy nor power but they were fighting for their homes and their liberties, their wives and their children, and their all, yea, for their rites of worship and their church.

46 And they were doing that which they felt was the duty which they owed to their God; for the Lord had said unto them, and also unto their fathers, that: Inasmuch as ye are not guilty of the first offense, neither the second, ye shall not suffer yourselves to be slain by the hands of your enemies.

47 And again, the Lord has said that: Ye shall defend your families even unto bloodshed. Therefore for this cause were the Nephites contending with the Lamanites, to defend themselves, and their families, and their lands, their country, and their rights, and their religion.

48 And it came to pass that when the men of Moroni saw the fierceness and the anger of the Lamanites, they were about to shrink and flee from them. And Moroni, perceiving their intent, sent forth and inspired their hearts with these thoughts—yea, the thoughts of their lands, their liberty, yea, their freedom from bondage.

49 And it came to pass that they turned upon the Lamanites, and they cried with one voice unto the Lord their God, for their liberty and their freedom from bondage.

50 And they began to stand against the Lamanites with power; and in that selfsame hour that they cried unto the Lord for their freedom, the Lamanites began to flee before them; and they fled even to the waters of Sidon.

51 Now, the Lamanites were more numerous, yea, by more than double the number of the Nephites; nevertheless, they were driven insomuch that they were gathered together in one body in the valley, upon the bank by the river Sidon.

52 Therefore the armies of Moroni encircled them about, yea, even on both sides of the river, for behold, on the east were the men of Lehi.

53 Therefore when Zerahemnah saw the men of Lehi on the east of the river Sidon, and the armies of Moroni on the west of the river Sidon, that they were encircled about by the Nephites, they were struck with terror.

54 Now Moroni, when he saw their terror, commanded his men that they should stop shedding their blood.

Teaching Tips from Prophets' Lips "It is imperative that we use our every capacity to stimulate students to think. They must not be recording devices that play back information for a class discussion or test with little thought of future use. When there is pondering and stimulation to incorporate a truth into life, it will be resident in the treasury of experience. Then it can be drawn upon to help students

Notes

> make correct decisions for a worthy, successful life. Ask carefully formulated questions that stimulate thought" (Elder Richard G. Scott, "To Understand and Live Truth," Address to CES Religious Educators, Feb 4, 2005, 3).

ALMA 44

The Conclusion of the Battle with Zerahemnah
About 74–73 BC

1–7, Moroni gives Zerahemnah the terms of peace; 8–14, Zerahemnah rejects the offer, and tries to kill Moroni but is stopped by a soldier; 15–24, some Lamanites surrender while the others continue to fight; Zerahemnah finally surrenders.

Note: This chapter is a continuation of the story from Alma 43. This chapter outlines the greatness of Captain Moroni.

1 And it came to pass that they did stop and withdrew a pace from them. And Moroni said unto Zerahemnah: Behold, Zerahemnah, that we do not desire to be men of blood. Ye know that ye are in our hands, yet we do not desire to slay you.

2 Behold, we have not come out to battle against you that we might shed your blood for power; neither do we desire to bring any one to the yoke of bondage. But this is the very cause for which ye have come against us; yea, and ye are angry with us because of our religion.

3 But now, ye behold that the Lord is with us; and ye behold that he has delivered you into our hands. And now I would that ye should understand that this is done unto us because of our religion and our faith in Christ. And now ye see that ye cannot destroy this our faith.

4 Now ye see that this is the true faith of God; yea, ye see that God will support, and keep, and preserve us, so long as we are faithful unto him, and unto our faith, and our religion; and never will the Lord suffer that we shall be destroyed except we should fall into transgression and deny our faith.

5 And now, Zerahemnah, I command you, in the name of that all-powerful God, who has strengthened our arms that we have gained power over you, by our faith, by our religion, and by our rites of worship, and by our church, and by the sacred support which we owe to our wives and our children, by that liberty which binds us to our lands and our country; yea, and also by the maintenance of the sacred word of God, to which we owe all our happiness; and by all that is most dear unto us—

6 Yea, and this is not all; I command you by all the desires which ye have for life, that ye deliver up your weapons of war unto us, and we will seek not your blood, but we will spare your lives, if ye will go your way and come not again to war against us.

7 And now, if ye do not this, behold, ye are in our hands, and I will command my men that they shall fall upon you, and inflict the wounds of death in your bodies, that ye may become extinct; and then we will see who shall have power over this people; yea, we will see who shall be brought into bondage.

8 And now it came to pass that when Zerahemnah had heard these sayings he came forth and delivered up his sword and his cimeter, and his bow into the hands of Moroni, and said unto him: Behold, here are our weapons of war; we will deliver them up unto you, but we will not suffer ourselves to take an oath unto you, which we know that we shall break, and also our children; but take our weapons of war, and suffer that we may depart into the wilderness; otherwise we will retain our swords, and we will perish or conquer.

9 Behold, we are not of your faith; we do not believe that it is God that has delivered us into your hands; but we believe that it is your cunning that has preserved you from our swords.

Notes

Behold, it is your breastplates and your shields that have preserved you.

10 And now when Zerahemnah had made an end of speaking these words, Moroni returned the sword and the weapons of war, which he had received, unto Zerahemnah, saying: Behold, we will end the conflict.

11 Now I cannot recall the words which I have spoken, therefore as the Lord liveth, ye shall not depart except ye depart with an oath that ye will not return again against us to war. Now as ye are in our hands we will spill your blood upon the ground, or ye shall submit to the conditions which I have proposed.

vv. 1–11 By following the examples of heroes from the Book of Mormon, we can know how to live.

- ⚡ Discuss with class members people they know who are inspirational leaders. Discuss what makes them great and ask if they would like to emulate them in any way.

- 🔍 Explain that Moroni was an excellent leader because of his desire to do right and not abuse his power. Encourage class members to read verses 1–11 and look for what Moroni says demonstrates this desire.

12 And now when Moroni had said these words, Zerahemnah retained his sword, and he was angry with Moroni, and he rushed forward that he might slay Moroni; but as he raised his sword, behold, one of Moroni's soldiers smote it even to the earth, and it broke by the hilt; and he also smote Zerahemnah that he took off his scalp and it fell to the earth. And Zerahemnah withdrew from before them into the midst of his soldiers.

13 And it came to pass that the soldier who stood by, who smote off the scalp of Zerahemnah, took up the scalp from off the ground by the hair, and laid it upon the point of his sword, and stretched it forth unto them, saying unto them with a loud voice:

14 Even as this scalp has fallen to the earth, which is the scalp of your chief, so shall ye fall to the earth except ye will deliver up your weapons of war and depart with a covenant of peace.

15 Now there were many, when they heard these words and saw the scalp which was upon the sword, that were struck with fear; and many came forth and threw down their weapons of war at the feet of Moroni, and entered into a covenant of peace. And as many as entered into a covenant they suffered to depart into the wilderness.

16 Now it came to pass that Zerahemnah was exceedingly wroth, and he did stir up the remainder of his soldiers to anger, to contend more powerfully against the Nephites.

17 And now Moroni was angry, because of the stubbornness of the Lamanites; therefore he commanded his people that they should fall upon them and slay them. And it came to pass that they began to slay them; yea, and the Lamanites did contend with their swords and their might.

18 But behold, their naked skins and their bare heads were exposed to the sharp swords of the Nephites; yea, behold they were pierced and smitten, yea, and did fall exceedingly fast before the swords of the Nephites; and they began to be swept down, even as the soldier of Moroni had prophesied.

19 Now Zerahemnah, when he saw that they were all about to be destroyed, cried mightily unto Moroni, promising that he would covenant and also his people with them, if they would spare the remainder of their lives, that they never would come to war again against them.

20 And it came to pass that Moroni caused that the work of death should cease again among the people. And he took the weapons of war from the Lamanites; and after they had entered into a covenant with him of peace they were suffered to depart into the wilderness.

21 Now the number of their dead was not numbered

Notes

because of the greatness of the number; yea, the number of their dead was exceedingly great, both on the Nephites and on the Lamanites.

22 And it came to pass that they did cast their dead into the waters of Sidon, and they have gone forth and are buried in the depths of the sea.

23 And the armies of the Nephites, or of Moroni, returned and came to their houses and their lands.

24 And thus ended the eighteenth year of the reign of the judges over the people of Nephi. And thus ended the record of Alma, which was written upon the plates of Nephi.

ALMA 45

Alma's Departure
About 73 BC

1–17, Alma teaches and prophesies to his son Helaman; 18–19, Alma departs the land and is never seen again; 20–24, Helaman begins to preach and build up the church.

1 Behold, now it came to pass that the people of Nephi were exceedingly rejoiced, because the Lord had again delivered them out of the hands of their enemies; therefore they gave thanks unto the Lord their God; yea, and they did fast much and pray much, and they did worship God with exceedingly great joy.

2 And it came to pass in the nineteenth year of the reign of the judges over the people of Nephi, that Alma came unto his son Helaman and said unto him: Believest thou the words which I spake unto thee concerning those records which have been kept?

3 And Helaman said unto him: Yea, I believe.

4 And Alma said again: Believest thou in Jesus Christ, who shall come?

5 And he said: Yea, I believe all the words which thou hast spoken.

6 And Alma said unto him again: Will ye keep my commandments?

7 And he said: Yea, I will keep thy commandments with all my heart.

8 Then Alma said unto him: Blessed art thou; and the Lord shall prosper thee in this land.

vv. 1–8 Leaders in the Lord's church must have faith in Christ and commitment to keep His commandments.

- Display a photograph of the current prophet. Tell the class that there are no wrong answers and ask, *If you had to choose a few important characteristics necessary to be the leader of the Church, what would you say?* Consider writing the answers on the board. Explain that in Alma 45, Alma will choose his son Helaman to be the next leader of the church.

- Invite a class member to read Alma 45:1–8 and have the class look for characteristics that Alma wanted to be sure Helaman possessed.

- Analyze: *Why do you think faith in Christ and a commitment to keep the commandments are the two characteristics that Alma focuses on? What impresses you about Helaman's answers?*

- Apply:
  - *Is it right or wrong to sometimes expect certain characteristics or competencies in those who are called to lead us?*
  - *Why might the two characteristics Alma asks about be sufficient in order for our leaders to be successful?*
  - *How have you seen these two characteristics benefit a leader you know?*

- Consider writing the following on the board or sharing it as part of your discussion: "The future is as bright as your faith" (Thomas S. Monson, "Be of Good Cheer," *Ensign*, May 2009, 92).

- Testify that when men and women have faith in Christ and are willing to keep the

Notes

commandments with all their hearts, that is all that is necessary for them to be successful leaders in Christ's church.

9 But behold, I have somewhat to prophesy unto thee; but what I prophesy unto thee ye shall not make known; yea, what I prophesy unto thee shall not be made known, even until the prophecy is fulfilled; therefore write the words which I shall say.

10 And these are the words: Behold, I perceive that this very people, the Nephites, according to the spirit of revelation which is in me, in four hundred years from the time that Jesus Christ shall manifest himself unto them, shall dwindle in unbelief.

11 Yea, and then shall they see wars and pestilences, yea, famines and bloodshed, even until the people of Nephi shall become extinct—

12 Yea, and this because they shall dwindle in unbelief and fall into the works of darkness, and lasciviousness, and all manner of iniquities; yea, I say unto you, that because they shall sin against so great light and knowledge, yea, I say unto you, that from that day, even the fourth generation shall not all pass away before this great iniquity shall come.

13 And when that great day cometh, behold, the time very soon cometh that those who are now, or the seed of those who are now numbered among the people of Nephi, shall no more be numbered among the people of Nephi.

14 But whosoever remaineth, and is not destroyed in that great and dreadful day, shall be numbered among the Lamanites, and shall become like unto them, all, save it be a few who shall be called the disciples of the Lord; and them shall the Lamanites pursue even until they shall become extinct. And now, because of iniquity, this prophecy shall be fulfilled.

15 And now it came to pass that after Alma had said these things to Helaman, he blessed him, and also his other sons; and he also blessed the earth for the righteous' sake.

16 And he said: Thus saith the Lord God—Cursed shall be the land, yea, this land, unto every nation, kindred, tongue, and people, unto destruction, which do wickedly, when they are fully ripe; and as I have said so shall it be; for this is the cursing and the blessing of God upon the land, for the Lord cannot look upon sin with the least degree of allowance.

vv. 9–16 The righteous must remain faithful to receive the promised blessings of the Lord.

- Explain that Alma 45:9–14 represents Alma's final prophecy regarding the destruction of the Nephites. Make two columns on the board. Label one, "Causes," and the other, "Effects." Invite class members to read Alma 45:9–14 and look for specific cause and effect relationships regarding the destruction of the Nephite people.

- Ask:
  - *If the Nephites were destroyed because of their iniquity, why weren't the Lamanites?*
  - *Were the Lamanites often just as wicked as the Nephites?*
  - *What is the difference between the two groups?* (see v. 12)

- Testify that the Lord expects much from His covenant people. If they will remain righteous, He will bless them. If they fall into transgression, they will lose the promised blessings.

17 And now, when Alma had said these words he blessed the church, yea, all those who should stand fast in the faith from that time henceforth.

18 And when Alma had done this he departed out of the land of Zarahemla, as if to go into the land of Melek. And it came to pass that he was never heard of more; as to his death or burial we know not of.

19 Behold, this we know, that he was a righteous man; and the saying went abroad in the church that he was taken up by the Spirit, or buried by the hand of the Lord, even as Moses. But behold,

Notes

the scriptures saith the Lord took Moses unto himself; and we suppose that he has also received Alma in the spirit, unto himself; therefore, for this cause we know nothing concerning his death and burial.

20 And now it came to pass in the commencement of the nineteenth year of the reign of the judges over the people of Nephi, that Helaman went forth among the people to declare the word unto them.

21 For behold, because of their wars with the Lamanites and the many little dissensions and disturbances which had been among the people, it became expedient that the word of God should be declared among them, yea, and that a regulation should be made throughout the church.

22 Therefore, Helaman and his brethren went forth to establish the church again in all the land, yea, in every city throughout all the land which was possessed by the people of Nephi. And it came to pass that they did appoint priests and teachers throughout all the land, over all the churches.

23 And now it came to pass that after Helaman and his brethren had appointed priests and teachers over the churches that there arose a dissension among them, and they would not give heed to the words of Helaman and his brethren;

24 But they grew proud, being lifted up in their hearts, because of their exceedingly great riches; therefore they grew rich in their own eyes, and would not give heed to their words, to walk uprightly before God.

Teaching Tips from Prophets' Lips "I have observed a common characteristic among the instructors who have had the greatest influence in my life. They have helped me to seek learning by faith. They refused to give me easy answers to hard questions. In fact, they did not give me any answers at all. Rather, they pointed the way and helped me take the steps to find my own answers. I certainly did not always appreciate this approach, but experience has enabled me to understand that an answer given by another person usually is not remembered for very long, if remembered at all. But an answer we discover or obtain through the exercise of faith, typically, is retained for a lifetime. The most important learnings of life are caught—not taught" (David A. Bednar, "Seek Learning by Faith," address to CES religious educators, February 3, 2006, 8).

ALMA 46
The Title of Liberty
About 73–72 BC

1–10, Amalickiah leads the people into dissensions against the church and the government; 11–20, Moroni raises a title of liberty in defense of religion, family, and freedom; 21–28, Moroni rallies the people to covenant with God.

1 And it came to pass that as many as would not hearken to the words of Helaman and his brethren were gathered together against their brethren.

2 And now behold, they were exceedingly wroth, insomuch that they were determined to slay them.

3 Now the leader of those who were wroth against their brethren was a large and a strong man; and his name was Amalickiah.

4 And Amalickiah was desirous to be a king; and those people who were wroth were also desirous that he should be their king; and they were the greater part of them the lower judges of the land, and they were seeking for power.

5 And they had been led by the flatteries of Amalickiah, that if they would support him and establish him to be their king that he would make them rulers over the people.

6 Thus they were led away by Amalickiah to dissensions, notwithstanding the preaching of Helaman and his brethren, yea, notwithstanding

Notes

their exceedingly great care over the church, for they were high priests over the church.

7 And there were many in the church who believed in the flattering words of Amalickiah, therefore they dissented even from the church; and thus were the affairs of the people of Nephi exceedingly precarious and dangerous, notwithstanding their great victory which they had had over the Lamanites, and their great rejoicings which they had had because of their deliverance by the hand of the Lord.

8 Thus we see how quick the children of men do forget the Lord their God, yea, how quick to do iniquity, and to be led away by the evil one.

9 Yea, and we also see the great wickedness one very wicked man can cause to take place among the children of men.

10 Yea, we see that Amalickiah, because he was a man of cunning device and a man of many flattering words, that he led away the hearts of many people to do wickedly; yea, and to seek to destroy the church of God, and to destroy the foundation of liberty which God had granted unto them, or which blessing God had sent upon the face of the land for the righteous' sake.

vv. 1–10 "Thus we see how quick the children of men do forget the Lord their God."

- Ask the following question or write it on the board: *What would you say are the top three things that Satan tries to get us to desire?* Ensure the class that there is no right answer, but encourage them to consider the question and discuss what they think. You could also invite them to answer this question with someone next to them.

- *What did the people desire who followed Amalickiah in Alma 45:24 and Alma 46:4–6.*

- *What are the three things Moroni wants us to learn from the dissension of Amalickiah in verses 8–10? They all start with "we see . . ." Write these three principles on the board.*

- Apply: *Which of these three principles do you think is most applicable to our time and why?* Invite the class to defend what they think and share their reasoning.

11 And now it came to pass that when Moroni, who was the chief commander of the armies of the Nephites, had heard of these dissensions, he was angry with Amalickiah.

12 And it came to pass that he rent his coat; and he took a piece thereof, and wrote upon it—In memory of our God, our religion, and freedom, and our peace, our wives, and our children—and he fastened it upon the end of a pole.

13 And he fastened on his head-plate, and his breastplate, and his shields, and girded on his armor about his loins; and he took the pole, which had on the end thereof his rent coat, (and he called it the title of liberty) and he bowed himself to the earth, and he prayed mightily unto his God for the blessings of liberty to rest upon his brethren, so long as there should a band of Christians remain to possess the land—

14 For thus were all the true believers of Christ, who belonged to the church of God, called by those who did not belong to the church.

15 And those who did belong to the church were faithful; yea, all those who were true believers in Christ took upon them, gladly, the name of Christ, or Christians as they were called, because of their belief in Christ who should come.

16 And therefore, at this time, Moroni prayed that the cause of the Christians, and the freedom of the land might be favored.

17 And it came to pass that when he had poured out his soul to God, he named all the land which was south of the land Desolation, yea, and in fine, all the land, both on the north and on the south—A chosen land, and the land of liberty.

18 And he said: Surely God shall not suffer that we, who are despised because we take upon us the name of Christ, shall be trodden down

Notes

and destroyed, until we bring it upon us by our own transgressions.

19 And when Moroni had said these words, he went forth among the people, waving the rent part of his garment in the air, that all might see the writing which he had written upon the rent part, and crying with a loud voice, saying:

20 Behold, whosoever will maintain this title upon the land, let them come forth in the strength of the Lord, and enter into a covenant that they will maintain their rights, and their religion, that the Lord God may bless them.

21 And it came to pass that when Moroni had proclaimed these words, behold, the people came running together with their armor girded about their loins, rending their garments in token, or as a covenant, that they would not forsake the Lord their God; or, in other words, if they should transgress the commandments of God, or fall into transgression, and be ashamed to take upon them the name of Christ, the Lord should rend them even as they had rent their garments.

vv. 11–22 The making and keeping of covenants will protect me in times of need.

- Ask class members if anyone knows the ancient Middle Eastern custom of making or "cutting" a covenant. Invite the class to turn to Genesis 15:8–10 and ask, *What did the Lord ask Abraham to do as He made a covenant with him?* You may have to help explain that the Lord asked Abraham to take these animals and cut them in half and put one half of the animal on one side and one half of the animal on the other side. Read the following information to the class: "After the individual making the covenant cut the animal (or animals) in two, he walked between the two pieces as if to say, 'If I do not keep my covenant, may I become as this animal'" (Old Testament Seminary Student Study Guide, (2002), 24–25).

- *What did Moroni and the people do in verses 11–22 to show the Lord that they were serious about their covenants?*

- Analyze: *Why do you think they rent their clothes? Is there anything in our latter-day church that similarly helps us remember our covenants?*

- Apply: *What do we do or should we do to show the Lord that we are serious about the covenants we have made with Him? How does keeping our covenants at all times protect us when we are in need?*

- Testify or have a class member testify of how they have been blessed and protected because of their covenants. Invite class members to make and keep sacred covenants with the Lord.

22 Now this was the covenant which they made, and they cast their garments at the feet of Moroni, saying: We covenant with our God, that we shall be destroyed, even as our brethren in the land northward, if we shall fall into transgression; yea, he may cast us at the feet of our enemies, even as we have cast our garments at thy feet to be trodden under foot, if we shall fall into transgression.

23 Moroni said unto them: Behold, we are a remnant of the seed of Jacob; yea, we are a remnant of the seed of Joseph, whose coat was rent by his brethren into many pieces; yea, and now behold, let us remember to keep the commandments of God, or our garments shall be rent by our brethren, and we be cast into prison, or be sold, or be slain.

24 Yea, let us preserve our liberty as a remnant of Joseph; yea, let us remember the words of Jacob, before his death, for behold, he saw that a part of the remnant of the coat of Joseph was preserved and had not decayed. And he said—Even as this remnant of garment of my son hath been preserved, so shall a remnant of the seed of my son be preserved by the hand of God, and be taken unto himself, while the remainder of the seed of Joseph shall perish, even as the remnant of his garment.

Notes

25 Now behold, this giveth my soul sorrow; nevertheless, my soul hath joy in my son, because of that part of his seed which shall be taken unto God.

26 Now behold, this was the language of Jacob.

27 And now who knoweth but what the remnant of the seed of Joseph, which shall perish as his garment, are those who have dissented from us? Yea, and even it shall be ourselves if we do not stand fast in the faith of Christ.

> ✋ To summarize the end of the chapter, put the following questions on the board with a space after each one: who? what? where? when? how? Invite class members to read verses 28–41 and answer each of the questions on the board to summarize what happened and how Amalickiah escaped.

28 And now it came to pass that when Moroni had said these words he went forth, and also sent forth in all the parts of the land where there were dissensions, and gathered together all the people who were desirous to maintain their liberty, to stand against Amalickiah and those who had dissented, who were called Amalickiahites.

29 And it came to pass that when Amalickiah saw that the people of Moroni were more numerous than the Amalickiahites—and he also saw that his people were doubtful concerning the justice of the cause in which they had undertaken—therefore, fearing that he should not gain the point, he took those of his people who would and departed into the land of Nephi.

30 Now Moroni thought it was not expedient that the Lamanites should have any more strength; therefore he thought to cut off the people of Amalickiah, or to take them and bring them back, and put Amalickiah to death; yea, for he knew that he would stir up the Lamanites to anger against them, and cause them to come to battle against them; and this he knew that Amalickiah would do that he might obtain his purposes.

31 Therefore Moroni thought it was expedient that he should take his armies, who had gathered themselves together, and armed themselves, and entered into a covenant to keep the peace—and it came to pass that he took his army and marched out with his tents into the wilderness, to cut off the course of Amalickiah in the wilderness.

32 And it came to pass that he did according to his desires, and marched forth into the wilderness, and headed the armies of Amalickiah.

33 And it came to pass that Amalickiah fled with a small number of his men, and the remainder were delivered up into the hands of Moroni and were taken back into the land of Zarahemla.

34 Now, Moroni being a man who was appointed by the chief judges and the voice of the people, therefore he had power according to his will with the armies of the Nephites, to establish and to exercise authority over them.

35 And it came to pass that whomsoever of the Amalickiahites that would not enter into a covenant to support the cause of freedom, that they might maintain a free government, he caused to be put to death; and there were but few who denied the covenant of freedom.

36 And it came to pass also, that he caused the title of liberty to be hoisted upon every tower which was in all the land, which was possessed by the Nephites; and thus Moroni planted the standard of liberty among the Nephites.

37 And they began to have peace again in the land; and thus they did maintain peace in the land until nearly the end of the nineteenth year of the reign of the judges.

38 And Helaman and the high priests did also maintain order in the church; yea, even for the space of four years did they have much peace and rejoicing in the church.

39 And it came to pass that there were many who died, firmly believing that their souls were redeemed by the Lord Jesus Christ; thus they went out of the world rejoicing.

Notes

40 And there were some who died with fevers, which at some seasons of the year were very frequent in the land—but not so much so with fevers, because of the excellent qualities of the many plants and roots which God had prepared to remove the cause of diseases, to which men were subject by the nature of the climate—

41 But there were many who died with old age; and those who died in the faith of Christ are happy in him, as we must needs suppose.

Index Topics: covenants

ALMA 47

Amalickiah Becomes the King of the Lamanites
About 72 BC

1–4, Amalickiah stirs up the Lamanites to battle and is given a portion of the Lamanite army to compel the other Lamanites to arms; 5–19, Through cunningness, intrigue, and murder, Amalickiah is appointed king over the entire Lamanite army; 20–36, Amalickiah kills the king of the Lamanites, frames the king's servants, marries the queen, and obtains the kingdom of the Lamanites.

Overarching Principle: Satan is the master of deceit, cunningness, and intrigue.

⚡ Bring a fishing pole and bait to class or bring pictures of these objects.

Ask, *How do these items relate to Satan?* Ask the class to explain how fishing is similar to the ways Satan tries to ensnare us. Write on the board, "Amalickiah is like Satan because . . ." Instruct class members to read verses 1–13 either as a class, individually, or in small groups, and as they read have them complete the statement by creating a list.

1 Now we will return in our record to Amalickiah and those who had fled with him into the wilderness; for, behold, he had taken those who went with him, and went up in the land of Nephi among the Lamanites, and did stir up the Lamanites to anger against the people of Nephi, insomuch that the king of the Lamanites sent a proclamation throughout all his land, among all his people, that they should gather themselves together again to go to battle against the Nephites.

2 And it came to pass that when the proclamation had gone forth among them they were exceedingly afraid; yea, they feared to displease the king, and they also feared to go to battle against the Nephites lest they should lose their lives. And it came to pass that they would not, or the more part of them would not, obey the commandments of the king.

3 And now it came to pass that the king was wroth because of their disobedience; therefore he gave Amalickiah the command of that part of his army which was obedient unto his commands, and commanded him that he should go forth and compel them to arms.

4 Now behold, this was the desire of Amalickiah; for he being a very subtle man to do evil therefore he laid the plan in his heart to dethrone the king of the Lamanites.

5 And now he had got the command of those parts of the Lamanites who were in favor of the king; and he sought to gain favor of those who were not obedient; therefore he went forward to the place which was called Onidah, for thither had all the Lamanites fled; for they discovered the army coming, and, supposing that they were coming to destroy them, therefore they fled to Onidah, to the place of arms.

6 And they had appointed a man to be a king and a leader over them, being fixed in their minds with a determined resolution that they would not be subjected to go against the Nephites.

7 And it came to pass that they had gathered

Notes

themselves together upon the top of the mount which was called Antipas, in preparation to battle.

8 Now it was not Amalickiah's intention to give them battle according to the commandments of the king; but behold, it was his intention to gain favor with the armies of the Lamanites, that he might place himself at their head and dethrone the king and take possession of the kingdom.

9 And behold, it came to pass that he caused his army to pitch their tents in the valley which was near the mount Antipas.

10 And it came to pass that when it was night he sent a secret embassy into the mount Antipas, desiring that the leader of those who were upon the mount, whose name was Lehonti, that he should come down to the foot of the mount, for he desired to speak with him.

11 And it came to pass that when Lehonti received the message he durst not go down to the foot of the mount. And it came to pass that Amalickiah sent again the second time, desiring him to come down. And it came to pass that Lehonti would not; and he sent again the third time.

12 And it came to pass that when Amalickiah found that he could not get Lehonti to come down off from the mount, he went up into the mount, nearly to Lehonti's camp; and he sent again the fourth time his message unto Lehonti, desiring that he would come down, and that he would bring his guards with him.

13 And it came to pass that when Lehonti had come down with his guards to Amalickiah, that Amalickiah desired him to come down with his army in the night-time, and surround those men in their camps over whom the king had given him command, and that he would deliver them up into Lehonti's hands, if he would make him (Amalickiah) a second leader over the whole army.

💬 Robert D. Hales taught, "As the Savior demonstrated with Herod, sometimes true disciples must show Christian courage by saying nothing at all. Once when I was golfing, I barely brushed up against a large cholla cactus, which seems to shoot needles like a porcupine. Thorns from that plant stuck all over my clothing, even though I had barely touched the cactus plant. Some situations are like that plant: they can only injure us. In such instances, we are better off to keep our distance and simply walk away. As we do, some may try to provoke us and engage us in argument. In the Book of Mormon, we read about Lehonti and his men camped upon a mount. The traitorous Amalickiah urged Lehonti to 'come down' and meet him in the valley. But when Lehonti left the high ground, he was poisoned 'by degrees' until he died, and his army fell into Amalickiah's hands. By arguments and accusations, some people bait us to leave the high ground. The high ground is where the light is. It's where we see the first light of morning and the last light in the evening. It is the safe ground. It is true and where knowledge is. Sometimes others want us to come down off the high ground and join them in a theological scrum in the mud. These few contentious individuals are set on picking religious fights, online or in person. We are always better staying on the higher ground of mutual respect and love" (Robert D. Hales, "Christian Courage: The Price of Discipleship," *Ensign*, Oct. 2008, 74).

❓ Apply: *What are additional examples of how others want us to come down off the high ground? What do they use to lure us in?*

14 And it came to pass that Lehonti came down with his men and surrounded the men of Amalickiah, so that before they awoke at the dawn of day they were surrounded by the armies of Lehonti.

15 And it came to pass that when they saw that they were surrounded, they pled with Amalickiah that he would suffer them to fall in with their brethren, that they might not be destroyed.

Notes

Now this was the very thing which Amalickiah desired.

16 And it came to pass that he delivered his men, contrary to the commands of the king. Now this was the thing that Amalickiah desired, that he might accomplish his designs in dethroning the king.

17 Now it was the custom among the Lamanites, if their chief leader was killed, to appoint the second leader to be their chief leader.

18 And it came to pass that Amalickiah caused that one of his servants should administer poison by degrees to Lehonti, that he died.

19 Now, when Lehonti was dead, the Lamanites appointed Amalickiah to be their leader and their chief commander.

20 And it came to pass that Amalickiah marched with his armies (for he had gained his desires) to the land of Nephi, to the city of Nephi, which was the chief city.

21 And the king came out to meet him with his guards, for he supposed that Amalickiah had fulfilled his commands, and that Amalickiah had gathered together so great an army to go against the Nephites to battle.

22 But behold, as the king came out to meet him Amalickiah caused that his servants should go forth to meet the king. And they went and bowed themselves before the king, as if to reverence him because of his greatness.

23 And it came to pass that the king put forth his hand to raise them, as was the custom with the Lamanites, as a token of peace, which custom they had taken from the Nephites.

24 And it came to pass that when he had raised the first from the ground, behold he stabbed the king to the heart; and he fell to the earth.

25 Now the servants of the king fled; and the servants of Amalickiah raised a cry, saying:

26 Behold, the servants of the king have stabbed him to the heart, and he has fallen and they have fled; behold, come and see.

27 And it came to pass that Amalickiah commanded that his armies should march forth and see what had happened to the king; and when they had come to the spot, and found the king lying in his gore, Amalickiah pretended to be wroth, and said: Whosoever loved the king, let him go forth, and pursue his servants that they may be slain.

28 And it came to pass that all they who loved the king, when they heard these words, came forth and pursued after the servants of the king.

29 Now when the servants of the king saw an army pursuing after them, they were frightened again, and fled into the wilderness, and came over into the land of Zarahemla and joined the people of Ammon.

30 And the army which pursued after them returned, having pursued after them in vain; and thus Amalickiah, by his fraud, gained the hearts of the people.

31 And it came to pass on the morrow he entered the city Nephi with his armies, and took possession of the city.

32 And now it came to pass that the queen, when she had heard that the king was slain—for Amalickiah had sent an embassy to the queen informing her that the king had been slain by his servants, that he had pursued them with his army, but it was in vain, and they had made their escape—

33 Therefore, when the queen had received this message she sent unto Amalickiah, desiring him that he would spare the people of the city; and she also desired him that he should come in unto her; and she also desired him that he should bring witnesses with him to testify concerning the death of the king.

34 And it came to pass that Amalickiah took the same servant that slew the king, and all them who were with him, and went in unto the queen, unto the place where she sat; and they all testified unto her that the king was slain by his own servants; and they said also: They have fled; does

Notes

not this testify against them? And thus they satisfied the queen concerning the death of the king.

35 And it came to pass that Amalickiah sought the favor of the queen, and took her unto him to wife; and thus by his fraud, and by the assistance of his cunning servants, he obtained the kingdom; yea, he was acknowledged king throughout all the land, among all the people of the Lamanites, who were composed of the Lamanites and the Lemuelites and the Ishmaelites, and all the dissenters of the Nephites, from the reign of Nephi down to the present time.

- Discuss with the class how Amalickiah is like Satan.
- Analyze: *What do you think Satan's number one tactic is to make us fall?*
- Apply: *What can we do to protect ourselves from Satan's deception and intrigue?*
- Invite class members to be aware of Satan's tactics so that they can avoid his deceptive and cunning ways.

36 Now these dissenters, having the same instruction and the same information of the Nephites, yea, having been instructed in the same knowledge of the Lord, nevertheless, it is strange to relate, not long after their dissensions they became more hardened and impenitent, and more wild, wicked and ferocious than the Lamanites—drinking in with the traditions of the Lamanites; giving way to indolence, and all manner of lasciviousness; yea, entirely forgetting the Lord their God.

vv. 35–36 Those who go against the Lord after knowing and tasting of His goodness become more hardened than those who have never known the Lord.

"Soon after the Prophet's arrival in Commerce (afterwards Nauvoo) from Missouri prison, Brother Isaac Behunin and myself made him a visit at his residence. His persecutions were the topic of conversation. He repeated many false, inconsistent and contradictory statements made by apostates, frightened members of the Church and outsiders. He also told how most of the officials who would fain have taken his life, when he was arrested, turned in his favor on forming his acquaintance. He laid the burden of the blame on false brethren. . . .

"When the Prophet had ended telling how he had been treated, Brother Behunin remarked: 'If I should leave this Church I would not do as those men have done: I would go to some remote place where Mormonism had never been heard of, settle down, and no one would ever learn that I knew anything about it.'

"The great Seer immediately replied: 'Brother Behunin, you don't know what you would do. No doubt these men once thought as you do. Before you joined this Church you stood on neutral ground. When the gospel was preached, good and evil were set before you. You could choose either or neither. There were two opposite masters inviting you to serve them. When you joined this Church you enlisted to serve God. When you did that you left the neutral ground, and you never can get back on to it. Should you forsake the Master you enlisted to serve, it will be by the instigation of the evil one, and you will follow his dictation and be his servant" (Daniel Tyler, in "Recollections of the Prophet Joseph Smith," *Juvenile Instructor*, August 15, 1892, 491–92).

Teaching Tips from Prophets' Lips "In contrast to the institutions of the world, which teach us to know something, the gospel of Jesus Christ challenges us to become something" (Dallin H. Oaks, "The Challenge to Become," *Ensign*, Nov. 2001, 32).

Index Topics: individual apostasy, tactics of Satan

Notes

ALMA 48

If All Men Were Like Unto Moroni
About 72 BC

1–6, Amalickiah manipulates the Lamanites to come to battle; 7–10, Moroni had been inspiring his people to be faithful and fortify their lands; 11–17, The character of Moroni; 18–20, Moroni is compared to other faithful men; 21–25, Out of necessity, the Nephites defend themselves.

1 And now it came to pass that, as soon as Amalickiah had obtained the kingdom he began to inspire the hearts of the Lamanites against the people of Nephi; yea, he did appoint men to speak unto the Lamanites from their towers, against the Nephites.

2 And thus he did inspire their hearts against the Nephites, insomuch that in the latter end of the nineteenth year of the reign of the judges, he having accomplished his designs thus far, yea, having been made king over the Lamanites, he sought also to reign over all the land, yea, and all the people who were in the land, the Nephites as well as the Lamanites.

3 Therefore he had accomplished his design, for he had hardened the hearts of the Lamanites and blinded their minds, and stirred them up to anger, insomuch that he had gathered together a numerous host to go to battle against the Nephites.

vv. 1–3 Satan uses the power of media to tempt us.

- *Because so many Lamanites were determined not to fight against the Nephites (Alma 47:6), how did Amalickiah convince the Lamanites to go against the Nephites again? Look for the answer in verses 1–3.*
- *Analyze: If Amalickiah is a symbol for Satan, what does this teach about Satan's tactics?*
- *Apply:*
  - *Instead of using towers to speak from, what types of media does Satan use to try to tempt us today?*
  - *What are messages he sends through the media?*
  - *How can we be immune from temptations coming from those sources?*
  - *What are some examples of good media with books, magazines, TV, Internet, etc?*

♥ Ask class members to think of one media choice they could change for the better, and have them write it down. Invite them to make that change.

4 For he was determined, because of the greatness of the number of his people, to overpower the Nephites and to bring them into bondage.

5 And thus he did appoint chief captains of the Zoramites, they being the most acquainted with the strength of the Nephites, and their places of resort, and the weakest parts of their cities; therefore he appointed them to be chief captains over his armies.

6 And it came to pass that they took their camp, and moved forth toward the land of Zarahemla in the wilderness.

7 Now it came to pass that while Amalickiah had thus been obtaining power by fraud and deceit, Moroni, on the other hand, had been preparing the minds of the people to be faithful unto the Lord their God.

8 Yea, he had been strengthening the armies of the Nephites, and erecting small forts, or places of resort; throwing up banks of earth round about to enclose his armies, and also building walls of stone to encircle them about, round about their cities and the borders of their lands; yea, all round about the land.

9 And in their weakest fortifications he did place the greater number of men; and thus he did fortify and strengthen the land which was possessed by the Nephites.

Notes

ALMA 48

vv. 7–9 Our strength as a people comes from obedience to God.

⚡ Consider:
- What is a nation's greatest source of protection?
- How important is a nation's military strength?
- In terms of protection and safety, how important is a nation's devotion to God?
- Which is the most important of the two?

💬 Less than a month after the September 11 attack on the United States where more than three thousand people were killed, President Gordon B. Hinckley said, "God our Eternal Father will watch over this nation and all of the civilized world who look to Him. He has declared, 'Blessed is the nation whose God is the Lord' (Psalm 33:12). Our safety lies in repentance. Our strength comes of obedience to the commandments of God" ("The Times in Which We Live," *Ensign*, Nov. 2001, 74).

🔍 In verses 7–9, look for what Captain Moroni focused on first—devotion to God or military strength.

❓ Analyze:
- Why is devotion to God even more important than military fortifications?
- Why did Captain Moroni do both?
- How did Moroni's preparations also show his faith in God?

❓ Apply: *How do these principles apply today?*

❤ Bear your testimony of how God protects nations who put their trust in Him. Invite class members to always strive to be obedient to God.

10 And thus he was preparing to support their liberty, their lands, their wives, and their children, and their peace, and that they might live unto the Lord their God, and that they might maintain that which was called by their enemies the cause of Christians.

11 And Moroni was a strong and a mighty man; he was a man of a perfect understanding; yea, a man that did not delight in bloodshed; a man whose soul did joy in the liberty and the freedom of his country, and his brethren from bondage and slavery;

12 Yea, a man whose heart did swell with thanksgiving to his God, for the many privileges and blessings which he bestowed upon his people; a man who did labor exceedingly for the welfare and safety of his people.

13 Yea, and he was a man who was firm in the faith of Christ, and he had sworn with an oath to defend his people, his rights, and his country, and his religion, even to the loss of his blood.

14 Now the Nephites were taught to defend themselves against their enemies, even to the shedding of blood if it were necessary; yea, and they were also taught never to give an offense, yea, and never to raise the sword except it were against an enemy, except it were to preserve their lives.

15 And this was their faith, that by so doing God would prosper them in the land, or in other words, if they were faithful in keeping the commandments of God that he would prosper them in the land; yea, warn them to flee, or to prepare for war, according to their danger;

16 And also, that God would make it known unto them whither they should go to defend themselves against their enemies, and by so doing, the Lord would deliver them; and this was the faith of Moroni, and his heart did glory in it; not in the shedding of blood but in doing good, in preserving his people, yea, in keeping the commandments of God, yea, and resisting iniquity.

17 Yea, verily, verily I say unto you, if all men had been, and were, and ever would be, like unto Moroni, behold, the very powers of hell would have been shaken forever; yea, the devil would never have power over the hearts of the children of men.

18 Behold, he was a man like unto Ammon, the son of Mosiah, yea, and even the other sons of Mosiah, yea, and also Alma and his sons, for they were all men of God.

Notes

19 Now behold, Helaman and his brethren were no less serviceable unto the people than was Moroni; for they did preach the word of God, and they did baptize unto repentance all men whosoever would hearken unto their words.

20 And thus they went forth, and the people did humble themselves because of their words, insomuch that they were highly favored of the Lord, and thus they were free from wars and contentions among themselves, yea, even for the space of four years.

vv. 11–20 Characteristics of great people.

- ⚡ Ask class members to write down someone they admire and why. Ask them to share their responses.

- ✋ Divide the board into three columns. Write at the top of one column "Verses 11–13, 17" then "Verses 14–16" in the next column, and "Verses 18–20" in the last column. Divide your class into three groups and assign each group one of the columns. Ask them to look for things they admire about the people in their assigned verses and create a list. Have each group (or representatives from each group) go to the front of the room and list what they found in their verses.

- ♥ Invite class members to try and implement characteristics of great people in their lives.

21 But, as I have said, in the latter end of the nineteenth year, yea, notwithstanding their peace amongst themselves, they were compelled reluctantly to contend with their brethren, the Lamanites.

22 Yea, and in fine, their wars never did cease for the space of many years with the Lamanites, notwithstanding their much reluctance.

23 Now, they were sorry to take up arms against the Lamanites, because they did not delight in the shedding of blood; yea, and this was not all—they were sorry to be the means of sending so many of their brethren out of this world into an eternal world, unprepared to meet their God.

24 Nevertheless, they could not suffer to lay down their lives, that their wives and their children should be massacred by the barbarous cruelty of those who were once their brethren, yea, and had dissented from their church, and had left them and had gone to destroy them by joining the Lamanites.

25 Yea, they could not bear that their brethren should rejoice over the blood of the Nephites, so long as there were any who should keep the commandments of God, for the promise of the Lord was, if they should keep his commandments they should prosper in the land.

Index Topics: media, temptations, obedience

ALMA 49

Fortified Cities
About 72 BC

1–4, The city of Ammonihah is fortified with great mounds of earth; 5–11, The Lamanite armies are prepared with breastplates and other protections, but are unable to attack the city; 12–24, The captains of the Lamanites swear to take the city of Noah; more than a thousand are killed in the attack, but not one Nephite; 25–27, The Lamanites flee to their own lands; Amalickiah swears to drink Moroni's blood; 28–30, The Nephites praise the Lord and prosper.

1 And now it came to pass in the eleventh month of the nineteenth year, on the tenth day of the month, the armies of the Lamanites were seen approaching towards the land of Ammonihah.

2 And behold, the city had been rebuilt, and Moroni had stationed an army by the borders of the city, and they had cast up dirt round about to shield them from the arrows and

Notes

the stones of the Lamanites; for behold, they fought with stones and with arrows.

3 Behold, I said that the city of Ammonihah had been rebuilt. I say unto you, yea, that it was in part rebuilt; and because the Lamanites had destroyed it once because of the iniquity of the people, they supposed that it would again become an easy prey for them.

4 But behold, how great was their disappointment; for behold, the Nephites had dug up a ridge of earth round about them, which was so high that the Lamanites could not cast their stones and their arrows at them that they might take effect, neither could they come upon them save it was by their place of entrance.

vv. 1–4 We must put defenses in place to protect our families.

- Review with the class by asking some of the following questions:
  - *Previously, how did Moroni help his individual soldiers in battle?*
  - *What lessons does this teach about the spiritual battles we face each day?*
  - *How can we put on those protections in our lives?*
  - *Now that Moroni has helped his individual soldiers, what should he do next to help his people?*

- *In verses 1–4, look for what Moroni had his soldiers and people do to defend themselves against the attacking armies.*

- Apply: Discuss the fortifications used by Moroni to analyze how we can fortify ourselves and our families against the temptations of Satan.

- Gordon B. Hinckley stated, "Why do we have this proclamation on the family now? Because the family is under attack. All across the world families are falling apart" (*Teachings of Gordon B. Hinckley*, 209).

- Invite class members to write down how they can help make their homes a place of security and a place where the Spirit can dwell. Challenge them to do those things.

5 Now at this time the chief captains of the Lamanites were astonished exceedingly, because of the wisdom of the Nephites in preparing their places of security.

6 Now the leaders of the Lamanites had supposed, because of the greatness of their numbers, yea, they supposed that they should be privileged to come upon them as they had hitherto done; yea, and they had also prepared themselves with shields, and with breastplates; and they had also prepared themselves with garments of skins, yea, very thick garments to cover their nakedness.

7 And being thus prepared they supposed that they should easily overpower and subject their brethren to the yoke of bondage, or slay and massacre them according to their pleasure.

vv. 6–7 We must be constantly strengthening ourselves and our families spiritually.

- *In verses 6–7, look for a lesson about the enemy and spiritual warfare.*

- Henry B. Eyring stated, "The spiritual strength sufficient for our youth to stand firm just a few years ago will soon not be enough. Many of them are remarkable in their spiritual maturity and in their faith. But even the best of them are sorely tested. And the testing will become more severe" ("We Must Raise Our Sights," *Ensign*, Sept. 2004).

- Ask:
  - *If the enemy is always getting better, what must we do in our spiritual warfare?*
  - *Why can't we let ourselves become complacent?*
  - *What evidence do you see that shows that Satan is better able to attack us than previous generations?*

Notes

Artist's rendering of Bécan fortifications [AD 100–250]; From Sorenson, John L. Images of Ancient America: Visualizing the Book of Mormon, p. 133 (Andrea Darais, artist).

8 But behold, to their uttermost astonishment, they were prepared for them, in a manner which never had been known among the children of Lehi. Now they were prepared for the Lamanites, to battle after the manner of the instructions of Moroni.

9 And it came to pass that the Lamanites, or the Amalickiahites, were exceedingly astonished at their manner of preparation for war.

10 Now, if king Amalickiah had come down out of the land of Nephi, at the head of his army, perhaps he would have caused the Lamanites to have attacked the Nephites at the city of Ammonihah; for behold, he did care not for the blood of his people.

11 But behold, Amalickiah did not come down himself to battle. And behold, his chief captains durst not attack the Nephites at the city of Ammonihah, for Moroni had altered the management of affairs among the Nephites, insomuch that the Lamanites were disappointed in their places of retreat and they could not come upon them.

12 Therefore they retreated into the wilderness, and took their camp and marched towards the land of Noah, supposing that to be the next best place for them to come against the Nephites.

13 For they knew not that Moroni had fortified, or had built forts of security, for every city in all the land round about; therefore, they marched forward to the land of Noah with a firm determination; yea, their chief captains came forward and took an oath that they would destroy the people of that city.

14 But behold, to their astonishment, the city of Noah, which had hitherto been a weak place, had now, by the means of Moroni, become strong, yea, even to exceed the strength of the city Ammonihah.

15 And now, behold, this was wisdom in Moroni; for he had supposed that they would be frightened at the city Ammonihah; and as the city of Noah had hitherto been the weakest part of the land, therefore they would march thither to battle; and thus it was according to his desires.

v. 15 We can overcome our weaknesses and make them areas of strength.

- Have class members search for Ether 12:27 and ask, *How can a weakness become a strength?* Have them write Ether 12:27 next to Alma 49:15.

- *In Alma 49:15, look for how Moroni made a weak thing become strong.*

- How does this relate with our spiritual warfare? What things can you do to make a weak area strong?

- Invite class members to think of their greatest weakness and to devise a strategy to eliminate that weakness.

16 And behold, Moroni had appointed Lehi to be chief captain over the men of that city; and it was that same Lehi who fought with the Lamanites in the valley on the east of the river Sidon.

17 And now behold it came to pass, that when the Lamanites had found that Lehi commanded the city they were again disappointed, for they feared Lehi exceedingly; nevertheless their chief captains had sworn with an oath to attack the

Notes

city; therefore, they brought up their armies.

18 Now behold, the Lamanites could not get into their forts of security by any other way save by the entrance, because of the highness of the bank which had been thrown up, and the depth of the ditch which had been dug round about, save it were by the entrance.

19 And thus were the Nephites prepared to destroy all such as should attempt to climb up to enter the fort by any other way, by casting over stones and arrows at them.

20 Thus they were prepared, yea, a body of their strongest men, with their swords and their slings, to smite down all who should attempt to come into their place of security by the place of entrance; and thus were they prepared to defend themselves against the Lamanites.

21 And it came to pass that the captains of the Lamanites brought up their armies before the place of entrance, and began to contend with the Nephites, to get into their place of security; but behold, they were driven back from time to time, insomuch that they were slain with an immense slaughter.

22 Now when they found that they could not obtain power over the Nephites by the pass, they began to dig down their banks of earth that they might obtain a pass to their armies, that they might have an equal chance to fight; but behold, in these attempts they were swept off by the stones and arrows which were thrown at them; and instead of filling up their ditches by pulling down the banks of earth, they were filled up in a measure with their dead and wounded bodies.

23 Thus the Nephites had all power over their enemies; and thus the Lamanites did attempt to destroy the Nephites until their chief captains were all slain; yea, and more than a thousand of the Lamanites were slain; while, on the other hand, there was not a single soul of the Nephites which was slain.

24 There were about fifty who were wounded, who had been exposed to the arrows of the Lamanites through the pass, but they were shielded by their shields, and their breastplates, and their head-plates, insomuch that their wounds were upon their legs, many of which were very severe.

25 And it came to pass, that when the Lamanites saw that their chief captains were all slain they fled into the wilderness. And it came to pass that they returned to the land of Nephi, to inform their king, Amalickiah, who was a Nephite by birth, concerning their great loss.

v. 25 Apostates oppose the Church.

- Have class members read verse 25 and ask if it is odd for the Lamanites to have a Nephite for their leader. Explain that in the war chapters, each leader of the Lamanites is a Nephite by birth.

26 And it came to pass that he was exceedingly angry with his people, because he had not obtained his desire over the Nephites; he had not subjected them to the yoke of bondage.

27 Yea, he was exceedingly wroth, and he did curse God, and also Moroni, swearing with an oath that he would drink his blood; and this because Moroni had kept the commandments of God in preparing for the safety of his people.

28 And it came to pass, that on the other hand, the people of Nephi did thank the Lord their God, because of his matchless power in delivering them from the hands of their enemies.

v. 28 We should give thanks to God when He blesses us.

- Discuss the following with class members. *Have you ever done something for someone that they were ungrateful for?*
- *Look for how the people of Nephi expressed their gratitude toward God in verse 28.*
- Encourage class members to consider the blessings in their lives and to continually thank God for their many blessings.

Notes

29 And thus ended the nineteenth year of the reign of the judges over the people of Nephi.

30 Yea, and there was continual peace among them, and exceedingly great prosperity in the church because of their heed and diligence which they gave unto the word of God, which was declared unto them by Helaman, and Shiblon, and Corianton, and Ammon and his brethren, yea, and by all those who had been ordained by the holy order of God, being baptized unto repentance, and sent forth to preach among the people.

Teaching Tips from Prophets' Lips "All knowledge is not of equal significance. There is no democracy of facts! They are not of equal importance. Something might be factual but unimportant, as Elder Spencer Condie has observed. For instance, today I wear a dark blue suit. That is true, but it is unimportant. The world does not quite understand this. As we brush against truth, we sense that it has a hierarchy of importance. We are dealing with some things of transcending importance. Some truths are salvationally significant, and others are not" (Neal A. Maxwell, "The Inexhaustible Gospel," *Ensign*, Apr. 1993, 69).

Index Topics: families, temptations, weaknesses, apostasy, gratitude

ALMA 50

Moroni's Fortifications of the Land
About 72–67 BC

1–17, Moroni's continual fortification of their lands; 18–23, The happiness of the Nephites is described; 24–36, Contention arises with Moriantion and his people and is halted by Moroni and Teancum; 37–40, Nephihah the chief judge dies, and Pahoran his son becomes chief judge.

1 And now it came to pass that Moroni did not stop making preparations for war, or to defend his people against the Lamanites; for he caused that his armies should commence in the commencement of the twentieth year of the reign of the judges, that they should commence in digging up heaps of earth round about all the cities, throughout all the land which was possessed by the Nephites.

2 And upon the top of these ridges of earth he caused that there should be timbers, yea, works of timbers built up to the height of a man, round about the cities.

3 And he caused that upon those works of timbers there should be a frame of pickets built upon the timbers round about; and they were strong and high.

4 And he caused towers to be erected that overlooked those works of pickets, and he caused places of security to be built upon those towers, that the stones and the arrows of the Lamanites could not hurt them.

5 And they were prepared that they could cast stones from the top thereof, according to their pleasure and their strength, and slay him who should attempt to approach near the walls of the city.

6 Thus Moroni did prepare strongholds against the coming of their enemies, round about every city in all the land.

7 And it came to pass that Moroni caused that his armies should go forth into the east wilderness; yea, and they went forth and drove all the Lamanites who were in the east wilderness into their own lands, which were south of the land of Zarahemla.

8 And the land of Nephi did run in a straight course from the east sea to the west.

9 And it came to pass that when Moroni had driven all the Lamanites out of the east wilderness, which was north of the lands of their own possessions, he caused that the inhabitants who were in the land of Zarahemla and in the land

Notes

round about should go forth into the east wilderness, even to the borders by the seashore, and possess the land.

10 And he also placed armies on the south, in the borders of their possessions, and caused them to erect fortifications that they might secure their armies and their people from the hands of their enemies.

11 And thus he cut off all the strongholds of the Lamanites in the east wilderness, yea, and also on the west, fortifying the line between the Nephites and the Lamanites, between the land of Zarahemla and the land of Nephi, from the west sea, running by the head of the river Sidon—the Nephites possessing all the land northward, yea, even all the land which was northward of the land Bountiful, according to their pleasure.

12 Thus Moroni, with his armies, which did increase daily because of the assurance of protection which his works did bring forth unto them, did seek to cut off the strength and the power of the Lamanites from off the lands of their possessions, that they should have no power upon the lands of their possession.

13 And it came to pass that the Nephites began the foundation of a city, and they called the name of the city Moroni; and it was by the east sea; and it was on the south by the line of the possessions of the Lamanites.

14 And they also began a foundation for a city between the city of Moroni and the city of Aaron, joining the borders of Aaron and Moroni; and they called the name of the city, or the land, Nephihah.

15 And they also began in that same year to build many cities on the north, one in a particular manner which they called Lehi, which was in the north by the borders of the seashore.

16 And thus ended the twentieth year.

17 And in these prosperous circumstances were the people of Nephi in the commencement of the twenty and first year of the reign of the judges over the people of Nephi.

18 And they did prosper exceedingly, and they became exceedingly rich; yea, and they did multiply and wax strong in the land.

19 And thus we see how merciful and just are all the dealings of the Lord, to the fulfilling of all his words unto the children of men; yea, we can behold that his words are verified, even at this time, which he spake unto Lehi, saying:

20 Blessed art thou and thy children; and they shall be blessed, inasmuch as they shall keep my commandments they shall prosper in the land. But remember, inasmuch as they will not keep my commandments they shall be cut off from the presence of the Lord.

21 And we see that these promises have been verified to the people of Nephi; for it has been their quarrelings and their contentions, yea, their murderings, and their plunderings, their idolatry, their whoredoms, and their abominations, which were among themselves, which brought upon them their wars and their destructions.

22 And those who were faithful in keeping the commandments of the Lord were delivered at all times, whilst thousands of their wicked brethren have been consigned to bondage, or to perish by the sword, or to dwindle in unbelief, and mingle with the Lamanites.

23 But behold there never was a happier time among the people of Nephi, since the days of Nephi, than in the days of Moroni, yea, even at this time, in the twenty and first year of the reign of the judges.

vv. 1–23 Despite the wickedness of the world, we can be happy and righteous.

⚡ To help teach the idea that people can flourish despite difficult and wicked times, research types of desert flowers on the Internet. You may want to bring some pictures to class and explain your findings. Ask class members if they have ever felt like they were in a "desert" because of the temptations and wickedness of the world. Explain that they will learn some

Notes

principles from Moroni that will give those surrounded by wickedness a sense of optimism.

🔍 *Contrast the state of the people in verse 1 with verse 23.* (The people were at war and making preparations to defend themselves, yet they were happy.) Discuss with the class whether they would be happy if they lived in a constant state of war and threat of invasion. Explain that the continual temptations of Satan in today's world could be likened unto the wartime conditions the Nephites were living in. *What did they do to remain happy despite these hardships?* (See the following 🔍 icon)

🔍 Assign the following verses to the class and invite class members to look for what Moroni did to protect his people against the constant threat of invasion and create a list with the class.

Alma 50:1–6

Alma 50:7–11

Alma 50:12–16

❓ **Analyze:** *Based on the list we have created, how could these actions help give the Nephites peace despite the constant threat of invasion?*

❓ **Apply:** *How could we liken this list to our day?* Take some time to discuss what Moroni did to protect his people and what we can do to protect ourselves.

♥ Read Alma 50:19–22 with your class and discuss the blessings that will come to us if we are faithful. You may want to consider asking a class member to share a personal experience or testimony of the blessings that come from keeping the commandments. It is often wise to give class members time to prepare; therefore, consider making the assignment before the class begins.

💬 Elder Russell M. Nelson taught us that, "The hope of the world is the Prince of Peace—our Creator, Savior, Jehovah, and Judge. He offers us the good life, the abundant life, and eternal life. Peaceful—even prosperous—living can come to those who abide His precepts" ("Blessed Are the Peacemakers," *Ensign*, Nov. 2002, 42).

24 And it came to pass that the twenty and second year of the reign of the judges also ended in peace; yea, and also the twenty and third year.

25 And it came to pass that in the commencement of the twenty and fourth year of the reign of the judges, there would also have been peace among the people of Nephi had it not been for a contention which took place among them concerning the land of Lehi, and the land of Morianton, which joined upon the borders of Lehi; both of which were on the borders by the seashore.

26 For behold, the people who possessed the land of Morianton did claim a part of the land of Lehi; therefore there began to be a warm contention between them, insomuch that the people of Morianton took up arms against their brethren, and they were determined by the sword to slay them.

27 But behold, the people who possessed the land of Lehi fled to the camp of Moroni, and appealed unto him for assistance; for behold they were not in the wrong.

28 And it came to pass that when the people of Morianton, who were led by a man whose name was Morianton, found that the people of Lehi had fled to the camp of Moroni, they were exceedingly fearful lest the army of Moroni should come upon them and destroy them.

29 Therefore, Morianton put it into their hearts that they should flee to the land which was northward, which was covered with large bodies of water, and take possession of the land which was northward.

30 And behold, they would have carried this plan into effect, (which would have been a cause to have been lamented) but behold, Morianton being a man of much passion, therefore he was angry with one of his maid servants, and he fell upon her and beat her much.

Notes

31 And it came to pass that she fled, and came over to the camp of Moroni, and told Moroni all things concerning the matter, and also concerning their intentions to flee into the land northward.

32 Now behold, the people who were in the land Bountiful, or rather Moroni, feared that they would hearken to the words of Morianton and unite with his people, and thus he would obtain possession of those parts of the land, which would lay a foundation for serious consequences among the people of Nephi, yea, which consequences would lead to the overthrow of their liberty.

33 Therefore Moroni sent an army, with their camp, to head the people of Morianton, to stop their flight into the land northward.

34 And it came to pass that they did not head them until they had come to the borders of the land Desolation; and there they did head them, by the narrow pass which led by the sea into the land northward, yea, by the sea, on the west and on the east.

35 And it came to pass that the army which was sent by Moroni, which was led by a man whose name was Teancum, did meet the people of Morianton; and so stubborn were the people of Morianton, (being inspired by his wickedness and his flattering words) that a battle commenced between them, in the which Teancum did slay Morianton and defeat his army, and took them prisoners, and returned to the camp of Moroni. And thus ended the twenty and fourth year of the reign of the judges over the people of Nephi.

36 And thus were the people of Morianton brought back. And upon their covenanting to keep the peace they were restored to the land of Morianton, and a union took place between them and the people of Lehi; and they were also restored to their lands.

vv. 25–36 The people of Morianton fight against the people of Lehi, flee northward, and are finally defeated by Moroni and Teancum.

37 And it came to pass that in the same year that the people of Nephi had peace restored unto them, that Nephihah, the second chief judge, died, having filled the judgment-seat with perfect uprightness before God.

38 Nevertheless, he had refused Alma to take possession of those records and those things which were esteemed by Alma and his fathers to be most sacred; therefore Alma had conferred them upon his son, Helaman.

39 Behold, it came to pass that the son of Nephihah was appointed to fill the judgment-seat, in the stead of his father; yea, he was appointed chief judge and governor over the people, with an oath and sacred ordinance to judge righteously, and to keep the peace and the freedom of the people, and to grant unto them their sacred privileges to worship the Lord their God, yea, to support and maintain the cause of God all his days, and to bring the wicked to justice according to their crime.

40 Now behold, his name was Pahoran. And Pahoran did fill the seat of his father, and did commence his reign in the end of the twenty and fourth year, over the people of Nephi.

vv. 37–40 Pahoran is established as the new chief judge.

ALMA 51

King-men versus Freemen
About 67–66 BC

1–8, Certain men desire to raise up a king in the stead of the chief judge, but the voice of the people choose Pahoran to remain in power; 9–12, The Lamanites come again against the Nephites and the king-men refuse to fight; 13–21, Moroni marches against the king-men to stop their rebellion; 22–28, The Lamanites overtake many outlying Nephite cities; 29–37, Teancum gives battle to the Lamanites, sneaks into the tent of Amalickiah by night, and kills him.

Notes

1 And now it came to pass in the commencement of the twenty and fifth year of the reign of the judges over the people of Nephi, they having established peace between the people of Lehi and the people of Morianton concerning their lands, and having commenced the twenty and fifth year in peace;

2 Nevertheless, they did not long maintain an entire peace in the land, for there began to be a contention among the people concerning the chief judge Pahoran; for behold, there were a part of the people who desired that a few particular points of the law should be altered.

3 But behold, Pahoran would not alter nor suffer the law to be altered; therefore, he did not hearken to those who had sent in their voices with their petitions concerning the altering of the law.

4 Therefore, those who were desirous that the law should be altered were angry with him, and desired that he should no longer be chief judge over the land; therefore there arose a warm dispute concerning the matter, but not unto bloodshed.

5 And it came to pass that those who were desirous that Pahoran should be dethroned from the judgment-seat were called king-men, for they were desirous that the law should be altered in a manner to overthrow the free government and to establish a king over the land.

6 And those who were desirous that Pahoran should remain chief judge over the land took upon them the name of freemen; and thus was the division among them, for the freemen had sworn or covenanted to maintain their rights and the privileges of their religion by a free government.

7 And it came to pass that this matter of their contention was settled by the voice of the people. And it came to pass that the voice of the people came in favor of the freemen, and Pahoran retained the judgment-seat, which caused much rejoicing among the brethren of Pahoran and also many of the people of liberty, who also put the king-men to silence, that they durst not oppose but were obliged to maintain the cause of freedom.

8 Now those who were in favor of kings were those of high birth, and they sought to be kings; and they were supported by those who sought power and authority over the people.

vv. 1–8 The King-men seek to dethrone Pahoran.

Display a newspaper to the class that has a prominent headline. Tell class members that today they will be the editors of *The Nephite Times*. Divide them into small groups and assign each group the following sets of verses. (You may assign more than one group to each set of verses.):

vv. 1–8

vv. 9–12

vv. 13–21

vv. 22–28

vv. 29–37

Instruct the groups to devise a headline for the story described in those verses, and to choose a few verses as supporting statements. Encourage them to use as many verses as possible to support and inspire their headline. When the groups share, discuss why they chose to describe the events the way they did.

9 But behold, this was a critical time for such contentions to be among the people of Nephi; for behold, Amalickiah had again stirred up the hearts of the people of the Lamanites against the people of the Nephites, and he was gathering together soldiers from all parts of his land, and arming them, and preparing for war with all diligence; for he had sworn to drink the blood of Moroni.

10 But behold, we shall see that his promise which he made was rash; nevertheless, he did prepare himself and his armies to come to battle against the Nephites.

Notes

11 Now his armies were not so great as they had hitherto been, because of the many thousands who had been slain by the hand of the Nephites; but notwithstanding their great loss, Amalickiah had gathered together a wonderfully great army, insomuch that he feared not to come down to the land of Zarahemla.

12 Yea, even Amalickiah did himself come down, at the head of the Lamanites. And it was in the twenty and fifth year of the reign of the judges; and it was at the same time that they had begun to settle the affairs of their contentions concerning the chief judge, Pahoran.

13 And it came to pass that when the men who were called king-men had heard that the Lamanites were coming down to battle against them, they were glad in their hearts; and they refused to take up arms, for they were so wroth with the chief judge, and also with the people of liberty, that they would not take up arms to defend their country.

14 And it came to pass that when Moroni saw this, and also saw that the Lamanites were coming into the borders of the land, he was exceedingly wroth because of the stubbornness of those people whom he had labored with so much diligence to preserve; yea, he was exceedingly wroth; his soul was filled with anger against them.

15 And it came to pass that he sent a petition, with the voice of the people, unto the governor of the land, desiring that he should read it, and give him (Moroni) power to compel those dissenters to defend their country or to put them to death.

16 For it was his first care to put an end to such contentions and dissensions among the people; for behold, this had been hitherto a cause of all their destruction. And it came to pass that it was granted according to the voice of the people.

17 And it came to pass that Moroni commanded that his army should go against those king-men, to pull down their pride and their nobility and level them with the earth, or they should take up arms and support the cause of liberty.

18 And it came to pass that the armies did march forth against them; and they did pull down their pride and their nobility, insomuch that as they did lift their weapons of war to fight against the men of Moroni they were hewn down and leveled to the earth.

19 And it came to pass that there were four thousand of those dissenters who were hewn down by the sword; and those of their leaders who were not slain in battle were taken and cast into prison, for there was no time for their trials at this period.

20 And the remainder of those dissenters, rather than be smitten down to the earth by the sword, yielded to the standard of liberty, and were compelled to hoist the title of liberty upon their towers, and in their cities, and to take up arms in defence of their country.

21 And thus Moroni put an end to those king-men, that there were not any known by the appellation of king-men; and thus he put an end to the stubbornness and the pride of those people who professed the blood of nobility; but they were brought down to humble themselves like unto their brethren, and to fight valiantly for their freedom from bondage.

22 Behold, it came to pass that while Moroni was thus breaking down the wars and contentions among his own people, and subjecting them to peace and civilization, and making regulations to prepare for war against the Lamanites, behold, the Lamanites had come into the land of Moroni, which was in the borders by the seashore.

23 And it came to pass that the Nephites were not sufficiently strong in the city of Moroni; therefore Amalickiah did drive them, slaying many. And it came to pass that Amalickiah took possession of the city, yea, possession of all their fortifications.

24 And those who fled out of the city of Moroni came to the city of Nephihah; and also the people of the city of Lehi gathered themselves together, and made preparations and

Notes

were ready to receive the Lamanites to battle.

25 But it came to pass that Amalickiah would not suffer the Lamanites to go against the city of Nephihah to battle, but kept them down by the seashore, leaving men in every city to maintain and defend it.

26 And thus he went on, taking possession of many cities, the city of Nephihah, and the city of Lehi, and the city of Morianton, and the city of Omner, and the city of Gid, and the city of Mulek, all of which were on the east borders by the seashore.

27 And thus had the Lamanites obtained, by the cunning of Amalickiah, so many cities, by their numberless hosts, all of which were strongly fortified after the manner of the fortifications of Moroni; all of which afforded strongholds for the Lamanites.

28 And it came to pass that they marched to the borders of the land Bountiful, driving the Nephites before them and slaying many.

29 But it came to pass that they were met by Teancum, who had slain Morianton and had headed his people in his flight.

30 And it came to pass that he headed Amalickiah also, as he was marching forth with his numerous army that he might take possession of the land Bountiful, and also the land northward.

31 But behold he met with a disappointment by being repulsed by Teancum and his men, for they were great warriors; for every man of Teancum did exceed the Lamanites in their strength and in their skill of war, insomuch that they did gain advantage over the Lamanites.

32 And it came to pass that they did harass them, insomuch that they did slay them even until it was dark. And it came to pass that Teancum and his men did pitch their tents in the borders of the land Bountiful; and Amalickiah did pitch his tents in the borders on the beach by the seashore, and after this manner were they driven.

33 And it came to pass that when the night had come, Teancum and his servant stole forth and went out by night, and went into the camp of Amalickiah; and behold, sleep had overpowered them because of their much fatigue, which was caused by the labors and heat of the day.

34 And it came to pass that Teancum stole privily into the tent of the king, and put a javelin to his heart; and he did cause the death of the king immediately that he did not awake his servants.

35 And he returned again privily to his own camp, and behold, his men were asleep, and he awoke them and told them all the things that he had done.

36 And he caused that his armies should stand in readiness, lest the Lamanites had awakened and should come upon them.

37 And thus endeth the twenty and fifth year of the reign of the judges over the people of Nephi; and thus endeth the days of Amalickiah.

Teaching Tips from Prophets' Lips "Teach the doctrines of salvation; supply spiritual food; bear testimony of our Lord's divine Sonship—anything short of such a course is unworthy of a true minister who has been called by revelation. Only when the Church is fed the bread of life are its members kept in paths of righteousness" (Bruce R. McConkie, *Doctrinal New Testament Commentary*, 3 vols. [1966–73], 2:178).

ALMA 52

Ammoron Becomes King of the Lamanites
About 66–64 BC

1–11, Ammoron, the brother of Amalickiah, is appointed king in his brother's stead and continues the battle against Teancum; 12–26, Moroni and Teancum join forces to take the city of Mulek with a planned decoy; 27–40, A battle between the Lamanites and the armies of Moroni takes place outside of the city of Bountiful in which the Lamanites surrender.

Notes

ALMA 52

1 And now, it came to pass in the twenty and sixth year of the reign of the judges over the people of Nephi, behold, when the Lamanites awoke on the first morning of the first month, behold, they found Amalickiah was dead in his own tent; and they also saw that Teancum was ready to give them battle on that day.

2 And now, when the Lamanites saw this they were affrighted; and they abandoned their design in marching into the land northward, and retreated with all their army into the city of Mulek, and sought protection in their fortifications.

3 And it came to pass that the brother of Amalickiah was appointed king over the people; and his name was Ammoron; thus king Ammoron, the brother of king Amalickiah, was appointed to reign in his stead.

4 And it came to pass that he did command that his people should maintain those cities, which they had taken by the shedding of blood; for they had not taken any cities save they had lost much blood.

5 And now, Teancum saw that the Lamanites were determined to maintain those cities which they had taken, and those parts of the land which they had obtained possession of; and also seeing the enormity of their number, Teancum thought it was not expedient that he should attempt to attack them in their forts.

6 But he kept his men round about, as if making preparations for war; yea, and truly he was preparing to defend himself against them, by casting up walls round about and preparing places of resort.

7 And it came to pass that he kept thus preparing for war until Moroni had sent a large number of men to strengthen his army.

8 And Moroni also sent orders unto him that he should retain all the prisoners who fell into his hands; for as the Lamanites had taken many prisoners, that he should retain all the prisoners of the Lamanites as a ransom for those whom the Lamanites had taken.

9 And he also sent orders unto him that he should fortify the land Bountiful, and secure the narrow pass which led into the land northward, lest the Lamanites should obtain that point and should have power to harass them on every side.

10 And Moroni also sent unto him, desiring him that he would be faithful in maintaining that quarter of the land, and that he would seek every opportunity to scourge the Lamanites in that quarter, as much as was in his power, that perhaps he might take again by stratagem or some other way those cities which had been taken out of their hands; and that he also would fortify and strengthen the cities round about, which had not fallen into the hands of the Lamanites.

11 And he also said unto him, I would come unto you, but behold, the Lamanites are upon us in the borders of the land by the west sea; and behold, I go against them, therefore I cannot come unto you.

12 Now, the king (Ammoron) had departed out of the land of Zarahemla, and had made known unto the queen concerning the death of his brother, and had gathered together a large number of men, and had marched forth against the Nephites on the borders by the west sea.

13 And thus he was endeavoring to harass the Nephites, and to draw away a part of their forces to that part of the land, while he had commanded those whom he had left to possess the cities which he had taken, that they should also harass the Nephites on the borders by the east sea, and should take possession of their lands as much as it was in their power, according to the power of their armies.

14 And thus were the Nephites in those dangerous circumstances in the ending of the twenty and sixth year of the reign of the judges over the people of Nephi.

15 But behold, it came to pass in the twenty and seventh year of the reign of the judges, that Teancum, by the command of Moroni—who had established armies to protect the south and the west borders of the land, and had begun

Notes

his march towards the land Bountiful, that he might assist Teancum with his men in retaking the cities which they had lost—

16 And it came to pass that Teancum had received orders to make an attack upon the city of Mulek, and retake it if it were possible.

17 And it came to pass that Teancum made preparations to make an attack upon the city of Mulek, and march forth with his army against the Lamanites; but he saw that it was impossible that he could overpower them while they were in their fortifications; therefore he abandoned his designs and returned again to the city Bountiful, to wait for the coming of Moroni, that he might receive strength to his army.

18 And it came to pass that Moroni did arrive with his army at the land of Bountiful, in the latter end of the twenty and seventh year of the reign of the judges over the people of Nephi.

19 And in the commencement of the twenty and eighth year, Moroni and Teancum and many of the chief captains held a council of war—what they should do to cause the Lamanites to come out against them to battle; or that they might by some means flatter them out of their strongholds, that they might gain advantage over them and take again the city of Mulek.

20 And it came to pass they sent embassies to the army of the Lamanites, which protected the city of Mulek, to their leader, whose name was Jacob, desiring him that he would come out with his armies to meet them upon the plains between the two cities. But behold, Jacob, who was a Zoramite, would not come out with his army to meet them upon the plains.

21 And it came to pass that Moroni, having no hopes of meeting them upon fair grounds, therefore, he resolved upon a plan that he might decoy the Lamanites out of their strongholds.

vv. 1–40 Moroni defeats his enemies by strategy.

⚡ Remind class members of Teancum's actions in Alma 51:31–35. Ask, *Based on this account, what kind of man is Teancum? Why might some consider him brave?*

❓ Analyze: Invite class members to read Alma 52:5, 17. Ask, *If Teancum is truly brave, how do you explain his actions in these verses? How are bravery and careful planning related?* Invite class members to note Mosiah 4:27 in their scriptures. Ask, *How could this scripture be related to Teancum and Moroni's actions in war?*

✋ Invite a class member to read aloud Alma 52:19. Explain that Moroni and Teancum created a strategy to defeat the Lamanites. Use the charts provided in this chapter to help class members understand Moroni's plan. Consider reproducing the charts on the chalk board or on posters. To increase class participation, display all five charts with the scripture references covered. Then invite the class to read Alma 52:19–40 and analyze your display to decide which verses describe the actions taken by Moroni as presented in each of the charts.

22 Therefore he caused that Teancum should take a small number of men and march down near the seashore; and Moroni and his army, by night, marched in the wilderness, on the west of the city Mulek; and thus, on the morrow, when the guards of the Lamanites had discovered Teancum, they ran and told it unto Jacob, their leader.

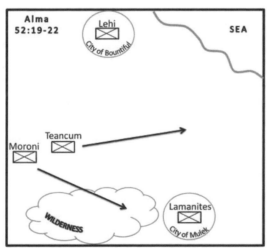

Notes

23 And it came to pass that the armies of the Lamanites did march forth against Teancum, supposing by their numbers to overpower Teancum because of the smallness of his numbers. And as Teancum saw the armies of the Lamanites coming out against him he began to retreat down by the seashore, northward.

24 And it came to pass that when the Lamanites saw that he began to flee, they took courage and pursued them with vigor. And while Teancum was thus leading away the Lamanites who were pursuing them in vain, behold, Moroni commanded that a part of his army who were with him should march forth into the city, and take possession of it.

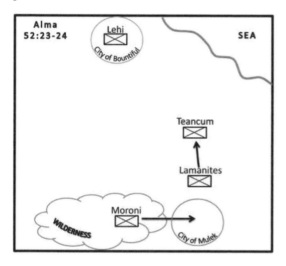

25 And thus they did, and slew all those who had been left to protect the city, yea, all those who would not yield up their weapons of war.

26 And thus Moroni had obtained possession of the city Mulek with a part of his army, while he marched with the remainder to meet the Lamanites when they should return from the pursuit of Teancum.

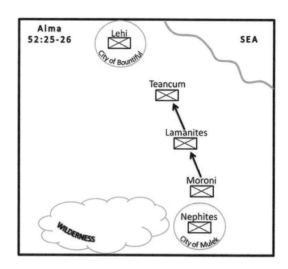

27 And it came to pass that the Lamanites did pursue Teancum until they came near the city Bountiful, and then they were met by Lehi and a small army, which had been left to protect the city Bountiful.

28 And now behold, when the chief captains of the Lamanites had beheld Lehi with his army coming against them, they fled in much confusion, lest perhaps they should not obtain the city Mulek before Lehi should overtake them; for they were wearied because of their march, and the men of Lehi were fresh.

29 Now the Lamanites did not know that Moroni had been in their rear with his army; and all they feared was Lehi and his men.

30 Now Lehi was not desirous to overtake them till they should meet Moroni and his army.

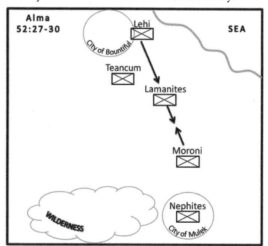

Notes

31 And it came to pass that before the Lamanites had retreated far they were surrounded by the Nephites, by the men of Moroni on one hand, and the men of Lehi on the other, all of whom were fresh and full of strength; but the Lamanites were wearied because of their long march.

32 And Moroni commanded his men that they should fall upon them until they had given up their weapons of war.

33 And it came to pass that Jacob, being their leader, being also a Zoramite, and having an unconquerable spirit, he led the Lamanites forth to battle with exceeding fury against Moroni.

34 Moroni being in their course of march, therefore Jacob was determined to slay them and cut his way through to the city of Mulek. But behold, Moroni and his men were more powerful; therefore they did not give way before the Lamanites.

35 And it came to pass that they fought on both hands with exceeding fury; and there were many slain on both sides; yea, and Moroni was wounded and Jacob was killed.

36 And Lehi pressed upon their rear with such fury with his strong men, that the Lamanites in the rear delivered up their weapons of war; and the remainder of them, being much confused, knew not whither to go or to strike.

37 Now Moroni seeing their confusion, he said unto them: If ye will bring forth your weapons of war and deliver them up, behold we will forbear shedding your blood.

38 And it came to pass that when the Lamanites had heard these words, their chief captains, all those who were not slain, came forth and threw down their weapons of war at the feet of Moroni, and also commanded their men that they should do the same.

39 But behold, there were many that would not; and those who would not deliver up their swords were taken and bound, and their weapons of war were taken from them, and they were compelled to march with their brethren forth into the land Bountiful.

40 And now the number of prisoners who were taken exceeded more than the number of those who had been slain, yea, more than those who had been slain on both sides.

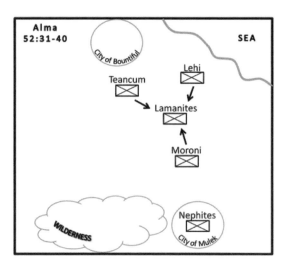

- **Apply:** *How can the principles of careful planning and strategy apply to our personal battles against sin and personal shortcomings? What are some examples of well-thought out plans or strategies that bring a person closer to Jesus Christ?*

- Testify that each of us should strive to carefully plan and ponder the best way to defeat sin and shortcomings in our lives, and that as we do, the Lord will bless us with success.

ALMA 53

"True at All Times in Whatsoever Thing They Were Entrusted"
About 64–63 BC

1–9, The Nephites prepare to continue to defend themselves by having the Lamanite prisoners fortify their cities; 10–15, The people of Ammon consider breaking their oath to help the Nephite army; 16–23,

Notes

ALMA 53

Two thousand sons of the people of Ammon covenant to defend their country.

1 And it came to pass that they did set guards over the prisoners of the Lamanites, and did compel them to go forth and bury their dead, yea, and also the dead of the Nephites who were slain; and Moroni placed men over them to guard them while they should perform their labors.

2 And Moroni went to the city of Mulek with Lehi, and took command of the city and gave it unto Lehi. Now behold, this Lehi was a man who had been with Moroni in the more part of all his battles; and he was a man like unto Moroni, and they rejoiced in each other's safety; yea, they were beloved by each other, and also beloved by all the people of Nephi.

3 And it came to pass that after the Lamanites had finished burying their dead and also the dead of the Nephites, they were marched back into the land Bountiful; and Teancum, by the orders of Moroni, caused that they should commence laboring in digging a ditch round about the land, or the city, Bountiful.

4 And he caused that they should build a breastwork of timbers upon the inner bank of the ditch; and they cast up dirt out of the ditch against the breastwork of timbers; and thus they did cause the Lamanites to labor until they had encircled the city of Bountiful round about with a strong wall of timbers and earth, to an exceeding height.

5 And this city became an exceeding stronghold ever after; and in this city they did guard the prisoners of the Lamanites; yea, even within a wall which they had caused them to build with their own hands. Now Moroni was compelled to cause the Lamanites to labor, because it was easy to guard them while at their labor; and he desired all his forces when he should make an attack upon the Lamanites.

6 And it came to pass that Moroni had thus gained a victory over one of the greatest of the armies of the Lamanites, and had obtained possession of the city of Mulek, which was one of the strongest holds of the Lamanites in the land of Nephi; and thus he had also built a stronghold to retain his prisoners.

7 And it came to pass that he did no more attempt a battle with the Lamanites in that year, but he did employ his men in preparing for war, yea, and in making fortifications to guard against the Lamanites, yea, and also delivering their women and their children from famine and affliction, and providing food for their armies.

8 And now it came to pass that the armies of the Lamanites, on the west sea, south, while in the absence of Moroni on account of some intrigue amongst the Nephites, which caused dissensions amongst them, had gained some ground over the Nephites, yea, insomuch that they had obtained possession of a number of their cities in that part of the land.

9 And thus because of iniquity amongst themselves, yea, because of dissensions and intrigue among themselves they were placed in the most dangerous circumstances.

10 And now behold, I have somewhat to say concerning the people of Ammon, who, in the beginning, were Lamanites; but by Ammon and his brethren, or rather by the power and word of God, they had been converted unto the Lord; and they had been brought down into the land of Zarahemla, and had ever since been protected by the Nephites.

vv. 1–10 Summary

- Put the following questions on the board (without the verses) and invite class members to search the scriptures or recall the answers from memory. These questions help summarize the first part of the chapter:

    Moroni was a successful leader because . . . (possible answer in v. 7).

    They would have easily gained and maintained victory if it was not for . . . (v. 9).

Notes

The people who buried their weapons and promised they would not fight again were called... (v. 10).

11 And because of their oath they had been kept from taking up arms against their brethren; for they had taken an oath that they never would shed blood more; and according to their oath they would have perished; yea, they would have suffered themselves to have fallen into the hands of their brethren, had it not been for the pity and the exceeding love which Ammon and his brethren had had for them.

12 And for this cause they were brought down into the land of Zarahemla; and they ever had been protected by the Nephites.

13 But it came to pass that when they saw the danger, and the many afflictions and tribulations which the Nephites bore for them, they were moved with compassion and were desirous to take up arms in the defence of their country.

14 But behold, as they were about to take their weapons of war, they were overpowered by the persuasions of Helaman and his brethren, for they were about to break the oath which they had made.

15 And Helaman feared lest by so doing they should lose their souls; therefore all those who had entered into this covenant were compelled to behold their brethren wade through their afflictions, in their dangerous circumstances at this time.

v. 10–15 When we choose not to keep covenants we cannot receive the blessings, and in some instances we suffer a penalty as a consequence of our disobedience.

- *When has someone broken a promise to you? What did you feel when this happened?*
- *What promise were the people of Ammon about to break? According to the scriptures, why were they about to do this?*
- *Analyze: Note with class members that the people of Ammon had a righteous desire to help the Nephites and ask, Why then does Helaman compel them not to break their oath? What does this teach us about our promises and covenants with God?*
- *Invite class members to finish the following phrases. (Stress that there is no specific answer to each of these phrases.)*

    Covenants provide . . .

    Covenants allow . . .

    Covenants bring . . .

    Covenants require . . .

- *Remind class members of the covenants they have made with the Lord and invite them to receive the blessings associated with their covenants.*

16 But behold, it came to pass they had many sons, who had not entered into a covenant that they would not take their weapons of war to defend themselves against their enemies; therefore they did assemble themselves together at this time, as many as were able to take up arms, and they called themselves Nephites.

17 And they entered into a covenant to fight for the liberty of the Nephites, yea, to protect the land unto the laying down of their lives; yea, even they covenanted that they never would give up their liberty, but they would fight in all cases to protect the Nephites and themselves from bondage.

18 Now behold, there were two thousand of those young men, who entered into this covenant and took their weapons of war to defend their country.

19 And now behold, as they never had hitherto been a disadvantage to the Nephites, they became now at this period of time also a great support; for they took their weapons of war, and they would that Helaman should be their leader.

20 And they were all young men, and they were

Notes

exceedingly valiant for courage, and also for strength and activity; but behold, this was not all—they were men who were true at all times in whatsoever thing they were entrusted.

21 Yea, they were men of truth and soberness, for they had been taught to keep the commandments of God and to walk uprightly before him.

22 And now it came to pass that Helaman did march at the head of his two thousand stripling soldiers, to the support of the people in the borders of the land on the south by the west sea.

23 And thus ended the twenty and eighth year of the reign of the judges over the people of Nephi.

vv. 16–23 The youth of the rising generation provide strength and vitality to the Church in the latter days.

- Display a picture of the youth of the Church in some capacity. This could be a picture of missionaries or perhaps even a personal picture that you have. Ask the class, *What are the benefits and strengths the youth add to the Church today?*

- Invite class members to note all of the characteristics of the two thousand young men of the people of Ammon that were willing to fight for the liberty of their people.

- Analyze: *Which characteristic stands out to you as you read about these young men? Why?*

- Elder Gary E. Stevenson recounted a story about a personal friend. "Some years ago, John was accepted at a prestigious Japanese university. He would be part of the international student program with many other top students from around the world. . . .

"Soon after John's arrival, word of a party to be held on the rooftop of a private residence spread among the foreign student population. That evening, John and two friends made their way to the advertised address. . .

"As the night wore on, the atmosphere changed. The noise, music volume, and alcohol amplified, as did John's uneasiness. Then suddenly someone began organizing the students into a large circle with the intent of sharing marijuana cigarettes. John grimaced and quickly informed his two friends that it was time to leave. Almost in ridicule, one of them replied, 'John, this is easy—we'll just stand in the circle, and when it is our turn, we'll just pass it along rather than smoke it. That way we won't have to embarrass ourselves in front of everyone by leaving.' This sounded easy to John, but it did not sound right. He knew he had to announce his intention and act. In a moment he mustered his courage and told them that they could do as they wished, but he was leaving. One friend decided to stay and joined the circle; the other reluctantly followed John down the stairs to board the elevator. Much to their surprise, when the elevator doors opened, Japanese police officers poured out and hurried to ascend the stairs to the rooftop. John and his friend boarded the elevator and departed.

"When the police appeared at the top of the stairs, the students quickly threw the illegal drugs off the roof so they wouldn't be caught. After securing the stairway, however, the officers lined up everyone on the roof and asked each student to extend both hands. The officers then walked down the line, carefully smelling each student's thumbs and index fingers. All who had held the marijuana, whether they had smoked it or not, were presumed guilty, and there were huge consequences. Almost without exception, the students who had remained on the rooftop were expelled from their respective universities, and those convicted of a crime were likely deported from Japan. Dreams of an education, years of preparation, and the possibility of future employment in Japan were dashed in a moment.

"Now let me tell you what happened to these three friends. The friend who stayed on the roof was expelled from the university in Japan to which he had worked so hard to be

Notes

accepted and was required to return home. The friend who left the party that night with John finished school in Japan and went on to earn degrees from two top-tier universities in the United States. His career took him back to Asia, where he has enjoyed immense professional success. He remains grateful to this day for John's courageous example. As for John, the consequences in his life have been immeasurable. His time in Japan that year led him to a happy marriage and the subsequent birth of two sons. He has been a very successful businessman and recently became a professor at a Japanese university. Imagine how different his life would have been had he not had the courage to leave the party on that important evening in Japan.

"Young men, there will be times when you, like John, will have to demonstrate your righteous courage in plain view of your peers, the consequence of which may be ridicule and embarrassment. Additionally, in your world, skirmishes with the adversary will also be fought on a silent, solitary battlefield in front of a screen. Technology with its substantial benefits also brings challenges not faced by generations before you" ("Be Valiant in Courage, Strength, and Activity," *Ensign*, Nov. 2012, 53).

❤ Invite class members to be true at all times. Consider having them write down one characteristic that they would like to emulate from the two thousand young men.

> **Teaching Tips from Prophets' Lips** "Let us make this clear. Even though what we teach is true, it is not of God unless it is taught by the power of the Spirit. There is no conversion, no spiritual experience, unless the Spirit of the Lord is involved" (Bruce R. McConkie, as cited in *Teaching, No Greater Call*, 9).

Index Topics: covenants, peer pressure

ALMA 54

Letters between Moroni and Ammoron
About 63 BC

1–3, Ammoron and Moroni desire to exchange prisoners; 4–14, Moroni's letter to Ammoron; 15–24, Ammoron's response to Moroni.

1 And now it came to pass in the commencement of the twenty and ninth year of the judges, that Ammoron sent unto Moroni desiring that he would exchange prisoners.

2 And it came to pass that Moroni felt to rejoice exceedingly at this request, for he desired the provisions which were imparted for the support of the Lamanite prisoners for the support of his own people; and he also desired his own people for the strengthening of his army.

3 Now the Lamanites had taken many women and children, and there was not a woman nor a child among all the prisoners of Moroni, or the prisoners whom Moroni had taken; therefore Moroni resolved upon a stratagem to obtain as many prisoners of the Nephites from the Lamanites as it were possible.

vv. 4–24 The words of Moroni and Ammoron to each other.

✋ This chapter is important in that it helps class members understand the story line that continues in the next chapters. One way to quickly teach the letters of Moroni and Ammoron is to choose two class members to read their letters in a dramatic voice they think might represent the authors. Consider giving two class members with theatrical abilities advanced notice of the assignment to allow them some time to prepare. Assign one class member verses 5–14, and the other verses 16–24. As the teacher, read verses 4 and 15 as an introduction to their dramatic readings. If such an activity does not seem effective or

Notes

appropriate, a simple reading by class members will suffice.

4 Therefore he wrote an epistle, and sent it by the servant of Ammoron, the same who had brought an epistle to Moroni. Now these are the words which he wrote unto Ammoron, saying:

5 Behold, Ammoron, I have written unto you somewhat concerning this war which ye have waged against my people, or rather which thy brother hath waged against them, and which ye are still determined to carry on after his death.

6 Behold, I would tell you somewhat concerning the justice of God, and the sword of his almighty wrath, which doth hang over you except ye repent and withdraw your armies into your own lands, or the land of your possessions, which is the land of Nephi.

7 Yea, I would tell you these things if ye were capable of hearkening unto them; yea, I would tell you concerning that awful hell that awaits to receive such murderers as thou and thy brother have been, except ye repent and withdraw your murderous purposes, and return with your armies to your own lands.

8 But as ye have once rejected these things, and have fought against the people of the Lord, even so I may expect you will do it again.

9 And now behold, we are prepared to receive you; yea, and except you withdraw your purposes, behold, ye will pull down the wrath of that God whom you have rejected upon you, even to your utter destruction.

10 But, as the Lord liveth, our armies shall come upon you except ye withdraw, and ye shall soon be visited with death, for we will retain our cities and our lands; yea, and we will maintain our religion and the cause of our God.

In verses 11–14, look for the terms Moroni proposes to Ammoron.

11 But behold, it supposeth me that I talk to you concerning these things in vain; or it supposeth me that thou art a child of hell; therefore I will close my epistle by telling you that I will not exchange prisoners, save it be on conditions that ye will deliver up a man and his wife and his children, for one prisoner; if this be the case that ye will do it, I will exchange.

12 And behold, if ye do not this, I will come against you with my armies; yea, even I will arm my women and my children, and I will come against you, and I will follow you even into your own land, which is the land of our first inheritance; yea, and it shall be blood for blood, yea, life for life; and I will give you battle even until you are destroyed from off the face of the earth.

13 Behold, I am in my anger, and also my people; ye have sought to murder us, and we have only sought to defend ourselves. But behold, if ye seek to destroy us more we will seek to destroy you; yea, and we will seek our land, the land of our first inheritance.

14 Now I close my epistle. I am Moroni; I am a leader of the people of the Nephites.

In verses 15–18, look for Ammoron's justifications for warring with the Nephites.

15 Now it came to pass that Ammoron, when he had received this epistle, was angry; and he wrote another epistle unto Moroni, and these are the words which he wrote, saying:

16 I am Ammoron, the king of the Lamanites; I am the brother of Amalickiah whom ye have murdered. Behold, I will avenge his blood upon you, yea, and I will come upon you with my armies for I fear not your threatenings.

17 For behold, your fathers did wrong their brethren, insomuch that they did rob them of their right to the government when it rightly belonged unto them.

18 And now behold, if ye will lay down your arms,

Notes

and subject yourselves to be governed by those to whom the government doth rightly belong, then will I cause that my people shall lay down their weapons and shall be at war no more.

19 Behold, ye have breathed out many threatenings against me and my people; but behold, we fear not your threatenings.

20 Nevertheless, I will grant to exchange prisoners according to your request, gladly, that I may preserve my food for my men of war; and we will wage a war which shall be eternal, either to the subjecting the Nephites to our authority or to their eternal extinction.

21 And as concerning that God whom ye say we have rejected, behold, we know not such a being; neither do ye; but if it so be that there is such a being, we know not but that he hath made us as well as you.

22 And if it so be that there is a devil and a hell, behold will he not send you there to dwell with my brother whom ye have murdered, whom ye have hinted that he hath gone to such a place? But behold these things matter not.

23 I am Ammoron, and a descendant of Zoram, whom your fathers pressed and brought out of Jerusalem.

24 And behold now, I am a bold Lamanite; behold, this war hath been waged to avenge their wrongs, and to maintain and to obtain their rights to the government; and I close my epistle to Moroni.

❓ *Did Ammoron agree to Moroni's conditions? (v. 20) This becomes a point of interest in the next chapter.*

ALMA 55

Moroni's Refusal to Exchange Prisoners

About 63–62 BC

1–2, Moroni receives Ammoron's letter and refuses to exchange prisoners; 3–15, Moroni sends Laman to the Lamanites with wine; they become drunk and fall asleep; 16–24, Moroni arms the Nephite prisoners; when the Lamanites awake they surrender without a fight; 25–35, The Nephites continue to strengthen themselves.

1 Now it came to pass that when Moroni had received this epistle he was more angry, because he knew that Ammoron had a perfect knowledge of his fraud; yea, he knew that Ammoron knew that it was not a just cause that had caused him to wage a war against the people of Nephi.

2 And he said: Behold, I will not exchange prisoners with Ammoron save he will withdraw his purpose, as I have stated in my epistle; for I will not grant unto him that he shall have any more power than what he hath got.

vv. 1–2 Moroni's reaction to Ammoron's letter.

🔍 *Look for the reasons Moroni became angry at Ammoron's letter and refused to exchange prisoners.*

3 Behold, I know the place where the Lamanites do guard my people whom they have taken prisoners; and as Ammoron would not grant unto me mine epistle, behold, I will give unto him according to my words; yea, I will seek death among them until they shall sue for peace.

4 And now it came to pass that when Moroni had said these words, he caused that a search should be made among his men, that perhaps he might find a man who was a descendant of Laman among them.

5 And it came to pass that they found one, whose name was Laman; and he was one of the servants of the king who was murdered by Amalickiah.

6 Now Moroni caused that Laman and a small number of his men should go forth unto the guards who were over the Nephites.

7 Now the Nephites were guarded in the city

Notes

of Gid; therefore Moroni appointed Laman and caused that a small number of men should go with him.

8 And when it was evening Laman went to the guards who were over the Nephites, and behold, they saw him coming and they hailed him; but he saith unto them: Fear not; behold, I am a Lamanite. Behold, we have escaped from the Nephites, and they sleep; and behold we have taken of their wine and brought with us.

9 Now when the Lamanites heard these words they received him with joy; and they said unto him: Give us of your wine, that we may drink; we are glad that ye have thus taken wine with you for we are weary.

10 But Laman said unto them: Let us keep of our wine till we go against the Nephites to battle. But this saying only made them more desirous to drink of the wine;

11 For, said they: We are weary, therefore let us take of the wine, and by and by we shall receive wine for our rations, which will strengthen us to go against the Nephites.

12 And Laman said unto them: You may do according to your desires.

13 And it came to pass that they did take of the wine freely; and it was pleasant to their taste, therefore they took of it more freely; and it was strong, having been prepared in its strength.

14 And it came to pass they did drink and were merry, and by and by they were all drunken.

15 And now when Laman and his men saw that they were all drunken, and were in a deep sleep, they returned to Moroni and told him all the things that had happened.

16 And now this was according to the design of Moroni. And Moroni had prepared his men with weapons of war; and he went to the city Gid, while the Lamanites were in a deep sleep and drunken, and cast in weapons of war unto the prisoners, insomuch that they were all armed;

17 Yea, even to their women, and all those of their children, as many as were able to use a weapon of war, when Moroni had armed all those prisoners; and all those things were done in a profound silence.

18 But had they awakened the Lamanites, behold they were drunken and the Nephites could have slain them.

19 But behold, this was not the desire of Moroni; he did not delight in murder or bloodshed, but he delighted in the saving of his people from destruction; and for this cause he might not bring upon him injustice, he would not fall upon the Lamanites and destroy them in their drunkenness.

💡 Note with the class that Moroni did not desire to slay the Lamanites despite their vulnerable condition.

20 But he had obtained his desires; for he had armed those prisoners of the Nephites who were within the wall of the city, and had given them power to gain possession of those parts which were within the walls.

21 And then he caused the men who were with him to withdraw a pace from them, and surround the armies of the Lamanites.

22 Now behold this was done in the night-time, so that when the Lamanites awoke in the morning they beheld that they were surrounded by the Nephites without, and that their prisoners were armed within.

23 And thus they saw that the Nephites had power over them; and in these circumstances they found that it was not expedient that they should fight with the Nephites; therefore their chief captains demanded their weapons of war, and they brought them forth and cast them at the feet of the Nephites, pleading for mercy.

24 Now behold, this was the desire of Moroni. He took them prisoners of war, and took possession of the city, and caused that all the prisoners should be liberated, who were Nephites; and

Notes

they did join the army of Moroni, and were a great strength to his army.

vv. 3–24 Moroni plots with Laman to entice the Lamanites in the city of Gid to become drunk. They fall asleep; Moroni enters the city and arms the prisoners. Once the Lamanites wake, they surrender without a fight.

25 And it came to pass that he did cause the Lamanites, whom he had taken prisoners, that they should commence a labor in strengthening the fortifications round about the city Gid.

26 And it came to pass that when he had fortified the city Gid, according to his desires, he caused that his prisoners should be taken to the city Bountiful; and he also guarded that city with an exceedingly strong force.

27 And it came to pass that they did, notwithstanding all the intrigues of the Lamanites, keep and protect all the prisoners whom they had taken, and also maintain all the ground and the advantage which they had retaken.

28 And it came to pass that the Nephites began again to be victorious, and to reclaim their rights and their privileges. 29 Many times did the Lamanites attempt to encircle them about by night, but in these attempts they did lose many prisoners.

30 And many times did they attempt to administer of their wine to the Nephites, that they might destroy them with poison or with drunkenness.

31 But behold, the Nephites were not slow to remember the Lord their God in this their time of affliction. They could not be taken in their snares; yea, they would not partake of their wine, save they had first given to some of the Lamanite prisoners.

32 And they were thus cautious that no poison should be administered among them; for if their wine would poison a Lamanite it would also poison a Nephite; and thus they did try all their liquors.

vv. 29–32 Continual vigilance in protecting yourself against the world's influence is required to remain safe in troubled times.

🔎 After reviewing the story of how the Nephites freed their prisoners in verses 3–24, invite class members to look for what the Lamanites tried as retaliation.

❓ Analyze: *Why does it make sense for the Nephites to be cautious in how they protected themselves against the Lamanites?*

❓ Apply: *What can we do today to be cautious in protecting ourselves against the world's influence?*

33 And now it came to pass that it was expedient for Moroni to make preparations to attack the city Morianton; for behold, the Lamanites had, by their labors, fortified the city Morianton until it had become an exceeding stronghold.

34 And they were continually bringing new forces into that city, and also new supplies of provisions.

35 And thus ended the twenty and ninth year of the reign of the judges over the people of Nephi.

Teaching Tips from Prophets' Lips "In all of this we do well. But we ought to do more. The inspired teacher, the one who teaches by the power of the Spirit, is expected to bear testimony that the doctrine he teaches is true" (Bruce R. McConkie, as cited in *Teaching, No Greater Call*, 10).

ALMA 56
The Stripling Warriors
About 66–64 BC

1–9, The sons of the Anti-Nephi-Lehi's join the battle under Helaman's direction; 10–29, Helaman joins the forces of Antipas; 30–44, Helaman's soldiers serve as a decoy for the Lamanite army; 45–48, The faithfulness of the stripling warriors; 49–57, Helaman's army fights against the Lamanites and none are killed.

Notes

ALMA 56

Overarching Principle: Making and keeping sacred covenants may be hard, but God will pour out blessings if we are faithful.

⚡ To help teach the overarching principle, you can use the following activity. Before class you will need to create a small square for a volunteer to stand in (you can use tape, sticks, or chairs), and you will need to bring a spray bottle filled with water, which you will hide discreetly. Invite a class member to stand in the square and ask that person if he is willing to remain in the square regardless of what happens to him. When he agrees, begin spraying him with the spray bottle until he steps out of the square. Have a discussion about why he stepped out and use this activity to help the class visualize how keeping covenants (staying within the square) could be very difficult when faced with trials (getting squirted with water). Be sure to emphasize that the Lord will bless us if we stay faithful. As you study what happens with the stripling warriors, consider teaching the blessings that come from "staying within the square."

1 And now it came to pass in the commencement of the thirtieth year of the reign of the judges, on the second day in the first month, Moroni received an epistle from Helaman, stating the affairs of the people in that quarter of the land.

2 And these are the words which he wrote, saying: My dearly beloved brother, Moroni, as well in the Lord as in the tribulations of our warfare; behold, my beloved brother, I have somewhat to tell you concerning our warfare in this part of the land.

3 Behold, two thousand of the sons of those men whom Ammon brought down out of the land of Nephi—now ye have known that these were descendants of Laman, who was the eldest son of our father Lehi;

4 Now I need not rehearse unto you concerning their traditions or their unbelief, for thou knowest concerning all these things—

5 Therefore it sufficeth me that I tell you that two thousand of these young men have taken their weapons of war, and would that I should be their leader; and we have come forth to defend our country.

6 And now ye also know concerning the covenant which their fathers made, that they would not take up their weapons of war against their brethren to shed blood.

7 But in the twenty and sixth year, when they saw our afflictions and our tribulations for them, they were about to break the covenant which they had made and take up their weapons of war in our defence.

8 But I would not suffer them that they should break this covenant which they had made, supposing that God would strengthen us, insomuch that we should not suffer more because of the fulfilling the oath which they had taken.

9 But behold, here is one thing in which we may have great joy. For behold, in the twenty and sixth year, I, Helaman, did march at the head of these two thousand young men to the city of Judea, to assist Antipas, whom ye had appointed a leader over the people of that part of the land.

vv. 1–9 We should always be true to our covenants.

⚡ Refer to the spray bottle object lesson above.

🔎 The first nine verses of this chapter describe why the stripling warriors volunteered to fight. Invite class members to read these verses looking for this reason. (Note: if you spent some time on this principle in Alma chapter 53, you may want to simply summarize this section).

🔎 Review what covenants their parents made and what challenges they faced as a result. See Alma 24:13–18, 20–23. (You may want to ask someone before class to prepare a summary of these verses and share it with the class.)

Notes

ALMA 56

> *Why did Helaman not want them to break their covenants? (v. 8)*
>
> **Analyze:** *Why do you think they were considering breaking the covenant now?*
>
> **Apply:** *How have you felt the strength of God as you have kept your covenants? How have your covenants been a blessing in your life?*
>
> ♥ Consider sharing your own experience and testimony of the blessings that come from keeping covenants.

10 And I did join my two thousand sons, (for they are worthy to be called sons) to the army of Antipas, in which strength Antipas did rejoice exceedingly; for behold, his army had been reduced by the Lamanites because their forces had slain a vast number of our men, for which cause we have to mourn.

11 Nevertheless, we may console ourselves in this point, that they have died in the cause of their country and of their God, yea, and they are happy.

12 And the Lamanites had also retained many prisoners, all of whom are chief captains, for none other have they spared alive. And we suppose that they are now at this time in the land of Nephi; it is so if they are not slain.

13 And now these are the cities of which the Lamanites have obtained possession by the shedding of the blood of so many of our valiant men:

14 The land of Manti, or the city of Manti, and the city of Zeezrom, and the city of Cumeni, and the city of Antiparah.

15 And these are the cities which they possessed when I arrived at the city of Judea; and I found Antipas and his men toiling with their might to fortify the city.

16 Yea, and they were depressed in body as well as in spirit, for they had fought valiantly by day and toiled by night to maintain their cities; and thus they had suffered great afflictions of every kind.

17 And now they were determined to conquer in this place or die; therefore you may well suppose that this little force which I brought with me, yea, those sons of mine, gave them great hopes and much joy.

18 And now it came to pass that when the Lamanites saw that Antipas had received a greater strength to his army, they were compelled by the orders of Ammoron to not come against the city of Judea, or against us, to battle.

19 And thus were we favored of the Lord; for had they come upon us in this our weakness they might have perhaps destroyed our little army; but thus were we preserved.

20 They were commanded by Ammoron to maintain those cities which they had taken. And thus ended the twenty and sixth year. And in the commencement of the twenty and seventh year we had prepared our city and ourselves for defence.

21 Now we were desirous that the Lamanites should come upon us; for we were not desirous to make an attack upon them in their strongholds.

22 And it came to pass that we kept spies out round about, to watch the movements of the Lamanites, that they might not pass us by night nor by day to make an attack upon our other cities which were on the northward.

23 For we knew in those cities they were not sufficiently strong to meet them; therefore we were desirous, if they should pass by us, to fall upon them in their rear, and thus bring them up in the rear at the same time they were met in the front. We supposed that we could overpower them; but behold, we were disappointed in this our desire.

24 They durst not pass by us with their whole army, neither durst they with a part, lest they should not be sufficiently strong and they should fall.

25 Neither durst they march down against the city of Zarahemla; neither durst they cross the head of Sidon, over to the city of Nephihah.

26 And thus, with their forces, they were determined to maintain those cities which they had taken.

Notes

ALMA 56

27 And now it came to pass in the second month of this year, there was brought unto us many provisions from the fathers of those my two thousand sons.

28 And also there were sent two thousand men unto us from the land of Zarahemla. And thus we were prepared with ten thousand men, and provisions for them, and also for their wives and their children.

29 And the Lamanites, thus seeing our forces increase daily, and provisions arrive for our support, they began to be fearful, and began to sally forth, if it were possible to put an end to our receiving provisions and strength.

30 Now when we saw that the Lamanites began to grow uneasy on this wise, we were desirous to bring a stratagem into effect upon them; therefore Antipas ordered that I should march forth with my little sons to a neighboring city, as if we were carrying provisions to a neighboring city.

31 And we were to march near the city of Antiparah, as if we were going to the city beyond, in the borders by the seashore.

32 And it came to pass that we did march forth, as if with our provisions, to go to that city.

33 And it came to pass that Antipas did march forth with a part of his army, leaving the remainder to maintain the city. But he did not march forth until I had gone forth with my little army, and came near the city Antiparah.

34 And now, in the city Antiparah were stationed the strongest army of the Lamanites; yea, the most numerous.

35 And it came to pass that when they had been informed by their spies, they came forth with their army and marched against us.

36 And it came to pass that we did flee before them, northward. And thus we did lead away the most powerful army of the Lamanites;

37 Yea, even to a considerable distance, insomuch that when they saw the army of Antipas pursuing them, with their might, they did not turn to the right nor to the left, but pursued their march in a straight course after us; and, as we suppose, it was their intent to slay us before Antipas should overtake them, and this that they might not be surrounded by our people.

38 And now Antipas, beholding our danger, did speed the march of his army. But behold, it was night; therefore they did not overtake us, neither did Antipas overtake them; therefore we did camp for the night.

39 And it came to pass that before the dawn of the morning, behold, the Lamanites were pursuing us. Now we were not sufficiently strong to contend with them; yea, I would not suffer that my little sons should fall into their hands; therefore we did continue our march, and we took our march into the wilderness.

40 Now they durst not turn to the right nor to the left lest they should be surrounded; neither would I turn to the right nor to the left lest they should overtake me, and we could not stand against them, but be slain, and they would make their escape; and thus we did flee all that day into the wilderness, even until it was dark.

41 And it came to pass that again, when the light of the morning came we saw the Lamanites upon us, and we did flee before them.

42 But it came to pass that they did not pursue us far before they halted; and it was in the morning of the third day of the seventh month.

43 And now, whether they were overtaken by Antipas we knew not, but I said unto my men: Behold, we know not but they have halted for the purpose that we should come against them, that they might catch us in their snare;

vv. 10–43 Helaman's army serves as a decoy to draw the Lamanites after them. Once the Lamanites follow them, Antipas pursues the Lamanites in an effort to surround them.

- You may need to summarize this part of the storyline for the class, highlighting the key verses.

Notes

44 Therefore what say ye, my sons, will ye go against them to battle?

45 And now I say unto you, my beloved brother Moroni, that never had I seen so great courage, nay, not amongst all the Nephites.

46 For as I had ever called them my sons (for they were all of them very young) even so they said unto me: Father, behold our God is with us, and he will not suffer that we should fall; then let us go forth; we would not slay our brethren if they would let us alone; therefore let us go, lest they should overpower the army of Antipas.

47 Now they never had fought, yet they did not fear death; and they did think more upon the liberty of their fathers than they did upon their lives; yea, they had been taught by their mothers, that if they did not doubt, God would deliver them.

48 And they rehearsed unto me the words of their mothers, saying: We do not doubt our mothers knew it.

vv. 44–48 "The standard for what should happen in our homes."

- *Despite having never fought before, why were the young men so confident that the Lord would protect them?*

- Apply: *What are some life lessons you have learned in the home?*

- Referring to the two thousand sons of Helaman, Elder D. Todd Christofferson said, "Here we find a standard for what should happen in our homes and in the Church. Our teaching should draw upon our own faith and focus first and foremost on instilling faith in God in the rising generation. We must declare the essential need to keep the commandments of God and to walk uprightly before Him in soberness, or in other words, with reverence. Each must be persuaded that service and sacrifice for the well-being and happiness of others are far superior to making one's own comfort and possessions the highest priority. This requires more than an occasional reference to one or another gospel principle. There must be constant teaching, mostly by example" ("Moral Discipline," *Ensign*, Nov. 2009, 107).

- Refer to the last phrase from Elder Christofferson's quote, "mostly by example," and discuss with the class what this means for parents specifically. Note that in the story of the stripling warriors, the young men were influenced by the teachings of their mothers, with no reference to fathers. Recall what happened to some of these warriors' fathers in Alma 24:20–23. Not only did the sons of Helaman receive excellent instructions regarding faith and trust in God from their mothers, but they were also taught by *example* from their fathers about the sacred importance of keeping covenants.

49 And it came to pass that I did return with my two thousand against these Lamanites who had pursued us. And now behold, the armies of Antipas had overtaken them, and a terrible battle had commenced.

50 The army of Antipas being weary, because of their long march in so short a space of time, were about to fall into the hands of the Lamanites; and had I not returned with my two thousand they would have obtained their purpose.

51 For Antipas had fallen by the sword, and many of his leaders, because of their weariness, which was occasioned by the speed of their march—therefore the men of Antipas, being confused because of the fall of their leaders, began to give way before the Lamanites.

52 And it came to pass that the Lamanites took courage, and began to pursue them; and thus were the Lamanites pursuing them with great vigor when Helaman came upon their rear with his two thousand, and began to slay them exceedingly, insomuch that the whole army of the Lamanites halted and turned upon Helaman.

53 Now when the people of Antipas saw that the

Notes

Lamanites had turned them about, they gathered together their men and came again upon the rear of the Lamanites.

54 And now it came to pass that we, the people of Nephi, the people of Antipas, and I with my two thousand, did surround the Lamanites, and did slay them; yea, insomuch that they were compelled to deliver up their weapons of war and also themselves as prisoners of war.

55 And now it came to pass that when they had surrendered themselves up unto us, behold, I numbered those young men who had fought with me, fearing lest there were many of them slain.

56 But behold, to my great joy, there had not one soul of them fallen to the earth; yea, and they had fought as if with the strength of God; yea, never were men known to have fought with such miraculous strength; and with such mighty power did they fall upon the Lamanites, that they did frighten them; and for this cause did the Lamanites deliver themselves up as prisoners of war.

vv. 49–56 Be a covenant keeper.

- Read verses 49–56 with the class and look for how the battle ends for the Nephites, specifically for the stripling warriors.

- Analyze: *Why were the young men so miraculously protected? What does this story teach about the protecting nature of covenants?*

- Apply: *How is this story relevant for us today? What does it mean for us to keep our covenants?*

- Encourage class members to consider ways they can be better covenant keepers. Elder M. Russell Ballard, in referencing this story said, "These inexperienced young men were so spiritually and physically prepared, and so powerful, that they frightened their foes into surrendering! Although all two thousand of the young men were wounded in battle at one time or another, not one was killed. . . . Today we are fighting a battle that in many ways is more perilous, more fraught with danger than the battle between the Nephites and the Lamanites. Our enemy is cunning and resourceful. We fight against Lucifer, the father of all lies, the enemy of all that is good and right and holy. . . . Resolve and commit to yourselves and to God that from this moment forward you will strive diligently to keep your hearts, hands, and minds pure and unsullied from any kind of moral transgression. . . . We expect you to be covenant makers and covenant keepers" ("The Greatest Generation of Missionaries," *Ensign*, Nov. 2002, 46). Refer back to the activity at the beginning of this lesson with the square and spray bottle and encourage your class to stay true to their covenants regardless of what they are faced with.

57 And as we had no place for our prisoners, that we could guard them to keep them from the armies of the Lamanites, therefore we sent them to the land of Zarahemla, and a part of those men who were not slain of Antipas, with them; and the remainder I took and joined them to my stripling Ammonites, and took our march back to the city of Judea.

ALMA 57
"They Do Put Their Trust in God Continually"
About 63 BC

1–12, Helaman continues his letter to Moroni; he takes the city of Antiparah and Cumeni; 13–23, Helaman's stripling soldiers engage in a long battle again; 24–27, Not a single soldier of Helaman's two thousand and sixty were killed; 28–36, Gid recounts his loss of Lamanite prisoners.

Overarching Principle: Constant diligence and obedience to God brings miraculous blessings.

Notes

⚡ Invite a member of your class who has a well-developed musical talent (playing the piano, violin, etc.) and who is willing, to perform briefly for the class. Ask,

- *Could you play like you just did after one day of practice?*
- *How did you develop the skill?*
- *How often did you listen to your instructor when learning?*

Explain that playing a musical instrument requires the same character traits displayed by the armies of Helaman and that those same traits can lead a person to eternal life. Write "diligence" and "obedience" on the board.

Note: Consider dividing the class into three groups and assigning each group one of the principles and activities below. For convenience, use the ideas in this chapter to create small worksheets. After class members have completed the activities, regroup and discuss what they have learned.

1 And now it came to pass that I received an epistle from Ammoron, the king, stating that if I would deliver up those prisoners of war whom we had taken that he would deliver up the city of Antiparah unto us.

2 But I sent an epistle unto the king, that we were sure our forces were sufficient to take the city of Antiparah by our force; and by delivering up the prisoners for that city we should suppose ourselves unwise, and that we would only deliver up our prisoners on exchange.

3 And Ammoron refused mine epistle, for he would not exchange prisoners; therefore we began to make preparations to go against the city of Antiparah.

4 But the people of Antiparah did leave the city, and fled to their other cities, which they had possession of, to fortify them; and thus the city of Antiparah fell into our hands.

5 And thus ended the twenty and eighth year of the reign of the judges.

6 And it came to pass that in the commencement of the twenty and ninth year, we received a supply of provisions, and also an addition to our army, from the land of Zarahemla, and from the land round about, to the number of six thousand men, besides sixty of the sons of the Ammonites who had come to join their brethren, my little band of two thousand. And now behold, we were strong, yea, and we had also plenty of provisions brought unto us.

7 And it came to pass that it was our desire to wage a battle with the army which was placed to protect the city Cumeni.

8 And now behold, I will show unto you that we soon accomplished our desire; yea, with our strong force, or with a part of our strong force, we did surround, by night, the city Cumeni, a little before they were to receive a supply of provisions.

9 And it came to pass that we did camp round about the city for many nights; but we did sleep upon our swords, and keep guards, that the Lamanites could not come upon us by night and slay us, which they attempted many times; but as many times as they attempted this their blood was spilt.

10 At length their provisions did arrive, and they were about to enter the city by night. And we, instead of being Lamanites, were Nephites; therefore, we did take them and their provisions.

11 And notwithstanding the Lamanites being cut off from their support after this manner, they were still determined to maintain the city; therefore it became expedient that we should take those provisions and send them to Judea, and our prisoners to the land of Zarahemla.

12 And it came to pass that not many days had passed away before the Lamanites began to lose all hopes of succor; therefore they yielded up the city unto our hands; and thus we had accomplished our designs in obtaining the city Cumeni.

Notes

ALMA 57

vv. 1–12 Constant diligence and effort bring success. (Group 1)

🔎 *Read Alma 57:1–12 and look for any examples of diligence on the part of Helaman's armies. Diligence can be defined as "constant effort to accomplish what is undertaken" (Webster, 1828).*

❓ Analyze: *Why do you think the Nephites were so diligent? What would have happened if they were lazy or negligent in anyway?*

❓ Apply: *In what spiritual situations could this same principle be important? Can you think of an example of someone you know who has received spiritual blessings because of their diligence?*

13 But it came to pass that our prisoners were so numerous that, notwithstanding the enormity of our numbers, we were obliged to employ all our force to keep them, or to put them to death.

14 For behold, they would break out in great numbers, and would fight with stones, and with clubs, or whatsoever thing they could get into their hands, insomuch that we did slay upwards of two thousand of them after they had surrendered themselves prisoners of war.

15 Therefore it became expedient for us, that we should put an end to their lives, or guard them, sword in hand, down to the land of Zarahemla; and also our provisions were not any more than sufficient for our own people, notwithstanding that which we had taken from the Lamanites.

16 And now, in those critical circumstances, it became a very serious matter to determine concerning these prisoners of war; nevertheless, we did resolve to send them down to the land of Zarahemla; therefore we selected a part of our men, and gave them charge over our prisoners to go down to the land of Zarahemla.

17 But it came to pass that on the morrow they did return. And now behold, we did not inquire of them concerning the prisoners; for behold, the Lamanites were upon us, and they returned in season to save us from falling into their hands. For behold, Ammoron had sent to their support a new supply of provisions and also a numerous army of men.

18 And it came to pass that those men whom we sent with the prisoners did arrive in season to check them, as they were about to overpower us.

19 But behold, my little band of two thousand and sixty fought most desperately; yea, they were firm before the Lamanites, and did administer death unto all those who opposed them.

20 And as the remainder of our army were about to give way before the Lamanites, behold, those two thousand and sixty were firm and undaunted.

21 Yea, and they did obey and observe to perform every word of command with exactness; yea, and even according to their faith it was done unto them; and I did remember the words which they said unto me that their mothers had taught them.

22 And now behold, it was these my sons, and those men who had been selected to convey the prisoners, to whom we owe this great victory; for it was they who did beat the Lamanites; therefore they were driven back to the city of Manti.

23 And we retained our city Cumeni, and were not all destroyed by the sword; nevertheless, we had suffered great loss.

vv. 13–23 Obedience with exactness. (Group 2)

🔎 *Read Alma 57:13–23 and look for what Helaman acknowledges as the quality that led to their success.*

❓ Analyze:
- *What phrase is used to describe the obedience of the stripling warriors?*
- *What do you think "with exactness" means?*
- *What would be the opposite of this phrase?*
- *What would that look like on the battlefield and what consequences would be felt?*

👥 Invite class members to devise several modern situations when a member of the

Notes

ALMA 57

Church could choose to obey a commandment with exactness or with incompleteness. Have them describe their examples and discuss the consequences of these two types of obedience.

24 And it came to pass that after the Lamanites had fled, I immediately gave orders that my men who had been wounded should be taken from among the dead, and caused that their wounds should be dressed.

25 And it came to pass that there were two hundred, out of my two thousand and sixty, who had fainted because of the loss of blood; nevertheless, according to the goodness of God, and to our great astonishment, and also the joy of our whole army, there was not one soul of them who did perish; yea, and neither was there one soul among them who had not received many wounds.

26 And now, their preservation was astonishing to our whole army, yea, that they should be spared while there was a thousand of our brethren who were slain. And we do justly ascribe it to the miraculous power of God, because of their exceeding faith in that which they had been taught to believe—that there was a just God, and whosoever did not doubt, that they should be preserved by his marvelous power.

27 Now this was the faith of these of whom I have spoken; they are young, and their minds are firm, and they do put their trust in God continually.

vv. 24–27 God has the power to preserve His people in miraculous ways. (Group 3)

- Read Alma 57:24–27 and look for a miracle provided by God.
- Analyze:
  - *What do you think the likelihood of not a single stripling warrior being slain was?*
  - *Why might some be tempted to ascribe this miracle to fighting skills and diligence in battle only?*
  - *In verse 26, to what does Helaman ascribe the miracle?*
- Refer back to the example of musical talent from the beginning of the lesson. Testify that while diligence and obedience can bring great success on their own, true miracles come by the power of God to those who have faith to diligently obey His will.

28 And now it came to pass that after we had thus taken care of our wounded men, and had buried our dead and also the dead of the Lamanites, who were many, behold, we did inquire of Gid concerning the prisoners whom they had started to go down to the land of Zarahemla with.

29 Now Gid was the chief captain over the band who was appointed to guard them down to the land.

30 And now, these are the words which Gid said unto me: Behold, we did start to go down to the land of Zarahemla with our prisoners. And it came to pass that we did meet the spies of our armies, who had been sent out to watch the camp of the Lamanites.

31 And they cried unto us, saying—Behold, the armies of the Lamanites are marching towards the city of Cumeni; and behold, they will fall upon them, yea, and will destroy our people.

32 And it came to pass that our prisoners did hear their cries, which caused them to take courage; and they did rise up in rebellion against us.

33 And it came to pass because of their rebellion we did cause that our swords should come upon them. And it came to pass that they did in a body run upon our swords, in the which, the greater number of them were slain; and the remainder of them broke through and fled from us.

34 And behold, when they had fled and we could not overtake them, we took our march with speed towards the city Cumeni; and behold, we did arrive in time that we might assist our brethren in preserving the city.

Notes

35 And behold, we are again delivered out of the hands of our enemies. And blessed is the name of our God; for behold, it is he that has delivered us; yea, that has done this great thing for us.

36 Now it came to pass that when I, Helaman, had heard these words of Gid, I was filled with exceeding joy because of the goodness of God in preserving us, that we might not all perish; yea, and I trust that the souls of them who have been slain have entered into the rest of their God.

> **Teaching Tips from Prophets' Lips** "I ask every man and woman occupying a place of responsibility whose duty it is to teach the gospel of Jesus Christ to live it and keep the commandments of God, so that their example will teach it" (Heber J. Grant, *Gospel Standards*, comp. G. Homer Durham [1941], 72).

ALMA 58

"God Will Deliver Us"
About 63–62 BC

1–9, Helaman, Gid, and Teomner await further provisions and strength, but only receive minimal support; 10–12, They look to the Lord and take strength and courage in Him; 13–41, Helaman, Gid, and Teomner use stratagem to obtain the city of Manti, and the Lamanites withdraw from that part of the land.

1 And behold, now it came to pass that our next object was to obtain the city of Manti; but behold, there was no way that we could lead them out of the city by our small bands. For behold, they remembered that which we had hitherto done; therefore we could not decoy them away from their strongholds.

2 And they were so much more numerous than was our army that we durst not go forth and attack them in their strongholds.

3 Yea, and it became expedient that we should employ our men to the maintaining those parts of the land which we had regained of our possessions; therefore it became expedient that we should wait, that we might receive more strength from the land of Zarahemla and also a new supply of provisions.

4 And it came to pass that I thus did send an embassy to the governor of our land, to acquaint him concerning the affairs of our people. And it came to pass that we did wait to receive provisions and strength from the land of Zarahemla.

5 But behold, this did profit us but little; for the Lamanites were also receiving great strength from day to day, and also many provisions; and thus were our circumstances at this period of time.

6 And the Lamanites were sallying forth against us from time to time, resolving by stratagem to destroy us; nevertheless we could not come to battle with them, because of their retreats and their strongholds.

7 And it came to pass that we did wait in these difficult circumstances for the space of many months, even until we were about to perish for the want of food.

8 But it came to pass that we did receive food, which was guarded to us by an army of two thousand men to our assistance; and this is all the assistance which we did receive, to defend ourselves and our country from falling into the hands of our enemies, yea, to contend with an enemy which was innumerable.

9 And now the cause of these our embarrassments, or the cause why they did not send more strength unto us, we knew not; therefore we were grieved and also filled with fear, lest by any means the judgments of God should come upon our land, to our overthrow and utter destruction.

10 Therefore we did pour out our souls in prayer to God, that he would strengthen us and deliver us out of the hands of our enemies, yea, and also give us strength that we might retain our cities,

Notes

and our lands, and our possessions, for the support of our people.

11 Yea, and it came to pass that the Lord our God did visit us with assurances that he would deliver us; yea, insomuch that he did speak peace to our souls, and did grant unto us great faith, and did cause us that we should hope for our deliverance in him.

12 And we did take courage with our small force which we had received, and were fixed with a determination to conquer our enemies, and to maintain our lands, and our possessions, and our wives, and our children, and the cause of our liberty.

vv. 1–12 If we humble ourselves before the Lord, He will make weak things become strong (see Ether 12:27).

- Write on the board, "If we humble ourselves before the Lord, He will make weak things become strong." Invite class members to silently read verses 1–12 and look for how these verses teach this principle. Write the following questions on the board to help them as they read:

    • What was the Nephites' weakness?
    • What scriptural phrases show that the Nephite army and their leaders were humble?
    • What were the immediate results of their humility?

    Have class members share some of the scriptural phrases that show the Nephites' humility, as well as the immediate result.

- Analyze: *Why do you think the Lord did not simply provide more provisions and men at the beginning?*

- *When has the Lord strengthened you in a time of weakness?* Testify that the Lord will strengthen us as we turn to Him in humility. Invite class members to read Ether 12:27 and look for where the strength comes from. Testify of the grace of Christ and that through His grace we can become strong. Invite class members to look for the hand of the Lord in the Nephites' victory.

13 And thus we did go forth with all our might against the Lamanites, who were in the city of Manti; and we did pitch our tents by the wilderness side, which was near to the city.

14 And it came to pass that on the morrow, that when the Lamanites saw that we were in the borders by the wilderness which was near the city, that they sent out their spies round about us that they might discover the number and the strength of our army.

15 And it came to pass that when they saw that we were not strong, according to our numbers, and fearing that we should cut them off from their support except they should come out to battle against us and kill us, and also supposing that they could easily destroy us with their numerous hosts, therefore they began to make preparations to come out against us to battle.

16 And when we saw that they were making preparations to come out against us, behold, I caused that Gid, with a small number of men, should secrete himself in the wilderness, and also that Teomner and a small number of men should secrete themselves also in the wilderness.

17 Now Gid and his men were on the right and the others on the left; and when they had thus secreted themselves, behold, I remained, with the remainder of my army, in that same place where we had first pitched our tents against the time that the Lamanites should come out to battle.

18 And it came to pass that the Lamanites did come out with their numerous army against us. And when they had come and were about to fall upon us with the sword, I caused that my men, those who were with me, should retreat into the wilderness.

19 And it came to pass that the Lamanites did follow after us with great speed, for they were exceedingly desirous to overtake us that they might slay us; therefore they did follow us into

Notes

the wilderness; and we did pass by in the midst of Gid and Teomner, insomuch that they were not discovered by the Lamanites.

20 And it came to pass that when the Lamanites had passed by, or when the army had passed by, Gid and Teomner did rise up from their secret places, and did cut off the spies of the Lamanites that they should not return to the city.

21 And it came to pass that when they had cut them off, they ran to the city and fell upon the guards who were left to guard the city, insomuch that they did destroy them and did take possession of the city.

22 Now this was done because the Lamanites did suffer their whole army, save a few guards only, to be led away into the wilderness.

23 And it came to pass that Gid and Teomner by this means had obtained possession of their strongholds. And it came to pass that we took our course, after having traveled much in the wilderness towards the land of Zarahemla.

24 And when the Lamanites saw that they were marching towards the land of Zarahemla, they were exceedingly afraid, lest there was a plan laid to lead them on to destruction; therefore they began to retreat into the wilderness again, yea, even back by the same way which they had come.

25 And behold, it was night and they did pitch their tents, for the chief captains of the Lamanites had supposed that the Nephites were weary because of their march; and supposing that they had driven their whole army therefore they took no thought concerning the city of Manti.

26 Now it came to pass that when it was night, I caused that my men should not sleep, but that they should march forward by another way towards the land of Manti.

27 And because of this our march in the nighttime, behold, on the morrow we were beyond the Lamanites, insomuch that we did arrive before them at the city of Manti.

28 And thus it came to pass, that by this stratagem we did take possession of the city of Manti without the shedding of blood.

29 And it came to pass that when the armies of the Lamanites did arrive near the city, and saw that we were prepared to meet them, they were astonished exceedingly and struck with great fear, insomuch that they did flee into the wilderness.

30 Yea, and it came to pass that the armies of the Lamanites did flee out of all this quarter of the land. But behold, they have carried with them many women and children out of the land.

vv. 13–30 Visualizing.

- Set up a visual of the two armies using small plastic "army men" or something similar. Before class starts, have these army men divided into two armies—a larger group in a city (use blocks, or something similar to represent the fortifications of the city), and a smaller group next to the city. Note: You could use just about any item to represent the different armies; the key is to help the scriptures come to life so the class can visualize the story.
- Read the story with the class and move the "army men" accordingly throughout the story to help the class visualize what is taking place.

31 And those cities which had been taken by the Lamanites, all of them are at this period of time in our possession; and our fathers and our women and our children are returning to their homes, all save it be those who have been taken prisoners and carried off by the Lamanites.

32 But behold, our armies are small to maintain so great a number of cities and so great possessions.

33 But behold, we trust in our God who has given us victory over those lands, insomuch that we have obtained those cities and those lands, which were our own.

34 Now we do not know the cause that the government does not grant us more strength; neither

Notes

do those men who came up unto us know why we have not received greater strength.

35 Behold, we do not know but what ye are unsuccessful, and ye have drawn away the forces into that quarter of the land; if so, we do not desire to murmur.

36 And if it is not so, behold, we fear that there is some faction in the government, that they do not send more men to our assistance; for we know that they are more numerous than that which they have sent.

37 But, behold, it mattereth not—we trust God will deliver us, notwithstanding the weakness of our armies, yea, and deliver us out of the hands of our enemies.

v. 37 If we trust in God, He will deliver us.

♥ *How does verse 37 add to our understanding that the Lord will make weak things strong unto us?* Invite class members to humbly put their trust in God and testify of His power to deliver us from all the trials, temptations, sufferings, and hardships of our lives.

38 Behold, this is the twenty and ninth year, in the latter end, and we are in the possession of our lands; and the Lamanites have fled to the land of Nephi.

39 And those sons of the people of Ammon, of whom I have so highly spoken, are with me in the city of Manti; and the Lord has supported them, yea, and kept them from falling by the sword, insomuch that even one soul has not been slain.

40 But behold, they have received many wounds; nevertheless they stand fast in that liberty wherewith God has made them free; and they are strict to remember the Lord their God from day to day; yea, they do observe to keep his statutes, and his judgments, and his commandments continually; and their faith is strong in the prophecies concerning that which is to come.

41 And now, my beloved brother, Moroni, may the Lord our God, who has redeemed us and made us free, keep you continually in his presence; yea, and may he favor this people, even that ye may have success in obtaining the possession of all that which the Lamanites have taken from us, which was for our support. And now, behold, I close mine epistle. I am Helaman, the son of Alma.

Index Topics: humility, trusting God

ALMA 59

Prepare and Prevent
About 62 BC

1–4, Moroni rejoices in the success of Helaman and his armies; 5–8, The city of Nephihah is attacked and the people of Nephihah flee to Moroni; 9–13, Moroni expresses his frustration with the government's indifference.

1 Now it came to pass in the thirtieth year of the reign of the judges over the people of Nephi, after Moroni had received and had read Helaman's epistle, he was exceedingly rejoiced because of the welfare, yea, the exceeding success which Helaman had had, in obtaining those lands which were lost.

2 Yea, and he did make it known unto all his people, in all the land round about in that part where he was, that they might rejoice also.

3 And it came to pass that he immediately sent an epistle to Pahoran, desiring that he should cause men to be gathered together to strengthen Helaman, or the armies of Helaman, insomuch that he might with ease maintain that part of the land which he had been so miraculously prospered in regaining.

4 And it came to pass when Moroni had sent this epistle to the land of Zarahemla, he began again to lay a plan that he might obtain the remainder of those possessions and cities which the Lamanites had taken from them.

Notes

ALMA 59

5 And it came to pass that while Moroni was thus making preparations to go against the Lamanites to battle, behold, the people of Nephihah, who were gathered together from the city of Moroni and the city of Lehi and the city of Morianton, were attacked by the Lamanites.

6 Yea, even those who had been compelled to flee from the land of Manti, and from the land round about, had come over and joined the Lamanites in this part of the land.

7 And thus being exceedingly numerous, yea, and receiving strength from day to day, by the command of Ammoron they came forth against the people of Nephihah, and they did begin to slay them with an exceedingly great slaughter.

8 And their armies were so numerous that the remainder of the people of Nephihah were obliged to flee before them; and they came even and joined the army of Moroni.

9 And now as Moroni had supposed that there should be men sent to the city of Nephihah, to the assistance of the people to maintain that city, and knowing that it was easier to keep the city from falling into the hands of the Lamanites than to retake it from them, he supposed that they would easily maintain that city.

10 Therefore he retained all his force to maintain those places which he had recovered.

11 And now, when Moroni saw that the city of Nephihah was lost he was exceedingly sorrowful, and began to doubt, because of the wickedness of the people, whether they should not fall into the hands of their brethren.

12 Now this was the case with all his chief captains. They doubted and marveled also because of the wickedness of the people, and this because of the success of the Lamanites over them.

13 And it came to pass that Moroni was angry with the government, because of their indifference concerning the freedom of their country.

vv. 1–13 It is better to prepare and prevent rather than repair and repent.

⚡ Read or write the following definition and invite class members to guess what is being defined. "The care and servicing by personnel for the purpose of maintaining equipment and facilities in satisfactory operating condition by providing for systematic inspection, detection, and correction of incipient failures either before they occur or before they develop into major defects." Answer—preventative maintenance. After the answer is given ask, *How does preventative maintenance relate with the gospel of Jesus Christ?*

🔍 Summarize what happened to the land of Nephihah and ask, *What verses in this chapter best fit the description of preventive maintenance?* (vv. 9–10) Share the principle, "It is better to prepare and prevent rather than repair and repent." Consider writing the principle on the board and inviting class members to note the principle in their scriptures.

❓ Analyze: *What might a plan to "maintain" ourselves spiritually look like? Why is it important to practice spiritual "preventative maintenance"?*

💗 Invite class members to write down three items that they feel they need to do to prepare and prevent spiritually. Remind the class to be specific about when and how they will do these things. Testify that as we do the small and simple things of the gospel we will prepare and prevent and we will have strength and power to overcome our enemy, Satan.

Teaching Tips from Prophets' Lips "There can be no failure in the work of the Lord when [we] do [our] best. We are but instruments; this is the Lord's work. This is His Church, His gospel plan. These are His children we are working with. He will not permit us to fail if we do our part. He will magnify us even beyond our own talents and abilities when necessary. This I know. I am sure many of you have experienced it as I have. It is one of the sweetest experiences that can come to a human being" (Ezra Taft Benson, *The Teachings of Ezra Taft Benson* [1988], 372).

Notes

Index Topics: preparation

ALMA 60

Moroni's Condemning Letter to Pahoran
About 62 BC

1–13, Moroni describes the army's suffering because of the government's neglect; 14–24, Internal strife has been the central cause of the Nephites' difficulties; 25–36, Moroni threatens to stir up insurrections toward the chief judge and traitors.

1 And it came to pass that he wrote again to the governor of the land, who was Pahoran, and these are the words which he wrote, saying: Behold, I direct mine epistle to Pahoran, in the city of Zarahemla, who is the chief judge and the governor over the land, and also to all those who have been chosen by this people to govern and manage the affairs of this war.

2 For behold, I have somewhat to say unto them by the way of condemnation; for behold, ye yourselves know that ye have been appointed to gather together men, and arm them with swords, and with cimeters, and all manner of weapons of war of every kind, and send forth against the Lamanites, in whatsoever parts they should come into our land.

3 And now behold, I say unto you that myself, and also my men, and also Helaman and his men, have suffered exceedingly great sufferings; yea, even hunger, thirst, and fatigue, and all manner of afflictions of every kind.

4 But behold, were this all we had suffered we would not murmur nor complain.

5 But behold, great has been the slaughter among our people; yea, thousands have fallen by the sword, while it might have otherwise been if ye had rendered unto our armies sufficient strength and succor for them. Yea, great has been your neglect towards us.

6 And now behold, we desire to know the cause of this exceedingly great neglect; yea, we desire to know the cause of your thoughtless state.

7 Can you think to sit upon your thrones in a state of thoughtless stupor, while your enemies are spreading the work of death around you? Yea, while they are murdering thousands of your brethren—

8 Yea, even they who have looked up to you for protection, yea, have placed you in a situation that ye might have succored them, yea, ye might have sent armies unto them, to have strengthened them, and have saved thousands of them from falling by the sword.

9 But behold, this is not all—ye have withheld your provisions from them, insomuch that many have fought and bled out their lives because of their great desires which they had for the welfare of this people; yea, and this they have done when they were about to perish with hunger, because of your exceedingly great neglect towards them.

10 And now, my beloved brethren—for ye ought to be beloved; yea, and ye ought to have stirred yourselves more diligently for the welfare and the freedom of this people; but behold, ye have neglected them insomuch that the blood of thousands shall come upon your heads for vengeance; yea, for known unto God were all their cries, and all their sufferings—

v. 10 If we neglect our own welfare and freedom, we may be guilty of serious wrongs.

- Ask class members, *What is the difference between a sin of omission and one of commission?* (Sin of omission is neglecting to do something you should; commission is doing something you should not.)

- *Read verse 10 and look for what Moroni accuses the Nephite government to be guilty of.*

- "All that is necessary for the triumph of evil is that good men do nothing" (Edmund Burke).

Notes

- Invite class members to note the cross-reference Doctrine and Covenants 58:26–28 in their scriptures. Read the verses and challenge your class to seek opportunities to do good instead of waiting to be asked.

11 Behold, could ye suppose that ye could sit upon your thrones, and because of the exceeding goodness of God ye could do nothing and he would deliver you? Behold, if ye have supposed this ye have supposed in vain.

12 Do ye suppose that, because so many of your brethren have been killed it is because of their wickedness? I say unto you, if ye have supposed this ye have supposed in vain; for I say unto you, there are many who have fallen by the sword; and behold it is to your condemnation;

13 For the Lord suffereth the righteous to be slain that his justice and judgment may come upon the wicked; therefore ye need not suppose that the righteous are lost because they are slain; but behold, they do enter into the rest of the Lord their God.

v. 13 God allows the righteous to die for His grand purposes.

- Ask, *Why does God allow the righteous to die sometimes?*
- Look for the answer in verse 13.
- Analyze:
  - *Why doesn't God stop every bad thing from happening?*
  - *What does this have to do with the agency of man?*
  - *In the pre-earth life, who wanted to remove man's agency? (Moses 4:3)*
- Near the end of World War II, J. Reuben Clark Jr. stated, "In this terrible war now waging thousands of our righteous young men in all parts of the world and in many countries are subject to a call into the military service of their own countries. Some of these, so serving, have already been called back to their heavenly home; others will almost surely be called to follow. But 'behold,' as Moroni said, the righteous of them who serve and are slain 'do enter into the rest of the Lord their God' (Alma 60:13), and of them the Lord has said 'those that die in me shall not taste of death, for it shall be sweet unto them' (Doctrine and Covenants 42:46). Their salvation and exaltation in the world to come will be secure. That in their work of destruction they will be striking at their brethren will not be held against them. That sin, as Moroni of old said, is to the condemnation of those who 'sit in their places of power in a state of thoughtless stupor' (Alma 60:7), those rulers in the world who in a frenzy of hate and lust for unrighteous power and dominion over their fellow men, have put into motion eternal forces they do not comprehend and cannot control. God, in his own due time, will pass sentence upon them" (General Conference, April 1945, Friday Afternoon, J. Reuben Clark Jr.).

14 And now behold, I say unto you, I fear exceedingly that the judgments of God will come upon this people, because of their exceeding slothfulness, yea, even the slothfulness of our government, and their exceedingly great neglect towards their brethren, yea, towards those who have been slain.

15 For were it not for the wickedness which first commenced at our head, we could have withstood our enemies that they could have gained no power over us.

16 Yea, had it not been for the war which broke out among ourselves; yea, were it not for these king-men, who caused so much bloodshed among ourselves; yea, at the time we were contending among ourselves, if we had united our strength as we hitherto have done; yea, had it not been for the desire of power and authority which those king-men had over us; had they been true to the cause of our freedom, and united with us, and gone forth against our enemies, instead of taking

Notes

ALMA 60

up their swords against us, which was the cause of so much bloodshed among ourselves; yea, if we had gone forth against them in the strength of the Lord, we should have dispersed our enemies, for it would have been done, according to the fulfilling of his word.

17 But behold, now the Lamanites are coming upon us, taking possession of our lands, and they are murdering our people with the sword, yea, our women and our children, and also carrying them away captive, causing them that they should suffer all manner of afflictions, and this because of the great wickedness of those who are seeking for power and authority, yea, even those king-men.

18 But why should I say much concerning this matter? For we know not but what ye yourselves are seeking for authority. We know not but what ye are also traitors to your country.

vv. 15–18 We must defend our country from enemies within.

> ⚡ Ask your class to listen to the oath sworn upon enlistment in the US Armed Forces.
>
> "I, _____, do solemnly swear that I will support and defend the Constitution of the United States against all enemies, foreign and domestic; that I will bear true faith and allegiance to the same; and that I will obey the orders of the President of the United States and the orders of the officers appointed over me, according to regulations and the Uniform Code of Military Justice. So help me God." Ask, *What two types of enemies are they to defend against?*
>
> 🔎 *In verses 15–18, look for which type of enemy the Nephites had the most problems with.*

19 Or is it that ye have neglected us because ye are in the heart of our country and ye are surrounded by security, that ye do not cause food to be sent unto us, and also men to strengthen our armies?

20 Have ye forgotten the commandments of the Lord your God? Yea, have ye forgotten the captivity of our fathers? Have ye forgotten the many times we have been delivered out of the hands of our enemies?

21 Or do ye suppose that the Lord will still deliver us, while we sit upon our thrones and do not make use of the means which the Lord has provided for us?

22 Yea, will ye sit in idleness while ye are surrounded with thousands of those, yea, and tens of thousands, who do also sit in idleness, while there are thousands round about in the borders of the land who are falling by the sword, yea, wounded and bleeding?

23 Do ye suppose that God will look upon you as guiltless while ye sit still and behold these things? Behold I say unto you, Nay. Now I would that ye should remember that God has said that the inward vessel shall be cleansed first, and then shall the outer vessel be cleansed also.

24 And now, except ye do repent of that which ye have done, and begin to be up and doing, and send forth food and men unto us, and also unto Helaman, that he may support those parts of our country which he has regained, and that we may also recover the remainder of our possessions in these parts, behold it will be expedient that we contend no more with the Lamanites until we have first cleansed our inward vessel, yea, even the great head of our government.

vv. 23–24 We must first try to cleanse the inward vessel in order to cleanse the outer vessel.

> ⚡ Show the class a mug, dirty on both the inside and out. Discuss if it is best to clean the outside or inside of the cup, if you could only choose one.
>
> 🔎 *In verses 23–24, look for which is best to clean and why.*
>
> ❓ Analyze:
> • Which sins are outwardly visible to others?

Notes

144

- *What are some sins that are not visible to others?*
- *Why would it be important to work on the non-visible sins first?*

25 And except ye grant mine epistle, and come out and show unto me a true spirit of freedom, and strive to strengthen and fortify our armies, and grant unto them food for their support, behold I will leave a part of my freemen to maintain this part of our land, and I will leave the strength and the blessings of God upon them, that none other power can operate against them—

26 And this because of their exceeding faith, and their patience in their tribulations—

27 And I will come unto you, and if there be any among you that has a desire for freedom, yea, if there be even a spark of freedom remaining, behold I will stir up insurrections among you, even until those who have desires to usurp power and authority shall become extinct.

28 Yea, behold I do not fear your power nor your authority, but it is my God whom I fear; and it is according to his commandments that I do take my sword to defend the cause of my country, and it is because of your iniquity that we have suffered so much loss.

29 Behold it is time, yea, the time is now at hand, that except ye do bestir yourselves in the defence of your country and your little ones, the sword of justice doth hang over you; yea, and it shall fall upon you and visit you even to your utter destruction.

30 Behold, I wait for assistance from you; and, except ye do administer unto our relief, behold, I come unto you, even in the land of Zarahemla, and smite you with the sword, insomuch that ye can have no more power to impede the progress of this people in the cause of our freedom.

31 For behold, the Lord will not suffer that ye shall live and wax strong in your iniquities to destroy his righteous people.

32 Behold, can you suppose that the Lord will spare you and come out in judgment against the Lamanites, when it is the tradition of their fathers that has caused their hatred, yea, and it has been redoubled by those who have dissented from us, while your iniquity is for the cause of your love of glory and the vain things of the world?

33 Ye know that ye do transgress the laws of God, and ye do know that ye do trample them under your feet. Behold, the Lord saith unto me: If those whom ye have appointed your governors do not repent of their sins and iniquities, ye shall go up to battle against them.

34 And now behold, I, Moroni, am constrained, according to the covenant which I have made to keep the commandments of my God; therefore I would that ye should adhere to the word of God, and send speedily unto me of your provisions and of your men, and also to Helaman.

35 And behold, if ye will not do this I come unto you speedily; for behold, God will not suffer that we should perish with hunger; therefore he will give unto us of your food, even if it must be by the sword. Now see that ye fulfil the word of God.

36 Behold, I am Moroni, your chief captain. I seek not for power, but to pull it down. I seek not for honor of the world, but for the glory of my God, and the freedom and welfare of my country. And thus I close mine epistle.

Index Topics: sin, death, patriotism

ALMA 61

Pahoran's Response to Moroni
About 62 BC

1–8, Pahoran describes the actions of traitorous Nephites to overthrow the free government; 9–21, Pahoran invites Moroni to return to Zarahemla and

Notes

together fight against the Nephites that have become traitors.

1 Behold, now it came to pass that soon after Moroni had sent his epistle unto the chief governor, he received an epistle from Pahoran, the chief governor. And these are the words which he received:

2 I, Pahoran, who am the chief governor of this land, do send these words unto Moroni, the chief captain over the army. Behold, I say unto you, Moroni, that I do not joy in your great afflictions, yea, it grieves my soul.

3 But behold, there are those who do joy in your afflictions, yea, insomuch that they have risen up in rebellion against me, and also those of my people who are freemen, yea, and those who have risen up are exceedingly numerous.

4 And it is those who have sought to take away the judgment-seat from me that have been the cause of this great iniquity; for they have used great flattery, and they have led away the hearts of many people, which will be the cause of sore affliction among us; they have withheld our provisions, and have daunted our freemen that they have not come unto you.

5 And behold, they have driven me out before them, and I have fled to the land of Gideon, with as many men as it were possible that I could get.

6 And behold, I have sent a proclamation throughout this part of the land; and behold, they are flocking to us daily, to their arms, in the defence of their country and their freedom, and to avenge our wrongs.

7 And they have come unto us, insomuch that those who have risen up in rebellion against us are set at defiance, yea, insomuch that they do fear us and durst not come out against us to battle.

8 They have got possession of the land, or the city, of Zarahemla; they have appointed a king over them, and he hath written unto the king of the Lamanites, in the which he hath joined an alliance with him; in the which alliance he hath agreed to maintain the city of Zarahemla, which maintenance he supposeth will enable the Lamanites to conquer the remainder of the land, and he shall be placed king over this people when they shall be conquered under the Lamanites.

9 And now, in your epistle you have censured me, but it mattereth not; I am not angry, but do rejoice in the greatness of your heart. I, Pahoran, do not seek for power, save only to retain my judgment-seat that I may preserve the rights and the liberty of my people. My soul standeth fast in that liberty in the which God hath made us free.

v. 9 We can decide to not become offended.

- Ask class members to think of a time they were offended and had hurt feelings. Explain that chapter 61 is Pahoran's response to Moroni's harsh letter. In it Pahoran explains that he is innocent of what Moroni is accusing him of.

- In verse 9, look for Pahoran's attitude toward Moroni.

- Analyze:
  • Why didn't Pahoran take offense at what Moroni said?
  • Is taking offense a choice or not? Why?
  • Why do many people choose to be offended instead of letting other's actions or words go?
  • What benefits come from letting go of offenses?

- Elder David A. Bednar taught, "You and I cannot control the intentions or behavior of other people. However, we do determine how we will act. Please remember that you and I are agents endowed with moral agency, and we can choose not to be offended" ("And Nothing Shall Offend Them," *Ensign,* Nov. 2006, 91).

- Challenge your class to become the kind of people that quickly let go of offenses when they come.

10 And now, behold, we will resist wickedness even unto bloodshed. We would not shed the blood

Notes

of the Lamanites if they would stay in their own land.

11 We would not shed the blood of our brethren if they would not rise up in rebellion and take the sword against us.

12 We would subject ourselves to the yoke of bondage if it were requisite with the justice of God, or if he should command us so to do.

13 But behold he doth not command us that we shall subject ourselves to our enemies, but that we should put our trust in him, and he will deliver us.

14 Therefore, my beloved brother, Moroni, let us resist evil, and whatsoever evil we cannot resist with our words, yea, such as rebellions and dissensions, let us resist them with our swords, that we may retain our freedom, that we may rejoice in the great privilege of our church, and in the cause of our Redeemer and our God.

15 Therefore, come unto me speedily with a few of your men, and leave the remainder in the charge of Lehi and Teancum; give unto them power to conduct the war in that part of the land, according to the Spirit of God, which is also the spirit of freedom which is in them.

16 Behold I have sent a few provisions unto them, that they may not perish until ye can come unto me.

17 Gather together whatsoever force ye can upon your march hither, and we will go speedily against those dissenters, in the strength of our God according to the faith which is in us.

18 And we will take possession of the city of Zarahemla, that we may obtain more food to send forth unto Lehi and Teancum; yea, we will go forth against them in the strength of the Lord, and we will put an end to this great iniquity.

19 And now, Moroni, I do joy in receiving your epistle, for I was somewhat worried concerning what we should do, whether it should be just in us to go against our brethren.

20 But ye have said, except they repent the Lord hath commanded you that ye should go against them.

21 See that ye strengthen Lehi and Teancum in the Lord; tell them to fear not, for God will deliver them, yea, and also all those who stand fast in that liberty wherewith God hath made them free. And now I close mine epistle to my beloved brother, Moroni.

Teaching Tips from Prophets' Lips "Think about those you teach. Consider their lives, the decisions they face, and the directions they are going. Be open to teaching ideas as you do such things as study the scriptures or observe the beauties of nature. You can even find teaching ideas in activities such as cleaning your house, going to work, or going to the store. Virtually any experience can provide you with just the example, enrichment, or clarification you need for a gospel lesson" (*Teaching, No Greater Call,* 23).

Index Topics: taking offense

ALMA 62

Peace Is Established
About 62–57 BC

1–11, Moroni marches to the aid of Pahoran, defeats the king-men, and establishes Pahoran on the judgment seat again; 12–29, Moroni recaptures the city of Nephihah; 30–34, the Nephites continue to drive the Lamanites out of their lands; 35–39, Teancum slays Ammoron and he is also killed, the war ends; 40–52, Moroni retires as general and Helaman returns to the ministry.

1 And now it came to pass that when Moroni had received this epistle his heart did take courage, and was filled with exceedingly great joy because of the faithfulness of Pahoran, that he was not also a traitor to the freedom and cause of his country.

2 But he did also mourn exceedingly because of the iniquity of those who had driven Pahoran

Notes

from the judgment-seat, yea, in fine because of those who had rebelled against their country and also their God.

3 And it came to pass that Moroni took a small number of men, according to the desire of Pahoran, and gave Lehi and Teancum command over the remainder of his army, and took his march towards the land of Gideon.

4 And he did raise the standard of liberty in whatsoever place he did enter, and gained whatsoever force he could in all his march towards the land of Gideon.

5 And it came to pass that thousands did flock unto his standard, and did take up their swords in the defence of their freedom, that they might not come into bondage.

6 And thus, when Moroni had gathered together whatsoever men he could in all his march, he came to the land of Gideon; and uniting his forces with those of Pahoran they became exceedingly strong, even stronger than the men of Pachus, who was the king of those dissenters who had driven the freemen out of the land of Zarahemla and had taken possession of the land.

7 And it came to pass that Moroni and Pahoran went down with their armies into the land of Zarahemla, and went forth against the city, and did meet the men of Pachus, insomuch that they did come to battle.

8 And behold, Pachus was slain and his men were taken prisoners, and Pahoran was restored to his judgment-seat.

9 And the men of Pachus received their trial, according to the law, and also those king-men who had been taken and cast into prison; and they were executed according to the law; yea, those men of Pachus and those king-men, whosoever would not take up arms in the defence of their country, but would fight against it, were put to death.

v. 9 Traitors were put to death.

💡 Note that instead of remaining imprisoned, the traitors were executed if they refused to take up arms in defense of their country.

10 And thus it became expedient that this law should be strictly observed for the safety of their country; yea, and whosoever was found denying their freedom was speedily executed according to the law.

11 And thus ended the thirtieth year of the reign of the judges over the people of Nephi; Moroni and Pahoran having restored peace to the land of Zarahemla, among their own people, having inflicted death upon all those who were not true to the cause of freedom.

vv. 1–11 Moroni marches to the aid of Pahoran, defeats the king-men, and establishes Pahoran on the judgment seat again.

12 And it came to pass in the commencement of the thirty and first year of the reign of the judges over the people of Nephi, Moroni immediately caused that provisions should be sent, and also an army of six thousand men should be sent unto Helaman, to assist him in preserving that part of the land.

13 And he also caused that an army of six thousand men, with a sufficient quantity of food, should be sent to the armies of Lehi and Teancum. And it came to pass that this was done to fortify the land against the Lamanites.

14 And it came to pass that Moroni and Pahoran, leaving a large body of men in the land of Zarahemla, took their march with a large body of men towards the land of Nephihah, being determined to overthrow the Lamanites in that city.

15 And it came to pass that as they were marching towards the land, they took a large body of men of the Lamanites, and slew many of them, and took their provisions and their weapons of war.

16 And it came to pass after they had taken them, they caused them to enter into a covenant that

Notes

they would no more take up their weapons of war against the Nephites.

17 And when they had entered into this covenant they sent them to dwell with the people of Ammon, and they were in number about four thousand who had not been slain.

18 And it came to pass that when they had sent them away they pursued their march towards the land of Nephihah. And it came to pass that when they had come to the city of Nephihah, they did pitch their tents in the plains of Nephihah, which is near the city of Nephihah.

19 Now Moroni was desirous that the Lamanites should come out to battle against them, upon the plains; but the Lamanites, knowing of their exceedingly great courage, and beholding the greatness of their numbers, therefore they durst not come out against them; therefore they did not come to battle in that day.

20 And when the night came, Moroni went forth in the darkness of the night, and came upon the top of the wall to spy out in what part of the city the Lamanites did camp with their army.

21 And it came to pass that they were on the east, by the entrance; and they were all asleep. And now Moroni returned to his army, and caused that they should prepare in haste strong cords and ladders, to be let down from the top of the wall into the inner part of the wall.

22 And it came to pass that Moroni caused that his men should march forth and come upon the top of the wall, and let themselves down into that part of the city, yea, even on the west, where the Lamanites did not camp with their armies.

23 And it came to pass that they were all let down into the city by night, by the means of their strong cords and their ladders; thus when the morning came they were all within the walls of the city.

24 And now, when the Lamanites awoke and saw that the armies of Moroni were within the walls, they were affrighted exceedingly, insomuch that they did flee out by the pass.

25 And now when Moroni saw that they were fleeing before him, he did cause that his men should march forth against them, and slew many, and surrounded many others, and took them prisoners; and the remainder of them fled into the land of Moroni, which was in the borders by the seashore.

26 Thus had Moroni and Pahoran obtained the possession of the city of Nephihah without the loss of one soul; and there were many of the Lamanites who were slain.

27 Now it came to pass that many of the Lamanites that were prisoners were desirous to join the people of Ammon and become a free people.

28 And it came to pass that as many as were desirous, unto them it was granted according to their desires.

29 Therefore, all the prisoners of the Lamanites did join the people of Ammon, and did begin to labor exceedingly, tilling the ground, raising all manner of grain, and flocks and herds of every kind; and thus were the Nephites relieved from a great burden; yea, insomuch that they were relieved from all the prisoners of the Lamanites.

vv. 12–29 Moroni recaptures the city of Nephihah.

30 Now it came to pass that Moroni, after he had obtained possession of the city of Nephihah, having taken many prisoners, which did reduce the armies of the Lamanites exceedingly, and having regained many of the Nephites who had been taken prisoners, which did strengthen the army of Moroni exceedingly; therefore Moroni went forth from the land of Nephihah to the land of Lehi.

31 And it came to pass that when the Lamanites saw that Moroni was coming against them, they were again frightened and fled before the army of Moroni.

32 And it came to pass that Moroni and his army did pursue them from city to city, until they were

Notes

met by Lehi and Teancum; and the Lamanites fled from Lehi and Teancum, even down upon the borders by the seashore, until they came to the land of Moroni.

33 And the armies of the Lamanites were all gathered together, insomuch that they were all in one body in the land of Moroni. Now Ammoron, the king of the Lamanites, was also with them.

34 And it came to pass that Moroni and Lehi and Teancum did encamp with their armies round about in the borders of the land of Moroni, insomuch that the Lamanites were encircled about in the borders by the wilderness on the south, and in the borders by the wilderness on the east.

vv. 30–34 The Nephites continue to drive the Lamanites from their lands.

35 And thus they did encamp for the night. For behold, the Nephites and the Lamanites also were weary because of the greatness of the march; therefore they did not resolve upon any stratagem in the night-time, save it were Teancum; for he was exceedingly angry with Ammoron, insomuch that he considered that Ammoron, and Amalickiah his brother, had been the cause of this great and lasting war between them and the Lamanites, which had been the cause of so much war and bloodshed, yea, and so much famine.

v. 35

- Note that Teancum acted out of anger which may be a reason for his being caught and killed.

36 And it came to pass that Teancum in his anger did go forth into the camp of the Lamanites, and did let himself down over the walls of the city. And he went forth with a cord, from place to place, insomuch that he did find the king; and he did cast a javelin at him, which did pierce him near the heart. But behold, the king did awaken his servants before he died, insomuch that they did pursue Teancum, and slew him.

37 Now it came to pass that when Lehi and Moroni knew that Teancum was dead they were exceedingly sorrowful; for behold, he had been a man who had fought valiantly for his country, yea, a true friend to liberty; and he had suffered very many exceedingly sore afflictions. But behold, he was dead, and had gone the way of all the earth.

38 Now it came to pass that Moroni marched forth on the morrow, and came upon the Lamanites, insomuch that they did slay them with a great slaughter; and they did drive them out of the land; and they did flee, even that they did not return at that time against the Nephites.

39 And thus ended the thirty and first year of the reign of the judges over the people of Nephi; and thus they had had wars, and bloodsheds, and famine, and affliction, for the space of many years.

vv. 35–39 Teancum slays Ammoron but is caught and killed; the war ends.

40 And there had been murders, and contentions, and dissensions, and all manner of iniquity among the people of Nephi; nevertheless for the righteous' sake, yea, because of the prayers of the righteous, they were spared.

41 But behold, because of the exceedingly great length of the war between the Nephites and the Lamanites many had become hardened, because of the exceedingly great length of the war; and many were softened because of their afflictions, insomuch that they did humble themselves before God, even in the depth of humility.

42 And it came to pass that after Moroni had fortified those parts of the land which were most exposed to the Lamanites, until they were sufficiently strong, he returned to the city of Zarahemla; and also Helaman returned to the place of his inheritance; and there was once more peace established among the people of Nephi.

43 And Moroni yielded up the command of his armies into the hands of his son, whose name was Moronihah; and he retired to his own house

Notes

that he might spend the remainder of his days in peace.

44 And Pahoran did return to his judgment-seat; and Helaman did take upon him again to preach unto the people the word of God; for because of so many wars and contentions it had become expedient that a regulation should be made again in the church.

45 Therefore, Helaman and his brethren went forth, and did declare the word of God with much power unto the convincing of many people of their wickedness, which did cause them to repent of their sins and to be baptized unto the Lord their God.

46 And it came to pass that they did establish again the church of God, throughout all the land.

47 Yea, and regulations were made concerning the law. And their judges, and their chief judges were chosen.

48 And the people of Nephi began to prosper again in the land, and began to multiply and to wax exceedingly strong again in the land. And they began to grow exceedingly rich.

49 But notwithstanding their riches, or their strength, or their prosperity, they were not lifted up in the pride of their eyes; neither were they slow to remember the Lord their God; but they did humble themselves exceedingly before him.

50 Yea, they did remember how great things the Lord had done for them, that he had delivered them from death, and from bonds, and from prisons, and from all manner of afflictions, and he had delivered them out of the hands of their enemies.

51 And they did pray unto the Lord their God continually, insomuch that the Lord did bless them, according to his word, so that they did wax strong and prosper in the land.

vv. 41–51 During times of trial, hearts can become hardened; however, God is able to soften our hearts.

To help class members visualize the principle from these verses, bring a piece of bread to class that has become hardened (you may want to leave the piece of bread out overnight before so it will be hard). Discuss with the class why bread turns hard if it is exposed to air and whether it is possible for the bread to soften again. Draw on the board a picture of a slice of bread and a heart, with an equal sign between the two of them. Note with the class that just as bread can become hardened so can our hearts. The intent of this lesson is to discover ways a person can soften their hearts once they have become hardened.

Read verse 41 and look for why the people's hearts had become hardened because of the war.

Analyze: *Why do you think the length of the war would harden hearts? What other factors could have hardened the hearts of people?* (Consider writing their answers on the board.)

Read verses 44–51 and look for what the Nephites did—specifically Helaman—to soften their hearts. (Consider making a list on the board.)

Apply: *How is this story and principle relevant in our day?*

52 And it came to pass that all these things were done. And Helaman died, in the thirty and fifth year of the reign of the judges over the people of Nephi.

Notes

ALMA 63

Hagoth's Migration
About 56–52 BC

1–3, Shiblon takes possession of the records from Helaman; Moroni dies; 4–8, Hagoth and a large company of people build ships and leave for the land northward; 9–17, Moronihah, Moroni's son, defeats an army of the Lamanites.

1 And it came to pass in the commencement of the thirty and sixth year of the reign of the judges over the people of Nephi, that Shiblon took possession of those sacred things which had been delivered unto Helaman by Alma.

2 And he was a just man, and he did walk uprightly before God; and he did observe to do good continually, to keep the commandments of the Lord his God; and also did his brother.

3 And it came to pass that Moroni died also. And thus ended the thirty and sixth year of the reign of the judges.

vv. 1–3 A farewell to Captain Moroni and Helaman.

- Alma 62:52 through Alma 63:3 records the changes in leadership among the Nephite armies. Invite class members to review some of the lessons that they were taught by the actions and example of Captain Moroni and Helaman—particularly review Alma 46:12–13, 21 and Alma 48:11–13, 17. Either vocally or in their notebooks, ask your class to create a farewell message or eulogy for Moroni or Helaman.

4 And it came to pass that in the thirty and seventh year of the reign of the judges, there was a large company of men, even to the amount of five thousand and four hundred men, with their wives and their children, departed out of the land of Zarahemla into the land which was northward.

5 And it came to pass that Hagoth, he being an exceedingly curious man, therefore he went forth and built him an exceedingly large ship, on the borders of the land Bountiful, by the land Desolation, and launched it forth into the west sea, by the narrow neck which led into the land northward.

6 And behold, there were many of the Nephites who did enter therein and did sail forth with much provisions, and also many women and children; and they took their course northward. And thus ended the thirty and seventh year.

7 And in the thirty and eighth year, this man built other ships. And the first ship did also return, and many more people did enter into it; and they also took much provisions, and set out again to the land northward.

8 And it came to pass that they were never heard of more. And we suppose that they were drowned in the depths of the sea. And it came to pass that one other ship also did sail forth; and whither she did go we know not.

9 And it came to pass that in this year there were many people who went forth into the land northward. And thus ended the thirty and eighth year.

vv. 4–9 Hagoth facilitated several large Nephite migrations.

- Regarding these verses Elder Spencer W. Kimball taught, "Not long before the birth of Christ, a great man by the name of Hagoth left continental America with colonies of people. . . . It has been thought by many people that they went to the Pacific islands. And the scripture would so indicate: But great are the promises of the Lord unto them who are upon the isles of the sea; wherefore as it says isles, there must needs be more than this, and they are inhabited also by our brethren (2 Nephi 10:21). Elder Cowley and I visited some of these peoples on the 'isles of the sea' and found them developing and progressing and doing well" (Conference Report, April 1947).

Notes

10 And it came to pass in the thirty and ninth year of the reign of the judges, Shiblon died also, and Corianton had gone forth to the land northward in a ship, to carry forth provisions unto the people who had gone forth into that land.

11 Therefore it became expedient for Shiblon to confer those sacred things, before his death, upon the son of Helaman, who was called Helaman, being called after the name of his father.

12 Now behold, all those engravings which were in the possession of Helaman were written and sent forth among the children of men throughout all the land, save it were those parts which had been commanded by Alma should not go forth.

13 Nevertheless, these things were to be kept sacred, and handed down from one generation to another; therefore, in this year, they had been conferred upon Helaman, before the death of Shiblon.

14 And it came to pass also in this year that there were some dissenters who had gone forth unto the Lamanites; and they were stirred up again to anger against the Nephites.

15 And also in this same year they came down with a numerous army to war against the people of Moronihah, or against the army of Moronihah, in the which they were beaten and driven back again to their own lands, suffering great loss.

16 And thus ended the thirty and ninth year of the reign of the judges over the people of Nephi.

17 And thus ended the account of Alma, and Helaman his son, and also Shiblon, who was his son.

Teaching Tips from Prophets' Lips "But audiovisual aids are just that—they are aids. They are not a substitute for a lesson. Use them in the way that you would use spice in cooking—to flavor, to heighten, to accentuate, to enrich. A map or a painting or a video clip or a key point written on the board—these can often make the difference between a good lesson and a great lesson. But no one wants a meal of spices only. So my plea to one and all is please do not overdo visual aids. They are not a substitute for the teacher, they are not a substitute for the course material, and they are not a substitute for the Spirit of the Lord. Use them when you need them" (Jeffrey R. Holland, "Teaching and Learning in the Church", *Ensign*, June 2007, 88–105).

Notes

THE BOOK OF HELAMAN

HELAMAN SUMMARY

Time Period: About 52–1 BC (51 years)

Contributors: Mormon, Helaman, Nephi, Samuel the Lamanite

Source: Large plates of Nephi

Abridged by: Mormon

Synopsis:

Chapters 1–4: The political and social unrest caused by wickedness and secret combinations arises among the Nephites

Chapters 5–6: Helaman counsels Nephi and Lehi and a record of their ministries among the Nephites and Lamanites

Chapters 7–11: Nephi's ministry and prophecies to the people of Zarahemla. He receives the sealing power of the priesthood

Chapter 12: Mormon comments on the unsteadiness of men

Chapters 13–15: The prophecy of Samuel the Lamanite

Chapter 16: The Nephites response to Samuel's prophecies

An account of the Nephites. Their wars and contentions, and their dissensions. And also the prophecies of many holy prophets, before the coming of Christ, according to the records of Helaman, who was the son of Helaman, and also according to the records of his sons, even down to the coming of Christ. Many of the Lamanites are converted. An account of their conversion. An account of the righteousness of the Lamanites, and the wickedness and abominations of the Nephites, according to the record of Helaman and his sons, even down to the coming of Christ, which is called the book of Helaman, and so forth.

Notes

HELAMAN 1

The Chief Judge Is Murdered
About 52–50 BC

1–5, Pahoran dies and there is a contention in the land as to which of his sons should be elected in his stead; the voice of the people choose Pahoran; 6–13, Paanchi, Kishkumen, and a secret band of others plot and murder Pahoran; Pacumeni replaces him as chief judge; 14–24, The Lamanites, led by Coriantumr,

HELAMAN 1

invade and capture Zarahemla, and kill Pacumeni; 25–34, Moronihah regains control of the city of Zarahemla.

Overarching principle: Unity through the principles of the gospel of Jesus Christ strengthens the Lord's people against evil influences.

⚡ Gather many small sticks that are easily breakable (popsicle sticks can also work). Divide them into two groups: one that has several separate sticks and one bundled together with a string so that they will be too difficult to break. Many will be familiar with this exercise, so you may either invite a class member to attempt to break a single stick and then try the bundle, or simply ask the class about the varying strength of the two arrangements. Display the sticks where they are visible and inform class members that you will refer to the sticks throughout your discussion of Helaman chapter 1.

1 And now behold, it came to pass in the commencement of the fortieth year of the reign of the judges over the people of Nephi, there began to be a serious difficulty among the people of the Nephites.

2 For behold, Pahoran had died, and gone the way of all the earth; therefore there began to be a serious contention concerning who should have the judgment-seat among the brethren, who were the sons of Pahoran.

3 Now these are their names who did contend for the judgment-seat, who did also cause the people to contend: Pahoran, Paanchi, and Pacumeni.

4 Now these are not all the sons of Pahoran (for he had many), but these are they who did contend for the judgment-seat; therefore, they did cause three divisions among the people.

5 Nevertheless, it came to pass that Pahoran was appointed by the voice of the people to be chief judge and a governor over the people of Nephi.

6 And it came to pass that Pacumeni, when he saw that he could not obtain the judgment-seat, he did unite with the voice of the people.

7 But behold, Paanchi, and that part of the people that were desirous that he should be their governor, was exceedingly wroth; therefore, he was about to flatter away those people to rise up in rebellion against their brethren.

8 And it came to pass as he was about to do this, behold, he was taken, and was tried according to the voice of the people, and condemned unto death; for he had raised up in rebellion and sought to destroy the liberty of the people.

9 Now when those people who were desirous that he should be their governor saw that he was condemned unto death, therefore they were angry, and behold, they sent forth one Kishkumen, even to the judgment-seat of Pahoran, and murdered Pahoran as he sat upon the judgment-seat.

10 And he was pursued by the servants of Pahoran; but behold, so speedy was the flight of Kishkumen that no man could overtake him.

11 And he went unto those that sent him, and they all entered into a covenant, yea, swearing by their everlasting Maker, that they would tell no man that Kishkumen had murdered Pahoran.

12 Therefore, Kishkumen was not known among the people of Nephi, for he was in disguise at the time that he murdered Pahoran. And Kishkumen and his band, who had covenanted with him, did mingle themselves among the people, in a manner that they all could not be found; but as many as were found were condemned unto death.

13 And now behold, Pacumeni was appointed, according to the voice of the people, to be a chief judge and a governor over the people, to reign in the stead of his brother Pahoran; and it was according to his right. And all this was done in the fortieth year of the reign of the judges; and it had an end.

vv. 1–13 We should seek to be peacemakers rather than seeking to satisfy our pride.

Notes

- Display a brief version of the beatitudes from 3 Nephi 12:3–10 or Matthew 5: 3–10 for the class to read.
  - Blessed are the poor in spirit
  - Blessed are they that mourn
  - Blessed are the meek
  - Blessed are they who hunger and thirst after righteousness
  - Blessed are the merciful
  - Blessed are the pure in heart
  - Blessed are the peacemakers

- Invite class members to read the story of Pahoran's three sons in Helaman 1:1–9 and look for examples of individuals seeking to exemplify the Savior's teachings from the beatitudes or individuals who disregard the Savior's teachings. Have a class member summarize the story, and then discuss the class members' findings.

- Analyze:
  - *What was presumably the goal of Pahoran's sons when they sought the judgment seat?*
  - *How did Pacumeni's (v. 6) and Paanchi's (v. 7) goals differ after the people had chosen Pahoran?*
  - *Which of the stick arrangement best represent Paanchi's choices? Pacumeni's?*

- Apply:
  - *In what modern situations could this story apply?*
  - *How might someone seek their own interests rather than the interest of the community?*
  - *How can following the teachings of Christ (like the beatitudes) help us to be unified as a people?*

- Point out the end results of Paanchi's selfish desires and compare them to the results of Pacumeni's choices. Explain that Paanchi's rebellion lead to the choices of Kishkumen and his band, which in turn constitute the formation of the Gadianton robbers—a burden to the Nephites for decades to come (see Helaman 2:13).

- Testify that those who follow the teachings of Christ by being peacemakers, meek, merciful, and pure in heart will be blessed by the Lord and do much good among their fellow men.

14 And it came to pass in the forty and first year of the reign of the judges, that the Lamanites had gathered together an innumerable army of men, and armed them with swords, and with cimeters and with bows, and with arrows, and with head-plates, and with breastplates, and with all manner of shields of every kind.

15 And they came down again that they might pitch battle against the Nephites. And they were led by a man whose name was Coriantumr; and he was a descendant of Zarahemla; and he was a dissenter from among the Nephites; and he was a large and a mighty man.

16 Therefore, the king of the Lamanites, whose name was Tubaloth, who was the son of Ammoron, supposing that Coriantumr, being a mighty man, could stand against the Nephites, with his strength and also with his great wisdom, insomuch that by sending him forth he should gain power over the Nephites—

17 Therefore he did stir them up to anger, and he did gather together his armies, and he did appoint Coriantumr to be their leader, and did cause that they should march down to the land of Zarahemla to battle against the Nephites.

18 And it came to pass that because of so much contention and so much difficulty in the government, that they had not kept sufficient guards in the land of Zarahemla; for they had supposed that the Lamanites durst not come into the heart of their lands to attack that great city Zarahemla.

19 But it came to pass that Coriantumr did march forth at the head of his numerous host, and came upon the inhabitants of the city, and their march was with such exceedingly great speed that there was no time for the Nephites to gather together their armies.

20 Therefore Coriantumr did cut down the watch by the entrance of the city, and did march forth

Notes

with his whole army into the city, and they did slay every one who did oppose them, insomuch that they did take possession of the whole city.

21 And it came to pass that Pacumeni, who was the chief judge, did flee before Coriantumr, even to the walls of the city. And it came to pass that Coriantumr did smite him against the wall, insomuch that he died. And thus ended the days of Pacumeni.

vv. 14–21 Disunity creates weakness.

🔎 *Who leads the armies of the Lamanites into battle?*

❓ *Analyze:*
- *How is Coriantumr a product of disunity?*
- *What word represents that concept in these verses? (Depending on your class, you may need to define the word "dissenter.")*
- *Why weren't the Nephites able to withstand the Lamanites like they had just a few years prior (see verse 18)?*

As you discuss these questions, slowly untie the bundle of sticks you have displayed. Then ask, *How do verses 19–21 show disunity?* If time permits, invite class members to find any other examples of disunity in the verses. Break a few of the sticks as you explain that the Nephites lost the battle to Coriantumr due to their lack of unity.

❓ *Apply: When have you seen disunity create weakness? What do you think can be done to create unity in a family, class, church, or community?*

22 And now when Coriantumr saw that he was in possession of the city of Zarahemla, and saw that the Nephites had fled before them, and were slain, and were taken, and were cast into prison, and that he had obtained the possession of the strongest hold in all the land, his heart took courage insomuch that he was about to go forth against all the land.

23 And now he did not tarry in the land of Zarahemla, but he did march forth with a large army, even towards the city of Bountiful; for it was his determination to go forth and cut his way through with the sword, that he might obtain the north parts of the land.

24 And, supposing that their greatest strength was in the center of the land, therefore he did march forth, giving them no time to assemble themselves together save it were in small bodies; and in this manner they did fall upon them and cut them down to the earth.

25 But behold, this march of Coriantumr through the center of the land gave Moronihah great advantage over them, notwithstanding the greatness of the number of the Nephites who were slain.

26 For behold, Moronihah had supposed that the Lamanites durst not come into the center of the land, but that they would attack the cities round about in the borders as they had hitherto done; therefore Moronihah had caused that their strong armies should maintain those parts round about by the borders.

27 But behold, the Lamanites were not frightened according to his desire, but they had come into the center of the land, and had taken the capital city which was the city of Zarahemla, and were marching through the most capital parts of the land, slaying the people with a great slaughter, both men, women, and children, taking possession of many cities and of many strongholds.

28 But when Moronihah had discovered this, he immediately sent forth Lehi with an army round about to head them before they should come to the land Bountiful.

29 And thus he did; and he did head them before they came to the land Bountiful, and gave unto them battle, insomuch that they began to retreat back towards the land of Zarahemla.

30 And it came to pass that Moronihah did head them in their retreat, and did give unto them battle, insomuch that it became an exceedingly bloody battle; yea, many were slain, and among the number who were slain Coriantumr was also found.

Notes

31 And now, behold, the Lamanites could not retreat either way, neither on the north, nor on the south, nor on the east, nor on the west, for they were surrounded on every hand by the Nephites.

32 And thus had Coriantumr plunged the Lamanites into the midst of the Nephites, insomuch that they were in the power of the Nephites, and he himself was slain, and the Lamanites did yield themselves into the hands of the Nephites.

33 And it came to pass that Moronihah took possession of the city of Zarahemla again, and caused that the Lamanites who had been taken prisoners should depart out of the land in peace.

34 And thus ended the forty and first year of the reign of the judges.

vv. 22–34 Friends united in righteousness can help one another combat sin and wickedness.

✋ Invite class members to read verses 22–27 to themselves. Then ask for a volunteer to draw a very simple diagram on the board to show the Lamanite plan of attack. (It could be as simple as the one shown.) Ask, *According to verse 26, what particular problem could the Lamanites encounter with this approach?*

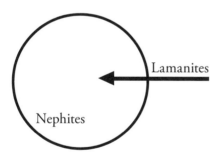

🔍 *Read verses 22–34 and look for what actions the Nephites take to defeat the Lamanites. Find a phrase that shows that Moronihah understood that he could not defeat the Lamanites alone, but that he needed support to be successful.*

❓ Analyze:
- Why do you think that Moronihah immediately began unifying their strategies and armies?
- How do you think Moronihah felt to have the support of Lehi and his armies?
- How might things have turned out differently if Moronihah couldn't have relied on Lehi or vice versa?

At this point in your discussion, begin bundling the sticks back together.

❓ Apply: *When have you been grateful to have a righteous friend in your life? At what times in your life have you been available to righteously support a friend in need?*

❤ Hold up the retied bundle of sticks. Invite class members to become a righteous friend to someone else and build gospel-centered unity in their families and communities.

Teaching Tips from Prophets' Lips "As you come to know and understand each person, you will be better prepared to teach lessons that speak to their individual situations. This understanding will help you to find ways to help each person participate in discussions and other learning activities. You will know who will be able to handle certain questions, who might be able to contribute a faith-promoting story or personal experience, or who has had an experience that supports the purpose of a certain lesson. You will be better able to assess the responses given in discussions and adapt your lessons" (*Teaching, No Greater Call*, 34).

HELAMAN 2
Secret Combinations
About 50–49 BC

1–5, Helaman is appointed to the judgment seat and Gadianton seeks to murder him through secret works; 6–9, One of the servants of Helaman is apprised of the

Notes

HELAMAN 2

murder plot and is able to kill Kishkumen, 10–14, Gadianton and his band flee before Helaman are able to apprehend them.

1 And it came to pass in the forty and second year of the reign of the judges, after Moronihah had established again peace between the Nephites and the Lamanites, behold there was no one to fill the judgment-seat; therefore there began to be a contention again among the people concerning who should fill the judgment-seat.

2 And it came to pass that Helaman, who was the son of Helaman, was appointed to fill the judgment-seat, by the voice of the people.

3 But behold, Kishkumen, who had murdered Pahoran, did lay wait to destroy Helaman also; and he was upheld by his band, who had entered into a covenant that no one should know his wickedness.

4 For there was one Gadianton, who was exceedingly expert in many words, and also in his craft, to carry on the secret work of murder and of robbery; therefore he became the leader of the band of Kishkumen.

5 Therefore he did flatter them, and also Kishkumen, that if they would place him in the judgment-seat he would grant unto those who belonged to his band that they should be placed in power and authority among the people; therefore Kishkumen sought to destroy Helaman.

6 And it came to pass as he went forth towards the judgment-seat to destroy Helaman, behold one of the servants of Helaman, having been out by night, and having obtained, through disguise, a knowledge of those plans which had been laid by this band to destroy Helaman—

7 And it came to pass that he met Kishkumen, and he gave unto him a sign; therefore Kishkumen made known unto him the object of his desire, desiring that he would conduct him to the judgment-seat that he might murder Helaman.

8 And when the servant of Helaman had known all the heart of Kishkumen, and how that it was his object to murder, and also that it was the object of all those who belonged to his band to murder, and to rob, and to gain power, (and this was their secret plan, and their combination) the servant of Helaman said unto Kishkumen: Let us go forth unto the judgment-seat.

9 Now this did please Kishkumen exceedingly, for he did suppose that he should accomplish his design; but behold, the servant of Helaman, as they were going forth unto the judgment-seat, did stab Kishkumen even to the heart, that he fell dead without a groan. And he ran and told Helaman all the things which he had seen, and heard, and done.

10 And it came to pass that Helaman did send forth to take this band of robbers and secret murderers, that they might be executed according to the law.

11 But behold, when Gadianton had found that Kishkumen did not return he feared lest that he should be destroyed; therefore he caused that his band should follow him. And they took their flight out of the land, by a secret way, into the wilderness; and thus when Helaman sent forth to take them they could nowhere be found.

12 And more of this Gadianton shall be spoken hereafter. And thus ended the forty and second year of the reign of the judges over the people of Nephi.

13 And behold, in the end of this book ye shall see that this Gadianton did prove the overthrow, yea, almost the entire destruction of the people of Nephi.

14 Behold I do not mean the end of the book of Helaman, but I mean the end of the book of Nephi, from which I have taken all the account which I have written.

vv. 1–14 Secret combinations introduced by Gadianton did "prove the overthrow . . . almost the entire destruction of the people of Nephi."

⚡ As you begin class, ask or write on the board the following question: *What was the main*

Notes

thing that caused the entire destruction of the people of Nephi? Invite class members to read Helaman 2:13 for the answer.

✋ To summarize Helaman 2, provide a handout with the phrases below without writing the attached verses. Cut the phrases into word strips and give them to several small groups of class members. Invite class members to use their scriptures to put the events in order. You may also choose to have the groups see if they can put the events in order first without scriptures and then check to see if they are correct.

- Contention concerning who should fill the judgment seat (v. 1)
- Helaman, son of Helaman, appointed to the judgment seat (v. 2)
- Entered into a covenant (v. 3)
- Gadianton becomes the leader of the band of Kishkumen (v. 4)
- Kishkumen seeks to destroy Helaman (v. 5)
- A servant of Helaman obtains knowledge of the plans to murder Helaman (v. 6)
- The servant of Helaman stabs Kishkumen in the heart (v. 9)
- Helaman sends his servants to apprehend the band of Kishkumen (v. 10)
- Gadianton and his band flee into the wilderness by a secret way and cannot be found (v. 11)

❓ Analyze: *What is it about secret combinations that caused the entire destruction of the people of Nephi?* In order to help clarify and discuss secret combinations, ask the following: *What would you say is the opposite of secret combinations?*

❓ Apply: *How do we stop or minimize the works of secret combinations? If the Book of Mormon is written for our day, why do you think Mormon feels that it is important to teach us about the effects of secret combinations?*

❤ Invite class members to look for how secret combinations destroyed the people of Nephi and how we can avoid such combinations.

Index Topics: secret combinations

HELAMAN 3
Prosperity Leading to Pride
About 49–39 BC

1–12, Many migrate to other lands; 13–16, Mormon describes how many records were destroyed; 17–32, War and contention are replaced with peace and prosperity through the preaching of the gospel; 33–37, Pride begins to separate the true followers of Christ from others.

Overarching Principle: By repenting and remaining humble, I can avoid the pride cycle.

⚡ Before class, draw the accompanying diagram of circles and arrows on the board without labeling each circle. Ask, *What is a cycle?* As class members answer this question consider suggesting some common cycles (e.g. the water cycle, the seasons, clocks, calendars, etc.). Ask, *Are there any such cycles in the Book of Mormon that could be explained by the diagram on the board?* Depending on the experience level of class members you may need to aid them considerably or very little at all. Consider slowly labeling each circle as you discuss the responses of the class members. Taking time to ensure understanding, ask them for examples of each stage in the cycle. A possible example of a pride cycle could resemble the one on the following page.

❓ Analyze:
- *Why can "peace & prosperity" often lead to "pride" in a people?* (Continue around the circle drawing asking questions to help establish any cause and effect relationships between the stages.)
- *Are there any more recent examples of such a cycle?*
- *How could this cycle occur in a person's life?*
- *Have you ever seen this cycle in your own life?*
- *How can someone break such a cycle in their life?*

Notes

HELAMAN 3

- ❤ Explain that this is a common cycle throughout the Book of Mormon and is demonstrated in Helaman 3. You will refer back to this cycle throughout the Book of Helaman.

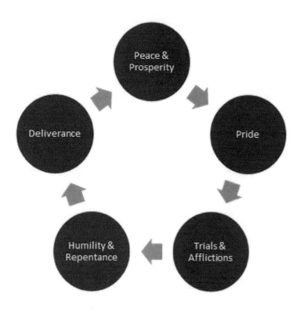

- ❓ Analyze:
  - *Where do the Nephites fall on the pride cycle?*
  - *Why did many people want to escape it?*
  - *How can "a little pride" lead to dissensions and contentions?*
- ❓ Apply: *According to these verses, what is the solution to eliminate contention?*
- 💬 Ezra Taft Benson taught, "Pride is the universal sin, the great vice. . . . The antidote for pride is humility" ("Beware of Pride," General Conference, Apr. 1989).
- ❤ Encourage class members to be humble, so as to avoid the great difficulties that come with pride.

1 And now it came to pass in the forty and third year of the reign of the judges, there was no contention among the people of Nephi save it were a little pride which was in the church, which did cause some little dissensions among the people, which affairs were settled in the ending of the forty and third year.

2 And there was no contention among the people in the forty and fourth year; neither was there much contention in the forty and fifth year.

3 And it came to pass in the forty and sixth, yea, there was much contention and many dissensions; in the which there were an exceedingly great many who departed out of the land of Zarahemla, and went forth unto the land northward to inherit the land.

vv. 1–3 Pride leads to contention.

🔍 *In verses 1–3, mark any words that explain what led to the dissensions and contentions.*

4 And they did travel to an exceedingly great distance, insomuch that they came to large bodies of water and many rivers.

5 Yea, and even they did spread forth into all parts of the land, into whatever parts it had not been rendered desolate and without timber, because of the many inhabitants who had before inherited the land.

6 And now no part of the land was desolate, save it were for timber; but because of the greatness of the destruction of the people who had before inhabited the land it was called desolate.

7 And there being but little timber upon the face of the land, nevertheless the people who went forth became exceedingly expert in the working of cement; therefore they did build houses of cement, in the which they did dwell.

8 And it came to pass that they did multiply and spread, and did go forth from the land southward to the land northward, and did spread insomuch that they began to cover the face of the whole earth, from the sea south to the sea north, from the sea west to the sea east.

9 And the people who were in the land northward did dwell in tents, and in houses of cement, and they did suffer whatsoever tree should spring up

Notes

upon the face of the land that it should grow up, that in time they might have timber to build their houses, yea, their cities, and their temples, and their synagogues, and their sanctuaries, and all manner of their buildings.

10 And it came to pass as timber was exceedingly scarce in the land northward, they did send forth much by the way of shipping.

11 And thus they did enable the people in the land northward that they might build many cities, both of wood and of cement.

12 And it came to pass that there were many of the people of Ammon, who were Lamanites by birth, did also go forth into this land.

13 And now there are many records kept of the proceedings of this people, by many of this people, which are particular and very large, concerning them.

14 But behold, a hundredth part of the proceedings of this people, yea, the account of the Lamanites and of the Nephites, and their wars, and contentions, and dissensions, and their preaching, and their prophecies, and their shipping and their building of ships, and their building of temples, and of synagogues and their sanctuaries, and their righteousness, and their wickedness, and their murders, and their robbings, and their plundering, and all manner of abominations and whoredoms, cannot be contained in this work.

15 But behold, there are many books and many records of every kind, and they have been kept chiefly by the Nephites.

16 And they have been handed down from one generation to another by the Nephites, even until they have fallen into transgression and have been murdered, plundered, and hunted, and driven forth, and slain, and scattered upon the face of the earth, and mixed with the Lamanites until they are no more called the Nephites, becoming wicked, and wild, and ferocious, yea, even becoming Lamanites.

vv. 13–16 The Book of Mormon is the best of the Nephites' records.

In Helaman 3:14, Mormon explains that his abridgment on the gold plates covers only a small part of their records. If you have not already done so, consider using the lesson idea from Words of Mormon 1:3–5 to teach this concept.

17 And now I return again to mine account; therefore, what I have spoken had passed after there had been great contentions, and disturbances, and wars, and dissensions, among the people of Nephi.

18 The forty and sixth year of the reign of the judges ended;

19 And it came to pass that there was still great contention in the land, yea, even in the forty and seventh year, and also in the forty and eighth year.

20 Nevertheless Helaman did fill the judgment-seat with justice and equity; yea, he did observe to keep the statutes, and the judgments, and the commandments of God; and he did do that which was right in the sight of God continually; and he did walk after the ways of his father, insomuch that he did prosper in the land.

21 And it came to pass that he had two sons. He gave unto the eldest the name of Nephi, and unto the youngest, the name of Lehi. And they began to grow up unto the Lord.

22 And it came to pass that the wars and contentions began to cease, in a small degree, among the people of the Nephites, in the latter end of the forty and eighth year of the reign of the judges over the people of Nephi.

23 And it came to pass in the forty and ninth year of the reign of the judges, there was continual peace established in the land, all save it were the secret combinations which Gadianton the robber had established in the more settled parts of the land, which at that time were not known unto

Notes

those who were at the head of government; therefore they were not destroyed out of the land.

24 And it came to pass that in this same year there was exceedingly great prosperity in the church, insomuch that there were thousands who did join themselves unto the church and were baptized unto repentance.

25 And so great was the prosperity of the church, and so many the blessings which were poured out upon the people, that even the high priests and the teachers were themselves astonished beyond measure.

26 And it came to pass that the work of the Lord did prosper unto the baptizing and uniting to the church of God, many souls, yea, even tens of thousands.

27 Thus we may see that the Lord is merciful unto all who will, in the sincerity of their hearts, call upon his holy name.

28 Yea, thus we see that the gate of heaven is open unto all, even to those who will believe on the name of Jesus Christ, who is the Son of God.

29 Yea, we see that whosoever will may lay hold upon the word of God, which is quick and powerful, which shall divide asunder all the cunning and the snares and the wiles of the devil, and lead the man of Christ in a strait and narrow course across that everlasting gulf of misery which is prepared to engulf the wicked—

30 And land their souls, yea, their immortal souls, at the right hand of God in the kingdom of heaven, to sit down with Abraham, and Isaac, and with Jacob, and with all our holy fathers, to go no more out.

vv. 24–30 By being constantly nourished by the word of God, we can prosper and avoid much heartache.

- Look for what stage of the pride cycle the Nephites are experiencing in verses 24–28.

- Read verse 29 and look for what brought repentance and humility to the Nephites.

- Explain that the scriptures often teach through symbolic imagery. Break your class into groups of two to three and give each group a piece of paper. Have them find as many examples of symbolic imagery as they can in verse 29 and draw what is depicted. You may need to explain that a snare is a trap, wiles are tricks, and a gulf is a deep ravine or chasm. Have them prepare to show their art work and explain why they drew what they did.

- *How does the word of God keep us humble? How can we stay constantly nourished by the word of God?*

- Invite class members to do those things so they can stay constantly nourished by the word of God and avoid many of the miseries of life.

31 And in this year there was continual rejoicing in the land of Zarahemla, and in all the regions round about, even in all the land which was possessed by the Nephites.

32 And it came to pass that there was peace and exceedingly great joy in the remainder of the forty and ninth year; yea, and also there was continual peace and great joy in the fiftieth year of the reign of the judges.

33 And in the fifty and first year of the reign of the judges there was peace also, save it were the pride which began to enter into the church—not into the church of God, but into the hearts of the people who professed to belong to the church of God—

34 And they were lifted up in pride, even to the persecution of many of their brethren. Now this was a great evil, which did cause the more humble part of the people to suffer great persecutions, and to wade through much affliction.

35 Nevertheless they did fast and pray oft, and did wax stronger and stronger in their humility, and firmer and firmer in the faith of Christ, unto the filling their souls with joy and consolation,

Notes

yea, even to the purifying and the sanctification of their hearts, which sanctification cometh because of their yielding their hearts unto God.

vv. 33–35 We must be members of the Lord's church in word and deed.

- 🔎 *Look for what Mormon is subtly teaching about being a member of the church of God in verses 33.*

- ✋ At the top of the board write, "*Professed Members*" and "*True Members*," then have class members list attributes of each group from verses 33–35.

- ❓ Analyze: *Which of these attributes listed under the "true members" heading do you think would prevent people from being prideful?*

- 💬 Gordon B. Hinckley stated, "We of this generation are the end harvest of all that has gone before. It is not enough to simply be known as a member of this Church. A solemn obligation rests upon us. Let us face it and work at it. We must live as true followers of the Christ, with charity toward all, returning good for evil, teaching by example the ways of the Lord, and accomplishing the vast service He has outlined for us" ("The Dawning of a Brighter Day," *Ensign*, May 2004, 84).

- ❤ Invite class members to be true members of the Church in word and deed by choosing one element listed on the board under "true members" and implementing it in their lives.

36 And it came to pass that the fifty and second year ended in peace also, save it were the exceedingly great pride which had gotten into the hearts of the people; and it was because of their exceedingly great riches and their prosperity in the land; and it did grow upon them from day to day.

37 And it came to pass in the fifty and third year of the reign of the judges, Helaman died, and his eldest son Nephi began to reign in his stead. And it came to pass that he did fill the judgment-seat with justice and equity; yea, he did keep the commandments of God, and did walk in the ways of his father.

v. 36 We must be careful to be faithful, even in times of prosperity.

- ❓ Referring back to the pride cycle illustration, ask:
  - *What should we do when we are in a time of peace and prosperity?*
  - *Why is it so difficult to stay humble in those times?*
  - *Why is it easy to forget about God when everything is going well?*

- 💬 Share the following quote by Ezra Taft Benson, "Every generation has its tests and its chance to stand and prove itself. Would you like to know of one of our toughest tests? Hear the warning words of President Brigham Young, 'The worst fear I have about this people is that they will get rich in this country, forget God and His people, wax fat, and kick themselves out of the Church and go to hell. This people will stand mobbing, robbing, poverty, and all manner of persecution and be true. But my greatest fear is that they cannot stand wealth.'

  "Ours then seems to be the toughest test of all for the evils are more subtle, more clever. It all seems less menacing and it is harder to detect. While every test of righteousness represents a struggle, this particular test seems like no test at all, no struggle and so could be the most deceiving of all tests.

  "Do you know what peace and prosperity can do to a people—It can put them to sleep" ("Our Obligation and Challenge" [address delivered at regional representatives seminar] Sept. 30, 1977, 2–3; quoted by Elder David A. Bednar in BYU-Idaho Education Week Devotional, July 30, 2010).

- ❤ Challenge class members to be faithful even in times of peace and prosperity. Ask them to take a few minutes and ponder where they

Notes

personally are on the pride cycle and what the Lord would like them do. If appropriate, have them write down their responses in a personal journal. Testify that the Lord has the power to help us break harmful cycles in our own lives.

> **Teaching Tips from Prophets' Lips** "Who will do the teaching? The Comforter. Be sure you don't believe you are the 'true teacher.' That is a serious mistake.... Be careful you do not get in the way. The major role of a teacher is to prepare the way such that the people will have a spiritual experience with the Lord. You are an instrument, not the teacher. The Lord is the One who knows the needs of those being taught. He is the One who can impress someone's heart and cause them to change" (Gene R. Cook, address delivered to religious educators, 1 Sept. 1989).

Index Topics: pride, wealth, scriptures, humility

HELAMAN 4

The Nephites Become Weak
About 38–30 BC

1–10, The Nephites and Lamanites engage in war again; 11–19, The sufferings of the Nephites are a result of their pride and wickedness; 20–26, The Nephites begin to recognize their faults.

Note: The state of the Nephites as described in Helaman chapter 4 sets the context for the mission that Nephi and Lehi serve in the following chapter.

Overarching Principle: The Nephites became weak because of their transgressions. Strength comes through keeping the commandments and relying on the Lord.

Note: That each bolded heading in this chapter will help you teach the whole chapter sequentially.

1 And it came to pass in the fifty and fourth year there were many dissensions in the church, and there was also a contention among the people, insomuch that there was much bloodshed.

2 And the rebellious part were slain and driven out of the land, and they did go unto the king of the Lamanites.

3 And it came to pass that they did endeavor to stir up the Lamanites to war against the Nephites; but behold, the Lamanites were exceedingly afraid, insomuch that they would not hearken to the words of those dissenters.

4 But it came to pass in the fifty and sixth year of the reign of the judges, there were dissenters who went up from the Nephites unto the Lamanites; and they succeeded with those others in stirring them up to anger against the Nephites; and they were all that year preparing for war.

5 And in the fifty and seventh year they did come down against the Nephites to battle, and they did commence the work of death; yea, insomuch that in the fifty and eighth year of the reign of the judges they succeeded in obtaining possession of the land of Zarahemla; yea, and also all the lands, even unto the land which was near the land Bountiful.

6 And the Nephites and the armies of Moronihah were driven even into the land of Bountiful;

7 And there they did fortify against the Lamanites, from the west sea, even unto the east; it being a day's journey for a Nephite, on the line which they had fortified and stationed their armies to defend their north country.

8 And thus those dissenters of the Nephites, with the help of a numerous army of the Lamanites, had obtained all the possession of the Nephites which was in the land southward. And all this was done in the fifty and eighth and ninth years of the reign of the judges.

9 And it came to pass in the sixtieth year of the reign of the judges, Moronihah did succeed with his armies in obtaining many parts of the land;

Notes

HELAMAN 4

yea, they regained many cities which had fallen into the hands of the Lamanites.

10 And it came to pass in the sixty and first year of the reign of the judges they succeeded in regaining even the half of all their possessions.

vv. 1–10 The Nephites again engage in war with the Lamanites.

- The information in these first ten verses establishes context for the rest of the chapter. You may want to summarize these verses by relaying the story yourself or assigning a class member to do so.

11 Now this great loss of the Nephites, and the great slaughter which was among them, would not have happened had it not been for their wickedness and their abomination which was among them; yea, and it was among those also who professed to belong to the church of God.

12 And it was because of the pride of their hearts, because of their exceeding riches, yea, it was because of their oppression to the poor, withholding their food from the hungry, withholding their clothing from the naked, and smiting their humble brethren upon the cheek, making a mock of that which was sacred, denying the spirit of prophecy and of revelation, murdering, plundering, lying, stealing, committing adultery, rising up in great contentions, and deserting away into the land of Nephi, among the Lamanites—

13 And because of this their great wickedness, and their boastings in their own strength, they were left in their own strength; therefore they did not prosper, but were afflicted and smitten, and driven before the Lamanites, until they had lost possession of almost all their lands.

14 But behold, Moronihah did preach many things unto the people because of their iniquity, and also Nephi and Lehi, who were the sons of Helaman, did preach many things unto the people, yea, and did prophesy many things unto them concerning their iniquities, and what should come unto them if they did not repent of their sins.

15 And it came to pass that they did repent, and inasmuch as they did repent they did begin to prosper.

16 For when Moronihah saw that they did repent he did venture to lead them forth from place to place, and from city to city, even until they had regained the one-half of their property and the one-half of all their lands.

17 And thus ended the sixty and first year of the reign of the judges.

vv. 11–17 The Nephite problem: When people are prideful and forget the Lord, they are left to their own strength.

- Invite class members to read verses 11–17 looking for the reason the Nephites were experiencing difficult trials. Create a list on the board.

- Apply: Refer to the list you just created and ask, *Which items on this list are prevalent today?* Discuss the answers.

18 And it came to pass in the sixty and second year of the reign of the judges, that Moronihah could obtain no more possessions over the Lamanites.

19 Therefore they did abandon their design to obtain the remainder of their lands, for so numerous were the Lamanites that it became impossible for the Nephites to obtain more power over them; therefore Moronihah did employ all his armies in maintaining those parts which he had taken.

20 And it came to pass, because of the greatness of the number of the Lamanites the Nephites were in great fear, lest they should be overpowered, and trodden down, and slain, and destroyed.

21 Yea, they began to remember the prophecies of Alma, and also the words of Mosiah; and they saw that they had been a stiffnecked people, and

Notes

that they had set at naught the commandments of God;

22 And that they had altered and trampled under their feet the laws of Mosiah, or that which the Lord commanded him to give unto the people; and they saw that their laws had become corrupted, and that they had become a wicked people, insomuch that they were wicked even like unto the Lamanites.

23 And because of their iniquity the church had begun to dwindle; and they began to disbelieve in the spirit of prophecy and in the spirit of revelation; and the judgments of God did stare them in the face.

24 And they saw that they had become weak, like unto their brethren, the Lamanites, and that the Spirit of the Lord did no more preserve them; yea, it had withdrawn from them because the Spirit of the Lord doth not dwell in unholy temples—

25 Therefore the Lord did cease to preserve them by his miraculous and matchless power, for they had fallen into a state of unbelief and awful wickedness; and they saw that the Lamanites were exceedingly more numerous than they, and except they should cleave unto the Lord their God they must unavoidably perish.

26 For behold, they saw that the strength of the Lamanites was as great as their strength, even man for man. And thus had they fallen into this great transgression; yea, thus had they become weak, because of their transgression, in the space of not many years.

vv. 18–26 The Nephite Realization: When the Lord withdraws His divine help, people become weak and fall into a state of unbelief.

- As a class, read verses 22–25 looking for what the Nephites are now realizing about themselves. Consider making a list on the board.

- What is the reason for the Nephites' weakness according to verse 26?

- Analyze: *Why do you think that once the Lord withdraws His strength people become weak? What could be done to prevent this weakening process?*

- Apply: *How do we see similar problems happening today? How can we avoid the same weakening process the Nephites experienced?*

- Robert D. Hales taught, "If we are not obedient to the laws, principles, and ordinances of the gospel, the Holy Ghost will withdraw. He cannot be with us if we are angry in our hearts, contentious with our companions, or critical of the Lord's anointed. He departs whenever we are rebellious, are immoral, dress or act immodestly, are unclean or profane in mind or body, are slothful in priesthood callings and duties, or commit other sins, for the Spirit of the Lord doth not dwell in unholy temples." (Robert D. Hales, "Receiving a Testimony of the Restored Gospel of Jesus Christ," *Ensign*, Nov. 2003, 31)

- Consider asking for personal examples from class members of when they have felt the Lord has protected and helped them individually. You may also want to bear testimony from your own experiences. Encourage class members to turn to the Lord and keep His commandments.

HELAMAN 5
Remember Our Redeemer
About 30 BC

1–11, Nephi and Lehi remember the words of their father, Helaman; 12, We must build our foundation on Christ, 13–22, Nephi and Lehi teach with great power and are cast into prison; 23–36, While in prison, Nephi and Lehi are miraculously freed and encircled by fire as witnessed by those present; 37–52, Many Lamanites are converted because of this experience.

Notes

Note: Helaman chapter 4 details the wickedness of the Nephites because they have chosen to forget the Lord and were left to their own strength. Helaman chapter 5 offers a stark contrast between forgetting and remembering. Consider teaching chapter 5 as a solution to the problems presented in chapter 4.

Overarching Principle: As we build ourselves upon the rock of our Redeemer, we will remember Him and receive His power, protection, and guidance.

1 And it came to pass that in this same year, behold, Nephi delivered up the judgment-seat to a man whose name was Cezoram.

2 For as their laws and their governments were established by the voice of the people, and they who chose evil were more numerous than they who chose good, therefore they were ripening for destruction, for the laws had become corrupted.

3 Yea, and this was not all; they were a stiffnecked people, insomuch that they could not be governed by the law nor justice, save it were to their destruction.

4 And it came to pass that Nephi had become weary because of their iniquity; and he yielded up the judgment-seat, and took it upon him to preach the word of God all the remainder of his days, and his brother Lehi also, all the remainder of his days;

vv. 1–4 The wickedness of the Nephites force Nephi to give up the judgment-seat to preach the word of God with Lehi.

Invite class members to read verses 1–4 to look for the spiritual state of the Nephites.

Note: Helaman chapter 4 gives a more detailed account of their spiritual state.

5 For they remembered the words which their father Helaman spake unto them. And these are the words which he spake:

6 Behold, my sons, I desire that ye should remember to keep the commandments of God; and I would that ye should declare unto the people these words. Behold, I have given unto you the names of our first parents who came out of the land of Jerusalem; and this I have done that when you remember your names ye may remember them; and when ye remember them ye may remember their works; and when ye remember their works ye may know how that it is said, and also written, that they were good.

7 Therefore, my sons, I would that ye should do that which is good, that it may be said of you, and also written, even as it has been said and written of them.

8 And now my sons, behold I have somewhat more to desire of you, which desire is, that ye may not do these things that ye may boast, but that ye may do these things to lay up for yourselves a treasure in heaven, yea, which is eternal, and which fadeth not away; yea, that ye may have that precious gift of eternal life, which we have reason to suppose hath been given to our fathers.

9 O remember, remember, my sons, the words which king Benjamin spake unto his people; yea, remember that there is no other way nor means whereby man can be saved, only through the atoning blood of Jesus Christ, who shall come; yea, remember that he cometh to redeem the world.

10 And remember also the words which Amulek spake unto Zeezrom, in the city of Ammonihah; for he said unto him that the Lord surely should come to redeem his people, but that he should not come to redeem them in their sins, but to redeem them from their sins.

11 And he hath power given unto him from the Father to redeem them from their sins because of repentance; therefore he hath sent his angels to declare the tidings of the conditions of repentance, which bringeth unto the power of the Redeemer, unto the salvation of their souls.

12 And now, my sons, remember, remember that it

Notes

is upon the rock of our Redeemer, who is Christ, the Son of God, that ye must build your foundation; that when the devil shall send forth his mighty winds, yea, his shafts in the whirlwind, yea, when all his hail and his mighty storm shall beat upon you, it shall have no power over you to drag you down to the gulf of misery and endless wo, because of the rock upon which ye are built, which is a sure foundation, a foundation whereon if men build they cannot fall.

vv. 5–12 It is essential to remember spiritual lessons and experiences throughout our lives.

⚡ To help introduce the importance of remembering, consider playing a memory game for a few minutes with your class. You could create one by printing various matching pairs of pictures. Tape the pictures to the board with the backside facing the class, then invite the members of your class to take turns guessing which pictures make a matching pair by flipping them over one at a time. If a class member makes a match, remove the pictures from the board. If the pictures do not match, turn them back over and allow the next class member to take a turn.

🔍 Create the following chart on the board or as a handout for the class to complete. This handout will help class members look for three areas in which our ability to remember has significant impact on our spiritual growth.

What Should We Remember?	
What parents teach (Hel. 5:5–8)	
What prophets teach (Hel. 5:9–11)	
Our dependence on Christ (Hel. 5:12)	

Allow class members enough time to complete the chart individually, as a group, or as a class

❓ Analyze: Once the chart has been completed and the class has identified principles about remembering, consider asking questions like the following to analyze what has been identified:

- Why do you think it would be helpful to remember council from parents?
- Notice that two prophets were quoted in verses 9–11. What was their common message and what does that common message teach about the role of prophets?
- Why is it significant for us to remember our dependence on Christ?

❓ Apply:

- What lessons from your parents do you remember?
- What lessons do you hope to teach your children?
- What recent message from our prophet has brought you closer to Christ?
- What have you done to show your dependence on Christ?
- What can sometimes cause us to forget these messages?

💬 Henry B. Eyring stated, "Peril comes from the forces of wickedness. Those forces are increasing. And so it will become harder, not easier, to keep the covenants we must make to live the gospel of Jesus Christ. For those of us who are concerned about such a future for ourselves . . . there is hope in the promise the Lord has given us of a place of safety in the storms ahead. Here is a word picture of that place. You have read about it in scripture. It has been repeatedly described by living prophets. A loving father told his sons of it this way as he tried to strengthen them against the storms of temptation: [He quotes Helaman 5:12] . . . It has never been more important than it is now to understand how to build on that sure foundation" (Henry B. Eyring, "As a Child," *Ensign*, May 2006, 17).

♥ To help class members understand the benefits of remembering, continue this lesson

Notes

through the next principle statement in bold below.

13 And it came to pass that these were the words which Helaman taught to his sons; yea, he did teach them many things which are not written, and also many things which are written.

14 And they did remember his words; and therefore they went forth, keeping the commandments of God, to teach the word of God among all the people of Nephi, beginning at the city Bountiful;

15 And from thenceforth to the city of Gid; and from the city of Gid to the city of Mulek;

16 And even from one city to another, until they had gone forth among all the people of Nephi who were in the land southward; and from thence into the land of Zarahemla, among the Lamanites.

17 And it came to pass that they did preach with great power, insomuch that they did confound many of those dissenters who had gone over from the Nephites, insomuch that they came forth and did confess their sins and were baptized unto repentance, and immediately returned to the Nephites to endeavor to repair unto them the wrongs which they had done.

18 And it came to pass that Nephi and Lehi did preach unto the Lamanites with such great power and authority, for they had power and authority given unto them that they might speak, and they also had what they should speak given unto them—

19 Therefore they did speak unto the great astonishment of the Lamanites, to the convincing them, insomuch that there were eight thousand of the Lamanites who were in the land of Zarahemla and round about baptized unto repentance, and were convinced of the wickedness of the traditions of their fathers.

vv. 13–19 The spiritual strength that results from remembrance.

Note: This is a continuation of the lesson above.

Look for what resulted from Nephi and Lehi remembering what their father had taught them in verses 13–19.

Apply: *What can we do to better remember the spiritual lessons we have been taught?*

Consider with class members what blessings would come to their lives if they would remember the principles or doctrines taught by prophets and parents. Invite them to continue to build their foundation on the Lord so they can withstand the fiery darts of the adversary.

20 And it came to pass that Nephi and Lehi did proceed from thence to go to the land of Nephi.

21 And it came to pass that they were taken by an army of the Lamanites and cast into prison; yea, even in that same prison in which Ammon and his brethren were cast by the servants of Limhi.

22 And after they had been cast into prison many days without food, behold, they went forth into the prison to take them that they might slay them.

23 And it came to pass that Nephi and Lehi were encircled about as if by fire, even insomuch that they durst not lay their hands upon them for fear lest they should be burned. Nevertheless, Nephi and Lehi were not burned; and they were as standing in the midst of fire and were not burned.

24 And when they saw that they were encircled about with a pillar of fire, and that it burned them not, their hearts did take courage.

25 For they saw that the Lamanites durst not lay their hands upon them; neither durst they come near unto them, but stood as if they were struck dumb with amazement.

26 And it came to pass that Nephi and Lehi did stand forth and began to speak unto them, saying: Fear not, for behold, it is God that has shown unto you this marvelous thing, in the

Notes

HELAMAN 5

which is shown unto you that ye cannot lay your hands on us to slay us.

27 And behold, when they had said these words, the earth shook exceedingly, and the walls of the prison did shake as if they were about to tumble to the earth; but behold, they did not fall. And behold, they that were in the prison were Lamanites and Nephites who were dissenters.

vv. 20–27 Nephi and Lehi are cast into prison.

> These verses tell the story of Nephi and Lehi's imprisonment. The following verses relate their miraculous escape and heavenly vision. Consider summarizing these verses or asking a class member to do so.

28 And it came to pass that they were overshadowed with a cloud of darkness, and an awful solemn fear came upon them.

29 And it came to pass that there came a voice as if it were above the cloud of darkness, saying: Repent ye, repent ye, and seek no more to destroy my servants whom I have sent unto you to declare good tidings.

30 And it came to pass when they heard this voice, and beheld that it was not a voice of thunder, neither was it a voice of a great tumultuous noise, but behold, it was a still voice of perfect mildness, as if it had been a whisper, and it did pierce even to the very soul—

31 And notwithstanding the mildness of the voice, behold the earth shook exceedingly, and the walls of the prison trembled again, as if it were about to tumble to the earth; and behold the cloud of darkness, which had overshadowed them, did not disperse—

32 And behold the voice came again, saying: Repent ye, repent ye, for the kingdom of heaven is at hand; and seek no more to destroy my servants. And it came to pass that the earth shook again, and the walls trembled.

33 And also again the third time the voice came, and did speak unto them marvelous words which cannot be uttered by man; and the walls did tremble again, and the earth shook as if it were about to divide asunder.

34 And it came to pass that the Lamanites could not flee because of the cloud of darkness which did overshadow them; yea, and also they were immovable because of the fear which did come upon them.

35 Now there was one among them who was a Nephite by birth, who had once belonged to the church of God but had dissented from them.

36 And it came to pass that he turned him about, and behold, he saw through the cloud of darkness the faces of Nephi and Lehi; and behold, they did shine exceedingly, even as the faces of angels. And he beheld that they did lift their eyes to heaven; and they were in the attitude as if talking or lifting their voices to some being whom they beheld.

37 And it came to pass that this man did cry unto the multitude, that they might turn and look. And behold, there was power given unto them that they did turn and look; and they did behold the faces of Nephi and Lehi.

38 And they said unto the man: Behold, what do all these things mean, and who is it with whom these men do converse?

39 Now the man's name was Aminadab. And Aminadab said unto them: They do converse with the angels of God.

40 And it came to pass that the Lamanites said unto him: What shall we do, that this cloud of darkness may be removed from overshadowing us?

41 And Aminadab said unto them: You must repent, and cry unto the voice, even until ye shall have faith in Christ, who was taught unto you by Alma, and Amulek, and Zeezrom; and when ye shall do this, the cloud of darkness shall be removed from overshadowing you.

Notes

vv. 28–41 Faith in the Lord Jesus Christ and repentance bring us from darkness into light.

⚡ If possible, turn the lights in the room where you are teaching on and off. Do this a few times, and then briefly discuss the contrast between light and dark. Explain that class members will see in verses 29–41 how we can be symbolically removed from darkness and brought into light as we exercise faith in the Lord Jesus Christ and repent.

🔍 *Read and contrast the experience of the prison guards (verses 28–34) with that of Nephi and Lehi (verse 36).*

❓ Analyze: *What contrast do you see between these two groups of people? Why would the group that needs repenting be in darkness?*

❓ Apply: *How does sin lead to darkness?*

🔍 Explain that one of the guards, named Aminadab, was a Nephite dissenter (verse 35). Look for what he invites the rest of the guards to do in verses 37–41.

❓ Analyze: *Why do you think faith in Jesus Christ and repentance would remove the cloud of darkness?*

♥ To help class members understand the importance of this principle, encourage them to consider how much added light can come into our life if we all exercise faith in Jesus Christ and repent of our sins. As a final application of the story, read verses 42–52 with the class. Consider asking someone to share their testimony of the power of faith and repentance.

42 And it came to pass that they all did begin to cry unto the voice of him who had shaken the earth; yea, they did cry even until the cloud of darkness was dispersed.

43 And it came to pass that when they cast their eyes about, and saw that the cloud of darkness was dispersed from overshadowing them, behold, they saw that they were encircled about, yea every soul, by a pillar of fire.

44 And Nephi and Lehi were in the midst of them; yea, they were encircled about; yea, they were as if in the midst of a flaming fire, yet it did harm them not, neither did it take hold upon the walls of the prison; and they were filled with that joy which is unspeakable and full of glory.

45 And behold, the Holy Spirit of God did come down from heaven, and did enter into their hearts, and they were filled as if with fire, and they could speak forth marvelous words.

46 And it came to pass that there came a voice unto them, yea, a pleasant voice, as if it were a whisper, saying:

47 Peace, peace be unto you, because of your faith in my Well Beloved, who was from the foundation of the world.

48 And now, when they heard this they cast up their eyes as if to behold from whence the voice came; and behold, they saw the heavens open; and angels came down out of heaven and ministered unto them.

49 And there were about three hundred souls who saw and heard these things; and they were bidden to go forth and marvel not, neither should they doubt.

50 And it came to pass that they did go forth, and did minister unto the people, declaring throughout all the regions round about all the things which they had heard and seen, insomuch that the more part of the Lamanites were convinced of them, because of the greatness of the evidences which they had received.

51 And as many as were convinced did lay down their weapons of war, and also their hatred and the tradition of their fathers.

52 And it came to pass that they did yield up unto the Nephites the lands of their possession.

Teaching Tips from Prophets' Lips "The crowning, convincing, converting power of gospel teaching is manifest, when an inspired teacher says, 'I know by the power of the Holy

Notes

> Ghost, by the revelations of the Holy Spirit to my soul, that the doctrines I have taught are true'" (Bruce R. McConkie, *The Promised Messiah* [1978], 516–17).

Index Topics: repentance, remember, pride cycle

HELAMAN 6

Times of Change
About 23 BC

1–6, The Lamanites become a righteous people; 7–14, The Lamanites and Nephites open channels of commerce and travel; 15–20, The chief judge is murdered by the band of Gadianton; 21–30, Satan builds up the secret band of Gadianton; 31–42, Because of wickedness, the Spirit of the Lord withdraws from the Nephites.

1 And it came to pass that when the sixty and second year of the reign of the judges had ended, all these things had happened and the Lamanites had become, the more part of them, a righteous people, insomuch that their righteousness did exceed that of the Nephites, because of their firmness and their steadiness in the faith.

2 For behold, there were many of the Nephites who had become hardened and impenitent and grossly wicked, insomuch that they did reject the word of God and all the preaching and prophesying which did come among them.

3 Nevertheless, the people of the church did have great joy because of the conversion of the Lamanites, yea, because of the church of God, which had been established among them. And they did fellowship one with another, and did rejoice one with another, and did have great joy.

4 And it came to pass that many of the Lamanites did come down into the land of Zarahemla, and did declare unto the people of the Nephites the manner of their conversion, and did exhort them to faith and repentance.

5 Yea, and many did preach with exceedingly great power and authority, unto the bringing down many of them into the depths of humility, to be the humble followers of God and the Lamb.

6 And it came to pass that many of the Lamanites did go into the land northward; and also Nephi and Lehi went into the land northward, to preach unto the people. And thus ended the sixty and third year.

7 And behold, there was peace in all the land, insomuch that the Nephites did go into whatsoever part of the land they would, whether among the Nephites or the Lamanites.

8 And it came to pass that the Lamanites did also go whithersoever they would, whether it were among the Lamanites or among the Nephites; and thus they did have free intercourse one with another, to buy and to sell, and to get gain, according to their desire.

9 And it came to pass that they became exceedingly rich, both the Lamanites and the Nephites; and they did have an exceeding plenty of gold, and of silver, and of all manner of precious metals, both in the land south and in the land north.

10 Now the land south was called Lehi, and the land north was called Mulek, which was after the son of Zedekiah; for the Lord did bring Mulek into the land north, and Lehi into the land south.

11 And behold, there was all manner of gold in both these lands, and of silver, and of precious ore of every kind; and there were also curious workmen, who did work all kinds of ore and did refine it; and thus they did become rich.

12 They did raise grain in abundance, both in the north and in the south; and they did flourish exceedingly, both in the north and in the south. And they did multiply and wax exceedingly strong in the land. And they did raise many flocks and herds, yea, many fatlings.

Notes

13 Behold their women did toil and spin, and did make all manner of cloth, of fine-twined linen and cloth of every kind, to clothe their nakedness. And thus the sixty and fourth year did pass away in peace.

14 And in the sixty and fifth year they did also have great joy and peace, yea, much preaching and many prophecies concerning that which was to come. And thus passed away the sixty and fifth year.

vv. 1–14 The Nephite society undergoes great changes.

⚡ Bring in some new items: examples of food or entertainment, prices of products, pictures of clothing or other examples of things that have dramatically changed from what they were one hundred years ago. Begin a discussion on changes in society and ask,

- *How influential are some of these changes?*
- *What caused such changes?*
- *Are these kinds of changes temporal or eternal?*

Point out the approximate date of Helaman chapter 6 and note that it has been one hundred years since King Benjamin gave his famous address. Explain that this chapter, when compared to Benjamin's time, will show some radical changes in Nephite society.

👥 Invite class members to form small groups. Have each group read Helaman 6:1–14 and find as many instances as they can showing a difference from the time of King Benjamin. Write the following questions on the board and have the groups discuss them.

❓ Analyze:
- *What was the cause of all the change?*
- *What was the result of all the change?*
- *How might things have been different without the influence of the gospel?*

15 And it came to pass that in the sixty and sixth year of the reign of the judges, behold, Cezoram was murdered by an unknown hand as he sat upon the judgment-seat. And it came to pass that in the same year, that his son, who had been appointed by the people in his stead, was also murdered. And thus ended the sixty and sixth year.

16 And in the commencement of the sixty and seventh year the people began to grow exceedingly wicked again.

17 For behold, the Lord had blessed them so long with the riches of the world that they had not been stirred up to anger, to wars, nor to bloodshed; therefore they began to set their hearts upon their riches; yea, they began to seek to get gain that they might be lifted up one above another; therefore they began to commit secret murders, and to rob and to plunder, that they might get gain.

18 And now behold, those murderers and plunderers were a band who had been formed by Kishkumen and Gadianton. And now it had come to pass that there were many, even among the Nephites, of Gadianton's band. But behold, they were more numerous among the more wicked part of the Lamanites. And they were called Gadianton's robbers and murderers.

19 And it was they who did murder the chief judge Cezoram, and his son, while in the judgment-seat; and behold, they were not found.

20 And now it came to pass that when the Lamanites found that there were robbers among them they were exceedingly sorrowful; and they did use every means in their power to destroy them off the face of the earth.

21 But behold, Satan did stir up the hearts of the more part of the Nephites, insomuch that they did unite with those bands of robbers, and did enter into their covenants and their oaths, that they would protect and preserve one another in whatsoever difficult circumstances they should be placed, that they should not suffer for their murders, and their plunderings, and their stealings.

22 And it came to pass that they did have their

Notes

signs, yea, their secret signs, and their secret words; and this that they might distinguish a brother who had entered into the covenant, that whatsoever wickedness his brother should do he should not be injured by his brother, nor by those who did belong to his band, who had taken this covenant.

23 And thus they might murder, and plunder, and steal, and commit whoredoms and all manner of wickedness, contrary to the laws of their country and also the laws of their God.

24 And whosoever of those who belonged to their band should reveal unto the world of their wickedness and their abominations, should be tried, not according to the laws of their country, but according to the laws of their wickedness, which had been given by Gadianton and Kishkumen.

25 Now behold, it is these secret oaths and covenants which Alma commanded his son should not go forth unto the world, lest they should be a means of bringing down the people unto destruction.

26 Now behold, those secret oaths and covenants did not come forth unto Gadianton from the records which were delivered unto Helaman; but behold, they were put into the heart of Gadianton by that same being who did entice our first parents to partake of the forbidden fruit—

27 Yea, that same being who did plot with Cain, that if he would murder his brother Abel it should not be known unto the world. And he did plot with Cain and his followers from that time forth.

28 And also it is that same being who put it into the hearts of the people to build a tower sufficiently high that they might get to heaven. And it was that same being who led on the people who came from that tower into this land; who spread the works of darkness and abominations over all the face of the land, until he dragged the people down to an entire destruction, and to an everlasting hell.

29 Yea, it is that same being who put it into the heart of Gadianton to still carry on the work of darkness, and of secret murder; and he has brought it forth from the beginning of man even down to this time.

30 And behold, it is he who is the author of all sin. And behold, he doth carry on his works of darkness and secret murder, and doth hand down their plots, and their oaths, and their covenants, and their plans of awful wickedness, from generation to generation according as he can get hold upon the hearts of the children of men.

vv. 15–30 Works of darkness and secret combinations are counterfeit versions of God's work and they bring wickedness and destruction upon the children of men.

- Bring a mirror to class. Ask a class member what he or she sees when looking in the mirror. Ask,
  - *Is it the same image?*
  - *Is it exactly the same?*
  - *How is it different?*

  Explain that while a mirror reflects a very similar image, it is in fact the opposite. To illustrate this point, place different items in front of the mirror like paintings, written documents, etc.

- Read Helaman 6:15–20 and look for an organization that is the opposite of God's organization.

- *While they clearly oppose God's church on the earth, are there any similarities between the Gadianton robbers and God's church? In what ways might the Gadianton robbers be considered a counterfeit version of God's church?*

- Invite class members to read Helaman 6:21–30 and make a list of "mirror-opposite" or counterfeit versions of God's plan for His children. Make a list on the board. Consider writing elements of God's true plan next to the qualities possessed by the Gadianton robbers. For example, "led by Satan—led by

Notes

God," "seeks to do wickedness—seeks to do righteousness," "secretly make dark oaths—openly witness their covenants," etc. Discuss the findings as a class.

- Verses 21–26 represent another chiastic passage within the Book of Mormon. (See the discussion of Alma 36 for an explanation of the most prominent example of chiastic structure.) This literary technique is used here most likely to identify the goal of secret combinations. The crux of the chiasmus centers on doing "wickedness" (v. 22). In addition, some have pointed out the literary repetition of the phrase "that same being." It is used five times in three verses (vv. 26–29). This seems to be another emphasis by Mormon that Satan is the author of such organizations and secret combinations. (See Donald W. Parry, *The Book of Mormon Text Reformatted according to Parallelistic Patterns*, p. 353 and Hugh W. Nibley, *Teachings of the Book of Mormon*, Semester 3, p. 245 for more information.)

31 And now behold, he had got great hold upon the hearts of the Nephites; yea, insomuch that they had become exceedingly wicked; yea, the more part of them had turned out of the way of righteousness, and did trample under their feet the commandments of God, and did turn unto their own ways, and did build up unto themselves idols of their gold and their silver.

32 And it came to pass that all these iniquities did come unto them in the space of not many years, insomuch that a more part of it had come unto them in the sixty and seventh year of the reign of the judges over the people of Nephi.

33 And they did grow in their iniquities in the sixty and eighth year also, to the great sorrow and lamentation of the righteous.

34 And thus we see that the Nephites did begin to dwindle in unbelief, and grow in wickedness and abominations, while the Lamanites began to grow exceedingly in the knowledge of their God; yea, they did begin to keep his statutes and commandments, and to walk in truth and uprightness before him.

35 And thus we see that the Spirit of the Lord began to withdraw from the Nephites, because of the wickedness and the hardness of their hearts.

36 And thus we see that the Lord began to pour out his Spirit upon the Lamanites, because of their easiness and willingness to believe in his words.

37 And it came to pass that the Lamanites did hunt the band of robbers of Gadianton; and they did preach the word of God among the more wicked part of them, insomuch that this band of robbers was utterly destroyed from among the Lamanites.

38 And it came to pass on the other hand, that the Nephites did build them up and support them, beginning at the more wicked part of them, until they had overspread all the land of the Nephites, and had seduced the more part of the righteous until they had come down to believe in their works and partake of their spoils, and to join with them in their secret murders and combinations.

39 And thus they did obtain the sole management of the government, insomuch that they did trample under their feet and smite and rend and turn their backs upon the poor and the meek, and the humble followers of God.

40 And thus we see that they were in an awful state, and ripening for an everlasting destruction.

41 And it came to pass that thus ended the sixty and eighth year of the reign of the judges over the people of Nephi.

vv. 31–41 As a people, we should seek to reject the works of darkness.

- Write the phrase "And thus we see . . ." on the board four times. Explain that Mormon uses this phrase to introduce a prophetic

Notes

commentary regarding the history of his people. He uses the phrase four times in Helaman 6.

🔎 *Read Helaman 6:31–41 and find the four "and thus we see . . ." lessons of Mormon in this chapter.* Invite a class member to write the four lessons on the board.

❓ Analyze:
- *What are your first impressions of these four lessons?*
- *How do you think Mormon felt looking back at this part of Nephite history?*
- *How would you summarize the major difference between the Nephites and Lamanites at this point in the Book of Mormon?*

❓ Apply: *What message do these lessons give to members of the Church in our day?*

❤ Testify that our society will be blessed as we support righteousness and reject wickedness.

HELAMAN 7

"Except Ye Repent Ye Shall Perish"
About 23–21 BC

1–9, Nephi's words are rejected and he mourns the wickedness of the people; 10–29, Nephi prays upon a tower and cries repentance to the people of Nephi.

1 Behold, now it came to pass in the sixty and ninth year of the reign of the judges over the people of the Nephites, that Nephi, the son of Helaman, returned to the land of Zarahemla from the land northward.

2 For he had been forth among the people who were in the land northward, and did preach the word of God unto them, and did prophesy many things unto them;

3 And they did reject all his words, insomuch that he could not stay among them, but returned again unto the land of his nativity.

4 And seeing the people in a state of such awful wickedness, and those Gadianton robbers filling the judgment-seats—having usurped the power and authority of the land; laying aside the commandments of God, and not in the least aright before him; doing no justice unto the children of men;

5 Condemning the righteous because of their righteousness; letting the guilty and the wicked go unpunished because of their money; and moreover to be held in office at the head of government, to rule and do according to their wills, that they might get gain and glory of the world, and, moreover, that they might the more easily commit adultery, and steal, and kill, and do according to their own wills—

6 Now this great iniquity had come upon the Nephites, in the space of not many years; and when Nephi saw it, his heart was swollen with sorrow within his breast; and he did exclaim in the agony of his soul:

7 Oh, that I could have had my days in the days when my father Nephi first came out of the land of Jerusalem, that I could have joyed with him in the promised land; then were his people easy to be entreated, firm to keep the commandments of God, and slow to be led to do iniquity; and they were quick to hearken unto the words of the Lord—

vv. 1–7 One of the roles of a prophet is to plead for and in behalf of his people.

⚡ Place a picture of Nephi on the garden tower praying, or draw a tower on the board before class begins. At the beginning of class, ask class members what they know about the visual or what they think they will learn from it.

💡 In order to explain the state of the Nephites, consider contrasting their current wickedness in verse 5 with their previous righteousness in verse 7.

❓ Analyze: *Today, how do we compare to the wickedness of the Nephites in verse 7?*

Notes

♥ Invite class members to learn from the mistakes of the Nephites so that they do not have to repeat the same mistakes.

8 Yea, if my days could have been in those days, then would my soul have had joy in the righteousness of my brethren.

9 But behold, I am consigned that these are my days, and that my soul shall be filled with sorrow because of this the wickedness of my brethren.

10 And behold, now it came to pass that it was upon a tower, which was in the garden of Nephi, which was by the highway which led to the chief market, which was in the city of Zarahemla; therefore, Nephi had bowed himself upon the tower which was in his garden, which tower was also near unto the garden gate by which led the highway.

11 And it came to pass that there were certain men passing by and saw Nephi as he was pouring out his soul unto God upon the tower; and they ran and told the people what they had seen, and the people came together in multitudes that they might know the cause of so great mourning for the wickedness of the people.

12 And now, when Nephi arose he beheld the multitudes of people who had gathered together.

13 And it came to pass that he opened his mouth and said unto them: Behold, why have ye gathered yourselves together? That I may tell you of your iniquities?

14 Yea, because I have got upon my tower that I might pour out my soul unto my God, because of the exceeding sorrow of my heart, which is because of your iniquities!

15 And because of my mourning and lamentation ye have gathered yourselves together, and do marvel; yea, and ye have great need to marvel; yea, ye ought to marvel because ye are given away that the devil has got so great hold upon your hearts.

16 Yea, how could you have given way to the enticing of him who is seeking to hurl away your souls down to everlasting misery and endless wo?

17 O repent ye, repent ye! Why will ye die? Turn ye, turn ye unto the Lord your God. Why has he forsaken you?

18 It is because you have hardened your hearts; yea, ye will not hearken unto the voice of the good shepherd; yea, ye have provoked him to anger against you.

19 And behold, instead of gathering you, except ye will repent, behold, he shall scatter you forth that ye shall become meat for dogs and wild beasts.

20 O, how could you have forgotten your God in the very day that he has delivered you?

21 But behold, it is to get gain, to be praised of men, yea, and that ye might get gold and silver. And ye have set your hearts upon the riches and the vain things of this world, for the which ye do murder, and plunder, and steal, and bear false witness against your neighbor, and do all manner of iniquity.

22 And for this cause wo shall come unto you except ye shall repent. For if ye will not repent, behold, this great city, and also all those great cities which are round about, which are in the land of our possession, shall be taken away that ye shall have no place in them; for behold, the Lord will not grant unto you strength, as he has hitherto done, to withstand against your enemies.

23 For behold, thus saith the Lord: I will not show unto the wicked of my strength, to one more than the other, save it be unto those who repent of their sins, and hearken unto my words. Now therefore, I would that ye should behold, my brethren, that it shall be better for the Lamanites than for you except ye shall repent.

24 For behold, they are more righteous than you, for they have not sinned against that great knowledge which ye have received; therefore the Lord will be merciful unto them; yea, he will

Notes

lengthen out their days and increase their seed, even when thou shalt be utterly destroyed except thou shalt repent.

25 Yea, wo be unto you because of that great abomination which has come among you; and ye have united yourselves unto it, yea, to that secret band which was established by Gadianton!

26 Yea, wo shall come unto you because of that pride which ye have suffered to enter your hearts, which has lifted you up beyond that which is good because of your exceedingly great riches!

27 Yea, wo be unto you because of your wickedness and abominations!

28 And except ye repent ye shall perish; yea, even your lands shall be taken from you, and ye shall be destroyed from off the face of the earth.

29 Behold now, I do not say that these things shall be, of myself, because it is not of myself that I know these things; but behold, I know that these things are true because the Lord God has made them known unto me, therefore I testify that they shall be.

vv. 13–29 One of the roles of a prophet is to teach the consequence of sin and disobedience.

- *What would be the most difficult responsibility as a prophet of God?* After accepting several responses, share the principle stated above and consider discussing how difficult it would be for a prophet of God to have to teach the consequence of sin.
- *What were the consequences that awaited the people of Nephi if they did not repent?* Direct class members to the following verses to answer this question: vv.18, 22, 24, and 28.
- Analyze: *Why do you think the consequences were so drastic?*
- *What were the sins of the people of Nephi according to Nephi in verses 21 and 25?*
- Apply: *What do we learn from the fact that the Lord warns the wicked and invites them to repent?*
- *What has the Lord's prophet warned us about recently? What consequences did he say would happen if we did not heed his words?* Consider giving each class member a copy of the most recent general conference address from the prophet in order to answer these questions. Invite all to heed to the warnings of a prophet of God.

Teaching Tips from Prophets' Lips "You cannot force spiritual things. . . . You can no more force the Spirit to respond than you can force a bean to sprout, or an egg to hatch before its time. You can create a climate to foster growth, nourish, and protect; but you cannot force or compel: you must await the growth" (Boyd K. Packer, "Candle of the Lord," *Ensign*, Jan. 1983, 53).

Index Topics: prophets

HELAMAN 8

Prophets Testify of Things to Come
About 23–21 BC

1–9, Those listening to Nephi contend with one another about the truthfulness of Nephi's words; 10–25, All prophets have testified of things to come; 26–28, Nephi announces the murder of the chief judge.

1 And now it came to pass that when Nephi had said these words, behold, there were men who were judges, who also belonged to the secret band of Gadianton, and they were angry, and they cried out against him, saying unto the people: Why do ye not seize upon this man and bring him forth, that he may be condemned according to the crime which he has done?

2 Why seest thou this man, and hearest him revile against this people and against our law?

Notes

HELAMAN 8

3 For behold, Nephi had spoken unto them concerning the corruptness of their law; yea, many things did Nephi speak which cannot be written; and nothing did he speak which was contrary to the commandments of God.

4 And those judges were angry with him because he spake plainly unto them concerning their secret works of darkness; nevertheless, they durst not lay their own hands upon him, for they feared the people lest they should cry out against them.

5 Therefore they did cry unto the people, saying: Why do you suffer this man to revile against us? For behold he doth condemn all this people, even unto destruction; yea, and also that these our great cities shall be taken from us, that we shall have no place in them.

6 And now we know that this is impossible, for behold, we are powerful, and our cities great, therefore our enemies can have no power over us.

7 And it came to pass that thus they did stir up the people to anger against Nephi, and raised contentions among them; for there were some who did cry out: Let this man alone, for he is a good man, and those things which he saith will surely come to pass except we repent;

8 Yea, behold, all the judgments will come upon us which he has testified unto us; for we know that he has testified aright unto us concerning our iniquities. And behold they are many, and he knoweth as well all things which shall befall us as he knoweth of our iniquities;

9 Yea, and behold, if he had not been a prophet he could not have testified concerning those things.

10 And it came to pass that those people who sought to destroy Nephi were compelled because of their fear, that they did not lay their hands on him; therefore he began again to speak unto them, seeing that he had gained favor in the eyes of some, insomuch that the remainder of them did fear.

vv. 1–10 The wicked take the truth to be hard.

✋ In order to help class members understand the storyline, explain that in the previous chapter, Nephi had testified of the Nephites wickedness and invited them to repent. Explain that different class members will be reading direct quotes from the scriptures of those who agree or disagree with Nephi. Type the quotes from the following verses for class members to read:

Those who disagree with Nephi: vv. 1, 2, 5, 6

Those in favor of Nephi: vv. 7, 8, 9

Explain the background of what happens in chapter 7, and invite those who have been given the quotes to stand up and read their parts in whatever order you wish.

⚡ *How would these reactions make you feel if you were Nephi?*

11 Therefore he was constrained to speak more unto them saying: Behold, my brethren, have ye not read that God gave power unto one man, even Moses, to smite upon the waters of the Red Sea, and they parted hither and thither, insomuch that the Israelites, who were our fathers, came through upon dry ground, and the waters closed upon the armies of the Egyptians and swallowed them up?

12 And now behold, if God gave unto this man such power, then why should ye dispute among yourselves, and say that he hath given unto me no power whereby I may know concerning the judgments that shall come upon you except ye repent?

13 But, behold, ye not only deny my words, but ye also deny all the words which have been spoken by our fathers, and also the words which were spoken by this man, Moses, who had such great power given unto him, yea, the words which he hath spoken concerning the coming of the Messiah.

14 Yea, did he not bear record that the Son of God

Notes

should come? And as he lifted up the brazen serpent in the wilderness, even so shall he be lifted up who should come.

15 And as many as should look upon that serpent should live, even so as many as should look upon the Son of God with faith, having a contrite spirit, might live, even unto that life which is eternal.

16 And now behold, Moses did not only testify of these things, but also all the holy prophets, from his days even to the days of Abraham.

17 Yea, and behold, Abraham saw of his coming, and was filled with gladness and did rejoice.

18 Yea, and behold I say unto you, that Abraham not only knew of these things, but there were many before the days of Abraham who were called by the order of God; yea, even after the order of his Son; and this that it should be shown unto the people, a great many thousand years before his coming, that even redemption should come unto them.

19 And now I would that ye should know, that even since the days of Abraham there have been many prophets that have testified these things; yea, behold, the prophet Zenos did testify boldly; for the which he was slain.

20 And behold, also Zenock, and also Ezias, and also Isaiah, and Jeremiah, (Jeremiah being that same prophet who testified of the destruction of Jerusalem) and now we know that Jerusalem was destroyed according to the words of Jeremiah. O then why not the Son of God come, according to his prophecy?

21 And now will you dispute that Jerusalem was destroyed? Will ye say that the sons of Zedekiah were not slain, all except it were Mulek? Yea, and do ye not behold that the seed of Zedekiah are with us, and they were driven out of the land of Jerusalem? But behold, this is not all—

22 Our father Lehi was driven out of Jerusalem because he testified of these things. Nephi also testified of these things, and also almost all of our fathers, even down to this time; yea, they have testified of the coming of Christ, and have looked forward, and have rejoiced in his day which is to come.

23 And behold, he is God, and he is with them, and he did manifest himself unto them, that they were redeemed by him; and they gave unto him glory, because of that which is to come.

24 And now, seeing ye know these things and cannot deny them except ye shall lie, therefore in this ye have sinned, for ye have rejected all these things, notwithstanding so many evidences which ye have received; yea, even ye have received all things, both things in heaven, and all things which are in the earth, as a witness that they are true.

25 But behold, ye have rejected the truth, and rebelled against your holy God; and even at this time, instead of laying up for yourselves treasures in heaven, where nothing doth corrupt, and where nothing can come which is unclean, ye are heaping up for yourselves wrath against the day of judgment.

26 Yea, even at this time ye are ripening, because of your murders and your fornication and wickedness, for everlasting destruction; yea, and except ye repent it will come unto you soon.

27 Yea, behold it is now even at your doors; yea, go ye in unto the judgment-seat, and search; and behold, your judge is murdered, and he lieth in his blood; and he hath been murdered by his brother, who seeketh to sit in the judgment-seat.

28 And behold, they both belong to your secret band, whose author is Gadianton and the evil one who seeketh to destroy the souls of men.

vv. 11–28 Prophets testify of things to come.

⚡ Put the following diagram on the board.

Notes

HELAMAN 9

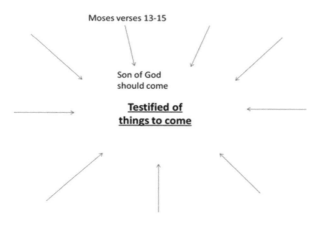

- One of the things Nephi is trying to prove to the people is that a prophet of God can testify of things to come, just as he is testifying that destruction is coming if they do not repent.

- Invite class members to find all of the prophets who testified of things to come in verses 11–28 and what they testified would happen. Write the names of each of the prophets on the diagram. Also include what each prophet of God testified of. Make sure to include Nephi's assertion that the chief judge had just been murdered in verses 26–28.

- Apply: *When have you heard or read about a prophet of God testifying of things to come? Have you seen that prophesy fulfilled?*

- Testify that all things prophets long ago have testified of have come to pass, and that all things that prophets today testify of will come to pass.

Index Topics: prophets

HELAMAN 9

Nephi Reveals the Murderer
About 23–21 BC

1–5, Five are sent to verify Nephi's words and find the chief judge dead; 6–18, The five are mistakenly assumed to be the murderers but are later confirmed not to be; 19–37, Nephi states how to obtain the confession from the true murderer; 38–41, There are diverse opinions of Nephi.

Overarching Principle: Through God, prophets can reveal what is unknown.

vv. 1–41 "Stump or Be Stumped" principle.

- To teach the important storyline of this chapter, play the game "Stump or Be Stumped." To play, you will give the class a few minutes to read a set of verses. While they are studying the verses, they need to either create a question to try to stump you, or know the verses well enough that they can answer any question you can give to stump them. After they are ready, randomly call on a class member to Stump or Be Stumped. The first set of verses could be 1–5, then 6–18, and finally 19–41. Questions are provided in the lesson below, or you can come up with your own questions. Make sure you take time to discuss any important insights or principles that are discovered.

1 Behold, now it came to pass that when Nephi had spoken these words, certain men who were among them ran to the judgment-seat; yea, even there were five who went, and they said among themselves, as they went:

2 Behold, now we will know of a surety whether this man be a prophet and God hath commanded him to prophesy such marvelous things unto us. Behold, we do not believe that he hath; yea, we do not believe that he is a prophet; nevertheless, if this thing which he has said concerning the chief judge be true, that he be dead, then will we believe that the other words which he has spoken are true.

3 And it came to pass that they ran in their might, and came in unto the judgment-seat; and behold, the chief judge had fallen to the earth, and did lie in his blood.

Notes

HELAMAN 9

4 And now behold, when they saw this they were astonished exceedingly, insomuch that they fell to the earth; for they had not believed the words which Nephi had spoken concerning the chief judge.

5 But now, when they saw they believed, and fear came upon them lest all the judgments which Nephi had spoken should come upon the people; therefore they did quake, and had fallen to the earth.

? Analyze:
- How many men went to check on the chief judge? (v. 1)
- (T or F) The men did not believe Nephi was a prophet. (v. 2)
- Once they saw the chief judge, what did they physically do? (v. 5)

6 Now, immediately when the judge had been murdered—he being stabbed by his brother by a garb of secrecy, and he fled, and the servants ran and told the people, raising the cry of murder among them;

7 And behold the people did gather themselves together unto the place of the judgment-seat—and behold, to their astonishment they saw those five men who had fallen to the earth.

8 And now behold, the people knew nothing concerning the multitude who had gathered together at the garden of Nephi; therefore they said among themselves: These men are they who have murdered the judge, and God has smitten them that they could not flee from us.

9 And it came to pass that they laid hold on them, and bound them and cast them into prison. And there was a proclamation sent abroad that the judge was slain, and that the murderers had been taken and were cast into prison.

10 And it came to pass that on the morrow the people did assemble themselves together to mourn and to fast, at the burial of the great chief judge who had been slain.

11 And thus also those judges who were at the garden of Nephi, and heard his words, were also gathered together at the burial.

12 And it came to pass that they inquired among the people, saying: Where are the five who were sent to inquire concerning the chief judge whether he was dead? And they answered and said: Concerning this five whom ye say ye have sent, we know not; but there are five who are the murderers, whom we have cast into prison.

13 And it came to pass that the judges desired that they should be brought; and they were brought, and behold they were the five who were sent; and behold the judges inquired of them to know concerning the matter, and they told them all that they had done, saying:

14 We ran and came to the place of the judgment-seat, and when we saw all things even as Nephi had testified, we were astonished insomuch that we fell to the earth; and when we were recovered from our astonishment, behold they cast us into prison.

15 Now, as for the murder of this man, we know not who has done it; and only this much we know, we ran and came according as ye desired, and behold he was dead, according to the words of Nephi.

16 And now it came to pass that the judges did expound the matter unto the people, and did cry out against Nephi, saying: Behold, we know that this Nephi must have agreed with some one to slay the judge, and then he might declare it unto us, that he might convert us unto his faith, that he might raise himself to be a great man, chosen of God, and a prophet.

17 And now behold, we will detect this man, and he shall confess his fault and make known unto us the true murderer of this judge.

18 And it came to pass that the five were liberated on the day of the burial. Nevertheless, they did rebuke the judges in the words which they had spoken against Nephi, and did contend with them one by one, insomuch that they did confound them.

Notes

HELAMAN 9

❓ Analyze:
- *What did the servants of the chief judge do? (v. 6)*
- *How many days passed before the burial of the chief judge? (v. 10)*
- *How many individuals did the people think murdered the chief judge? (v. 12)*
- *What did the judges say was the reason that Nephi knew about the chief judge's death? (v. 16)*
- *Who confounded the judges? (v. 18)*

19 Nevertheless, they caused that Nephi should be taken and bound and brought before the multitude, and they began to question him in divers ways that they might cross him, that they might accuse him to death—

20 Saying unto him: Thou art confederate; who is this man that hath done this murder? Now tell us, and acknowledge thy fault; saying, Behold here is money; and also we will grant unto thee thy life if thou wilt tell us, and acknowledge the agreement which thou hast made with him.

21 But Nephi said unto them: O ye fools, ye uncircumcised of heart, ye blind, and ye stiffnecked people, do ye know how long the Lord your God will suffer you that ye shall go on in this your way of sin?

22 O ye ought to begin to howl and mourn, because of the great destruction which at this time doth await you, except ye shall repent.

23 Behold ye say that I have agreed with a man that he should murder Seezoram, our chief judge. But behold, I say unto you, that this is because I have testified unto you that ye might know concerning this thing; yea, even for a witness unto you, that I did know of the wickedness and abominations which are among you.

24 And because I have done this, ye say that I have agreed with a man that he should do this thing; yea, because I showed unto you this sign ye are angry with me, and seek to destroy my life.

25 And now behold, I will show unto you another sign, and see if ye will in this thing seek to destroy me.

26 Behold I say unto you: Go to the house of Seantum, who is the brother of Seezoram, and say unto him—

27 Has Nephi, the pretended prophet, who doth prophesy so much evil concerning this people, agreed with thee, in the which ye have murdered Seezoram, who is your brother?

28 And behold, he shall say unto you, Nay.

29 And ye shall say unto him: Have ye murdered your brother?

30 And he shall stand with fear, and wist not what to say. And behold, he shall deny unto you; and he shall make as if he were astonished; nevertheless, he shall declare unto you that he is innocent.

31 But behold, ye shall examine him, and ye shall find blood upon the skirts of his cloak.

32 And when ye have seen this, ye shall say: From whence cometh this blood? Do we not know that it is the blood of your brother?

33 And then shall he tremble, and shall look pale, even as if death had come upon him.

34 And then shall ye say: Because of this fear and this paleness which has come upon your face, behold, we know that thou art guilty.

35 And then shall greater fear come upon him; and then shall he confess unto you, and deny no more that he has done this murder.

36 And then shall he say unto you, that I, Nephi, know nothing concerning the matter save it were given unto me by the power of God. And then shall ye know that I am an honest man, and that I am sent unto you from God.

37 And it came to pass that they went and did, even according as Nephi had said unto them. And behold, the words which he had said were true; for according to the words he did deny; and also according to the words he did confess.

38 And he was brought to prove that he himself

Notes

HELAMAN 10

was the very murderer, insomuch that the five were set at liberty, and also was Nephi.

39 And there were some of the Nephites who believed on the words of Nephi; and there were some also, who believed because of the testimony of the five, for they had been converted while they were in prison.

40 And now there were some among the people, who said that Nephi was a prophet.

41 And there were others who said: Behold, he is a god, for except he was a god he could not know of all things. For behold, he has told us the thoughts of our hearts, and also has told us things; and even he has brought unto our knowledge the true murderer of our chief judge.

Analyze:
- What two things did they offer Nephi if he would confess? (v. 20)
- What are some of the accusations Nephi makes against the judges? (v. 21)
- Why did Nephi give them another sign? (v. 25)
- (T or F) Seezoram accused Nephi of being involved with the murder. (vv. 27–28, 36)
- Where did they find blood on Seezoram?
- What did they have to do to get Seezoram to finally confess? (vv. 34–35)
- Why did some say Nephi was a god? (v. 41)

> **Teaching Tips from Prophets' Lips** "You teachers have a great mission. As teachers you stand upon the highest peak in education, for what teaching can compare in priceless value and in far-reaching effect with that which deals with man as he was in the eternity of yesterday, as he is in the mortality of today, and as he will be in the forever of tomorrow" (J. Reuben Clark, *The Charted Course of the Church in Education*, rev. ed. [1994], 9).

Index Topics: prophets

HELAMAN 10

Nephi Is Given the Sealing Power
About 21–20 BC

1–11, As Nephi returns home, the Lord speaks to him and endows him with the sealing power; 12–19, He returns to teaching but is rejected, and the people begin to fight among themselves.

1 And it came to pass that there arose a division among the people, insomuch that they divided hither and thither and went their ways, leaving Nephi alone, as he was standing in the midst of them.

2 And it came to pass that Nephi went his way towards his own house, pondering upon the things which the Lord had shown unto him.

3 And it came to pass as he was thus pondering—being much cast down because of the wickedness of the people of the Nephites, their secret works of darkness, and their murderings, and their plunderings, and all manner of iniquities—and it came to pass as he was thus pondering in his heart, behold, a voice came unto him saying:

vv. 1–3 Without charity we cannot be effective missionaries.

⚡ Ask class members to imagine they are missionaries and have worked hard to share the gospel with the people in an area, but they have received nothing but rejection and persecution. Give class members a minute or two to think of one word to describe how they might feel, and allow everyone a chance to share their one word. Have a scribe write the words on the board.

🔍 Have each class member come up with another word to describe how they think Alma feels as you read verses 1–3. Have the scribe also write these on the board.

Analyze: *What do your findings teach about effective missionaries?*

Apply: *How can a missionary develop this love*

Notes

for the people? How can we develop this trait now?

- Have class members note a cross-reference, Moroni 7:48, in their scriptures. Invite them to turn to this verse, looking for another way to develop this love and encourage them to develop it in their own lives.

4 Blessed art thou, Nephi, for those things which thou hast done; for I have beheld how thou hast with unwearyingness declared the word, which I have given unto thee, unto this people. And thou hast not feared them, and hast not sought thine own life, but hast sought my will, and to keep my commandments.

5 And now, because thou hast done this with such unwearyingness, behold, I will bless thee forever; and I will make thee mighty in word and in deed, in faith and in works; yea, even that all things shall be done unto thee according to thy word, for thou shalt not ask that which is contrary to my will.

6 Behold, thou art Nephi, and I am God. Behold, I declare it unto thee in the presence of mine angels, that ye shall have power over this people, and shall smite the earth with famine, and with pestilence, and destruction, according to the wickedness of this people.

7 Behold, I give unto you power, that whatsoever ye shall seal on earth shall be sealed in heaven; and whatsoever ye shall loose on earth shall be loosed in heaven; and thus shall ye have power among this people.

8 And thus, if ye shall say unto this temple it shall be rent in twain, it shall be done.

9 And if ye shall say unto this mountain, Be thou cast down and become smooth, it shall be done.

10 And behold, if ye shall say that God shall smite this people, it shall come to pass.

11 And now behold, I command you, that ye shall go and declare unto this people, that thus saith the Lord God, who is the Almighty: Except ye repent ye shall be smitten, even unto destruction.

vv. 4–11 God gives us spiritual gifts as we prove faithful and dependable.

- *What are some of the powerful spiritual gifts God can give to a person?*
- *Look for what gift Nephi is given in verses 6–10.*
- Analyze:
  - *What makes this gift particularly powerful?*
  - *What phrase do we use to describe the power given to Nephi today? (See chapter heading)*
  - *What was the purpose of "the sealing power" in verses 6–10? How does that relate to how it is used in the Church today?*
- *Look for what kind of a person God would entrust with this power in verses 4–6.* Have a scribe list attributes the class comes up with.
- Have your class name other spiritual gifts. Explain that as they prove themselves faithful, God will entrust them with more spiritual gifts, as He did with Nephi.

12 And behold, now it came to pass that when the Lord had spoken these words unto Nephi, he did stop and did not go unto his own house, but did return unto the multitudes who were scattered about upon the face of the land, and began to declare unto them the word of the Lord which had been spoken unto him, concerning their destruction if they did not repent.

13 Now behold, notwithstanding that great miracle which Nephi had done in telling them concerning the death of the chief judge, they did harden their hearts and did not hearken unto the words of the Lord.

14 Therefore Nephi did declare unto them the word of the Lord, saying: Except ye repent, thus saith the Lord, ye shall be smitten even unto destruction.

15 And it came to pass that when Nephi had

Notes

declared unto them the word, behold, they did still harden their hearts and would not hearken unto his words; therefore they did revile against him, and did seek to lay their hands upon him that they might cast him into prison.

16 But behold, the power of God was with him, and they could not take him to cast him into prison, for he was taken by the Spirit and conveyed away out of the midst of them.

17 And it came to pass that thus he did go forth in the Spirit, from multitude to multitude, declaring the word of God, even until he had declared it unto them all, or sent it forth among all the people.

18 And it came to pass that they would not hearken unto his words; and there began to be contentions, insomuch that they were divided against themselves and began to slay one another with the sword.

19 And thus ended the seventy and first year of the reign of the judges over the people of Nephi.

vv. 16–19 Often afflictions are required to lead people to repentance.

- 🔍 *In verses 16–17, determine which stage of the pride cycle the Nephites are experiencing. Which stage seems apparent in verse 18?*

- ♥ Remind class members that often afflictions lead people to repentance. Ask, *What should the Nephites have done in verse 16? How can we do the same?*

Index Topics: repentance, charity, spiritual gifts, sealing power, temples

HELAMAN 11

A Temporary Period of Peace
About 20–6 BC

1–6, Because of the numerous wars and wickedness, Nephi asks the Lord to send a famine in the land; 7–17, The people acknowledge their wrongs and ask Nephi to stop the famine; he prays to God to send rain; 18–23, The people enjoy a period of temporary peace; 24–38, Gadianton robbers return to power and the people forget the Lord their God.

Overarching Principle: Dependence on God can fade quickly when prayers are answered.

- ⚡ Explain that Helaman 11 depicts how quickly people forget the Lord, and why this is so. Discuss with the class times when people typically turn to the Lord for help and times when people may not feel the need to call upon God.

- 💬 Share the following quote from President Henry B. Eyring that he stated one month after the attack in New York on September 11, 2001: "You have probably noticed, as I have in recent days, that prayers have not only become more numerous but more heartfelt. . . . The great increase in heartfelt prayer, and the public acceptance of it, has been remarkable to me and to others. More than once in recent days someone has said to me with great intensity and with a sound of worry in the voice, 'I hope that the change lasts.' That worry is justified. Our own personal experience and God's record of His dealing with His children teaches us that. Dependence on God can fade quickly when prayers are answered. And when the trouble lessens, so do the prayers. The Book of Mormon repeats that sad story over and over again" ("Prayer," *Ensign*, Nov. 2001, 17).

- ❓ Analyze: *What is President Henry B. Eyring's point?*

- 🔍 Invite class members to look for how Helaman 11 proves what President Henry B. Eyring is suggesting.

Note: The lesson ideas in this chapter will assist you in helping the class members find what the people of Nephi did that caused them to fall away

Notes

from God. Helaman 12 teaches why people fall away from God so easily and quickly. You may want to consider teaching these two chapters together.

1 And now it came to pass in the seventy and second year of the reign of the judges that the contentions did increase, insomuch that there were wars throughout all the land among all the people of Nephi.

2 And it was this secret band of robbers who did carry on this work of destruction and wickedness. And this war did last all that year; and in the seventy and third year it did also last.

3 And it came to pass that in this year Nephi did cry unto the Lord, saying:

4 O Lord, do not suffer that this people shall be destroyed by the sword; but O Lord, rather let there be a famine in the land, to stir them up in remembrance of the Lord their God, and perhaps they will repent and turn unto thee.

vv. 1–4 The Lord sends a famine to stir the people up in remembrance.

- Read verses 1–4 with the class to set the context for what is going to happen to the people of Nephi.

- Analyze: *Why would Nephi desire a famine rather than a sword or other calamity in order to help stir people up to remembrance?*

5 And so it was done, according to the words of Nephi. And there was a great famine upon the land, among all the people of Nephi. And thus in the seventy and fourth year the famine did continue, and the work of destruction did cease by the sword but became sore by famine.

6 And this work of destruction did also continue in the seventy and fifth year. For the earth was smitten that it was dry, and did not yield forth grain in the season of grain; and the whole earth was smitten, even among the Lamanites as well as among the Nephites, so that they were smitten that they did perish by thousands in the more wicked parts of the land.

7 And it came to pass that the people saw that they were about to perish by famine, and they began to remember the Lord their God; and they began to remember the words of Nephi.

8 And the people began to plead with their chief judges and their leaders, that they would say unto Nephi: Behold, we know that thou art a man of God, and therefore cry unto the Lord our God that he turn away from us this famine, lest all the words which thou hast spoken concerning our destruction be fulfilled.

9 And it came to pass that the judges did say unto Nephi, according to the words which had been desired. And it came to pass that when Nephi saw that the people had repented and did humble themselves in sackcloth, he cried again unto the Lord, saying:

10 O Lord, behold this people repenteth; and they have swept away the band of Gadianton from amongst them insomuch that they have become extinct, and they have concealed their secret plans in the earth.

11 Now, O Lord, because of this their humility wilt thou turn away thine anger, and let thine anger be appeased in the destruction of those wicked men whom thou hast already destroyed.

12 O Lord, wilt thou turn away thine anger, yea, thy fierce anger, and cause that this famine may cease in this land.

13 O Lord, wilt thou hearken unto me, and cause that it may be done according to my words, and send forth rain upon the face of the earth, that she may bring forth her fruit, and her grain in the season of grain.

14 O Lord, thou didst hearken unto my words when I said, Let there be a famine, that the pestilence of the sword might cease; and I know that thou wilt, even at this time, hearken unto my words, for thou saidst that: If this people repent I will spare them.

Notes

HELAMAN 11

15 Yea, O Lord, and thou seest that they have repented, because of the famine and the pestilence and destruction which has come unto them.

16 And now, O Lord, wilt thou turn away thine anger, and try again if they will serve thee? And if so, O Lord, thou canst bless them according to thy words which thou hast said.

17 And it came to pass that in the seventy and sixth year the Lord did turn away his anger from the people, and caused that rain should fall upon the earth, insomuch that it did bring forth her fruit in the season of her fruit. And it came to pass that it did bring forth her grain in the season of her grain.

vv. 5–17 The Lord sends rain in response to the people's repentance and Nephi's pleading.

- What do the people of Nephi finally ask for in verses 7–9? What does Nephi pray for in verses 10–16?
- Analyze:
  - What phrases impress you from Nephi's prayer?
  - What does that teach about a prophet's desire for the people he serves?
  - What do we learn from Helaman about the role of a prophet of God? Consider how he both requested the famine and also requested the abatement of the famine.

18 And behold, the people did rejoice and glorify God, and the whole face of the land was filled with rejoicing; and they did no more seek to destroy Nephi, but they did esteem him as a great prophet, and a man of God, having great power and authority given unto him from God.

19 And behold, Lehi, his brother, was not a whit behind him as to things pertaining to righteousness.

20 And thus it did come to pass that the people of Nephi began to prosper again in the land, and began to build up their waste places, and began to multiply and spread, even until they did cover the whole face of the land, both on the northward and on the southward, from the sea west to the sea east.

21 And it came to pass that the seventy and sixth year did end in peace. And the seventy and seventh year began in peace; and the church did spread throughout the face of all the land; and the more part of the people, both the Nephites and the Lamanites, did belong to the church; and they did have exceedingly great peace in the land; and thus ended the seventy and seventh year.

22 And also they had peace in the seventy and eighth year, save it were a few contentions concerning the points of doctrine which had been laid down by the prophets.

vv. 18–22 The Nephites enjoy a period of temporary peace. The Lord is very quick to bless us despite our mistakes.

- Invite class members to read verses 18–22 and look for what the Nephites experience after their repentance.
- Note with the class how quickly God forgives and blesses His people.
- The rest of the chapter will relate what the Nephites do after they have been forgiven and blessed by God.

23 And in the seventy and ninth year there began to be much strife. But it came to pass that Nephi and Lehi, and many of their brethren who knew concerning the true points of doctrine, having many revelations daily, therefore they did preach unto the people, insomuch that they did put an end to their strife in that same year.

24 And it came to pass that in the eightieth year of the reign of the judges over the people of Nephi, there were a certain number of the dissenters from the people of Nephi, who had some years

Notes

before gone over unto the Lamanites, and taken upon themselves the name of Lamanites, and also a certain number who were real descendants of the Lamanites, being stirred up to anger by them, or by those dissenters, therefore they commenced a war with their brethren.

25 And they did commit murder and plunder; and then they would retreat back into the mountains, and into the wilderness and secret places, hiding themselves that they could not be discovered, receiving daily an addition to their numbers, inasmuch as there were dissenters that went forth unto them.

26 And thus in time, yea, even in the space of not many years, they became an exceedingly great band of robbers; and they did search out all the secret plans of Gadianton; and thus they became robbers of Gadianton.

27 Now behold, these robbers did make great havoc, yea, even great destruction among the people of Nephi, and also among the people of the Lamanites.

28 And it came to pass that it was expedient that there should be a stop put to this work of destruction; therefore they sent an army of strong men into the wilderness and upon the mountains to search out this band of robbers, and to destroy them.

29 But behold, it came to pass that in that same year they were driven back even into their own lands. And thus ended the eightieth year of the reign of the judges over the people of Nephi.

30 And it came to pass in the commencement of the eighty and first year they did go forth again against this band of robbers, and did destroy many; and they were also visited with much destruction.

31 And they were again obliged to return out of the wilderness and out of the mountains unto their own lands, because of the exceeding greatness of the numbers of those robbers who infested the mountains and the wilderness.

32 And it came to pass that thus ended this year. And the robbers did still increase and wax strong, insomuch that they did defy the whole armies of the Nephites, and also of the Lamanites; and they did cause great fear to come unto the people upon all the face of the land.

33 Yea, for they did visit many parts of the land, and did do great destruction unto them; yea, did kill many, and did carry away others captive into the wilderness, yea, and more especially their women and their children.

34 Now this great evil, which came unto the people because of their iniquity, did stir them up again in remembrance of the Lord their God.

35 And thus ended the eighty and first year of the reign of the judges.

36 And in the eighty and second year they began again to forget the Lord their God. And in the eighty and third year they began to wax strong in iniquity. And in the eighty and fourth year they did not mend their ways.

37 And it came to pass in the eighty and fifth year they did wax stronger and stronger in their pride, and in their wickedness; and thus they were ripening again for destruction.

38 And thus ended the eighty and fifth year.

- Invite the class to read verses 23–38 looking for the decline of the Nephites. Consider making a list on the board of their findings.

- Analyze: Refer to President Henry B. Eyring's quote at the beginning of this chapter. *How does this chapter prove what President Henry B. Eyring's states?*

- Apply: *What can we do to make sure we don't make the same mistake?*

- Encourage class members to consider how they can individually apply this lesson by striving to remember what the Lord has done for them.

Notes

> **Teaching Tips from Prophets' Lips** "We all understand that the success of the gospel message depends upon its being taught and then understood and then lived in such a way that its promise of happiness and salvation can be realized" (Jeffrey R. Holland, "Teaching and Learning in the Church," *Ensign*, June 2007, 88–105).

HELAMAN 12

The Unsteadiness of the Children of Men

About 6 BC

1–26, Moroni expounds on the unsteady nature of fallen man when compared to the Lord.

1 And thus we can behold how false, and also the unsteadiness of the hearts of the children of men; yea, we can see that the Lord in his great infinite goodness doth bless and prosper those who put their trust in him.

2 Yea, and we may see at the very time when he doth prosper his people, yea, in the increase of their fields, their flocks and their herds, and in gold, and in silver, and in all manner of precious things of every kind and art; sparing their lives, and delivering them out of the hands of their enemies; softening the hearts of their enemies that they should not declare wars against them; yea, and in fine, doing all things for the welfare and happiness of his people; yea, then is the time that they do harden their hearts, and do forget the Lord their God, and do trample under their feet the Holy One—yea, and this because of their ease, and their exceedingly great prosperity.

3 And thus we see that except the Lord doth chasten his people with many afflictions, yea, except he doth visit them with death and with terror, and with famine and with all manner of pestilence, they will not remember him.

4 O how foolish, and how vain, and how evil, and devilish, and how quick to do iniquity, and how slow to do good, are the children of men; yea, how quick to hearken unto the words of the evil one, and to set their hearts upon the vain things of the world!

5 Yea, how quick to be lifted up in pride; yea, how quick to boast, and do all manner of that which is iniquity; and how slow are they to remember the Lord their God, and to give ear unto his counsels, yea, how slow to walk in wisdom's paths!

6 Behold, they do not desire that the Lord their God, who hath created them, should rule and reign over them; notwithstanding his great goodness and his mercy towards them, they do set at naught his counsels, and they will not that he should be their guide.

vv. 1–6 Men are unstable and foolish, but the Lord is merciful and good.

- *What do you think Mormon's opinion of his people was after abridging the Nephite records? What might have been difficult for him to read and write about?* Explain that Helaman 12 contains a small sermon by the prophet Mormon as he reviewed Nephite history.

- Divide the class into six groups and assign each group one verse from Helaman 12:1–6. Have class members rewrite each verse in their own words, emphasizing the lessons that Mormon teaches in this chapter. Discuss each verse.

- Apply: *How do Mormon's teachings apply to us today?*

7 O how great is the nothingness of the children of men; yea, even they are less than the dust of the earth.

8 For behold, the dust of the earth moveth hither and thither, to the dividing asunder, at the command of our great and everlasting God.

Notes

9 Yea, behold at his voice do the hills and the mountains tremble and quake.

10 And by the power of his voice they are broken up, and become smooth, yea, even like unto a valley.

11 Yea, by the power of his voice doth the whole earth shake;

12 Yea, by the power of his voice, do the foundations rock, even to the very center.

13 Yea, and if he say unto the earth—Move—it is moved.

14 Yea, if he say unto the earth—Thou shalt go back, that it lengthen out the day for many hours—it is done;

15 And thus, according to his word the earth goeth back, and it appeareth unto man that the sun standeth still; yea, and behold, this is so; for surely it is the earth that moveth and not the sun.

> Moroni is probably referencing—and clarifying—the Old Testament story found in Joshua 10:12–14. These verses show a sophisticated understanding of astronomy among the Nephites.

16 And behold, also, if he say unto the waters of the great deep—Be thou dried up—it is done.

17 Behold, if he say unto this mountain—Be thou raised up, and come over and fall upon that city, that it be buried up—behold it is done.

18 And behold, if a man hide up a treasure in the earth, and the Lord shall say—Let it be accursed, because of the iniquity of him who hath hid it up—behold, it shall be accursed.

19 And if the Lord shall say—Be thou accursed, that no man shall find thee from this time henceforth and forever—behold, no man getteth it henceforth and forever.

20 And behold, if the Lord shall say unto a man—Because of thine iniquities, thou shalt be accursed forever—it shall be done.

21 And if the Lord shall say—Because of thine iniquities thou shalt be cut off from my presence—he will cause that it shall be so.

22 And wo unto him to whom he shall say this, for it shall be unto him that will do iniquity, and he cannot be saved; therefore, for this cause, that men might be saved, hath repentance been declared.

23 Therefore, blessed are they who will repent and hearken unto the voice of the Lord their God; for these are they that shall be saved.

24 And may God grant, in his great fulness, that men might be brought unto repentance and good works, that they might be restored unto grace for grace, according to their works.

25 And I would that all men might be saved. But we read that in the great and last day there are some who shall be cast out, yea, who shall be cast off from the presence of the Lord;

26 Yea, who shall be consigned to a state of endless misery, fulfilling the words which say: They that have done good shall have everlasting life; and they that have done evil shall have everlasting damnation. And thus it is. Amen.

vv. 16–26 Man is nothing and God is great. Men can be brought back to God through grace and repentance.

Analyze: Invite class members to study verses 16–26 and ask,

- What do you think Mormon's opinion is of mankind?
- What is his opinion of God?
- How can we ever be reconciled with God?
- What do verses 23–26 teach about that reconciliation?

Notes

HELAMAN 13

Samuel the Lamanite Begins to Preach

About 6 BC

1–7, Samuel the Lamanite comes to Zarahemla to preach to the wicked Nephites; 8–16, Samuel prophecies destruction to those who will not repent; 17–39, The riches of the people will become cursed because they have rejected true prophets and lifted up false prophets.

1 And now it came to pass in the eighty and sixth year, the Nephites did still remain in wickedness, yea, in great wickedness, while the Lamanites did observe strictly to keep the commandments of God, according to the law of Moses.

2 And it came to pass that in this year there was one Samuel, a Lamanite, came into the land of Zarahemla, and began to preach unto the people. And it came to pass that he did preach, many days, repentance unto the people, and they did cast him out, and he was about to return to his own land.

3 But behold, the voice of the Lord came unto him, that he should return again, and prophesy unto the people whatsoever things should come into his heart.

4 And it came to pass that they would not suffer that he should enter into the city; therefore he went and got upon the wall thereof, and stretched forth his hand and cried with a loud voice, and prophesied unto the people whatsoever things the Lord put into his heart.

5 And he said unto them: Behold, I, Samuel, a Lamanite, do speak the words of the Lord which he doth put into my heart; and behold he hath put it into my heart to say unto this people that the sword of justice hangeth over this people; and four hundred years pass not away save the sword of justice falleth upon this people.

6 Yea, heavy destruction awaiteth this people, and it surely cometh unto this people, and nothing can save this people save it be repentance and faith on the Lord Jesus Christ, who surely shall come into the world, and shall suffer many things and shall be slain for his people.

vv. 1–6 Samuel obeyed the Lord's call to preach to the Nephites.

🔎 Invite class members to read verses 1–6, then ask one class member to summarize the main points.

❓ Analyze:

- *What difficulty must there have been for Samuel to preach to the Nephites?*
- *Why might Samuel have been fearful of going to the Nephites?*
- *What actions show that Samuel was obedient and faithful to the Lord rather than to man?*
- *What does the fact that a Lamanite is now preaching to Nephites teach about how the Lord feels about His children from all nations?*

7 And behold, an angel of the Lord hath declared it unto me, and he did bring glad tidings to my soul. And behold, I was sent unto you to declare it unto you also, that ye might have glad tidings; but behold ye would not receive me.

8 Therefore, thus saith the Lord: Because of the hardness of the hearts of the people of the Nephites, except they repent I will take away my word from them, and I will withdraw my Spirit from them, and I will suffer them no longer, and I will turn the hearts of their brethren against them.

9 And four hundred years shall not pass away before I will cause that they shall be smitten; yea, I will visit them with the sword and with famine and with pestilence.

10 Yea, I will visit them in my fierce anger, and there shall be those of the fourth generation who shall live, of your enemies, to behold your utter destruction; and this shall surely come except ye

Notes

repent, saith the Lord; and those of the fourth generation shall visit your destruction.

11 But if ye will repent and return unto the Lord your God I will turn away mine anger, saith the Lord; yea, thus saith the Lord, blessed are they who will repent and turn unto me, but wo unto him that repenteth not.

12 Yea, wo unto this great city of Zarahemla; for behold, it is because of those who are righteous that it is saved; yea, wo unto this great city, for I perceive, saith the Lord, that there are many, yea, even the more part of this great city, that will harden their hearts against me, saith the Lord.

13 But blessed are they who will repent, for them will I spare. But behold, if it were not for the righteous who are in this great city, behold, I would cause that fire should come down out of heaven and destroy it.

14 But behold, it is for the righteous' sake that it is spared. But behold, the time cometh, saith the Lord, that when ye shall cast out the righteous from among you, then shall ye be ripe for destruction; yea, wo be unto this great city, because of the wickedness and abominations which are in her.

vv. 7–14 The Lord honors His righteous saints.

- Analyze:
  - Has the Lord ever destroyed a city?
  - Why would He do that?
  - Why do you think more cities aren't destroyed?

- In verses 7–10, what will the Lord do, according to Samuel, if the people do not repent?

- According to verses 12–14, why hasn't the Lord destroyed the people yet?

- If time permits, consider drawing a parallel between Sodom and Gomorrah and Zarahemla. Genesis 18:23–33 records Abraham's discussion about the destruction of the city and how many righteous would be required for the Lord to spare the inhabitants.

- Apply: *How might these verses change your perspective about living in a wicked world? What can the righteous do to help prepare a people to be blessed by the Lord?*

- Challenge class members to play a part in the world around them and preserve their communities through personal righteousness.

15 Yea, and wo be unto the city of Gideon, for the wickedness and abominations which are in her.

16 Yea, and wo be unto all the cities which are in the land round about, which are possessed by the Nephites, because of the wickedness and abominations which are in them.

17 And behold, a curse shall come upon the land, saith the Lord of Hosts, because of the people's sake who are upon the land, yea, because of their wickedness and their abominations.

18 And it shall come to pass, saith the Lord of Hosts, yea, our great and true God, that whoso shall hide up treasures in the earth shall find them again no more, because of the great curse of the land, save he be a righteous man and shall hide it up unto the Lord.

19 For I will, saith the Lord, that they shall hide up their treasures unto me; and cursed be they who hide not up their treasures unto me; for none hideth up their treasures unto me save it be the righteous; and he that hideth not up his treasures unto me, cursed is he, and also the treasure, and none shall redeem it because of the curse of the land.

20 And the day shall come that they shall hide up their treasures, because they have set their hearts upon riches; and because they have set their hearts upon their riches, and will hide up their treasures when they shall flee before their enemies; because they will not hide them up unto me, cursed be they and also their treasures; and in that day shall they be smitten, saith the Lord.

21 Behold ye, the people of this great city, and hearken unto my words; yea, hearken unto the words which the Lord saith; for behold, he saith

Notes

HELAMAN 13

that ye are cursed because of your riches, and also are your riches cursed because ye have set your hearts upon them, and have not hearkened unto the words of him who gave them unto you.

22 Ye do not remember the Lord your God in the things with which he hath blessed you, but ye do always remember your riches, not to thank the Lord your God for them; yea, your hearts are not drawn out unto the Lord, but they do swell with great pride, unto boasting, and unto great swelling, envyings, strifes, malice, persecutions, and murders, and all manner of iniquities.

23 For this cause hath the Lord God caused that a curse should come upon the land, and also upon your riches, and this because of your iniquities.

24 Yea, wo unto this people, because of this time which has arrived, that ye do cast out the prophets, and do mock them, and cast stones at them, and do slay them, and do all manner of iniquity unto them, even as they did of old time.

25 And now when ye talk, ye say: If our days had been in the days of our fathers of old, we would not have slain the prophets; we would not have stoned them, and cast them out.

26 Behold ye are worse than they; for as the Lord liveth, if a prophet come among you and declareth unto you the word of the Lord, which testifieth of your sins and iniquities, ye are angry with him, and cast him out and seek all manner of ways to destroy him; yea, you will say that he is a false prophet, and that he is a sinner, and of the devil, because he testifieth that your deeds are evil.

27 But behold, if a man shall come among you and shall say: Do this, and there is no iniquity; do that and ye shall not suffer; yea, he will say: Walk after the pride of your own hearts; yea, walk after the pride of your eyes, and do whatsoever your heart desireth—and if a man shall come among you and say this, ye will receive him, and say that he is a prophet.

28 Yea, ye will lift him up, and ye will give unto him of your substance; ye will give unto him of your gold, and of your silver, and ye will clothe him with costly apparel; and because he speaketh flattering words unto you, and he saith that all is well, then ye will not find fault with him.

29 O ye wicked and ye perverse generation; ye hardened and ye stiffnecked people, how long will ye suppose that the Lord will suffer you? Yea, how long will ye suffer yourselves to be led by foolish and blind guides? Yea, how long will ye choose darkness rather than light?

vv. 24–29 We will be judged according to how we treat the Lord's prophets.

⚡ Write the names Noah, Moses, Peter, and Joseph Smith on the board. Call on a few class members and ask questions like, *Do you think you would have boarded the Ark when Noah asked?* or *Would you have followed Moses in the wilderness?*

🔍 Read Helaman 13:24–29 and find a sin that the Nephites have committed.

❓ The Nephites claimed to be willing to follow prophets of old. Why do you think it was easier for the Nephites to accept ancient prophets than to accept living prophets? Which would have been more beneficial to the Nephites?

💬 President Ezra Taft Benson taught, "The living prophet is more important to us than a dead prophet. God's revelation to Adam did not instruct Noah how to build the Ark. Noah needed his own revelation. Therefore the most important prophet so far as you and I are concerned is the one living in our day and age to whom the Lord is currently revealing His will for us. Therefore the most important reading we can do is any of the words of the prophet contained each month in our Church magazines. Our instructions about what we should do for each six months are found in the general conference addresses which are printed in the Church magazine. Beware of those who would set up the dead prophets against the living prophets, for the living prophets always take precedence" (Ezra Taft

Notes

Benson, "Fourteen Fundamentals in Following the Prophet", *Ensign*, June 1981).

❓ Apply:
- *In what ways might we fall into the same sin as the Nephites today?*
- *Since we generally don't threaten prophets physically today, in what ways could we reject the living prophet?*
- *If we don't outright reject the living prophet, are there ways we do the same thing as the Nephites in verse 28?*

30 Yea, behold, the anger of the Lord is already kindled against you; behold, he hath cursed the land because of your iniquity.

31 And behold, the time cometh that he curseth your riches, that they become slippery, that ye cannot hold them; and in the days of your poverty ye cannot retain them.

32 And in the days of your poverty ye shall cry unto the Lord; and in vain shall ye cry, for your desolation is already come upon you, and your destruction is made sure; and then shall ye weep and howl in that day, saith the Lord of Hosts. And then shall ye lament, and say:

33 O that I had repented, and had not killed the prophets, and stoned them, and cast them out. Yea, in that day ye shall say: O that we had remembered the Lord our God in the day that he gave us our riches, and then they would not have become slippery that we should lose them; for behold, our riches are gone from us.

34 Behold, we lay a tool here and on the morrow it is gone; and behold, our swords are taken from us in the day we have sought them for battle.

35 Yea, we have hid up our treasures and they have slipped away from us, because of the curse of the land.

36 O that we had repented in the day that the word of the Lord came unto us; for behold the land is cursed, and all things are become slippery, and we cannot hold them.

37 Behold, we are surrounded by demons, yea, we are encircled about by the angels of him who hath sought to destroy our souls. Behold, our iniquities are great. O Lord, canst thou not turn away thine anger from us? And this shall be your language in those days.

38 But behold, your days of probation are past; ye have procrastinated the day of your salvation until it is everlastingly too late, and your destruction is made sure; yea, for ye have sought all the days of your lives for that which ye could not obtain; and ye have sought for happiness in doing iniquity, which thing is contrary to the nature of that righteousness which is in our great and Eternal Head.

39 O ye people of the land, that ye would hear my words! And I pray that the anger of the Lord be turned away from you, and that ye would repent and be saved.

vv. 38–39 A firm warning from Samuel.

✏ Invite class members to note Alma 34:32–34 and Alma 41:10 next to verse 38. Read these verses and ask, *How have you seen these teachings thus far in the Book of Mormon? How have you seen these teachings in our day?*

Teaching Tips from Prophets' Lips "A gospel teacher will never be satisfied with just delivering a message or preaching a sermon. A superior gospel teacher wants to assist in the Lord's work to bring eternal life to His children" (Dallin H. Oaks, "Gospel Teaching," *Ensign*, Nov. 1999, 80).

HELAMAN 14

The Signs of the Savior's Birth and Death
About 6 BC

Notes

HELAMAN 14

1–8, Samuel the Lamanite prophesies of the signs of Christ birth; 9–13, Samuel pleads with the Nephites to hear and know the judgments of God and the conditions of repentance; 14–19, Christ brings to pass the resurrection of the dead and the conditions of repentance; 20–27, Signs of Christ's death are set forth; 28–30, All are given knowledge and are free to do good or evil.

1 And now it came to pass that Samuel, the Lamanite, did prophesy a great many more things which cannot be written.

2 And behold, he said unto them: Behold, I give unto you a sign; for five years more cometh, and behold, then cometh the Son of God to redeem all those who shall believe on his name.

3 And behold, this will I give unto you for a sign at the time of his coming; for behold, there shall be great lights in heaven, insomuch that in the night before he cometh there shall be no darkness, insomuch that it shall appear unto man as if it was day.

4 Therefore, there shall be one day and a night and a day, as if it were one day and there were no night; and this shall be unto you for a sign; for ye shall know of the rising of the sun and also of its setting; therefore they shall know of a surety that there shall be two days and a night; nevertheless the night shall not be darkened; and it shall be the night before he is born.

💡 Notice that the sign of the Savior's birth may be similar to a sign at the Lord's Second Coming according to Zechariah 14:6–7.

5 And behold, there shall a new star arise, such an one as ye never have beheld; and this also shall be a sign unto you.

6 And behold this is not all, there shall be many signs and wonders in heaven.

7 And it shall come to pass that ye shall all be amazed, and wonder, insomuch that ye shall fall to the earth.

8 And it shall come to pass that whosoever shall believe on the Son of God, the same shall have everlasting life.

9 And behold, thus hath the Lord commanded me, by his angel, that I should come and tell this thing unto you; yea, he hath commanded that I should prophesy these things unto you; yea, he hath said unto me: Cry unto this people, repent and prepare the way of the Lord.

10 And now, because I am a Lamanite, and have spoken unto you the words which the Lord hath commanded me, and because it was hard against you, ye are angry with me and do seek to destroy me, and have cast me out from among you.

11 And ye shall hear my words, for, for this intent have I come up upon the walls of this city, that ye might hear and know of the judgments of God which do await you because of your iniquities, and also that ye might know the conditions of repentance;

12 And also that ye might know of the coming of Jesus Christ, the Son of God, the Father of heaven and of earth, the Creator of all things from the beginning; and that ye might know of the signs of his coming, to the intent that ye might believe on his name.

13 And if ye believe on his name ye will repent of all your sins, that thereby ye may have a remission of them through his merits.

14 And behold, again, another sign I give unto you, yea, a sign of his death.

15 For behold, he surely must die that salvation may come; yea, it behooveth him and becometh expedient that he dieth, to bring to pass the resurrection of the dead, that thereby men may be brought into the presence of the Lord.

16 Yea, behold, this death bringeth to pass the resurrection, and redeemeth all mankind from the first death—that spiritual death; for all mankind, by the fall of Adam being cut off from the presence of the Lord, are considered as dead, both as to things temporal and to things spiritual.

Notes

17 But behold, the resurrection of Christ redeemeth mankind, yea, even all mankind, and bringeth them back into the presence of the Lord.

18 Yea, and it bringeth to pass the condition of repentance, that whosoever repenteth the same is not hewn down and cast into the fire; but whosoever repenteth not is hewn down and cast into the fire; and there cometh upon them again a spiritual death, yea, a second death, for they are cut off again as to things pertaining to righteousness.

19 Therefore repent ye, repent ye, lest by knowing these things and not doing them ye shall suffer yourselves to come under condemnation, and ye are brought down unto this second death.

20 But behold, as I said unto you concerning another sign, a sign of his death, behold, in that day that he shall suffer death the sun shall be darkened and refuse to give his light unto you; and also the moon and the stars; and there shall be no light upon the face of this land, even from the time that he shall suffer death, for the space of three days, to the time that he shall rise again from the dead.

21 Yea, at the time that he shall yield up the ghost there shall be thunderings and lightnings for the space of many hours, and the earth shall shake and tremble; and the rocks which are upon the face of this earth, which are both above the earth and beneath, which ye know at this time are solid, or the more part of it is one solid mass, shall be broken up;

22 Yea, they shall be rent in twain, and shall ever after be found in seams and in cracks, and in broken fragments upon the face of the whole earth, yea, both above the earth and beneath.

23 And behold, there shall be great tempests, and there shall be many mountains laid low, like unto a valley, and there shall be many places which are now called valleys which shall become mountains, whose height is great.

24 And many highways shall be broken up, and many cities shall become desolate.

25 And many graves shall be opened, and shall yield up many of their dead; and many saints shall appear unto many.

26 And behold, thus hath the angel spoken unto me; for he said unto me that there should be thunderings and lightnings for the space of many hours.

27 And he said unto me that while the thunder and the lightning lasted, and the tempest, that these things should be, and that darkness should cover the face of the whole earth for the space of three days.

28 And the angel said unto me that many shall see greater things than these, to the intent that they might believe that these signs and these wonders should come to pass upon all the face of this land, to the intent that there should be no cause for unbelief among the children of men—

29 And this to the intent that whosoever will believe might be saved, and that whosoever will not believe, a righteous judgment might come upon them; and also if they are condemned they bring upon themselves their own condemnation.

30 And now remember, remember, my brethren, that whosoever perisheth, perisheth unto himself; and whosoever doeth iniquity, doeth it unto himself; for behold, ye are free; ye are permitted to act for yourselves; for behold, God hath given unto you a knowledge and he hath made you free.

31 He hath given unto you that ye might know good from evil, and he hath given unto you that ye might choose life or death; and ye can do good and be restored unto that which is good, or have that which is good restored unto you; or ye can do evil, and have that which is evil restored unto you.

vv. 1–30 Signs are given so that we might believe and be saved.

⚡ Put the following questions on the board and invite class members to prepare to answer

Notes

one of the questions. After they have had time to ponder, invite them to share their responses.

1. Why does the Lord provide signs of His Second Coming?

2. What is the role of a prophet in preparing us for the Second Coming?

Display a picture of Christ's birth and His death on the cross. Explain to class members that we will be discussing the signs and warnings of these two events to help us prepare for Christ's Second Coming.

- Put the following scripture references on the board: vv. 6–8, 12, 27–29 and ask, *According to these scriptures, why does the Lord provide signs of His Second Coming?*

- Analyze: *What do these repeated signs teach us about the nature of God? Why?*

- According to verse 10–11, what is the role of a prophet in times when signs are being given?

- As individuals or small groups, complete the following activity: List all the doctrines that Samuel the Lamanite taught to the people of Nephi to help them prepare for Christ's coming in verses 15–19 and 30–31. Remind the class that a doctrine is truth that is eternal and unchanging. Have class members share with each other what they found and/or make a list on the board. Testify that these doctrines are the same truths that will help us prepare for the Second Coming.

- Apply: *What do we learn from His first coming that will help us prepare for His second coming?*

- Invite class members to write down what they can do to prepare and/or help others prepare for the Second Coming of Christ.

Index Topics: Second Coming, role of prophets

HELAMAN 15

Samuel Concludes His Prophecies
About 6 BC

1–3, Samuel explains that the Nephites must repent or face destruction; 4–10, As the Lamanites have repented, they have been steadfast in the faith; 11–17, Prophecies of the Lamanites in the latter times.

1 And now, my beloved brethren, behold, I declare unto you that except ye shall repent your houses shall be left unto you desolate.

2 Yea, except ye repent, your women shall have great cause to mourn in the day that they shall give suck; for ye shall attempt to flee and there shall be no place for refuge; yea, and wo unto them which are with child, for they shall be heavy and cannot flee; therefore, they shall be trodden down and shall be left to perish.

3 Yea, wo unto this people who are called the people of Nephi except they shall repent, when they shall see all these signs and wonders which shall be showed unto them; for behold, they have been a chosen people of the Lord; yea, the people of Nephi hath he loved, and also hath he chastened them; yea, in the days of their iniquities hath he chastened them because he loveth them.

4 But behold my brethren, the Lamanites hath he hated because their deeds have been evil continually, and this because of the iniquity of the tradition of their fathers. But behold, salvation hath come unto them through the preaching of the Nephites; and for this intent hath the Lord prolonged their days.

vv. 3–4 "The Lamanites hath he hated."

- Hate is not a word that is generally associated with God, yet it is used in verse 4. Note with your class that in Alma 24:14 the Lord "loveth" the Lamanites even before they repented. The Lord doesn't hate people, but He hates their unrighteous deeds as noted in Helaman 15:4.

Notes

5 And I would that ye should behold that the more part of them are in the path of their duty, and they do walk circumspectly before God, and they do observe to keep his commandments and his statutes and his judgments according to the law of Moses.

6 Yea, I say unto you, that the more part of them are doing this, and they are striving with unwearied diligence that they may bring the remainder of their brethren to the knowledge of the truth; therefore there are many who do add to their numbers daily.

7 And behold, ye do know of yourselves, for ye have witnessed it, that as many of them as are brought to the knowledge of the truth, and to know of the wicked and abominable traditions of their fathers, and are led to believe the holy scriptures, yea, the prophecies of the holy prophets, which are written, which leadeth them to faith on the Lord, and unto repentance, which faith and repentance bringeth a change of heart unto them—

8 Therefore, as many as have come to this, ye know of yourselves are firm and steadfast in the faith, and in the thing wherewith they have been made free.

9 And ye know also that they have buried their weapons of war, and they fear to take them up lest by any means they should sin; yea, ye can see that they fear to sin—for behold they will suffer themselves that they be trodden down and slain by their enemies, and will not lift their swords against them, and this because of their faith in Christ.

10 And now, because of their steadfastness when they do believe in that thing which they do believe, for because of their firmness when they are once enlightened, behold, the Lord shall bless them and prolong their days, notwithstanding their iniquity—

vv. 5–10 How can we be "firm and steadfast" in the faith?

⚡ Write the words "Firm and Steadfast" on the board and ask your class to name things that are firm and steadfast in the world. Write their answers on the board. Depending on the age of class members, you may consider defining these words first.

🔎 *Look for what is described as firm and steadfast in verse 8.*

👥 Break the class into small groups. Have each group read verses 5–10 and note as many things as they can find that made the Lamanites firm and steadfast. Then have the group members share what they found.

❤ Invite class members to be firm and steadfast by applying some of the insights that were learned as a class.

11 Yea, even if they should dwindle in unbelief the Lord shall prolong their days, until the time shall come which hath been spoken of by our fathers, and also by the prophet Zenos, and many other prophets, concerning the restoration of our brethren, the Lamanites, again to the knowledge of the truth—

12 Yea, I say unto you, that in the latter times the promises of the Lord have been extended to our brethren, the Lamanites; and notwithstanding the many afflictions which they shall have, and notwithstanding they shall be driven to and fro upon the face of the earth, and be hunted, and shall be smitten and scattered abroad, having no place for refuge, the Lord shall be merciful unto them.

13 And this is according to the prophecy, that they shall again be brought to the true knowledge, which is the knowledge of their Redeemer, and their great and true shepherd, and be numbered among his sheep.

14 Therefore I say unto you, it shall be better for them than for you except ye repent.

15 For behold, had the mighty works been shown unto them which have been shown unto you, yea, unto them who have dwindled in unbelief

Notes

because of the traditions of their fathers, ye can see of yourselves that they never would again have dwindled in unbelief.

16 Therefore, saith the Lord: I will not utterly destroy them, but I will cause that in the day of my wisdom they shall return again unto me, saith the Lord.

17 And now behold, saith the Lord, concerning the people of the Nephites: If they will not repent, and observe to do my will, I will utterly destroy them, saith the Lord, because of their unbelief notwithstanding the many mighty works which I have done among them; and as surely as the Lord liveth shall these things be, saith the Lord.

> **Teaching Tips from Prophets' Lips** "Giving students experiences with the Spirit is far more important than talking about it. And just know that each person experiences the Spirit a little differently. . . . I think it is so individual that I would be a little careful in trying to say too much specifically. I think experience with it . . . might be better than if you keep saying, 'Do you feel the Spirit?' I think that can be counterproductive" ("Elder Richard G. Scott and Elder Henry B. Eyring Discussion" [CES satellite training broadcast, Aug. 2003], 8).

HELAMAN 16

"They Could Not Hit Him"
About 6–1 BC

1–5, Samuel finishes his preaching and some believe; those who do not believe begin to cast stones and arrows at him; they are unable to hit him, causing more to believe; 6–8, Samuel jumps from the wall and flees into the wilderness; 9–25, The people's continual decline into wickedness.

1 And now, it came to pass that there were many who heard the words of Samuel, the Lamanite, which he spake upon the walls of the city. And as many as believed on his word went forth and sought for Nephi; and when they had come forth and found him they confessed unto him their sins and denied not, desiring that they might be baptized unto the Lord.

2 But as many as there were who did not believe in the words of Samuel were angry with him; and they cast stones at him upon the wall, and also many shot arrows at him as he stood upon the wall; but the Spirit of the Lord was with him, insomuch that they could not hit him with their stones neither with their arrows.

3 Now when they saw that they could not hit him, there were many more who did believe on his words, insomuch that they went away unto Nephi to be baptized.

4 For behold, Nephi was baptizing, and prophesying, and preaching, crying repentance unto the people, showing signs and wonders, working miracles among the people, that they might know that the Christ must shortly come—

5 Telling them of things which must shortly come, that they might know and remember at the time of their coming that they had been made known unto them beforehand, to the intent that they might believe; therefore as many as believed on the words of Samuel went forth unto him to be baptized, for they came repenting and confessing their sins.

6 But the more part of them did not believe in the words of Samuel; therefore when they saw that they could not hit him with their stones and their arrows, they cried unto their captains, saying: Take this fellow and bind him, for behold he hath a devil; and because of the power of the devil which is in him we cannot hit him with our stones and our arrows; therefore take him and bind him, and away with him.

7 And as they went forth to lay their hands on him, behold, he did cast himself down from the wall, and did flee out of their lands, yea, even unto his own country, and began to preach and to prophesy among his own people.

Notes

8 And behold, he was never heard of more among the Nephites; and thus were the affairs of the people.

vv. 1–8 How do we react when a prophet of God speaks? We should act in faith based on his teachings.

- ⚡ Display a picture of Samuel the Lamanite. Briefly discuss with class members how the people reacted to Samuel's teachings and prophecies.

- 🔍 Read verses 1–8 with the class and look for the two different Nephite reactions to Samuel.

- ❓ Analyze: *What do these two reactions teach about how we respond to a prophet's teachings?*

- ❓ Apply: *What are some modern-day applications of these types of reactions?*

- 💬 Elder Neal A. Maxwell stated, "Happily, even though the world worsens around us, there will be many, many fine and wonderful men and women of all races and creeds—and of no religious creeds at all—who will continue to lead decent and useful lives. . . . So let us look at ourselves. For the Church, the scriptures suggest both an accelerated sifting and accelerated spiritual and numerical growth—with all this preceding the time when the people of God will be 'armed with righteousness'—not weapons—and when the Lord's glory will be poured out upon them" ("For I Will Lead You Along," *Ensign*, May 1988, 8).

9 And thus ended the eighty and sixth year of the reign of the judges over the people of Nephi.

10 And thus ended also the eighty and seventh year of the reign of the judges, the more part of the people remaining in their pride and wickedness, and the lesser part walking more circumspectly before God.

11 And these were the conditions also, in the eighty and eighth year of the reign of the judges.

12 And there was but little alteration in the affairs of the people, save it were the people began to be more hardened in iniquity, and do more and more of that which was contrary to the commandments of God, in the eighty and ninth year of the reign of the judges.

13 But it came to pass in the ninetieth year of the reign of the judges, there were great signs given unto the people, and wonders; and the words of the prophets began to be fulfilled.

14 And angels did appear unto men, wise men, and did declare unto them glad tidings of great joy; thus in this year the scriptures began to be fulfilled.

15 Nevertheless, the people began to harden their hearts, all save it were the most believing part of them, both of the Nephites and also of the Lamanites, and began to depend upon their own strength and upon their own wisdom, saying:

16 Some things they may have guessed right, among so many; but behold, we know that all these great and marvelous works cannot come to pass, of which has been spoken.

17 And they began to reason and to contend among themselves, saying:

18 That it is not reasonable that such a being as a Christ shall come; if so, and he be the Son of God, the Father of heaven and of earth, as it has been spoken, why will he not show himself unto us as well as unto them who shall be at Jerusalem?

19 Yea, why will he not show himself in this land as well as in the land of Jerusalem?

20 But behold, we know that this is a wicked tradition, which has been handed down unto us by our fathers, to cause us that we should believe in some great and marvelous thing which should come to pass, but not among us, but in a land which is far distant, a land which we know not; therefore they can keep us in ignorance, for we cannot witness with our own eyes that they are true.

21 And they will, by the cunning and the

Notes

mysterious arts of the evil one, work some great mystery which we cannot understand, which will keep us down to be servants to their words, and also servants unto them, for we depend upon them to teach us the word; and thus will they keep us in ignorance if we will yield ourselves unto them, all the days of our lives.

22 And many more things did the people imagine up in their hearts, which were foolish and vain; and they were much disturbed, for Satan did stir them up to do iniquity continually; yea, he did go about spreading rumors and contentions upon all the face of the land, that he might harden the hearts of the people against that which was good and against that which should come.

23 And notwithstanding the signs and the wonders which were wrought among the people of the Lord, and the many miracles which they did, Satan did get great hold upon the hearts of the people upon all the face of the land.

24 And thus ended the ninetieth year of the reign of the judges over the people of Nephi.

25 And thus ended the book of Helaman, according to the record of Helaman and his sons.

vv. 13–25 Satan seeks to undermine God's efforts to inspire people to believe. The "more believing part" will remain faithful.

- Explain that in various sports or professional fields there are varying strategies to distract an opponent. For instance, in politics, a congressman can use a filibuster to prevent a vote, or a football quarterback can fake a hand-off in order to pass the ball. Consider using these examples or your own to discuss with the class an opponent's strategy of distraction. Use this discussion to help the class understand Satan's tactics with the people of Nephi after Samuel prophecies.

- Use the following chart as a means of helping the class identify Satan's distractions:

God's attempt to help the people believe	Satan's attempt at distracting them
Hel. 16:13–14	Hel. 16:15–23
God's attempt to help us believe in our day	Satan's attempt at distracting us in our day

- Analyze: Once the class has discovered Satan's attempts, discuss with them how they work and why he uses them.

- Apply: Discuss with the class how Satan is using these same tactics in our day.

- Elder Hales taught, "In ancient America, Samuel the Lamanite prophesied that on the night of the Savior's birth 'there [would] be great lights in heaven, . . . insomuch that it shall appear unto man as if it was day.' Many believed Samuel and went to find Nephi, confessed their sins, repented, and were baptized. 'And angels did appear unto [them], and did declare unto them glad tidings of great joy.' But for the most part, the Nephites 'harden[ed] their hearts' and became blind to the 'signs and wonders' of the times. . . . In those days as in ours, some naysayers, called anti-Christs, convinced others that there was no need for a Savior and His Atonement. . . . Those who believed on the words of the prophets recognized the Savior throughout His life and ministry and were blessed to follow Him. . . . Brothers and sisters, the prophecies of Christ's *first* coming were fulfilled, 'every whit.' . . . But there are still many prophecies yet to be fulfilled! In this and other conferences, we hear living prophets prophesy and testify of Christ's *Second* Coming.

Notes

They also witness of the signs and wonders all about us, telling us that Christ will surely come again. Are we choosing to believe their words? Or despite their witnesses and warnings, are we waiting for evidence—are we 'walking in darkness at noon-day,' refusing to see by the light of modern prophecy, and denying that the Light of the World will return to rule and reign among us?" (Robert D. Hales, "Finding Faith in the Lord Jesus Christ," *Ensign*, Nov. 2004, 73).

♥ Encourage class members to not become distracted from following the prophets. Consider asking class members to consider times when they have followed the council of a prophet and it blessed them.

Index Topics: prophets, temptations

Notes

THE THIRD BOOK OF NEPHI

The Son of Nephi Who Was the Son of Helaman

THIRD NEPHI SUMMARY

Time Period: About AD 1–35 (35 years)

Contributors: Jesus Christ, Nephi, Isaiah, Malachi, Mormon

Source: Large plates of Nephi

Synopsis:

Chapter 1: The sign of Christ's birth is given

Chapters 2–5: The people's struggle against the Gadianton robbers, repentance, and deliverance

Chapters 6–7: The wickedness and overthrowing of the Nephite government

Chapter 8: The destructions in America at Christ's death

Chapters 9–10: The voice of Christ speaks to the survivors

Chapters 11–30: Christ reveals Himself, teaches, heals, and blesses in His ministry to the people in America

And Helaman was the son of Helaman, who was the son of Alma, who was the son of Alma, being a descendant of Nephi who was the son of Lehi, who came out of Jerusalem in the first year of the reign of Zedekiah, the king of Judah.

3 NEPHI 1

The Sign of Christ's Birth
About AD 1–4

1–3, Helaman departs out of the land, leaving all the records with his son Nephi; 4–9, The unbelievers set a day aside to kill all believers; 10–14, Jesus Christ tells Nephi He will be born the following day; 15–21, The sign of Jesus's birth appears in the heavens; 22–30, Description of Nephi's missionary efforts after the sign.

Overarching Principle: Jesus Christ ensures that all prophesies are fulfilled in order to help bring people unto Him so they can become converted.

⚡ To help class members understand the importance of the fulfillment of prophecies in the gospel of Jesus Christ, write the following phrase on the board: "What does it mean that

Notes

a prophesy is fulfilled?" Discuss this concept with the class. Once the word fulfillment is defined, consider asking, *What does a fulfilled prophecy prove about a prophet?*

💡 Note with the class that the word *fulfill* is found at least ten times throughout 3 Nephi 1.

Note: Each of the lesson outlines throughout this chapter will help teach the overarching principle.

1 Now it came to pass that the ninety and first year had passed away and it was six hundred years from the time that Lehi left Jerusalem; and it was in the year that Lachoneus was the chief judge and the governor over the land.

2 And Nephi, the son of Helaman, had departed out of the land of Zarahemla, giving charge unto his son Nephi, who was his eldest son, concerning the plates of brass, and all the records which had been kept, and all those things which had been kept sacred from the departure of Lehi out of Jerusalem.

3 Then he departed out of the land, and whither he went, no man knoweth; and his son Nephi did keep the records in his stead, yea, the record of this people.

4 And it came to pass that in the commencement of the ninety and second year, behold, the prophecies of the prophets began to be fulfilled more fully; for there began to be greater signs and greater miracles wrought among the people.

5 But there were some who began to say that the time was past for the words to be fulfilled, which were spoken by Samuel, the Lamanite.

6 And they began to rejoice over their brethren, saying: Behold the time is past, and the words of Samuel are not fulfilled; therefore, your joy and your faith concerning this thing hath been vain.

7 And it came to pass that they did make a great uproar throughout the land; and the people who believed began to be very sorrowful, lest by any means those things which had been spoken might not come to pass.

8 But behold, they did watch steadfastly for that day and that night and that day which should be as one day as if there were no night, that they might know that their faith had not been vain.

9 Now it came to pass that there was a day set apart by the unbelievers, that all those who believed in those traditions should be put to death except the sign should come to pass, which had been given by Samuel the prophet.

vv. 4–9 The believers and unbelievers' reaction to Samuel the Lamanite's prophesies.

🔎 *Read verses 4–9 and look for what is happening among the Nephites during this time.*

❓ Analyze: *Since the signs were being fulfilled, what should the people's reaction be? Why do you think some people are doubting?*

❓ Apply: Encourage the class to consider what they would do if they were in the same situation.

10 Now it came to pass that when Nephi, the son of Nephi, saw this wickedness of his people, his heart was exceedingly sorrowful.

11 And it came to pass that he went out and bowed himself down upon the earth, and cried mightily to his God in behalf of his people, yea, those who were about to be destroyed because of their faith in the tradition of their fathers.

12 And it came to pass that he cried mightily unto the Lord all that day; and behold, the voice of the Lord came unto him, saying:

13 Lift up your head and be of good cheer; for behold, the time is at hand, and on this night shall the sign be given, and on the morrow come I into the world, to show unto the world that I will fulfil all that which I have caused to be spoken by the mouth of my holy prophets.

14 Behold, I come unto my own, to fulfil all things which I have made known unto the children of men from the foundation of the world, and to do the will, both of the Father and of the Son—of

Notes

the Father because of me, and of the Son because of my flesh. And behold, the time is at hand, and this night shall the sign be given.

vv. 10–14 Jesus Christ's assurance.

🔍 *What does Nephi do as a result of the "day being set apart by unbelievers"? What does God give as an answer to Nephi's prayer?*

❓ Analyze: *In verses 13–14, what is Christ's reason to come into the world? What does this teach us about His role in the plan of salvation?*

💬 Neal A. Maxwell taught, "When the earlier coming of Jesus was imminent, signs abounded. Still, for some, there were 'doubtings.' (3 Nephi 8:4) But the faithful prevailed and were vindicated.

There were determined detractors then, mocking the faith of believers, briefly creating 'a great uproar,' even rejoicing over the seeming prospect that the faith of Christ's followers would be in vain. (See 3 Nephi 1:5–7.) It was not. Members kept the faith, and the faith kept them!" (Neal A. Maxwell, "The Great Plan of the Eternal God," *Ensign*, May 1984, 23).

15 And it came to pass that the words which came unto Nephi were fulfilled, according as they had been spoken; for behold, at the going down of the sun there was no darkness; and the people began to be astonished because there was no darkness when the night came.

16 And there were many, who had not believed the words of the prophets, who fell to the earth and became as if they were dead, for they knew that the great plan of destruction which they had laid for those who believed in the words of the prophets had been frustrated; for the sign which had been given was already at hand.

17 And they began to know that the Son of God must shortly appear; yea, in fine, all the people upon the face of the whole earth from the west to the east, both in the land north and in the land south, were so exceedingly astonished that they fell to the earth.

18 For they knew that the prophets had testified of these things for many years, and that the sign which had been given was already at hand; and they began to fear because of their iniquity and their unbelief.

19 And it came to pass that there was no darkness in all that night, but it was as light as though it was mid-day. And it came to pass that the sun did rise in the morning again, according to its proper order; and they knew that it was the day that the Lord should be born, because of the sign which had been given.

20 And it had come to pass, yea, all things, every whit, according to the words of the prophets.

21 And it came to pass also that a new star did appear, according to the word.

vv. 15–21 The prophecy is fulfilled.

⚡ Read or summarize verses 15–21 where Samuel the Lamanite's prophecy regarding Christ's birth is fulfilled.

22 And it came to pass that from this time forth there began to be lyings sent forth among the people, by Satan, to harden their hearts, to the intent that they might not believe in those signs and wonders which they had seen; but notwithstanding these lyings and deceivings the more part of the people did believe, and were converted unto the Lord.

23 And it came to pass that Nephi went forth among the people, and also many others, baptizing unto repentance, in the which there was a great remission of sins. And thus the people began again to have peace in the land.

24 And there were no contentions, save it were a few that began to preach, endeavoring to prove by the scriptures that it was no more expedient to observe the law of Moses. Now in this thing they

Notes

did err, having not understood the scriptures.

25 But it came to pass that they soon became converted, and were convinced of the error which they were in, for it was made known unto them that the law was not yet fulfilled, and that it must be fulfilled in every whit; yea, the word came unto them that it must be fulfilled; yea, that one jot or tittle should not pass away till it should all be fulfilled; therefore in this same year were they brought to a knowledge of their error and did confess their faults.

26 And thus the ninety and second year did pass away, bringing glad tidings unto the people because of the signs which did come to pass, according to the words of the prophecy of all the holy prophets.

vv. 22–26 How we choose to respond to prophetic prophecy may determine our conversion to the gospel.

- ⚡ Once you have identified the magnificent fulfillment of Samuel the Lamanite's prophecy, discuss with the class how believable it would be for anyone who witnessed it.
- 🔍 Make two columns on the board. Label one column "Reaction 1" and the other column "Reaction 2." Invite class members to look for two different reactions to the sign of Christ's birth in verses 22–26. Write their responses on the board.
- ❓ Analyze: *Why did some people still not believe? What did those who believed do as a result of the sign?*
- ❓ Apply: *Though we will not experience an exact parallel to this story, how is it relevant in our day?*

27 And it came to pass that the ninety and third year did also pass away in peace, save it were for the Gadianton robbers, who dwelt upon the mountains, who did infest the land; for so strong were their holds and their secret places that the people could not overpower them; therefore they did commit many murders, and did do much slaughter among the people.

28 And it came to pass that in the ninety and fourth year they began to increase in a great degree, because there were many dissenters of the Nephites who did flee unto them, which did cause much sorrow unto those Nephites who did remain in the land.

29 And there was also a cause of much sorrow among the Lamanites; for behold, they had many children who did grow up and began to wax strong in years, that they became for themselves, and were led away by some who were Zoramites, by their lyings and their flattering words, to join those Gadianton robbers.

30 And thus were the Lamanites afflicted also, and began to decrease as to their faith and righteousness, because of the wickedness of the rising generation.

vv. 27–30 The Gadiaton robbers once again infest the land.

- 💡 Note with the class that the Gadianton robbers once again begin to infest the land. Over the next few chapters they will successfully overthrow the Nephite form of government.

Teaching Tips from Prophets' Lips "Become acquainted with the lessons the scriptures teach. Learn the background and setting of the Master's parables and the prophets' admonitions. Study them as though they were speaking to you, for such is the truth" (Thomas S. Monson, "Be Your Best Self," *Ensign*, May, 2009, 68).

Index Topics: prophecy

Notes

3 NEPHI 2

Wickedness and Apostasy among the Nephites
About AD 5–16

1–5, The Nephites begin to disbelieve in the signs and wonders regarding Christ's birth; 6–16, The Gadianton robbers return to power; 17–19, War between the robbers and the Nephites occurs.

1 And it came to pass that thus passed away the ninety and fifth year also, and the people began to forget those signs and wonders which they had heard, and began to be less and less astonished at a sign or a wonder from heaven, insomuch that they began to be hard in their hearts, and blind in their minds, and began to disbelieve all which they had heard and seen—

2 Imagining up some vain thing in their hearts, that it was wrought by men and by the power of the devil, to lead away and deceive the hearts of the people; and thus did Satan get possession of the hearts of the people again, insomuch that he did blind their eyes and lead them away to believe that the doctrine of Christ was a foolish and a vain thing.

3 And it came to pass that the people began to wax strong in wickedness and abominations; and they did not believe that there should be any more signs or wonders given; and Satan did go about, leading away the hearts of the people, tempting them and causing them that they should do great wickedness in the land.

vv. 1–3 Signs and wonders are quickly forgotten when they are not supplemented by faith and righteous living.

⚡ Ask:
- *When are signs and wonders effective methods of bringing individuals to the Lord?*
- *What makes them effective or ineffective?*
- *What are some examples from the scriptures of effective or ineffective signs and wonders?*

🔎 *Read verses 1–3 and look for what occurred amongst the people after the sign of Christ's birth was seen.*

❓ *What are some ways we can make sure that we do not forget the wonders God works in our lives?*

💬 President Henry B. Eyring taught, "Tonight, and tomorrow night, you might pray and ponder, asking the questions: Did God send a message that was just for me? Did I see His hand in my life or the lives of my children? I will do that. And then I will find a way to preserve that memory for the day that I, and those that I love, will need to remember how much God loves us and how much we need Him" ("O Remember, Remember," *Ensign*, Nov. 2007).

4 And thus did pass away the ninety and sixth year; and also the ninety and seventh year; and also the ninety and eighth year; and also the ninety and ninth year;

5 And also an hundred years had passed away since the days of Mosiah, who was king over the people of the Nephites.

6 And six hundred and nine years had passed away since Lehi left Jerusalem.

7 And nine years had passed away from the time when the sign was given, which was spoken of by the prophets, that Christ should come into the world.

8 Now the Nephites began to reckon their time from this period when the sign was given, or from the coming of Christ; therefore, nine years had passed away.

9 And Nephi, who was the father of Nephi, who had the charge of the records, did not return to the land of Zarahemla, and could nowhere be found in all the land.

10 And it came to pass that the people did still remain in wickedness, notwithstanding the much preaching and prophesying which was

Notes

sent among them; and thus passed away the tenth year also; and the eleventh year also passed away in iniquity.

11 And it came to pass in the thirteenth year there began to be wars and contentions throughout all the land; for the Gadianton robbers had become so numerous, and did slay so many of the people, and did lay waste so many cities, and did spread so much death and carnage throughout the land, that it became expedient that all the people, both the Nephites and the Lamanites, should take up arms against them.

12 Therefore, all the Lamanites who had become converted unto the Lord did unite with their brethren, the Nephites, and were compelled, for the safety of their lives and their women and their children, to take up arms against those Gadianton robbers, yea, and also to maintain their rights, and the privileges of their church and of their worship, and their freedom and their liberty.

13 And it came to pass that before this thirteenth year had passed away the Nephites were threatened with utter destruction because of this war, which had become exceedingly sore.

14 And it came to pass that those Lamanites who had united with the Nephites were numbered among the Nephites;

15 And their curse was taken from them, and their skin became white like unto the Nephites;

16 And their young men and their daughters became exceedingly fair, and they were numbered among the Nephites, and were called Nephites. And thus ended the thirteenth year.

17 And it came to pass in the commencement of the fourteenth year, the war between the robbers and the people of Nephi did continue and did become exceedingly sore; nevertheless, the people of Nephi did gain some advantage of the robbers, insomuch that they did drive them back out of their lands into the mountains and into their secret places.

18 And thus ended the fourteenth year. And in the fifteenth year they did come forth against the people of Nephi; and because of the wickedness of the people of Nephi, and their many contentions and dissensions, the Gadianton robbers did gain many advantages over them.

19 And thus ended the fifteenth year, and thus were the people in a state of many afflictions; and the sword of destruction did hang over them, insomuch that they were about to be smitten down by it, and this because of their iniquity.

vv. 4–19 After rejecting the signs of the Lord and His prophets, society quickly falls into a state of sin.

- Invite class members to pair themselves with a partner in the class. Instruct one partner to read verses 4–19 and summarize what is happening among the wicked, and instruct the other partner to read the same verses looking for what the righteous are doing. Ask the partnerships to compare, contrast, and share their findings.

- Analyze: *Why do you think the Nephites fell into a state of sin so quickly?*

Topic Index: signs, wickedness

3 NEPHI 3

"A Defense and a Refuge from the Storm"
About AD 16–18

1–10, Lachoneus receives an epistle from Giddianhi, the Gadianton leader, demanding that the Nephities surrender; 11–33, Lachoneus gathers his people together, appoints chief captains, and prepares fortifications.

Notes

Overarching Principle: In the last days the saints must gather together for a defense and a refuge from the storm.

- ⚡ Ask the class where you should go during the following natural disasters: a tornado, an earthquake, a tsunami, a hurricane, and a flood. Ask, *Where should the saints gather during the storm of wickedness in the last days?*

- 🔎 Direct class members to Doctrine and Covenants 115:4–6 and invite them to find the answer to the question above. Help them discover that we are to gather together in Zion and upon her stakes.

- 💬 Bruce D. Porter taught, "The Lord will stand by His Church and people and keep them in safety until His coming. There will be peace in Zion and in her stakes, for He has proclaimed 'that the gathering together upon the land of Zion, and upon her stakes, may be for a defense, and for a refuge from the storm, and from wrath when it shall be poured out without mixture upon the whole earth' (Doctrine and Covenants 115:6). The Church stands as a bulwark of safety for its members. Though conditions in the world may become very vexing at times, faithful Latter-day Saints will find sanctuary in the stakes of Zion" (Bruce D Porter, "Beautiful Morning", *Ensign*, Oct. 2013, 85).

1 And now it came to pass that in the sixteenth year from the coming of Christ, Lachoneus, the governor of the land, received an epistle from the leader and the governor of this band of robbers; and these were the words which were written, saying:

2 Lachoneus, most noble and chief governor of the land, behold, I write this epistle unto you, and do give unto you exceedingly great praise because of your firmness, and also the firmness of your people, in maintaining that which ye suppose to be your right and liberty; yea, ye do stand well, as if ye were supported by the hand of a god, in the defence of your liberty, and your property, and your country, or that which ye do call so.

3 And it seemeth a pity unto me, most noble Lachoneus, that ye should be so foolish and vain as to suppose that ye can stand against so many brave men who are at my command, who do now at this time stand in their arms, and do await with great anxiety for the word—Go down upon the Nephites and destroy them.

4 And I, knowing of their unconquerable spirit, having proved them in the field of battle, and knowing of their everlasting hatred towards you because of the many wrongs which ye have done unto them, therefore if they should come down against you they would visit you with utter destruction.

5 Therefore I have written this epistle, sealing it with mine own hand, feeling for your welfare, because of your firmness in that which ye believe to be right, and your noble spirit in the field of battle.

6 Therefore I write unto you, desiring that ye would yield up unto this my people, your cities, your lands, and your possessions, rather than that they should visit you with the sword and that destruction should come upon you.

7 Or in other words, yield yourselves up unto us, and unite with us and become acquainted with our secret works, and become our brethren that ye may be like unto us—not our slaves, but our brethren and partners of all our substance.

8 And behold, I swear unto you, if ye will do this, with an oath, ye shall not be destroyed; but if ye will not do this, I swear unto you with an oath, that on the morrow month I will command that my armies shall come down against you, and they shall not stay their hand and shall spare not, but shall slay you, and shall let fall the sword upon you even until ye shall become extinct.

9 And behold, I am Giddianhi; and I am the governor of this the secret society of Gadianton; which society and the works thereof I know to be good; and they are of ancient date and they have been handed down unto us.

10 And I write this epistle unto you, Lachoneus,

Notes

3 NEPHI 3

and I hope that ye will deliver up your lands and your possessions, without the shedding of blood, that this my people may recover their rights and government, who have dissented away from you because of your wickedness in retaining from them their rights of government, and except ye do this, I will avenge their wrongs. I am Giddianhi.

✋ Consider having someone in the class stand up and read verses 2–10 as if they were Giddianhi. Additionally, help class members understand the context by reminding them that it has been sixteen years since the sign of Christ's birth and that His coming to the Americas is in AD 34, eighteen years away.

11 And now it came to pass when Lachoneus received this epistle he was exceedingly astonished, because of the boldness of Giddianhi demanding the possession of the land of the Nephites, and also of threatening the people and avenging the wrongs of those that had received no wrong, save it were they had wronged themselves by dissenting away unto those wicked and abominable robbers.

12 Now behold, this Lachoneus, the governor, was a just man, and could not be frightened by the demands and the threatenings of a robber; therefore he did not hearken to the epistle of Giddianhi, the governor of the robbers, but he did cause that his people should cry unto the Lord for strength against the time that the robbers should come down against them.

13 Yea, he sent a proclamation among all the people, that they should gather together their women, and their children, their flocks and their herds, and all their substance, save it were their land, unto one place.

14 And he caused that fortifications should be built round about them, and the strength thereof should be exceedingly great. And he caused that armies, both of the Nephites and of the Lamanites, or of all them who were numbered among the Nephites, should be placed as guards round about to watch them, and to guard them from the robbers day and night.

15 Yea, he said unto them: As the Lord liveth, except ye repent of all your iniquities, and cry unto the Lord, ye will in nowise be delivered out of the hands of those Gadianton robbers.

16 And so great and marvelous were the words and prophecies of Lachoneus that they did cause fear to come upon all the people; and they did exert themselves in their might to do according to the words of Lachoneus.

17 And it came to pass that Lachoneus did appoint chief captains over all the armies of the Nephites, to command them at the time that the robbers should come down out of the wilderness against them.

18 Now the chiefest among all the chief captains and the great commander of all the armies of the Nephites was appointed, and his name was Gidgiddoni.

19 Now it was the custom among all the Nephites to appoint for their chief captains, (save it were in their times of wickedness) some one that had the spirit of revelation and also prophecy; therefore, this Gidgiddoni was a great prophet among them, as also was the chief judge.

20 Now the people said unto Gidgiddoni: Pray unto the Lord, and let us go up upon the mountains and into the wilderness, that we may fall upon the robbers and destroy them in their own lands.

21 But Gidgiddoni saith unto them: The Lord forbid; for if we should go up against them the Lord would deliver us into their hands; therefore we will prepare ourselves in the center of our lands, and we will gather all our armies together, and we will not go against them, but we will wait till they shall come against us; therefore as the Lord liveth, if we do this he will deliver them into our hands.

22 And it came to pass in the seventeenth year, in the latter end of the year, the proclamation

Notes

of Lachoneus had gone forth throughout all the face of the land, and they had taken their horses, and their chariots, and their cattle, and all their flocks, and their herds, and their grain, and all their substance, and did march forth by thousands and by tens of thousands, until they had all gone forth to the place which had been appointed that they should gather themselves together, to defend themselves against their enemies.

23 And the land which was appointed was the land of Zarahemla, and the land which was between the land Zarahemla and the land Bountiful, yea, to the line which was between the land Bountiful and the land Desolation.

24 And there were a great many thousand people who were called Nephites, who did gather themselves together in this land. Now Lachoneus did cause that they should gather themselves together in the land southward, because of the great curse which was upon the land northward.

25 And they did fortify themselves against their enemies; and they did dwell in one land, and in one body, and they did fear the words which had been spoken by Lachoneus, insomuch that they did repent of all their sins; and they did put up their prayers unto the Lord their God, that he would deliver them in the time that their enemies should come down against them to battle.

26 And they were exceedingly sorrowful because of their enemies. And Gidgiddoni did cause that they should make weapons of war of every kind, and they should be strong with armor, and with shields, and with bucklers, after the manner of his instruction.

🔍 Have class members read verses 14–26 individually and look for how the preparations of the Nephites are like the preparations we must do to protect ourselves from the wickedness around us. Then have class members share with one another what they found.

❓ What was the individual responsibility of each person as they sought protection?

🔍 Look for what President Uchtdorf teaches that we need to do to personally find safety in the following quote.

💬 "We recognize that we are living in a time of turmoil, disaster, and war. We and many others feel strongly the great need for a 'defense, and for a refuge from the storm, and from wrath when it shall be poured out without mixture upon the whole earth' (Doctrine and Covenants 115:6). How do we find such a place of safety? The prophet of God, even President Hinckley, has taught: 'Our safety lies in the virtue of our lives. Our strength lies in our righteousness'" (Dieter F. Uchtdorf, "Christlike Attributes—the Wind beneath Our Wings," Ensign, Nov. 2005, 102).

❓ Apply: *As we consider the storm of wickedness in the last days, how do these quotes give you hope and strength?*

♥ Invite class members to prepare for wickedness in the last days through personal righteousness. Testify that we will find safety in the last days as we stand by His Church.

Teaching Tips from Prophets' Lips "One cannot honestly study the scriptures without learning gospel principles because the scriptures have been written to preserve principles for our benefit" (Marion G. Romney, "The Message of the Old Testament" [CES symposium on the Old Testament, Aug. 17, 1979], 3.)

Index Topics: Second Coming, last days

3 NEPHI 4
The Nephites Overcome the Gadianton Robbers
About AD 19–22

1–13, Gadianton robbers come down to battle but are defeated by the Nephites; 14–22, The Gadianton robbers are unsuccessful at laying a siege around the

Notes

Nephites; 23–29, The robbers flee but are overtaken and made prisoners by Gidgiddoni; 30–33, The people rejoice and praise the Lord for their deliverance.

1 And it came to pass that in the latter end of the eighteenth year those armies of robbers had prepared for battle, and began to come down and to sally forth from the hills, and out of the mountains, and the wilderness, and their strongholds, and their secret places, and began to take possession of the lands, both which were in the land south and which were in the land north, and began to take possession of all the lands which had been deserted by the Nephites, and the cities which had been left desolate.

2 But behold, there were no wild beasts nor game in those lands which had been deserted by the Nephites, and there was no game for the robbers save it were in the wilderness.

3 And the robbers could not exist save it were in the wilderness, for the want of food; for the Nephites had left their lands desolate, and had gathered their flocks and their herds and all their substance, and they were in one body.

4 Therefore, there was no chance for the robbers to plunder and to obtain food, save it were to come up in open battle against the Nephites; and the Nephites being in one body, and having so great a number, and having reserved for themselves provisions, and horses and cattle, and flocks of every kind, that they might subsist for the space of seven years, in the which time they did hope to destroy the robbers from off the face of the land; and thus the eighteenth year did pass away.

5 And it came to pass that in the nineteenth year Giddianhi found that it was expedient that he should go up to battle against the Nephites, for there was no way that they could subsist save it were to plunder and rob and murder.

6 And they durst not spread themselves upon the face of the land insomuch that they could raise grain, lest the Nephites should come upon them and slay them; therefore Giddianhi gave commandment unto his armies that in this year they should go up to battle against the Nephites.

7 And it came to pass that they did come up to battle; and it was in the sixth month; and behold, great and terrible was the day that they did come up to battle; and they were girded about after the manner of robbers; and they had a lamb-skin about their loins, and they were dyed in blood, and their heads were shorn, and they had head-plates upon them; and great and terrible was the appearance of the armies of Giddianhi, because of their armor, and because of their being dyed in blood.

8 And it came to pass that the armies of the Nephites, when they saw the appearance of the army of Giddianhi, had all fallen to the earth, and did lift their cries to the Lord their God, that he would spare them and deliver them out of the hands of their enemies.

9 And it came to pass that when the armies of Giddianhi saw this they began to shout with a loud voice, because of their joy, for they had supposed that the Nephites had fallen with fear because of the terror of their armies.

10 But in this thing they were disappointed, for the Nephites did not fear them; but they did fear their God and did supplicate him for protection; therefore, when the armies of Giddianhi did rush upon them they were prepared to meet them; yea, in the strength of the Lord they did receive them.

11 And the battle commenced in this the sixth month; and great and terrible was the battle thereof, yea, great and terrible was the slaughter thereof, insomuch that there never was known so great a slaughter among all the people of Lehi since he left Jerusalem.

12 And notwithstanding the threatenings and the oaths which Giddianhi had made, behold, the Nephites did beat them, insomuch that they did fall back from before them.

🔎 Mormon mentions three things that were "great

Notes

and terrible." Invite class members to find these three things in verses 5–12 as a way to summarize the war the Nephites had with the Gadianton robbers.

13 And it came to pass that Gidgiddoni commanded that his armies should pursue them as far as the borders of the wilderness, and that they should not spare any that should fall into their hands by the way; and thus they did pursue them and did slay them, to the borders of the wilderness, even until they had fulfilled the commandment of Gidgiddoni.

14 And it came to pass that Giddianhi, who had stood and fought with boldness, was pursued as he fled; and being weary because of his much fighting he was overtaken and slain. And thus was the end of Giddianhi the robber.

15 And it came to pass that the armies of the Nephites did return again to their place of security. And it came to pass that this nineteenth year did pass away, and the robbers did not come again to battle; neither did they come again in the twentieth year.

16 And in the twenty and first year they did not come up to battle, but they came up on all sides to lay siege round about the people of Nephi; for they did suppose that if they should cut off the people of Nephi from their lands, and should hem them in on every side, and if they should cut them off from all their outward privileges, that they could cause them to yield themselves up according to their wishes.

17 Now they had appointed unto themselves another leader, whose name was Zemnarihah; therefore it was Zemnarihah that did cause that this siege should take place.

18 But behold, this was an advantage to the Nephites; for it was impossible for the robbers to lay siege sufficiently long to have any effect upon the Nephites, because of their much provision which they had laid up in store,

19 And because of the scantiness of provisions among the robbers; for behold, they had nothing save it were meat for their subsistence, which meat they did obtain in the wilderness;

20 And it came to pass that the wild game became scarce in the wilderness insomuch that the robbers were about to perish with hunger.

21 And the Nephites were continually marching out by day and by night, and falling upon their armies, and cutting them off by thousands and by tens of thousands.

22 And thus it became the desire of the people of Zemnarihah to withdraw from their design, because of the great destruction which came upon them by night and by day.

23 And it came to pass that Zemnarihah did give command unto his people that they should withdraw themselves from the siege, and march into the furthermost parts of the land northward.

24 And now, Gidgiddoni being aware of their design, and knowing of their weakness because of the want of food, and the great slaughter which had been made among them, therefore he did send out his armies in the night-time, and did cut off the way of their retreat, and did place his armies in the way of their retreat.

25 And this did they do in the night-time, and got on their march beyond the robbers, so that on the morrow, when the robbers began their march, they were met by the armies of the Nephites both in their front and in their rear.

26 And the robbers who were on the south were also cut off in their places of retreat. And all these things were done by command of Gidgiddoni.

27 And there were many thousands who did yield themselves up prisoners unto the Nephites, and the remainder of them were slain.

💡 Consider summarizing the battle between the Nephites and the Gadianton robbers by drawing a simple diagram of what occurred.

Notes

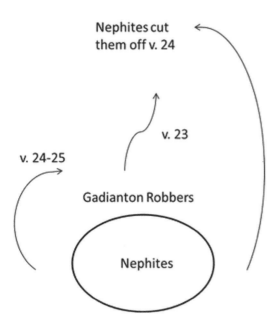

28 And their leader, Zemnarihah, was taken and hanged upon a tree, yea, even upon the top thereof until he was dead. And when they had hanged him until he was dead they did fell the tree to the earth, and did cry with a loud voice, saying:

29 May the Lord preserve his people in righteousness and in holiness of heart, that they may cause to be felled to the earth all who shall seek to slay them because of power and secret combinations, even as this man hath been felled to the earth.

30 And they did rejoice and cry again with one voice, saying: May the God of Abraham, and the God of Isaac, and the God of Jacob, protect this people in righteousness, so long as they shall call on the name of their God for protection.

31 And it came to pass that they did break forth, all as one, in singing, and praising their God for the great thing which he had done for them, in preserving them from falling into the hands of their enemies.

32 Yea, they did cry: Hosanna to the Most High God. And they did cry: Blessed be the name of the Lord God Almighty, the Most High God.

33 And their hearts were swollen with joy, unto the gushing out of many tears, because of the great goodness of God in delivering them out of the hands of their enemies; and they knew it was because of their repentance and their humility that they had been delivered from an everlasting destruction.

vv. 30–33 Protection can come when we call upon the name of God.

♥ Invite the class to privately write down or think of one or two trials that they are experiencing. After they have done this, invite them to seek for what the Lord would have them do to overcome this trial as they study 3 Nephi 4.

🔎 In verses 30–33, what lessons did the people of Nephi learn from this experience?

❓ Apply: *What lessons are applicable to us as we seek the protection of the Lord?*

Index Topics: prayer, gratitude

3 NEPHI 5

"I Am a Disciple of Jesus Christ"
About AD 22–26

1–8, The Nephites all believe and help those who had rebelled come back to the ways of righteousness; 9–19, Mormon abridges the records; 20–26, The house of Jacob will be gathered in.

1 And now behold, there was not a living soul among all the people of the Nephites who did doubt in the least the words of all the holy prophets who had spoken; for they knew that it must needs be that they must be fulfilled.

2 And they knew that it must be expedient that Christ had come, because of the many signs which had been given, according to the words of the prophets; and because of the things which had come to pass already they knew that it must

Notes

needs be that all things should come to pass according to that which had been spoken.

3 Therefore they did forsake all their sins, and their abominations, and their whoredoms, and did serve God with all diligence day and night.

vv. 1–3 Pride cycle.

- Refer back to the pride cycle idea in Helaman 3. Have class members identify where the Nephites fall on the pride cycle as they read verses 1–3.

4 And now it came to pass that when they had taken all the robbers prisoners, insomuch that none did escape who were not slain, they did cast their prisoners into prison, and did cause the word of God to be preached unto them; and as many as would repent of their sins and enter into a covenant that they would murder no more were set at liberty.

5 But as many as there were who did not enter into a covenant, and who did still continue to have those secret murders in their hearts, yea, as many as were found breathing out threatenings against their brethren were condemned and punished according to the law.

6 And thus they did put an end to all those wicked, and secret, and abominable combinations, in the which there was so much wickedness, and so many murders committed.

vv. 4–6 How to change a society.

- Explain to class members that many of the Gadianton robbers were captured and imprisoned during the war. In verses 4–6, look for what the Nephites did to reform these prisoners.

- Boyd K. Packard explained, "True doctrine, understood, changes attitudes and behavior. The study of the doctrines of the gospel will improve behavior quicker than a study of behavior will improve behavior" ("Do Not Fear," *Ensign*, May 2004, 79).

7 And thus had the twenty and second year passed away, and the twenty and third year also, and the twenty and fourth, and the twenty and fifth; and thus had twenty and five years passed away.

8 And there had many things transpired which, in the eyes of some, would be great and marvelous; nevertheless, they cannot all be written in this book; yea, this book cannot contain even a hundredth part of what was done among so many people in the space of twenty and five years;

9 But behold there are records which do contain all the proceedings of this people; and a shorter but true account was given by Nephi.

10 Therefore I have made my record of these things according to the record of Nephi, which was engraven on the plates which were called the plates of Nephi.

11 And behold, I do make the record on plates which I have made with mine own hands.

12 And behold, I am called Mormon, being called after the land of Mormon, the land in which Alma did establish the church among the people, yea, the first church which was established among them after their transgression.

13 Behold, I am a disciple of Jesus Christ, the Son of God. I have been called of him to declare his word among his people, that they might have everlasting life.

v. 13 We are disciples of Jesus Christ as we seek to follow Him.

- List the words "Learner," "Adherent," "Apprentice," and "Follower" on the board. Ask class members to come up with one word that encompasses the meaning of those four words.

- Have them compare their results with an answer in verse 13.

- Point out each of the words on the board and ask class members how a disciple of Jesus Christ fulfills the meaning of that word.

- Encourage class members to be disciples of

Notes

Jesus Christ by incorporating each of those traits listed on the board in their own lives.

14 And it hath become expedient that I, according to the will of God, that the prayers of those who have gone hence, who were the holy ones, should be fulfilled according to their faith, should make a record of these things which have been done—

15 Yea, a small record of that which hath taken place from the time that Lehi left Jerusalem, even down until the present time.

16 Therefore I do make my record from the accounts which have been given by those who were before me, until the commencement of my day;

17 And then I do make a record of the things which I have seen with mine own eyes.

18 And I know the record which I make to be a just and a true record; nevertheless there are many things which, according to our language, we are not able to write.

19 And now I make an end of my saying, which is of myself, and proceed to give my account of the things which have been before me.

20 I am Mormon, and a pure descendant of Lehi. I have reason to bless my God and my Savior Jesus Christ, that he brought our fathers out of the land of Jerusalem, (and no one knew it save it were himself and those whom he brought out of that land) and that he hath given me and my people so much knowledge unto the salvation of our souls.

21 Surely he hath blessed the house of Jacob, and hath been merciful unto the seed of Joseph.

22 And insomuch as the children of Lehi have kept his commandments he hath blessed them and prospered them according to his word.

23 Yea, and surely shall he again bring a remnant of the seed of Joseph to the knowledge of the Lord their God.

24 And as surely as the Lord liveth, will he gather in from the four quarters of the earth all the remnant of the seed of Jacob, who are scattered abroad upon all the face of the earth.

25 And as he hath covenanted with all the house of Jacob, even so shall the covenant wherewith he hath covenanted with the house of Jacob be fulfilled in his own due time, unto the restoring all the house of Jacob unto the knowledge of the covenant that he hath covenanted with them.

26 And then shall they know their Redeemer, who is Jesus Christ, the Son of God; and then shall they be gathered in from the four quarters of the earth unto their own lands, from whence they have been dispersed; yea, as the Lord liveth so shall it be. Amen.

Teaching Tips from Prophets' Lips "A true teacher, once he has taught the facts [of the gospel] . . . takes [the students] a step further to gain the spiritual witness and the understanding in their hearts that brings about the action and the doing" ("Teaching by Faith" [an evening with Elder Robert D. Hales, Feb. 1, 2002], 5).

Index Topics: discipleship

3 NEPHI 6

The Nephites Fall into Sin
About AD 26–30

1–9, The Nephites return to their lands, rebuild, and prosper; 10–19, They become prideful and sinful, and the church is broken up; 20–30, Leaders kill the prophets and conspire to overthrow the liberty of the people.

1 And now it came to pass that the people of the Nephites did all return to their own lands in the twenty and sixth year, every man, with his family, his flocks and his herds, his horses and his cattle, and all things whatsoever did belong unto them.

Notes

2 And it came to pass that they had not eaten up all their provisions; therefore they did take with them all that they had not devoured, of all their grain of every kind, and their gold, and their silver, and all their precious things, and they did return to their own lands and their possessions, both on the north and on the south, both on the land northward and on the land southward.

3 And they granted unto those robbers who had entered into a covenant to keep the peace of the land, who were desirous to remain Lamanites, lands, according to their numbers, that they might have, with their labors, wherewith to subsist upon; and thus they did establish peace in all the land.

4 And they began again to prosper and to wax great; and the twenty and sixth and seventh years passed away, and there was great order in the land; and they had formed their laws according to equity and justice.

5 And now there was nothing in all the land to hinder the people from prospering continually, except they should fall into transgression.

6 And now it was Gidgiddoni, and the judge, Lachoneus, and those who had been appointed leaders, who had established this great peace in the land.

7 And it came to pass that there were many cities built anew, and there were many old cities repaired.

8 And there were many highways cast up, and many roads made, which led from city to city, and from land to land, and from place to place.

9 And thus passed away the twenty and eighth year, and the people had continual peace.

10 But it came to pass in the twenty and ninth year there began to be some disputings among the people; and some were lifted up unto pride and boastings because of their exceedingly great riches, yea, even unto great persecutions;

11 For there were many merchants in the land, and also many lawyers, and many officers.

12 And the people began to be distinguished by ranks, according to their riches and their chances for learning; yea, some were ignorant because of their poverty, and others did receive great learning because of their riches.

13 Some were lifted up in pride, and others were exceedingly humble; some did return railing for railing, while others would receive railing and persecution and all manner of afflictions, and would not turn and revile again, but were humble and penitent before God.

14 And thus there became a great inequality in all the land, insomuch that the church began to be broken up; yea, insomuch that in the thirtieth year the church was broken up in all the land save it were among a few of the Lamanites who were converted unto the true faith; and they would not depart from it, for they were firm, and steadfast, and immovable, willing with all diligence to keep the commandments of the Lord.

15 Now the cause of this iniquity of the people was this—Satan had great power, unto the stirring up of the people to do all manner of iniquity, and to the puffing them up with pride, tempting them to seek for power, and authority, and riches, and the vain things of the world.

16 And thus Satan did lead away the hearts of the people to do all manner of iniquity; therefore they had enjoyed peace but a few years.

vv. 1–16 Pride results from comparing ourselves to others.

⚡ Draw circles with arrows to represent the pride cycle (see lesson ideas for Helaman 3). Quiz your class and have them say and write what goes into each circle of the pride cycle.

❓ *How quick does it take to go through the pride cycle? Why do you think they go through the pride cycle so quickly?*

👥 List the following on the left side of the board.

AD 26 (vv. 1–3)

Notes

AD 27–28 (vv. 4–9)

AD 29 (vv. 10–14)

AD 30 (vv. 14–16)

Break your class into four groups and assign each of them one of the years. Give them three minutes to read their verses and ask them to summarize what happened in that time period, and how it relates to the pride cycle. Ask a representative from each group to write the summary to the right of their verses, and point out where the Nephites are in relation to the pride cycle.

In verses 10–14, look for how comparison is part of pride. C. S. Lewis stated, "Pride gets no pleasure out of having something, only out of having more of it than the next man. We say that people are proud of being rich, or clever, or good-looking, but they are not. They are proud of being richer, or cleverer, or better-looking than others. If every one else became equally rich, or clever, or good-looking there would be nothing to be proud about. It is the comparison that makes you proud: the pleasure of being above the rest. Once the element of competition has gone, pride has gone. That is why I say that Pride is essentially competitive in a way the other vices are not" (*Mere Christianity*, New York: Macmillan, 1952, 109–10).

17 And thus, in the commencement of the thirtieth year—the people having been delivered up for the space of a long time to be carried about by the temptations of the devil whithersoever he desired to carry them, and to do whatsoever iniquity he desired they should—and thus in the commencement of this, the thirtieth year, they were in a state of awful wickedness.

18 Now they did not sin ignorantly, for they knew the will of God concerning them, for it had been taught unto them; therefore they did wilfully rebel against God.

v. 18 We must not "willfully rebel" against God.

⚡ Write on the board the words, "willful rebellion" and "sinning." Ask:
- *Is there a difference between sinning and willfully rebelling?*
- *What is that difference?*
- *Which is worse and why?*

🔍 Look for a characteristic of "willful rebellion" in verse 18.

❓ Why would someone willfully rebel against God? What leads us to willfully rebel against God?

❤ Ask class members to evaluate their lives and consider areas where they might be sinning deliberately or doing things that will lead to willful rebellion. Challenge them to strive to overcome rebellion against God.

19 And now it was in the days of Lachoneus, the son of Lachoneus, for Lachoneus did fill the seat of his father and did govern the people that year.

20 And there began to be men inspired from heaven and sent forth, standing among the people in all the land, preaching and testifying boldly of the sins and iniquities of the people, and testifying unto them concerning the redemption which the Lord would make for his people, or in other words, the resurrection of Christ; and they did testify boldly of his death and sufferings.

21 Now there were many of the people who were exceedingly angry because of those who testified of these things; and those who were angry were chiefly the chief judges, and they who had been high priests and lawyers; yea, all those who were lawyers were angry with those who testified of these things.

22 Now there was no lawyer nor judge nor high priest that could have power to condemn any one to death save their condemnation was signed by the governor of the land.

23 Now there were many of those who testified of the things pertaining to Christ who testified boldly, who were taken and put to death secretly by the judges, that the knowledge of their death

Notes

came not unto the governor of the land until after their death.

24 Now behold, this was contrary to the laws of the land, that any man should be put to death except they had power from the governor of the land—

25 Therefore a complaint came up unto the land of Zarahemla, to the governor of the land, against these judges who had condemned the prophets of the Lord unto death, not according to the law.

26 Now it came to pass that they were taken and brought up before the judge, to be judged of the crime which they had done, according to the law which had been given by the people.

27 Now it came to pass that those judges had many friends and kindreds; and the remainder, yea, even almost all the lawyers and the high priests, did gather themselves together, and unite with the kindreds of those judges who were to be tried according to the law.

28 And they did enter into a covenant one with another, yea, even into that covenant which was given by them of old, which covenant was given and administered by the devil, to combine against all righteousness.

29 Therefore they did combine against the people of the Lord, and enter into a covenant to destroy them, and to deliver those who were guilty of murder from the grasp of justice, which was about to be administered according to the law.

30 And they did set at defiance the law and the rights of their country; and they did covenant one with another to destroy the governor, and to establish a king over the land, that the land should no more be at liberty but should be subject unto kings.

Index Topics: pride, sin

3 NEPHI 7

The Collapse of the Nephite Government
About AD 30–33

1–14, The Nephite government collapses and is replaced by tribal entities; 15–26, Nephi continues to preach repentance to the people with some success.

Overarching Principle: It is possible to live righteously in troubled times.

1 Now behold, I will show unto you that they did not establish a king over the land; but in this same year, yea, the thirtieth year, they did destroy upon the judgment-seat, yea, did murder the chief judge of the land.

2 And the people were divided one against another; and they did separate one from another into tribes, every man according to his family and his kindred and friends; and thus they did destroy the government of the land.

3 And every tribe did appoint a chief or a leader over them; and thus they became tribes and leaders of tribes.

4 Now behold, there was no man among them save he had much family and many kindreds and friends; therefore their tribes became exceedingly great.

5 Now all this was done, and there were no wars as yet among them; and all this iniquity had come upon the people because they did yield themselves unto the power of Satan.

6 And the regulations of the government were destroyed, because of the secret combination of the friends and kindreds of those who murdered the prophets.

7 And they did cause a great contention in the land, insomuch that the more righteous part of the people had nearly all become wicked; yea, there were but few righteous men among them.

Notes

8 And thus six years had not passed away since the more part of the people had turned from their righteousness, like the dog to his vomit, or like the sow to her wallowing in the mire.

9 Now this secret combination, which had brought so great iniquity upon the people, did gather themselves together, and did place at their head a man whom they did call Jacob;

10 And they did call him their king; therefore he became a king over this wicked band; and he was one of the chiefest who had given his voice against the prophets who testified of Jesus.

11 And it came to pass that they were not so strong in number as the tribes of the people, who were united together save it were their leaders did establish their laws, every one according to his tribe; nevertheless they were enemies; notwithstanding they were not a righteous people, yet they were united in the hatred of those who had entered into a covenant to destroy the government.

12 Therefore, Jacob seeing that their enemies were more numerous than they, he being the king of the band, therefore he commanded his people that they should take their flight into the northernmost part of the land, and there build up unto themselves a kingdom, until they were joined by dissenters, (for he flattered them that there would be many dissenters) and they become sufficiently strong to contend with the tribes of the people; and they did so.

13 And so speedy was their march that it could not be impeded until they had gone forth out of the reach of the people. And thus ended the thirtieth year; and thus were the affairs of the people of Nephi.

14 And it came to pass in the thirty and first year that they were divided into tribes, every man according to his family, kindred and friends; nevertheless they had come to an agreement that they would not go to war one with another; but they were not united as to their laws, and their manner of government, for they were established according to the minds of those who were their chiefs and their leaders. But they did establish very strict laws that one tribe should not trespass against another, insomuch that in some degree they had peace in the land; nevertheless, their hearts were turned from the Lord their God, and they did stone the prophets and did cast them out from among them.

vv. 1–14 The collapse of the Nephite government.

- With your class, briefly review and summarize the following warnings given by prophets regarding the Gadianton robbers: Helaman 2:12–13; Helaman 7:4; 3 Nephi 2:18; 3 Nephi 3:15. Discuss the continual increase in power and influence of the Gadianton robbers.

- Read verses 1–14 with your class looking for the final effect of the Gadianton robbers upon the Nephites.

- Analyze: *What could the Nephites have done differently years before that could have prevented this chaos?*

- Apply: Liken the dissolution of the government to encroaching sin in our lives. *What will be the end result of sin if we don't eliminate it? What could we learn from this story that is applicable to us striving to avoid sin?*

15 And it came to pass that Nephi—having been visited by angels and also the voice of the Lord, therefore having seen angels, and being eye-witness, and having had power given unto him that he might know concerning the ministry of Christ, and also being eye-witness to their quick return from righteousness unto their wickedness and abominations;

16 Therefore, being grieved for the hardness of their hearts and the blindness of their minds—went forth among them in that same year, and began to testify, boldly, repentance and remission of sins through faith on the Lord Jesus Christ.

17 And he did minister many things unto them;

Notes

and all of them cannot be written, and a part of them would not suffice, therefore they are not written in this book. And Nephi did minister with power and with great authority.

18 And it came to pass that they were angry with him, even because he had greater power than they, for it were not possible that they could disbelieve his words, for so great was his faith on the Lord Jesus Christ that angels did minister unto him daily.

19 And in the name of Jesus did he cast out devils and unclean spirits; and even his brother did he raise from the dead, after he had been stoned and suffered death by the people.

20 And the people saw it, and did witness of it, and were angry with him because of his power; and he did also do many more miracles, in the sight of the people, in the name of Jesus.

21 And it came to pass that the thirty and first year did pass away, and there were but few who were converted unto the Lord; but as many as were converted did truly signify unto the people that they had been visited by the power and Spirit of God, which was in Jesus Christ, in whom they believed.

22 And as many as had devils cast out from them, and were healed of their sicknesses and their infirmities, did truly manifest unto the people that they had been wrought upon by the Spirit of God, and had been healed; and they did show forth signs also and did do some miracles among the people.

vv. 15–22 It is possible to remain righteous despite the wickedness around us.

- To help the class visualize the above stated principle, bring a bowl of dirty water to class and place it where everyone can see it. You will also need a cup of clean water. Discuss with the class whether the water inside the cup would remain clean if it were put inside the bowl of dirty water. After some discussion, place the entire cup of clean water inside the bowl of dirty water. The water inside the cup still remains clean because of the protection of the glass. Explain that the principles in this chapter can act as a protective barrier between us and the wickedness of the world.

- Review the wicked, troubled times of the Nephites in this chapter. Invite class members to read verses 15–22, looking for principles about how to stay clean despite living in a wicked, troubled world. Consider making a list on the board.

- Apply: *How could these principles help us with the challenges we face in our day?*

- Elder David A. Bednar counseled priesthood holders, "In this momentous season of the earth's history, you and I as bearers of the priesthood need to be righteous men and effective instruments in the hands of God. We need to rise up as men of God. You and I would do well to learn from and heed the example of Nephi, the grandson of Helaman and the first of the twelve disciples called by the Savior at the beginning of His ministry among the Nephites. "And [Nephi] did minister many things unto them. . . . And Nephi did minister with power and with great authority (see 3 Nephi 7:17)" ("The Powers of Heaven," *Ensign*, May 2012, 51).

- Encourage class members to follow Nephi's example.

23 Thus passed away the thirty and second year also. And Nephi did cry unto the people in the commencement of the thirty and third year; and he did preach unto them repentance and remission of sins.

24 Now I would have you to remember also, that there were none who were brought unto repentance who were not baptized with water.

25 Therefore, there were ordained of Nephi, men unto this ministry, that all such as should come unto them should be baptized with water, and this as a witness and a testimony before God,

Notes

and unto the people, that they had repented and received a remission of their sins.

26 And there were many in the commencement of this year that were baptized unto repentance; and thus the more part of the year did pass away.

> **Teaching Tips from Prophets' Lips** "Will you pray for guidance in how to have truth sink deep into the minds and hearts of your students so as to be used throughout life? As you prayerfully seek ways to do that, I know that the Lord will guide you" ("To Understand and Live Truth," [an evening with Elder Richard G. Scott, Feb. 4, 2005], 2).

3 NEPHI 8

Darkness and Destruction
About AD 32–34

1–4, The people look for the sign given by Samuel; 5–19, Tempests, lightning, and earthquakes are given as a sign; 20–25, Darkness and mourning fill the land.

1 And now it came to pass that according to our record, and we know our record to be true, for behold, it was a just man who did keep the record—for he truly did many miracles in the name of Jesus; and there was not any man who could do a miracle in the name of Jesus save he were cleansed every whit from his iniquity—

2 And now it came to pass, if there was no mistake made by this man in the reckoning of our time, the thirty and third year had passed away;

3 And the people began to look with great earnestness for the sign which had been given by the prophet Samuel, the Lamanite, yea, for the time that there should be darkness for the space of three days over the face of the land.

4 And there began to be great doubtings and disputations among the people, notwithstanding so many signs had been given.

5 And it came to pass in the thirty and fourth year, in the first month, on the fourth day of the month, there arose a great storm, such an one as never had been known in all the land.

6 And there was also a great and terrible tempest; and there was terrible thunder, insomuch that it did shake the whole earth as if it was about to divide asunder.

7 And there were exceedingly sharp lightnings, such as never had been known in all the land.

8 And the city of Zarahemla did take fire.

v. 8 The prophecy of Zarahemla.

- Note with your class that Samuel the Lamanite prophesied that Zarahemla would be destroyed by fire in Helaman 13:12–13.

9 And the city of Moroni did sink into the depths of the sea, and the inhabitants thereof were drowned.

10 And the earth was carried up upon the city of Moronihah, that in the place of the city there became a great mountain.

11 And there was a great and terrible destruction in the land southward.

12 But behold, there was a more great and terrible destruction in the land northward; for behold, the whole face of the land was changed, because of the tempest and the whirlwinds, and the thunderings and the lightnings, and the exceedingly great quaking of the whole earth;

13 And the highways were broken up, and the level roads were spoiled, and many smooth places became rough.

14 And many great and notable cities were sunk, and many were burned, and many were shaken till the buildings thereof had fallen to the earth, and the inhabitants thereof were slain, and the places were left desolate.

15 And there were some cities which remained; but the damage thereof was exceedingly great,

Notes

and there were many in them who were slain.

16 And there were some who were carried away in the whirlwind; and whither they went no man knoweth, save they know that they were carried away.

17 And thus the face of the whole earth became deformed, because of the tempests, and the thunderings, and the lightnings, and the quaking of the earth.

18 And behold, the rocks were rent in twain; they were broken up upon the face of the whole earth, insomuch that they were found in broken fragments, and in seams and in cracks, upon all the face of the land.

19 And it came to pass that when the thunderings, and the lightnings, and the storm, and the tempest, and the quakings of the earth did cease—for behold, they did last for about the space of three hours; and it was said by some that the time was greater; nevertheless, all these great and terrible things were done in about the space of three hours—and then behold, there was darkness upon the face of the land.

20 And it came to pass that there was thick darkness upon all the face of the land, insomuch that the inhabitants thereof who had not fallen could feel the vapor of darkness;

21 And there could be no light, because of the darkness, neither candles, neither torches; neither could there be fire kindled with their fine and exceedingly dry wood, so that there could not be any light at all;

💡 It may be interesting to note at this point that Jesus Christ is known as the Light of the World, and that this might symbolically represent His death. After three days of darkness the light returned, just as after three days in the tomb the Son of God was resurrected.

22 And there was not any light seen, neither fire, nor glimmer, neither the sun, nor the moon, nor the stars, for so great were the mists of darkness which were upon the face of the land.

23 And it came to pass that it did last for the space of three days that there was no light seen; and there was great mourning and howling and weeping among all the people continually; yea, great were the groanings of the people, because of the darkness and the great destruction which had come upon them.

24 And in one place they were heard to cry, saying: O that we had repented before this great and terrible day, and then would our brethren have been spared, and they would not have been burned in that great city Zarahemla.

25 And in another place they were heard to cry and mourn, saying: O that we had repented before this great and terrible day, and had not killed and stoned the prophets, and cast them out; then would our mothers and our fair daughters, and our children have been spared, and not have been buried up in that great city Moronihah. And thus were the howlings of the people great and terrible.

vv. 1–25 The Nephites were visited with terrible destruction at the time of the Christ's crucifixion.

⚡ If possible, consider procuring audio recordings of storm sounds (free versions are available online). Depending on your circumstances and the age group of class members, you may also consider bringing a few portable fans to class. Ask class members to close their eyes if they feel comfortable to do so, and invite a class member with a loud voice to read 3 Nephi 8 in its entirety. When the reader begins verse 5, turn off the lights and turn on the audio recording and fans. When the reader has completed reading the chapter, encourage a discussion about what it must have been like for the Nephites to experience the events described.

❓ *According to the last few verses of 3 Nephi 8, what seems to be more devastating to the*

Notes

people than the storm itself? Why do you think that is?

✏ If journals or notebooks are available, invite class members to answer this question: If the Lord were to return today, would I say, "O that I had repented before this great and terrible day"? (see v. 25).

3 NEPHI 9

A Voice Is Heard
About AD 34

1–12, A voice from the darkness laments and describes the destruction of the Nephites and their cities; 13–22, The voice of Christ invites those who are spared to come unto Him and be healed.

1 And it came to pass that there was a voice heard among all the inhabitants of the earth, upon all the face of this land, crying:

2 Wo, wo, wo unto this people; wo unto the inhabitants of the whole earth except they shall repent; for the devil laugheth, and his angels rejoice, because of the slain of the fair sons and daughters of my people; and it is because of their iniquity and abominations that they are fallen!

3 Behold, that great city Zarahemla have I burned with fire, and the inhabitants thereof.

4 And behold, that great city Moroni have I caused to be sunk in the depths of the sea, and the inhabitants thereof to be drowned.

5 And behold, that great city Moronihah have I covered with earth, and the inhabitants thereof, to hide their iniquities and their abominations from before my face, that the blood of the prophets and the saints shall not come any more unto me against them.

6 And behold, the city of Gilgal have I caused to be sunk, and the inhabitants thereof to be buried up in the depths of the earth;

7 Yea, and the city of Onihah and the inhabitants thereof, and the city of Mocum and the inhabitants thereof, and the city of Jerusalem and the inhabitants thereof; and waters have I caused to come up in the stead thereof, to hide their wickedness and abominations from before my face, that the blood of the prophets and the saints shall not come up any more unto me against them.

8 And behold, the city of Gadiandi, and the city of Gadiomnah, and the city of Jacob, and the city of Gimgimno, all these have I caused to be sunk, and made hills and valleys in the places thereof; and the inhabitants thereof have I buried up in the depths of the earth, to hide their wickedness and abominations from before my face, that the blood of the prophets and the saints should not come up any more unto me against them.

9 And behold, that great city Jacobugath, which was inhabited by the people of king Jacob, have I caused to be burned with fire because of their sins and their wickedness, which was above all the wickedness of the whole earth, because of their secret murders and combinations; for it was they that did destroy the peace of my people and the government of the land; therefore I did cause them to be burned, to destroy them from before my face, that the blood of the prophets and the saints should not come up unto me any more against them.

vv. 1–9 The Savior laments the destruction of His people.

🔍 Explain that in the midst of darkness and destruction the Savior's voice is heard by the surviving Nephites. Read 3 Nephi 9:1–2 and compare and contrast the feelings of the Lord and the feelings of the devil concerning the destruction of the Nephites.

❓ Analyze:
- *If these destructions cause the Lord to cry over His people, why did He allow them to happen?*
- *Why do you think the devil is laughing?*
- *What does that teach about Satan? What does this teach about God?*

Notes

💡 It is interesting to compare the concepts in these verses with those in Moses 7:24–37.

10 And behold, the city of Laman, and the city of Josh, and the city of Gad, and the city of Kishkumen, have I caused to be burned with fire, and the inhabitants thereof, because of their wickedness in casting out the prophets, and stoning those whom I did send to declare unto them concerning their wickedness and their abominations.

11 And because they did cast them all out, that there were none righteous among them, I did send down fire and destroy them, that their wickedness and abominations might be hid from before my face, that the blood of the prophets and the saints whom I sent among them might not cry unto me from the ground against them.

12 And many great destructions have I caused to come upon this land, and upon this people, because of their wickedness and their abominations.

13 O all ye that are spared because ye were more righteous than they, will ye not now return unto me, and repent of your sins, and be converted, that I may heal you?

14 Yea, verily I say unto you, if ye will come unto me ye shall have eternal life. Behold, mine arm of mercy is extended towards you, and whosoever will come, him will I receive; and blessed are those who come unto me.

15 Behold, I am Jesus Christ the Son of God. I created the heavens and the earth, and all things that in them are. I was with the Father from the beginning. I am in the Father, and the Father in me; and in me hath the Father glorified his name.

16 I came unto my own, and my own received me not. And the scriptures concerning my coming are fulfilled.

17 And as many as have received me, to them have I given to become the sons of God; and even so will I to as many as shall believe on my name, for behold, by me redemption cometh, and in me is the law of Moses fulfilled.

18 I am the light and the life of the world. I am Alpha and Omega, the beginning and the end.

vv. 13–18 Those who come unto Christ can be healed by Him.

⚡ Ask class members if they remember ever receiving a grade in school "on a curve." See if someone would be willing to explain that concept. If necessary, explain that "curved grading" takes a certain percentage of the top scores on a test and raises those to an A grade—even if the actual scoring would have been assigned to a much lower grade. In this way, an individual's grade is based largely on the performance of others in the class. Ask, *Do you think the Lord ever "grades on a curve"?*

🔍 *Read verses 10–13 and look for phrases that could lead someone to believe that the Lord metaphorically graded the Nephites on a curve.* (Some Nephites were spared because they were "more righteous" than others, not necessarily because they were independently righteous.)

❓ Analyze: *Even though some of the Nephites were not destroyed because they were more righteous than others, what blessings had yet to be fulfilled for them?* (see v. 13). *What requirements still needed to be met by the surviving Nephites to reap the full blessings of the Atonement?*

♥ Explain that we should not be satisfied with temporal salvation only. Testify that coming unto Christ through repentance and conversion will always be required in order to reap the full blessings and healing power of the Atonement of Christ and that He never lowers that standard. Share your testimony of the truthfulness of verses 15–18.

19 And ye shall offer up unto me no more the shedding of blood; yea, your sacrifices and your burnt

Notes

offerings shall be done away, for I will accept none of your sacrifices and your burnt offerings.

20 And ye shall offer for a sacrifice unto me a broken heart and a contrite spirit. And whoso cometh unto me with a broken heart and a contrite spirit, him will I baptize with fire and with the Holy Ghost, even as the Lamanites, because of their faith in me at the time of their conversion, were baptized with fire and with the Holy Ghost, and they knew it not.

21 Behold, I have come unto the world to bring redemption unto the world, to save the world from sin.

22 Therefore, whoso repenteth and cometh unto me as a little child, him will I receive, for of such is the kingdom of God. Behold, for such I have laid down my life, and have taken it up again; therefore repent, and come unto me ye ends of the earth, and be saved.

vv. 19–22 Baptism by fire and by the Holy Ghost can be a subtle process that comes upon those with broken hearts and contrite spirits.

- Bring a large soft feather to class. (Peacock feathers work well.) Show the feather to the class and invite a volunteer to the front of the room to participate in an object lesson. Tell the volunteer to close his or her eyes and hold out his or her left hand. Ask them to indicate when they feel the feather on their left hand. You may need to practice this on your own hand prior to the lesson. Avoid rubbing the feather against the hairs of the arm as it will make the feather easier to detect and lessen the effect of the object lesson. If done correctly, the volunteer will not be able to detect when the feather has touched his or her skin. When ready, invite the volunteer to look as you continue touching the feather to his or her wrist. Lead a short discussion regarding the feather and why the results of the object lesson might be surprising.

- *Read 3 Nephi 9:19–22 and look for something similar to the feather from this object lesson. (The Lord baptized the Lamanites with fire and the Holy Ghost and they knew it not.)*

- Analyze:
  - *What does it mean to be baptized by fire and with the Holy Ghost?*
  - *What does the Lord require us to sacrifice to gain this spiritual gift?*
  - *Why does the baptism of fire seem like it would be a very noticeable occurrence?*
  - *Why do you think the Lamanites were unaware that they had experienced this blessing?*
  - *Why do we often find that the workings of the Spirit are difficult to discern?*

- Apply:
  - *How might similar occurrences happen in the lives of Church members today?*
  - *How long might it take for someone to acquire a broken heart and contrite spirit?*
  - *What types of actions does that require?*
  - *If the baptism of fire is sometimes a gradual process, what could we do that would help us monitor our growth?*

- Boyd K. Packer taught, "There may be more power in your testimony than even you realize. . . . Several years ago I met one of our sons in the mission field in a distant part of the world. He had been there for a year. His first question was this: 'Dad, what can I do to grow spiritually? I have tried so hard to grow spiritually and I just haven't made any progress.' That was his perception: to me it was otherwise. I could hardly believe the maturity, the spiritual growth that he had gained in just one year. He 'knew it not' for it had come as growth, not as a startling spiritual experience" ("The Candle of the Lord," *Ensign*, Jan. 1983).

- Testify that although it can be a gradual process, those who come unto Christ will receive the power of the Holy Ghost in their lives and be sanctified.

Notes

Teaching Tips from Prophets' Lips "Our ultimate reassurance is in the honest prompting of the Lord—the prompting that you are the Lord's instrument, this is His class, this is His Church, these are His people. Then honestly respond to that Spirit" (Jeffrey R. Holland, "Teaching and Learning in the Church," *Ensign*, June 2007, 88–105).

3 NEPHI 10

"Return unto Me with Full Purpose of Heart"
About AD 34–35

1–3, After a long silence in the land, the Lord's voice is heard again; 4–7, The Lord invites all to repent and return unto Him; 8–19, All of these things are the fulfillment of many of the holy prophets' words.

1 And now behold, it came to pass that all the people of the land did hear these sayings, and did witness of it. And after these sayings there was silence in the land for the space of many hours;

2 For so great was the astonishment of the people that they did cease lamenting and howling for the loss of their kindred which had been slain; therefore there was silence in all the land for the space of many hours.

3 And it came to pass that there came a voice again unto the people, and all the people did hear, and did witness of it, saying:

4 O ye people of these great cities which have fallen, who are descendants of Jacob, yea, who are of the house of Israel, how oft have I gathered you as a hen gathereth her chickens under her wings, and have nourished you.

5 And again, how oft would I have gathered you as a hen gathereth her chickens under her wings, yea, O ye people of the house of Israel, who have fallen; yea, O ye people of the house of Israel, ye that dwell at Jerusalem, as ye that have fallen; yea, how oft would I have gathered you as a hen gathereth her chickens, and ye would not.

6 O ye house of Israel whom I have spared, how oft will I gather you as a hen gathereth her chickens under her wings, if ye will repent and return unto me with full purpose of heart.

7 But if not, O house of Israel, the places of your dwellings shall become desolate until the time of the fulfilling of the covenant to your fathers.

vv. 1–7 If we will repent and return unto the Lord with full purpose of heart, the Lord will forgive us.

- ⚡ Bring a picture of a hen and her brood. Ask, *How does this picture relate with the destruction of the people of Nephi?*

- 🔎 Look in verse 6 for the metaphor of the hen and her brood.

- ❓ Analyze:
  - *How does the analogy of a hen gathering her chickens represent protection?*
  - *Why does the Lord use the metaphor of a hen gathering her chickens under her wings?*
  - *What does this teach us about the Lord's desire to protect us?*

- 🔎 Look for how many times the Lord will allow us to repent and return unto Him according to verse 6.

- 🔎 Invite class members to turn to Doctrine and Covenants 43:25 to discover how the Lord warns us today that we need to repent and return unto Him.

- ❓ Apply: *How do you know the Lord will forgive us as we return unto Him?* Invite class members to recall any spiritual memories they may have had that demonstrate this love of the Lord.

- ♥ Testify of the Lord's desire to protect us and forgive us. Invite class members to return to Him.

8 And now it came to pass that after the people had heard these words, behold, they began to

Notes

weep and howl again because of the loss of their kindred and friends.

9 And it came to pass that thus did the three days pass away. And it was in the morning, and the darkness dispersed from off the face of the land, and the earth did cease to tremble, and the rocks did cease to rend, and the dreadful groanings did cease, and all the tumultuous noises did pass away.

10 And the earth did cleave together again, that it stood; and the mourning, and the weeping, and the wailing of the people who were spared alive did cease; and their mourning was turned into joy, and their lamentations into the praise and thanksgiving unto the Lord Jesus Christ, their Redeemer.

11 And thus far were the scriptures fulfilled which had been spoken by the prophets.

12 And it was the more righteous part of the people who were saved, and it was they who received the prophets and stoned them not; and it was they who had not shed the blood of the saints, who were spared—

13 And they were spared and were not sunk and buried up in the earth; and they were not drowned in the depths of the sea; and they were not burned by fire, neither were they fallen upon and crushed to death; and they were not carried away in the whirlwind; neither were they overpowered by the vapor of smoke and of darkness.

14 And now, whoso readeth, let him understand; he that hath the scriptures, let him search them, and see and behold if all these deaths and destructions by fire, and by smoke, and by tempests, and by whirlwinds, and by the opening of the earth to receive them, and all these things are not unto the fulfilling of the prophecies of many of the holy prophets.

15 Behold, I say unto you, Yea, many have testified of these things at the coming of Christ, and were slain because they testified of these things.

16 Yea, the prophet Zenos did testify of these things, and also Zenock spake concerning these things, because they testified particularly concerning us, who are the remnant of their seed.

17 Behold, our father Jacob also testified concerning a remnant of the seed of Joseph. And behold, are not we a remnant of the seed of Joseph? And these things which testify of us, are they not written upon the plates of brass which our father Lehi brought out of Jerusalem?

18 And it came to pass that in the ending of the thirty and fourth year, behold, I will show unto you that the people of Nephi who were spared, and also those who had been called Lamanites, who had been spared, did have great favors shown unto them, and great blessings poured out upon their heads, insomuch that soon after the ascension of Christ into heaven he did truly manifest himself unto them—

19 Showing his body unto them, and ministering unto them; and an account of his ministry shall be given hereafter. Therefore for this time I make an end of my sayings.

vv. 8–19 The prophecies of all the prophets are fulfilled.

What is the main point that Mormon is trying to make in verses 10–17?

Apply: The teachings of 3 Nephi invite us to look to the past to see the future. Both modern and ancient apostles have testified of the Second Coming. Ask, What do these verses teach us about preparing for the Second Coming? What lesson can we learn from this as we prepare for the Lord's Second Coming?

Index Topics: repentance, prophets (roles of)

Notes

3 NEPHI 11

Jesus Appears to the Nephites
About AD 34

1–7, The Father testifies of His Son to the people; 8–17, Jesus testifies of His Atonement and invites the people to feel the prints from His crucifixion; 18–27, He teaches about baptism; 28–30, He teaches about contention; 31–41, He details His doctrine.

Note: Jesus Christ did show himself unto the people of Nephi, as the multitude were gathered together in the land Bountiful, and did minister unto them; and on this wise did he show himself unto them.

- Inform class members that the record of the first day of Christ's visit is comprised of chapters 11–18. Invite them to annotate this at the beginning of chapter 11.

1 And now it came to pass that there were a great multitude gathered together, of the people of Nephi, round about the temple which was in the land Bountiful; and they were marveling and wondering one with another, and were showing one to another the great and marvelous change which had taken place.

2 And they were also conversing about this Jesus Christ, of whom the sign had been given concerning his death.

3 And it came to pass that while they were thus conversing one with another, they heard a voice as if it came out of heaven; and they cast their eyes round about, for they understood not the voice which they heard; and it was not a harsh voice, neither was it a loud voice; nevertheless, and notwithstanding it being a small voice it did pierce them that did hear to the center, insomuch that there was no part of their frame that it did not cause to quake; yea, it did pierce them to the very soul, and did cause their hearts to burn.

4 And it came to pass that again they heard the voice, and they understood it not.

5 And again the third time they did hear the voice, and did open their ears to hear it; and their eyes were towards the sound thereof; and they did look steadfastly towards heaven, from whence the sound came.

6 And behold, the third time they did understand the voice which they heard; and it said unto them:

7 Behold my Beloved Son, in whom I am well pleased, in whom I have glorified my name—hear ye him.

vv. 1–7 We need to remove distractions in order to hear and understand the Lord's voice.

- Invite five class members to the front of the room. Give four of them excerpts of news articles and the fifth a copy of 3 Nephi 11:1–7. Have the five read their text simultaneously at the same volume. Do not inform the class regarding the content of the readings. After a few seconds of reading, have the readers stop, and ask the class if they could tell what was being read. If needed, prompt them by asking if they heard a scriptural passage from the readers. If they did, ask them what they heard in the passage. Ask the five to continue reading, and have the class attempt to understand what the scriptural passage is about. After a few more seconds, ask class members what they learned from the scripture. Ask them what needed to happen to better understand the scripture. Discuss how removing the distractions allowed them to clearly hear and understand the scriptural passage.

- Have four of the readers sit down and ask the one left to read verses 1–7 again and have the class to look for what the people did in order to understand what was being spoken to them.

- Analyze: *Why did the Nephites need to hear the message three times? What did the*

Notes

3 NEPHI 11

Nephites do to better understand the message? (v. 5). Consider writing the answers on the board to aid discussion.

❓ **Apply:** *How does a person today do the three actions described in verse 5? What kinds of distractions do we need to remove when reading the scriptures in order to hear the Lord's voice more clearly?*

✏️ Invite class members to write down some of the distractions they could remove to help them more effectively read the scriptures and understand the promptings of the Spirit.

---

8 And it came to pass, as they understood they cast their eyes up again towards heaven; and behold, they saw a Man descending out of heaven; and he was clothed in a white robe; and he came down and stood in the midst of them; and the eyes of the whole multitude were turned upon him, and they durst not open their mouths, even one to another, and wist not what it meant, for they thought it was an angel that had appeared unto them.

9 And it came to pass that he stretched forth his hand and spake unto the people, saying:

10 Behold, I am Jesus Christ, whom the prophets testified shall come into the world.

11 And behold, I am the light and the life of the world; and I have drunk out of that bitter cup which the Father hath given me, and have glorified the Father in taking upon me the sins of the world, in the which I have suffered the will of the Father in all things from the beginning.

12 And it came to pass that when Jesus had spoken these words the whole multitude fell to the earth; for they remembered that it had been prophesied among them that Christ should show himself unto them after his ascension into heaven.

13 And it came to pass that the Lord spake unto them saying:

14 Arise and come forth unto me, that ye may thrust your hands into my side, and also that ye may feel the prints of the nails in my hands and in my feet, that ye may know that I am the God of Israel, and the God of the whole earth, and have been slain for the sins of the world.

vv. 10–14 "A lot, in a little."

⚡ Write on the board "A lot, in a little." Ask class members how DNA is an example of the statement on the board. You may need to explain that the DNA in a single cell has the blueprints for almost all the physical characteristics of an individual.

🔍 Explain that 3 Nephi 11:10–14 gives the first words of Christ when He descended among the Nephites, and that His teachings are another example of "a lot, in a little." Invite class members to read verses 10–14 to themselves and try to find as many insights in those verses as they can. Have them share what they found.

❓ Consider following up with questions like:
- *How is Jesus the Light and Life of the world?*
- *Why did He describe His Atonement as a "bitter cup"?*
- *How does sin make it bitter?*
- *How did Jesus glorify His Father by this act?*
- *Why do you think Jesus wanted each person to personally feel His wounds?*
- *Why does Jesus describe Himself as "God"?*

💬 To help explain why Jesus also uses the title of God, share the following quote by Bruce R. McConkie: "Christ-Messiah is God! Such is the plain and pure pronouncement of all the prophets of all the ages. In our desire to avoid the false and absurd conclusions contained in the creeds of Christendom, we are wont to shy away from this pure and unadorned verity; we go to great lengths to use language that shows there is both a Father and a Son, that they are separate Persons and are not somehow mystically intertwined as an essence or spirit that is everywhere present. Such an approach is perhaps essential in reasoning with the Gentiles of sectarianism; it helps to overthrow the fallacies formulated

Notes

in their creeds. But having so done, if we are to envision our Lord's true status and glory, we must come back to the pronouncement of pronouncements, the doctrine of doctrines, the message of messages, which is that Christ is God. And if it were not so, he could not save us" (*The Promised Messiah* [1978], 98).

15 And it came to pass that the multitude went forth, and thrust their hands into his side, and did feel the prints of the nails in his hands and in his feet; and this they did do, going forth one by one until they had all gone forth, and did see with their eyes and did feel with their hands, and did know of a surety and did bear record, that it was he, of whom it was written by the prophets, that should come.

16 And when they had all gone forth and had witnessed for themselves, they did cry out with one accord, saying:

17 Hosanna! Blessed be the name of the Most High God! And they did fall down at the feet of Jesus, and did worship him.

v. 15 The Atonement was personal in nature.

Analyze: *Why do you think the people felt Christ's wounds "one by one"? When Jesus experienced the "bitter cup" did He suffer for us individually?*

Share the following quote by Merrill J. Bateman: "For many years I thought of the Savior's experience in the garden and on the cross as places where a large mass of sin was heaped upon Him. Through the words of Alma, Abinadi, Isaiah, and other prophets, however, my view has changed. Instead of an impersonal mass of sin, there was a long line of people, as Jesus felt 'our infirmities' (Hebrews 4:15), '[bore] our griefs, . . . carried our sorrows . . . [and] was bruised for our iniquities' (Isaiah 53:4–5). The Atonement was an intimate, personal experience in which Jesus came to know how to help each of us. The Pearl of Great Price teaches that Moses was shown all the inhabitants of the earth, which were 'numberless as the sand upon the sea shore' (Moses 1:28). If Moses beheld every soul, then it seems reasonable that the Creator of the universe has the power to become intimately acquainted with each of us. He learned about your weaknesses and mine. He experienced your pains and sufferings. He experienced mine. I testify that He knows us. He understands the way in which we deal with temptations. He knows our weaknesses. But more than that, more than just knowing us, He knows how to help us if we come to Him in faith" ("A Pattern for All," *Ensign*, Nov. 2005, 76).

18 And it came to pass that he spake unto Nephi (for Nephi was among the multitude) and he commanded him that he should come forth.

19 And Nephi arose and went forth, and bowed himself before the Lord and did kiss his feet.

20 And the Lord commanded him that he should arise. And he arose and stood before him.

21 And the Lord said unto him: I give unto you power that ye shall baptize this people when I am again ascended into heaven.

22 And again the Lord called others, and said unto them likewise; and he gave unto them power to baptize. And he said unto them: On this wise shall ye baptize; and there shall be no disputations among you.

23 Verily I say unto you, that whoso repenteth of his sins through your words, and desireth to be baptized in my name, on this wise shall ye baptize them—Behold, ye shall go down and stand in the water, and in my name shall ye baptize them.

24 And now behold, these are the words which ye shall say, calling them by name, saying:

25 Having authority given me of Jesus Christ, I baptize you in the name of the Father, and of the Son, and of the Holy Ghost. Amen.

Notes

26 And then shall ye immerse them in the water, and come forth again out of the water.

27 And after this manner shall ye baptize in my name; for behold, verily I say unto you, that the Father, and the Son, and the Holy Ghost are one; and I am in the Father, and the Father in me, and the Father and I are one.

28 And according as I have commanded you thus shall ye baptize. And there shall be no disputations among you, as there have hitherto been; neither shall there be disputations among you concerning the points of my doctrine, as there have hitherto been.

29 For verily, verily I say unto you, he that hath the spirit of contention is not of me, but is of the devil, who is the father of contention, and he stirreth up the hearts of men to contend with anger, one with another.

vv. 22–29 We must avoid contention to be true followers of Christ.

⚡ Hold up a policy manual of some kind. Ask, *Why does the Church have policy manuals and handbooks of instructions?*

🔍 *In verse 22, look for why Jesus gives the people instructions on how to properly baptize. In verses 28–29, look for why it is important to avoid contention.*

❓ Analyze: *Why would the devil want contention? Why does contention lead to anger?*

✏️ Invite class members to think to themselves of situations that might often spark anger and contention in their lives. Have them write down a plan of what to do next time they are in one of those situations so that they can avoid contention and anger.

30 Behold, this is not my doctrine, to stir up the hearts of men with anger, one against another; but this is my doctrine, that such things should be done away.

31 Behold, verily, verily, I say unto you, I will declare unto you my doctrine.

32 And this is my doctrine, and it is the doctrine which the Father hath given unto me; and I bear record of the Father, and the Father beareth record of me, and the Holy Ghost beareth record of the Father and me; and I bear record that the Father commandeth all men, everywhere, to repent and believe in me.

33 And whoso believeth in me, and is baptized, the same shall be saved; and they are they who shall inherit the kingdom of God.

34 And whoso believeth not in me, and is not baptized, shall be damned.

35 Verily, verily, I say unto you, that this is my doctrine, and I bear record of it from the Father; and whoso believeth in me believeth in the Father also; and unto him will the Father bear record of me, for he will visit him with fire and with the Holy Ghost.

36 And thus will the Father bear record of me, and the Holy Ghost will bear record unto him of the Father and me; for the Father, and I, and the Holy Ghost are one.

37 And again I say unto you, ye must repent, and become as a little child, and be baptized in my name, or ye can in nowise receive these things.

38 And again I say unto you, ye must repent, and be baptized in my name, and become as a little child, or ye can in nowise inherit the kingdom of God.

39 Verily, verily, I say unto you, that this is my doctrine, and whoso buildeth upon this buildeth upon my rock, and the gates of hell shall not prevail against them.

40 And whoso shall declare more or less than this, and establish it for my doctrine, the same cometh of evil, and is not built upon my rock; but he buildeth upon a sandy foundation, and the gates of hell stand open to receive such when the floods come and the winds beat upon them.

41 Therefore, go forth unto this people, and declare the words which I have spoken, unto the ends of the earth.

Notes

vv. 31–40 The doctrine of Christ.

🔎 Have class members read verses 31–40 and underline each time "my doctrine" is said. Have them write 2 Nephi 32:5–6 in their margins. Explain that in those verses, Nephi said that when the Lord would come, He would give further details on His doctrine. Have class members read verses 31–40 and try to identify various points of the doctrine of Christ.

> **Teaching Tips from Prophets' Lips** "The best measure of the effectiveness of what occurs in the classroom is to observe that the truths are being understood and applied in a student's life" (Richard G. Scott, "To Understand and Live Truth," 3).

Index Topics: revelation, atonement, anger

3 NEPHI 12

The Sermon on the Mount to the Nephites

About AD 34

1–12, Jesus teaches the beatitudes; 13–16, Jesus teaches the importance of example; 17–48, Jesus teaches the fulfillment of the law of Moses and what is to supersede it.

Note: 3 Nephi 12–14 contain the Savior's teachings from the Sermon on the Mount found in Matthew 5–7.

Overarching Principle: A guide on how to be a disciple of Christ.

⚡ Similar to the lesson idea in Nephi 11, bring an instruction manual or some other type of guidebook. Discuss with class members the importance of using the manual as a reference. Explain that the Sermon on the Mount could be viewed as a guidebook on being a disciple of Christ. This chapter will outline three specific guidelines: how to receive blessings, how to be an example, and how to treat other people.

✏️ You may want to consider creating three columns on the board, one for each guideline you will identify, and encourage the class to make a list on their own.

1 And it came to pass that when Jesus had spoken these words unto Nephi, and to those who had been called, (now the number of them who had been called, and received power and authority to baptize, was twelve) and behold, he stretched forth his hand unto the multitude, and cried unto them, saying: Blessed are ye if ye shall give heed unto the words of these twelve whom I have chosen from among you to minister unto you, and to be your servants; and unto them I have given power that they may baptize you with water; and after that ye are baptized with water, behold, I will baptize you with fire and with the Holy Ghost; therefore blessed are ye if ye shall believe in me and be baptized, after that ye have seen me and know that I am.

2 And again, more blessed are they who shall believe in your words because that ye shall testify that ye have seen me, and that ye know that I am. Yea, blessed are they who shall believe in your words, and come down into the depths of humility and be baptized, for they shall be visited with fire and with the Holy Ghost, and shall receive a remission of their sins.

3 Yea, blessed are the poor in spirit who come unto me, for theirs is the kingdom of heaven.

4 And again, blessed are all they that mourn, for they shall be comforted.

5 And blessed are the meek, for they shall inherit the earth.

6 And blessed are all they who do hunger and thirst after righteousness, for they shall be filled with the Holy Ghost.

Notes

7 And blessed are the merciful, for they shall obtain mercy.

8 And blessed are all the pure in heart, for they shall see God.

9 And blessed are all the peacemakers, for they shall be called the children of God.

10 And blessed are all they who are persecuted for my name's sake, for theirs is the kingdom of heaven.

11 And blessed are ye when men shall revile you and persecute, and shall say all manner of evil against you falsely, for my sake;

vv. 1–11 How to receive blessings from God.

- Refer to the hook icon below the overarching principle at the beginning of this lesson.

- Invite class members to search in verses 1–11 for each "blessed" statement offered by the Savior. Depending on class size and age of class members, you may want to consider breaking the class into groups and allow them to work together.

- Write the "blessed" statements on the board as they are identified under the appropriate column.

- Analyze: Depending on time, discuss a few of these beatitudes with the class.

- The Greek word for "blessed" can be translated as "happy." Consider discussing how each of the beatitudes can lead to happiness.

12 For ye shall have great joy and be exceedingly glad, for great shall be your reward in heaven; for so persecuted they the prophets who were before you.

13 Verily, verily, I say unto you, I give unto you to be the salt of the earth; but if the salt shall lose its savor wherewith shall the earth be salted? The salt shall be thenceforth good for nothing, but to be cast out and to be trodden under foot of men.

14 Verily, verily, I say unto you, I give unto you to be the light of this people. A city that is set on a hill cannot be hid.

15 Behold, do men light a candle and put it under a bushel? Nay, but on a candlestick, and it giveth light to all that are in the house;

16 Therefore let your light so shine before this people, that they may see your good works and glorify your Father who is in heaven.

17 Think not that I am come to destroy the law or the prophets. I am not come to destroy but to fulfil;

18 For verily I say unto you, one jot nor one tittle hath not passed away from the law, but in me it hath all been fulfilled.

19 And behold, I have given you the law and the commandments of my Father, that ye shall believe in me, and that ye shall repent of your sins, and come unto me with a broken heart and a contrite spirit. Behold, ye have the commandments before you, and the law is fulfilled.

20 Therefore come unto me and be ye saved; for verily I say unto you, that except ye shall keep my commandments, which I have commanded you at this time, ye shall in no case enter into the kingdom of heaven.

vv. 12–20 How to live as an example.

- Refer to the hook icon below the overarching principle at the beginning of this lesson. You may also want to bring two salt shakers, one with salt and another with a salt and dirt mixture.

- Invite class members to read verses 12–20 looking for principles of being an example and how they relate to the salt shakers.

- Write what the class discovers on the board under the appropriate column.

- Analyze: Analyze with the class the various uses of salt and how those uses could represent our being an example.

- President Boyd K. Packer has counseled, "A worthy Latter-day Saint family is a standard to the world. Not only are we to maintain the highest of standards, but each of us is

Notes

to be a standard, a defense, a refuge. We are to 'let [our] light so shine before men, that they may see [our] good works, and glorify [our] Father which is in heaven'" ("A Defense and A Refuge," *Ensign*, Nov. 2006, 87).

21 Ye have heard that it hath been said by them of old time, and it is also written before you, that thou shalt not kill, and whosoever shall kill shall be in danger of the judgment of God;

22 But I say unto you, that whosoever is angry with his brother shall be in danger of his judgment. And whosoever shall say to his brother, Raca, shall be in danger of the council; and whosoever shall say, Thou fool, shall be in danger of hell fire.

23 Therefore, if ye shall come unto me, or shall desire to come unto me, and rememberest that thy brother hath aught against thee—

24 Go thy way unto thy brother, and first be reconciled to thy brother, and then come unto me with full purpose of heart, and I will receive you.

25 Agree with thine adversary quickly while thou art in the way with him, lest at any time he shall get thee, and thou shalt be cast into prison.

26 Verily, verily, I say unto thee, thou shalt by no means come out thence until thou hast paid the uttermost senine. And while ye are in prison can ye pay even one senine? Verily, verily, I say unto you, Nay.

27 Behold, it is written by them of old time, that thou shalt not commit adultery;

28 But I say unto you, that whosoever looketh on a woman, to lust after her, hath committed adultery already in his heart.

29 Behold, I give unto you a commandment, that ye suffer none of these things to enter into your heart;

30 For it is better that ye should deny yourselves of these things, wherein ye will take up your cross, than that ye should be cast into hell.

31 It hath been written, that whosoever shall put away his wife, let him give her a writing of divorcement.

32 Verily, verily, I say unto you, that whosoever shall put away his wife, saving for the cause of fornication, causeth her to commit adultery; and whoso shall marry her who is divorced committeth adultery.

33 And again it is written, thou shalt not forswear thyself, but shalt perform unto the Lord thine oaths;

34 But verily, verily, I say unto you, swear not at all; neither by heaven, for it is God's throne;

35 Nor by the earth, for it is his footstool;

36 Neither shalt thou swear by thy head, because thou canst not make one hair black or white;

37 But let your communication be Yea, yea; Nay, nay; for whatsoever cometh of more than these is evil.

38 And behold, it is written, an eye for an eye, and a tooth for a tooth;

39 But I say unto you, that ye shall not resist evil, but whosoever shall smite thee on thy right cheek, turn to him the other also;

40 And if any man will sue thee at the law and take away thy coat, let him have thy cloak also;

41 And whosoever shall compel thee to go a mile, go with him twain.

42 Give to him that asketh thee, and from him that would borrow of thee turn thou not away.

43 And behold it is written also, that thou shalt love thy neighbor and hate thine enemy;

44 But behold I say unto you, love your enemies, bless them that curse you, do good to them that hate you, and pray for them who despitefully use you and persecute you;

45 That ye may be the children of your Father who is in heaven; for he maketh his sun to rise on the evil and on the good.

Notes

vv. 21–45 How to treat other people.

- ⚡ Refer to the hook icon below the overarching principle at the beginning of this lesson. Consider having the class write "old" by what was taught from the law of Moses and "new" by the higher law of Christ.

- ✏️ Consider writing on the board what the class finds in this section under its appropriate column.

- 🔍 The following categories can be used to help class members search for principles on how to treat other people.

  How to treat those you disagree with (vv. 21–26)

  How to treat your spouse (vv. 27–32)

  How to communicate with others (vv. 33–37)

  How to treat your enemies (vv. 38–41)

- ❓ Analyze: Encourage class members to find and discuss principles from each of the Savior's teachings. Ask, *Why does the Savior have such high expectations?*

- ❓ Apply: *What have you learned today that can help you become a more devoted follower of Jesus Christ?*

46 Therefore those things which were of old time, which were under the law, in me are all fulfilled.

47 Old things are done away, and all things have become new.

48 Therefore I would that ye should be perfect even as I, or your Father who is in heaven is perfect.

v. 48 "Be perfect even as I."

- 🔍 Note with the class Jesus's concluding invitation found in verse 48.

- 💡 The Greek word for "perfect" doesn't necessarily indicate having no errors, but rather being brought to an end, finished, or completed.

- 💡 Compare the difference in verse 48 with Matthew 5:48. Jesus includes Himself in this invitation to the Nephites, since He now has a perfected, glorified body.

- 💬 President Thomas S. Monson taught, "Although we come into mortality 'trailing clouds of glory,' life moves relentlessly forward. Youth follows childhood, and maturity comes ever so imperceptibly. From experience we learn the need to reach heavenward for assistance as we make our way along life's pathway. God, our Father, and Jesus Christ, our Lord, have marked the way to perfection. They beckon us to follow eternal verities and to become perfect, as They are perfect. The Apostle Paul likened life to a race. To the Hebrews he urged, 'Let us lay aside . . . the sin which doth so easily beset us, and let us run with patience the race that is set before us' (see Hebrews 12:1)" ("The Race of Life," *Ensign*, May 2012, 93).

- ❤️ Encourage class members to choose one way they can be more Christlike.

3 NEPHI 13

Where Your Treasure Is, There Shall Be Your Heart
About AD 34

1–4, Jesus teaches how to give alms properly; 5–13, Jesus teaches principles of prayer; 14–24, Jesus teaches about priorities; 25–34, Jesus offers instruction to the twelve disciples.

Note: 3 Nephi 12–14 contain the Savior's teachings from the Sermon on the Mount found in Matthew 5–7.

Overarching Principle: True disciples of Christ do what they are asked for the right reasons.

- ⚡ Discuss the following questions with the class:
  - *When are times we do right things for the wrong reasons?*

Notes

- *If we are doing things for the wrong reason, why do we do them?*

Consider asking for a few brief examples or share one yourself. Allow class members to discuss these two questions, and then use that discussion to introduce the overarching principle above. Explain that Jesus will address the correct and incorrect reasons for living the commandments we have been asked to live.

✎ The following chart may be useful to allow class members to search for principles from this chapter:

Giving alms or sevice (3 Ne. 13:1–4)	
How to	How not to

Prayer and fasting (3 Ne. 13:5–18)	
How to	How not to

Priorities (3 Ne. 13:19–23)	
How to	How not to

Jesus's conclusion (3 Ne. 13:24)

1 Verily, verily, I say that I would that ye should do alms unto the poor; but take heed that ye do not your alms before men to be seen of them; otherwise ye have no reward of your Father who is in heaven.

2 Therefore, when ye shall do your alms do not sound a trumpet before you, as will hypocrites do in the synagogues and in the streets, that they may have glory of men. Verily I say unto you, they have their reward.

3 But when thou doest alms let not thy left hand know what thy right hand doeth;

4 That thine alms may be in secret; and thy Father who seeth in secret, himself shall reward thee openly.

vv. 1–4 Giving alms or service.

🔍 Refer to the chart at the beginning of this lesson.

5 And when thou prayest thou shalt not do as the hypocrites, for they love to pray, standing in the synagogues and in the corners of the streets, that they may be seen of men. Verily I say unto you, they have their reward.

6 But thou, when thou prayest, enter into thy closet, and when thou hast shut thy door, pray to thy Father who is in secret; and thy Father, who seeth in secret, shall reward thee openly.

7 But when ye pray, use not vain repetitions, as the heathen, for they think that they shall be heard for their much speaking.

8 Be not ye therefore like unto them, for your Father knoweth what things ye have need of before ye ask him.

9 After this manner therefore pray ye: Our Father who art in heaven, hallowed be thy name.

10 Thy will be done on earth as it is in heaven.

11 And forgive us our debts, as we forgive our debtors.

12 And lead us not into temptation, but deliver us from evil.

13 For thine is the kingdom, and the power, and the glory, forever. Amen.

14 For, if ye forgive men their trespasses your heavenly Father will also forgive you;

Notes

15 But if ye forgive not men their trespasses neither will your Father forgive your trespasses.

16 Moreover, when ye fast be not as the hypocrites, of a sad countenance, for they disfigure their faces that they may appear unto men to fast. Verily I say unto you, they have their reward.

17 But thou, when thou fastest, anoint thy head, and wash thy face;

18 That thou appear not unto men to fast, but unto thy Father, who is in secret; and thy Father, who seeth in secret, shall reward thee openly.

vv. 5–18 Prayer and Fasting.

- Refer to the chart at the beginning of this lesson.

19 Lay not up for yourselves treasures upon earth, where moth and rust doth corrupt, and thieves break through and steal;

20 But lay up for yourselves treasures in heaven, where neither moth nor rust doth corrupt, and where thieves do not break through nor steal.

21 For where your treasure is, there will your heart be also.

22 The light of the body is the eye; if, therefore, thine eye be single, thy whole body shall be full of light.

23 But if thine eye be evil, thy whole body shall be full of darkness. If, therefore, the light that is in thee be darkness, how great is that darkness!

vv. 19–23 Priorities.

- Refer to the chart at the beginning of this lesson.

24 No man can serve two masters; for either he will hate the one and love the other, or else he will hold to the one and despise the other. Ye cannot serve God and Mammon.

v. 24 No man can serve two masters.

- Verse 24 could be a conclusion to Jesus's sermon in this chapter. Use the chart to allow the class to analyze the meaning of verse 24 in context of the whole chapter.

- Encourage class members to consider ways they can meaningfully improve the way they choose to obey God's commandments.

25 And now it came to pass that when Jesus had spoken these words he looked upon the twelve whom he had chosen, and said unto them: Remember the words which I have spoken. For behold, ye are they whom I have chosen to minister unto this people. Therefore I say unto you, take no thought for your life, what ye shall eat, or what ye shall drink; nor yet for your body, what ye shall put on. Is not the life more than meat, and the body than raiment?

26 Behold the fowls of the air, for they sow not, neither do they reap nor gather into barns; yet your heavenly Father feedeth them. Are ye not much better than they?

27 Which of you by taking thought can add one cubit unto his stature?

28 And why take ye thought for raiment? Consider the lilies of the field how they grow; they toil not, neither do they spin;

29 And yet I say unto you, that even Solomon, in all his glory, was not arrayed like one of these.

30 Wherefore, if God so clothe the grass of the field, which today is, and tomorrow is cast into the oven, even so will he clothe you, if ye are not of little faith.

31 Therefore take no thought, saying, What shall we eat? or, What shall we drink? or, Wherewithal shall we be clothed?

32 For your heavenly Father knoweth that ye have need of all these things.

33 But seek ye first the kingdom of God and his righteousness, and all these things shall be added unto you.

34 Take therefore no thought for the morrow, for

Notes

the morrow shall take thought for the things of itself. Sufficient is the day unto the evil thereof.

vv. 25–34 Counsel to missionaries.

🔎 *Notice in verse 25 who it is that the Savior now addresses in the next nine verses.*

💡 Note with the class that the twelve disciples will become missionaries, charged to teach the resurrected Savior to their people.

🔎 *Read verses 25–34 and ask, What advice and counsel does Jesus offer these newly called missionaries?*

❓ **Apply:** *How could this same counsel be applicable to today?*

💬 In speaking to senior couple missionaries, Elder Robert D. Hales taught, "In considering missionary opportunities, many couples throughout the world have an abundant desire to serve but lack abundant means. If this is your situation, remember that the right mission call may not be to a far-off country with a strange sounding name. The right call for you may be within your stake or area. 'Your heavenly Father knoweth that ye have need of all these things.' Counsel with your extended family and your bishop or branch president. As the Lord's servants understand your temporal situation, you will be able to receive the eternal blessings of full-time missionary service." ("Couple Missionaries: Blessings from Sacrifice and Service," *Ensign*, May 2005, 39)

> **Teaching Tips from Prophets' Lips** "As we explain that which we already know there seems to come to us an unfolding of additional truths, and enlargement of our understandings, new connections and applications" (*The Teachings of Spencer W. Kimball* [1982], 530).

3 NEPHI 14

The Sermon on the Mount to the Nephites
About AD 34

1–6, Jesus teaches about judging; 7–11, Jesus teaches the doctrine of asking and reciving; 12–14, Baptism is the straight gate by which we enter heaven; 15–27, Jesus concludes the Sermon on the Mount with invitations to action.

Note: 3 Nephi 12–14 contain the Savior's teachings from the Sermon on the Mount found in Matthew 5–7.

1 And now it came to pass that when Jesus had spoken these words he turned again to the multitude, and did open his mouth unto them again, saying: Verily, verily, I say unto you, Judge not, that ye be not judged.

2 For with what judgment ye judge, ye shall be judged; and with what measure ye mete, it shall be measured to you again.

3 And why beholdest thou the mote that is in thy brother's eye, but considerest not the beam that is in thine own eye?

4 Or how wilt thou say to thy brother: Let me pull the mote out of thine eye—and behold, a beam is in thine own eye?

5 Thou hypocrite, first cast the beam out of thine own eye; and then shalt thou see clearly to cast the mote out of thy brother's eye.

vv. 1–5 "Judge not, that ye be not judged."

⚡ Write the following phrases on the board: "That's the pot calling the kettle black!" and "People in glass houses shouldn't throw stones." Ask, *What do these two phrases have in common?*

🔎 *Read 3 Nephi 14:1–5 and look for the metaphor that Jesus uses to teach a similar principle to the phrases on the board.*

Notes

💬 Invite a class member to read the following story from President Thomas S. Monson:

"A young couple, Lisa and John, moved into a new neighborhood. One morning while they were eating breakfast, Lisa looked out the window and watched her next-door neighbor hanging out her wash.

"'That laundry's not clean!' Lisa exclaimed. 'Our neighbor doesn't know how to get clothes clean!'

"John looked on but remained silent.

"Every time her neighbor would hang her wash to dry, Lisa would make the same comments.

"A few weeks later Lisa was surprised to glance out her window and see a nice, clean wash hanging in her neighbor's yard. She said to her husband, 'Look, John—she's finally learned how to wash correctly! I wonder how she did it.'

"John replied, 'Well, dear, I have the answer for you. You'll be interested to know that I got up early this morning and washed our windows!'" ("Charity Never Faileth," *Ensign*, November 2010, 125).

❓ Analyze: *Why is it so easy to judge others? What can we do to overcome the tendency to judge unrighteously?*

6 Give not that which is holy unto the dogs, neither cast ye your pearls before swine, lest they trample them under their feet, and turn again and rend you.

7 Ask, and it shall be given unto you; seek, and ye shall find; knock, and it shall be opened unto you.

8 For every one that asketh, receiveth; and he that seeketh, findeth; and to him that knocketh, it shall be opened.

9 Or what man is there of you, who, if his son ask bread, will give him a stone?

10 Or if he ask a fish, will he give him a serpent?

11 If ye then, being evil, know how to give good gifts unto your children, how much more shall your Father who is in heaven give good things to them that ask him?

vv. 7–11 The Lord hears and answers our prayers.

⚡ *What do you think is the most repeated message of scripture?*

💬 President Boyd K. Packer has taught, "No message is repeated more times in scripture than the simple thought: 'Ask, and ye shall receive.'" ("Prayers and Answers," *Ensign*, Nov. 1979, 20)

❓ Read verses 7–11 and ask, *According to these verses, what is it about God that leads Him to answer our prayers? How does prayer change for you when you realize that you are talking to your spiritual Father?*

♥ Invite class members to share experiences of times when their prayers have been heard and answered by the Lord. Bear your testimony that the Father will hear and answer our prayers.

12 Therefore, all things whatsoever ye would that men should do to you, do ye even so to them, for this is the law and the prophets.

13 Enter ye in at the strait gate; for wide is the gate, and broad is the way, which leadeth to destruction, and many there be who go in thereat;

14 Because strait is the gate, and narrow is the way, which leadeth unto life, and few there be that find it.

15 Beware of false prophets, who come to you in sheep's clothing, but inwardly they are ravening wolves.

16 Ye shall know them by their fruits. Do men gather grapes of thorns, or figs of thistles?

17 Even so every good tree bringeth forth good fruit; but a corrupt tree bringeth forth evil fruit.

18 A good tree cannot bring forth evil fruit,

Notes

neither a corrupt tree bring forth good fruit.

19 Every tree that bringeth not forth good fruit is hewn down, and cast into the fire.

20 Wherefore, by their fruits ye shall know them.

21 Not everyone that saith unto me, Lord, Lord, shall enter into the kingdom of heaven; but he that doeth the will of my Father who is in heaven.

22 Many will say to me in that day: Lord, Lord, have we not prophesied in thy name, and in thy name have cast out devils, and in thy name done many wonderful works?

23 And then will I profess unto them: I never knew you; depart from me, ye that work iniquity.

24 Therefore, whoso heareth these sayings of mine and doeth them, I will liken him unto a wise man, who built his house upon a rock—

25 And the rain descended, and the floods came, and the winds blew, and beat upon that house; and it fell not, for it was founded upon a rock.

26 And every one that heareth these sayings of mine and doeth them not shall be likened unto a foolish man, who built his house upon the sand—

27 And the rain descended, and the floods came, and the winds blew, and beat upon that house; and it fell, and great was the fall of it.

vv. 15–27 The gospel of Christ is a gospel of action.

Divide the class into three sections and invite class members to work with one or two individuals near them. Assign the first group verses 16–20, the second group verses 21–23, and the third group verses 24–27. Invite group members to complete the following steps. Consider writing the instructions on the board:

Read and summarize the verses you are assigned.

- Ask yourselves, "What principle is Jesus teaching in these verses?"
- Ask yourselves, "Why is acting on what we know such an important part of the gospel? How does it further the plan of salvation?"
- Think of one or two modern examples of how to apply these teachings.

Invite class members to share their findings, being sure to summarize the verses they read.

Invite class members to apply the principle from verses 15–27 to what they have learned from 3 Nephi 12–14. Ask them to select one or two 'take-home' ideas from what they have learned in class. Have them write those ideas as goals for the coming week on a piece of paper or journal. Then, invite class members to place the goals somewhere to remind them to be "doers of the word and not hearers only."

3 NEPHI 15

Endure to the End

About AD 34

1–11, Jesus tells the multitude He has come to fulfill the law of Moses unto eternal life; 12–24, Jesus tells of other sheep He has that are not of this fold.

1 And now it came to pass that when Jesus had ended these sayings he cast his eyes round about on the multitude, and said unto them: Behold, ye have heard the things which I taught before I ascended to my Father; therefore, whoso remembereth these sayings of mine and doeth them, him will I raise up at the last day.

2 And it came to pass that when Jesus had said these words he perceived that there were some among them who marveled, and wondered what he would concerning the law of Moses; for they understood not the saying that old things had passed away, and that all things had become new.

Notes

3 NEPHI 15

3 And he said unto them: Marvel not that I said unto you that old things had passed away, and that all things had become new.

4 Behold, I say unto you that the law is fulfilled that was given unto Moses.

5 Behold, I am he that gave the law, and I am he who covenanted with my people Israel; therefore, the law in me is fulfilled, for I have come to fulfil the law; therefore it hath an end.

6 Behold, I do not destroy the prophets, for as many as have not been fulfilled in me, verily I say unto you, shall all be fulfilled.

7 And because I said unto you that old things have passed away, I do not destroy that which hath been spoken concerning things which are to come.

8 For behold, the covenant which I have made with my people is not all fulfilled; but the law which was given unto Moses hath an end in me.

9 Behold, I am the law, and the light. Look unto me, and endure to the end, and ye shall live; for unto him that endureth to the end will I give eternal life.

10 Behold, I have given unto you the commandments; therefore keep my commandments. And this is the law and the prophets, for they truly testified of me.

vv. 1–10 Christ will give us eternal life if we look unto Him and endure to the end.

- Show a picture of Moses and a picture of the Savior. Explain that during this lesson we will compare Moses and the Savior.

- *Look in verses 2–3 for what the people were struggling to understand.*

- Notice in verse 2 that the Savior, who is the Master teacher, perceived their needs and questions and then began to address them.

- Analyze: *Why was it so hard for the Nephites to change from the law of Moses to the higher law of Christ?*

- *Look in verses 9–10 for what the Savior expects of all of us in order to obtain eternal life.*

- Analyze: *How do these requirements relate with the first part of the chapter where the Savior speaks of the law of Moses being done away with?*

- Look for President Monson's advice on what it means to endure to the end: "Finally, may you endure. What does it mean to endure? I love this definition: to withstand with courage. Courage may be necessary for you to believe; it will at times be necessary as you obey. It will most certainly be required as you endure until that day when you will leave this mortal existence. I have spoken over the years with many individuals who have told me, 'I have so many problems, such real concerns. I'm overwhelmed with the challenges of life. What can I do?' I have offered to them, and I now offer to you, this specific suggestion: seek heavenly guidance one day at a time. Life by the yard is hard; by the inch it's a cinch. Each of us can be true for just one day—and then one more and then one more after that—until we've lived a lifetime guided by the Spirit, a lifetime close to the Lord, a lifetime of good deeds and righteousness. The Savior promised, 'Look unto me, and endure to the end, and ye shall live; for unto him that endureth to the end will I give eternal life.' For this purpose have you come into mortality, my young friends. There is nothing more important than the goal you strive to attain—even eternal life in the kingdom of your Father" ("Believe, Obey, Endure," *Ensign*, May 2012, 129).

- Invite class members to share what they liked from President Monson's quote. Testify that the counsel President Monson has given is true.

- Have class members write down the phrase, "Life by the yard is hard; by the inch it's a cinch" on a piece of paper. Then invite them to write what they can do or need to do to implement this suggestion in their lives.

Notes

Encourage a few class members to share what they wrote down if appropriate.

11 And now it came to pass that when Jesus had spoken these words, he said unto those twelve whom he had chosen:

12 Ye are my disciples; and ye are a light unto this people, who are a remnant of the house of Joseph.

13 And behold, this is the land of your inheritance; and the Father hath given it unto you.

14 And not at any time hath the Father given me commandment that I should tell it unto your brethren at Jerusalem.

15 Neither at any time hath the Father given me commandment that I should tell unto them concerning the other tribes of the house of Israel, whom the Father hath led away out of the land.

16 This much did the Father command me, that I should tell unto them:

17 That other sheep I have which are not of this fold; them also I must bring, and they shall hear my voice; and there shall be one fold, and one shepherd.

18 And now, because of stiffneckedness and unbelief they understood not my word; therefore I was commanded to say no more of the Father concerning this thing unto them.

19 But, verily, I say unto you that the Father hath commanded me, and I tell it unto you, that ye were separated from among them because of their iniquity; therefore it is because of their iniquity that they know not of you.

20 And verily, I say unto you again that the other tribes hath the Father separated from them; and it is because of their iniquity that they know not of them.

21 And verily I say unto you, that ye are they of whom I said: Other sheep I have which are not of this fold; them also I must bring, and they shall hear my voice; and there shall be one fold, and one shepherd.

22 And they understood me not, for they supposed it had been the Gentiles; for they understood not that the Gentiles should be converted through their preaching.

23 And they understood me not that I said they shall hear my voice; and they understood me not that the Gentiles should not at any time hear my voice—that I should not manifest myself unto them save it were by the Holy Ghost.

24 But behold, ye have both heard my voice, and seen me; and ye are my sheep, and ye are numbered among those whom the Father hath given me.

vv. 11–20 Those who are unbelieving are unable to understand the Lord's word.

- Ask class members to find the New Testament verse that accompanies verse 21 (John 10:16).

- Ask class members to look for why the Savior did not tell those at Jerusalem who His other sheep were in verses 11–20.

- Have class members turn to someone next to them and give what they think is the best definition for the word stiffneckedness. Have a few individuals share some responses.

- Invite class members to reflect on what we may not understand because of stiffneckedness and unbelief. Invite them to believe the Lord in order to be given more of His word.

Teaching Tips from Prophets' Lips "Testimony—real testimony, born of the Spirit and confirmed by the Holy Ghost—changes lives" (M. Russell Ballard, "Pure Testimony," *Ensign*, Nov. 2004, 40).

Index Topics: eternal life, endure to the end

Notes

3 NEPHI 16

I Will Remember My Covenant
About AD 34

1–7, The truth of the gospel shall come to the Gentiles in the last days; 8–20, The Lord shall remember His covenant with all of the house of Israel.

1 And verily, verily, I say unto you that I have other sheep, which are not of this land, neither of the land of Jerusalem, neither in any parts of that land round about whither I have been to minister.

2 For they of whom I speak are they who have not as yet heard my voice; neither have I at any time manifested myself unto them.

3 But I have received a commandment of the Father that I shall go unto them, and that they shall hear my voice, and shall be numbered among my sheep, that there may be one fold and one shepherd; therefore I go to show myself unto them.

4 And I command you that ye shall write these sayings after I am gone, that if it so be that my people at Jerusalem, they who have seen me and been with me in my ministry, do not ask the Father in my name, that they may receive a knowledge of you by the Holy Ghost, and also of the other tribes whom they know not of, that these sayings which ye shall write shall be kept and shall be manifested unto the Gentiles, that through the fulness of the Gentiles, the remnant of their seed, who shall be scattered forth upon the face of the earth because of their unbelief, may be brought in, or may be brought to a knowledge of me, their Redeemer.

5 And then will I gather them in from the four quarters of the earth; and then will I fulfil the covenant which the Father hath made unto all the people of the house of Israel.

6 And blessed are the Gentiles, because of their belief in me, in and of the Holy Ghost, which witnesses unto them of me and of the Father.

7 Behold, because of their belief in me, saith the Father, and because of the unbelief of you, O house of Israel, in the latter day shall the truth come unto the Gentiles, that the fulness of these things shall be made known unto them.

vv. 1–7 The last shall be first and the first shall be last.

⚡ Write on the board the following phrase: "The last shall be first and the first shall be last" (1 Nephi 13:42). Also, attach with magnets three papers to the board that have the following words on them: "Jews", "Gentiles", "Jews". Explain that you will use these papers to help show what this phrase means. Ask the class to find for themselves what this phrase means by finding a verse anywhere in the Book of Mormon that explains this phrase. Invite them to use their index and look up words such as first, gathering, and covenant. After the class has had a sufficient time to search, ask a few of them to share what they found.

❓ After and/or during your discussion, consider asking the following questions to help the class understand what the phrase on the board means:
- *Who was given the gospel first?* (The Jews)
- *Who was given the gospel last?* (The Gentiles)
- *What is the covenant that is referred to?* (Abrahamic covenant)

💡 As you teach this principle, use the papers that are on the board to visually help the class understand. For example, when you talk about the Jews being "first," put that paper first, etc., as below.

JEWS – GENTILES – JEWS.

8 But wo, saith the Father, unto the unbelieving of the Gentiles—for notwithstanding they have come forth upon the face of this land, and have scattered my people who are of the house of Israel; and my people who are of the house of

Notes

Israel have been cast out from among them, and have been trodden under feet by them;

9 And because of the mercies of the Father unto the Gentiles, and also the judgments of the Father upon my people who are of the house of Israel, verily, verily, I say unto you, that after all this, and I have caused my people who are of the house of Israel to be smitten, and to be afflicted, and to be slain, and to be cast out from among them, and to become hated by them, and to become a hiss and a byword among them—

10 And thus commandeth the Father that I should say unto you: At that day when the Gentiles shall sin against my gospel, and shall reject the fulness of my gospel, and shall be lifted up in the pride of their hearts above all nations, and above all the people of the whole earth, and shall be filled with all manner of lyings, and of deceits, and of mischiefs, and all manner of hypocrisy, and murders, and priestcrafts, and whoredoms, and of secret abominations; and if they shall do all those things, and shall reject the fulness of my gospel, behold, saith the Father, I will bring the fulness of my gospel from among them.

11 And then will I remember my covenant which I have made unto my people, O house of Israel, and I will bring my gospel unto them.

12 And I will show unto thee, O house of Israel, that the Gentiles shall not have power over you; but I will remember my covenant unto you, O house of Israel, and ye shall come unto the knowledge of the fulness of my gospel.

13 But if the Gentiles will repent and return unto me, saith the Father, behold they shall be numbered among my people, O house of Israel.

14 And I will not suffer my people, who are of the house of Israel, to go through among them, and tread them down, saith the Father.

15 But if they will not turn unto me, and hearken unto my voice, I will suffer them, yea, I will suffer my people, O house of Israel, that they shall go through among them, and shall tread them down, and they shall be as salt that hath lost its savor, which is thenceforth good for nothing but to be cast out, and to be trodden under foot of my people, O house of Israel.

16 Verily, verily, I say unto you, thus hath the Father commanded me—that I should give unto this people this land for their inheritance.

17 And then the words of the prophet Isaiah shall be fulfilled, which say:

18 Thy watchmen shall lift up the voice; with the voice together shall they sing, for they shall see eye to eye when the Lord shall bring again Zion.

19 Break forth into joy, sing together, ye waste places of Jerusalem; for the Lord hath comforted his people, he hath redeemed Jerusalem.

20 The Lord hath made bare his holy arm in the eyes of all the nations; and all the ends of the earth shall see the salvation of God.

vv. 8–20 God will keep His covenant with the remnants of the house of Israel.

💬 Begin by sharing the following quote wherein Elder Russell M. Nelson referred to two specific themes in the Book of Mormon. The first theme that he invited all of us to notice was that of Jesus Christ. He then stated, "And look for a second undergirding theme: God will keep His covenants with the remnants of the house of Israel" ("A Testimony of the Book of Mormon," *Ensign*, April 1999, 71). Consider writing the last part about covenants on the board.

🔎 *Look for the word "covenant" in verses 5, 11, and 12.*

❓ *Why do you think it is important for all of us to remember this second undergirding theme that Elder Nelson stated?* Remind the class that the Book of Mormon was written for our day. You may consider following up with the question, *What is the Lord trying to tell us as we study and ponder this theme?*

❓ Analyze:
- *According to 3 Nephi 16, will there ever come a time when the Gentiles will lose*

Notes

the promised blessings of the fulness of the gospel? (v. 10)
• What can we do to retain the promised blessings? (vv. 13–15)
• How do the words of Isaiah in verses 17–20 add to our understanding of the gathering of Israel?

♥ Invite class members to remember that the Lord will keep His covenants with all of us. All that He has promised to us can be ours as we remain worthy of His promises.

Index Topics: gathering of Israel

3 NEPHI 17

Jesus Heals at the Temple
About AD 34

1–5, Because of His compassion, Jesus delays His departure; 6–10, He heals each individual; 11–18, He has the children brought to Him and prays with all the children; 19–25, Jesus blesses each child and angels minister to them.

Overarching Principle: By attending the temple, we can be taught and healed by the Savior.

⚡ Have written on the board, "Jesus taught and healed in the temple; Jesus still does today." Point out the phrase on the board and ask class members what lesson this is teaching. Share how this chapter is about Jesus teaching and healing in the temple.

1 Behold, now it came to pass that when Jesus had spoken these words he looked round about again on the multitude, and he said unto them: Behold, my time is at hand.

2 I perceive that ye are weak, that ye cannot understand all my words which I am commanded of the Father to speak unto you at this time.

3 Therefore, go ye unto your homes, and ponder upon the things which I have said, and ask of the Father, in my name, that ye may understand, and prepare your minds for the morrow, and I come unto you again.

4 But now I go unto the Father, and also to show myself unto the lost tribes of Israel, for they are not lost unto the Father, for he knoweth whither he hath taken them.

5 And it came to pass that when Jesus had thus spoken, he cast his eyes round about again on the multitude, and beheld they were in tears, and did look steadfastly upon him as if they would ask him to tarry a little longer with them.

6 And he said unto them: Behold, my bowels are filled with compassion towards you.

7 Have ye any that are sick among you? Bring them hither. Have ye any that are lame, or blind, or halt, or maimed, or leprous, or that are withered, or that are deaf, or that are afflicted in any manner? Bring them hither and I will heal them, for I have compassion upon you; my bowels are filled with mercy.

8 For I perceive that ye desire that I should show unto you what I have done unto your brethren at Jerusalem, for I see that your faith is sufficient that I should heal you.

9 And it came to pass that when he had thus spoken, all the multitude, with one accord, did go forth with their sick and their afflicted, and their lame, and with their blind, and with their dumb, and with all them that were afflicted in any manner; and he did heal them every one as they were brought forth unto him.

vv. 1–9 Jesus has great compassion for all of us.

⚡ Ask class members to define the word, "compassion."

🔍 Read verses 1–9 and mark portions that show the Savior's compassion. Have class members share what they found.

Notes

- ❓ *Can you think of a time you have felt the Savior's compassion for you?*
- ♥ Testify of the Savior's compassion for all of us. Ask class members to continue looking for the Lord's compassion throughout the chapter.

10 And they did all, both they who had been healed and they who were whole, bow down at his feet, and did worship him; and as many as could come for the multitude did kiss his feet, insomuch that they did bathe his feet with their tears.

11 And it came to pass that he commanded that their little children should be brought.

12 So they brought their little children and set them down upon the ground round about him, and Jesus stood in the midst; and the multitude gave way till they had all been brought unto him.

13 And it came to pass that when they had all been brought, and Jesus stood in the midst, he commanded the multitude that they should kneel down upon the ground.

14 And it came to pass that when they had knelt upon the ground, Jesus groaned within himself, and said: Father, I am troubled because of the wickedness of the people of the house of Israel.

15 And when he had said these words, he himself also knelt upon the earth; and behold he prayed unto the Father, and the things which he prayed cannot be written, and the multitude did bear record who heard him.

vv. 11–15 Jesus can heal us from abuses we suffer.

- 🔎 *Try to determine how verses 11–13 and 15 relate to verse 14.*
- ❓ Analyze: *Why is Jesus suddenly talking about the wickedness of the house of Israel in verse 14 when he has invited the children forward and is about to bless them?*
- 💡 Explain that these children had been witnesses of the great wickedness that had happened before Jesus's coming. In the previous verses he healed physically but perhaps He is healing emotionally also. Notice that in this healing there is prayer (vv. 15–18), blessing (v. 21), and ministry of angels (vv. 23–24).
- ♥ Testify to class members that today the Lord also heals people who have been hurt by others' wickedness and abuses. Through the Lord we can become healed of all things.

16 And after this manner do they bear record: The eye hath never seen, neither hath the ear heard, before, so great and marvelous things as we saw and heard Jesus speak unto the Father;

17 And no tongue can speak, neither can there be written by any man, neither can the hearts of men conceive so great and marvelous things as we both saw and heard Jesus speak; and no one can conceive of the joy which filled our souls at the time we heard him pray for us unto the Father.

18 And it came to pass that when Jesus had made an end of praying unto the Father, he arose; but so great was the joy of the multitude that they were overcome.

19 And it came to pass that Jesus spake unto them, and bade them arise.

20 And they arose from the earth, and he said unto them: Blessed are ye because of your faith. And now behold, my joy is full.

21 And when he had said these words, he wept, and the multitude bare record of it, and he took their little children, one by one, and blessed them, and prayed unto the Father for them.

22 And when he had done this he wept again;

vv. 16–22 The Lord's compassion.

- 🔎 As you did with verses 1–9, have class members again look for signs of Christ's compassion in verses 16–19. Perhaps share Hebrews 4:15. Ask class members how the temple relates with what is occurring.

Notes

23 And he spake unto the multitude, and said unto them: Behold your little ones.

24 And as they looked to behold they cast their eyes towards heaven, and they saw the heavens open, and they saw angels descending out of heaven as it were in the midst of fire; and they came down and encircled those little ones about, and they were encircled about with fire; and the angels did minister unto them.

25 And the multitude did see and hear and bear record; and they know that their record is true for they all of them did see and hear, every man for himself; and they were in number about two thousand and five hundred souls; and they did consist of men, women, and children.

Teaching Tips from Prophets' Lips "As President J. Reuben Clark Jr. once said, 'Never let your faith be difficult to detect.' May I repeat that? 'Never let your faith be difficult to detect.'" (Jeffrey R. Holland, "Teaching and Learning in the Church." *Ensign*, June 2007, 88–105)

Index Topics: God's love

3 NEPHI 18

Jesus Administers the Sacrament with the Nephites
About AD 34

1–16, Jesus administers the sacrament and teaches concerning it; 17–25, Jesus teaches the multitudes concerning prayer and meeting together often; 26–34, Jesus teaches his disciples about not suffering the unworthy to partake of the sacrament; 35–39, Jesus gives the authority to give the gift of the Holy Ghost and departs.

1 And it came to pass that Jesus commanded his disciples that they should bring forth some bread and wine unto him.

2 And while they were gone for bread and wine, he commanded the multitude that they should sit themselves down upon the earth.

3 And when the disciples had come with bread and wine, he took of the bread and brake and blessed it; and he gave unto the disciples and commanded that they should eat.

4 And when they had eaten and were filled, he commanded that they should give unto the multitude.

5 And when the multitude had eaten and were filled, he said unto the disciples: Behold there shall one be ordained among you, and to him will I give power that he shall break bread and bless it and give it unto the people of my church, unto all those who shall believe and be baptized in my name.

vv. 1–5 Most priesthood ordinances need to be done under the direction of one who holds the proper priesthood keys.

- Consider beginning class with a sacrament hymn. After the hymn, ask questions like, *Would it be okay if we administered the sacrament right now in class? Why or why not? If there are people here with the correct priesthood office, why would or wouldn't it be okay?*

- *In verses 1–5, look for a good reason why it would not be appropriate to administer the sacrament in class.* Note: This assumes that the bishop is not there in class at the time.

- "The ordinance of the sacrament of the Lord's Supper must be done under the direction of the proper priesthood authority. Merely breaking the bread, reciting the prayers, and partaking of the ordinances—even if done by someone who holds the priesthood—does not mean it is a valid sacramental ordinance. Authority or permission to perform this sacred rite can only be given by the one who holds the keys of the priesthood. On a ward level, this means that only the bishop has the right and authority to grant permission for the sacrament to be administered. Through

Notes

his keys of priesthood authority priesthood holders are thus empowered to perform this important ordinance and make is emblems available to members of the ward" (Joseph F. McConkie and Robert L. Millet, *Doctrinal Commentary on the Book of Mormon*, vol. 4, 121).

6 And this shall ye always observe to do, even as I have done, even as I have broken bread and blessed it and given it unto you.

7 And this shall ye do in remembrance of my body, which I have shown unto you. And it shall be a testimony unto the Father that ye do always remember me. And if ye do always remember me ye shall have my Spirit to be with you.

8 And it came to pass that when he said these words, he commanded his disciples that they should take of the wine of the cup and drink of it, and that they should also give unto the multitude that they might drink of it.

9 And it came to pass that they did so, and did drink of it and were filled; and they gave unto the multitude, and they did drink, and they were filled.

10 And when the disciples had done this, Jesus said unto them: Blessed are ye for this thing which ye have done, for this is fulfilling my commandments, and this doth witness unto the Father that ye are willing to do that which I have commanded you.

11 And this shall ye always do to those who repent and are baptized in my name; and ye shall do it in remembrance of my blood, which I have shed for you, that ye may witness unto the Father that ye do always remember me. And if ye do always remember me ye shall have my Spirit to be with you.

12 And I give unto you a commandment that ye shall do these things. And if ye shall always do these things blessed are ye, for ye are built upon my rock.

13 But whoso among you shall do more or less than these are not built upon my rock, but are built upon a sandy foundation; and when the rain descends, and the floods come, and the winds blow, and beat upon them, they shall fall, and the gates of hell are ready open to receive them.

vv. 7–13 Remembering the Savior helps us to always have His spirit with us.

⚡ *Why is it important to have the Lord's spirit with us?*

🔎 *In verses 7–13, look for what helps us have the Lord's spirit.*

💬 Spencer W. Kimball stated, "When you look in the dictionary for the most important word, do you know what it is? It could be 'remember.' Because all of [us] have made covenants . . . our greatest need is to remember. That is why everyone goes to sacrament meeting every Sabbath day—to take the sacrament and listen to the priests pray that [we] '. . . may always remember him and keep his commandments which he has given [us].' . . . 'Remember' is the word" ("Circles of Exaltation" [address to religious educators, Brigham Young University, 28 June 1968], 8).

❤ *What can we do to help us remember the Savior during the week? What reminders can help us?* Challenge class members to try to remember the Savior each day.

14 Therefore blessed are ye if ye shall keep my commandments, which the Father hath commanded me that I should give unto you.

15 Verily, verily, I say unto you, ye must watch and pray always, lest ye be tempted by the devil, and ye be led away captive by him.

16 And as I have prayed among you even so shall ye pray in my church, among my people who do repent and are baptized in my name. Behold I am the light; I have set an example for you.

17 And it came to pass that when Jesus had spoken these words unto his disciples, he turned again unto the multitude and said unto them:

Notes

18 Behold, verily, verily, I say unto you, ye must watch and pray always lest ye enter into temptation; for Satan desireth to have you, that he may sift you as wheat.

19 Therefore ye must always pray unto the Father in my name;

20 And whatsoever ye shall ask the Father in my name, which is right, believing that ye shall receive, behold it shall be given unto you.

21 Pray in your families unto the Father, always in my name, that your wives and your children may be blessed.

22 And behold, ye shall meet together oft; and ye shall not forbid any man from coming unto you when ye shall meet together, but suffer them that they may come unto you and forbid them not;

23 But ye shall pray for them, and shall not cast them out; and if it so be that they come unto you oft ye shall pray for them unto the Father, in my name.

24 Therefore, hold up your light that it may shine unto the world. Behold I am the light which ye shall hold up—that which ye have seen me do. Behold ye see that I have prayed unto the Father, and ye all have witnessed.

25 And ye see that I have commanded that none of you should go away, but rather have commanded that ye should come unto me, that ye might feel and see; even so shall ye do unto the world; and whosoever breaketh this commandment suffereth himself to be led into temptation.

26 And now it came to pass that when Jesus had spoken these words, he turned his eyes again upon the disciples whom he had chosen, and said unto them:

27 Behold verily, verily, I say unto you, I give unto you another commandment, and then I must go unto my Father that I may fulfil other commandments which he hath given me.

28 And now behold, this is the commandment which I give unto you, that ye shall not suffer any one knowingly to partake of my flesh and blood unworthily, when ye shall minister it;

29 For whoso eateth and drinketh my flesh and blood unworthily eateth and drinketh damnation to his soul; therefore if ye know that a man is unworthy to eat and drink of my flesh and blood ye shall forbid him.

vv. 26–29 Only the presiding leaders have the authority to stop one from partaking of the sacrament. We should also stop ourselves if unworthy.

- Ask, *Who determines an individual's worthiness to partake of the sacrament? What role, if any, do members of the congregation play in such matters?*

- *Look for what verses 28–29 say we should do in that situation.*

- Explain that verses 26–29 are not addressed to the general membership of the Church. Point out that in verse 26, it shows that Jesus is giving instructions to the disciples who were the general leaders of the Church. Only the bishop in the ward has the authority to prevent someone from taking the sacrament.

- Elder Dallin H. Oaks taught, "We should not presume to exercise and act upon judgments that are outside our personal responsibilities. Some time ago I attended an adult Sunday School class in a small town in Utah. The subject was the sacrament, and the class was being taught by the bishop. During class discussion a member asked, 'What if you see an unworthy person partaking of the sacrament? What do you do?' The bishop answered, 'You do nothing. I may need to do something.' That wise answer illustrates my point about stewardship in judging." ("Judge Not and Judging," in *Speeches of the Year* [1998], 4)

- Apply: *Can we stop ourselves from partaking the sacrament? Cross-reference 1 Corinthians 11:27–29 for additional insights to that question.*

Notes

- ♥ Challenge class members to examine themselves for worthiness each week and to continually communicate with their bishop in order to refrain from partaking the sacrament unworthily.

30 Nevertheless, ye shall not cast him out from among you, but ye shall minister unto him and shall pray for him unto the Father, in my name; and if it so be that he repenteth and is baptized in my name, then shall ye receive him, and shall minister unto him of my flesh and blood.

31 But if he repent not he shall not be numbered among my people, that he may not destroy my people, for behold I know my sheep, and they are numbered.

32 Nevertheless, ye shall not cast him out of your synagogues, or your places of worship, for unto such shall ye continue to minister; for ye know not but what they will return and repent, and come unto me with full purpose of heart, and I shall heal them; and ye shall be the means of bringing salvation unto them.

33 Therefore, keep these sayings which I have commanded you that ye come not under condemnation; for wo unto him whom the Father condemneth.

v. 32 We should seek to bring back those who have stopped going to church.

- ♥ After reading the verse, ask class members to think of a time they might have helped someone less active come back to activity. Share an experience of your own, and/or ask class members to share.

34 And I give you these commandments because of the disputations which have been among you. And blessed are ye if ye have no disputations among you.

35 And now I go unto the Father, because it is expedient that I should go unto the Father for your sakes.

36 And it came to pass that when Jesus had made an end of these sayings, he touched with his hand the disciples whom he had chosen, one by one, even until he had touched them all, and spake unto them as he touched them.

37 And the multitude heard not the words which he spake, therefore they did not bear record; but the disciples bare record that he gave them power to give the Holy Ghost. And I will show unto you hereafter that this record is true.

38 And it came to pass that when Jesus had touched them all, there came a cloud and overshadowed the multitude that they could not see Jesus.

39 And while they were overshadowed he departed from them, and ascended into heaven. And the disciples saw and did bear record that he ascended again into heaven.

Index Topics: sacrament, priesthood keys, church attendance, Holy Ghost, helping less active members

3 NEPHI 19

Jesus Prays with the Multitude
About AD 34

1–3, Jesus ascends to heaven; 4, The twelve disciples called by Jesus are named; 5–9, The twelve disciples teach and pray with the people; 10–14, The people are baptized, filled with the Holy Ghost, and are ministered to by angels; 15–23, Jesus appears and prays with them; 24–36, Jesus separates Himself from the multitude and prays to the Father.

1 And now it came to pass that when Jesus had ascended into heaven, the multitude did disperse, and every man did take his wife and his children and did return to his own home.

2 And it was noised abroad among the people immediately, before it was yet dark, that the multitude had seen Jesus, and that he had ministered

Notes

unto them, and that he would also show himself on the morrow unto the multitude.

3 Yea, and even all the night it was noised abroad concerning Jesus; and insomuch did they send forth unto the people that there were many, yea, an exceedingly great number, did labor exceedingly all that night, that they might be on the morrow in the place where Jesus should show himself unto the multitude.

vv. 1–3 We should labor to help others learn about and come unto Jesus.

- Read verses 1–3 looking for what the people do after Jesus leaves that is similar to missionary work.
- Analyze: *Why do you think the people were so eager to share their experiences of that day with others?*
- Apply: *How does this story relate to missionary work?*
- Note with the class that when we have spiritual experiences, our natural desire is to want to have other people share that same experience.

4 And it came to pass that on the morrow, when the multitude was gathered together, behold, Nephi and his brother whom he had raised from the dead, whose name was Timothy, and also his son, whose name was Jonas, and also Mathoni, and Mathonihah, his brother, and Kumen, and Kumenonhi, and Jeremiah, and Shemnon, and Jonas, and Zedekiah, and Isaiah—now these were the names of the disciples whom Jesus had chosen—and it came to pass that they went forth and stood in the midst of the multitude.

v. 4 Mormon names the twelve apostles called by the Lord.

5 And behold, the multitude was so great that they did cause that they should be separated into twelve bodies.

6 And the twelve did teach the multitude; and behold, they did cause that the multitude should kneel down upon the face of the earth, and should pray unto the Father in the name of Jesus.

7 And the disciples did pray unto the Father also in the name of Jesus. And it came to pass that they arose and ministered unto the people.

8 And when they had ministered those same words which Jesus had spoken—nothing varying from the words which Jesus had spoken—behold, they knelt again and prayed to the Father in the name of Jesus.

9 And they did pray for that which they most desired; and they desired that the Holy Ghost should be given unto them.

10 And when they had thus prayed they went down unto the water's edge, and the multitude followed them.

11 And it came to pass that Nephi went down into the water and was baptized.

12 And he came up out of the water and began to baptize. And he baptized all those whom Jesus had chosen.

13 And it came to pass when they were all baptized and had come up out of the water, the Holy Ghost did fall upon them, and they were filled with the Holy Ghost and with fire.

14 And behold, they were encircled about as if it were by fire; and it came down from heaven, and the multitude did witness it, and did bear record; and angels did come down out of heaven and did minister unto them.

15 And it came to pass that while the angels were ministering unto the disciples, behold, Jesus came and stood in the midst and ministered unto them.

16 And it came to pass that he spake unto the multitude, and commanded them that they should kneel down again upon the earth, and also that his disciples should kneel down upon the earth.

Notes

17 And it came to pass that when they had all knelt down upon the earth, he commanded his disciples that they should pray.

18 And behold, they began to pray; and they did pray unto Jesus, calling him their Lord and their God.

19 And it came to pass that Jesus departed out of the midst of them, and went a little way off from them and bowed himself to the earth, and he said:

20 Father, I thank thee that thou hast given the Holy Ghost unto these whom I have chosen; and it is because of their belief in me that I have chosen them out of the world.

21 Father, I pray thee that thou wilt give the Holy Ghost unto all them that shall believe in their words.

22 Father, thou hast given them the Holy Ghost because they believe in me; and thou seest that they believe in me because thou hearest them, and they pray unto me; and they pray unto me because I am with them.

23 And now Father, I pray unto thee for them, and also for all those who shall believe on their words, that they may believe in me, that I may be in them as thou, Father, art in me, that we may be one.

24 And it came to pass that when Jesus had thus prayed unto the Father, he came unto his disciples, and behold, they did still continue, without ceasing, to pray unto him; and they did not multiply many words, for it was given unto them what they should pray, and they were filled with desire.

v. 24 The Spirit and prayer.

♦ Cross reference verse 24 with D&C 50:30 and Romans 8:26. Note that in all three of these verses the spirit can teach us what to pray for.

25 And it came to pass that Jesus blessed them as they did pray unto him; and his countenance did smile upon them, and the light of his countenance did shine upon them, and behold they were as white as the countenance and also the garments of Jesus; and behold the whiteness thereof did exceed all the whiteness, yea, even there could be nothing upon earth so white as the whiteness thereof.

26 And Jesus said unto them: Pray on; nevertheless they did not cease to pray.

27 And he turned from them again, and went a little way off and bowed himself to the earth; and he prayed again unto the Father, saying:

28 Father, I thank thee that thou hast purified those whom I have chosen, because of their faith, and I pray for them, and also for them who shall believe on their words, that they may be purified in me, through faith on their words, even as they are purified in me.

29 Father, I pray not for the world, but for those whom thou hast given me out of the world, because of their faith, that they may be purified in me, that I may be in them as thou, Father, art in me, that we may be one, that I may be glorified in them.

30 And when Jesus had spoken these words he came again unto his disciples; and behold they did pray steadfastly, without ceasing, unto him; and he did smile upon them again; and behold they were white, even as Jesus.

31 And it came to pass that he went again a little way off and prayed unto the Father;

32 And tongue cannot speak the words which he prayed, neither can be written by man the words which he prayed.

33 And the multitude did hear and do bear record; and their hearts were open and they did understand in their hearts the words which he prayed.

34 Nevertheless, so great and marvelous were the words which he prayed that they cannot be written, neither can they be uttered by man.

Notes

vv. 15–34 How to engage in meaningful prayer.

⚡ Share the following quote from Elder David A. Bednar. "Simply saying prayers is quite a different thing from engaging in meaningful prayer." ("Ask in Faith," *Ensign,* May 2008, 94) Discuss how the class interprets that quote.

👥 Explain to class members that they will learn principles of engaging in meaningful prayer from Jesus's example in 3 Nephi 19. Divide the class in half. Assign one half of the class the first bullet point; assign the other half the second bullet point:

- Read verses 15–34, looking for principles of how to engage in meaningful prayer.
- Read verses 15–34, looking for what Jesus's prayer teaches about His character.

Encourage class members to be prepared to share their findings.

❓ Analyze: Once completed, discuss their findings as a class, asking appropriate questions to stimulate discussion and thought.

💬 Elder David A. Bednar taught, "The most meaningful and spiritual prayers I have experienced contained many expressions of thanks and few, if any, requests. As I am blessed now to pray with apostles and prophets, I find among these modern-day leaders of the Savior's Church the same characteristic that describes Captain Moroni in the Book of Mormon: these are men whose hearts swell with thanksgiving to God for the many privileges and blessings which He bestows upon His people (see Alma 48:12). Also, they do not multiply many words, for it is given unto them what they should pray, and they are filled with desire (see 3 Nephi 19:24). The prayers of prophets are childlike in their simplicity and powerful because of their sincerity." ("Pray Always," *Ensign,* Nov. 2008, 43)

❓ Apply: *What have you learned about prayer today that is applicable to you?*

♥ In your lesson preparation, consider reading the entire talk "Ask in Faith" given in April 2008 conference by Elder David A. Bednar and share principles from his talk regarding how to engage in meaningful prayer.

35 And it came to pass that when Jesus had made an end of praying he came again to the disciples, and said unto them: So great faith have I never seen among all the Jews; wherefore I could not show unto them so great miracles, because of their unbelief.

36 Verily I say unto you, there are none of them that have seen so great things as ye have seen; neither have they heard so great things as ye have heard.

Teaching Tips from Prophets' Lips "Our students may not know that they are fainting from famine, but the words of God will slake a thirst they did not know they had, and the Holy Ghost will take it down into their hearts" (Henry B. Eyring, "We Must Raise Our Sights" [CES conference on the Book of Mormon, Aug. 14, 2001], 3).

3 NEPHI 20

Jesus Expounds the Scriptures
About AD 34

1–9, Again, Jesus administers the sacrament to the people; 10–17, The gathering of His people and the role of the Gentiles; 18–22, The role of His gathered people and the New Jerusalem; 23–26, Jesus is prophesied of by the prophet Moses; 27–46, Jesus quotes and expounds upon passages from Isaiah 44, 51, and 52.

1 And it came to pass that he commanded the multitude that they should cease to pray, and also his disciples. And he commanded them that they should not cease to pray in their hearts.

2 And he commanded them that they should arise and stand up upon their feet. And they arose up and stood upon their feet.

Notes

3 NEPHI 20

3 And it came to pass that he brake bread again and blessed it, and gave to the disciples to eat.

4 And when they had eaten he commanded them that they should break bread, and give unto the multitude.

5 And when they had given unto the multitude he also gave them wine to drink, and commanded them that they should give unto the multitude.

6 Now, there had been no bread, neither wine, brought by the disciples, neither by the multitude;

7 But he truly gave unto them bread to eat, and also wine to drink.

8 And he said unto them: He that eateth this bread eateth of my body to his soul; and he that drinketh of this wine drinketh of my blood to his soul; and his soul shall never hunger nor thirst, but shall be filled.

9 Now, when the multitude had all eaten and drunk, behold, they were filled with the Spirit; and they did cry out with one voice, and gave glory to Jesus, whom they both saw and heard.

vv. 7–9 The Lord can fulfill our spiritual thirst in life.

- Compare in verses 8–9 how Jesus taught the woman at the well (John 4:10–15) that whoever drinks of His water would never thirst.

10 And it came to pass that when they had all given glory unto Jesus, he said unto them: Behold now I finish the commandment which the Father hath commanded me concerning this people, who are a remnant of the house of Israel.

11 Ye remember that I spake unto you, and said that when the words of Isaiah should be fulfilled—behold they are written, ye have them before you, therefore search them—

12 And verily, verily, I say unto you, that when they shall be fulfilled then is the fulfilling of the covenant which the Father hath made unto his people, O house of Israel.

13 And then shall the remnants, which shall be scattered abroad upon the face of the earth, be gathered in from the east and from the west, and from the south and from the north; and they shall be brought to the knowledge of the Lord their God, who hath redeemed them.

14 And the Father hath commanded me that I should give unto you this land, for your inheritance.

15 And I say unto you, that if the Gentiles do not repent after the blessing which they shall receive, after they have scattered my people—

16 Then shall ye, who are a remnant of the house of Jacob, go forth among them; and ye shall be in the midst of them who shall be many; and ye shall be among them as a lion among the beasts of the forest, and as a young lion among the flocks of sheep, who, if he goeth through both treadeth down and teareth in pieces, and none can deliver.

17 Thy hand shall be lifted up upon thine adversaries, and all thine enemies shall be cut off.

v. 16 Remnant of Jacob will be as a lion treading down its enemies.

- The message in 3 Nephi 20:16 is one that is repeated a few times by Jesus (3 Nephi 16:14–15; 21:12–21; 25:3) and Mormon (Mormon 5:24). Micah also gave this prophecy (Micah 5:7–15). It is not clear how this prophecy will be fulfilled. You may want to invite class members to note these cross references in their scriptures.

18 And I will gather my people together as a man gathereth his sheaves into the floor.

19 For I will make my people with whom the Father hath covenanted, yea, I will make thy horn iron, and I will make thy hoofs brass. And thou shalt beat in pieces many people; and I will consecrate their gain unto the Lord, and their substance unto the Lord of the whole earth. And behold, I am he who doeth it.

Notes

20 And it shall come to pass, saith the Father, that the sword of my justice shall hang over them at that day; and except they repent it shall fall upon them, saith the Father, yea, even upon all the nations of the Gentiles.

21 And it shall come to pass that I will establish my people, O house of Israel.

22 And behold, this people will I establish in this land, unto the fulfilling of the covenant which I made with your father Jacob; and it shall be a New Jerusalem. And the powers of heaven shall be in the midst of this people; yea, even I will be in the midst of you.

v. 22 The New Jerusalem.

Bruce R. McConkie stated, "The New Jerusalem is a center place, a center city which shall be built up and established as the headquarters of The Church of Jesus Christ of Latter-day Saints. Its location will be independence, Jackson County, Missouri (see D&C 57:3). 'We believe . . . that Zion (the New Jerusalem) will be built upon the American continent' (Articles of Faith 1:10). Zion, the New Jerusalem, on American soil! And we hasten to add, so also shall there be Zions in all lands and New Jerusalems in the mountains of the Lord in all the earth. But the American Zion shall be the capital city, the source whence the law shall go forth to govern all the earth. It shall be the city of the Great King. His throne shall be there, and from there he shall reign gloriously over all the earth." (*The Millennial Messiah*, 301–2.) Concerning the New Jerusalem, see also Ether 13:3–12.

23 Behold, I am he of whom Moses spake, saying: A prophet shall the Lord your God raise up unto you of your brethren, like unto me; him shall ye hear in all things whatsoever he shall say unto you. And it shall come to pass that every soul who will not hear that prophet shall be cut off from among the people.

24 Verily I say unto you, yea, and all the prophets from Samuel and those that follow after, as many as have spoken, have testified of me.

25 And behold, ye are the children of the prophets; and ye are of the house of Israel; and ye are of the covenant which the Father made with your fathers, saying unto Abraham: And in thy seed shall all the kindreds of the earth be blessed.

26 The Father having raised me up unto you first, and sent me to bless you in turning away every one of you from his iniquities; and this because ye are the children of the covenant—

27 And after that ye were blessed then fulfilleth the Father the covenant which he made with Abraham, saying: In thy seed shall all the kindreds of the earth be blessed—unto the pouring out of the Holy Ghost through me upon the Gentiles, which blessing upon the Gentiles shall make them mighty above all, unto the scattering of my people, O house of Israel.

v. 27 Those who embrace the gospel become part of the house of Israel.

Joseph Fielding Smith wrote, "Is it necessary that we be of the house of Israel in order to accept the gospel and all the blessings pertaining to it? If so, how do we become of the house of Israel, by adoption or by direct lineage? Every person who embraces the gospel becomes of the house of Israel. In other words, they become members of the chosen lineage, or Abraham's children through Isaac and Jacob unto whom the promises were made. The great majority of those who become members of the Church are literal descendants of Abraham through Ephraim, son of Joseph. Those who are not literal descendants of Abraham and Israel must become such, and when they are baptized and confirmed they are grafted into the tree and are entitled to all the rights and privileges as heirs" (*Doctrines of Salvation*, 3:245–46).

Notes

vv. 28–46 Jesus teaches from the words of Isaiah.

◊ In verses 28–46, before Jesus quotes, the Isaiah reference will be noted.

Isaiah 51:23

28 And they shall be a scourge unto the people of this land. Nevertheless, when they shall have received the fulness of my gospel, then if they shall harden their hearts against me I will return their iniquities upon their own heads, saith the Father.

Isaiah 44:21

29 And I will remember the covenant which I have made with my people; and I have covenanted with them that I would gather them together in mine own due time, that I would give unto them again the land of their fathers for their inheritance, which is the land of Jerusalem, which is the promised land unto them forever, saith the Father.

30 And it shall come to pass that the time cometh, when the fulness of my gospel shall be preached unto them;

31 And they shall believe in me, that I am Jesus Christ, the Son of God, and shall pray unto the Father in my name.

Isaiah 52:8–9

32 Then shall their watchmen lift up their voice, and with the voice together shall they sing; for they shall see eye to eye.

33 Then will the Father gather them together again, and give unto them Jerusalem for the land of their inheritance.

Isaiah 54:1

34 Then shall they break forth into joy—Sing together, ye waste places of Jerusalem; for the Father hath comforted his people, he hath redeemed Jerusalem.

35 The Father hath made bare his holy arm in the eyes of all the nations; and all the ends of the earth shall see the salvation of the Father; and the Father and I are one.

Isaiah 52:1–3

36 And then shall be brought to pass that which is written: Awake, awake again, and put on thy strength, O Zion; put on thy beautiful garments, O Jerusalem, the holy city, for henceforth there shall no more come into thee the uncircumcised and the unclean.

37 Shake thyself from the dust; arise, sit down, O Jerusalem; loose thyself from the bands of thy neck, O captive daughter of Zion.

38 For thus saith the Lord: Ye have sold yourselves for naught, and ye shall be redeemed without money.

39 Verily, verily, I say unto you, that my people shall know my name; yea, in that day they shall know that I am he that doth speak.

Isaiah 52:7

40 And then shall they say: How beautiful upon the mountains are the feet of him that bringeth good tidings unto them, that publisheth peace; that bringeth good tidings unto them of good, that publisheth salvation; that saith unto Zion: Thy God reigneth!

Isaiah 52:11–15

41 And then shall a cry go forth: Depart ye, depart ye, go ye out from thence, touch not that which is unclean; go ye out of the midst of her; be ye clean that bear the vessels of the Lord.

42 For ye shall not go out with haste nor go by flight; for the Lord will go before you, and the God of Israel shall be your rearward.

Notes

43 Behold, my servant shall deal prudently; he shall be exalted and extolled and be very high.

44 As many were astonished at thee—his visage was so marred, more than any man, and his form more than the sons of men—

45 So shall he sprinkle many nations; the kings shall shut their mouths at him, for that which had not been told them shall they see; and that which they had not heard shall they consider.

46 Verily, verily, I say unto you, all these things shall surely come, even as the Father hath commanded me. Then shall this covenant which the Father hath covenanted with his people be fulfilled; and then shall Jerusalem be inhabited again with my people, and it shall be the land of their inheritance.

Index Topics: house of Israel

3 NEPHI 21

Israel and the Gentiles
About AD 34

1–10, The Book of Mormon and the restoration of the gospel are signs that Israel is being gathered together again; 11–21, Judgments will come upon the Gentiles if they do not believe; 22–29, Blessings will come upon both those Gentiles who repent and Israel unto the building up of the New Jerusalem.

1 And verily I say unto you, I give unto you a sign, that ye may know the time when these things shall be about to take place—that I shall gather in, from their long dispersion, my people, O house of Israel, and shall establish again among them my Zion;

2 And behold, this is the thing which I will give unto you for a sign—for verily I say unto you that when these things which I declare unto you, and which I shall declare unto you hereafter of myself, and by the power of the Holy Ghost which shall be given unto you of the Father, shall be made known unto the Gentiles that they may know concerning this people who are a remnant of the house of Jacob, and concerning this my people who shall be scattered by them;

3 Verily, verily, I say unto you, when these things shall be made known unto them of the Father, and shall come forth of the Father, from them unto you;

vv. 1–3 The coming forth of the Book of Mormon signals the gathering of scattered Israel.

⚡ Display several road signs. Explain that they are signals to drivers regarding changes on the road ahead (stop signs, sharp turns, railroad crossings, etc.). Ask, *Does the Lord give signs to his people regarding His works that are ahead of us?*

🔎 *Look for what, in verses 1–3, signals the gathering of Israel again.* Direct class members to the chapter heading of the Book of Mormon if they need help.

4 For it is wisdom in the Father that they should be established in this land, and be set up as a free people by the power of the Father, that these things might come forth from them unto a remnant of your seed, that the covenant of the Father may be fulfilled which he hath covenanted with his people, O house of Israel;

5 Therefore, when these works and the works which shall be wrought among you hereafter shall come forth from the Gentiles, unto your seed which shall dwindle in unbelief because of iniquity;

6 For thus it behooveth the Father that it should come forth from the Gentiles, that he may show forth his power unto the Gentiles, for this cause that the Gentiles, if they will not harden their hearts, that they may repent and come unto me and be baptized in my name and know of the true points of my doctrine, that they may be numbered among my people, O house of Israel;

Notes

7 And when these things come to pass that thy seed shall begin to know these things—it shall be a sign unto them, that they may know that the work of the Father hath already commenced unto the fulfilling of the covenant which he hath made unto the people who are of the house of Israel.

8 And when that day shall come, it shall come to pass that kings shall shut their mouths; for that which had not been told them shall they see; and that which they had not heard shall they consider.

9 For in that day, for my sake shall the Father work a work, which shall be a great and a marvelous work among them; and there shall be among them those who will not believe it, although a man shall declare it unto them.

10 But behold, the life of my servant shall be in my hand; therefore they shall not hurt him, although he shall be marred because of them. Yet I will heal him, for I will show unto them that my wisdom is greater than the cunning of the devil.

11 Therefore it shall come to pass that whosoever will not believe in my words, who am Jesus Christ, which the Father shall cause him to bring forth unto the Gentiles, and shall give unto him power that he shall bring them forth unto the Gentiles, (it shall be done even as Moses said) they shall be cut off from among my people who are of the covenant.

12 And my people who are a remnant of Jacob shall be among the Gentiles, yea, in the midst of them as a lion among the beasts of the forest, as a young lion among the flocks of sheep, who, if he go through both treadeth down and teareth in pieces, and none can deliver.

v. 12 Remnant of Jacob as a lion treading down.

See 3 Nephi 20:16 about the prophecy of the remnant of Jacob treading down the Gentiles.

13 Their hand shall be lifted up upon their adversaries, and all their enemies shall be cut off.

14 Yea, wo be unto the Gentiles except they repent; for it shall come to pass in that day, saith the Father, that I will cut off thy horses out of the midst of thee, and I will destroy thy chariots;

15 And I will cut off the cities of thy land, and throw down all thy strongholds;

16 And I will cut off witchcrafts out of thy land, and thou shalt have no more soothsayers;

17 Thy graven images I will also cut off, and thy standing images out of the midst of thee, and thou shalt no more worship the works of thy hands;

18 And I will pluck up thy groves out of the midst of thee; so will I destroy thy cities.

19 And it shall come to pass that all lyings, and deceivings, and envyings, and strifes, and priestcrafts, and whoredoms, shall be done away.

20 For it shall come to pass, saith the Father, that at that day whosoever will not repent and come unto my Beloved Son, them will I cut off from among my people, O house of Israel;

21 And I will execute vengeance and fury upon them, even as upon the heathen, such as they have not heard.

22 But if they will repent and hearken unto my words, and harden not their hearts, I will establish my church among them, and they shall come in unto the covenant and be numbered among this the remnant of Jacob, unto whom I have given this land for their inheritance;

23 And they shall assist my people, the remnant of Jacob, and also as many of the house of Israel as shall come, that they may build a city, which shall be called the New Jerusalem.

24 And then shall they assist my people that they may be gathered in, who are scattered upon all the face of the land, in unto the New Jerusalem.

25 And then shall the power of heaven come down among them; and I also will be in the midst.

Notes

26 And then shall the work of the Father commence at that day, even when this gospel shall be preached among the remnant of this people. Verily I say unto you, at that day shall the work of the Father commence among all the dispersed of my people, yea, even the tribes which have been lost, which the Father hath led away out of Jerusalem.

27 Yea, the work shall commence among all the dispersed of my people, with the Father to prepare the way whereby they may come unto me, that they may call on the Father in my name.

28 Yea, and then shall the work commence, with the Father among all nations in preparing the way whereby his people may be gathered home to the land of their inheritance.

29 And they shall go out from all nations; and they shall not go out in haste, nor go by flight, for I will go before them, saith the Father, and I will be their rearward.

vv. 23–29 "And then . . ."

- Have class members find all the instances that the phrase "and then" is used in verses 23–29. Explain that those words can help establish chronology with the event described prior to the Lord's return. Have class members mark the phrase and then put the events in order on the board.

- Testify that the coming forth of the Book of Mormon is a signal to us of the wonderful promises that the Lord will soon fulfill.

> **Teaching Tips from Prophets' Lips** Elder Boyd K. Packer taught: "If you are teaching a class, . . . [students] will not return with any enthusiasm unless they are being taught something. They must learn something to want to return. They will come willingly, even eagerly, to a class . . . in which they are fed" (*Teach Ye Diligently*, 182).

Index Topics: gathering of Israel

3 NEPHI 22
"With Great Mercies I Will Gather Thee"
About AD 34

1–3, Stakes of Zion are to be established and strengthened; 4–12, The Lord will gather those of the covenant in kindness and mercy; 13–17, Righteousness shall be established and the kingdom of God will prosper.

- To teach the context of this chapter read the following quote from Bruce R. McConkie: "When I speak of the kingdom, I mean the Church of Jesus Christ of Latter-day Saints, which, in the most complete, real, literal, and accurate sense, is the kingdom of God on earth. For a text I will read some words originally written by the great prophet Isaiah, words which later were quoted by the resurrected Christ as he ministered among the Nephites. When Jesus quoted these words, he put them in their perspective, in their context. He had just announced that the restitution of all things was to take place; that the gospel was to come again in its fulness; that Israel was to be gathered; and that the kingdom of God on earth was to be established in the last days. Then he quoted these words from Isaiah, words which are addressed to the Church and which specifically describe the stability, growth, and eventual destiny of the Church" ("God's Kingdom on Earth," *Ensign*, Oct. 1958, 115).

- Invite class members to look for the stability, growth, and eventual destiny of the Church as you look at 3 Nephi 22.

1 And then shall that which is written come to pass: Sing, O barren, thou that didst not bear; break forth into singing, and cry aloud, thou that didst not travail with child; for more are the children of the desolate than the children of the married wife, saith the Lord.

Notes

2 Enlarge the place of thy tent, and let them stretch forth the curtains of thy habitations; spare not, lengthen thy cords and strengthen thy stakes;

3 For thou shalt break forth on the right hand and on the left, and thy seed shall inherit the Gentiles and make the desolate cities to be inhabited.

4 Fear not, for thou shalt not be ashamed; neither be thou confounded, for thou shalt not be put to shame; for thou shalt forget the shame of thy youth, and shalt not remember the reproach of thy youth, and shalt not remember the reproach of thy widowhood any more.

5 For thy maker, thy husband, the Lord of Hosts is his name; and thy Redeemer, the Holy One of Israel—the God of the whole earth shall he be called.

6 For the Lord hath called thee as a woman forsaken and grieved in spirit, and a wife of youth, when thou wast refused, saith thy God.

7 For a small moment have I forsaken thee, but with great mercies will I gather thee.

8 In a little wrath I hid my face from thee for a moment, but with everlasting kindness will I have mercy on thee, saith the Lord thy Redeemer.

9 For this, the waters of Noah unto me, for as I have sworn that the waters of Noah should no more go over the earth, so have I sworn that I would not be wroth with thee.

10 For the mountains shall depart and the hills be removed, but my kindness shall not depart from thee, neither shall the covenant of my peace be removed, saith the Lord that hath mercy on thee.

> "The everlasting covenant is the gospel. This promise is, then, an assurance that the gospel of Jesus Christ will remain in and be administered by the Church and kingdom as set up and established in this day" (Bruce R. McConkie, "God's Kingdom on Earth," *Ensign*, Oct. 1958, 115).

11 O thou afflicted, tossed with tempest, and not comforted! Behold, I will lay thy stones with fair colors, and lay thy foundations with sapphires.

12 And I will make thy windows of agates, and thy gates of carbuncles, and all thy borders of pleasant stones.

13 And all thy children shall be taught of the Lord; and great shall be the peace of thy children.

14 In righteousness shalt thou be established; thou shalt be far from oppression for thou shalt not fear, and from terror for it shall not come near thee.

15 Behold, they shall surely gather together against thee, not by me; whosoever shall gather together against thee shall fall for thy sake.

16 Behold, I have created the smith that bloweth the coals in the fire, and that bringeth forth an instrument for his work; and I have created the waster to destroy.

17 No weapon that is formed against thee shall prosper; and every tongue that shall revile against thee in judgment thou shalt condemn. This is the heritage of the servants of the Lord, and their righteousness is of me, saith the Lord.

> "But there is one great thing about this dispensation which differs from all the dispensations of the past. It is that this time, with the opening of the heavens and the revealing of the gospel in our day, there came the positive, unqualified assurance that the gospel was to remain on earth; that the kingdom was to be secure; that the Church of Jesus Christ of Latter-day Saints was to remain among men to prepare a people for the second coming of the Son of man" (Bruce R. McConkie, "God's Kingdom on Earth," *Ensign*, Oct. 1958, 115).

vv. 1–22 In the last days, the Lord will gather His people and set up His Kingdom to never again be removed.

⚡ Ask the class, *What is the current number of members of the Church? How many temples*

Notes

are on the earth? Testify that the Church will continue to grow and progress until the Lord returns.

✋ Divide the class into two groups. Inform class members that each group will be reading the same verses but looking for something different. Instruct the groups that they will be reading over the verses individually before meeting and discussing what they found as a group. Each group will be given a "look for," a guiding question, and an example of what they can expect to find. Inform class members that not all of the answers will come immediately or easily, but that as they seek to understand and help one another, they will find what the Lord would have them understand from His words.

Group One:

Look for the relationship of the Lord as the husband (bridegroom) of the Church.

Guiding question: *What characteristics of the Savior do we come to understand through the imagery of the husband and father?*

Example: In verse 4 the Lord uses the image of the forsaken wife to show that the Lord will remember Israel, "shalt not remember the reproach of thy widowhood anymore." The Lord will show great love and mercy to the Church in the last days.

Group Two:

Look for the permanence of the Church of Jesus Christ in the last days.

Guiding questions: *Why does the Savior want us to understand the permanence and greatness of the Church in the last days? How might that knowledge help us in the last days?*

Example: In verse 2 the Lord speaks of the growth and strength of the church, "Enlarge the place of thy tent . . . lengthen thy cords . . . strengthen thy stakes."

After the groups have discussed what they have found, have each group share with the class what they found and guide the class accordingly.

❤ Testify of the Savior's love and mercy and that the Church of Jesus Christ is the only true church. Testify that this church will never be taken off the earth and that it is our role to prepare the Church and the world for the Second Coming of the Savior.

Index Topics: gathering, Church in the last days

3 NEPHI 23
"Search the Prophets"
About AD 34

1–6, Jesus certifies the words of Isaiah, Himself, and the prophets; 7–14, Jesus has Nephi insert a prophecy of Samuel the Lamanite that had been excluded.

1 And now, behold, I say unto you, that ye ought to search these things. Yea, a commandment I give unto you that ye search these things diligently; for great are the words of Isaiah.

2 For surely he spake as touching all things concerning my people which are of the house of Israel; therefore it must needs be that he must speak also to the Gentiles.

3 And all things that he spake have been and shall be, even according to the words which he spake.

vv. 1–3 Scripture from all prophets is the word of God.

⚡ Ask your class, *Who did Jesus quote in the last chapter? Wouldn't Jesus have better things to say than what Isaiah said?* To have your class find out why Jesus spent the time quoting Isaiah, have them mark D&C 1:37–38 near these verses in 3 Nephi and refer to the scripture to find the answer.

Notes

- ♥ Testify to class members of how important it is to study all scripture because it is God's word.

4 Therefore give heed to my words; write the things which I have told you; and according to the time and the will of the Father they shall go forth unto the Gentiles.

5 And whosoever will hearken unto my words and repenteth and is baptized, the same shall be saved. Search the prophets, for many there be that testify of these things.

6 And now it came to pass that when Jesus had said these words he said unto them again, after he had expounded all the scriptures unto them which they had received, he said unto them: Behold, other scriptures I would that ye should write, that ye have not.

7 And it came to pass that he said unto Nephi: Bring forth the record which ye have kept.

8 And when Nephi had brought forth the records, and laid them before him, he cast his eyes upon them and said:

9 Verily I say unto you, I commanded my servant Samuel, the Lamanite, that he should testify unto this people, that at the day that the Father should glorify his name in me that there were many saints who should arise from the dead, and should appear unto many, and should minister unto them. And he said unto them: Was it not so?

10 And his disciples answered him and said: Yea, Lord, Samuel did prophesy according to thy words, and they were all fulfilled.

11 And Jesus said unto them: How be it that ye have not written this thing, that many saints did arise and appear unto many and did minister unto them?

12 And it came to pass that Nephi remembered that this thing had not been written.

13 And it came to pass that Jesus commanded that it should be written; therefore it was written according as he commanded.

14 And now it came to pass that when Jesus had expounded all the scriptures in one, which they had written, he commanded them that they should teach the things which he had expounded unto them.

vv. 1–14 We should study the word of God diligently.

- Divide the board into three columns. Write one of the following sets of verses at the top of each of the three columns: vv. 1–3, vv. 4–6 & 14, vv. 7–13. Divide the class into three groups and ask them to prepare to answer the following questions:

  • Which prophet's words are important in the verses?

  • What do the verses say we should do with scripture?

  You may need to explain to the second group that Jesus is also a prophet. Have a member from each group come to the board and write the answer to the two questions in their column on the board.

- Analyze: *With the list of what we are to do with the scriptures, which one has helped you the most to learn and come closer to God? Why?*

- ♥ Testify of the importance of all prophets and the scriptures they wrote. Challenge class members to search, remember, and expound scripture.

Index Topics: scripture study

> **Teaching Tips from Prophets' Lips** "As you prepare a lesson, look in it for converting principles. . . . A converting principle is one that leads to obedience to the will of God" (Henry B. Eyring, "Converting Principles" [remarks at an evening with Elder L. Tom Perry, Feb. 2, 1996], 1).

Notes

3 NEPHI 24

Jesus Quotes Malachi 3
About AD 34

1–7, The wickedness of the people leading up to the Second Coming is described; 8–11, The payment of tithing will open the windows of heaven; 12–18, The Lord discerns between the righteous and the wicked.

Overarching Principle: What we must do to prepare for the Second Coming.

1 And it came to pass that he commanded them that they should write the words which the Father had given unto Malachi, which he should tell unto them. And it came to pass that after they were written he expounded them. And these are the words which he did tell unto them, saying: Thus said the Father unto Malachi—Behold, I will send my messenger, and he shall prepare the way before me, and the Lord whom ye seek shall suddenly come to his temple, even the messenger of the covenant, whom ye delight in; behold, he shall come, saith the Lord of Hosts.

2 But who may abide the day of his coming, and who shall stand when he appeareth? For he is like a refiner's fire, and like fuller's soap.

3 And he shall sit as a refiner and purifier of silver; and he shall purify the sons of Levi, and purge them as gold and silver, that they may offer unto the Lord an offering in righteousness.

vv. 1–3 At His Second Coming, the Lord will cleanse the wicked from the earth.

- ⚡ To help class members visualize what the Lord is trying to teach in these three verses, bring a bar of soap, a very dirty sock, and a match to show the class. Ask if anyone would like to wear the dirty sock and why or why not. Ask, *What needs to happen before the sock is ready to be worn?* Show the class the soap and discuss how the soap could help. Finally, if the soap does not clean the sock, show the match and explain that if the sock was simply too dirty, a final option may be to destroy it.

- 🔍 Invite class members to read verses 1–3 looking for what the three objects have to do with what Jesus is teaching.

- 💡 Fuller's soap was used anciently to cleanse wool before making it into clothing. You may want to conduct an Internet search on "fuller's soap old testament" to learn more about the properties of fuller's soap so you can draw your own parallels with the class.

Note: The lesson outline continues below.

4 Then shall the offering of Judah and Jerusalem be pleasant unto the Lord, as in the days of old, and as in former years.

5 And I will come near to you to judgment; and I will be a swift witness against the sorcerers, and against the adulterers, and against false swearers, and against those that oppress the hireling in his wages, the widow and the fatherless, and that turn aside the stranger, and fear not me, saith the Lord of Hosts.

6 For I am the Lord, I change not; therefore ye sons of Jacob are not consumed.

7 Even from the days of your fathers ye are gone away from mine ordinances, and have not kept them. Return unto me and I will return unto you, saith the Lord of Hosts. But ye say: Wherein shall we return?

8 Will a man rob God? Yet ye have robbed me. But ye say: Wherein have we robbed thee? In tithes and offerings.

9 Ye are cursed with a curse, for ye have robbed me, even this whole nation.

10 Bring ye all the tithes into the storehouse, that there may be meat in my house; and prove me now herewith, saith the Lord of Hosts, if I will not open you the windows of heaven, and pour you out a blessing that there shall not be room enough to receive it.

Notes

11 And I will rebuke the devourer for your sakes, and he shall not destroy the fruits of your ground; neither shall your vine cast her fruit before the time in the fields, saith the Lord of Hosts.

12 And all nations shall call you blessed, for ye shall be a delightsome land, saith the Lord of Hosts.

13 Your words have been stout against me, saith the Lord. Yet ye say: What have we spoken against thee?

14 Ye have said: It is vain to serve God, and what doth it profit that we have kept his ordinances and that we have walked mournfully before the Lord of Hosts?

15 And now we call the proud happy; yea, they that work wickedness are set up; yea, they that tempt God are even delivered.

16 Then they that feared the Lord spake often one to another, and the Lord hearkened and heard; and a book of remembrance was written before him for them that feared the Lord, and that thought upon his name.

17 And they shall be mine, saith the Lord of Hosts, in that day when I make up my jewels; and I will spare them as a man spareth his own son that serveth him.

18 Then shall ye return and discern between the righteous and the wicked, between him that serveth God and him that serveth him not.

vv. 4–18 As we keep the Lord's commandments and ordinances, we will become cleansed and be prepared for the Second Coming.

- This is a continuation from the lesson outline above, so you can continue to reference the objects used at the beginning.

- Explain to your class that they will be looking for what is required to be ready for the Second Coming and how some people may not be ready for it. Write the following on the board and encourage class members to search the following scriptures to find principles of being ready for the Second Coming of the Lord. Write their findings on the board.

Those that will be ready for the Second Coming	Those that will not be ready for the Second Coming
3 Ne. 24:7, 10–11, 16–17	3 Ne. 24:7–8, 13–15

- Analyze: Once identified, ask questions that will allow a discussion of what Jesus is saying about preparation. Consider asking the following questions or using your own:

  - *In what ways are "they that work wickedness set up"? (see v. 15)*
  - *What do you think the Lord means when He says, "Return unto me and I will return unto you?"*
  - *What does tithing have to do with preparation for the Second Coming?*

Note: You probably do not want to focus all your time exclusively on tithing, since tithing is just one mode of preparation for the Second Coming in this chapter. However, Malachi does teach the wonderful blessings that result from paying tithing. The following quotes may be helpful to emphasis the importance of the principle of tithing.

- Dallin H. Oaks stated, "Here we see that the law of tithing is not a remote Old Testament practice, but a commandment directly from the Savior to the people of our day. The Lord reaffirmed that law in modern revelation, commanding his people to pay 'one-tenth of all their interest annually' and declaring that 'this shall be a standing law unto them forever' (see D&C 119:4)" (Dallin H. Oaks, "Tithing," *Ensign*, May 1994, 33).

- Heber J. Grant stated, "I bear witness—and I know that the witness I bear is true—that the men and the women who have been absolutely honest with God, who have paid

Notes

their tithing, . . . God has given them wisdom whereby they have been able to utilize the remaining nine-tenths, and it has been of greater value to them, and they have accomplished more with it than they would if they had not been honest with the Lord" (Heber J. Grant, in Conference Report, April 1912, 30).

- Apply: Have class members read verse 18 and ask, *How does this lesson apply to you?*

3 NEPHI 25

Jesus Quotes Malachi 4
About AD 34

1, The proud and wicked will be burned at the Second Coming; 2–4, The righteous shall be spared at His coming; 5–6, Elijah will come to turn the hearts of the fathers to the children before the great and dreadful day of the Lord.

Note: Jesus continues to quote from the writings of Malachi, who continues his discourse regarding the Second Coming of the Savior. 3 Nephi 24 and 25 could be taught together using the same overarching principle.

Overarching Principle: What we must do to prepare for the Second Coming.

1 For behold, the day cometh that shall burn as an oven; and all the proud, yea, and all that do wickedly, shall be stubble; and the day that cometh shall burn them up, saith the Lord of Hosts, that it shall leave them neither root nor branch.

2 But unto you that fear my name, shall the Son of Righteousness arise with healing in his wings; and ye shall go forth and grow up as calves in the stall.

3 And ye shall tread down the wicked; for they shall be ashes under the soles of your feet in the day that I shall do this, saith the Lord of Hosts.

4 Remember ye the law of Moses, my servant, which I commanded unto him in Horeb for all Israel, with the statutes and judgments.

5 Behold, I will send you Elijah the prophet before the coming of the great and dreadful day of the Lord;

6 And he shall turn the heart of the fathers to the children, and the heart of the children to their fathers, lest I come and smite the earth with a curse.

vv. 1–6 The three P's of Malachi 4: Peril, Preparation, and Prophecy.

- Place or write a big letter 'P' on the board or cut one out of poster board to hold up in front of the class. In conjuction with the previous chapter, discuss with the class why the Lord would want people to be ready for the Second Coming. Ask, *If he wants everyone ready, then why not just tell us when he is coming?* Explain the importance of personal preparation and tell the class they will look for the three P's of Malachi—Peril, Preparation, and Prophecy.

- Consider dividing the class into groups and invite them to look for each of the three P's:

  Peril—v. 1

  Preparation—vv. 2–4

  Prophecy—vv. 5–6

- Analyze: Note with the class that Malachi refers to all those who will be unprepared as one group, being "all they that do wickedly." Ask, *What specific sin does Malachi address? Why do you think Malachi would emphasize that particular sin?*

- The phrase "calves in the stall" in verse 2 has interesting significance in this verse particularly as it applies to the Second Coming. The phrase has reference to stall-fed cows, or cows that are well taken care of. Amidst all the chaos of the Second Coming, if we fear the name of God, then we will be protected and fed as cows in the stall.

Notes

- 💡 The prophecy of Malachi, that Elijah would come to turn the hearts of the fathers to the children and the heart of the children to the fathers, is unique in that it is one of the only prophecies to be found in the Bible (Malachi 4), Book of Mormon (3 Nephi 25), Doctrine and Covenants (Section 2), and the Pearl of Great Price (JSH 1:39).

- 💬 Regarding Malachi's prophecy about Elijah, Elder D. Todd Christofferson said, "Our work for the dead bears witness that Jesus Christ will come again to this earth. In the final verses of the Old Testament, Jehovah declared, 'Behold, I will send you Elijah the prophet before the coming of the great and dreadful day of the Lord: And he shall turn the heart of the fathers to the children, and the heart of the children to their fathers, lest I come and smite the earth with a curse.' In an inspired commentary on this scripture, the Prophet Joseph Smith stated, 'The earth will be smitten with a curse unless there is a welding link of some kind or other between the fathers and the children, upon some subject or other—and behold what is that subject? It is the baptism for the dead (see D&C 128:18).' The vicarious ordinances we perform in temples, beginning with baptism, make possible an eternal welding link between generations that fulfills the purpose of the earth's creation. Without this, 'the whole earth would be utterly wasted at [Christ's] coming' (see D&C 2:3). Elijah has, in fact, come as promised to confer the priesthood power that turns hearts and establishes the welding links between the fathers and the children so that once again what is bound on earth 'shall be bound in heaven' (see Matthew 16:19). When he came, Elijah declared, 'The keys of this dispensation are committed into your hands; and by this ye may know that the great and dreadful day of the Lord is near, even at the doors' (see D&C 110). We are anxiously about the task of searching out our fathers and mothers of generations past and binding them to us and us to them. Is not this the strongest possible evidence of our conviction that Jesus Christ will come again to reign upon the earth? We know He will, and we know what He expects we will have done in preparation for His return" ("The Redemption of the Dead and the Testimony of Jesus," *Ensign*, Nov. 2000, 12).

- ♥ Consider asking class members to share experiences regarding family history or temple work.

Teaching Tips from Prophets' Lips "To ask and to answer questions is at the heart of all learning and all teaching" (Henry B. Eyring, "The Lord Will Multiply the Harvest" [an evening with Elder Henry B. Eyring, Feb. 6, 1998], 5–6).

3 NEPHI 26
The Lord Concludes His Visit
About AD 34

1–5, Jesus expounds the scriptures unto the multitude; 6–12, Many things cannot be written until the faith of the Lord's people has been tried; 13–16, Jesus teaches and ministers unto the people and then ascends into heaven; 17–21, Jesus's disciples continue His ministry on the earth.

1 And now it came to pass that when Jesus had told these things he expounded them unto the multitude; and he did expound all things unto them, both great and small.

2 And he saith: These scriptures, which ye had not with you, the Father commanded that I should give unto you; for it was wisdom in him that they should be given unto future generations.

3 And he did expound all things, even from the beginning until the time that he should come in his glory—yea, even all things which should come upon the face of the earth, even until the elements should melt with fervent

Notes

heat, and the earth should be wrapt together as a scroll, and the heavens and the earth should pass away;

4 And even unto the great and last day, when all people, and all kindreds, and all nations and tongues shall stand before God, to be judged of their works, whether they be good or whether they be evil—

5 If they be good, to the resurrection of everlasting life; and if they be evil, to the resurrection of damnation; being on a parallel, the one on the one hand and the other on the other hand, according to the mercy, and the justice, and the holiness which is in Christ, who was before the world began.

6 And now there cannot be written in this book even a hundredth part of the things which Jesus did truly teach unto the people;

7 But behold the plates of Nephi do contain the more part of the things which he taught the people.

8 And these things have I written, which are a lesser part of the things which he taught the people; and I have written them to the intent that they may be brought again unto this people, from the Gentiles, according to the words which Jesus hath spoken.

9 And when they shall have received this, which is expedient that they should have first, to try their faith, and if it shall so be that they shall believe these things then shall the greater things be made manifest unto them.

10 And if it so be that they will not believe these things, then shall the greater things be withheld from them, unto their condemnation.

11 Behold, I was about to write them, all which were engraven upon the plates of Nephi, but the Lord forbade it, saying: I will try the faith of my people.

12 Therefore I, Mormon, do write the things which have been commanded me of the Lord. And now I, Mormon, make an end of my sayings, and proceed to write the things which have been commanded me.

vv. 1–12 The Lord can reveal all knowledge, but we must be faithful to what we have received in order to receive more.

- ⚡ Have you ever had a question that no one could answer? How did that feel? What would you do to be able to receive an answer to that question?

- 🔍 Read 3 Nephi 26:1–3 and look for what questions Jesus would have been able to answer for the Nephites.

- ❓ Analyze:
  - What would that have been like to hear the Savior expound all things?
  - How much of Jesus's teachings did Mormon record in 3 Nephi (see v. 6)?
  - Why do you think he didn't write more?
  - Read 3 Nephi 26:7–12 and find the reasons Mormon says he didn't write all of Jesus's teachings.

- ❓ Analyze: *What do you think the phrase "try the faith of my people" refers to? What might happen to faith if we had all of the answers?*

- ❓ Apply: *What does verse 9 teach about receiving answers to your personal questions? Have you had an experience when you have received more knowledge by faithfully studying that which you already have?*

- ♥ Testify that the Lord will reveal truth to us as we are faithful to the truths we have already received.

13 Therefore, I would that ye should behold that the Lord truly did teach the people, for the space of three days; and after that he did show himself unto them oft, and did break bread oft, and bless it, and give it unto them.

14 And it came to pass that he did teach and minister unto the children of the multitude of whom hath been spoken, and he did loose their tongues, and they did speak unto their fathers great and

Notes

marvelous things, even greater than he had revealed unto the people; and he loosed their tongues that they could utter.

15 And it came to pass that after he had ascended into heaven—the second time that he showed himself unto them, and had gone unto the Father, after having healed all their sick, and their lame, and opened the eyes of their blind and unstopped the ears of the deaf, and even had done all manner of cures among them, and raised a man from the dead, and had shown forth his power unto them, and had ascended unto the Father—

16 Behold, it came to pass on the morrow that the multitude gathered themselves together, and they both saw and heard these children; yea, even babes did open their mouths and utter marvelous things; and the things which they did utter were forbidden that there should not any man write them.

17 And it came to pass that the disciples whom Jesus had chosen began from that time forth to baptize and to teach as many as did come unto them; and as many as were baptized in the name of Jesus were filled with the Holy Ghost.

18 And many of them saw and heard unspeakable things, which are not lawful to be written.

19 And they taught, and did minister one to another; and they had all things common among them, every man dealing justly, one with another.

20 And it came to pass that they did do all things even as Jesus had commanded them.

21 And they who were baptized in the name of Jesus were called the church of Christ.

vv. 13–21 Christ established His church in the Americas the same way He did in Palestine.

- Invite class members to read 3 Nephi 26:13–21 and find as many similarities between Jesus's ministry in the old and new worlds as they can. Make a list on the board. If time permits, consider comparing the class's findings with Acts 2:37–47.

- Testify that Christ's gospel is the same yesterday, today, and forever.

3 NEPHI 27

"What Manner of Men Ought Ye to Be?"

About AD 34–35

1–11, Jesus Christ appears to His disciples and He instructs them to name the church according to His name; 12–27, Christ invites all to do the things He did and become like Him; 28–33, He foretells what will happen to those of the fourth generation.

1 And it came to pass that as the disciples of Jesus were journeying and were preaching the things which they had both heard and seen, and were baptizing in the name of Jesus, it came to pass that the disciples were gathered together and were united in mighty prayer and fasting.

2 And Jesus again showed himself unto them, for they were praying unto the Father in his name; and Jesus came and stood in the midst of them, and said unto them: What will ye that I shall give unto you?

3 And they said unto him: Lord, we will that thou wouldst tell us the name whereby we shall call this church; for there are disputations among the people concerning this matter.

4 And the Lord said unto them: Verily, verily, I say unto you, why is it that the people should murmur and dispute because of this thing?

5 Have they not read the scriptures, which say ye must take upon you the name of Christ, which is my name? For by this name shall ye be called at the last day;

6 And whoso taketh upon him my name, and endureth to the end, the same shall be saved at the last day.

7 Therefore, whatsoever ye shall do, ye shall do it

Notes

in my name; therefore ye shall call the church in my name; and ye shall call upon the Father in my name that he will bless the church for my sake.

8 And how be it my church save it be called in my name? For if a church be called in Moses' name then it be Moses' church; or if it be called in the name of a man then it be the church of a man; but if it be called in my name then it is my church, if it so be that they are built upon my gospel.

💬 "Obedient to revelation, we call ourselves 'The Church of Jesus Christ of Latter-day Saints' rather than the Mormon Church. It is one thing for others to refer to the Church as the Mormon Church or to us as Mormons; it is quite another for us to do so.

"The First Presidency stated: 'The use of the revealed name, The Church of Jesus Christ of Latter-day Saints (D&C 115:4), is increasingly important in our responsibility to proclaim the name of the Savior throughout all the world. Accordingly, we ask that when we refer to the Church we use its full name wherever possible. . . . "When referring to Church members, we suggest 'members of The Church of Jesus Christ of Latter-day Saints.' As a shortened reference, 'Latter-day Saints' is preferred" [First Presidency letter, Feb. 23, 2001] (Boyd K. Packer, "Guided by the Holy Spirit," *Ensign,* May 2011, 33).

♥ Invite class members to frequently use the correct name of the Church as revealed.

9 Verily I say unto you, that ye are built upon my gospel; therefore ye shall call whatsoever things ye do call, in my name; therefore if ye call upon the Father, for the church, if it be in my name the Father will hear you;

10 And if it so be that the church is built upon my gospel then will the Father show forth his own works in it.

11 But if it be not built upon my gospel, and is built upon the works of men, or upon the works of the devil, verily I say unto you they have joy in their works for a season, and by and by the end cometh, and they are hewn down and cast into the fire, from whence there is no return.

12 For their works do follow them, for it is because of their works that they are hewn down; therefore remember the things that I have told you.

13 Behold I have given unto you my gospel, and this is the gospel which I have given unto you—that I came into the world to do the will of my Father, because my Father sent me.

14 And my Father sent me that I might be lifted up upon the cross; and after that I had been lifted up upon the cross, that I might draw all men unto me, that as I have been lifted up by men even so should men be lifted up by the Father, to stand before me, to be judged of their works, whether they be good or whether they be evil—

15 And for this cause have I been lifted up; therefore, according to the power of the Father I will draw all men unto me, that they may be judged according to their works.

vv. 14–15 Christ has been lifted up that He might draw all men unto Him.

⚡ Show a picture of the Savior's crucifixion and write on the board, "Christ has been lifted up that . . ." Invite class members to finish the phrase.

🔍 *Look for the end of the phrase in verses 14–15.*

❓ Analyze:
- *What does the phrase "draw all men unto me" mean?*
- *Why do both of the verses (14 and 15) end with the phrase, "judged of their works?"*
- *What is the connection between being judged by our works and Christ being lifted up that he might draw all men unto Him?*

💬 Speaking of the Savior, Kent F. Richards taught, "Perhaps His most significant work is in the ongoing labor with each of us

Notes

individually to lift, to bless, to strengthen, to sustain, to guide, and to forgive us" (Kent F. Richards, "The Atonement Covers All Pain," *Ensign*, May 2011, 17).

- Invite all to Christ and to access His Atonement in order to be lifted up by the Savior.

16 And it shall come to pass, that whoso repenteth and is baptized in my name shall be filled; and if he endureth to the end, behold, him will I hold guiltless before my Father at that day when I shall stand to judge the world.

17 And he that endureth not unto the end, the same is he that is also hewn down and cast into the fire, from whence they can no more return, because of the justice of the Father.

18 And this is the word which he hath given unto the children of men. And for this cause he fulfilleth the words which he hath given, and he lieth not, but fulfilleth all his words.

19 And no unclean thing can enter into his kingdom; therefore nothing entereth into his rest save it be those who have washed their garments in my blood, because of their faith, and the repentance of all their sins, and their faithfulness unto the end.

20 Now this is the commandment: Repent, all ye ends of the earth, and come unto me and be baptized in my name, that ye may be sanctified by the reception of the Holy Ghost, that ye may stand spotless before me at the last day.

21 Verily, verily, I say unto you, this is my gospel; and ye know the things that ye must do in my church; for the works which ye have seen me do that shall ye also do; for that which ye have seen me do even that shall ye do;

22 Therefore, if ye do these things blessed are ye, for ye shall be lifted up at the last day.

vv. 16–22 We must *be* as the Savior.

- Note that this lesson will help formulate a distinction between "doing" and "being." Have class members answer the following question: *Is it more important to be like Christ as stated in verse 27, or do the things he did as stated in verse 21?* Invite class members to review the two verses as they think about the answer.

- According to verses 16–21, what are the things we are to DO? According to verse 19, what is the one thing that we are to BE?

- Analyze:
  - What is the relationship between doing and being?
  - If you do the things that Christ does, that mean you have become like He is?
  - If you have become like Christ, does that mean that you will always do as He would do?

- Use the following quote by Lynn G. Robbins to guide the discussion: "To *be* and to *do* are inseparable. As interdependent doctrines they reinforce and promote each other. Faith inspires one to pray, for example, and prayer in turn strengthens one's faith. . . . While He recognized the importance of *do*, the Savior identified *be* as a 'weightier matter.' . . . Because *be* begets *do* and is the motive behind *do*, teaching be will improve behavior more effectively than focusing on do will improve behavior" (Lynn G. Robbins, "What Manner of Men and Women Ought Ye to Be?" *Ensign*, May 2011, 103).

- Elder Dallin H. Oaks has also taught, "The Final Judgement is not just an evaluation of a sum total of good and evil acts—what we have *done*. It is an acknowledgment of the final effect of our acts and thoughts—what we have *become*. It is not enough for anyone just to go through the motions. The commandments, ordinances, and covenants of the gospel are not a list of deposits required to be made in some heavenly account. The gospel of Jesus Christ is a plan that shows us how to become what our Heavenly Father desires us to become" ("The Challenge to Become," *Ensign*, Nov. 2000, 32).

- Invite class members to *be* like the Savior and

Notes

not simply *do* the things that He asks of us. Help them understand that a check-list mentality may keep us from truly becoming like the Savior.

23 Write the things which ye have seen and heard, save it be those which are forbidden.

24 Write the works of this people, which shall be, even as hath been written, of that which hath been.

25 For behold, out of the books which have been written, and which shall be written, shall this people be judged, for by them shall their works be known unto men.

26 And behold, all things are written by the Father; therefore out of the books which shall be written shall the world be judged.

27 And know ye that ye shall be judges of this people, according to the judgment which I shall give unto you, which shall be just. Therefore, what manner of men ought ye to be? Verily I say unto you, even as I am.

28 And now I go unto the Father. And verily I say unto you, whatsoever things ye shall ask the Father in my name shall be given unto you.

29 Therefore, ask, and ye shall receive; knock, and it shall be opened unto you; for he that asketh, receiveth; and unto him that knocketh, it shall be opened.

💡 You could connect verses 28–29 with verses 1–5, where the disciples show an example of what it means to ask, seek, and knock.

30 And now, behold, my joy is great, even unto fulness, because of you, and also this generation; yea, and even the Father rejoiceth, and also all the holy angels, because of you and this generation; for none of them are lost.

31 Behold, I would that ye should understand; for I mean them who are now alive of this generation; and none of them are lost; and in them I have fulness of joy.

32 But behold, it sorroweth me because of the fourth generation from this generation, for they are led away captive by him even as was the son of perdition; for they will sell me for silver and for gold, and for that which moth doth corrupt and which thieves can break through and steal. And in that day will I visit them, even in turning their works upon their own heads.

33 And it came to pass that when Jesus had ended these sayings he said unto his disciples: Enter ye in at the strait gate; for strait is the gate, and narrow is the way that leads to life, and few there be that find it; but wide is the gate, and broad the way which leads to death, and many there be that travel therein, until the night cometh, wherein no man can work.

Teaching Tips from Prophets' Lips "It is your duty to teach that Jesus Christ is the Redeemer of the world, that Joseph Smith was a Prophet of God, and that to him in this last dispensation there appeared God the Father and his Son in person. Do you believe it? Do you feel it? Does that testimony radiate from your being? . . . If so, that radiation will give life to the people whom you go to teach. If not, there will be a dearth, a drought, a lack of that spiritual environment in which the Saints grow. . . . You can teach effectively only that which you yourselves feel" (David O. McKay, *Gospel Ideals* [1953], 190).

Index Topics: becoming, atonement

3 NEPHI 28

The Three Nephites
About AD 34–35

1–3, Nine of the Nephite disciples desire to return to God's kingdom when they die; 4–10, Three of the Nephite disciples request to tarry on the earth until the end; 11–24, Mormon explains some of the actions of the three Nephites; 25–40, Mormon explains the

Notes

three Nephites' responsibilities with the house of Israel, and he also explains transfiguration.

1 And it came to pass when Jesus had said these words, he spake unto his disciples, one by one, saying unto them: What is it that ye desire of me, after that I am gone to the Father?

2 And they all spake, save it were three, saying: We desire that after we have lived unto the age of man, that our ministry, wherein thou hast called us, may have an end, that we may speedily come unto thee in thy kingdom.

3 And he said unto them: Blessed are ye because ye desired this thing of me; therefore, after that ye are seventy and two years old ye shall come unto me in my kingdom; and with me ye shall find rest.

4 And when he had spoken unto them, he turned himself unto the three, and said unto them: What will ye that I should do unto you, when I am gone unto the Father?

5 And they sorrowed in their hearts, for they durst not speak unto him the thing which they desired.

6 And he said unto them: Behold, I know your thoughts, and ye have desired the thing which John, my beloved, who was with me in my ministry, before that I was lifted up by the Jews, desired of me.

7 Therefore, more blessed are ye, for ye shall never taste of death; but ye shall live to behold all the doings of the Father unto the children of men, even until all things shall be fulfilled according to the will of the Father, when I shall come in my glory with the powers of heaven.

8 And ye shall never endure the pains of death; but when I shall come in my glory ye shall be changed in the twinkling of an eye from mortality to immortality; and then shall ye be blessed in the kingdom of my Father.

9 And again, ye shall not have pain while ye shall dwell in the flesh, neither sorrow save it be for the sins of the world; and all this will I do because of the thing which ye have desired of me, for ye have desired that ye might bring the souls of men unto me, while the world shall stand.

10 And for this cause ye shall have fulness of joy; and ye shall sit down in the kingdom of my Father; yea, your joy shall be full, even as the Father hath given me fulness of joy; and ye shall be even as I am, and I am even as the Father; and the Father and I are one;

11 And the Holy Ghost beareth record of the Father and me; and the Father giveth the Holy Ghost unto the children of men, because of me.

vv. 1–11 A fulness of joy comes as we seek to bring the souls of men unto God.

- *What would you say to the Savior if He asked you, "What is it that ye desire of me, after that I am gone to the Father?" Note that this is what He asked His disciples as found in verse 1.*

- *What did the disciples say in verses 2–6?*

- Analyze: *If you had to choose between the two choices, what would you choose and why? What does the Savior say is the better choice? (v. 7).*

- *What was one of the most important results of the choice to stay on the earth according to verse 10?*

- Apply: *Why is it that joy comes as we seek to bring souls to God?*

- Invite class members to testify by asking the following questions, *Can someone please share an experience when they found joy as a direct result of bringing souls to God?* If needed explain that this experience is not limited to missionary work, but could include helping family, friends, and those who are inactive in the Church.

12 And it came to pass that when Jesus had spoken these words, he touched every one of them with his finger save it were the three who were to tarry, and then he departed.

Notes

13 And behold, the heavens were opened, and they were caught up into heaven, and saw and heard unspeakable things.

14 And it was forbidden them that they should utter; neither was it given unto them power that they could utter the things which they saw and heard;

15 And whether they were in the body or out of the body, they could not tell; for it did seem unto them like a transfiguration of them, that they were changed from this body of flesh into an immortal state, that they could behold the things of God.

16 But it came to pass that they did again minister upon the face of the earth; nevertheless they did not minister of the things which they had heard and seen, because of the commandment which was given them in heaven.

17 And now, whether they were mortal or immortal, from the day of their transfiguration, I know not;

18 But this much I know, according to the record which hath been given—they did go forth upon the face of the land, and did minister unto all the people, uniting as many to the church as would believe in their preaching; baptizing them, and as many as were baptized did receive the Holy Ghost.

19 And they were cast into prison by them who did not belong to the church. And the prisons could not hold them, for they were rent in twain.

20 And they were cast down into the earth; but they did smite the earth with the word of God, insomuch that by his power they were delivered out of the depths of the earth; and therefore they could not dig pits sufficient to hold them.

21 And thrice they were cast into a furnace and received no harm.

22 And twice were they cast into a den of wild beasts; and behold they did play with the beasts as a child with a suckling lamb, and received no harm.

23 And it came to pass that thus they did go forth among all the people of Nephi, and did preach the gospel of Christ unto all people upon the face of the land; and they were converted unto the Lord, and were united unto the church of Christ, and thus the people of that generation were blessed, according to the word of Jesus.

24 And now I, Mormon, make an end of speaking concerning these things for a time.

25 Behold, I was about to write the names of those who were never to taste of death, but the Lord forbade; therefore I write them not, for they are hid from the world.

26 But behold, I have seen them, and they have ministered unto me.

27 And behold they will be among the Gentiles, and the Gentiles shall know them not.

28 They will also be among the Jews, and the Jews shall know them not.

29 And it shall come to pass, when the Lord seeth fit in his wisdom that they shall minister unto all the scattered tribes of Israel, and unto all nations, kindreds, tongues and people, and shall bring out of them unto Jesus many souls, that their desire may be fulfilled, and also because of the convincing power of God which is in them.

30 And they are as the angels of God, and if they shall pray unto the Father in the name of Jesus they can show themselves unto whatsoever man it seemeth them good.

31 Therefore, great and marvelous works shall be wrought by them, before the great and coming day when all people must surely stand before the judgment-seat of Christ;

32 Yea even among the Gentiles shall there be a great and marvelous work wrought by them, before that judgment day.

33 And if ye had all the scriptures which give an account of all the marvelous works of Christ, ye would, according to the words of Christ, know that these things must surely come.

Notes

34 And wo be unto him that will not hearken unto the words of Jesus, and also to them whom he hath chosen and sent among them; for whoso receiveth not the words of Jesus and the words of those whom he hath sent receiveth not him; and therefore he will not receive them at the last day;

35 And it would be better for them if they had not been born. For do ye suppose that ye can get rid of the justice of an offended God, who hath been trampled under feet of men, that thereby salvation might come?

36 And now behold, as I spake concerning those whom the Lord hath chosen, yea, even three who were caught up into the heavens, that I knew not whether they were cleansed from mortality to immortality—

37 But behold, since I wrote, I have inquired of the Lord, and he hath made it manifest unto me that there must needs be a change wrought upon their bodies, or else it needs be that they must taste of death;

38 Therefore, that they might not taste of death there was a change wrought upon their bodies, that they might not suffer pain nor sorrow save it were for the sins of the world.

39 Now this change was not equal to that which shall take place at the last day; but there was a change wrought upon them, insomuch that Satan could have no power over them, that he could not tempt them; and they were sanctified in the flesh, that they were holy, and that the powers of the earth could not hold them.

40 And in this state they were to remain until the judgment day of Christ; and at that day they were to receive a greater change, and to be received into the kingdom of the Father to go no more out, but to dwell with God eternally in the heavens.

vv. 7–40 Description of the state of the three Nephites.

👥 Divide the class into six groups and give each group one of the following sets of verses: 7–9, 15–17, 18–22, 23–26, 27–30, and 37–40. Invite each group to find any description of the three Nephites and then to write it on the board. After all groups have written their descriptions on the board, discuss the results as a class.

Index Topics: desires, joy, the three Nephites

3 NEPHI 29

"Wo unto Him That Spurneth"
About AD 34–35

1–3, As the Book of Mormon goes forth, it shows that God is fulfilling His covenants unto Israel; 4–9, We must not spurn at the Lord's doings.

1 And now behold, I say unto you that when the Lord shall see fit, in his wisdom, that these sayings shall come unto the Gentiles according to his word, then ye may know that the covenant which the Father hath made with the children of Israel, concerning their restoration to the lands of their inheritance, is already beginning to be fulfilled.

2 And ye may know that the words of the Lord, which have been spoken by the holy prophets, shall all be fulfilled; and ye need not say that the Lord delays his coming unto the children of Israel.

3 And ye need not imagine in your hearts that the words which have been spoken are vain, for behold, the Lord will remember his covenant which he hath made unto his people of the house of Israel.

4 And when ye shall see these sayings coming forth among you, then ye need not any longer spurn at the doings of the Lord, for the sword of his justice is in his right hand; and behold, at that day, if ye shall spurn at his doings he will cause that it shall soon overtake you.

Notes

5 Wo unto him that spurneth at the doings of the Lord; yea, wo unto him that shall deny the Christ and his works!

6 Yea, wo unto him that shall deny the revelations of the Lord, and that shall say the Lord no longer worketh by revelation, or by prophecy, or by gifts, or by tongues, or by healings, or by the power of the Holy Ghost!

7 Yea, and wo unto him that shall say at that day, to get gain, that there can be no miracle wrought by Jesus Christ; for he that doeth this shall become like unto the son of perdition, for whom there was no mercy, according to the word of Christ!

8 Yea, and ye need not any longer hiss, nor spurn, nor make game of the Jews, nor any of the remnant of the house of Israel; for behold, the Lord remembereth his covenant unto them, and he will do unto them according to that which he hath sworn.

9 Therefore ye need not suppose that ye can turn the right hand of the Lord unto the left, that he may not execute judgment unto the fulfilling of the covenant which he hath made unto the house of Israel.

vv. 3–8 We are not to spurn at the doings of the Lord.

- Before class, prepare three pieces of paper. On the first write, "The correct definition of the word, *spurn* is 'To reject with disdain; to kick; to drive back or away, as with the foot.'" (Webster 1828 edition). On the other two papers write, "You need to create a definition of the word, *spurn,* and try to convince the class you are giving the correct definition." In class, ask for three volunteers and explain the game to them. Give the volunteers a minute to prepare, and then invite them to present their definitions to the class. After presenting, allow the class the chance to guess who has presented the correct definition. Tally how many votes each person gets. Finally, tell the person with the correct definition to step forward.

- Write the correct definition of "spurn" on the board and have class members underline each usage of the word in verses 3–8.

- Invite class members to look for each of the times spurn (or a form of the word) is used, and make a list on the board of the things we are not to spurn.

- *Why do you think the Lord cares about our attitude towards the things listed on the board? How might spurning those things drive the spirit out of our lives?*

- Challenge class members not to spurn those things they listed.

Teaching Tips from Prophets' Lips "As a teacher, you can prepare an environment that invites the Spirit to attend your teaching. Then the Spirit can bear witness of the truthfulness of the principles you teach" (*Teaching, No Greater Call*, p. 45).

3 NEPHI 30

"Hearken, O Ye Gentiles"
About AD 34–35

1–2, Mormon writes the words the Lord commands to be written to the Gentiles.

1 Hearken, O ye Gentiles, and hear the words of Jesus Christ, the Son of the living God, which he hath commanded me that I should speak concerning you, for, behold he commandeth me that I should write, saying:

2 Turn, all ye Gentiles, from your wicked ways; and repent of your evil doings, of your lyings and deceivings, and of your whoredoms, and of your secret abominations, and your idolatries, and of your murders, and your priestcrafts, and your envyings, and your strifes, and from all your wickedness and abominations, and come unto me, and be baptized in my name, that ye may receive a remission of your sins, and be filled

Notes

with the Holy Ghost, that ye may be numbered with my people who are of the house of Israel.

vv. 1–2 The people of the world must repent.

⚡ *Who is chapter 30 written to?* (Direct the class to the chapter heading.)

🔍 *Look for and list how the Lord wants the Gentiles to repent in verse 2.*

✋ List each of the things that are mentioned. Ask class members to put each term into modern language and then ask if there is a problem in the world today with that particular sin.

❓ *What does it mean to be "numbered with my people who are of the house of Israel"?* (Take a moment to discuss the concept of a covenant people and the blessings that come from keeping covenants.) Then ask, *How do these sins prohibit us from being part of the covenant people? What two specific blessings are offered to those who are numbered with the Lord's people in verse 2?*

♥ Testify that all people, Jew or Gentile, who repent of their sins and are baptized in Christ's name can be numbered among the covenant people.

Notes

THE FOURTH BOOK OF NEPHI

Who Is the Son of Nephi—One of the Disciples of Jesus Christ

FOURTH NEPHI SUMMARY

Time Period: About AD 35–321

Contributor: Mormon who is summarizing almost a 300-year period of history

Source: Large plates of Nephi

Abridged by: Mormon

An account of the people of Nephi, according to his record.

4 NEPHI 1

Three Generations of Peace
About AD 35–321

1–11, Peace and prosperity continue in the land, all were converted unto the Lord; 12–18, There were no manner of -ites in the land, the people were completely unified; 19–30, Pride and riches begin to disunify the people; 31–41, Various churches are established that begin to persecute the church of Christ; 42–46, Gadiantion robbers are introduced into society and the people become completely wicked; 47–49, Ammaron hides the golden plate records and finishes his record.

Overarching Principle: If Christ and His gospel are central in our lives we will experience peace, prosperity, and the ability to view everyone equally. When we allow something else to become central in our lives we become prideful, pompous, and we may be set at variance with our fellow man.

- ⚡ To help establish the concept of Christ and His gospel being central in our lives, consider beginning your lesson with the following object lesson. Bring a dartboard to class or draw one on the board. Discuss with the class how to play darts—especially the goal of hitting the bullseye and the importance of keeping an eye on the target. Place a picture of Jesus Christ in the center of the target and discuss what it would mean to have Christ as the center of our lives and focus. (Note: Out of respect for the Savior, do not throw darts at this target.) Move the picture of Christ away from the center to an outer ring of the dartboard and then place a picture of a worldly object in the center and discuss the implications of the placement of the two pictures on the dartboard. After teaching this object

Notes

lesson, you can refer to it throughout the rest of the chapter.

1 And it came to pass that the thirty and fourth year passed away, and also the thirty and fifth, and behold the disciples of Jesus had formed a church of Christ in all the lands round about. And as many as did come unto them, and did truly repent of their sins, were baptized in the name of Jesus; and they did also receive the Holy Ghost.

2 And it came to pass in the thirty and sixth year, the people were all converted unto the Lord, upon all the face of the land, both Nephites and Lamanites, and there were no contentions and disputations among them, and every man did deal justly one with another.

3 And they had all things common among them; therefore there were not rich and poor, bond and free, but they were all made free, and partakers of the heavenly gift.

4 And it came to pass that the thirty and seventh year passed away also, and there still continued to be peace in the land.

5 And there were great and marvelous works wrought by the disciples of Jesus, insomuch that they did heal the sick, and raise the dead, and cause the lame to walk, and the blind to receive their sight, and the deaf to hear; and all manner of miracles did they work among the children of men; and in nothing did they work miracles save it were in the name of Jesus.

6 And thus did the thirty and eighth year pass away, and also the thirty and ninth, and forty and first, and the forty and second, yea, even until forty and nine years had passed away, and also the fifty and first, and the fifty and second; yea, and even until fifty and nine years had passed away.

7 And the Lord did prosper them exceedingly in the land; yea, insomuch that they did build cities again where there had been cities burned.

8 Yea, even that great city Zarahemla did they cause to be built again.

9 But there were many cities which had been sunk, and waters came up in the stead thereof; therefore these cities could not be renewed.

10 And now, behold, it came to pass that the people of Nephi did wax strong, and did multiply exceedingly fast, and became an exceedingly fair and delightsome people.

vv. 1–10 The people of Nephi grow and prosper after Christ leaves.

💡 Consider summarizing the preceding verses in your own words. Note with the class why they experienced so much prosperity.

11 And they were married, and given in marriage, and were blessed according to the multitude of the promises which the Lord had made unto them.

12 And they did not walk any more after the performances and ordinances of the law of Moses; but they did walk after the commandments which they had received from their Lord and their God, continuing in fasting and prayer, and in meeting together oft both to pray and to hear the word of the Lord.

13 And it came to pass that there was no contention among all the people, in all the land; but there were mighty miracles wrought among the disciples of Jesus.

14 And it came to pass that the seventy and first year passed away, and also the seventy and second year, yea, and in fine, till the seventy and ninth year had passed away; yea, even an hundred years had passed away, and the disciples of Jesus, whom he had chosen, had all gone to the paradise of God, save it were the three who should tarry; and there were other disciples ordained in their stead; and also many of that generation had passed away.

15 And it came to pass that there was no contention in the land, because of the love of God which did dwell in the hearts of the people.

Notes

16 And there were no envyings, nor strifes, nor tumults, nor whoredoms, nor lyings, nor murders, nor any manner of lasciviousness; and surely there could not be a happier people among all the people who had been created by the hand of God.

17 There were no robbers, nor murderers, neither were there Lamanites, nor any manner of -ites; but they were in one, the children of Christ, and heirs to the kingdom of God.

18 And how blessed were they! For the Lord did bless them in all their doings; yea, even they were blessed and prospered until an hundred and ten years had passed away; and the first generation from Christ had passed away, and there was no contention in all the land.

19 And it came to pass that Nephi, he that kept this last record, (and he kept it upon the plates of Nephi) died, and his son Amos kept it in his stead; and he kept it upon the plates of Nephi also.

vv. 11–19 If Christ and His gospel are central in our lives, we will experience peace, prosperity, and view everyone equally.

- Use the dart object lesson found at the beginning of this chapter.

- Write, "Keeping Christ Central" on the board and leave the room so the class can create a list underneath it.

- Invite class members to look for evidence that Christ and His gospel were central in the people of Nephi's lives. Consider writing the class's findings on the board.

- Analyze: *What does the phrase, "nor any manner of -ites" mean? (see v. 17) What impresses you about what the people were doing?* Continue analyzing and sharing insights regarding these principles.

- Elder Jeffrey R. Holland stated, "We may not yet be the Zion of which our prophets foretold and toward which the poets and priests of Israel have pointed us, but we long for it and we keep working toward it. I do not know whether a full implementation of such a society can be realized until Christ comes, but I know that when He did come to the Nephites, His majestic teachings and ennobling spirit led to the happiest of all times, a time in which 'there were no contentions and disputations among them, and every man did deal justly one with another. And they had all things common among them; therefore there were not rich and poor, bond and free, but they were all made free, and partakers of the heavenly gift.' That blessed circumstance was, I suppose, achieved on only one other occasion of which we know—the city of Enoch, where 'they were of one heart and one mind, and dwelt in righteousness; and there was no poor among them.' (see Moses 7:18.)

"The Prophet Joseph Smith had such a grand view of our possibilities, a view given him by the revelations of God. He knew that the real task was in being more Christlike—caring the way the Savior cared, loving the way he loved, 'every man seeking the interest of his neighbor,' the scripture says, 'and doing all things with an eye single to the glory of God'" ("A Handful of Meal and a Little Oil," *Ensign*, May 1996, 31).

- Apply: *How does the example of the Nephites apply to us in our day? Even though we may not reach this type of complete righteousness as a people, what is our individual responsibility to create this type of situation?*

20 And he kept it eighty and four years, and there was still peace in the land, save it were a small part of the people who had revolted from the church and taken upon them the name of Lamanites; therefore there began to be Lamanites again in the land.

21 And it came to pass that Amos died also, (and it was an hundred and ninety and four years from the coming of Christ) and his son Amos kept the record in his stead; and he also kept it upon the

Notes

plates of Nephi; and it was also written in the book of Nephi, which is this book.

22 And it came to pass that two hundred years had passed away; and the second generation had all passed away save it were a few.

> Notice that Satan will often times seek to destroy the Church through the next generation. If he cannot destroy us, he will seek to destroy the generations that follow us.

23 And now I, Mormon, would that ye should know that the people had multiplied, insomuch that they were spread upon all the face of the land, and that they had become exceedingly rich, because of their prosperity in Christ.

24 And now, in this two hundred and first year there began to be among them those who were lifted up in pride, such as the wearing of costly apparel, and all manner of fine pearls, and of the fine things of the world.

25 And from that time forth they did have their goods and their substance no more common among them.

26 And they began to be divided into classes; and they began to build up churches unto themselves to get gain, and began to deny the true church of Christ.

27 And it came to pass that when two hundred and ten years had passed away there were many churches in the land; yea, there were many churches which professed to know the Christ, and yet they did deny the more parts of his gospel, insomuch that they did receive all manner of wickedness, and did administer that which was sacred unto him to whom it had been forbidden because of unworthiness.

28 And this church did multiply exceedingly because of iniquity, and because of the power of Satan who did get hold upon their hearts.

29 And again, there was another church which denied the Christ; and they did persecute the true church of Christ, because of their humility and their belief in Christ; and they did despise them because of the many miracles which were wrought among them.

30 Therefore they did exercise power and authority over the disciples of Jesus who did tarry with them, and they did cast them into prison; but by the power of the word of God, which was in them, the prisons were rent in twain, and they went forth doing mighty miracles among them.

31 Nevertheless, and notwithstanding all these miracles, the people did harden their hearts, and did seek to kill them, even as the Jews at Jerusalem sought to kill Jesus, according to his word.

32 And they did cast them into furnaces of fire, and they came forth receiving no harm.

33 And they also cast them into dens of wild beasts, and they did play with the wild beasts even as a child with a lamb; and they did come forth from among them, receiving no harm.

34 Nevertheless, the people did harden their hearts, for they were led by many priests and false prophets to build up many churches, and to do all manner of iniquity. And they did smite upon the people of Jesus; but the people of Jesus did not smite again. And thus they did dwindle in unbelief and wickedness, from year to year, even until two hundred and thirty years had passed away.

35 And now it came to pass in this year, yea, in the two hundred and thirty and first year, there was a great division among the people.

36 And it came to pass that in this year there arose a people who were called the Nephites, and they were true believers in Christ; and among them there were those who were called by the Lamanites—Jacobites, and Josephites, and Zoramites;

37 Therefore the true believers in Christ, and the true worshipers of Christ, (among whom were the three disciples of Jesus who should tarry) were called Nephites, and Jacobites, and Josephites, and Zoramites.

38 And it came to pass that they who rejected the

Notes

gospel were called Lamanites, and Lemuelites, and Ishmaelites; and they did not dwindle in unbelief, but they did wilfully rebel against the gospel of Christ; and they did teach their children that they should not believe, even as their fathers, from the beginning, did dwindle.

39 And it was because of the wickedness and abomination of their fathers, even as it was in the beginning. And they were taught to hate the children of God, even as the Lamanites were taught to hate the children of Nephi from the beginning.

40 And it came to pass that two hundred and forty and four years had passed away, and thus were the affairs of the people. And the more wicked part of the people did wax strong, and became exceedingly more numerous than were the people of God.

41 And they did still continue to build up churches unto themselves, and adorn them with all manner of precious things. And thus did two hundred and fifty years pass away, and also two hundred and sixty years.

42 And it came to pass that the wicked part of the people began again to build up the secret oaths and combinations of Gadianton.

43 And also the people who were called the people of Nephi began to be proud in their hearts, because of their exceeding riches, and become vain like unto their brethren, the Lamanites.

44 And from this time the disciples began to sorrow for the sins of the world.

45 And it came to pass that when three hundred years had passed away, both the people of Nephi and the Lamanites had become exceedingly wicked one like unto another.

vv. 20–45 When we allow something else to become central in our lives we become prideful, pompous, and we may be set at variance with our fellow man.

⚡ Use the object lesson found at the beginning of this chapter, and consider using these verses as a continuation of the principle from verses 11–19.

✏ Next to the list you created from verses 11–19, write, "Displacing Christ as Central" on the board and leave room so the class can create a list underneath it.

🔍 Invite class members to read verses 20–45 looking for evidence that the people of Nephi began to displace Christ and His gospel as a central part of their lives. If you feel the amount of verses is too long to read, consider splitting them into groups.

❓ Analyze:
- *How was this displacement a slow process?*
- *What is so detrimental about a slow and steady decline in spirituality?*
- *What was the first thing to displace Christ? (v. 24)*
- *What does that teach us?*

❓ Apply: *How do we see the bad example of the Nephites in our day?*

♥ Encourage class members to consider times then they felt like Christ and His gospel were at the center of their lives. Ask for class members to share the blessings they received as they lived the principles from verses 11–19. Consider sharing your own testimony or experience.

46 And it came to pass that the robbers of Gadianton did spread over all the face of the land; and there were none that were righteous save it were the disciples of Jesus. And gold and silver did they lay up in store in abundance, and did traffic in all manner of traffic.

47 And it came to pass that after three hundred and five years had passed away, (and the people did still remain in wickedness) Amos died; and his brother, Ammaron, did keep the record in his stead.

48 And it came to pass that when three hundred and twenty years had passed away, Ammaron, being constrained by the Holy Ghost, did hide up

Notes

the records which were sacred—yea, even all the sacred records which had been handed down from generation to generation, which were sacred—even until the three hundred and twentieth year from the coming of Christ.

49 And he did hide them up unto the Lord, that they might come again unto the remnant of the house of Jacob, according to the prophecies and the promises of the Lord. And thus is the end of the record of Ammaron.

vv. 47–49 Ammaron hides the records.

○ Note with the class that Ammaron was the keeper of all the Nephite records. He soon entrusted those records to Mormon in the next book.

Teaching Tips from Prophets' Lips "As you prayerfully prepare to teach, as you study the scriptures, and even as you perform your daily tasks, open your mind and heart to the Lord's guidance. You may receive "sudden strokes of ideas" from the Spirit (*Teachings of the Prophet Joseph Smith*, sel. Joseph Fielding Smith [1976], 151).

Notes

THE BOOK OF MORMON

MORMON SUMMARY

Time Period: About AD 322–421

Contributors & Authorship: Mormon, Moroni

Source: Large plates of Nephi

Synopsis:

Chapters 1–6: Mormon is given charge of the plates, commands the Nephite armies, preaches repentance, and witnesses the Nephite nation's destruction

Chapter 7: Mormon invites latter-day Lamanites to accept the gospel of Christ

Chapters 8–9: Moroni gives account of his father's death and speaks to the generations of those who will have the Book of Mormon

MORMON 1

Mormon—A True Disciple of Christ

About AD 321–326

1–5, Ammoron commissions Mormon to retrieve the plates; 6–14, Wickedness and bloodshed prevail over the entire land; 15–19, Mormon is forbidden to preach because of the wickedness of the Nephites.

1 And now I, Mormon, make a record of the things which I have both seen and heard, and call it the Book of Mormon.

2 And about the time that Ammaron hid up the records unto the Lord, he came unto me, (I being about ten years of age, and I began to be learned somewhat after the manner of the learning of my people) and Ammaron said unto me: I perceive that thou art a sober child, and art quick to observe;

3 Therefore, when ye are about twenty and four years old I would that ye should remember the things that ye have observed concerning this people; and when ye are of that age go to the land Antum, unto a hill which shall be called Shim; and there have I deposited unto the Lord all the sacred engravings concerning this people.

4 And behold, ye shall take the plates of Nephi unto yourself, and the remainder shall ye leave in the place where they are; and ye shall engrave on

Notes

the plates of Nephi all the things that ye have observed concerning this people.

5 And I, Mormon, being a descendant of Nephi, (and my father's name was Mormon) I remembered the things which Ammaron commanded me.

vv. 1–5 "Quick to observe."

💬 Consider using the following quote independently, or with the lesson ideas below: "In my study of the Book of Mormon I have been especially impressed with a particular description of Mormon, the principal compiler of the Nephite record. . . . Please note that the root word observe is used three times in these verses. And Mormon, even in his youth, is described as being 'quick to observe' (Mormon 1:2). As you study and learn and . . . I hope you also are learning about and becoming quick to observe. Your future success and happiness will in large measure be determined by this spiritual capacity. . . . Thus when we are quick to observe, we promptly look or notice and obey. Both of these fundamental elements—looking and obeying—are essential to being quick to observe. And the prophet Mormon is an impressive example of this gift in action" (David A. Bednar, "Quick to Observe," BYU 2005–2006 Speeches, [Provo, 10 May, 2005]).

6 And it came to pass that I, being eleven years old, was carried by my father into the land southward, even to the land of Zarahemla.

7 The whole face of the land had become covered with buildings, and the people were as numerous almost, as it were the sand of the sea.

8 And it came to pass in this year there began to be a war between the Nephites, who consisted of the Nephites and the Jacobites and the Josephites and the Zoramites; and this war was between the Nephites, and the Lamanites and the Lemuelites and the Ishmaelites.

9 Now the Lamanites and the Lemuelites and the Ishmaelites were called Lamanites, and the two parties were Nephites and Lamanites.

10 And it came to pass that the war began to be among them in the borders of Zarahemla, by the waters of Sidon.

11 And it came to pass that the Nephites had gathered together a great number of men, even to exceed the number of thirty thousand. And it came to pass that they did have in this same year a number of battles, in which the Nephites did beat the Lamanites and did slay many of them.

12 And it came to pass that the Lamanites withdrew their design, and there was peace settled in the land; and peace did remain for the space of about four years, that there was no bloodshed.

13 But wickedness did prevail upon the face of the whole land, insomuch that the Lord did take away his beloved disciples, and the work of miracles and of healing did cease because of the iniquity of the people.

14 And there were no gifts from the Lord, and the Holy Ghost did not come upon any, because of their wickedness and unbelief.

15 And I, being fifteen years of age and being somewhat of a sober mind, therefore I was visited of the Lord, and tasted and knew of the goodness of Jesus.

16 And I did endeavor to preach unto this people, but my mouth was shut, and I was forbidden that I should preach unto them; for behold they had wilfully rebelled against their God; and the beloved disciples were taken away out of the land, because of their iniquity.

17 But I did remain among them, but I was forbidden to preach unto them, because of the hardness of their hearts; and because of the hardness of their hearts the land was cursed for their sake.

18 And these Gadianton robbers, who were among the Lamanites, did infest the land, insomuch that the inhabitants thereof began to hide up their treasures in the earth; and they became

Notes

slippery, because the Lord had cursed the land, that they could not hold them, nor retain them again.

19 And it came to pass that there were sorceries, and witchcrafts, and magics; and the power of the evil one was wrought upon all the face of the land, even unto the fulfilling of all the words of Abinadi, and also Samuel the Lamanite.

vv. 1–19 Mormon was a mighty man of faith despite his wicked surroundings.

- On the board write, "Are you a Mormon?" Ask individual class members to answer this question. Some class members will likely begin a discussion about membership in the Church and what we should be called as members. To aid the discussion explain that President Boyd K. Packer discussed the importance of the name of the Church when he explained that "obedient to revelation, we call ourselves The Church of Jesus Christ of Latter-day Saints rather than the Mormon Church" ("Guided by the Holy Spirit," *Liahona* and *Ensign*, May 2011, 30). State to the class, *I know you are members of the Church of Jesus Christ of Latter-day Saints, but let's find out whether or not you are a 'Mormon.'* Note that this activity will teach the class how to follow Mormon's example of living in wicked times.

- Explain that in Mormon 1:1–19 we will finally be introduced to Mormon—the abridger of the Book of Mormon. Throughout the Book of Mormon one can read his commentary and teachings, but these chapters give us insight into his personal life. Other references when Mormon speaks directly include Words of Mormon, Helaman 12, 3 Nephi 5:10–26, 3 Nephi 30, Moroni 7–8, and many more.

- Write the following verses on the board: 1:1–19, Mormon 2:1, 9, 12–15, 19, and Mormon 3:12, 20–22. Instruct class members to search these verses looking for attributes and characteristics that made Mormon a great individual. After giving the class some time, write their findings on the board and discuss them asking questions like, *What would that characteristic look like in today's world?* or *How might an individual be like Mormon in our time?* Explain that we can be "Mormons" as we take on the attributes of this great disciple of Jesus Christ.

- Read 3 Nephi 5:13 to the class. Testify that we can be better disciples of Jesus Christ as we overcome our wicked surroundings as Mormon did.

Teaching Tips from Prophets' Lips "Listen for the truth, hearken to the doctrine, and let the manifestation of the spirit come as it may in all of its many and varied forms. Stay with solid principles; teach from a pure heart. Then the Spirit will penetrate your mind and heart and every mind and heart of your students" (Howard W. Hunter, *Eternal Investments* [address to religious educators, 10 Feb. 1989], 3).

MORMON 2

Sorrowing of the Damned
About AD 327–350

1–7, Mormon is appointed leader of the Nephite armies at the age of sixteen—they commence war with the Lamanites; 8–15, The wickedness of the people leads Mormon to sorrow for their souls; 16–2, The Nephites begin to lose their battles—Mormon recounts their warfare and laments their iniquity.

1 And it came to pass in that same year there began to be a war again between the Nephites and the Lamanites. And notwithstanding I being young, was large in stature; therefore the people of Nephi appointed me that I should be their leader, or the leader of their armies.

2 Therefore it came to pass that in my sixteenth year I did go forth at the head of an army of the Nephites, against the Lamanites; therefore three

Notes

hundred and twenty and six years had passed away.

3 And it came to pass that in the three hundred and twenty and seventh year the Lamanites did come upon us with exceedingly great power, insomuch that they did frighten my armies; therefore they would not fight, and they began to retreat towards the north countries.

4 And it came to pass that we did come to the city of Angola, and we did take possession of the city, and make preparations to defend ourselves against the Lamanites. And it came to pass that we did fortify the city with our might; but notwithstanding all our fortifications the Lamanites did come upon us and did drive us out of the city.

5 And they did also drive us forth out of the land of David.

6 And we marched forth and came to the land of Joshua, which was in the borders west by the seashore.

7 And it came to pass that we did gather in our people as fast as it were possible, that we might get them together in one body.

8 But behold, the land was filled with robbers and with Lamanites; and notwithstanding the great destruction which hung over my people, they did not repent of their evil doings; therefore there was blood and carnage spread throughout all the face of the land, both on the part of the Nephites and also on the part of the Lamanites; and it was one complete revolution throughout all the face of the land.

9 And now, the Lamanites had a king, and his name was Aaron; and he came against us with an army of forty and four thousand. And behold, I withstood him with forty and two thousand. And it came to pass that I beat him with my army that he fled before me. And behold, all this was done, and three hundred and thirty years had passed away.

10 And it came to pass that the Nephites began to repent of their iniquity, and began to cry even as had been prophesied by Samuel the prophet; for behold no man could keep that which was his own, for the thieves, and the robbers, and the murderers, and the magic art, and the witchcraft which was in the land.

11 Thus there began to be a mourning and a lamentation in all the land because of these things, and more especially among the people of Nephi.

12 And it came to pass that when I, Mormon, saw their lamentation and their mourning and their sorrow before the Lord, my heart did begin to rejoice within me, knowing the mercies and the long-suffering of the Lord, therefore supposing that he would be merciful unto them that they would again become a righteous people.

13 But behold this my joy was vain, for their sorrowing was not unto repentance, because of the goodness of God; but it was rather the sorrowing of the damned, because the Lord would not always suffer them to take happiness in sin.

14 And they did not come unto Jesus with broken hearts and contrite spirits, but they did curse God, and wish to die. Nevertheless they would struggle with the sword for their lives.

15 And it came to pass that my sorrow did return unto me again, and I saw that the day of grace was passed with them, both temporally and spiritually; for I saw thousands of them hewn down in open rebellion against their God, and heaped up as dung upon the face of the land. And thus three hundred and forty and four years had passed away.

vv. 1–15 Only godly sorrow leads to true repentance.

- Discuss with your class, *Is it ever right to rejoice because someone else is sorrowing? Why or why not?*

- Invite class members to find partners, being careful that no one is left alone. Have one partner read Mormon 2:10–15 and the

Notes

second partner read 2 Corinthians 7:8–11. Consider writing the following questions on the board and inviting each partner to answer them from their assigned verses separately, then invite them to compare and contrast their findings as a partnership. After the group activity, ask if anyone would like to share what they learned with the class.

❓ Analyze:
- *Why are Mormon (2:10–15) or Paul (2 Corinthians 7:8–11) rejoicing?*
- *Why are the people sorrowing?*
- *What is the result of the sorrowing of the people?*
- *In your own words, summarize why the sorrowing leads to the results in the verses you read.*

❓ Apply:
- *Do not answer aloud, but think about the last time you felt sorrow for sin. Why did you feel bad?*
- *Was it because you were caught or because you knew the thing was wrong?*
- *Why does the Lord need us to feel sorrow for our sins?*

💬 Regarding suffering for sin, Elder Dallin H. Oaks taught, "Why is it necessary for us to suffer on the way to repentance for serious transgressions? We tend to think of the results of repentance as simply cleansing us from sin. But that is an incomplete view of the matter. A person who sins is like a tree that bends easily in the wind. On a windy and rainy day, the tree bends so deeply against the ground that the leaves become soiled with mud, like sin. If we focus only on cleaning the leaves, the weakness in the tree that allowed it to bend and soil its leaves may remain. Similarly, a person who is merely sorry to be soiled by sin will sin again in the next high wind. The susceptibility to repetition continues until the tree has been strengthened.

"When a person has gone through the process that results in what the scriptures call a broken heart and a contrite spirit, the Savior does more than cleanse that person from sin. He also gives him or her new strength. That strengthening is essential for us to realize the purpose of the cleansing, which is to return to our Heavenly Father. To be admitted to his presence, we must be more than clean. We must also be changed from a morally weak person who has sinned into a strong person with the spiritual stature to dwell in the presence of God" (Dallin H. Oaks, "Sin and Suffering," *Ensign*, July 1992).

16 And it came to pass that in the three hundred and forty and fifth year the Nephites did begin to flee before the Lamanites; and they were pursued until they came even to the land of Jashon, before it was possible to stop them in their retreat.

17 And now, the city of Jashon was near the land where Ammaron had deposited the records unto the Lord, that they might not be destroyed. And behold I had gone according to the word of Ammaron, and taken the plates of Nephi, and did make a record according to the words of Ammaron.

18 And upon the plates of Nephi I did make a full account of all the wickedness and abominations; but upon these plates I did forbear to make a full account of their wickedness and abominations, for behold, a continual scene of wickedness and abominations has been before mine eyes ever since I have been sufficient to behold the ways of man.

19 And wo is me because of their wickedness; for my heart has been filled with sorrow because of their wickedness, all my days; nevertheless, I know that I shall be lifted up at the last day.

vv. 16–29 When surrounded by wickedness, we may sorrow for those around us but retain hope for the future.

❓ Analyze: *What words would you use to describe Mormon's feelings and actions in verses 16–19? What actions or phrases*

Notes

could describe Mormon as hopeful despite his situation?

❓ *Apply: How does knowing what happens after this life help you to endure the trials of the world?*

20 And it came to pass that in this year the people of Nephi again were hunted and driven. And it came to pass that we were driven forth until we had come northward to the land which was called Shem.

21 And it came to pass that we did fortify the city of Shem, and we did gather in our people as much as it were possible, that perhaps we might save them from destruction.

22 And it came to pass in the three hundred and forty and sixth year they began to come upon us again.

23 And it came to pass that I did speak unto my people, and did urge them with great energy, that they would stand boldly before the Lamanites and fight for their wives, and their children, and their houses, and their homes.

24 And my words did arouse them somewhat to vigor, insomuch that they did not flee from before the Lamanites, but did stand with boldness against them.

25 And it came to pass that we did contend with an army of thirty thousand against an army of fifty thousand. And it came to pass that we did stand before them with such firmness that they did flee from before us.

26 And it came to pass that when they had fled we did pursue them with our armies, and did meet them again, and did beat them; nevertheless the strength of the Lord was not with us; yea, we were left to ourselves, that the Spirit of the Lord did not abide in us; therefore we had become weak like unto our brethren.

27 And my heart did sorrow because of this the great calamity of my people, because of their wickedness and their abominations. But behold, we did go forth against the Lamanites and the robbers of Gadianton, until we had again taken possession of the lands of our inheritance.

28 And the three hundred and forty and ninth year had passed away. And in the three hundred and fiftieth year we made a treaty with the Lamanites and the robbers of Gadianton, in which we did get the lands of our inheritance divided.

29 And the Lamanites did give unto us the land northward, yea, even to the narrow passage which led into the land southward. And we did give unto the Lamanites all the land southward.

MORMON 3

Repent and Be Spared
AD 360–362

1–3, Mormon calls on his people to repent, but it is in vain; 4–16, The Nephites win a battle against the Lamanites in the land of Desolation; they glory in their victory and Mormon refuses to be their military leader; 17–22, Mormon writes to persuade all men to repent.

1 And it came to pass that the Lamanites did not come to battle again until ten years more had passed away. And behold, I had employed my people, the Nephites, in preparing their lands and their arms against the time of battle.

2 And it came to pass that the Lord did say unto me: Cry unto this people—Repent ye, and come unto me, and be ye baptized, and build up again my church, and ye shall be spared.

3 And I did cry unto this people, but it was in vain; and they did not realize that it was the Lord that had spared them, and granted unto them a chance for repentance. And behold they did harden their hearts against the Lord their God.

Notes

> Point out that unless we realize all that the Lord has done for us, we will harden our hearts against the Lord.

4 And it came to pass that after this tenth year had passed away, making, in the whole, three hundred and sixty years from the coming of Christ, the king of the Lamanites sent an epistle unto me, which gave unto me to know that they were preparing to come again to battle against us.

5 And it came to pass that I did cause my people that they should gather themselves together at the land Desolation, to a city which was in the borders, by the narrow pass which led into the land southward.

6 And there we did place our armies, that we might stop the armies of the Lamanites, that they might not get possession of any of our lands; therefore we did fortify against them with all our force.

7 And it came to pass that in the three hundred and sixty and first year the Lamanites did come down to the city of Desolation to battle against us; and it came to pass that in that year we did beat them, insomuch that they did return to their own lands again.

8 And in the three hundred and sixty and second year they did come down again to battle. And we did beat them again, and did slay a great number of them, and their dead were cast into the sea.

9 And now, because of this great thing which my people, the Nephites, had done, they began to boast in their own strength, and began to swear before the heavens that they would avenge themselves of the blood of their brethren who had been slain by their enemies.

10 And they did swear by the heavens, and also by the throne of God, that they would go up to battle against their enemies, and would cut them off from the face of the land.

11 And it came to pass that I, Mormon, did utterly refuse from this time forth to be a commander and a leader of this people, because of their wickedness and abomination.

12 Behold, I had led them, notwithstanding their wickedness I had led them many times to battle, and had loved them, according to the love of God which was in me, with all my heart; and my soul had been poured out in prayer unto my God all the day long for them; nevertheless, it was without faith, because of the hardness of their hearts.

> Speaking of Mormon, Glenn L. Pace taught, "This prophet had Christlike love for a fallen people. Can we be content with loving less? We must press forward with the pure love of Christ to spread the good news of the gospel. As we do so and fight the war of good against evil, light against darkness, and truth against falsehood, we must not neglect our responsibility of dressing the wounds of those who have fallen in battle. There is no room in the kingdom for fatalism" ("A Thousand Times," *Ensign*, Nov. 1990, 8).

13 And thrice have I delivered them out of the hands of their enemies, and they have repented not of their sins.

14 And when they had sworn by all that had been forbidden them by our Lord and Savior Jesus Christ, that they would go up unto their enemies to battle, and avenge themselves of the blood of their brethren, behold the voice of the Lord came unto me, saying:

15 Vengeance is mine, and I will repay; and because this people repented not after I had delivered them, behold, they shall be cut off from the face of the earth.

16 And it came to pass that I utterly refused to go up against mine enemies; and I did even as the Lord had commanded me; and I did stand as an idle witness to manifest unto the world the things which I saw and heard, according to the

Notes

manifestations of the Spirit which had testified of things to come.

17 Therefore I write unto you, Gentiles, and also unto you, house of Israel, when the work shall commence, that ye shall be about to prepare to return to the land of your inheritance;

18 Yea, behold, I write unto all the ends of the earth; yea, unto you, twelve tribes of Israel, who shall be judged according to your works by the twelve whom Jesus chose to be his disciples in the land of Jerusalem.

19 And I write also unto the remnant of this people, who shall also be judged by the twelve whom Jesus chose in this land; and they shall be judged by the other twelve whom Jesus chose in the land of Jerusalem.

20 And these things doth the Spirit manifest unto me; therefore I write unto you all. And for this cause I write unto you, that ye may know that ye must all stand before the judgment-seat of Christ, yea, every soul who belongs to the whole human family of Adam; and ye must stand to be judged of your works, whether they be good or evil;

21 And also that ye may believe the gospel of Jesus Christ, which ye shall have among you; and also that the Jews, the covenant people of the Lord, shall have other witness besides him whom they saw and heard, that Jesus, whom they slew, was the very Christ and the very God.

22 And I would that I could persuade all ye ends of the earth to repent and prepare to stand before the judgment-seat of Christ.

vv. 17–22 All will stand before the judgment seat of Christ.

- Bring a gavel, or show a picture of one and ask, *Who will be our judge when we die, Heavenly Father or Jesus Christ?* Invite class members to find the answer in Mormon chapter 3.

- Summarize the situation of the Nephites, including the fact that they have hardened their hearts and have refused to repent.

- Write the word "Therefore . . ." on the board and have them mark this word in verse 17. Indicate that Mormon, knowing that his people are about to be destroyed, turns to those who will read the Book of Mormon, the Gentiles and the remnant of the House of Israel, to give them a message. *How would you summarize Mormon's message as found verses 18–22?*

- Ask,
  - Why do you think Mormon stresses the doctrine of judgment at this time?
  - What does it mean to prepare to stand before God?
  - Are we ever ready?

- Invite class members to prepare to stand before Christ our Judge. Invite them to allow the doctrine of the Judgment to influence the way they live in this life.

Teaching Tips from Prophets' Lips "I get concerned when it appears that strong emotion or free-flowing tears are equated with the presence of the Spirit. Certainly the Spirit of the Lord can bring strong emotional feelings, including tears, but that outward manifestation ought not to be confused with the presence of the Spirit itself" (Howard W. Hunter, *Eternal Investments* [address to religious educators, 10 Feb. 1989], 3).

Index Topics: judgment

MORMON 4
The Wicked Punish the Wicked
About AD 363–375

1–5, The Nephites go to battle against the Lamanites and are smitten; 6–15, A scene of continual violence and wickedness, including human sacrifice; 16–22, The Lamanites attack again and the Nephites never again gain advantage over the Lamanites; 23, Mormon takes the records with him as they flee.

Notes

1 And now it came to pass that in the three hundred and sixty and third year the Nephites did go up with their armies to battle against the Lamanites, out of the land Desolation.

2 And it came to pass that the armies of the Nephites were driven back again to the land of Desolation. And while they were yet weary, a fresh army of the Lamanites did come upon them; and they had a sore battle, insomuch that the Lamanites did take possession of the city Desolation, and did slay many of the Nephites, and did take many prisoners.

3 And the remainder did flee and join the inhabitants of the city Teancum. Now the city Teancum lay in the borders by the seashore; and it was also near the city Desolation.

4 And it was because the armies of the Nephites went up unto the Lamanites that they began to be smitten; for were it not for that, the Lamanites could have had no power over them.

5 But, behold, the judgments of God will overtake the wicked; and it is by the wicked that the wicked are punished; for it is the wicked that stir up the hearts of the children of men unto bloodshed.

v. 5 Punishments usually result from the natural consequence of sin, rather than the hand of God.

- Write "Punishment for Sin" and the suggested answers below on the board and ask, *Where do the punishments from sin usually come from?*
  - From God
  - Natural consequences of our sins
  - Consequences of others sinning

6 And it came to pass that the Lamanites did make preparations to come against the city Teancum.

7 And it came to pass in the three hundred and sixty and fourth year the Lamanites did come against the city Teancum, that they might take possession of the city Teancum also.

8 And it came to pass that they were repulsed and driven back by the Nephites. And when the Nephites saw that they had driven the Lamanites they did again boast of their own strength; and they went forth in their own might, and took possession again of the city Desolation.

9 And now all these things had been done, and there had been thousands slain on both sides, both the Nephites and the Lamanites.

10 And it came to pass that the three hundred and sixty and sixth year had passed away, and the Lamanites came again upon the Nephites to battle; and yet the Nephites repented not of the evil they had done, but persisted in their wickedness continually.

11 And it is impossible for the tongue to describe, or for man to write a perfect description of the horrible scene of the blood and carnage which was among the people, both of the Nephites and of the Lamanites; and every heart was hardened, so that they delighted in the shedding of blood continually.

v. 11 We should avoid watching violence or delighting in it.

- *Look in verse 11 for the horrific scene Mormon is describing.*

- Read the following questions to class members and ask them to each write down their response in a journal or on a piece of paper:
  - *How have you felt when you have seen movies or video games that are violent in nature?*
  - *What does it mean to "delight in the shedding of blood"? How can an individual get to that point?*
  - *What happens to a society that is consistently immersed in violence, both real and depicted?*
  - *How might you describe the harden hearts in verse 11 using modern language?*
  - *How does violence harden peoples' hearts?*

- Review the questions you asked and discuss

Notes

the answers and implications with your class. Ask, *Like Mormon, we may not be able to completely avoid violence, but what can we do to lessen its impact on our lives?*

12 And there never had been so great wickedness among all the children of Lehi, nor even among all the house of Israel, according to the words of the Lord, as was among this people.

13 And it came to pass that the Lamanites did take possession of the city Desolation, and this because their number did exceed the number of the Nephites.

14 And they did also march forward against the city Teancum, and did drive the inhabitants forth out of her, and did take many prisoners both women and children, and did offer them up as sacrifices unto their idol gods.

15 And it came to pass that in the three hundred and sixty and seventh year, the Nephites being angry because the Lamanites had sacrificed their women and their children, that they did go against the Lamanites with exceedingly great anger, insomuch that they did beat again the Lamanites, and drive them out of their lands.

16 And the Lamanites did not come again against the Nephites until the three hundred and seventy and fifth year.

17 And in this year they did come down against the Nephites with all their powers; and they were not numbered because of the greatness of their number.

18 And from this time forth did the Nephites gain no power over the Lamanites, but began to be swept off by them even as a dew before the sun.

19 And it came to pass that the Lamanites did come down against the city Desolation; and there was an exceedingly sore battle fought in the land Desolation, in the which they did beat the Nephites.

20 And they fled again from before them, and they came to the city Boaz; and there they did stand against the Lamanites with exceeding boldness, insomuch that the Lamanites did not beat them until they had come again the second time.

21 And when they had come the second time, the Nephites were driven and slaughtered with an exceedingly great slaughter; their women and their children were again sacrificed unto idols.

vv. 12–21 Signs of great wickedness in a society.

🔎 *In verse 12, look for how wicked the people had become.*

✋ Divide the class in half and have the one half look for signs of the Nephites' wickedness in verses 13–16, and the other half look for the Nephites' wickedness in verses 17–21. Have them share what they found. As they share ask, *How do we see similar wickedness in the world today?*

22 And it came to pass that the Nephites did again flee from before them, taking all the inhabitants with them, both in towns and villages.

23 And now I, Mormon, seeing that the Lamanites were about to overthrow the land, therefore I did go to the hill Shim, and did take up all the records which Ammaron had hid up unto the Lord.

Index Topics: sin, violence

MORMON 5

"An Awful Scene of Blood and Carnage"
About AD 375–384

1–2, Mormon returns to command the armies of the Nephites despite his oath and their wickedness; 3–8, Mormon describes the carnage of the battles between

Notes

the Nephites and Lamanites; 9–15, The Book of Mormon shall come forth to help the people of Israel believe and remember the covenants of God; 16–24, "Therefore, repent ye, and humble yourselves before [God]."

1 And it came to pass that I did go forth among the Nephites, and did repent of the oath which I had made that I would no more assist them; and they gave me command again of their armies, for they looked upon me as though I could deliver them from their afflictions.

2 But behold, I was without hope, for I knew the judgments of the Lord which should come upon them; for they repented not of their iniquities, but did struggle for their lives without calling upon that Being who created them.

3 And it came to pass that the Lamanites did come against us as we had fled to the city of Jordan; but behold, they were driven back that they did not take the city at that time.

4 And it came to pass that they came against us again, and we did maintain the city. And there were also other cities which were maintained by the Nephites, which strongholds did cut them off that they could not get into the country which lay before us, to destroy the inhabitants of our land.

5 But it came to pass that whatsoever lands we had passed by, and the inhabitants thereof were not gathered in, were destroyed by the Lamanites, and their towns, and villages, and cities were burned with fire; and thus three hundred and seventy and nine years passed away.

6 And it came to pass that in the three hundred and eightieth year the Lamanites did come again against us to battle, and we did stand against them boldly; but it was all in vain, for so great were their numbers that they did tread the people of the Nephites under their feet.

7 And it came to pass that we did again take to flight, and those whose flight was swifter than the Lamanites' did escape, and those whose flight did not exceed the Lamanites' were swept down and destroyed.

8 And now behold, I, Mormon, do not desire to harrow up the souls of men in casting before them such an awful scene of blood and carnage as was laid before mine eyes; but I, knowing that these things must surely be made known, and that all things which are hid must be revealed upon the house-tops—

vv. 1–8 "An awful scene of blood and carnage."

- Consider summarizing verses 1–8 or allowing class members to read a handful of verses that you feel encapsulate Mormon's message from 1–8. Doing so helps class members understand the context of the rest of this chapter.

9 And also that a knowledge of these things must come unto the remnant of these people, and also unto the Gentiles, who the Lord hath said should scatter this people, and this people should be counted as naught among them—therefore I write a small abridgment, daring not to give a full account of the things which I have seen, because of the commandment which I have received, and also that ye might not have too great sorrow because of the wickedness of this people.

10 And now behold, this I speak unto their seed, and also to the Gentiles who have care for the house of Israel, that realize and know from whence their blessings come.

11 For I know that such will sorrow for the calamity of the house of Israel; yea, they will sorrow for the destruction of this people; they will sorrow that this people had not repented that they might have been clasped in the arms of Jesus.

12 Now these things are written unto the remnant of the house of Jacob; and they are written after this manner, because it is known of God that wickedness will not bring them forth unto them; and they are to be hid up unto the

Notes

Lord that they may come forth in his own due time.

13 And this is the commandment which I have received; and behold, they shall come forth according to the commandment of the Lord, when he shall see fit, in his wisdom.

14 And behold, they shall go unto the unbelieving of the Jews; and for this intent shall they go—that they may be persuaded that Jesus is the Christ, the Son of the living God; that the Father may bring about, through his most Beloved, his great and eternal purpose, in restoring the Jews, or all the house of Israel, to the land of their inheritance, which the Lord their God hath given them, unto the fulfilling of his covenant;

15 And also that the seed of this people may more fully believe his gospel, which shall go forth unto them from the Gentiles; for this people shall be scattered, and shall become a dark, a filthy, and a loathsome people, beyond the description of that whichever hath been amongst us, yea, even that which hath been among the Lamanites, and this because of their unbelief and idolatry.

vv. 9–15 God manifests His love to us through covenants, despite our unworthiness.

- One purpose of the Book of Mormon as stated in the title page, written by Moroni, is that the Book of Mormon "is to show unto the remnant of the house of Israel what great things the Lord hath done for their fathers; and that they may know the covenants of the Lord, that they are not cast off forever." It is noteworthy that the phrase "covenant(s) of the Lord" appears 48 times in the Book of Mormon, which underscores the fact that the contributors to the Book of Mormon were focused on the covenants of the Lord.

- Analyze: Consider with your class how a people who are as wicked as the Nephites would be interested in the covenants of the Lord.

- Elder Jeffrey R. Holland taught, "To all of you who think you are lost or without hope, or who think you have done too much that was too wrong for too long, to every one of you who worry that you are stranded somewhere on the wintry plains of life and have wrecked your handcart in the process, this conference calls out Jehovah's unrelenting refrain, '[My] hand is stretched out still. 'I shall lengthen out mine arm unto them,' He said, '[and even if they] deny me; nevertheless, I will be merciful unto them, . . . if they will repent and come unto me; for mine arm is lengthened out all the day long, saith the Lord God of Hosts.' His mercy endureth forever, and His hand is stretched out still. His is the pure love of Christ, the charity that never faileth, that compassion which endures even when all other strength disappears" ("Prophets in the Land Again," *Ensign*, Nov. 2006, 107).

- Help class members feel the importance of the covenants of the Lord by discussing when they have felt God's love, despite their unworthiness.

16 For behold, the Spirit of the Lord hath already ceased to strive with their fathers; and they are without Christ and God in the world; and they are driven about as chaff before the wind.

17 They were once a delightsome people, and they had Christ for their shepherd; yea, they were led even by God the Father.

18 But now, behold, they are led about by Satan, even as chaff is driven before the wind, or as a vessel is tossed about upon the waves, without sail or anchor, or without anything wherewith to steer her; and even as she is, so are they.

19 And behold, the Lord hath reserved their blessings, which they might have received in the land, for the Gentiles who shall possess the land.

20 But behold, it shall come to pass that they shall be driven and scattered by the Gentiles; and after they have been driven and scattered by the Gentiles, behold, then will the Lord remember

Notes

the covenant which he made unto Abraham and unto all the house of Israel.

21 And also the Lord will remember the prayers of the righteous, which have been put up unto him for them.

22 And then, O ye Gentiles, how can ye stand before the power of God, except ye shall repent and turn from your evil ways?

23 Know ye not that ye are in the hands of God? Know ye not that he hath all power, and at his great command the earth shall be rolled together as a scroll?

24 Therefore, repent ye, and humble yourselves before him, lest he shall come out in justice against you—lest a remnant of the seed of Jacob shall go forth among you as a lion, and tear you in pieces, and there is none to deliver.

vv. 16–24 "Repent ye, and humble yourselves before [God]" in order to escape His judgments.

- Explain that when an individual is debating or asserting his or her position, they will use certain words that indicate their conclusion or final statement. One of these cue words is *therefore*. An example would be, "cars run on gasoline and gasoline is expensive, therefore, it is expensive to run a car." Note with class members how the last verse of this chapter begins.

- Read verse 24 and look for what Mormon's conclusion or final point in this chapter is. Encourage a class member to explain it in their own words and write their answer on the board.

- Depending on the size of your class, break the class into small groups and invite each group to complete the following chart. Have them read Mormon 5:16–24 and look for principles that answer the following questions:

Why we should repent and humble ourselves	
What are the people of Nephi doing that would force Mormon to say, "Therefore, repent ye, and humble yourselves before him, lest he shall come out in justice against you."	Principles:
How are these principles applicable to us in our day?	

- Analyze: Discuss with the class the principles they found, taking time to answer any questions they might have from the verses.

- Apply: Spend time to discuss class members' own conclusions found at the bottom of the chart.

- Encourage class members to repent and humble themselves so they can escape the judgments of God.

Teaching Tips from Prophets' Lips "You are to teach the scriptures.... If your students are acquainted with the revelations, there is no question—personal or social or political or occupational—that need go unanswered. Therein is contained the fulness of the everlasting gospel. Therein we find principles of truth that will resolve every confusion and every problem and every dilemma that will face the human family or any individual in it" (Boyd K. Packer, *Teach the Scriptures* [address to religious educators, 14 Oct. 1977], 5).

MORMON 6

The Battle at Cumorah
About AD 385

1–5, Mormon arranges a battle at the land of Cumorah with the Lamanites; 6, He hides up all the records

Notes

MORMON 6

in the Hill Cumorah; 7–16, Virtually all the Nephite army is destroyed; 17–22, Mormon laments his fallen people.

Overarching Principle: Sin always leads to destruction.

⚡ Explain to class members that the concept of reverse engineering is to take a final product and disassemble it in order to understand how it is made or works. You may want to bring an object that could be easily disassembled and then put back together. Explain that they will reverse engineer the Nephite destruction.

1 And now I finish my record concerning the destruction of my people, the Nephites. And it came to pass that we did march forth before the Lamanites.

2 And I, Mormon, wrote an epistle unto the king of the Lamanites, and desired of him that he would grant unto us that we might gather together our people unto the land of Cumorah, by a hill which was called Cumorah, and there we could give them battle.

3 And it came to pass that the king of the Lamanites did grant unto me the thing which I desired.

4 And it came to pass that we did march forth to the land of Cumorah, and we did pitch our tents around about the hill Cumorah; and it was in a land of many waters, rivers, and fountains; and here we had hope to gain advantage over the Lamanites.

5 And when three hundred and eighty and four years had passed away, we had gathered in all the remainder of our people unto the land of Cumorah.

6 And it came to pass that when we had gathered in all our people in one to the land of Cumorah, behold I, Mormon, began to be old; and knowing it to be the last struggle of my people, and having been commanded of the Lord that I should not suffer the records which had been handed down by our fathers, which were sacred, to fall into the hands of the Lamanites, (for the Lamanites would destroy them) therefore I made this record out of the plates of Nephi, and hid up in the hill Cumorah all the records which had been entrusted to me by the hand of the Lord, save it were these few plates which I gave unto my son Moroni.

7 And it came to pass that my people, with their wives and their children, did now behold the armies of the Lamanites marching towards them; and with that awful fear of death which fills the breasts of all the wicked, did they await to receive them.

8 And it came to pass that they came to battle against us, and every soul was filled with terror because of the greatness of their numbers.

9 And it came to pass that they did fall upon my people with the sword, and with the bow, and with the arrow, and with the ax, and with all manner of weapons of war.

10 And it came to pass that my men were hewn down, yea, even my ten thousand who were with me, and I fell wounded in the midst; and they passed by me that they did not put an end to my life.

11 And when they had gone through and hewn down all my people save it were twenty and four of us, (among whom was my son Moroni) and we having survived the dead of our people, did behold on the morrow, when the Lamanites had returned unto their camps, from the top of the hill Cumorah, the ten thousand of my people who were hewn down, being led in the front by me.

12 And we also beheld the ten thousand of my people who were led by my son Moroni.

13 And behold, the ten thousand of Gidgiddonah had fallen, and he also in the midst.

14 And Lamah had fallen with his ten thousand; and Gilgal had fallen with his ten thousand; and

Notes

Limhah had fallen with his ten thousand; and Jeneum had fallen with his ten thousand; and Cumenihah, and Moronihah, and Antionum, and Shiblom, and Shem, and Josh, had fallen with their ten thousand each.

15 And it came to pass that there were ten more who did fall by the sword, with their ten thousand each; yea, even all my people, save it were those twenty and four who were with me, and also a few who had escaped into the south countries, and a few who had deserted over unto the Lamanites, had fallen; and their flesh, and bones, and blood lay upon the face of the earth, being left by the hands of those who slew them to molder upon the land, and to crumble and to return to their mother earth.

vv. 1–15 The entire destruction of the Nephite army.

- Explain that the final Nephite/Lamanite battle takes place at the Hill Cumorah. Read verses 1–15 as a class to look for two things: 1) How many people were destroyed, and 2) How many people were spared.

16 And my soul was rent with anguish, because of the slain of my people, and I cried:

17 O ye fair ones, how could ye have departed from the ways of the Lord! O ye fair ones, how could ye have rejected that Jesus, who stood with open arms to receive you!

18 Behold, if ye had not done this, ye would not have fallen. But behold, ye are fallen, and I mourn your loss.

19 O ye fair sons and daughters, ye fathers and mothers, ye husbands and wives, ye fair ones, how is it that ye could have fallen!

20 But behold, ye are gone, and my sorrows cannot bring your return.

21 And the day soon cometh that your mortal must put on immortality, and these bodies which are now moldering in corruption must soon become incorruptible bodies; and then ye must stand before the judgment-seat of Christ, to be judged according to your works; and if it so be that ye are righteous, then are ye blessed with your fathers who have gone before you.

22 O that ye had repented before this great destruction had come upon you. But behold, ye are gone, and the Father, yea, the Eternal Father of heaven, knoweth your state; and he doeth with you according to his justice and mercy.

vv. 16–22 Sin always leads to destruction.

- Use the object lesson from the beginning of the chapter to discuss reverse engineering the Nephite destruction. Be sure the class knows of the events that happen in verses 1–15 of this chapter.

- In your own preparation for this lesson, review the declining spirituality of the Nephites starting in 4 Nephi through Mormon 5. Consider finding principles you could share with the class or inviting class members to find their own principles.

- Apply: *How do we see the world following a similar path in our day?*

- Read verses 16–22 to look for Mormon's reaction when he sees his fallen people.

- Analyze: *If God knew of the future Nephite destruction, why didn't He warn them?*

- Henry B. Eyring taught, "There seems to be no end to the Savior's desire to lead us to safety. And there is constancy in the way He shows us the path. He calls by more than one means so that it will reach those willing to accept it. And those means always include sending the message by the mouths of His prophets whenever people have qualified to have the prophets of God among them. Those authorized servants are always charged with warning the people, telling them the way to safety" (Henry B. Eyring, "Finding Safety in Council," *Ensign*, May 1997, 24).

- Apply: *What can we learn from this tragic Nephite story?*

Notes

- Read Mormon's final plea in verse 22 as a class and discuss what he wished the people had done. Help class members feel the importance of repenting now rather than procrastinating the day of their repentance until the end.

- Elder Oaks taught, "As we look about us, we see many who are practicing deception. We hear of prominent officials who have lied about their secret acts. We learn of honored sports heroes who have lied about gambling on the outcome of their games or using drugs to enhance their performance. We see less well-known persons engaging in evil acts in secret they would never do in public. Perhaps they think no one will ever know. But God always knows. And He has repeatedly warned that the time will come when '[our] iniquities shall be spoken upon the housetops, and [our] secret acts shall be revealed'" (Dallin H. Oaks, "Be Not Deceived," *Ensign*, Nov. 2004, 45).

MORMON 7

To the Remnant of the House of Israel

About AD 385

1–4, The Nephite and Lamanite people are a remnant of the House of Israel and must repent; 5–8, Jesus is the Christ and the son of God who offers redemption to Israel; 9–10, The Bible and the Book of Mormon teach that Israel must be baptized and receive the Holy Ghost to be saved.

1 And now, behold, I would speak somewhat unto the remnant of this people who are spared, if it so be that God may give unto them my words, that they may know of the things of their fathers; yea, I speak unto you, ye remnant of the house of Israel; and these are the words which I speak:

2 Know ye that ye are of the house of Israel.

3 Know ye that ye must come unto repentance, or ye cannot be saved.

4 Know ye that ye must lay down your weapons of war, and delight no more in the shedding of blood, and take them not again, save it be that God shall command you.

5 Know ye that ye must come to the knowledge of your fathers, and repent of all your sins and iniquities, and believe in Jesus Christ, that he is the Son of God, and that he was slain by the Jews, and by the power of the Father he hath risen again, whereby he hath gained the victory over the grave; and also in him is the sting of death swallowed up.

6 And he bringeth to pass the resurrection of the dead, whereby man must be raised to stand before his judgment-seat.

7 And he hath brought to pass the redemption of the world, whereby he that is found guiltless before him at the judgment day hath it given unto him to dwell in the presence of God in his kingdom, to sing ceaseless praises with the choirs above, unto the Father, and unto the Son, and unto the Holy Ghost, which are one God, in a state of happiness which hath no end.

8 Therefore repent, and be baptized in the name of Jesus, and lay hold upon the gospel of Christ, which shall be set before you, not only in this record but also in the record which shall come unto the Gentiles from the Jews, which record shall come from the Gentiles unto you.

9 For behold, this is written for the intent that ye may believe that; and if ye believe that ye will believe this also; and if ye believe this ye will know concerning your fathers, and also the marvelous works which were wrought by the power of God among them.

10 And ye will also know that ye are a remnant of the seed of Jacob; therefore ye are numbered among the people of the first covenant; and if it so be that ye believe in Christ, and are baptized,

Notes

first with water, then with fire and with the Holy Ghost, following the example of our Savior, according to that which he hath commanded us, it shall be well with you in the day of judgment. Amen.

vv. 1–10 The Book of Mormon was written to a remnant of the house of Israel to teach them regarding covenants and bring them unto Jesus Christ.

- Ask, *What is the purpose of the Book of Mormon?* After some discussion, invite class members to turn back to the title page. If you have taught a consecutive course on the Book of Mormon, this is a good chance to review principles from the beginning of the course. Read the second paragraph from the title page and have class members look for the three purposes of the Book of Mormon. Write them on the board as the headings for three columns:

  - To show unto the remnant of the house of Israel what great things the Lord hath done for their fathers
  - That they may know the covenants of the Lord, that they are not cast off forever
  - To the convincing of the Jew and Gentile that Jesus is the Christ

- Invite class members to read Mormon 7:1–10 and assign each verse to one of the three purposes of the Book of Mormon as listed in the columns on the board. They may assign a verse to more than one column but must be able to explain their choices. Explain that the purpose of this activity is not to correctly assign a verse, but to discuss the principles in the verses.

- Apply: *What is our role as members of the Church in all of this? How do we fulfill this role and make Mormon's message known?*

> **Teaching Tips from Prophets' Lips** "I have spoken before about the importance of keeping the doctrine of the Church pure, and seeing that it is taught in all of our meetings. I worry about this. Small aberrations in doctrinal teaching can lead to large and evil falsehoods" (Gordon B. Hinckley, *Teachings of Gordon B. Hinckley* [1997], 620).

MORMON 8
"I Even Remain Alone"
About AD 400–421

1–3, Mormon is killed by Lamanites; 4–10, Moroni recounts his lone state; 11–34, He prophecies concerning the coming forth of the Book of Mormon; 35–41, Moroni explains his vision of those in the latter days.

Overarching theme: We must stand for truth in perilous times.

- Consider showing the Mormon Message entitled "Dare to Stand Alone," which recounts President Monson's example of when he was willing to say he was a Mormon even when he thought he was the only one. Also consider reading his talk in preparation for teaching this lesson (Thomas S. Monson, "Dare to Stand Alone," *Ensign*, Nov. 2011, 67).

1 Behold I, Moroni, do finish the record of my father, Mormon. Behold, I have but few things to write, which things I have been commanded by my father.

2 And now it came to pass that after the great and tremendous battle at Cumorah, behold, the Nephites who had escaped into the country southward were hunted by the Lamanites, until they were all destroyed.

3 And my father also was killed by them, and I even remain alone to write the sad tale of the destruction of my people. But behold, they are gone, and I fulfil the commandment of my father. And whether they will slay me, I know not.

Notes

4 Therefore I will write and hide up the records in the earth; and whither I go it mattereth not.

5 Behold, my father hath made this record, and he hath written the intent thereof. And behold, I would write it also if I had room upon the plates, but I have not; and ore I have none, for I am alone. My father hath been slain in battle, and all my kinsfolk, and I have not friends nor whither to go; and how long the Lord will suffer that I may live I know not.

6 Behold, four hundred years have passed away since the coming of our Lord and Savior.

7 And behold, the Lamanites have hunted my people, the Nephites, down from city to city and from place to place, even until they are no more; and great has been their fall; yea, great and marvelous is the destruction of my people, the Nephites.

8 And behold, it is the hand of the Lord which hath done it. And behold also, the Lamanites are at war one with another; and the whole face of this land is one continual round of murder and bloodshed; and no one knoweth the end of the war.

vv. 1–8 Standing for the right.

🔍 *Read through verses 1–8 and mark or take note of every word or phrase that Moroni uses to describe his situation.*

❓ *What do you think helped Moroni through this difficult time in his life?*

💬 Susan W. Tanner taught, "Moroni also knew firsthand about loneliness and discouragement. After a great and tremendous battle between the Nephites and the Lamanites where all of his people were destroyed, he lamented: 'I am alone. My father hath been slain in battle, and all my kinsfolk, and I have not friends nor whither to go; and how long the Lord will suffer that I may live I know not' (Mormon. 8:5). Can you sense Moroni's loneliness and discouragement? I realize that many of us also at times feel without friends and alone in a wicked world. Some of us feel we have not 'whither to go' as we face our trials. But you and I can not only survive but prevail, as did Moroni, in our efforts to stand for truth in perilous times. What did he do when facing a lonely and hostile world? He, in faithful obedience to his father's direction, finished the record on the gold plates. He became familiar with the writings of the prophets. Above all, he fought his way out of his discouragement by clinging to the Lord's promises for the future. He clung to the covenants that God had made with the house of Israel to bless them forever. Moroni exercised faith in the promised blessings for future generations (Susan W. Tanner, "Glad Tiding From Cumorah," *Ensign*, May 2005, 104).

❤ Testify that Moroni and all the ancient prophets stood for truth in order that we could have the truth in these last days.

9 And now, behold, I say no more concerning them, for there are none save it be the Lamanites and robbers that do exist upon the face of the land.

10 And there are none that do know the true God save it be the disciples of Jesus, who did tarry in the land until the wickedness of the people was so great that the Lord would not suffer them to remain with the people; and whether they be upon the face of the land no man knoweth.

11 But behold, my father and I have seen them, and they have ministered unto us.

12 And whoso receiveth this record, and shall not condemn it because of the imperfections which are in it, the same shall know of greater things than these. Behold, I am Moroni; and were it possible, I would make all things known unto you.

13 Behold, I make an end of speaking concerning this people. I am the son of Mormon, and my father was a descendant of Nephi.

14 And I am the same who hideth up this record

Notes

unto the Lord; the plates thereof are of no worth, because of the commandment of the Lord. For he truly saith that no one shall have them to get gain; but the record thereof is of great worth; and whoso shall bring it to light, him will the Lord bless.

15 For none can have power to bring it to light save it be given him of God; for God wills that it shall be done with an eye single to his glory, or the welfare of the ancient and long dispersed covenant people of the Lord.

💡 Note in verses 14–15 that Joseph Smith received similar instructions and warnings regarding the worth of the record in Joseph Smith—History verses 46 and 52.

16 And blessed be he that shall bring this thing to light; for it shall be brought out of darkness unto light, according to the word of God; yea, it shall be brought out of the earth, and it shall shine forth out of darkness, and come unto the knowledge of the people; and it shall be done by the power of God.

17 And if there be faults they be the faults of a man. But behold, we know no fault; nevertheless God knoweth all things; therefore, he that condemneth, let him be aware lest he shall be in danger of hell fire.

18 And he that saith: Show unto me, or ye shall be smitten—let him beware lest he commandeth that which is forbidden of the Lord.

19 For behold, the same that judgeth rashly shall be judged rashly again; for according to his works shall his wages be; therefore, he that smiteth shall be smitten again, of the Lord.

20 Behold what the scripture says—man shall not smite, neither shall he judge; for judgment is mine, saith the Lord, and vengeance is mine also, and I will repay.

21 And he that shall breath out wrath and strifes against the work of the Lord, and against the covenant people of the Lord who are the house of Israel, and shall say: We will destroy the work of the Lord, and the Lord will not remember his covenant which he hath made unto the house of Israel—the same is in danger to be hewn down and cast into the fire;

22 For the eternal purposes of the Lord shall roll on, until all his promises shall be fulfilled.

23 Search the prophecies of Isaiah. Behold, I cannot write them. Yea, behold I say unto you, that those saints who have gone before me, who have possessed this land, shall cry, yea, even from the dust will they cry unto the Lord; and as the Lord liveth he will remember the covenant which he hath made with them.

24 And he knoweth their prayers, that they were in behalf of their brethren. And he knoweth their faith, for in his name could they remove mountains; and in his name could they cause the earth to shake; and by the power of his word did they cause prisons to tumble to the earth; yea, even the fiery furnace could not harm them, neither wild beasts nor poisonous serpents, because of the power of his word.

25 And behold, their prayers were also in behalf of him that the Lord should suffer to bring these things forth.

26 And no one need say they shall not come, for they surely shall, for the Lord hath spoken it; for out of the earth shall they come, by the hand of the Lord, and none can stay it; and it shall come in a day when it shall be said that miracles are done away; and it shall come even as if one should speak from the dead.

💬 Sister Susan W. Tanner related the following, "Elder Jeffrey R. Holland explained that this joyful anticipation of past prophets, including Moroni, was because they had seen our day in vision. They saw strong, covenant-keeping young people like you who would carry out the Lord's work in this final dispensation. Elder Holland said, 'The leaders in those

Notes

ages past, were able to keep going, . . . not because they knew that *they* would succeed but because they knew that *you* would . . . a magnificent congregation of young [women] like you . . . in a determined effort to see the gospel prevail and triumph' " ("Terror, Triumph, and a Wedding Feast," Church Educational System fireside, Sept. 12, 2004). "We have that huge responsibility to fulfill Moroni's "joyful anticipation" (Glad Tiding From Cumorah, *Ensign*, April 2005, p. 104).

27 And it shall come in a day when the blood of saints shall cry unto the Lord, because of secret combinations and the works of darkness.

28 Yea, it shall come in a day when the power of God shall be denied, and churches become defiled and be lifted up in the pride of their hearts; yea, even in a day when leaders of churches and teachers shall rise in the pride of their hearts, even to the envying of them who belong to their churches.

29 Yea, it shall come in a day when there shall be heard of fires, and tempests, and vapors of smoke in foreign lands;

30 And there shall also be heard of wars, rumors of wars, and earthquakes in divers places.

31 Yea, it shall come in a day when there shall be great pollutions upon the face of the earth; there shall be murders, and robbing, and lying, and deceivings, and whoredoms, and all manner of abominations; when there shall be many who will say, Do this, or do that, and it mattereth not, for the Lord will uphold such at the last day. But wo unto such, for they are in the gall of bitterness and in the bonds of iniquity.

32 Yea, it shall come in a day when there shall be churches built up that shall say: Come unto me, and for your money you shall be forgiven of your sins.

33 O ye wicked and perverse and stiffnecked people, why have ye built up churches unto yourselves to get gain? Why have ye transfigured the holy word of God, that ye might bring damnation upon your souls? Behold, look ye unto the revelations of God; for behold, the time cometh at that day when all these things must be fulfilled.

34 Behold, the Lord hath shown unto me great and marvelous things concerning that which must shortly come, at that day when these things shall come forth among you.

35 Behold, I speak unto you as if ye were present, and yet ye are not. But behold, Jesus Christ hath shown you unto me, and I know your doing.

♥ Testify that the Moroni not only saw our day, but he also saw us.

36 And I know that ye do walk in the pride of your hearts; and there are none save a few only who do not lift themselves up in the pride of their hearts, unto the wearing of very fine apparel, unto envying, and strifes, and malice, and persecutions, and all manner of iniquities; and your churches, yea, even every one, have become polluted because of the pride of your hearts.

37 For behold, ye do love money, and your substance, and your fine apparel, and the adorning of your churches, more than ye love the poor and the needy, the sick and the afflicted.

38 O ye pollutions, ye hypocrites, ye teachers, who sell yourselves for that which will canker, why have ye polluted the holy church of God? Why are ye ashamed to take upon you the name of Christ? Why do ye not think that greater is the value of an endless happiness than that misery which never dies—because of the praise of the world?

39 Why do ye adorn yourselves with that which hath no life, and yet suffer the hungry, and the needy, and the naked, and the sick and the afflicted to pass by you, and notice them not?

40 Yea, why do ye build up your secret abominations to get gain, and cause that widows should mourn before the Lord, and also orphans to mourn before the Lord, and also the blood of their fathers and their husbands to cry unto the

Notes

Lord from the ground, for vengeance upon your heads?

41 Behold, the sword of vengeance hangeth over you; and the time soon cometh that he avengeth the blood of the saints upon you, for he will not suffer their cries any longer.

vv. 27–41 Standing for truth.

- 🔍 *Quickly scan through verses 27–41 and look for which description you think best describes our day.*

- ❓ Analyze: *Why do you think Moroni wanted us to know that he saw our day?*

- 💬 President Ezra Taft Benson stated that the Book of Mormon is of particular value to our time when he said: "The Book of Mormon was written for us today. God is the author of the book. It is a record of a fallen people, compiled by inspired men for our blessing today. Those people never had the book—it was meant for us. Mormon, the ancient prophet after whom the book is named, abridged centuries of records. God, who knows the end from the beginning, told him what to include in his abridgment that we would need for our day" ("The Book of Mormon Is the Word of God," *Ensign*, May 1975, 63).

- 💬 Elder Perry stated, "How often we read the record primarily as a history of a fallen people, failing to remember that it was compiled by inspired prophets for the purpose of helping us come unto Christ. The major writers of the Book of Mormon did not intend it to be a history book at all. In fact, Jacob said that his brother Nephi commanded him that he 'should not touch, save it were lightly, concerning the history of this people' (Jacob 1:2). Each time we read the book we should probably ask ourselves: 'Why did these writers choose these particular stories or events to include in the record? What value are they for us today?'" (L. Tom Perry, "Blessings Resulting from Reading the Book of Mormon," *Ensign*, Nov. 2005, 7).

- ❤️ Testify that what Moroni and other writers in the Book of Mormon wrote will prepare us to stand for truth in the perilous times in which we live because they saw our day.

Index Topics: last days, stand for truth

MORMON 9
God Is a God of Miracles
About AD 401–421

1–10, Moroni speaks directly to those who do not believe in Christ; 11–19, God is a god of miracles; 20–21, Miracles cease when faith ceases; 22–37, Moroni offers final words of exhortation.

Overarching theme: Doubt not, but be believing.

- ⚡ *What would you choose as the last topic in the Book of Mormon if you were Moroni?*

- 🔍 *Briefly read over this chapter for any clues that show that Moroni thinks these are his final words to the readers of this book. You may have the class also consider Mormon 8:1. Explain that these are not Moroni's last words but that he thinks that they may be as he is writing them.*

- 🔍 *According to verses 1 and 7, who is Moroni speaking to specifically?*

- ✋ Write the following verses on the board: 1–6, 7–11, 15–20, 21–25, 26–29, and 31–37. Invite the class members to choose one of the sets of verses and find one phrase that they think best summarizes what Moroni is trying to say to those unbelievers who deny the revelations of God. Depending on time, class members may look at more than one set of verses. After the class has had time to find a phrase, invite them to share with each other and the class. Write the discovered phrases on the board.

Notes

MORMON 9

♥ Point to the board and invite the class to look at what Moroni's message is to all those who would read the Book of Mormon. Invite them to pick a phrase that best applies to them. Invite the class to "doubt not, but be believing."

1 And now, I speak also concerning those who do not believe in Christ.

2 Behold, will ye believe in the day of your visitation—behold, when the Lord shall come, yea, even that great day when the earth shall be rolled together as a scroll, and the elements shall melt with fervent heat, yea, in that great day when ye shall be brought to stand before the Lamb of God—then will ye say that there is no God?

3 Then will ye longer deny the Christ, or can ye behold the Lamb of God? Do ye suppose that ye shall dwell with him under a consciousness of your guilt? Do ye suppose that ye could be happy to dwell with that holy Being, when your souls are racked with a consciousness of guilt that ye have ever abused his laws?

4 Behold, I say unto you that ye would be more miserable to dwell with a holy and just God, under a consciousness of your filthiness before him, than ye would to dwell with the damned souls in hell.

5 For behold, when ye shall be brought to see your nakedness before God, and also the glory of God, and the holiness of Jesus Christ, it will kindle a flame of unquenchable fire upon you.

6 O then ye unbelieving, turn ye unto the Lord; cry mightily unto the Father in the name of Jesus, that perhaps ye may be found spotless, pure, fair, and white, having been cleansed by the blood of the Lamb, at that great and last day.

7 And again I speak unto you who deny the revelations of God, and say that they are done away, that there are no revelations, nor prophecies, nor gifts, nor healing, nor speaking with tongues, and the interpretation of tongues;

8 Behold I say unto you, he that denieth these things knoweth not the gospel of Christ; yea, he has not read the scriptures; if so, he does not understand them.

9 For do we not read that God is the same yesterday, today, and forever, and in him there is no variableness neither shadow of changing?

10 And now, if ye have imagined up unto yourselves a god who doth vary, and in whom there is shadow of changing, then have ye imagined up unto yourselves a god who is not a God of miracles.

11 But behold, I will show unto you a God of miracles, even the God of Abraham, and the God of Isaac, and the God of Jacob; and it is that same God who created the heavens and the earth, and all things that in them are.

12 Behold, he created Adam, and by Adam came the fall of man. And because of the fall of man came Jesus Christ, even the Father and the Son; and because of Jesus Christ came the redemption of man.

13 And because of the redemption of man, which came by Jesus Christ, they are brought back into the presence of the Lord; yea, this is wherein all men are redeemed, because the death of Christ bringeth to pass the resurrection, which bringeth to pass a redemption from an endless sleep, from which sleep all men shall be awakened by the power of God when the trump shall sound; and they shall come forth, both small and great, and all shall stand before his bar, being redeemed and loosed from this eternal band of death, which death is a temporal death.

14 And then cometh the judgment of the Holy One upon them; and then cometh the time that he that is filthy shall be filthy still; and he that is righteous shall be righteous still; he that is happy shall be happy still; and he that is unhappy shall be unhappy still.

15 And now, O all ye that have imagined up unto yourselves a god who can do no miracles, I would ask of you, have all these things passed, of which

Notes

I have spoken? Has the end come yet? Behold I say unto you, Nay; and God has not ceased to be a God of miracles.

16 Behold, are not the things that God hath wrought marvelous in our eyes? Yea, and who can comprehend the marvelous works of God?

17 Who shall say that it was not a miracle that by his word the heaven and the earth should be; and by the power of his word man was created of the dust of the earth; and by the power of his word have miracles been wrought?

18 And who shall say that Jesus Christ did not do many mighty miracles? And there were many mighty miracles wrought by the hands of the apostles.

19 And if there were miracles wrought then, why has God ceased to be a God of miracles and yet be an unchangeable Being? And behold, I say unto you he changeth not; if so he would cease to be God; and he ceaseth not to be God, and is a God of miracles.

20 And the reason why he ceaseth to do miracles among the children of men is because that they dwindle in unbelief, and depart from the right way, and know not the God in whom they should trust.

21 Behold, I say unto you that whoso believeth in Christ, doubting nothing, whatsoever he shall ask the Father in the name of Christ it shall be granted him; and this promise is unto all, even unto the ends of the earth.

22 For behold, thus said Jesus Christ, the Son of God, unto his disciples who should tarry, yea, and also to all his disciples, in the hearing of the multitude: Go ye into all the world, and preach the gospel to every creature;

23 And he that believeth and is baptized shall be saved, but he that believeth not shall be damned;

24 And these signs shall follow them that believe—in my name shall they cast out devils; they shall speak with new tongues; they shall take up serpents; and if they drink any deadly thing it shall not hurt them; they shall lay hands on the sick and they shall recover;

25 And whosoever shall believe in my name, doubting nothing, unto him will I confirm all my words, even unto the ends of the earth.

26 And now, behold, who can stand against the works of the Lord? Who can deny his sayings? Who will rise up against the almighty power of the Lord? Who will despise the works of the Lord? Who will despise the children of Christ? Behold, all ye who are despisers of the works of the Lord, for ye shall wonder and perish.

27 O then despise not, and wonder not, but hearken unto the words of the Lord, and ask the Father in the name of Jesus for what things soever ye shall stand in need. Doubt not, but be believing, and begin as in times of old, and come unto the Lord with all your heart, and work out your own salvation with fear and trembling before him.

28 Be wise in the days of your probation; strip yourselves of all uncleanness; ask not, that ye may consume it on your lusts, but ask with a firmness unshaken, that ye will yield to no temptation, but that ye will serve the true and living God.

29 See that ye are not baptized unworthily; see that ye partake not of the sacrament of Christ unworthily; but see that ye do all things in worthiness, and do it in the name of Jesus Christ, the Son of the living God; and if ye do this, and endure to the end, ye will in nowise be cast out.

30 Behold, I speak unto you as though I spake from the dead; for I know that ye shall have my words.

31 Condemn me not because of mine imperfection, neither my father, because of his imperfection, neither them who have written before him; but rather give thanks unto God that he hath made manifest unto you our imperfections, that ye may learn to be more wise than we have been.

32 And now, behold, we have written this record according to our knowledge, in the characters which are called among us the reformed Egyptian,

Notes

being handed down and altered by us, according to our manner of speech.

33 And if our plates had been sufficiently large we should have written in Hebrew; but the Hebrew hath been altered by us also; and if we could have written in Hebrew, behold, ye would have had no imperfection in our record.

34 But the Lord knoweth the things which we have written, and also that none other people knoweth our language; and because that none other people knoweth our language, therefore he hath prepared means for the interpretation thereof.

35 And these things are written that we may rid our garments of the blood of our brethren, who have dwindled in unbelief.

36 And behold, these things which we have desired concerning our brethren, yea, even their restoration to the knowledge of Christ, are according to the prayers of all the saints who have dwelt in the land.

37 And may the Lord Jesus Christ grant that their prayers may be answered according to their faith; and may God the Father remember the covenant which he hath made with the house of Israel; and may he bless them forever, through faith on the name of Jesus Christ. Amen.

Teaching Tips from Prophets' Lips "What should be the source for teaching the great plan of the Eternal God? The scriptures, of course—particularly the Book of Mormon. This should also include the other modern-day revelations. These should be coupled with the words of the Apostles and prophets and the promptings of the Spirit" (Ezra Taft Benson, *Ensign*, May 1987, 85).

Notes

THE BOOK OF ETHER

ETHER SUMMARY

Time Period: Started between 2500 and 2200 BC and ended between 500 and 250 BC (over 1,700 years)

Contributors: Moroni, Ether, brother of Jared

Source: Twenty-four plates found by the people of Limhi (see Mosiah 28:11–19)

Abridged by: Moroni

Synopsis:

Chapters 1–3: An account of the Jaredites' departure from Babylon and preparations to cross the ocean

Chapter 4: The sealed two-thirds portion of the golden plates and faith are discussed

Chapter 5: Moroni's note to Joseph Smith concerning the plates

Chapters 6–11: The voyage of the Jaredites and development of their civilization in the promised land

Chapter 12: Ether preaches, and Moroni speaks of faith in God, gives an account of his father's death, and speaks to the generations of those who will have the Book of Mormon

Chapter 13: Ether prophesies of the destruction of the Jaredites and speaks of the New Jerusalem

Chapters 14–15: The Jaredites are all destroyed except Coriantumr

The record of the Jaredites, taken from the twenty-four plates found by the people of Limhi in the days of King Mosiah.

ETHER 1
The Jaredites Leave Babel

1–5, Moroni discusses his abridgment of the Jaredite record; 6–32, Ether's genealogy is given back to Jared; 33–37, The brother of Jared cries unto the Lord on behalf of his family and friends that their language is not confounded; 38–43, The Lord promises to bring them to a choice land and make them into a great nation.

Notes

1 And now I, Moroni, proceed to give an account of those ancient inhabitants who were destroyed by the hand of the Lord upon the face of this north country.

2 And I take mine account from the twenty and four plates which were found by the people of Limhi, which is called the Book of Ether.

3 And as I suppose that the first part of this record, which speaks concerning the creation of the world, and also of Adam, and an account from that time even to the great tower, and whatsoever things transpired among the children of men until that time, is had among the Jews—

4 Therefore I do not write those things which transpired from the days of Adam until that time; but they are had upon the plates; and whoso findeth them, the same will have power that he may get the full account.

v. 4 "The full account."

- From the time of Adam and Eve until the building of the Tower of Babel (approximately 1,800 years of history) is covered in Genesis chapters 1–10. Joseph Smith expounded this brief account in the Bible when completing the Joseph Smith Translation of those verses which is today known as Moses chapters 2–8. This greatly increases the information we have of this time and period and almost doubles the amount of scripture text compared to the Genesis account.

5 But behold, I give not the full account, but a part of the account I give, from the tower down until they were destroyed.

6 And on this wise do I give the account. He that wrote this record was Ether, and he was a descendant of Coriantor.

v. 6 The name "Ether."

- Hugh Nibley stated that the name "Ether" (Ether 1:6), or athira, means "the one who left a trace, the one who left his mark or left a record." In all Semitic languages it's the same, and it means "to leave a track, to trail somebody" (Hugh W. Nibley, *Teachings of the Book of Mormon*, Semester 4, 243).

7 Coriantor was the son of Moron.

8 And Moron was the son of Ethem.

9 And Ethem was the son of Ahah.

10 And Ahah was the son of Seth.

11 And Seth was the son of Shiblon.

12 And Shiblon was the son of Com.

13 And Com was the son of Coriantum.

14 And Coriantum was the son of Amnigaddah.

15 And Amnigaddah was the son of Aaron.

16 And Aaron was a descendant of Heth, who was the son of Hearthom.

17 And Hearthom was the son of Lib.

18 And Lib was the son of Kish.

19 And Kish was the son of Corom.

20 And Corom was the son of Levi.

21 And Levi was the son of Kim.

22 And Kim was the son of Morianton.

23 And Morianton was a descendant of Riplakish.

24 And Riplakish was the son of Shez.

25 And Shez was the son of Heth.

26 And Heth was the son of Com.

27 And Com was the son of Coriantum.

28 And Coriantum was the son of Emer.

29 And Emer was the son of Omer.

30 And Omer was the son of Shule.

31 And Shule was the son of Kib.

32 And Kib was the son of Orihah, who was the son of Jared;

vv. 6–32 "A descendant."

- Notice that the word "descendant" is used

Notes

twice in the verses, meaning the genealogy is not a perfect record of father to son.

33 Which Jared came forth with his brother and their families, with some others and their families, from the great tower, at the time the Lord confounded the language of the people, and swore in his wrath that they should be scattered upon all the face of the earth; and according to the word of the Lord the people were scattered.

34 And the brother of Jared being a large and mighty man, and a man highly favored of the Lord, Jared, his brother, said unto him: Cry unto the Lord, that he will not confound us that we may not understand our words.

v. 34 The brother of Jared's name.

Elder George Reynolds relates how the name of the brother of Jared was revealed to the Prophet Joseph Smith, "While residing at Kirtland, Elder Reynolds Cahoon had a son born to him. One day when President Joseph Smith was passing his door he called the Prophet in and asked him to bless and name the baby. Joseph did so and gave the boy the name of Mahonri Moriancumer. When he had finished the blessing, he laid the child on the bed, and turning to Elder Cahoon he said, the name I have given your son is the name of the brother of Jared; the Lord has just shown or revealed it to me. Elder William F. Cahoon, who was standing near heard the Prophet make this statement to his father; and this was the first time the name of the brother of Jared was known in the Church in this dispensation" ("The Jaredites," *The Juvenile Instructor,* 1 May 1892, 282).

Many believe that since Mahonri was a fairly common name in Joseph's day, the actual name of the brother of Jared was just "Moriancumer." Notice that a place was named after him in Ether 2:13.

35 And it came to pass that the brother of Jared did cry unto the Lord, and the Lord had compassion upon Jared; therefore he did not confound the language of Jared; and Jared and his brother were not confounded.

36 Then Jared said unto his brother: Cry again unto the Lord, and it may be that he will turn away his anger from them who are our friends, that he confound not their language.

37 And it came to pass that the brother of Jared did cry unto the Lord, and the Lord had compassion upon their friends and their families also, that they were not confounded.

38 And it came to pass that Jared spake again unto his brother, saying: Go and inquire of the Lord whether he will drive us out of the land, and if he will drive us out of the land, cry unto him whither we shall go. And who knoweth but the Lord will carry us forth into a land which is choice above all the earth? And if it so be, let us be faithful unto the Lord, that we may receive it for our inheritance.

39 And it came to pass that the brother of Jared did cry unto the Lord according to that which had been spoken by the mouth of Jared.

40 And it came to pass that the Lord did hear the brother of Jared, and had compassion upon him, and said unto him:

41 Go to and gather together thy flocks, both male and female, of every kind; and also of the seed of the earth of every kind; and thy families; and also Jared thy brother and his family; and also thy friends and their families, and the friends of Jared and their families.

42 And when thou hast done this thou shalt go at the head of them down into the valley which is northward. And there will I meet thee, and I will go before thee into a land which is choice above all the lands of the earth.

43 And there will I bless thee and thy seed, and raise up unto me of thy seed, and of the seed of thy brother, and they who shall go with thee, a great nation. And there shall be none greater than the nation which I will raise up unto me of

Notes

thy seed, upon all the face of the earth. And thus I will do unto thee because this long time ye have cried unto me.

vv. 33–43 We should cry unto the Lord in prayer.

- 🔎 Quickly skim through verses 33–43 and look for what word is used instead of the word "prayer."
- ❓ Analyze:
  - How is "crying" unto the Lord different than prayer?
  - In what situations might someone be more likely to "cry" unto the Lord?
  - How is the heart more involved when crying unto the Lord?
  - Would the Lord have given the brother of Jared the things he wanted if he would not have asked for them?
- ❓ Apply:
  - If appropriate to share, when is a time you found yourself crying unto the Lord?
  - Have you found yourself more likely to cry unto the Lord when you have a problem (v. 34) or when you want something? (v. 38)
  - Why is it easy to forget to pray when there is not a need or a desire? (See Ether 2:14)
- ♥ Challenge class members to cry unto the Lord in prayer by making their prayers heartfelt.

> **Teaching Tips from Prophets' Lips** "In presenting a lesson there are many ways for the undisciplined teacher to stray from the path that leads to his objective. One of the most common temptations is to speculate on matters about which the Lord has said very little. The disciplined teacher has the courage to say, 'I don't know,' and leave it at that. As President Joseph F. Smith said, 'It is no discredit to our intelligence or to our integrity to say frankly in the face of a hundred speculative questions, "I don't know" ' [*Gospel Doctrine*, 5th ed. (1939), 9]" (Joseph F. McConkie, "The Disciplined Teacher," *Instructor*, Sept. 1969, 334–35).

Index Topics: prayer

Notes

ETHER 2

"Choice above All Other Lands"

1–7, They prepare and begin their journey; 8–12, The people in the land of promise must serve God or be swept off; 13–15, The brother of Jared is chastened for not calling upon the Lord; 16–25, The vessels are constructed and Jared confers with the Lord over the problem of lighting.

1 And it came to pass that Jared and his brother, and their families, and also the friends of Jared and his brother and their families, went down into the valley which was northward, (and the name of the valley was Nimrod, being called after the mighty hunter) with their flocks which they had gathered together, male and female, of every kind.

2 And they did also lay snares and catch fowls of the air; and they did also prepare a vessel, in which they did carry with them the fish of the waters.

3 And they did also carry with them deseret, which, by interpretation, is a honey bee; and thus they did carry with them swarms of bees, and all manner of that which was upon the face of the land, seeds of every kind.

v. 3 Deseret.

- ⚡ As an opening hymn, you might want to sing, "In Our Lovely Deseret" (Hymn 307). Ask class members what "deseret" means. You may want to point out the symbol on the center of the Utah state flag and insignia. Ask why someone would want to make this symbol part of the state's identity. Have class members look in verse 3 for what the symbol means and teach that it is a symbol of industry. Ask why industry is an important trait.

4 And it came to pass that when they had come down into the valley of Nimrod the Lord came down and talked with the brother of Jared; and he was in a cloud, and the brother of Jared saw him not.

5 And it came to pass that the Lord commanded them that they should go forth into the wilderness, yea, into that quarter where there never had man been. And it came to pass that the Lord did go before them, and did talk with them as he stood in a cloud, and gave directions whither they should travel.

6 And it came to pass that they did travel in the wilderness, and did build barges, in which they did cross many waters, being directed continually by the hand of the Lord.

7 And the Lord would not suffer that they should stop beyond the sea in the wilderness, but he would that they should come forth even unto the land of promise, which was choice above all other lands, which the Lord God had preserved for a righteous people.

8 And he had sworn in his wrath unto the brother of Jared, that whoso should possess this land of promise, from that time henceforth and forever, should serve him, the true and only God, or they should be swept off when the fulness of his wrath should come upon them.

9 And now, we can behold the decrees of God concerning this land, that it is a land of promise; and whatsoever nation shall possess it shall serve God, or they shall be swept off when the fulness of his wrath shall come upon them. And the fulness of his wrath cometh upon them when they are ripened in iniquity.

10 For behold, this is a land which is choice above all other lands; wherefore he that doth possess it shall serve God or shall be swept off; for it is the everlasting decree of God. And it is not until the fulness of iniquity among the children of the land, that they are swept off.

11 And this cometh unto you, O ye Gentiles, that ye may know the decrees of God—that ye may repent, and not continue in your iniquities until the fulness come, that ye may not bring down the fulness of the wrath of God upon you as the inhabitants of the land have hitherto done.

12 Behold, this is a choice land, and whatsoever nation shall possess it shall be free from bondage, and from captivity, and from all other nations under heaven, if they will but serve the God of the land, who is Jesus Christ, who hath been manifested by the things which we have written.

vv. 8–12 If the people in the Americas become wicked as a people, they will be swept off from the land of promise.

- On a table or on the floor where it can be seen, lay out a map of the world or the Risk© game board. On it, lay out some of the small figures of the game, or something to represent people on the American continents. Have a small broom in hand and as verses 8–12 are taught, follow the actions with your boom.

- As a variation, you could also discuss how the people become "ripe" in their wickedness—how some bananas are in different degrees or ripeness (green, yellow, browning, black). As you discuss the different degrees of ripening in wickedness in the verses, refer to the bananas.

- *In verses 8–12, look for what will happen to the people in the Americas if they become too wicked.*

- Analyze:
  - *Is it difficult for God to sweep people from this land?*
  - *What words describe how bad they will be before being swept off?*
  - *Why will God sweep wickedness from this land?*
  - Show the bananas and ask, *"On a scale of 1–10, how ripe are we in our nation right now?"*
  - *In what areas do we need to repent as a nation?*

- List those areas on the board. Challenge class members to personally become free from those sins in their lives.

13 And now I proceed with my record; for behold, it came to pass that the Lord did bring Jared and

Notes

his brethren forth even to that great sea which divideth the lands. And as they came to the sea they pitched their tents; and they called the name of the place Moriancumer; and they dwelt in tents, and dwelt in tents upon the seashore for the space of four years.

14 And it came to pass at the end of four years that the Lord came again unto the brother of Jared, and stood in a cloud and talked with him. And for the space of three hours did the Lord talk with the brother of Jared, and chastened him because he remembered not to call upon the name of the Lord.

vv. 14–15 When we remember to pray to the Lord, it pleases Him.

- ⚡ Ask class members to share an experience of a significant chastisement they have received. Make sure they know to share only if it is appropriate.

- 🔍 *Look for how those times of chastisement might compare to the chastisement the brother of Jared received in verse 14.*

- ❓ Ask,
  - *Why is it so important to the Lord that we pray?*
  - *How do we benefit from prayer?*
  - *For you, when is it most difficult to remember to pray?*

- ✏️ Have class members write down when it is the most difficult time to remember to pray. Have them share if they feel comfortable.

- ❤️ Give each class member a popsicle stick and explain that it is actually a "Prayer Stick." Ask them to keep it with them all week as a reminder to pray often. Follow up with the class each day throughout the week if possible.

15 And the brother of Jared repented of the evil which he had done, and did call upon the name of the Lord for his brethren who were with him. And the Lord said unto him: I will forgive thee and thy brethren of their sins; but thou shalt not sin any more, for ye shall remember that my Spirit will not always strive with man; wherefore, if ye will sin until ye are fully ripe ye shall be cut off from the presence of the Lord. And these are my thoughts upon the land which I shall give you for your inheritance; for it shall be a land choice above all other lands.

16 And the Lord said: Go to work and build, after the manner of barges which ye have hitherto built. And it came to pass that the brother of Jared did go to work, and also his brethren, and built barges after the manner which they had built, according to the instructions of the Lord. And they were small, and they were light upon the water, even like unto the lightness of a fowl upon the water.

17 And they were built after a manner that they were exceedingly tight, even that they would hold water like unto a dish; and the bottom thereof was tight like unto a dish; and the sides thereof were tight like unto a dish; and the ends thereof were peaked; and the top thereof was tight like unto a dish; and the length thereof was the length of a tree; and the door thereof, when it was shut, was tight like unto a dish.

18 And it came to pass that the brother of Jared cried unto the Lord, saying: O Lord, I have performed the work which thou hast commanded me, and I have made the barges according as thou hast directed me.

19 And behold, O Lord, in them there is no light; whither shall we steer? And also we shall perish, for in them we cannot breathe, save it is the air which is in them; therefore we shall perish.

20 And the Lord said unto the brother of Jared: Behold, thou shalt make a hole in the top, and also in the bottom; and when thou shalt suffer for air thou shalt unstop the hole and receive air. And if it be so that the water come in upon thee, behold, ye shall stop the hole, that ye may not perish in the flood.

21 And it came to pass that the brother of Jared did so, according as the Lord had commanded.

Notes

22 And he cried again unto the Lord saying: O Lord, behold I have done even as thou hast commanded me; and I have prepared the vessels for my people, and behold there is no light in them. Behold, O Lord, wilt thou suffer that we shall cross this great water in darkness?

23 And the Lord said unto the brother of Jared: What will ye that I should do that ye may have light in your vessels? For behold, ye cannot have windows, for they will be dashed in pieces; neither shall ye take fire with you, for ye shall not go by the light of fire.

24 For behold, ye shall be as a whale in the midst of the sea; for the mountain waves shall dash upon you. Nevertheless, I will bring you up again out of the depths of the sea; for the winds have gone forth out of my mouth, and also the rains and the floods have I sent forth.

25 And behold, I prepare you against these things; for ye cannot cross this great deep save I prepare you against the waves of the sea, and the winds which have gone forth, and the floods which shall come. Therefore what will ye that I should prepare for you that ye may have light when ye are swallowed up in the depths of the sea?

vv. 16–25 God doesn't just give us all the answers because personal effort helps us grow.

- ⚡ Have class members skim verses 16–25 and ask a volunteer to summarize what happens in those verses. Afterward, show a mathematics book and ask,
  - *Why do math books have so many problems in them?*
  - *Wouldn't it be better if math books weren't so full of problems?*
  - *Would life be better without so many problems?*
  - *Would it be good if someone worked out all the problems for you in your math book?*
  - *How are problems in a math books and problems in life similar?*
  - *What is the purpose behind problems in life and in math books?*
- ❓ Analyze:
  - *When the brother of Jared came to the Lord with the problem of no light in the boats, why didn't God just quickly give him the solution?*
  - *What do we learn about the Lord from His first question in verse 23 to the brother of Jared?*
  - *What would happen if God quickly solved every problem for us when we asked in prayer?*
  - *Does this mean we shouldn't ask in prayer and just try to figure out everything on our own?*
  - *What does this story teach about faith?*
  - *What does this teach about spiritual growth as individuals?*
- ❤ Help class members know that we should always seek God's guidance through prayer. Point out that the purpose of prayer is not for God to solve all of our problems, but rather to help us work through our problems. With God's help, we can eventually overcome any problem.

Index Topics: prayer, spiritual growth, wickedness

ETHER 3
The Brother of Jared's Vision

1–12, The brother of Jared forms sixteen stones out of rock and requests the Lord to illuminate them with His touch; 13–18, Jesus Christ shows Himself to the brother of Jared and reveals doctrine about His physical and spiritual body; 19–28, Because of his faith, the brother of Jared has a perfect knowledge and is shown marvelous things, commanded to write them, and then seal his writings up.

Overarching Principle: When we exercise faith,

Notes

the Lord is able to turn our life into something more than we could do on our own.

Note: The storyline in Ether 3 is a continuation from Ether 2 and, depending on time, may best be taught together.

1 And it came to pass that the brother of Jared, (now the number of the vessels which had been prepared was eight) went forth unto the mount, which they called the mount Shelem, because of its exceeding height, and did molten out of a rock sixteen small stones; and they were white and clear, even as transparent glass; and he did carry them in his hands upon the top of the mount, and cried again unto the Lord, saying:

2 O Lord, thou hast said that we must be encompassed about by the floods. Now behold, O Lord, and do not be angry with thy servant because of his weakness before thee; for we know that thou art holy and dwellest in the heavens, and that we are unworthy before thee; because of the fall our natures have become evil continually; nevertheless, O Lord, thou hast given us a commandment that we must call upon thee, that from thee we may receive according to our desires.

3 Behold, O Lord, thou hast smitten us because of our iniquity, and hast driven us forth, and for these many years we have been in the wilderness; nevertheless, thou hast been merciful unto us. O Lord, look upon me in pity, and turn away thine anger from this thy people, and suffer not that they shall go forth across this raging deep in darkness; but behold these things which I have molten out of the rock.

4 And I know, O Lord, that thou hast all power, and can do whatsoever thou wilt for the benefit of man; therefore touch these stones, O Lord, with thy finger, and prepare them that they may shine forth in darkness; and they shall shine forth unto us in the vessels which we have prepared, that we may have light while we shall cross the sea.

5 Behold, O Lord, thou canst do this. We know that thou art able to show forth great power, which looks small unto the understanding of men.

vv. 1–5 Proper principles of prayer.

Note: This principle could be used as a continuation of the principle from Ether 1:33–43 or Ether 2:14–15.

- Write "Proper Principles of Prayer" on the board and invite class members to consider all the possible responses regarding what the proper principles of prayer could be. Consider writing their answers on the board. Explain that there are a few instances in all scripture where the words of a prophet's prayer are recorded, and Ether 3:1–5 is one of those times.

- *Invite class members to read verses 1–5 to identify principles of prayer and invite them to explain their answers.*

- Analyze: As class members discuss their findings, consider asking additional questions regarding their answers to help the class analyze the principles they found. You could ask questions like, *How do you think that affected the prayer of the brother of Jared?* or *How might that have changed how the Lord responded to the prayer?*

- Apply: *What can you do to make your prayers more meaningful?*

- Elder David A. Bednar taught the following regarding engaging in meaningful prayer. "Humble, earnest, and persistent prayer enables us to recognize and align ourselves with the will of our Heavenly Father. And in this the Savior provided the perfect example as He prayed in the Garden of Gethsemane, 'saying, Father, if thou be willing, remove this cup from me: nevertheless not my will, but thine, be done. . . . And being in an agony he prayed more earnestly' (see Luke 22:42, 44). The object of our prayers should not be to present a wish list or a series of requests but to secure for ourselves and for others blessings that God is eager to bestow, according

Notes

to His will and timing. Every sincere prayer is heard and answered by our Heavenly Father, but the answers we receive may not be what we expect or come to us when we want or in the way we anticipate . . . Prayer is a privilege and the soul's sincere desire. We can move beyond routine and 'checklist' prayers and engage in meaningful prayer as we appropriately ask in faith and act, as we patiently persevere through the trial of our faith, and as we humbly acknowledge and accept 'not my will, but Thine, be done' " ("Ask in Faith," *Ensign*, May 2008, 97).

- ♥ Discuss how Elder Bednar's quote could apply to the prayer of the brother of Jared and to our prayers. Consider asking class members to share a personal experience regarding prayer or share testimony about engaging in meaningful prayer.

6 And it came to pass that when the brother of Jared had said these words, behold, the Lord stretched forth his hand and touched the stones one by one with his finger. And the veil was taken from off the eyes of the brother of Jared, and he saw the finger of the Lord; and it was as the finger of a man, like unto flesh and blood; and the brother of Jared fell down before the Lord, for he was struck with fear.

7 And the Lord saw that the brother of Jared had fallen to the earth; and the Lord said unto him: Arise, why hast thou fallen?

8 And he saith unto the Lord: I saw the finger of the Lord, and I feared lest he should smite me; for I knew not that the Lord had flesh and blood.

9 And the Lord said unto him: Because of thy faith thou hast seen that I shall take upon me flesh and blood; and never has man come before me with such exceeding faith as thou hast; for were it not so ye could not have seen my finger. Sawest thou more than this?

10 And he answered: Nay; Lord, show thyself unto me.

11 And the Lord said unto him: Believest thou the words which I shall speak?

12 And he answered: Yea, Lord, I know that thou speakest the truth, for thou art a God of truth, and canst not lie.

13 And when he had said these words, behold, the Lord showed himself unto him, and said: Because thou knowest these things ye are redeemed from the fall; therefore ye are brought back into my presence; therefore I show myself unto you.

vv. 6–13 When we exercise faith, the Lord is able to turn our life into something more than we could on our own.

- ⚡ You will want to contrast the difference between light and dark to teach this principle. Consider using a bright flashlight or lamp as you discuss light and dark. Point out to your class the darkness of the barges mentioned in Ether 2:22, and how this contrasts with the light the Lord provides through touching the stones.

- 🔍 Explain to class members that the brother of Jared requested the Lord to touch the stones in order to illuminate them. Then invite class members to look for what happens as a result of his request in verse 6.

- ❓ Analyze: *If the brother of Jared requested the Lord to touch the stones, why do you think he was struck with fear when he witnessed it happen?*

- 🔍 Read verses 7–13 as a class. You may want to assign two individuals to read—one reading what the brother of Jared says, and the other reading what the Lord says. Ask, *Look for what principle of faith the Lord is teaching His prophet.*

- ❓ Analyze: Once class members have identified a principle of faith, help them analyze it by asking follow-up questions about their comments.

- ❓ Apply: *How does this principle of faith apply to us?*

Notes

ETHER 3

- ♥ Refer back to the contrast of light and dark activity you did at the beginning of the lesson and discuss how it applies. Ask class members when they felt they have acted in faith and received light from God.

- 💬 President Howard W. Hunter taught, "Whatever Jesus lays his hands upon lives. If Jesus lays his hands upon a marriage, it lives. If he is allowed to lay his hands on the family, it lives" ("Reading the Scriptures," *Ensign*, Nov. 1979, 6).

- 💡 Often our faith can grow as we read from the scriptures, particularly as we read about earlier prophets who exercised faith amid great trials. When asked by the Lord what to do about the darkness within the barges (see Ether 2:23), perhaps the brother of Jared turned to the story of Noah, who also built a vessel, as a means of inspiration. Cross-reference Genesis 6:16 and look at the LDS footnote for the word "window." Thus, scripture study may have aided the brother of Jared as he sought a solution to the difficulties facing his family.

14 Behold, I am he who was prepared from the foundation of the world to redeem my people. Behold, I am Jesus Christ. I am the Father and the Son. In me shall all mankind have life, and that eternally, even they who shall believe on my name; and they shall become my sons and my daughters.

15 And never have I showed myself unto man whom I have created, for never has man believed in me as thou hast. Seest thou that ye are created after mine own image? Yea, even all men were created in the beginning after mine own image.

16 Behold, this body, which ye now behold, is the body of my spirit; and man have I created after the body of my spirit; and even as I appear unto thee to be in the spirit will I appear unto my people in the flesh.

17 And now, as I, Moroni, said I could not make a full account of these things which are written, therefore it sufficeth me to say that Jesus showed himself unto this man in the spirit, even after the manner and in the likeness of the same body even as he showed himself unto the Nephites.

18 And he ministered unto him even as he ministered unto the Nephites; and all this, that this man might know that he was God, because of the many great works which the Lord had showed unto him.

19 And because of the knowledge of this man he could not be kept from beholding within the veil; and he saw the finger of Jesus, which, when he saw, he fell with fear; for he knew that it was the finger of the Lord; and he had faith no longer, for he knew, nothing doubting.

20 Wherefore, having this perfect knowledge of God, he could not be kept from within the veil; therefore he saw Jesus; and he did minister unto him.

vv. 14–20 The Doctrine of Jesus Christ.

- 🔍 Invite class members to read and mark verses 14–20, looking for every doctrine about Jesus Christ: His physical appearance, His role in our salvation, etc.

- ❓ Analyze: Use this opportunity to discuss the doctrine regarding Christ they have identified. Consider allowing class members to ask questions regarding these doctrines. You may need to research more information yourself beforehand so you can be ready to answer their questions.

- 💬 Robert D. Hales stated, "The Lord thus showed Himself twenty-five hundred years before He was actually born as a babe in Jerusalem. He then bore testimony of the fact that He would be Jesus the Christ, that He would come before His people, and that He would be the atoning sacrifice, that all mankind might live" (Robert D. Hales, "Lessons from the Atonement That Help Us Endure to the End," *Ensign*, Nov. 1985, 19).

Notes

💬 Russell M. Nelson taught, "Central to that plan was the Atonement of Jesus Christ. In premortal councils, He was foreordained by His Father to atone for our sins and break the bands of physical and spiritual death. [See John 17:5, 24; 1 Pet. 1:19–20; Mosiah 4:6–7; Mosiah 18:13; 3 Ne. 26:3–5; D&C 93:7–9; Moses 5:57; JST, Gen. 5:43; JST, Gen. 14:30–31.] Jesus declared, 'I . . . was prepared from the foundation of the world to redeem my people. . . . In me shall all mankind have life, and that eternally, even they who shall believe on my name.' [Ether 3:14] Later, Paul added that the Church is 'built upon the foundation of the apostles and prophets, Jesus Christ himself being the chief corner stone' [Eph. 2:20]" (Russell M. Nelson, "How Firm Our Foundation," *Ensign*, May 2002, 77).

❤ Testify of Christ's important role in the plan of salvation and of our dependence upon Him.

21 And it came to pass that the Lord said unto the brother of Jared: Behold, thou shalt not suffer these things which ye have seen and heard to go forth unto the world, until the time cometh that I shall glorify my name in the flesh; wherefore, ye shall treasure up the things which ye have seen and heard, and show it to no man.

22 And behold, when ye shall come unto me, ye shall write them and shall seal them up, that no one can interpret them; for ye shall write them in a language that they cannot be read.

23 And behold, these two stones will I give unto thee, and ye shall seal them up also with the things which ye shall write.

24 For behold, the language which ye shall write I have confounded; wherefore I will cause in my own due time that these stones shall magnify to the eyes of men these things which ye shall write.

25 And when the Lord had said these words, he showed unto the brother of Jared all the inhabitants of the earth which had been, and also all that would be; and he withheld them not from his sight, even unto the ends of the earth.

26 For he had said unto him in times before, that if he would believe in him that he could show unto him all things—it should be shown unto him; therefore the Lord could not withhold anything from him, for he knew that the Lord could show him all things.

27 And the Lord said unto him: Write these things and seal them up; and I will show them in mine own due time unto the children of men.

28 And it came to pass that the Lord commanded him that he should seal up the two stones which he had received, and show them not, until the Lord should show them unto the children of men.

vv. 21–28 Records sealed up.

💡 Note that the brother of Jared is commanded to seal up certain portions of his vision he will write. According to Moroni, the brother of Jared seals up this portion of his vision and it will come forth "in [the Lord's] own due time unto the children of men" (see verse 27).

Teaching Tips from Prophets' Lips "Always remember, there is no satisfactory substitute for the scriptures and the words of the living prophets. These should be your original sources. Read and ponder more what the Lord has said, and less about what others have written concerning what the Lord has said" (*The Gospel Teacher and His Message* [address to religious educators, 17 Sept. 1976], 6).

ETHER 4
When This Record Shall Come Forth

1–7, Moroni writes down what the brother of Jared saw and seals it up with the interpreters—they are to come forth in a time when the Gentiles repent; 8–19, The Book of Mormon helps us learn of Christ and His work.

Notes

ETHER 4

1 And the Lord commanded the brother of Jared to go down out of the mount from the presence of the Lord, and write the things which he had seen; and they were forbidden to come unto the children of men until after that he should be lifted up upon the cross; and for this cause did king Mosiah keep them, that they should not come unto the world until after Christ should show himself unto his people.

2 And after Christ truly had showed himself unto his people he commanded that they should be made manifest.

3 And now, after that, they have all dwindled in unbelief; and there is none save it be the Lamanites, and they have rejected the gospel of Christ; therefore I am commanded that I should hide them up again in the earth.

4 Behold, I have written upon these plates the very things which the brother of Jared saw; and there never were greater things made manifest than those which were made manifest unto the brother of Jared.

5 Wherefore the Lord hath commanded me to write them; and I have written them. And he commanded me that I should seal them up; and he also hath commanded that I should seal up the interpretation thereof; wherefore I have sealed up the interpreters, according to the commandment of the Lord.

6 For the Lord said unto me: They shall not go forth unto the Gentiles until the day that they shall repent of their iniquity, and become clean before the Lord.

7 And in that day that they shall exercise faith in me, saith the Lord, even as the brother of Jared did, that they may become sanctified in me, then will I manifest unto them the things which the brother of Jared saw, even to the unfolding unto them all my revelations, saith Jesus Christ, the Son of God, the Father of the heavens and of the earth, and all things that in them are.

vv. 1–7 The writings of the brother of Jared will come forth.

- Remind class members what the brother of Jared saw in vision (see Ether 3:25–28). Then have them look for what Moroni writes regarding the brother of Jared's vision and when those records will come forth.

- Share the following quote from President Joseph Fielding Smith. "The Lord has promised that we can have that hidden record [referring to Ether 4:2–3] when we are prepared to receive it. I will read it. [He then quotes Ether 4:6–7]. Now the Lord has placed us on probation as members of the Church. He has given us the Book of Mormon, which is the lesser part, to build up our faith through our obedience to the counsels which it contains, and when we ourselves, members of the Church, are willing to keep the commandments as they have been given to us and show our faith as the Nephites did for a short period of time, then the Lord is ready to bring forth the other record and give it to us, but we are not ready now to receive it. Why? Because we have not lived up to the requirements in this probationary state in the reading of the record which had been given to us and in following its counsels" ("The Book of Mormon, a Divine Record," in Conference Report, October 1961, pp. 18–20).

- Encourage class members to continue to study from the Book of Mormon.

8 And he that will contend against the word of the Lord, let him be accursed; and he that shall deny these things, let him be accursed; for unto them will I show no greater things, saith Jesus Christ; for I am he who speaketh.

9 And at my command the heavens are opened and are shut; and at my word the earth shall shake; and at my command the inhabitants thereof shall pass away, even so as by fire.

10 And he that believeth not my words believeth not my disciples; and if it so be that I do not

Notes

speak, judge ye; for ye shall know that it is I that speaketh, at the last day.

11 But he that believeth these things which I have spoken, him will I visit with the manifestations of my Spirit, and he shall know and bear record. For because of my Spirit he shall know that these things are true; for it persuadeth men to do good.

12 And whatsoever thing persuadeth men to do good is of me; for good cometh of none save it be of me. I am the same that leadeth men to all good; he that will not believe my words will not believe me—that I am; and he that will not believe me will not believe the Father who sent me. For behold, I am the Father, I am the light, and the life, and the truth of the world.

13 Come unto me, O ye Gentiles, and I will show unto you the greater things, the knowledge which is hid up because of unbelief.

14 Come unto me, O ye house of Israel, and it shall be made manifest unto you how great things the Father hath laid up for you, from the foundation of the world; and it hath not come unto you, because of unbelief.

15 Behold, when ye shall rend that veil of unbelief which doth cause you to remain in your awful state of wickedness, and hardness of heart, and blindness of mind, then shall the great and marvelous things which have been hid up from the foundation of the world from you—yea, when ye shall call upon the Father in my name, with a broken heart and a contrite spirit, then shall ye know that the Father hath remembered the covenant which he made unto your fathers, O house of Israel.

16 And then shall my revelations which I have caused to be written by my servant John be unfolded in the eyes of all the people. Remember, when ye see these things, ye shall know that the time is at hand that they shall be made manifest in very deed.

17 Therefore, when ye shall receive this record ye may know that the work of the Father has commenced upon all the face of the land.

18 Therefore, repent all ye ends of the earth, and come unto me, and believe in my gospel, and be baptized in my name; for he that believeth and is baptized shall be saved; but he that believeth not shall be damned; and signs shall follow them that believe in my name.

19 And blessed is he that is found faithful unto my name at the last day, for he shall be lifted up to dwell in the kingdom prepared for him from the foundation of the world. And behold it is I that hath spoken it. Amen.

vv. 8–19 The Book of Mormon helps us learn of Christ and His work.

- ⚡ Discuss with the class how meteorologists can predict the weather. Explain that they look for certain signs and patterns and then, based on their observation, they predict what the weather will be for the coming days.

- 🔎 *Read verse 17 and look for the sign we seek to know that God has commenced his work in the last days. Then read verses 8–16 and look for what impact the Book of Mormon will have on both the believing and unbelieving.*

- ❤ Invite a class member to testify of their experience with the Book of Mormon and how it has helped them come unto Jesus Christ and learn of His gospel.

ETHER 5

Moroni's Instructions to Joseph Smith

1–6, Moroni offers instructions to Joseph Smith regarding allowing three witnesses to see the plates.

1 And now I, Moroni, have written the words which were commanded me, according to my memory; and I have told you the things which I have sealed up; therefore touch them not in order that ye may translate; for that thing is forbidden you, except by and by it shall be wisdom in God.

Notes

ETHER 6

Arrival to the Promised Land

1–11, The Jaredites take their journey across the great waters to the promised land; 12–18, They arrive at the promised land and begin to spread upon the face of the earth; 19–30, The people desire a king; Orihah is anointed king.

1 And now I, Moroni, proceed to give the record of Jared and his brother.

2 For it came to pass after the Lord had prepared the stones which the brother of Jared had carried up into the mount, the brother of Jared came down out of the mount, and he did put forth the stones into the vessels which were prepared, one in each end thereof; and behold, they did give light unto the vessels.

3 And thus the Lord caused stones to shine in darkness, to give light unto men, women, and children, that they might not cross the great waters in darkness.

4 And it came to pass that when they had prepared all manner of food, that thereby they might subsist upon the water, and also food for their flocks and herds, and whatsoever beast or animal or fowl that they should carry with them—and it came to pass that when they had done all these things they got aboard of their vessels or barges, and set forth into the sea, commending themselves unto the Lord their God.

5 And it came to pass that the Lord God caused that there should be a furious wind blow upon the face of the waters, towards the promised land; and thus they were tossed upon the waves of the sea before the wind.

6 And it came to pass that they were many times buried in the depths of the sea, because of the mountain waves which broke upon them, and also the great and terrible tempests which were caused by the fierceness of the wind.

7 And it came to pass that when they were buried in the deep there was no water that could hurt

---

2 And behold, ye may be privileged that ye may show the plates unto those who shall assist to bring forth this work;

3 And unto three shall they be shown by the power of God; wherefore they shall know of a surety that these things are true.

4 And in the mouth of three witnesses shall these things be established; and the testimony of three, and this work, in the which shall be shown forth the power of God and also his word, of which the Father, and the Son, and the Holy Ghost bear record—and all this shall stand as a testimony against the world at the last day.

5 And if it so be that they repent and come unto the Father in the name of Jesus, they shall be received into the kingdom of God.

6 And now, if I have no authority for these things, judge ye; for ye shall know that I have authority when ye shall see me, and we shall stand before God at the last day. Amen.

◊ Ether 5 is a unique chapter in that it is written directly to Joseph Smith. Moroni knew at some future point a prophet would receive this record, and in Ether 5 he is giving instructions to that prophet regarding the sealed portion of the book and also who would be privileged to view the plates. Consider discussing with the class what such an experience may have been like for both Moroni and Joseph.

Teaching Tips from Prophets' Lips "It is that each person must learn the doctrines of the gospel for himself. No one else can do it for him. Each person stands alone where gospel scholarship is concerned; each has access to the same scriptures and is entitled to the guidance of the same Holy Spirit; each must pay the price set by a Divine Providence if he is to gain the pearl of great price" (Bruce R. McConkie, "Finding Answers to Gospel Questions," in *Charge to Religious Educators*, 3rd ed. [1994], 80).

Notes

them, their vessels being tight like unto a dish, and also they were tight like unto the ark of Noah; therefore when they were encompassed about by many waters they did cry unto the Lord, and he did bring them forth again upon the top of the waters.

8 And it came to pass that the wind did never cease to blow towards the promised land while they were upon the waters; and thus they were driven forth before the wind.

9 And they did sing praises unto the Lord; yea, the brother of Jared did sing praises unto the Lord, and he did thank and praise the Lord all the day long; and when the night came, they did not cease to praise the Lord.

10 And thus they were driven forth; and no monster of the sea could break them, neither whale that could mar them; and they did have light continually, whether it was above the water or under the water.

11 And thus they were driven forth, three hundred and forty and four days upon the water.

12 And they did land upon the shore of the promised land. And when they had set their feet upon the shores of the promised land they bowed themselves down upon the face of the land, and did humble themselves before the Lord, and did shed tears of joy before the Lord, because of the multitude of his tender mercies over them.

vv. 1–12

Compare the Jaredites' journey across the sea with the Nephites' journey across the sea. Consider using the following chart to compare the two journeys. Put this chart on the board or make a similar handout.

Jaredite Journey—Ether 6:1–12	Nephite Journey—1 Nephi 18:5–23

Invite class members to look for answers to the following questions to facilitate the chart completion.

- *How long did the journeys take (if recorded)?*
- *What did they do as they reached the promised land?*
- *What obstacles did they overcome to arrive at their destination?*
- *What was the role of the Lord in their journey?*

Apply: *What do these journeys teach us about our journey back to our Heavenly Father—"our promised land"?*

13 And it came to pass that they went forth upon the face of the land, and began to till the earth.

14 And Jared had four sons; and they were called Jacom, and Gilgah, and Mahah, and Orihah.

15 And the brother of Jared also begat sons and daughters.

16 And the friends of Jared and his brother were in number about twenty and two souls; and they also begat sons and daughters before they came to the promised land; and therefore they began to be many.

17 And they were taught to walk humbly before the Lord; and they were also taught from on high.

18 And it came to pass that they began to spread upon the face of the land, and to multiply and to till the earth; and they did wax strong in the land.

19 And the brother of Jared began to be old, and saw that he must soon go down to the grave; wherefore he said unto Jared: Let us gather together our people that we may number them, that we may know of them what they will desire of us before we go down to our graves.

20 And accordingly the people were gathered together. Now the number of the sons and the daughters of the brother of Jared were twenty and two souls; and the number of sons and daughters of Jared were twelve, he having four sons.

Notes

21 And it came to pass that they did number their people; and after that they had numbered them, they did desire of them the things which they would that they should do before they went down to their graves.

22 And it came to pass that the people desired of them that they should anoint one of their sons to be a king over them.

23 And now behold, this was grievous unto them. And the brother of Jared said unto them: Surely this thing leadeth into captivity.

24 But Jared said unto his brother: Suffer them that they may have a king. And therefore he said unto them: Choose ye out from among our sons a king, even whom ye will.

25 And it came to pass that they chose even the firstborn of the brother of Jared; and his name was Pagag. And it came to pass that he refused and would not be their king. And the people would that his father should constrain him, but his father would not; and he commanded them that they should constrain no man to be their king.

26 And it came to pass that they chose all the brothers of Pagag, and they would not.

27 And it came to pass that neither would the sons of Jared, even all save it were one; and Orihah was anointed to be king over the people.

28 And he began to reign, and the people began to prosper; and they became exceedingly rich.

29 And it came to pass that Jared died, and his brother also.

30 And it came to pass that Orihah did walk humbly before the Lord, and did remember how great things the Lord had done for his father, and also taught his people how great things the Lord had done for their fathers.

vv. 21–30 Having a king will lead to captivity.

⚡ Write on the board as many different forms of government you can think of, such as anarchy, democracy, dictatorship, socialism, communism, and fascism. Ask, *What have we learned about the role of government from the Book of Mormon?*

🔎 Read verses 21–30 and look for the following:
- *What type of government did the Jaredites desire?*
- *Whose idea was it to have a king?*
- *What does the Brother of Jared state will happen if they have a king, according to verse 23?*

❓ Analyze: *Why do you think the role of government is so important to the Lord?*

🔎 Direct the class to Doctrine and Covenants 101:77–80 and ask, *What does this scripture teach us about how the Lord feels about the role of government?*

Index Topics: government, mortal journey

ETHER 7

Shule Prevails in Righteousness

1–13, Corihor and Shule, the sons of Kib, create rival kingdoms but Shule prevails and reigns in righteousness; 14–21, The kingdom of Cohor, the nephew of Shule, is also defeated; 22–27, The people revile against the prophets but Shule gives power to the prophets to preach, and the people repent.

1 And it came to pass that Orihah did execute judgment upon the land in righteousness all his days, whose days were exceedingly many.

2 And he begat sons and daughters; yea, he begat thirty and one, among whom were twenty and three sons.

3 And it came to pass that he also begat Kib in his old age. And it came to pass that Kib reigned in his stead; and Kib begat Corihor.

4 And when Corihor was thirty and two years old he rebelled against his father, and went over and

Notes

dwelt in the land of Nehor; and he begat sons and daughters, and they became exceedingly fair; wherefore Corihor drew away many people after him.

v. 4 Beware of the deceitfulness of beauty.

🔎 *In verse 4, look for why wicked Corihor is able to draw so many people to him.*

❓ *How can outward beauty be deceptive?*

💬 Have your class consider the following quotes.

"Judge nothing by the appearance. The more beautiful the serpent, the more fatal its sting." –William Scott Downey

"That which is striking and beautiful is not always good, but that which is good is always beautiful." –Ninon de L'Enclos

❤ How does the Lord feel about outward appearances? Have your class find and read 1 Samuel 16:7.

5 And when he had gathered together an army he came up unto the land of Moron where the king dwelt, and took him captive, which brought to pass the saying of the brother of Jared that they would be brought into captivity.

6 Now the land of Moron, where the king dwelt, was near the land which is called Desolation by the Nephites.

7 And it came to pass that Kib dwelt in captivity, and his people under Corihor his son, until he became exceedingly old; nevertheless Kib begat Shule in his old age, while he was yet in captivity.

8 And it came to pass that Shule was angry with his brother; and Shule waxed strong, and became mighty as to the strength of a man; and he was also mighty in judgment.

9 Wherefore, he came to the hill Ephraim, and he did molten out of the hill, and made swords out of steel for those whom he had drawn away with him; and after he had armed them with swords he returned to the city Nehor, and gave battle unto his brother Corihor, by which means he obtained the kingdom and restored it unto his father Kib.

10 And now because of the thing which Shule had done, his father bestowed upon him the kingdom; therefore he began to reign in the stead of his father.

11 And it came to pass that he did execute judgment in righteousness; and he did spread his kingdom upon all the face of the land, for the people had become exceedingly numerous.

12 And it came to pass that Shule also begat many sons and daughters.

13 And Corihor repented of the many evils which he had done; wherefore Shule gave him power in his kingdom.

14 And it came to pass that Corihor had many sons and daughters. And among the sons of Corihor there was one whose name was Noah.

15 And it came to pass that Noah rebelled against Shule, the king, and also his father Corihor, and drew away Cohor his brother, and also all his brethren and many of the people.

16 And he gave battle unto Shule, the king, in which he did obtain the land of their first inheritance; and he became a king over that part of the land.

17 And it came to pass that he gave battle again unto Shule, the king; and he took Shule, the king, and carried him away captive into Moron.

18 And it came to pass as he was about to put him to death, the sons of Shule crept into the house of Noah by night and slew him, and broke down the door of the prison and brought out their father, and placed him upon his throne in his own kingdom.

19 Wherefore, the son of Noah did build up his kingdom in his stead; nevertheless they did not gain power any more over Shule the king, and the people who were under the reign of Shule the king did prosper exceedingly and wax great.

Notes

20 And the country was divided; and there were two kingdoms, the kingdom of Shule, and the kingdom of Cohor, the son of Noah.

21 And Cohor, the son of Noah, caused that his people should give battle unto Shule, in which Shule did beat them and did slay Cohor.

22 And now Cohor had a son who was called Nimrod; and Nimrod gave up the kingdom of Cohor unto Shule, and he did gain favor in the eyes of Shule; wherefore Shule did bestow great favors upon him, and he did do in the kingdom of Shule according to his desires.

23 And also in the reign of Shule there came prophets among the people, who were sent from the Lord, prophesying that the wickedness and idolatry of the people was bringing a curse upon the land, and they should be destroyed if they did not repent.

24 And it came to pass that the people did revile against the prophets, and did mock them. And it came to pass that king Shule did execute judgment against all those who did revile against the prophets.

25 And he did execute a law throughout all the land, which gave power unto the prophets that they should go whithersoever they would; and by this cause the people were brought unto repentance.

26 And because the people did repent of their iniquities and idolatries the Lord did spare them, and they began to prosper again in the land. And it came to pass that Shule begat sons and daughters in his old age.

27 And there were no more wars in the days of Shule; and he remembered the great things that the Lord had done for his fathers in bringing them across the great deep into the promised land; wherefore he did execute judgment in righteousness all his days.

vv. 23–27 When government allows the preaching of the gospel, society is blessed.

Look for what role King Shule played in preaching the gospel during his time.

Why is the protection of religious freedoms beneficial to a society?

Have class members note Ether 11:5–6 with these verses. Look up the verses and compare and contrast them with what King Shule did in his day.

Let class members know that it is a role of government to ensure that religious freedoms are protected. While every country has its unique government and laws, each should strive toward a protection of freedom of worship. Invite class members to ponder the significance of Article of Faith 11 in connection with this chapter. Then, express gratitude for the ability to meet as a class and discuss religious principles. Express your gratitude for living in a time and place where religious freedom is largely protected.

Teaching Tips from Prophets' Lips "The skilled teacher does not want students who leave the class talking about how magnificent and unusual the teacher is. This teacher wants students who leave talking about how magnificent the gospel is!" (Virginia H. Pearce, *Ensign,* Nov. 1996, 12).

Index Topics: government, prophets

ETHER 8

Secret Combinations among the Jaredites

1–10, Jared's kingdom is overthrown, he mourns his loss, and his daughter suggests to search out the ancient, secret plans of gaining power and glory; 11–18, Jared, his daughter, and Akish secretly conspire to kill the king, and thus secret combinations are introduced among the Jaredites; 19–26, Moroni denounces secret combinations as being of the devil.

Notes

1 And it came to pass that he begat Omer, and Omer reigned in his stead. And Omer begat Jared; and Jared begat sons and daughters.

2 And Jared rebelled against his father, and came and dwelt in the land of Heth. And it came to pass that he did flatter many people, because of his cunning words, until he had gained the half of the kingdom.

3 And when he had gained the half of the kingdom he gave battle unto his father, and he did carry away his father into captivity, and did make him serve in captivity;

4 And now, in the days of the reign of Omer he was in captivity the half of his days. And it came to pass that he begat sons and daughters, among whom were Esrom and Coriantumr;

5 And they were exceedingly angry because of the doings of Jared their brother, insomuch that they did raise an army and gave battle unto Jared. And it came to pass that they did give battle unto him by night.

6 And it came to pass that when they had slain the army of Jared they were about to slay him also; and he pled with them that they would not slay him, and he would give up the kingdom unto his father. And it came to pass that they did grant unto him his life.

7 And now Jared became exceedingly sorrowful because of the loss of the kingdom, for he had set his heart upon the kingdom and upon the glory of the world.

8 Now the daughter of Jared being exceedingly expert, and seeing the sorrows of her father, thought to devise a plan whereby she could redeem the kingdom unto her father.

9 Now the daughter of Jared was exceedingly fair. And it came to pass that she did talk with her father, and said unto him: Whereby hath my father so much sorrow? Hath he not read the record which our fathers brought across the great deep? Behold, is there not an account concerning them of old, that they by their secret plans did obtain kingdoms and great glory?

10 And now, therefore, let my father send for Akish, the son of Kimnor; and behold, I am fair, and I will dance before him, and I will please him, that he will desire me to wife; wherefore if he shall desire of thee that ye shall give unto him me to wife, then shall ye say: I will give her if ye will bring unto me the head of my father, the king.

vv. 1–10 The desire for power causes people to seek out evil things.

- Consider summarizing verses 1–10 in your own words or ask a class member to prepare a brief summary of the storyline of the first ten verses.

- *Look for why Jared's daughter suggests seeking out the secret plans "concerning them of old" in verses 7–10.*

- Analyze: Discuss with class members how the desire for power causes people to do evil.

- Ezra Taft Benson taught, "Selfishness is one of the more common faces of pride. 'How everything affects me' is the center of all that matters—self-conceit, self-pity, worldly self-fulfillment, self-gratification, and self-seeking. Pride results in secret combinations that are built up to get power, gain, and glory of the world. (See Helaman 7:5; Ether 8:9, 16, 22–23; Moses 5:31.) This fruit of the sin of pride, namely secret combinations, brought down both the Jaredite and the Nephite civilizations and has been and will yet be the cause of the fall of many nations" (Ezra Taft Benson, "Beware of Pride," *Ensign*, May 1989, 6).

11 And now Omer was a friend to Akish; wherefore, when Jared had sent for Akish, the daughter of Jared danced before him that she pleased him, insomuch that he desired her to wife. And it came to pass that he said unto Jared: Give her unto me to wife.

Notes

12 And Jared said unto him: I will give her unto you, if ye will bring unto me the head of my father, the king.

13 And it came to pass that Akish gathered in unto the house of Jared all his kinsfolk, and said unto them: Will ye swear unto me that ye will be faithful unto me in the thing which I shall desire of you?

14 And it came to pass that they all sware unto him, by the God of heaven, and also by the heavens, and also by the earth, and by their heads, that whoso should vary from the assistance which Akish desired should lose his head; and whoso should divulge whatsoever thing Akish made known unto them, the same should lose his life.

15 And it came to pass that thus they did agree with Akish. And Akish did administer unto them the oaths which were given by them of old who also sought power, which had been handed down even from Cain, who was a murderer from the beginning.

16 And they were kept up by the power of the devil to administer these oaths unto the people, to keep them in darkness, to help such as sought power to gain power, and to murder, and to plunder, and to lie, and to commit all manner of wickedness and whoredoms.

17 And it was the daughter of Jared who put it into his heart to search up these things of old; and Jared put it into the heart of Akish; wherefore, Akish administered it unto his kindred and friends, leading them away by fair promises to do whatsoever thing he desired.

18 And it came to pass that they formed a secret combination, even as they of old; which combination is most abominable and wicked above all, in the sight of God;

19 For the Lord worketh not in secret combinations, neither doth he will that man should shed blood, but in all things hath forbidden it, from the beginning of man.

vv. 11–19 Women can have great influence in the world.

⚡ Consider summarizing verses 11–19 in your own words, or ask a class member to prepare a brief summary of the storyline of these verses, or read all the verses aloud together.

🔎 *Beginning in verse 10, look for who instigated the secret combination plan.*

💬 Explain that a woman can have a very significant impact in the world. President James E. Faust, in speaking in the General Young Women's broadcast, taught about the important, positive role women can have by saying, "We frequently find that the influence of good women is underrated. It is an influence that is often subtle but yet has tremendous consequences. One woman can make a great difference for a whole nation. I cite two examples from the scriptures, one for evil and one for good. In the book of Ether, Jared's beautiful daughter enticed Akish to marry her through a seductive dance. Akish was to pay for her hand in marriage by murdering her grandfather, King Omer, so that her father could become the king. At her urging, Akish formed oath-bound secret combinations which caused the destruction of the Jaredite nation.

"On the other hand, Esther, a Jewess in the Old Testament, saved her people. When the Jews were in captivity, Esther was married to King Ahasuerus. The king signed a decree that all Jews were to be put to death. Esther's cousin Mordecai urged her to intercede with the king on behalf of her people by saying to her, 'Who knoweth whether thou art come to the kingdom for such a time as this?' (See Esther 4:14). Esther, at the peril of her own life, pled with the king that her people should be spared. The king listened to her entreaty, and they were saved. One woman can make a great difference, even for a nation.

"These are challenging times. I believe your spirits may have been reserved for these latter days; that you, like Esther, have come

Notes

to earth 'for such a time as this.' It may be that your most significant, everlasting achievements will be your righteous influence on others, that your divine feminine inner beauty and intuition will find expression in your quiet strength, gentleness, dignity, charm, graciousness, creativity, sensitivity, radiance, and spirituality. Enhance these sublime feminine gifts. They will make you appealing and even irresistible as you serve others as the handmaidens of God" ("The Virtues of Righteous Daughters of God," *Ensign*, May 2003, 111).

❤ Testify of the important, positive role women can play in society. Encourage class members to honor the virtue of womanhood.

20 And now I, Moroni, do not write the manner of their oaths and combinations, for it hath been made known unto me that they are had among all people, and they are had among the Lamanites.

21 And they have caused the destruction of this people of whom I am now speaking, and also the destruction of the people of Nephi.

22 And whatsoever nation shall uphold such secret combinations, to get power and gain, until they shall spread over the nation, behold, they shall be destroyed; for the Lord will not suffer that the blood of his saints, which shall be shed by them, shall always cry unto him from the ground for vengeance upon them and yet he avenge them not.

23 Wherefore, O ye Gentiles, it is wisdom in God that these things should be shown unto you, that thereby ye may repent of your sins, and suffer not that these murderous combinations shall get above you, which are built up to get power and gain—and the work, yea, even the work of destruction come upon you, yea, even the sword of the justice of the Eternal God shall fall upon you, to your overthrow and destruction if ye shall suffer these things to be.

24 Wherefore, the Lord commandeth you, when ye shall see these things come among you that ye shall awake to a sense of your awful situation, because of this secret combination which shall be among you; or wo be unto it, because of the blood of them who have been slain; for they cry from the dust for vengeance upon it, and also upon those who built it up.

25 For it cometh to pass that whoso buildeth it up seeketh to overthrow the freedom of all lands, nations, and countries; and it bringeth to pass the destruction of all people, for it is built up by the devil, who is the father of all lies; even that same liar who beguiled our first parents, yea, even that same liar who hath caused man to commit murder from the beginning; who hath hardened the hearts of men that they have murdered the prophets, and stoned them, and cast them out from the beginning.

26 Wherefore, I, Moroni, am commanded to write these things that evil may be done away, and that the time may come that Satan may have no power upon the hearts of the children of men, but that they may be persuaded to do good continually, that they may come unto the fountain of all righteousness and be saved.

vv. 20–26 Secret combinations are evil and overthrow the freedom of nations.

🔍 Read verses 20–26 with the class and look for what Moroni's conclusion is about secret combinations.

❓ Analyze: *In verse 22, Moroni warns about upholding secret combinations to get power and gain. What does this mean, and how do we as a nation and as individuals seek to not uphold these works?*

💡 Note Moroni's perspective as he is abridging this record. He has witnessed the destruction of his own people due to secret combinations and he is learning of the demise of the Jaredite nation as a result of secret combinations.

Notes

ETHER 9

The Cycle of Jaredite Righteousness and Wickedness

1–11, Omer is warned by God and flees from Akish who sought to kill him, Akish becomes king by killing Jared; 12–20, Omer is restored as king, and the people enjoy a period of peace and prosperity; 21–25, Various kings reign in righteousness; 26–35, The people fall into wickedness, are called to repentance by prophets, and are plagued with poisonous serpents.

Overarching Principle: When we are righteous, God blesses us; when we are wicked, God calls us to repentance.

- ⚡ To help teach why God calls people to repentance, bring an object that is clearly broken and display it in front of the class. Discuss together what options a person has with this object now that it is broken. Explain that one of the options would be to fix it. This can be related to people's wickedness and repentance—we are broken when we sin, and when God calls upon us to repent, He is trying to "fix" us. Ether 9 shows an example of how God tries to call His people to repentance.

1 And now I, Moroni, proceed with my record. Therefore, behold, it came to pass that because of the secret combinations of Akish and his friends, behold, they did overthrow the kingdom of Omer.

2 Nevertheless, the Lord was merciful unto Omer, and also to his sons and to his daughters who did not seek his destruction.

3 And the Lord warned Omer in a dream that he should depart out of the land; wherefore Omer departed out of the land with his family, and traveled many days, and came over and passed by the hill of Shim, and came over by the place where the Nephites were destroyed, and from thence eastward, and came to a place which was called Ablom, by the seashore, and there he pitched his tent, and also his sons and his daughters, and all his household, save it were Jared and his family.

4 And it came to pass that Jared was anointed king over the people, by the hand of wickedness; and he gave unto Akish his daughter to wife.

5 And it came to pass that Akish sought the life of his father-in-law; and he applied unto those whom he had sworn by the oath of the ancients, and they obtained the head of his father-in-law, as he sat upon his throne, giving audience to his people.

6 For so great had been the spreading of this wicked and secret society that it had corrupted the hearts of all the people; therefore Jared was murdered upon his throne, and Akish reigned in his stead.

7 And it came to pass that Akish began to be jealous of his son, therefore he shut him up in prison, and kept him upon little or no food until he had suffered death.

8 And now the brother of him that suffered death, (and his name was Nimrah) was angry with his father because of that which his father had done unto his brother.

9 And it came to pass that Nimrah gathered together a small number of men, and fled out of the land, and came over and dwelt with Omer.

10 And it came to pass that Akish begat other sons, and they won the hearts of the people, notwithstanding they had sworn unto him to do all manner of iniquity according to that which he desired.

11 Now the people of Akish were desirous for gain, even as Akish was desirous for power; wherefore, the sons of Akish did offer them money, by which means they drew away the more part of the people after them.

12 And there began to be a war between the sons of Akish and Akish, which lasted for the space of many years, yea, unto the destruction of nearly

Notes

all the people of the kingdom, yea, even all, save it were thirty souls, and they who fled with the house of Omer.

13 Wherefore, Omer was restored again to the land of his inheritance.

vv. 1–13 Akish reigns in wickedness.

💡 Consider summarizing verses 1–13 in your own words with class members. Note that these verses are the conclusion of the story from Ether 8.

14 And it came to pass that Omer began to be old; nevertheless, in his old age he begat Emer; and he anointed Emer to be king to reign in his stead.

15 And after that he had anointed Emer to be king he saw peace in the land for the space of two years, and he died, having seen exceedingly many days, which were full of sorrow. And it came to pass that Emer did reign in his stead, and did fill the steps of his father.

16 And the Lord began again to take the curse from off the land, and the house of Emer did prosper exceedingly under the reign of Emer; and in the space of sixty and two years they had become exceedingly strong, insomuch that they became exceedingly rich—

17 Having all manner of fruit, and of grain, and of silks, and of fine linen, and of gold, and of silver, and of precious things;

18 And also all manner of cattle, of oxen, and cows, and of sheep, and of swine, and of goats, and also many other kinds of animals which were useful for the food of man.

19 And they also had horses, and asses, and there were elephants and cureloms and cumoms; all of which were useful unto man, and more especially the elephants and cureloms and cumoms.

20 And thus the Lord did pour out his blessings upon this land, which was choice above all other lands; and he commanded that whoso should possess the land should possess it unto the Lord, or they should be destroyed when they were ripened in iniquity; for upon such, saith the Lord: I will pour out the fulness of my wrath.

21 And Emer did execute judgment in righteousness all his days, and he begat many sons and daughters; and he begat Coriantum, and he anointed Coriantum to reign in his stead.

22 And after he had anointed Coriantum to reign in his stead he lived four years, and he saw peace in the land; yea, and he even saw the Son of Righteousness, and did rejoice and glory in his day; and he died in peace.

23 And it came to pass that Coriantum did walk in the steps of his father, and did build many mighty cities, and did administer that which was good unto his people in all his days. And it came to pass that he had no children even until he was exceedingly old.

24 And it came to pass that his wife died, being an hundred and two years old. And it came to pass that Coriantum took to wife, in his old age, a young maid, and begat sons and daughters; wherefore he lived until he was an hundred and forty and two years old.

25 And it came to pass that he begat Com, and Com reigned in his stead; and he reigned forty and nine years, and he begat Heth; and he also begat other sons and daughters.

26 And the people had spread again over all the face of the land, and there began again to be an exceedingly great wickedness upon the face of the land, and Heth began to embrace the secret plans again of old, to destroy his father.

27 And it came to pass that he did dethrone his father, for he slew him with his own sword; and he did reign in his stead.

28 And there came prophets in the land again, crying repentance unto them—that they must prepare the way of the Lord or there should come a curse upon the face of the land; yea, even there should be a great famine, in which they should be destroyed if they did not repent.

Notes

29 But the people believed not the words of the prophets, but they cast them out; and some of them they cast into pits and left them to perish. And it came to pass that they did all these things according to the commandment of the king, Heth.

30 And it came to pass that there began to be a great dearth upon the land, and the inhabitants began to be destroyed exceedingly fast because of the dearth, for there was no rain upon the face of the earth.

31 And there came forth poisonous serpents also upon the face of the land, and did poison many people. And it came to pass that their flocks began to flee before the poisonous serpents, towards the land southward, which was called by the Nephites Zarahemla.

32 And it came to pass that there were many of them which did perish by the way; nevertheless, there were some which fled into the land southward.

33 And it came to pass that the Lord did cause the serpents that they should pursue them no more, but that they should hedge up the way that the people could not pass, that whoso should attempt to pass might fall by the poisonous serpents.

34 And it came to pass that the people did follow the course of the beasts, and did devour the carcasses of them which fell by the way, until they had devoured them all. Now when the people saw that they must perish they began to repent of their iniquities and cry unto the Lord.

35 And it came to pass that when they had humbled themselves sufficiently before the Lord he did send rain upon the face of the earth; and the people began to revive again, and there began to be fruit in the north countries, and in all the countries round about. And the Lord did show forth his power unto them in preserving them from famine.

vv. 14–35 When we are righteous, God blesses us; when we are wicked, God calls us to repentance.

⚡ Refer to the object lesson idea at the beginning of this chapter.

🔎 Break class members into two groups. Invite one group to read verses 14–25 and the other group to read 26–35. Invite each group to look for the following three things:

How are the people being either righteous or wicked?

What does the Lord do as a result of their actions?

Which verse or phrase is the most important or applicable for us?

❓ Analyze: Once class members have read their assigned verses and answered the three questions, begin to analyze the contrast between what the Lord does when people are righteous and what He does when they are wicked.

♥ Refer back to the object lesson and encourage class members to change what needs to be changed in their lives in order to receive blessings from the Lord.

> **Teaching Tips from Prophets' Lips** "Imagine hundreds of thousands of classrooms every Sunday, each with a teacher who understands that 'the learning has to be done by the pupil.' Therefore it is the pupil who has to be put into action. When a teacher takes the spotlight, becomes the star of the show, does all the talking, and otherwise takes over all of the activity, it is almost certain that he is interfering with the learning of the class members" (Asahel D. Woodruff, *Teaching the Gospel* (1962), 37).

ETHER 10

Succession of the Jaredite Kings

1–34, Various Jaredite kings rule—righteousness and wickedness increase and decrease in the land—some kings rule in captivity—conflict is nearly continuous.

Notes

ETHER 10

Overarching Principle: vv. 1–34 Jaredite kings rule in succession—some are righteous, others are wicked.

✋ Prior to class, prepare 12 large sheets of paper. On the back of each piece write one of the kings (or groups of kings) as found below. Divide the papers amongst the class as evenly as possible (12 groups of one or two are ideal, but you may double up on assigned papers if your class is small). Class members will read Ether 10:1–34 looking for their king or group of kings. Using the information from the scriptures, they will then flip the page over (so the name is on the back) and draw a picture depicting their king. You may choose to have a few standard symbols such as handcuffs or a chain for captivity, smiles or frowns for righteousness or wickedness, etc. The more detail that is included in the drawing, the better the activity will go. When class members have completed their drawings, display them in the front of the room. Then, invite the other class members to guess each king using the scriptures as their clues. Reveal the names on the backed as needed. Discuss any interesting details as you see appropriate.

Shez 1

Shez 2

Riplakish

Morianton

Kim

Levi

Corom

Kish

Lib

Hearthom

Heth, Aaron, Amnigaddah, and Coriantum

Com

1 And it came to pass that Shez, who was a descendant of Heth—for Heth had perished by the famine, and all his household save it were Shez—wherefore, Shez began to build up again a broken people.

2 And it came to pass that Shez did remember the destruction of his fathers, and he did build up a righteous kingdom; for he remembered what the Lord had done in bringing Jared and his brother across the deep; and he did walk in the ways of the Lord; and he begat sons and daughters.

3 And his eldest son, whose name was Shez, did rebel against him; nevertheless, Shez was smitten by the hand of a robber, because of his exceeding riches, which brought peace again unto his father.

4 And it came to pass that his father did build up many cities upon the face of the land, and the people began again to spread over all the face of the land. And Shez did live to an exceedingly old age; and he begat Riplakish. And he died, and Riplakish reigned in his stead.

5 And it came to pass that Riplakish did not do that which was right in the sight of the Lord, for he did have many wives and concubines, and did lay that upon men's shoulders which was grievous to be borne; yea, he did tax them with heavy taxes; and with the taxes he did build many spacious buildings.

6 And he did erect him an exceedingly beautiful throne; and he did build many prisons, and whoso would not be subject unto taxes he did cast into prison; and whoso was not able to pay taxes he did cast into prison; and he did cause that they should labor continually for their support; and whoso refused to labor he did cause to be put to death.

7 Wherefore he did obtain all his fine work, yea, even his fine gold he did cause to be refined in prison; and all manner of fine workmanship he did cause to be wrought in prison. And it came to pass that he did afflict the people with his whoredoms and abominations.

8 And when he had reigned for the space of forty and two years the people did rise up in rebellion

Notes

against him; and there began to be war again in the land, insomuch that Riplakish was killed, and his descendants were driven out of the land.

9 And it came to pass after the space of many years, Morianton, (he being a descendant of Riplakish) gathered together an army of outcasts, and went forth and gave battle unto the people; and he gained power over many cities; and the war became exceedingly sore, and did last for the space of many years; and he did gain power over all the land, and did establish himself king over all the land.

10 And after that he had established himself king he did ease the burden of the people, by which he did gain favor in the eyes of the people, and they did anoint him to be their king.

11 And he did do justice unto the people, but not unto himself because of his many whoredoms; wherefore he was cut off from the presence of the Lord.

12 And it came to pass that Morianton built up many cities, and the people became exceedingly rich under his reign, both in buildings, and in gold and silver, and in raising grain, and in flocks, and herds, and such things which had been restored unto them.

13 And Morianton did live to an exceedingly great age, and then he begat Kim; and Kim did reign in the stead of his father; and he did reign eight years, and his father died. And it came to pass that Kim did not reign in righteousness, wherefore he was not favored of the Lord.

14 And his brother did rise up in rebellion against him, by which he did bring him into captivity; and he did remain in captivity all his days; and he begat sons and daughters in captivity, and in his old age he begat Levi; and he died.

15 And it came to pass that Levi did serve in captivity after the death of his father, for the space of forty and two years. And he did make war against the king of the land, by which he did obtain unto himself the kingdom.

16 And after he had obtained unto himself the kingdom he did that which was right in the sight of the Lord; and the people did prosper in the land; and he did live to a good old age, and begat sons and daughters; and he also begat Corom, whom he anointed king in his stead.

17 And it came to pass that Corom did that which was good in the sight of the Lord all his days; and he begat many sons and daughters; and after he had seen many days he did pass away, even like unto the rest of the earth; and Kish reigned in his stead.

18 And it came to pass that Kish passed away also, and Lib reigned in his stead.

19 And it came to pass that Lib also did that which was good in the sight of the Lord. And in the days of Lib the poisonous serpents were destroyed. Wherefore they did go into the land southward, to hunt food for the people of the land, for the land was covered with animals of the forest. And Lib also himself became a great hunter.

20 And they built a great city by the narrow neck of land, by the place where the sea divides the land.

21 And they did preserve the land southward for a wilderness, to get game. And the whole face of the land northward was covered with inhabitants.

22 And they were exceedingly industrious, and they did buy and sell and traffic one with another, that they might get gain.

23 And they did work in all manner of ore, and they did make gold, and silver, and iron, and brass, and all manner of metals; and they did dig it out of the earth; wherefore, they did cast up mighty heaps of earth to get ore, of gold, and of silver, and of iron, and of copper. And they did work all manner of fine work.

24 And they did have silks, and fine-twined linen; and they did work all manner of cloth, that they might clothe themselves from their nakedness.

25 And they did make all manner of tools to till

Notes

the earth, both to plow and to sow, to reap and to hoe, and also to thrash.

26 And they did make all manner of tools with which they did work their beasts.

27 And they did make all manner of weapons of war. And they did work all manner of work of exceedingly curious workmanship.

28 And never could be a people more blessed than were they, and more prospered by the hand of the Lord. And they were in a land that was choice above all lands, for the Lord had spoken it.

29 And it came to pass that Lib did live many years, and begat sons and daughters; and he also begat Hearthom.

30 And it came to pass that Hearthom reigned in the stead of his father. And when Hearthom had reigned twenty and four years, behold, the kingdom was taken away from him. And he served many years in captivity, yea, even all the remainder of his days.

31 And he begat Heth, and Heth lived in captivity all his days. And Heth begat Aaron, and Aaron dwelt in captivity all his days; and he begat Amnigaddah, and Amnigaddah also dwelt in captivity all his days; and he begat Coriantum, and Coriantum dwelt in captivity all his days; and he begat Com.

32 And it came to pass that Com drew away the half of the kingdom. And he reigned over the half of the kingdom forty and two years; and he went to battle against the king, Amgid, and they fought for the space of many years, during which time Com gained power over Amgid, and obtained power over the remainder of the kingdom.

33 And in the days of Com there began to be robbers in the land; and they adopted the old plans, and administered oaths after the manner of the ancients, and sought again to destroy the kingdom.

34 Now Com did fight against them much; nevertheless, he did not prevail against them.

Notes

ETHER 11

Repent or Utter Destruction

1–8, Prophets prophesy of the destruction of the people except they should repent; the people begin to repent; 9–22, The prophets again warn the people to repent, but their words are rejected.

1 And there came also in the days of Com many prophets, and prophesied of the destruction of that great people except they should repent, and turn unto the Lord, and forsake their murders and wickedness.

2 And it came to pass that the prophets were rejected by the people, and they fled unto Com for protection, for the people sought to destroy them.

3 And they prophesied unto Com many things; and he was blessed in all the remainder of his days.

4 And he lived to a good old age, and begat Shiblom; and Shiblom reigned in his stead. And the brother of Shiblom rebelled against him, and there began to be an exceedingly great war in all the land.

5 And it came to pass that the brother of Shiblom caused that all the prophets who prophesied of the destruction of the people should be put to death;

v. 5 Supporting or rejecting the prophets.

○ Compare Ether 11:5 to Ether 7:23–27 for what results when a king supports and protects the prophets—even though the people are wicked.

6 And there was great calamity in all the land, for they had testified that a great curse should come upon the land, and also upon the people, and that there should be a great destruction among them, such an one as never had been upon the face of the earth, and their bones should become as heaps of earth upon the face of the land except they should repent of their wickedness.

7 And they hearkened not unto the voice of the Lord, because of their wicked combinations; wherefore, there began to be wars and contentions in all the land, and also many famines and pestilences, insomuch that there was a great destruction, such an one as never had been known upon the face of the earth; and all this came to pass in the days of Shiblom.

8 And the people began to repent of their iniquity; and inasmuch as they did the Lord did have mercy on them.

9 And it came to pass that Shiblom was slain, and Seth was brought into captivity, and did dwell in captivity all his days.

10 And it came to pass that Ahah, his son, did obtain the kingdom; and he did reign over the people all his days. And he did do all manner of iniquity in his days, by which he did cause the shedding of much blood; and few were his days.

11 And Ethem, being a descendant of Ahah, did obtain the kingdom; and he also did do that which was wicked in his days.

12 And it came to pass that in the days of Ethem there came many prophets, and prophesied again unto the people; yea, they did prophesy that the Lord would utterly destroy them from off the face of the earth except they repented of their iniquities.

13 And it came to pass that the people hardened their hearts, and would not hearken unto their words; and the prophets mourned and withdrew from among the people.

14 And it came to pass that Ethem did execute judgment in wickedness all his days; and he begat Moron. And it came to pass that Moron did reign in his stead; and Moron did that which was wicked before the Lord.

15 And it came to pass that there arose a rebellion among the people, because of that secret combination which was built up to get power and gain; and there arose a mighty man among them in iniquity, and gave battle unto Moron, in which he did overthrow the half of the kingdom; and he did maintain the half of the kingdom for many years.

16 And it came to pass that Moron did overthrow him, and did obtain the kingdom again.

17 And it came to pass that there arose another mighty man; and he was a descendant of the brother of Jared.

18 And it came to pass that he did overthrow Moron and obtain the kingdom; wherefore, Moron dwelt in captivity all the remainder of his days; and he begat Coriantor.

19 And it came to pass that Coriantor dwelt in captivity all his days.

20 And in the days of Coriantor there also came many prophets, and prophesied of great and marvelous things, and cried repentance unto the people, and except they should repent the Lord God would execute judgment against them to their utter destruction;

21 And that the Lord God would send or bring forth another people to possess the land, by his power, after the manner by which he brought their fathers.

22 And they did reject all the words of the prophets, because of their secret society and wicked abominations.

23 And it came to pass that Coriantor begat Ether, and he died, having dwelt in captivity all his days.

vv. 1–23 Our greatest safety comes as we listen to the prophets of God.

⚡ Write the names of all the kings that are listed in this chapter on the board and have the class identify which of these kings were righteous. The kings include: Com, Shiblom, Seth, Ahah, Ethem, Moron, and Coriantor. Inform the class that Ether 11 includes many generations of kings and covers a vast amount of years.

🔍 What do you think is the central message

Notes

of this chapter? Depending on the circumstances, you could invite class members to look in the following verses to answer this question: 1, 6, 12, and 20.

❓ Analyze:
- *How many times were the people warned that they needed to repent?*
- *Why did the Lord not destroy them after they did not listen to Him in the first generation?*
- *What does this teach us about the lord?*

❓ Apply: *How does this chapter apply to us when we are surrounded by wickedness, yet there are many that are righteous as well?*

♥ Testify that as we listen to the Lord's prophets, we will live in safety.

> **Teaching Tips from Prophets' Lips** "A teacher's goal is greater than just delivering a lecture about truth. It is to invite the Spirit and use techniques that will enhance the possibility that the learner will discover the truth [and] be motivated to apply it" (Virginia H. Pearce, *Ensign*, Nov. 1996, 12).

Index Topics: prophets

ETHER 12

"Seek This Jesus"

1–5, Ether invites all to repent through faith in the Lord; 6–22, Moroni teaches that faith is things hoped for and not seen; for you receive no witness until after the trial of your faith; 23–28, The Lord will make weak things become strong through our humility and His grace; 29–41, Moroni highlights the importance of charity and invites all to seek Christ.

1 And it came to pass that the days of Ether were in the days of Coriantumr; and Coriantumr was king over all the land.

2 And Ether was a prophet of the Lord; wherefore Ether came forth in the days of Coriantumr, and began to prophesy unto the people, for he could not be restrained because of the Spirit of the Lord which was in him.

3 For he did cry from the morning, even until the going down of the sun, exhorting the people to believe in God unto repentance lest they should be destroyed, saying unto them that by faith all things are fulfilled—

4 Wherefore, whoso believeth in God might with surety hope for a better world, yea, even a place at the right hand of God, which hope cometh of faith, maketh an anchor to the souls of men, which would make them sure and steadfast, always abounding in good works, being led to glorify God.

5 And it came to pass that Ether did prophesy great and marvelous things unto the people, which they did not believe, because they saw them not.

6 And now, I, Moroni, would speak somewhat concerning these things; I would show unto the world that faith is things which are hoped for and not seen; wherefore, dispute not because ye see not, for ye receive no witness until after the trial of your faith.

7 For it was by faith that Christ showed himself unto our fathers, after he had risen from the dead; and he showed not himself unto them until after they had faith in him; wherefore, it must needs be that some had faith in him, for he showed himself not unto the world.

8 But because of the faith of men he has shown himself unto the world, and glorified the name of the Father, and prepared a way that thereby others might be partakers of the heavenly gift, that they might hope for those things which they have not seen.

9 Wherefore, ye may also have hope, and be partakers of the gift, if ye will but have faith.

10 Behold it was by faith that they of old were called after the holy order of God.

11 Wherefore, by faith was the law of Moses given. But in the gift of his Son hath God prepared a

Notes

more excellent way; and it is by faith that it hath been fulfilled.

12 For if there be no faith among the children of men God can do no miracle among them; wherefore, he showed not himself until after their faith.

13 Behold, it was the faith of Alma and Amulek that caused the prison to tumble to the earth.

14 Behold, it was the faith of Nephi and Lehi that wrought the change upon the Lamanites, that they were baptized with fire and with the Holy Ghost.

15 Behold, it was the faith of Ammon and his brethren which wrought so great a miracle among the Lamanites.

16 Yea, and even all they who wrought miracles wrought them by faith, even those who were before Christ and also those who were after.

17 And it was by faith that the three disciples obtained a promise that they should not taste of death; and they obtained not the promise until after their faith.

18 And neither at any time hath any wrought miracles until after their faith; wherefore they first believed in the Son of God.

19 And there were many whose faith was so exceedingly strong, even before Christ came, who could not be kept from within the veil, but truly saw with their eyes the things which they had beheld with an eye of faith, and they were glad.

20 And behold, we have seen in this record that one of these was the brother of Jared; for so great was his faith in God, that when God put forth his finger he could not hide it from the sight of the brother of Jared, because of his word which he had spoken unto him, which word he had obtained by faith.

21 And after the brother of Jared had beheld the finger of the Lord, because of the promise which the brother of Jared had obtained by faith, the Lord could not withhold anything from his sight; wherefore he showed him all things, for he could no longer be kept without the veil.

22 And it is by faith that my fathers have obtained the promise that these things should come unto their brethren through the Gentiles; therefore the Lord hath commanded me, yea, even Jesus Christ.

vv. 1–22 We exercise faith when we act on true things that are hoped for and not seen.

- (This teaching suggestion will need to be done the class before.) Ask a class member to prepare to share an experience related to Ether 12:6. Ask that person to study the verse and share an experience accordingly. Depending on circumstances, you may need to give more specific directions. Explain that as you start class the next time, you will ask that person to share his or her experience.

- Put the following verses on the board: 3, 4, 6, 12, and 27 under the heading FAITH. Invite every class member to study these verses and write down every truth or doctrine that Ether and Moroni teach about faith. (You may want to point out that verses 3 and 4 were taught by Ether and verses 6, 12, and 27 were taught by Moroni.) When class members have completed their study, ask them to write down one concise statement about what they learned or relearned about the concept of faith. Encourage class members to then share with each other or with the class what they learned.

- Consider asking the following questions as you discuss the doctrine of faith: *From what you learned, why would you say that faith is the first principles of the gospel? What is the relationship between faith and hope?*

- Ask class members to look for something that impresses them that Richard G. Scott says in the following quote. " 'Faith is things which are hoped for and not seen; wherefore, dispute not because ye see not, for ye receive no witness until after the trial of your faith' (Ether 12:6). Thus, every time you try your faith—that is, act in worthiness on an impression—you will receive the confirming evidence of

Notes

the Spirit. As you walk to the boundary of your understanding into the twilight of uncertainty, exercising faith, you will be led to find solutions you would not obtain otherwise. With even your strongest faith, God will not always reward you immediately according to your desires. Rather, God will respond with what in His eternal plan is best for you, when it will yield the greatest advantage. Be thankful that sometimes God lets you struggle for a long time before that answer comes. That causes your faith to increase and your character to grow" ("The Transforming power of Faith and Character," *Ensign*, Nov. 2010, 44).

- *What do you think about Elder Scott's definition of "try your faith"? What impresses you most about what Elder Scott said?*

- Read verses 7–22 and invite class members to look for the following: *Which of the stories recounted by Moroni are the most meaningful illustrations of faith for you and why?*

- Invite class members to act in faith in order to receive the witness they seek. Ask for class members to share experiences of when they received a witness after a trial of their faith.

23 And I said unto him: Lord, the Gentiles will mock at these things, because of our weakness in writing; for Lord thou hast made us mighty in word by faith, but thou hast not made us mighty in writing; for thou hast made all this people that they could speak much, because of the Holy Ghost which thou hast given them;

24 And thou hast made us that we could write but little, because of the awkwardness of our hands. Behold, thou hast not made us mighty in writing like unto the brother of Jared, for thou madest him that the things which he wrote were mighty even as thou art, unto the overpowering of man to read them.

25 Thou hast also made our words powerful and great, even that we cannot write them; wherefore, when we write we behold our weakness, and stumble because of the placing of our words; and I fear lest the Gentiles shall mock at our words.

26 And when I had said this, the Lord spake unto me, saying: Fools mock, but they shall mourn; and my grace is sufficient for the meek, that they shall take no advantage of your weakness;

27 And if men come unto me I will show unto them their weakness. I give unto men weakness that they may be humble; and my grace is sufficient for all men that humble themselves before me; for if they humble themselves before me, and have faith in me, then will I make weak things become strong unto them.

28 Behold, I will show unto the Gentiles their weakness, and I will show unto them that faith, hope and charity bringeth unto me—the fountain of all righteousness.

29 And I, Moroni, having heard these words, was comforted, and said: O Lord, thy righteous will be done, for I know that thou workest unto the children of men according to their faith;

30 For the brother of Jared said unto the mountain Zerin, Remove—and it was removed. And if he had not had faith it would not have moved; wherefore thou workest after men have faith.

31 For thus didst thou manifest thyself unto thy disciples; for after they had faith, and did speak in thy name, thou didst show thyself unto them in great power.

32 And I also remember that thou hast said that thou hast prepared a house for man, yea, even among the mansions of thy Father, in which man might have a more excellent hope; wherefore man must hope, or he cannot receive an inheritance in the place which thou hast prepared.

33 And again, I remember that thou hast said that thou hast loved the world, even unto the laying down of thy life for the world, that thou mightest take it again to prepare a place for the children of men.

34 And now I know that this love which thou hast had for the children of men is charity; wherefore,

Notes

except men shall have charity they cannot inherit that place which thou hast prepared in the mansions of thy Father.

35 Wherefore, I know by this thing which thou hast said, that if the Gentiles have not charity, because of our weakness, that thou wilt prove them, and take away their talent, yea, even that which they have received, and give unto them who shall have more abundantly.

36 And it came to pass that I prayed unto the Lord that he would give unto the Gentiles grace, that they might have charity.

37 And it came to pass that the Lord said unto me: If they have not charity it mattereth not unto thee, thou hast been faithful; wherefore, thy garments shall be made clean. And because thou hast seen thy weakness thou shalt be made strong, even unto the sitting down in the place which I have prepared in the mansions of my Father.

38 And now I, Moroni, bid farewell unto the Gentiles, yea, and also unto my brethren whom I love, until we shall meet before the judgment-seat of Christ, where all men shall know that my garments are not spotted with your blood.

39 And then shall ye know that I have seen Jesus, and that he hath talked with me face to face, and that he told me in plain humility, even as a man telleth another in mine own language, concerning these things;

40 And only a few have I written, because of my weakness in writing.

41 And now, I would commend you to seek this Jesus of whom the prophets and apostles have written, that the grace of God the Father, and also the Lord Jesus Christ, and the Holy Ghost, which beareth record of them, may be and abide in you forever. Amen.

vv. 23–41 With the Lord's strength we are able to do that which we could never do alone.

⚡ Bring a basketball and a tennis ball to class. Explain that the tennis ball represents all of us and that the basketball represents the Lord. Explain that the tennis ball needs to "reach" the ceiling by simply dropping it (not throwing it) to the ground. Drop the tennis ball and demonstrate that it is likely impossible for the ball to bounce back to the ceiling on its own. Then take the tennis ball and place it directly on top of the basketball and drop them together. The basketball will cause the tennis ball to spring up and hit the ceiling. (Make sure you take time to try this on your own before doing it in class.) Share with the class that today you will be discussing the concept of grace.

🔎 *What weakness was Moroni worried about according to verses 23–26? What are the conditions by which we can access grace according to verse 27?* Consider having class members work together in pairs. Each will seek to find the answer to one of the questions and then teach the other what they found.

❓ *What is the definition of grace?* Consider using the Bible Dictionary to help in this discussion.

💬 Thomas S. Monson stated, "Should there be anyone who feels he is too weak to change the onward and downward course of his life, or should there be those who fail to resolve to do better because of that greatest of fears, the fear of failure, there is no more comforting assurance to be had than the words of the Lord: 'My grace,' said He, 'is sufficient for all men that humble themselves before me; for if they humble themselves before me, and have faith in me, then will I make weak things become strong unto them' " ("Your Eternal Voyage," *Ensign*, May 2000, 48).

💬 Robert D. Hales stated, "This change, called conversion, is possible only through the Savior. Jesus promised: 'If men come unto me I will show unto them their weakness. . . . And my grace is sufficient for all men that humble themselves before me; for if they humble themselves before me, and

Notes

have faith in me, then will I make weak things become strong unto them.' [Ether 12:27] As we are made new in Christ, our very natures change and we no longer want to go back to our old ways" ("Being a More Christian Christian," *Ensign*, May 2012, 92).

♥ Invite class members to "seek this Jesus" as stated in verse 41. Refer back to the tennis ball and basketball and testify that we are in need of the Savior's grace to return back to our Heavenly Father.

Topics: faith, hope, weaknesses

ETHER 13

The New Jerusalem

1–12, Ether and Moroni prophecy concerning the New Jerusalem; 13–19, Ether is cast out and views further destruction; 20–21, Ether prophesies to Coriantumr that if they do not repent, Coriantumr will live to see all of the people destroyed; 22–31, He does not repent and further destruction continues.

1 And now I, Moroni, proceed to finish my record concerning the destruction of the people of whom I have been writing.

2 For behold, they rejected all the words of Ether; for he truly told them of all things, from the beginning of man; and that after the waters had receded from off the face of this land it became a choice land above all other lands, a chosen land of the Lord; wherefore the Lord would have that all men should serve him who dwell upon the face thereof;

3 And that it was the place of the New Jerusalem, which should come down out of heaven, and the holy sanctuary of the Lord.

4 Behold, Ether saw the days of Christ, and he spake concerning a New Jerusalem upon this land.

5 And he spake also concerning the house of Israel, and the Jerusalem from whence Lehi should come—after it should be destroyed it should be built up again, a holy city unto the Lord; wherefore, it could not be a new Jerusalem for it had been in a time of old; but it should be built up again, and become a holy city of the Lord; and it should be built unto the house of Israel—

6 And that a New Jerusalem should be built up upon this land, unto the remnant of the seed of Joseph, for which things there has been a type.

7 For as Joseph brought his father down into the land of Egypt, even so he died there; wherefore, the Lord brought a remnant of the seed of Joseph out of the land of Jerusalem, that he might be merciful unto the seed of Joseph that they should perish not, even as he was merciful unto the father of Joseph that he should perish not.

8 Wherefore, the remnant of the house of Joseph shall be built upon this land; and it shall be a land of their inheritance; and they shall build up a holy city unto the Lord, like unto the Jerusalem of old; and they shall no more be confounded, until the end come when the earth shall pass away.

9 And there shall be a new heaven and a new earth; and they shall be like unto the old save the old have passed away, and all things have become new.

10 And then cometh the New Jerusalem; and blessed are they who dwell therein, for it is they whose garments are white through the blood of the Lamb; and they are they who are numbered among the remnant of the seed of Joseph, who were of the house of Israel.

11 And then also cometh the Jerusalem of old; and the inhabitants thereof, blessed are they, for they have been washed in the blood of the Lamb; and they are they who were scattered and gathered in from the four quarters of the earth, and from the north countries, and are partakers of the fulfilling of the covenant which God made with their father, Abraham.

12 And when these things come, bringeth to pass

Notes

ETHER 13

the scripture which saith, there are they who were first, who shall be last; and there are they who were last, who shall be first.

vv. 1–12 The New Jerusalem.

⚡ Write on the board, "New Jerusalem." Review the 10th Article of Faith with the class and discuss everything the class knows about Zion, or the New Jerusalem. Consider writing their answers on the board.

🔍 *Look in verses 1–5 for whether or not the New Jerusalem is the same as the Jerusalem in the land of Israel.*

💬 Joseph Fielding Smith wrote the following about the New Jerusalem: "The prevailing notion in the world is that this [the New Jerusalem] is the city of Jerusalem, the ancient city of the Jews which in the day of regeneration will be renewed, but this is not the case. We read in the Book of Ether that the Lord revealed to him many of the same things which were seen by John. Ether, as members of the Church will know, was the last of the prophets among the Jaredites, and the Lord had revealed to him much concerning the history of the Jews and their city of Jerusalem which stood in the days of the ministry of our Savior. In his vision, in many respects similar to that given to John, Ether saw the old city of Jerusalem and also the new city which has not yet been built, and he wrote of them as follows as reported in the writings of Moroni" (*Answers to Gospel Questions*, 2:103–106).

✋ Give class members some time to study verses 6–12 to find out as much information as they can about the New Jerusalem. Have them share what they found.

💬 Note with the class the phrase "a new heaven and earth" in verse 9. Bruce R. McConkie taught: "This earth was created in a new or paradisiacal state; then, incident to Adam's transgression, it fell to its present telestial state. At the Second Coming of our Lord, it will be renewed, regenerated, refreshed, transfigured, become again a new earth, a paradisiacal earth. Its millennial status will be a return to its pristine state of beauty and glory, the state that existed before the fall. . . . (Isaiah 65:17–25; Isaiah 66:22–24; Matthew 19:28; D&C 63:20–21; D&C 101:23–31.) This same designation applies also to the celestial heaven and earth that will prevail in the day when the Father and the Son make this planet their habitation (D&C 29:22–25; D&C 77:1; D&C 88:16–32; Revelation 21:10–27)" (*Doctrinal New Testament Commentary* 3:580).

13 And I was about to write more, but I am forbidden; but great and marvelous were the prophecies of Ether; but they esteemed him as naught, and cast him out; and he hid himself in the cavity of a rock by day, and by night he went forth viewing the things which should come upon the people.

14 And as he dwelt in the cavity of a rock he made the remainder of this record, viewing the destructions which came upon the people, by night.

15 And it came to pass that in that same year in which he was cast out from among the people there began to be a great war among the people, for there were many who rose up, who were mighty men, and sought to destroy Coriantumr by their secret plans of wickedness, of which hath been spoken.

16 And now Coriantumr, having studied, himself, in all the arts of war and all the cunning of the world, wherefore he gave battle unto them who sought to destroy him.

17 But he repented not, neither his fair sons nor daughters; neither the fair sons and daughters of Cohor; neither the fair sons and daughters of Corihor; and in fine, there were none of the fair sons and daughters upon the face of the whole earth who repented of their sins.

18 Wherefore, it came to pass that in the first year that Ether dwelt in the cavity of a rock, there

Notes

were many people who were slain by the sword of those secret combinations, fighting against Coriantumr that they might obtain the kingdom.

19 And it came to pass that the sons of Coriantumr fought much and bled much.

20 And in the second year the word of the Lord came to Ether, that he should go and prophesy unto Coriantumr that, if he would repent, and all his household, the Lord would give unto him his kingdom and spare the people—

21 Otherwise they should be destroyed, and all his household save it were himself. And he should only live to see the fulfilling of the prophecies which had been spoken concerning another people receiving the land for their inheritance; and Coriantumr should receive a burial by them; and every soul should be destroyed save it were Coriantumr.

vv. 20–21 The prophecy to Coriantumr.

- Have class members read verses 20–21 and ask if Coriantumr repented. Ask, *According to Ether's prophecy, who is to bury Coriantumr?*
- Have class members note Omni 1:21 with the verses and look for the answer.

22 And it came to pass that Coriantumr repented not, neither his household, neither the people; and the wars ceased not; and they sought to kill Ether, but he fled from before them and hid again in the cavity of the rock.

vv. 20–22 God is always loving.

- Look in verses 20–22 for the opportunity God is giving to Coriantumr.
- Analyze: *Why is God giving Coriantumr and his people another chance not to be destroyed? Why does God give people second chances despite their wickedness?*
- Break your class into three groups and ask them to look for the nature and disposition of God in their assigned verses:

Jeremiah 29:11–13

2 Peter 3:9

2 Nephi 26:23–27

- Afterward, have them share what they found. Bear testimony, and allow your class to bear testimony of the goodness of God, and His desire to redeem all of us.

23 And it came to pass that there arose up Shared, and he also gave battle unto Coriantumr; and he did beat him, insomuch that in the third year he did bring him into captivity.

24 And the sons of Coriantumr, in the fourth year, did beat Shared, and did obtain the kingdom again unto their father.

25 Now there began to be a war upon all the face of the land, every man with his band fighting for that which he desired.

26 And there were robbers, and in fine, all manner of wickedness upon all the face of the land.

27 And it came to pass that Coriantumr was exceedingly angry with Shared, and he went against him with his armies to battle; and they did meet in great anger, and they did meet in the valley of Gilgal; and the battle became exceedingly sore.

28 And it came to pass that Shared fought against him for the space of three days. And it came to pass that Coriantumr beat him, and did pursue him until he came to the plains of Heshlon.

29 And it came to pass that Shared gave him battle again upon the plains; and behold, he did beat Coriantumr, and drove him back again to the valley of Gilgal.

30 And Coriantumr gave Shared battle again in the valley of Gilgal, in which he beat Shared and slew him.

31 And Shared wounded Coriantumr in his thigh, that he did not go to battle again for the space of two years, in which time all the people upon the face of the land were shedding blood, and there was none to restrain them.

Notes

> **Teaching Tips from Prophets' Lips** "Meaningful discussions are fundamental to most gospel teaching. We invite the influence of the Spirit when we teach the gospel to one another and give respectful attention to one another" (*Teaching, No Greater Call*, p. 63).

Index Topics: repentance, New Jerusalem.

ETHER 14

Jaredite Destruction

1–9, The land is cursed and Coriantumr contends with Gilead; 10–16, Coriantumr contends with Lib; 17–31, Coriantumr contends with Shiz; the land is covered with the bodies of the dead.

1 And now there began to be a great curse upon all the land because of the iniquity of the people, in which, if a man should lay his tool or his sword upon his shelf, or upon the place whither he would keep it, behold, upon the morrow, he could not find it, so great was the curse upon the land.

2 Wherefore every man did cleave unto that which was his own, with his hands, and would not borrow neither would he lend; and every man kept the hilt of his sword in his right hand, in the defence of his property and his own life and of his wives and children.

3 And now, after the space of two years, and after the death of Shared, behold, there arose the brother of Shared and he gave battle unto Coriantumr, in which Coriantumr did beat him and did pursue him to the wilderness of Akish.

4 And it came to pass that the brother of Shared did give battle unto him in the wilderness of Akish; and the battle became exceedingly sore, and many thousands fell by the sword.

5 And it came to pass that Coriantumr did lay siege to the wilderness; and the brother of Shared did march forth out of the wilderness by night, and slew a part of the army of Coriantumr, as they were drunken.

6 And he came forth to the land of Moron, and placed himself upon the throne of Coriantumr.

7 And it came to pass that Coriantumr dwelt with his army in the wilderness for the space of two years, in which he did receive great strength to his army.

8 Now the brother of Shared, whose name was Gilead, also received great strength to his army, because of secret combinations.

9 And it came to pass that his high priest murdered him as he sat upon his throne.

10 And it came to pass that one of the secret combinations murdered him in a secret pass, and obtained unto himself the kingdom; and his name was Lib; and Lib was a man of great stature, more than any other man among all the people.

11 And it came to pass that in the first year of Lib, Coriantumr came up unto the land of Moron, and gave battle unto Lib.

12 And it came to pass that he fought with Lib, in which Lib did smite upon his arm that he was wounded; nevertheless, the army of Coriantumr did press forward upon Lib, that he fled to the borders upon the seashore.

13 And it came to pass that Coriantumr pursued him; and Lib gave battle unto him upon the seashore.

14 And it came to pass that Lib did smite the army of Coriantumr, that they fled again to the wilderness of Akish.

15 And it came to pass that Lib did pursue him until he came to the plains of Agosh. And Coriantumr had taken all the people with him as he fled before Lib in that quarter of the land whither he fled.

16 And when he had come to the plains of Agosh he gave battle unto Lib, and he smote upon him until he died; nevertheless, the brother of Lib did come against Coriantumr in the stead thereof,

Notes

and the battle became exceedingly sore, in the which Coriantumr fled again before the army of the brother of Lib.

17 Now the name of the brother of Lib was called Shiz. And it came to pass that Shiz pursued after Coriantumr, and he did overthrow many cities, and he did slay both women and children, and he did burn the cities.

18 And there went a fear of Shiz throughout all the land; yea, a cry went forth throughout the land—Who can stand before the army of Shiz? Behold, he sweepeth the earth before him!

19 And it came to pass that the people began to flock together in armies, throughout all the face of the land.

20 And they were divided; and a part of them fled to the army of Shiz, and a part of them fled to the army of Coriantumr.

21 And so great and lasting had been the war, and so long had been the scene of bloodshed and carnage, that the whole face of the land was covered with the bodies of the dead.

22 And so swift and speedy was the war that there was none left to bury the dead, but they did march forth from the shedding of blood to the shedding of blood, leaving the bodies of both men, women, and children strewed upon the face of the land, to become a prey to the worms of the flesh.

23 And the scent thereof went forth upon the face of the land, even upon all the face of the land; wherefore the people became troubled by day and by night, because of the scent thereof.

24 Nevertheless, Shiz did not cease to pursue Coriantumr; for he had sworn to avenge himself upon Coriantumr of the blood of his brother, who had been slain, and the word of the Lord which came to Ether that Coriantumr should not fall by the sword.

25 And thus we see that the Lord did visit them in the fulness of his wrath, and their wickedness and abominations had prepared a way for their everlasting destruction.

26 And it came to pass that Shiz did pursue Coriantumr eastward, even to the borders by the seashore, and there he gave battle unto Shiz for the space of three days.

27 And so terrible was the destruction among the armies of Shiz that the people began to be frightened, and began to flee before the armies of Coriantumr; and they fled to the land of Corihor, and swept off the inhabitants before them, all them that would not join them.

28 And they pitched their tents in the valley of Corihor; and Coriantumr pitched his tents in the valley of Shurr. Now the valley of Shurr was near the hill Comnor; wherefore, Coriantumr did gather his armies together upon the hill Comnor, and did sound a trumpet unto the armies of Shiz to invite them forth to battle.

29 And it came to pass that they came forth, but were driven again; and they came the second time, and they were driven again the second time. And it came to pass that they came again the third time, and the battle became exceedingly sore.

30 And it came to pass that Shiz smote upon Coriantumr that he gave him many deep wounds; and Coriantumr, having lost his blood, fainted, and was carried away as though he were dead.

31 Now the loss of men, women and children on both sides was so great that Shiz commanded his people that they should not pursue the armies of Coriantumr; wherefore, they returned to their camp.

vv. 1–31 The Jaredite destruction continues.

To help class members understand the context and story line, break them into four groups. Assign each group one of the following sets of verses: 1–9, 10–16, 17–25, 26–31. Have them study their verses and be prepared to have a summary that they will share with the class.

Analyze: Review with your class the pride cycle and ask,
- *Where are the Jaredites in the pride cycle?*
- *What do the Jaredites need to do next?*

Notes

- *What happens to people who do not repent?* (They are destroyed, not necessarily physically, but spiritually.)

ETHER 15

The Final Jaredite Destruction

1–10, Coriantumr desires to end the war but is still pursued and continually beaten by the army of Shiz; 11–14, The two armies spend four years making preparations to fight against each other; 15–34, the final Jaredite battle commences, and ends with Coriantumr surviving the battle.

1 And it came to pass when Coriantumr had recovered of his wounds, he began to remember the words which Ether had spoken unto him.

2 He saw that there had been slain by the sword already nearly two millions of his people, and he began to sorrow in his heart; yea, there had been slain two millions of mighty men, and also their wives and their children.

3 He began to repent of the evil which he had done; he began to remember the words which had been spoken by the mouth of all the prophets, and he saw them that they were fulfilled thus far, every whit; and his soul mourned and refused to be comforted.

4 And it came to pass that he wrote an epistle unto Shiz, desiring him that he would spare the people, and he would give up the kingdom for the sake of the lives of the people.

5 And it came to pass that when Shiz had received his epistle he wrote an epistle unto Coriantumr, that if he would give himself up, that he might slay him with his own sword, that he would spare the lives of the people.

6 And it came to pass that the people repented not of their iniquity; and the people of Coriantumr were stirred up to anger against the people of Shiz; and the people of Shiz were stirred up to anger against the people of Coriantumr; wherefore, the people of Shiz did give battle unto the people of Coriantumr.

7 And when Coriantumr saw that he was about to fall he fled again before the people of Shiz.

8 And it came to pass that he came to the waters of Ripliancum, which, by interpretation, is large, or to exceed all; wherefore, when they came to these waters they pitched their tents; and Shiz also pitched his tents near unto them; and therefore on the morrow they did come to battle.

9 And it came to pass that they fought an exceedingly sore battle, in which Coriantumr was wounded again, and he fainted with the loss of blood.

10 And it came to pass that the armies of Coriantumr did press upon the armies of Shiz that they beat them, that they caused them to flee before them; and they did flee southward, and did pitch their tents in a place which was called Ogath.

11 And it came to pass that the army of Coriantumr did pitch their tents by the hill Ramah; and it was that same hill where my father Mormon did hide up the records unto the Lord, which were sacred.

v. 11 Jaredite geography.

- The final Jaredite battle takes place at the foot of the same mountain as the Nephites' last war. The Jaredites called it Hill Ramah, and the Nephites called it Hill Cumorah. Cross reference Mormon 6:6.

12 And it came to pass that they did gather together all the people upon all the face of the land, who had not been slain, save it was Ether.

13 And it came to pass that Ether did behold all the doings of the people; and he beheld that the people who were for Coriantumr were gathered together to the army of Coriantumr; and the people who were for Shiz were gathered together to the army of Shiz.

14 Wherefore, they were for the space of four years gathering together the people, that they might

Notes

get all who were upon the face of the land, and that they might receive all the strength which it was possible that they could receive.

15 And it came to pass that when they were all gathered together, every one to the army which he would, with their wives and their children—both men, women and children being armed with weapons of war, having shields, and breastplates, and head-plates, and being clothed after the manner of war—they did march forth one against another to battle; and they fought all that day, and conquered not.

16 And it came to pass that when it was night they were weary, and retired to their camps; and after they had retired to their camps they took up a howling and a lamentation for the loss of the slain of their people; and so great were their cries, their howlings and lamentations, that they did rend the air exceedingly.

17 And it came to pass that on the morrow they did go again to battle, and great and terrible was that day; nevertheless, they conquered not, and when the night came again they did rend the air with their cries, and their howlings, and their mournings, for the loss of the slain of their people.

18 And it came to pass that Coriantumr wrote again an epistle unto Shiz, desiring that he would not come again to battle, but that he would take the kingdom, and spare the lives of the people.

19 But behold, the Spirit of the Lord had ceased striving with them, and Satan had full power over the hearts of the people; for they were given up unto the hardness of their hearts, and the blindness of their minds that they might be destroyed; wherefore they went again to battle.

v. 19 "The Spirit of the Lord had ceased striving with them."

Satan tries to convince us that repentance is a "crutch" for those who want to sin now and repent later. Verse 19 teaches that the Spirit of the Lord will cease striving with us, which may, in the long run, make it hard for us to change. Consider Coriantumr's desire to change in verse 1 and in verse 18, and contrast that with what happens in verse 19.

20 And it came to pass that they fought all that day, and when the night came they slept upon their swords.

21 And on the morrow they fought even until the night came.

22 And when the night came they were drunken with anger, even as a man who is drunken with wine; and they slept again upon their swords.

23 And on the morrow they fought again; and when the night came they had all fallen by the sword save it were fifty and two of the people of Coriantumr, and sixty and nine of the people of Shiz.

24 And it came to pass that they slept upon their swords that night, and on the morrow they fought again, and they contended in their might with their swords and with their shields, all that day.

25 And when the night came there were thirty and two of the people of Shiz, and twenty and seven of the people of Coriantumr.

26 And it came to pass that they ate and slept, and prepared for death on the morrow. And they were large and mighty men as to the strength of men.

27 And it came to pass that they fought for the space of three hours, and they fainted with the loss of blood.

28 And it came to pass that when the men of Coriantumr had received sufficient strength that they could walk, they were about to flee for their lives; but behold, Shiz arose, and also his men, and he swore in his wrath that he would slay Coriantumr or he would perish by the sword.

29 Wherefore, he did pursue them, and on the morrow he did overtake them; and they fought again with the sword. And it came to pass that when they had all fallen by the sword, save it were Coriantumr and Shiz, behold Shiz had fainted with the loss of blood.

Notes

30 And it came to pass that when Coriantumr had leaned upon his sword, that he rested a little, he smote off the head of Shiz.

31 And it came to pass that after he had smitten off the head of Shiz, that Shiz raised up on his hands and fell; and after that he had struggled for breath, he died.

32 And it came to pass that Coriantumr fell to the earth, and became as if he had no life.

33 And the Lord spake unto Ether, and said unto him: Go forth. And he went forth, and beheld that the words of the Lord had all been fulfilled; and he finished his record; (and the hundredth part I have not written) and he hid them in a manner that the people of Limhi did find them.

34 Now the last words which are written by Ether are these: Whether the Lord will that I be translated, or that I suffer the will of the Lord in the flesh, it mattereth not, if it so be that I am saved in the kingdom of God. Amen.

vv. 20–35 The words of the Lord will always be fulfilled.

- Review the highlights of verses 20–35 with class members and discuss how a mighty nation like the Jaredites could be destroyed the way they were.

- Invite class members to cross-reference Ether 2:7–10 and look for why this mighty nation was destroyed.

- Analyze: *What do you remember from Jaredite history that shows they were so wicked?*

- President Marion G. Romney visited the Hill Cumorah in New York and reflected on the following: "As I contemplated this tragic scene from the crest of Cumorah and viewed the beautiful land of the Restoration as it appears today, I cried in my soul, 'How could it have happened?' The answer came immediately as I remembered that some fifteen to twenty centuries before their destruction, as the small group of their ancestors was being divinely led from the tower of Babel, the Lord 'would that they should come forth even unto [this] land of promise, which was choice above all other lands, which the Lord God had preserved for a righteous people. And he had sworn in his wrath unto the brother of Jared [their prophet-leader], that whoso should possess this land . . . from that time henceforth and forever, should serve him, the true and only God, or they should be swept off when the fulness of his wrath should come upon them. And now, we can behold the decrees of God concerning this land,' wrote the ancient prophet-historian, 'that it is a land of promise; and whatsoever nation shall possess it shall serve God, or they shall be swept off when the fulness of his wrath shall come upon them. And the fulness of his wrath cometh upon them when they are ripened in iniquity. For behold, this is a land which is choice above all other lands; wherefore he that doth possess it shall serve God or shall be swept off; for it is the everlasting decree of God.' (see Ether 2:7–10.) Pursuant to this decree concerning the land of America, the Jaredites were swept off in the manner we have reviewed, because, rebelling against the laws of Jesus Christ—the God of the land—they 'ripened in iniquity' " ("America's Destiny," *Ensign*, November 1975, 35).

- Look for Ether's final words of the whole Jaredite story in verse 34.

- Apply: *What can we learn from the Jaredite story that is applicable in our day?*

- Refer to the paragraph in the "Family: A Proclamation to the World," which begins with "We warn" and discuss what the prophets of our day are saying to the world.

Teaching Tips from Prophets' Lips "Questions can encourage those present to participate in discussions. They can help learners understand a principle, think about it more deeply, and relate it to their lives. They can lead learners to turn to the scriptures for answers" (*Teaching, No Greater Call*, p. 63).

Notes

THE BOOK OF MORONI

MORONI SUMMARY

Time Period: About AD 400–421 (about 22 years)

Contributors & Authorship: Moroni, Mormon

Synopsis:

Chapter 1: Moroni prefaces his book

Chapters 2–5: Instructions concerning the administration of the gift of the Holy Ghost, ordaining to the priesthood, and sacrament

Chapter 6: The manner of Church meetings and conduct

Chapters 7–9: Letters from Mormon to Moroni

Chapter 10: Moroni's closing words to the Book of Mormon

MORONI 1

Will Not Deny the Christ
About AD 401–421

1–3, Moroni wanders for safety from the Lamanites because he will not deny the Christ; 4, He writes a few a more things to benefit the Lamanites in a future day.

1 Now I, Moroni, after having made an end of abridging the account of the people of Jared, I had supposed not to have written more, but I have not as yet perished; and I make not myself known to the Lamanites lest they should destroy me.

2 For behold, their wars are exceedingly fierce among themselves; and because of their hatred they put to death every Nephite that will not deny the Christ.

3 And I, Moroni, will not deny the Christ; wherefore, I wander whithersoever I can for the safety of mine own life.

4 Wherefore, I write a few more things, contrary to that which I had supposed; for I had supposed not to have written any more; but I write a few more things, that perhaps they may be of worth unto my brethren, the Lamanites, in some future day, according to the will of the Lord.

vv. 1–4 Moroni had the courage to stay true to his testimony regardless of the consequences.

Notes

- ⚡ Write the word "Martyr" on the board. Ask, *What does this word mean?* Explain that the Greek word from which martyr is derived literally means witness—particularly someone who gives their life as a witness to something. Ask, *What kinds of spiritual experiences would someone need to be willing to become a martyr?*

- 🔍 *Read verses 1–4 and find why the word martyr is relevant to Moroni chapter 1.*

- ❓ Ask, *What did Moroni know that made him strong in faith despite the threats against his life? How can testimony give an individual courage to stand up for God?*

- 💬 Explain that we most likely won't be asked to risk our lives for our testimonies but that we can do something else. Regarding true disciples of Christ, President Ezra Taft Benson said, "They do always those things that please the Lord. Not only would they die for the Lord, but, more important, they want to live for Him." (July 1989 *Ensign*, "Born of God")

- ❓ *Besides martyrdom, how can an individual "give his life" for the Lord?*

- ♥ Invite class members to ponder their dedication to and testimonies of Jesus Christ. Testify of the great blessings that come from having a firm testimony like Moroni.

> **Teaching Tips from Prophets' Lips** "When [we receive] the truth [we] will be saved by it. [We] will not be saved merely because someone taught it to [us], but because [we] received and acted upon it" (President Joseph F. Smith, in Conference Report, Apr. 1902, 86).

MORONI 2

The Words of Christ unto His Disciples
About AD 401–421

1–3, The words which Christ spoke when authorizing His disciples to bestow the gift of the Holy Ghost.

1 The words of Christ, which he spake unto his disciples, the twelve whom he had chosen, as he laid his hands upon them—

2 And he called them by name, saying: Ye shall call on the Father in my name, in mighty prayer; and after ye have done this ye shall have power that to him upon whom ye shall lay your hands, ye shall give the Holy Ghost; and in my name shall ye give it, for thus do mine apostles.

3 Now Christ spake these words unto them at the time of his first appearing; and the multitude heard it not, but the disciples heard it; and on as many as they laid their hands, fell the Holy Ghost.

vv. 1–3 The Lord gives His true servants the power to bestow the gift of the Holy Ghost on others.

- ⚡ Ask, *What are some things that differentiate our church from all others?*

- 🔍 *Read verses 1–3 and look for something that is unique about the true church of Jesus Christ.*

- 💬 Explain that Joseph Smith once had a meeting with Martin Van Buren, then president of the United States. When asked how our church was different from the others Joseph stated, "We have the correct mode of baptism, and the gift of the Holy Ghost by the laying on of hands. We consider that all other considerations were contained in the gift of the Holy Ghost." (*History of the Church*, 4:42)

- ♥ Invite class members to share experiences of how having the availability of the gift of the Holy Ghost has been a blessing in their lives. Bear your testimony of the power to give the gift of the Holy Ghost in the Church today.

Notes

MORONI 3

Ordination of Priests and Teachers
About AD 401–421

1–4, The process of ordaining priests and teachers is set forth.

1 The manner which the disciples, who were called the elders of the church, ordained priests and teachers—

2 After they had prayed unto the Father in the name of Christ, they laid their hands upon them, and said:

3 In the name of Jesus Christ I ordain you to be a priest (or if he be a teacher, I ordain you to be a teacher) to preach repentance and remission of sins through Jesus Christ, by the endurance of faith on his name to the end. Amen.

4 And after this manner did they ordain priests and teachers, according to the gifts and callings of God unto men; and they ordained them by the power of the Holy Ghost, which was in them.

vv. 1–4 The priesthood of God must be conferred by the laying on of hands.

- Put the following questions on the board and invite class members to answer what questions they know. Do this activity until all the questions have been answered or found.
  - What scripture in the Old Testament states that those who receive the priesthood must be called of God as was Aaron?
  - Can a priest confer the priesthood on another priest?
  - Find a scripture that mentions the importance of "laying on of hands."

- Russell M. Nelson taught, "Love for the Book of Mormon expands one's love for the Bible and vice versa. Scriptures of the Restoration do not compete with the Bible; they complement the Bible. We are indebted to martyrs who gave their lives so that we could have the Bible. It establishes the everlasting nature of the gospel and of the plan of happiness." (Russell M. Nelson, "Scriptural Witnesses," *Ensign*, November 2007, 45) Testify that one of these doctrines is that of the priesthood.

- Invite class members to read verses 1–4 and look for what the Book of Mormon teaches about the ordination of priests and teachers.

- Analyze: *What does the phrase "ordained them by the power of God" in verse 4 mean or signify? Why is it important that this information is taught within the Book of Mormon?*

- Testify of the power of the priesthood and the importance of the ordinance of the priesthood in these latter days.

Teaching Tips from Prophets' Lips "When missionaries and teachers draw upon the Spirit, they teach the appropriate principle, invite their learners to live that principle, and bear witness of the promised blessings that will certainly follow. Elder David A. Bednar shared these three simple elements of effective teaching in a recent training meeting: (1) key doctrine, (2) invitation to action, and (3) promised blessings" (Teaching Helps Save Lives, Russell T. Osguthorpe, Nov. 2009, 15).

Index Topics: Priesthood

MORONI 4

Sacrament Prayer for the Bread
About AD 401–421

1–3, Moroni explains and gives the sacrament prayer for the bread.

1 The manner of their elders and priests administering the flesh and blood of Christ unto the church; and they administered it according to the commandments of Christ; wherefore we know the manner to be true; and the elder or priest did minister it—

Notes

2 And they did kneel down with the church, and pray to the Father in the name of Christ, saying:

3 O God, the Eternal Father, we ask thee in the name of thy Son, Jesus Christ, to bless and sanctify this bread to the souls of all those who partake of it; that they may eat in remembrance of the body of thy Son, and witness unto thee, O God, the Eternal Father, that they are willing to take upon them the name of thy Son, and always remember him, and keep his commandments which he hath given them, that they may always have his Spirit to be with them. Amen.

v. 3 Power in the sacrament comes by consciously recommitting ourselves with the promises of the sacrament.

- *What verse of scripture do Church members hear or read more than any other?* After they have a chance to respond, direct the class to Moroni 4:3 and see if they have heard that more than the others. Select an average age of the class members and calculate how often a person that age, if a member all their lives, might have heard the sacrament prayer.

- Since class members hear the sacrament prayer so often, give everyone a piece of paper and see if they can write it from memory. If this seems too difficult for class members, consider making a fill-in-the-blank worksheet which provides some of the answers but leaves others blank. After they have had time to complete this activity, review it together.

- Analyze:
  - *In the prayer, what are the three promises we make to God when we take the sacrament?*
  - *What does it mean for us to "take upon [us] the name of thy Son"?*
  - *How do we "always remember Him"?*
  - *Why does the Lord want us to renew our promise to "keep His commandments" each week?*
  - *What does the Lord promise in return as we keep our commitments?*

- Have class members recall when they last partook of the sacrament. Ask them to consider whether or not they consciously recommitted themselves with these three promises. Ask,
  - *Why is it important to deliberately recommit yourself in these areas each week?*
  - *What power can come from consciously keeping these covenants instead of mindlessly taking the sacrament?*
  - *Why is it easy to get distracted when taking the sacrament?*

Challenge class members to avoid being distracted and to sincerely recommit themselves each week as they partake of the sacrament. Testify of the power they can experience in their lives from this. Inform the class that you will ask them about their experience the following week.

The following week, remind them of the lesson and ask them if their sacrament experience was different and, if so, in what way.

- Ask class members where the sacrament prayer is also found in scripture (D&C 20:77). Explain to them that there is one slight difference between the prayer in the Doctrine and Covenants and the prayer in Moroni. Have them search for the difference. If they don't see it, explain that after the words "commandments which He", the word "hath" is used in the Book of Mormon, but the word "has" is used in the Doctrine and Covenants. Explain that the official prayer that is printed in Church materials always uses the Doctrine and Covenants version.

Index Topics: sacrament

MORONI 5
The Sacrament Prayer for the Wine
About AD 401–421

Notes

1–2, The manner of administering the wine for the sacrament.

1 The manner of administering the wine—Behold, they took the cup, and said:

2 O God, the Eternal Father, we ask thee, in the name of thy Son, Jesus Christ, to bless and sanctify this wine to the souls of all those who drink of it, that they may do it in remembrance of the blood of thy Son, which was shed for them; that they may witness unto thee, O God, the Eternal Father, that they do always remember him, that they may have his Spirit to be with them. Amen.

- Consider using the lesson from Moroni 4 along with this chapter.

- One way to make the sacrament more meaningful is to repeat the sacrament prayer in your mind and replace the words 'we,' 'they,' and 'them,' with personal pronouns of 'I' and 'me.'

> **Teaching Tips from Prophets' Lips** President David O. McKay gave us this instruction on the importance of teaching: "Teaching is the noblest profession in the world. Upon the proper education of youth depend the permanency and purity of home, the safety and perpetuity of the nation. The parent gives the child an opportunity to live; the teacher enables the child to live well" (David O. McKay, *Gospel Ideals* [1953], 436).

MORONI 6

Baptism and Membership in the Church

About AD 401–421

1–9 Moroni explains the requirements of baptism and membership in the Church.

1 And now I speak concerning baptism. Behold, elders, priests, and teachers were baptized; and they were not baptized save they brought forth fruit meet that they were worthy of it.

2 Neither did they receive any unto baptism save they came forth with a broken heart and a contrite spirit, and witnessed unto the church that they truly repented of all their sins.

3 And none were received unto baptism save they took upon them the name of Christ, having a determination to serve him to the end.

4 And after they had been received unto baptism, and were wrought upon and cleansed by the power of the Holy Ghost, they were numbered among the people of the church of Christ; and their names were taken, that they might be remembered and nourished by the good word of God, to keep them in the right way, to keep them continually watchful unto prayer, relying alone upon the merits of Christ, who was the author and the finisher of their faith.

5 And the church did meet together oft, to fast and to pray, and to speak one with another concerning the welfare of their souls.

6 And they did meet together oft to partake of bread and wine, in remembrance of the Lord Jesus.

7 And they were strict to observe that there should be no iniquity among them; and whoso was found to commit iniquity, and three witnesses of the church did condemn them before the elders, and if they repented not, and confessed not, their names were blotted out, and they were not numbered among the people of Christ.

8 But as oft as they repented and sought forgiveness, with real intent, they were forgiven.

9 And their meetings were conducted by the church after the manner of the workings of the Spirit, and by the power of the Holy Ghost; for as the power of the Holy Ghost led them whether to preach, or to exhort, or to pray, or to supplicate, or to sing, even so it was done.

Notes

vv. 1–9 The requirements of baptism and membership in the Church.

- ⚡ Create two columns on the board—one labeled "Requirements of Baptism" and the other labeled "Requirements of Membership in the Church."

- 🔍 Read verses 1–9 and look for the requirements for each column.

- 💬 Gordon B. Hinckly stated, "In these days as in those days [referring to Moroni 6:4] converts are 'numbered among the people of the church . . . [to] be remembered and nourished by the good word of God, to keep them in the right way, to keep them continually watchful unto prayer.' Brethren, let us help them as they take their first steps as members." (Gordon B. Hinckley, "Converts and Young Men," *Ensign*, May 1997, 47)

- 💬 Elder Quentin L Cook has taught, "At baptism we promise to take upon us 'the name of [Jesus] Christ, having [the] determination to serve him to the end.' Such a covenant requires courageous effort, commitment, and integrity if we are to continue to sing the song of redeeming love and stay truly converted" ("Can Ye Feel So Now?" *Ensign*, November 2012, 9).

- ❤ Discuss what principles they discovered from these nine verses as a class and help them understand the importance of Church membership.

MORONI 7

Faith, Hope, and Charity
About AD 401–421

1–12, Mormon speaks of giving good gifts; 13–20, How to judge that which is righteous and that which is wicked; 21–48, How to lay hold of every good thing: faith, hope, and charity.

1 And now I, Moroni, write a few of the words of my father Mormon, which he spake concerning faith, hope, and charity; for after this manner did he speak unto the people, as he taught them in the synagogue which they had built for the place of worship.

- 💡 Note that in Moroni chapter 7, Moroni quotes his father Mormon's words regarding faith, hope, and charity.

2 And now I, Mormon, speak unto you, my beloved brethren; and it is by the grace of God the Father, and our Lord Jesus Christ, and his holy will, because of the gift of his calling unto me, that I am permitted to speak unto you at this time.

3 Wherefore, I would speak unto you that are of the church, that are the peaceable followers of Christ, and that have obtained a sufficient hope by which ye can enter into the rest of the Lord, from this time henceforth until ye shall rest with him in heaven.

4 And now my brethren, I judge these things of you because of your peaceable walk with the children of men.

5 For I remember the word of God which saith by their works ye shall know them; for if their works be good, then they are good also.

6 For behold, God hath said a man being evil cannot do that which is good; for if he offereth a gift, or prayeth unto God, except he shall do it with real intent it profiteth him nothing.

7 For behold, it is not counted unto him for righteousness.

8 For behold, if a man being evil giveth a gift, he doeth it grudgingly; wherefore it is counted unto him the same as if he had retained the gift; wherefore he is counted evil before God.

9 And likewise also is it counted evil unto a man, if he shall pray and not with real intent of heart; yea, and it profiteth him nothing, for God receiveth none such.

Notes

10 Wherefore, a man being evil cannot do that which is good; neither will he give a good gift.

11 For behold, a bitter fountain cannot bring forth good water; neither can a good fountain bring forth bitter water; wherefore, a man being a servant of the devil cannot follow Christ; and if he follow Christ he cannot be a servant of the devil.

12 Wherefore, all things which are good cometh of God; and that which is evil cometh of the devil; for the devil is an enemy unto God, and fighteth against him continually, and inviteth and enticeth to sin, and to do that which is evil continually.

13 But behold, that which is of God inviteth and enticeth to do good continually; wherefore, every thing which inviteth and enticeth to do good, and to love God, and to serve him, is inspired of God.

14 Wherefore, take heed, my beloved brethren, that ye do not judge that which is evil to be of God, or that which is good and of God to be of the devil.

15 For behold, my brethren, it is given unto you to judge, that ye may know good from evil; and the way to judge is as plain, that ye may know with a perfect knowledge, as the daylight is from the dark night.

16 For behold, the Spirit of Christ is given to every man, that he may know good from evil; wherefore, I show unto you the way to judge; for every thing which inviteth to do good, and to persuade to believe in Christ, is sent forth by the power and gift of Christ; wherefore ye may know with a perfect knowledge it is of God.

17 But whatsoever thing persuadeth men to do evil, and believe not in Christ, and deny him, and serve not God, then ye may know with a perfect knowledge it is of the devil; for after this manner doth the devil work, for he persuadeth no man to do good, no, not one; neither do his angels; neither do they who subject themselves unto him.

18 And now, my brethren, seeing that ye know the light by which ye may judge, which light is the light of Christ, see that ye do not judge wrongfully; for with that same judgment which ye judge ye shall also be judged.

19 Wherefore, I beseech of you, brethren, that ye should search diligently in the light of Christ that ye may know good from evil; and if ye will lay hold upon every good thing, and condemn it not, ye certainly will be a child of Christ.

20 And now, my brethren, how is it possible that ye can lay hold upon every good thing?

vv. 5–20 How to judge between good and evil.

⚡ Discuss the following quote. "Let's begin with what we know. Good comes from God; evil comes from the devil" (Neil L. Anderson, "Beware of the Evil Behind the Smiling Eyes," *Ensign*, April 2005, 46). Focus the discussion specifically on how we can know the difference between good and evil in a world where so many people call evil good and good evil.

✎ Consider using the following chart to help class members discover principles of judging good and evil.

Principles of judging between good and evil (Moroni 7:5–20)	
How to know if something or someone is good:	How to know if something or someone is evil:
Analyze your current choices. What choices have you made recently that were good? What choices may be considered evil based on these verses?	

❓ Analyze: Select one or two principles from the verses that you feel are the most important and analyze them with the class. Ask, *How could you simplify Mormon's criteria for judging between good and evil?*

Notes

❓ **Apply:** *Which of these principles are the most applicable to our day? What are some dilemmas that such criteria could help us work through?*

💬 President Thomas S. Monson has taught the following: "Each of us has come to this earth with all the tools necessary to make correct choices. The prophet Mormon tells us, 'The Spirit of Christ is given to every man, that he may know good from evil.' (See Mormon 7:16). We are surrounded—even at times bombarded—by the messages of the adversary. Listen to some of them; they are no doubt familiar to you: 'Just this once won't matter.' 'Don't worry; no one will know.' 'You can stop smoking or drinking or taking drugs any time you want.' 'Everybody's doing it, so it can't be that bad.' The lies are endless. Although in our journey we will encounter forks and turnings in the road, we simply cannot afford the luxury of a detour from which we may never return. Lucifer, that clever pied piper, plays his lilting melody and attracts the unsuspecting away from the safety of their chosen pathway, away from the counsel of loving parents, away from the security of God's teachings. He seeks not just the so-called refuse of humanity; he seeks all of us, including the very elect of God. King David listened, wavered, and then followed and fell. So did Cain in an earlier era and Judas Iscariot in a later one. Lucifer's methods are cunning; his victims, numerous" ("The Three R's of Choice," *Ensign*, November 2010, 70).

♥ Help class members understand the importance of discerning and choosing good over evil, and invite them to continue to make good choices.

21 And now I come to that faith, of which I said I would speak; and I will tell you the way whereby ye may lay hold on every good thing.

22 For behold, God knowing all things, being from everlasting to everlasting, behold, he sent angels to minister unto the children of men, to make manifest concerning the coming of Christ; and in Christ there should come every good thing.

23 And God also declared unto prophets, by his own mouth, that Christ should come.

24 And behold, there were divers ways that he did manifest things unto the children of men, which were good; and all things which are good cometh of Christ; otherwise men were fallen, and there could no good thing come unto them.

25 Wherefore, by the ministering of angels, and by every word which proceeded forth out of the mouth of God, men began to exercise faith in Christ; and thus by faith, they did lay hold upon every good thing; and thus it was until the coming of Christ.

26 And after that he came men also were saved by faith in his name; and by faith, they become the sons of God. And as surely as Christ liveth he spake these words unto our fathers, saying: Whatsoever thing ye shall ask the Father in my name, which is good, in faith believing that ye shall receive, behold, it shall be done unto you.

27 Wherefore, my beloved brethren, have miracles ceased because Christ hath ascended into heaven, and hath sat down on the right hand of God, to claim of the Father his rights of mercy which he hath upon the children of men?

28 For he hath answered the ends of the law, and he claimeth all those who have faith in him; and they who have faith in him will cleave unto every good thing; wherefore he advocateth the cause of the children of men; and he dwelleth eternally in the heavens.

29 And because he hath done this, my beloved brethren, have miracles ceased? Behold I say unto you, Nay; neither have angels ceased to minister unto the children of men.

30 For behold, they are subject unto him, to minister according to the word of his command, showing themselves unto them of strong faith and a firm mind in every form of godliness.

Notes

31 And the office of their ministry is to call men unto repentance, and to fulfil and to do the work of the covenants of the Father, which he hath made unto the children of men, to prepare the way among the children of men, by declaring the word of Christ unto the chosen vessels of the Lord, that they may bear testimony of him.

32 And by so doing, the Lord God prepareth the way that the residue of men may have faith in Christ, that the Holy Ghost may have place in their hearts, according to the power thereof; and after this manner bringeth to pass the Father, the covenants which he hath made unto the children of men.

33 And Christ hath said: If ye will have faith in me ye shall have power to do whatsoever thing is expedient in me.

34 And he hath said: Repent all ye ends of the earth, and come unto me, and be baptized in my name, and have faith in me, that ye may be saved.

35 And now, my beloved brethren, if this be the case that these things are true which I have spoken unto you, and God will show unto you, with power and great glory at the last day, that they are true, and if they are true has the day of miracles ceased?

36 Or have angels ceased to appear unto the children of men? Or has he withheld the power of the Holy Ghost from them? Or will he, so long as time shall last, or the earth shall stand, or there shall be one man upon the face thereof to be saved?

37 Behold I say unto you, Nay; for it is by faith that miracles are wrought; and it is by faith that angels appear and minister unto men; wherefore, if these things have ceased wo be unto the children of men, for it is because of unbelief, and all is vain.

38 For no man can be saved, according to the words of Christ, save they shall have faith in his name; wherefore, if these things have ceased, then has faith ceased also; and awful is the state of man, for they are as though there had been no redemption made.

39 But behold, my beloved brethren, I judge better things of you, for I judge that ye have faith in Christ because of your meekness; for if ye have not faith in him then ye are not fit to be numbered among the people of his church.

vv. 21–39 We are expected to learn of God by faith.

- Note in verse 25 the phrase, "men began to exercise faith in Christ." Invite class members to then study verses 21–39, looking for ways men begin and continue to exercise faith in Jesus Christ.

- Analyze: There are many principles of faith taught in these verses. Pick one or two that you feel are important and applicable to further analyze with the class. You might consider asking,
  - *What are some of the effects of faith that you read in these verses?*
  - *Why do you think faith was required?*
  - *Could God have accomplished the same things in other ways? Why or why not?*

- Apply: Note Mormon's preface to his discussion of faith in verse 21. Ask, *How could the principles of faith from these verses help us lay hold on every good thing?*

40 And again, my beloved brethren, I would speak unto you concerning hope. How is it that ye can attain unto faith, save ye shall have hope?

41 And what is it that ye shall hope for? Behold I say unto you that ye shall have hope through the atonement of Christ and the power of his resurrection, to be raised unto life eternal, and this because of your faith in him according to the promise.

42 Wherefore, if a man have faith he must needs have hope; for without faith there cannot be any hope.

43 And again, behold I say unto you that he cannot

Notes

have faith and hope, save he shall be meek, and lowly of heart.

vv. 40–43 "Ye shall have hope through the Atonement of Christ."

🔍 *Look for the relationship between faith and hope in verses 40–43.*

❓ Analyze: *In what ways does the Atonement of Christ give someone hope? Why are faith and hope connected?*

44 If so, his faith and hope is vain, for none is acceptable before God, save the meek and lowly in heart; and if a man be meek and lowly in heart, and confesses by the power of the Holy Ghost that Jesus is the Christ, he must needs have charity; for if he have not charity he is nothing; wherefore he must needs have charity.

45 And charity suffereth long, and is kind, and envieth not, and is not puffed up, seeketh not her own, is not easily provoked, thinketh no evil, and rejoiceth not in iniquity but rejoiceth in the truth, beareth all things, believeth all things, hopeth all things, endureth all things.

46 Wherefore, my beloved brethren, if ye have not charity, ye are nothing, for charity never faileth. Wherefore, cleave unto charity, which is the greatest of all, for all things must fail—

47 But charity is the pure love of Christ, and it endureth forever; and whoso is found possessed of it at the last day, it shall be well with him.

48 Wherefore, my beloved brethren, pray unto the Father with all the energy of heart, that ye may be filled with this love, which he hath bestowed upon all who are true followers of his Son, Jesus Christ; that ye may become the sons of God; that when he shall appear we shall be like him, for we shall see him as he is; that we may have this hope; that we may be purified even as he is pure. Amen.

vv. 44–48 Charity, the pure love of Christ.

🔍 *Mormon says that in order to have faith and hope, a person must have a specific attribute. What is the attribute according to verse 44?*

👥 Allow class members time to read verses 45–48, looking for both a definition of charity and an attribute of charity. Depending on the size and age of class members, consider allowing them time to discuss their findings with each other, or you can discuss their answers as a class. Invite them to think of individuals in their lives who have exhibited those findings.

❤ If appropriate, consider asking a class member to share a personal incident when they experienced faith, hope, or charity.

> **Teaching Tips from Prophets' Lips** "I believe there is no greater call in the Church than to be an effective teacher. Effective teaching by the Spirit can stir the souls of men with a desire to live the principles of the gospel of Jesus Christ more completely" (M. Russell Ballard, *Teaching—No Greater Call,* April 1983, 63).

MORONI 8

"Little Children Are Alive in Christ"

About AD 401–421

1–4, Moroni is called to the ministry; 5–26, Mormon warns against the gross error of baptism of little children; 27–31, The pride of the Nephites has led to their destruction.

1 An epistle of my father Mormon, written to me, Moroni; and it was written unto me soon after my calling to the ministry. And on this wise did he write unto me, saying:

2 My beloved son, Moroni, I rejoice exceedingly that your Lord Jesus Christ hath been mindful of you, and hath called you to his ministry, and to his holy work.

Notes

3 I am mindful of you always in my prayers, continually praying unto God the Father in the name of his Holy Child, Jesus, that he, through his infinite goodness and grace, will keep you through the endurance of faith on his name to the end.

4 And now, my son, I speak unto you concerning that which grieveth me exceedingly; for it grieveth me that there should disputations rise among you.

5 For, if I have learned the truth, there have been disputations among you concerning the baptism of your little children.

6 And now, my son, I desire that ye should labor diligently, that this gross error should be removed from among you; for, for this intent I have written this epistle.

7 For immediately after I had learned these things of you I inquired of the Lord concerning the matter. And the word of the Lord came to me by the power of the Holy Ghost, saying:

8 Listen to the words of Christ, your Redeemer, your Lord and your God. Behold, I came into the world not to call the righteous but sinners to repentance; the whole need no physician, but they that are sick; wherefore, little children are whole, for they are not capable of committing sin; wherefore the curse of Adam is taken from them in me, that it hath no power over them; and the law of circumcision is done away in me.

9 And after this manner did the Holy Ghost manifest the word of God unto me; wherefore, my beloved son, I know that it is solemn mockery before God, that ye should baptize little children.

10 Behold I say unto you that this thing shall ye teach—repentance and baptism unto those who are accountable and capable of committing sin; yea, teach parents that they must repent and be baptized, and humble themselves as their little children, and they shall all be saved with their little children.

11 And their little children need no repentance, neither baptism. Behold, baptism is unto repentance to the fulfilling the commandments unto the remission of sins.

12 But little children are alive in Christ, even from the foundation of the world; if not so, God is a partial God, and also a changeable God, and a respecter to persons; for how many little children have died without baptism!

13 Wherefore, if little children could not be saved without baptism, these must have gone to an endless hell.

14 Behold I say unto you, that he that supposeth that little children need baptism is in the gall of bitterness and in the bonds of iniquity; for he hath neither faith, hope, nor charity; wherefore, should he be cut off while in the thought, he must go down to hell.

15 For awful is the wickedness to suppose that God saveth one child because of baptism, and the other must perish because he hath no baptism.

16 Wo be unto them that shall pervert the ways of the Lord after this manner, for they shall perish except they repent. Behold, I speak with boldness, having authority from God; and I fear not what man can do; for perfect love casteth out all fear.

17 And I am filled with charity, which is everlasting love; wherefore, all children are alike unto me; wherefore, I love little children with a perfect love; and they are all alike and partakers of salvation.

18 For I know that God is not a partial God, neither a changeable being; but he is unchangeable from all eternity to all eternity.

19 Little children cannot repent; wherefore, it is awful wickedness to deny the pure mercies of God unto them, for they are all alive in him because of his mercy.

20 And he that saith that little children need baptism denieth the mercies of Christ, and setteth at naught the atonement of him and the power of his redemption.

Notes

21 Wo unto such, for they are in danger of death, hell, and an endless torment. I speak it boldly; God hath commanded me. Listen unto them and give heed, or they stand against you at the judgment-seat of Christ.

22 For behold that all little children are alive in Christ, and also all they that are without the law. For the power of redemption cometh on all them that have no law; wherefore, he that is not condemned, or he that is under no condemnation, cannot repent; and unto such baptism availeth nothing—

23 But it is mockery before God, denying the mercies of Christ, and the power of his Holy Spirit, and putting trust in dead works.

24 Behold, my son, this thing ought not to be; for repentance is unto them that are under condemnation and under the curse of a broken law.

25 And the first fruits of repentance is baptism; and baptism cometh by faith unto the fulfilling the commandments; and the fulfilling the commandments bringeth remission of sins;

26 And the remission of sins bringeth meekness, and lowliness of heart; and because of meekness and lowliness of heart cometh the visitation of the Holy Ghost, which Comforter filleth with hope and perfect love, which love endureth by diligence unto prayer, until the end shall come, when all the saints shall dwell with God.

vv. 5–26 Little children are alive in Christ.

- In verse 6, Mormon indicates the intent of his epistle. Invite class members to look at verses 5 and 7 and explain Mormon's intent.
- Read verses 12, 14, 18, 20, and 23 and look for the following: Those who believe in the baptism of little children do not believe in what?
- What are the consequences to those who believe in the baptism of little children according to verses 14, 16, and 21?
- Analyze: *Why do you think Mormon is so bold about the consequences of baptizing little children?*
- What is the principle we should learn from Mormon's epistle? Invite class members to read or reread and ponder parts of this chapter before asking them to respond with each other or the entire class.

27 Behold, my son, I will write unto you again if I go not out soon against the Lamanites. Behold, the pride of this nation, or the people of the Nephites, hath proven their destruction except they should repent.

28 Pray for them, my son, that repentance may come unto them. But behold, I fear lest the Spirit hath ceased striving with them; and in this part of the land they are also seeking to put down all power and authority which cometh from God; and they are denying the Holy Ghost.

29 And after rejecting so great a knowledge, my son, they must perish soon, unto the fulfilling of the prophecies which were spoken by the prophets, as well as the words of our Savior himself.

30 Farewell, my son, until I shall write unto you, or shall meet you again. Amen.

Index Topics: baptism

MORONI 9

"The Spirit of the Lord Hath Ceased Striving with Them"
About AD 401

1–6, Mormon labors diligently to persuade the Nephites to repent; 7–20, Horrible wickedness of both the Nephites and Lamanites set forth; 21–26, Mormon exhorts Moroni to be faithful in Christ.

1 My beloved son, I write unto you again that ye may know that I am yet alive; but I write somewhat of that which is grievous.

2 For behold, I have had a sore battle with the

Notes

Lamanites, in which we did not conquer; and Archeantus has fallen by the sword, and also Luram and Emron; yea, and we have lost a great number of our choice men.

3 And now behold, my son, I fear lest the Lamanites shall destroy this people; for they do not repent, and Satan stirreth them up continually to anger one with another.

4 Behold, I am laboring with them continually; and when I speak the word of God with sharpness they tremble and anger against me; and when I use no sharpness they harden their hearts against it; wherefore, I fear lest the Spirit of the Lord hath ceased striving with them.

5 For so exceedingly do they anger that it seemeth me that they have no fear of death; and they have lost their love, one towards another; and they thirst after blood and revenge continually.

6 And now, my beloved son, notwithstanding their hardness, let us labor diligently; for if we should cease to labor, we should be brought under condemnation; for we have a labor to perform whilst in this tabernacle of clay, that we may conquer the enemy of all righteousness, and rest our souls in the kingdom of God.

7 And now I write somewhat concerning the sufferings of this people. For according to the knowledge which I have received from Amoron, behold, the Lamanites have many prisoners, which they took from the tower of Sherrizah; and there were men, women, and children.

8 And the husbands and fathers of those women and children they have slain; and they feed the women upon the flesh of their husbands, and the children upon the flesh of their fathers; and no water, save a little, do they give unto them.

9 And notwithstanding this great abomination of the Lamanites, it doth not exceed that of our people in Moriantum. For behold, many of the daughters of the Lamanites have they taken prisoners; and after depriving them of that which was most dear and precious above all things, which is chastity and virtue—

10 And after they had done this thing, they did murder them in a most cruel manner, torturing their bodies even unto death; and after they have done this, they devour their flesh like unto wild beasts, because of the hardness of their hearts; and they do it for a token of bravery.

11 O my beloved son, how can a people like this, that are without civilization—

12 (And only a few years have passed away, and they were a civil and a delightsome people)

13 But O my son, how can a people like this, whose delight is in so much abomination—

14 How can we expect that God will stay his hand in judgment against us?

15 Behold, my heart cries: Wo unto this people. Come out in judgment, O God, and hide their sins, and wickedness, and abominations from before thy face!

16 And again, my son, there are many widows and their daughters who remain in Sherrizah; and that part of the provisions which the Lamanites did not carry away, behold, the army of Zenephi has carried away, and left them to wander whithersoever they can for food; and many old women do faint by the way and die.

17 And the army which is with me is weak; and the armies of the Lamanites are betwixt Sherrizah and me; and as many as have fled to the army of Aaron have fallen victims to their awful brutality.

18 O the depravity of my people! They are without order and without mercy. Behold, I am but a man, and I have but the strength of a man, and I cannot any longer enforce my commands.

19 And they have become strong in their perversion; and they are alike brutal, sparing none, neither old nor young; and they delight in everything save that which is good; and the suffering of our women and our children upon all the face of this land doth exceed everything; yea, tongue cannot tell, neither can it be written.

20 And now, my son, I dwell no longer upon this

Notes

horrible scene. Behold, thou knowest the wickedness of this people; thou knowest that they are without principle, and past feeling; and their wickedness doth exceed that of the Lamanites.

vv. 4–20 Wickedness and selfishness lead to becoming past feeling.

⚡ *What is a callous? What are the advantages and disadvantages of having a callous?*

🔎 *What phrase in verse 20 describes a callous?*

❓ *Analyze: Define what you think Mormon meant when he used the words 'past feeling'.*

❓ *Apply: How does someone become past feeling? How does that relate to the forming of a callous?*

🔎 *What actions prove that the Nephites and the Lamanites had become past feeling according to verses 4–19?*

❓ *Analyze: What principle do you think Moroni is trying to communicate by describing such a horrible scene of wickedness? Why is the placement of the chapter at the end of the Book of Mormon instructive?*

💬 Neal A. Maxwell taught, "Take away regard for the divinity in one's neighbor, and watch the decline in our regard for his property. Take away basic moral standards, and observe how quickly tolerance changes into permissiveness. Take away the sacred sense of belonging to a family or community, and observe how quickly citizens cease to care for big cities. Take away regard for the seventh commandment, and behold the current celebration of sex, the secular religion with its own liturgy of lust and supporting music. Its theology focuses on 'self.' Its hereafter is 'now.' Its chief ritual is 'sensation'—though, ironically, it finally desensitizes its obsessed adherents, who become "past feeling." (Eph. 4:19; Moro. 9:20) Thus, in all its various expressions, selfishness is really self-destruction in slow motion!" (Neal A. Maxwell, "Put Off the Natural Man, and Come Off Conqueror", *Ensign*, October 1990, 16)

21 Behold, my son, I cannot recommend them unto God lest he should smite me.

22 But behold, my son, I recommend thee unto God, and I trust in Christ that thou wilt be saved; and I pray unto God that he will spare thy life, to witness the return of his people unto him, or their utter destruction; for I know that they must perish except they repent and return unto him.

23 And if they perish it will be like unto the Jaredites, because of the wilfulness of their hearts, seeking for blood and revenge.

24 And if it so be that they perish, we know that many of our brethren have deserted over unto the Lamanites, and many more will also desert over unto them; wherefore, write somewhat a few things, if thou art spared and I shall perish and not see thee; but I trust that I may see thee soon; for I have sacred records that I would deliver up unto thee.

25 My son, be faithful in Christ; and may not the things which I have written grieve thee, to weigh thee down unto death; but may Christ lift thee up, and may his sufferings and death, and the showing his body unto our fathers, and his mercy and long-suffering, and the hope of his glory and of eternal life, rest in your mind forever.

vv. 21–25 We must be faithful despite facing a world of wickedness.

🔎 *What does Mormon teach Moroni about facing a world of wickedness?*

💬 Elder Neal A. Maxwell spoke to our need to find comfort in times of trial and great wickedness: "Furthermore, God will give us priceless, personal assurances through the Holy Ghost (see John 14:26; D&C 36:2). Whether in tranquil or turbulent times, our best source of comfort is the Comforter. Enoch wept over the wickedness in his time, and, at first, 'refuse[d] to be comforted' (see Moses 7:4, 44). But then came revelations, successively showing Jesus redeeming the world,

Notes

the latter-day Restoration, and the Second Coming. Enoch was told to 'lift up [his] heart, and be glad' (Moses 7:44). The doctrines and revelations can likewise lift us—even amid 'wars and rumors of wars' (Matt. 24:6; Mark 13:7; see also 1 Ne. 12:2; Morm. 8:30; D&C 45:26). Thus we need not grow weary in our minds (see Heb. 12:3; D&C 84:80). Our discipleship need not be dried out by discouragement or the heat of the day, nor should dismaying, societal symptoms 'weigh [us] down' (Moro. 9:25), including 'in-your-face,' carnal confrontiveness (see Alma 32:38)" (Neal A. Maxwell, "Encircled in the Arms of His Love," *Ensign*, October 2002, 16).

- ♥ Invite class members to not despair because of the wickedness of the world. Testify that all that is unfair about life can be made up through the Atonement of Jesus Christ.

26 And may the grace of God the Father, whose throne is high in the heavens, and our Lord Jesus Christ, who sitteth on the right hand of his power, until all things shall become subject unto him, be, and abide with you forever. Amen.

> **Teaching Tips from Prophets' Lips** "Please take a particular interest in strengthening and improving the quality of teaching in the Church. . . . I fear at times that all too often many of our members come to church, sit through a class or meeting, and then return home having been largely uninformed. . . . We all need to be touched and nurtured by the Spirit, and effective teaching is one of the most important ways this can happen" (*Ensign*, May 1981, p. 45).

MORONI 10

Moroni Concludes the Record
About AD 421

1–7, Moroni teaches how to know if the Book of Mormon is true; 8–26, The gifts of the Spirit and receiving spiritual manifestations; 27–34, Moroni's last words to receive these things and his invitation to come unto Christ.

1 Now I, Moroni, write somewhat as seemeth me good; and I write unto my brethren, the Lamanites; and I would that they should know that more than four hundred and twenty years have passed away since the sign was given of the coming of Christ.

2 And I seal up these records, after I have spoken a few words by way of exhortation unto you.

3 Behold, I would exhort you that when ye shall read these things, if it be wisdom in God that ye should read them, that ye would remember how merciful the Lord hath been unto the children of men, from the creation of Adam even down until the time that ye shall receive these things, and ponder it in your hearts.

4 And when ye shall receive these things, I would exhort you that ye would ask God, the Eternal Father, in the name of Christ, if these things are not true; and if ye shall ask with a sincere heart, with real intent, having faith in Christ, he will manifest the truth of it unto you, by the power of the Holy Ghost.

5 And by the power of the Holy Ghost ye may know the truth of all things.

vv. 3–5 If we seek sincerely, the Holy Ghost will reveal to us the truth of the Book of Mormon.

- ⚡ Invite some full-time missionaries (or recently returned missionaries) to be guests in your class. At the proper time, ask them to share what role Moroni 10:3–5 has played in their missions and how "Moroni's Promise" works.

- 🔍 *In verses 3–5, look for and underline what conditions must be met before we can receive a witness from the Holy Ghost that the Book of Mormon is true.* Some conditions that they should find are:

Notes

- "read these things"
- "remember how merciful the Lord hath been"
- "ponder it in your hearts"
- "ask God . . . if these things are true"
- "with a sincere heart"
- "with real intent"
- "having faith in Christ"

❓ After each point, ask questions like, *Why is that an important step to knowing that the Book of Mormon is true?*

💗 Invite class members to write, "Moroni's Promise" next to the verses. Explain to the class that you are going to ask them to write down their thoughts about their testimony of the Book of Mormon, but first you will have the missionaries share their testimonies about how they came to know the Book of Mormon is true. When the missionaries have finished, allow class members time to write. Afterward, ask for a volunteer or two to share their thoughts if they feel comfortable doing so. Express to the class that if they have not gained their own testimony yet, they may do so by studying the Book of Mormon and by completing the process taught by Moroni. Invite those who already have the testimony to refresh it again and again by studying the Book of Mormon.

6 And whatsoever thing is good is just and true; wherefore, nothing that is good denieth the Christ, but acknowledgeth that he is.

7 And ye may know that he is, by the power of the Holy Ghost; wherefore I would exhort you that ye deny not the power of God; for he worketh by power, according to the faith of the children of men, the same today and tomorrow, and forever.

8 And again, I exhort you, my brethren, that ye deny not the gifts of God, for they are many; and they come from the same God. And there are different ways that these gifts are administered; but it is the same God who worketh all in all; and they are given by the manifestations of the Spirit of God unto men, to profit them.

9 For behold, to one is given by the Spirit of God, that he may teach the word of wisdom;

10 And to another, that he may teach the word of knowledge by the same Spirit;

11 And to another, exceedingly great faith; and to another, the gifts of healing by the same Spirit;

12 And again, to another, that he may work mighty miracles;

13 And again, to another, that he may prophesy concerning all things;

14 And again, to another, the beholding of angels and ministering spirits;

15 And again, to another, all kinds of tongues;

16 And again, to another, the interpretation of languages and of divers kinds of tongues.

17 And all these gifts come by the Spirit of Christ; and they come unto every man severally, according as he will.

18 And I would exhort you, my beloved brethren, that ye remember that every good gift cometh of Christ.

vv. 8–18 The gifts of the Spirit will help bring us, and others, closer to God.

⚡ Ask class members to consider what spiritual gifts they have been given by God.

🔍 In verses 8–18, after each gift mentioned in a verse, ask a class member to state that spiritual gift in his or her own words. Ask for examples of that gift they have witnessed.

💬 Explain that Marvin J. Ashton shared some additional gifts of the Spirit when he taught: ". . . let me mention a few gifts that are not always evident or noteworthy but that are very important. Among these may be your gifts—gifts not so evident but nevertheless real and valuable. Let us review some of these less-conspicuous gifts: the gift of asking; the gift of listening; the gift of hearing and using a still, small voice; the gift of being able to weep; the gift of avoiding

Notes

contention; the gift of being agreeable; the gift of avoiding vain repetition; the gift of seeking that which is righteous; the gift of not passing judgment; the gift of looking to God for guidance; the gift of being a disciple; the gift of caring for others; the gift of being able to ponder; the gift of offering prayer; the gift of bearing a mighty testimony; and the gift of receiving the Holy Ghost" ("There Are Many Gifts," *Ensign*, November 1987, 20).

❓ Analyze:
- *Is it possible to develop spiritual gifts you don't currently possess?*
- *What must we do to develop and strengthen spiritual gifts?*
- *What does verse 17 teach about developing spiritual gifts?*

✏️ Give class members a chance to write down ways they can personally develop spiritual gifts in their lives.

19 And I would exhort you, my beloved brethren, that ye remember that he is the same yesterday, today, and forever, and that all these gifts of which I have spoken, which are spiritual, never will be done away, even as long as the world shall stand, only according to the unbelief of the children of men.

20 Wherefore, there must be faith; and if there must be faith there must also be hope; and if there must be hope there must also be charity.

21 And except ye have charity ye can in nowise be saved in the kingdom of God; neither can ye be saved in the kingdom of God if ye have not faith; neither can ye if ye have no hope.

22 And if ye have no hope ye must needs be in despair; and despair cometh because of iniquity.

23 And Christ truly said unto our fathers: If ye have faith ye can do all things which are expedient unto me.

24 And now I speak unto all the ends of the earth—that if the day cometh that the power and gifts of God shall be done away among you, it shall be because of unbelief.

25 And wo be unto the children of men if this be the case; for there shall be none that doeth good among you, no not one. For if there be one among you that doeth good, he shall work by the power and gifts of God.

26 And wo unto them who shall do these things away and die, for they die in their sins, and they cannot be saved in the kingdom of God; and I speak it according to the words of Christ; and I lie not.

27 And I exhort you to remember these things; for the time speedily cometh that ye shall know that I lie not, for ye shall see me at the bar of God; and the Lord God will say unto you: Did I not declare my words unto you, which were written by this man, like as one crying from the dead, yea, even as one speaking out of the dust?

28 I declare these things unto the fulfilling of the prophecies. And behold, they shall proceed forth out of the mouth of the everlasting God; and his word shall hiss forth from generation to generation.

29 And God shall show unto you, that that which I have written is true.

30 And again I would exhort you that ye would come unto Christ, and lay hold upon every good gift, and touch not the evil gift, nor the unclean thing.

31 And awake, and arise from the dust, O Jerusalem; yea, and put on thy beautiful garments, O daughter of Zion; and strengthen thy stakes and enlarge thy borders forever, that thou mayest no more be confounded, that the covenants of the Eternal Father which he hath made unto thee, O house of Israel, may be fulfilled.

32 Yea, come unto Christ, and be perfected in him, and deny yourselves of all ungodliness; and if ye shall deny yourselves of all ungodliness, and love God with all your might, mind and strength, then is his grace sufficient for you, that by his

Notes

grace ye may be perfect in Christ; and if by the grace of God ye are perfect in Christ, ye can in nowise deny the power of God.

33 And again, if ye by the grace of God are perfect in Christ, and deny not his power, then are ye sanctified in Christ by the grace of God, through the shedding of the blood of Christ, which is in the covenant of the Father unto the remission of your sins, that ye become holy, without spot.

34 And now I bid unto all, farewell. I soon go to rest in the paradise of God, until my spirit and body shall again reunite, and I am brought forth triumphant through the air, to meet you before the pleasing bar of the great Jehovah, the Eternal Judge of both quick and dead. Amen.

vv. 30–32 We can only become perfect in this life "in Christ" and not by our own merits.

- ⚡ *How perfect does a person have to be in order to enter heaven?* After some discussion, read together Alma 45:16 and Alma 11:37, and then ask the first question again about how perfect we have to be.
- ❓ *If these verses are true, how can anyone ever be good enough to make it to heaven?*
- 🔍 *In verse 32, look for how we can be perfect enough to enter the kingdom of God.*
- ❓ *What does it mean to be "perfect in Christ"?*
- 💡 For an insight of what judgment day is like for those who are "perfect in Christ," read D&C 45:3–5. Notice that it is Christ's merits and goodness that is mentioned to our Father in Heaven. It is His (not our) perfection that save us.
- ❓ *What do we need to do to become "perfect in Christ"?*
- ♥ Review the covenants we make with Christ in baptism and in the sacrament. Challenge class members to strive to make those promises a daily part of their lives.

Teaching Tips from Prophets' Lips "While we are all teachers, we must fully realize that it is the Holy Ghost who is the real teacher and witness of all truth. Those who do not fully understand this either try to take over for the Holy Ghost and do everything themselves, politely invite the Spirit to be with them but only in a supporting role, or believe they are turning all their teaching over to the Spirit when, in truth, they are actually just "winging it." All parents, leaders, and teachers have the responsibility to teach "by the Spirit." They should not teach "in front of the Spirit" or "behind the Spirit" but "by the Spirit" so the Spirit can teach the truth unrestrained" (Matthew O. Richardson, Teaching After the Manner of the Spirit," *Ensign*, Nov. 2011, 96).

Index Topics: testimony, spiritual gifts, perfection

Notes

INDEX

A
apostasy, individual, 103, 109

atonement, 60, 61, 75, 86, 235, 274, 370

B
baptism, 237, 358, 364

Book of Mormon, 163, 367; role of, 44, 262, 305, 325

C
charity, 186, 362

commandments, 166, 269

contention, 236

conversion, 13, 14, 23

covenant, 64–65, 98, 122, 129–30, 133, 300

D
death, 79

E
endure to the end, 246

F
faith, 52-57, 62, 94, 173, 319–21, 342, 361

faithful, 201, 291, 366

families, 107, 132

forgiveness, 19, 68, 231

G
Gadianton Robbers, 160, 215-18

God, belief in, 11; blessings of, 41; mercy of, 59, 60, 86, 192, 347; praise, 35, 109; trust in, 18, 140

H
heart, 151

hell, 67

Holy Ghost, 230, 354, 367

hope, 362

humble, 53, 161, 301

I
Israel, gathering of, 262, 265

Israel, house of, 260

J
Jesus Christ, 169, 228; appearance of, 233; come unto Him, 229, 256; compassion of, 234, 250-51; covenant of, 249; disciple of, 237–39; doctrine of, 237, 245, 322; prophecies of, 207-9, 227; strength of, 344, 170

joy, 36, 42, 111, 277

Judgment Day, 40, 81, 196, 296

judging others, 243

INDEX

M

missionary work, 7, 10, 11, 19–20, 26, 75

missionary, attributes of, 75, 243

N

New Jerusalem, 260, 346

O

obedience, 85, 105, 135, 141, 165, 194, 290

offense, 146

P

parenting, 67, 132

peace, 43, 148, 190

persecution, 37

plan of salvation, 40, 79

prayer, 51, 63, 73, 242, 244, 257, 316, 320

preparation, 10, 63

pride, 162, 167, 221

pride cycle, 161-62, 219

priesthood ordinances, 252, 355, 356–57

priorities, 283–85

promised land, 317, 326-27

prophet, reacting to, 203, 210, 340; prophecies of, 232, 352; role of, 32, 90, 178, 182

protection, spiritual, 87-91, 107, 128, 213, 218

R

rebellion, 27

religious freedom, 43, 142

remember, 170–71, 189, 253

repentance, 29, 62, 78, 141, 161, 173, 193, 231, 292, 336

resurrection, 79, 81

righteous, 95, 111, 225

S

scripture study, 267, 272

scriptures, power of, 21, 24, 48, 70, 164, 259, 266

Second Coming, 268, 270

secret combinations, 160, 176, 210, 333

service, 8, 9, 240

sin, 72, 77, 222; consequences of, 67, 83, 168, 180, 297, 302–3, 351, 366; quick to forget, 97, 188–90, 211

spirit world, 79

spiritual gifts, 187, 368

T

temple, 250

temptation, 104

testimony, 44

trials, 51, 188

U

unity, 156-59

W

weakness, 108, 138, 166, 193, 344

Y

youth, 123

ABOUT THE AUTHORS

JOHN S. BUSHMAN is proud to be the father of five, the son of two, and the husband of one. He grew up in Tempe, Arizona, and served a mission in the Philippines. Later, he got his bachelor's degree in psychology and his master's in instructional technology from ASU.

Second to the Lord and his family, his greatest love is teaching and studying the scriptures with the youth of the Church.

One of his other passions is writing. He is the author of *Impractical Grace,* a story about how God's grace can heal any wound in life. He has recently coauthored a book with his wife, *Table Talk,* a book of hundreds of questions and quotes to get family discussing the issues that matter most in life. Both of these books are published with Cedar Fort.

REED ROMNEY was born in Mesa, Arizona, and grew up in various cities including Philadelphia, Baltimore, Atlanta, Las Vegas, and even London. He served his mission in the Washington Spokane Spanish-speaking mission. He and his wife have been married for ten years and are the parents of three children. Reed currently lives in St. George, Utah, where he enjoys road biking nearly year-round.

Reed attended Brigham Young University and later earned a bachelor's degree from the University of Nevada, Las Vegas, in business finance, graduating *cum laude.* He then obtained a master's degree in business administration from Southern Utah University. He also owns and operates two businesses.

ABOUT THE AUTHORS

JOHN R. MANIS, or Jack as he is known to friends, was born to goodly parents in Las Vegas, Nevada. When he was twelve years old, he found a book giving life sketches of each of the major characters of the Book of Mormon. Since that day, he has been determined to understand as much as possible from the Book of Mormon and the truth it contains. Jack enjoys the support and companionship of his wonderful wife, three little boys, and his dog, Charlemagne.

CURT R. WAKEFIELD was born and raised in Idaho. He served a mission to Southern Italy and then attended BYU-Idaho, where he received his bachelor's degree in recreational leadership. He has a master's degree in professional communication from SUU and is currently pursuing a doctorate degree in educational psychology at UNLV. He currently lives in St. George, Utah. He and his amazing wife, Shawna, are the parents of four children. He loves to learn about learning and teaching, which is why he was so excited to be a part of this book.